RESEARCH HANDBOOK ON LAW AND POLITICAL SYSTEMS

RESEARCH HANDBOOKS IN LAW AND POLITICS

Research Handbooks within this series provide state-of-the-art analysis of discrete areas of research that sit at the intersection of law and political science. Through exploring the legal aspects of political science and the impact of politics on the formation and application of the law, this series acts as a platform for cutting-edge interdisciplinary research. The *Research Handbooks* explore legal and political science approaches to key topics and domains, such as: the actions of legal institutions, the application of the law, judicial politics, constitutions, global governance, law and political theory, democracy, diplomacy, and federalism, among others. Edited by leading scholars in their respective fields, volumes bring together authors with diverse expertise to provide rounded analysis of the substantive issue at hand. Due to the interdisciplinary nature of the series, the volumes within will not only act as valuable resources to those researching the nexus of law and politics, but also provide new insights for those whose area of focus sits within either of the respective fields. The research presented will make significant new contributions to existing debates within the broadening study of law and political science whilst also acting as a starting point for fresh analysis.

For a full list of Edward Elgar published titles, including the titles in this series, visit our website at www.e-elgar.com.

Research Handbook on Law and Political Systems

Edited by

Robert M. Howard

Professor of Political Science, Department of Political Science, Georgia State University, USA

Kirk A. Randazzo

Professor of Political Science, Chair, Department of Political Science, University of South Carolina, USA

Rebecca A. Reid

Associate Professor of Political Science, Department of Political Science and Public Administration, University of Texas at El Paso, USA

RESEARCH HANDBOOKS IN LAW AND POLITICS

Edward Elgar PUBLISHING

Cheltenham, UK • Northampton, MA, USA

Published by
Edward Elgar Publishing Limited
The Lypiatts
15 Lansdown Road
Cheltenham
Glos GL50 2JA
UK

Edward Elgar Publishing, Inc.
William Pratt House
9 Dewey Court
Northampton
Massachusetts 01060
USA

A catalogue record for this book
is available from the British Library

Library of Congress Control Number: 2023945125

This book is available electronically in the **Elgar**online
Law subject collection
http://dx.doi.org/10.4337/9781800378346

Printed on elemental chlorine free (ECF)
recycled paper containing 30% Post-Consumer Waste

ISBN 978 1 80037 833 9 (cased)
ISBN 978 1 80037 834 6 (eBook)

Printed and bound in the USA

Robert Howard dedicates this book to his grandchildren, Arthur, Lucius and Joseph, and please let's not stop there. You are all such a joy.

Kirk Randazzo would like to dedicate this book to his wife, Carol, and his two children, Sam (in heaven) and Anna. Thank you for your constant love and support.

Rebecca Reid dedicates this book to her parents. Thank you for your constant love and support.

Contents

List of contributors ix

1 Introduction to the *Research Handbook on Law and Political Systems* 1
Robert M. Howard, Rebecca A. Reid, and Kirk A. Randazzo

2 Court-curbing through legal reforms or coercion? 8
Aylin Aydin-Cakir

3 Majoritarians in robes 25
Todd Curry and Michael Romano

4 Gender, race, and politics in judicial process 40
Tao Dumas and Alexandra Mannix

5 Judges and politics in UK courts 57
Lewis Graham

6 Government transparency and judicial deference 71
Gbemende Johnson

7 A court of law or a court of judges? 85
Maoz Rosenthal and Shai Talmor

8 Planting seeds but bearing different fruit 99
Kyle Shen

9 Explaining congressional support for the federal judiciary 122
Jake S. Truscott and Teena Wilhelm

10 Instrumentalization of constitutional law in Central Asia 139
Alexei Trochev and Alisher Juzgenbayev

11 Politicization of courts in European democracies 169
Maria Popova and Christine Rothmayr Allison

12 Constitution-making and transnational expertise: lessons from the 2014 Tunisian Constitution 186
Alicia Pastor y Camarasa

13 The battle for judicial independence 200
Mónica Castillejos-Aragón

14 Public support and compliance with high courts around the world 212
Amanda Driscoll and Martín Gandur

15 Open justice at highest courts 234
Philipp Meyer

16 Courting dissent 254
Hayley Munir and Syed Rashid Munir

17 The theoretical and empirical relationship between legal pluralism and economic development 271
Valenta Kabo

18 The Caribbean Court of Justice 289
Harold A. Young

19 Law and violence against civilians 305
M.P. Broache

20 Strategic deference of the European Court of Justice 325
Joshua Boston and Dino Hadzic

21 Conclusion to the *Research Handbook on Law and Political Systems* 344
Kirk A. Randazzo, Rebecca A. Reid, and Robert M. Howard

Index 355

Contributors

Aylin Aydin-Cakir is a Lecturer of Political Science at Vrije Universiteit Amsterdam (VU). Before joining VU, she worked as Assistant Professor at Yeditepe University, Turkey (2014–2019). In 2017 she was awarded the Young Scientist Award by the Science Academy in Turkey. In 2019 she received the Re: Constitution fellowship from Stiftung Mercator, and she has been visiting scholar at Utrecht University, School of Law from 2020–2021. Her research interests focus on judicial politics, comparative political institutions, public trust in the judiciary, and constitution-making processes. Aydin-Cakir has published in various journals, such as *Political Research Quarterly*, *International Political Science Review*, *Law & Society Review*, *Democratization*, *International Journal of Constitutional Law*, and *Turkish Studies*.

Joshua Boston is an Assistant Professor in the Bowling Green State University Political Science Department, where he researches and teaches classes on political institutions. His research—centering on questions of judicial politics—examines (1) the internal politics of courts, (2) how courts fit into separation of powers systems, and (3) the effect of legal institutions on the public. Prof. Boston's published work can be found in the *Journal of Law & Courts*, *Political Science Quarterly*, *Congress & the Presidency*, and *Public Opinion Quarterly*.

M.P. Broache is an Assistant Professor in the Department of Political Science at the University of North Carolina at Greensboro. Professor Broache's research and teaching focus on international relations, international law, and political violence, with a substantive emphasis on the International Criminal Court and a regional focus on sub-Saharan Africa. Professor Broache has previously published work in *Foreign Policy Analysis*, *Journal of Human Rights*, *Journal of Global Security Studies*, *International Journal of Transitional Justice*, and the *Journal of the Middle East and Africa*.

Mónica Castillejos-Aragón is an internationally trained attorney and a lecturer in legal studies at University of California (UC) Berkeley Law School. She has reported extensively on courts and politics from a comparative perspective and international human rights. Her research focuses on the impacts on democracy and the rule of law, including the strengthening or stabilization of the rule of law and the consolidation of democratic institutions, including judiciaries across the globe. She served four years as a legal advisor to the United Nations Special Rapporteur on the Independence of Judges and Lawyers and contributed to the drafting of dozens of thematic reports and interventions on contemporary challenges to the independence of judges and lawyers worldwide, annually presented before the UN Human Rights Council, the General Assembly, and international tribunals. She clerked for four years at the Supreme Court of Mexico and conducted professional visits to judiciaries in the United States, India, and Colombia. She has worked for a number of human rights organizations and UN agencies, where she has attained wide-ranging experience engaging in rule of law, peacebuilding, and international justice projects in various parts of the world. Dr. Castillejos-Aragón received a J.S.D and LL.M from UC Berkeley School of Law, and an LL.B (*Licenciada en Derecho*) from ITAM Department of Law, Mexico.

Todd Curry is an Associate Professor of Political Science at the University of Texas at El Paso. His primary area of research is state supreme courts, where he advances an audience-based approach to explaining how judges behave on and off the bench. His recent book with Michael Romano, *Creating the Law: State Supreme Court Opinions and the Effect of Audiences*, examines how judges craft their opinions differently depending on if their constituency is watching or not.

Amanda Driscoll is an Associate Professor in the Department of Political Science at Florida State University, and an Associate Professor of Law at the Florida State University College of Law (by Courtesy). Her research and teaching interests center on comparative democratic institutions of modern Latin America, with particular regard for courts, the separation of powers, and the rule of law.

Tao Dumas is an Associate Professor of Political Science at The College of New Jersey. Her research focuses on the political role of U.S. courts and the ways lawyers shape and work within the legal system. She is particularly interested in how institutional differences across states condition winners and losers in the courts and how attorneys' experience, expertise, and demographic characteristics impact their legal practices. She also teaches prelaw classes and chairs the College's Prelaw Advisory Committee.

Martín Gandur is a Ph.D. Candidate in the Department of Political Science at Florida State University. His research interests include comparative judicial institutions, inter-branch relations, and public support for courts. He holds an M.S. in Political Science from Florida State University, an LL.M. (UCLA School of Law), and an LL.B. (Universidad Nacional de Tucumán, Argentina).

Lewis Graham is a Fellow in Law at Wadham College at the University of Oxford. He teaches, researches, and publishes in areas including judges and judging, administrative law, and human rights law. He is particularly interested in the examination of judicial politics and judicial behavior, both in the UK and elsewhere. He also maintains a research position at the University of Cambridge and is an associate consultant at the Public Law Project, a legal charity based in London. His monograph, an empirical examination into judicial behavior in the UK Supreme Court, is due to be published next year.

Dino Hadzic is an Assistant Professor of Political Science at Trinity College Dublin. He specializes in comparative politics and his research agenda primarily focuses on violent conflict, ethnic politics, and European politics. Professor Hadzic's published work has appeared in such journals as the *American Political Science Review*, the *Journal of Politics*, the *British Journal of Political Science*, *European Union Politics*, *Research and Politics*, and *Political Research Quarterly*.

Robert M. Howard is currently a Professor of Political Science at Georgia State University in Atlanta, Georgia. Dr. Howard received his bachelor's degree from Union College in Schenectady, New York, earned a law degree from Suffolk University in Boston, Massachusetts, and a master's and a Ph.D. in American Politics and Public Law from the State University of New York (SUNY) at Stony Brook. His main research interests are the impact of courts and litigation on social and public policy, and judicial decision-making by the Federal Courts. He is the author of numerous articles and books, including *Judging Law and Policy: Courts and Policymaking in the American Political System* and *Getting a Poor Return: Courts,*

Justice and Taxes. Dr. Howard has been the Editor of *Justice System Journal* as well as the Editor of the book series Law, Courts, and Politics.

Gbemende Johnson is currently an Associate Professor of Political Science at the University of Georgia. She received her doctorate in Political Science from Vanderbilt University. Gbemende Johnson's research interests are American institutions, judicial politics, and executive branch politics. She also has interests in race and politics and political theory. She has taught courses on American government, courts and judicial process, bureaucracy, the American presidency, and the politics of equality. Johnson's research has appeared in outlets such as the *American Journal of Political Science*, *Vanderbilt Law Review*, *Presidential Studies Quarterly*, and *Law and Society Review*. Her published research explores interactions between judicial–executive institutional actors, judicial decision-making, government transparency, and judicial diversity.

Alisher Juzgenbayev is a J.D./Ph.D. candidate at Northwestern University Pritzker School of Law and Department of Political Science. He studies the relationship between law and politics in post-communist countries and has published datasets on the High Courts of Kazakhstan and Kyrgyzstan at the Harvard Dataverse.

Valenta Kabo is a member of the faculty at the University of Michigan Ford School of Public Policy, where she teaches courses on politics and policy, the U.S. Supreme Court, and comparative law. Her primary research interests focus on how law shapes policy outcomes in areas such as comparative law, law and economics, and property rights and development. She earned her Ph.D. (Political Science and Public Policy), Master's in Public Policy, and J.D. from the University of Michigan. She also received postdoctoral training and concurrently served as program director at the Center for Public Policy in Diverse Societies. Dr. Kabo also has prior professional legal experience, having practiced immigration law.

Alexandra Mannix is currently enrolled in her second year of law school at George Mason University Antonin Scalia Law School. She is a candidate member of the *Journal of Law, Economics, and Policy*. Prior to law school, she attended Raritan Valley Community College, earning an associate degree in liberal arts magna cum laude, before matriculating at The College of New Jersey, where she earned a bachelor's degree in political science summa cum laude.

Philipp Meyer is a Postdoctoral Research Associate in the Department of Political Science, Leibniz University Hannover. He holds a Ph.D. in Political Science from Leibniz University Hannover and an M.A. in Comparative Politics from Otto-Friedrich-University Bamberg. He has published his research on judicial politics and court communication, among others, in *Political Communication*, *Public Relations Review* and *Journalism Studies*, and has been recognized for excellence in undergraduate teaching. Currently, he is working as a science manager at the German Research Foundation focusing on e-research technologies and the digital turn in science.

Hayley Munir is an Assistant Professor of Political Science at Albright College, where she specializes in judicial politics. Her research primarily focuses on judicial selection systems at the state level. In addition to her work on U.S. courts, she also studies judicial independence and legitimacy in the comparative context.

Syed Rashid Munir is an Assistant Professor of Politics at the Lahore University of Management Sciences in Lahore, Pakistan. His research interests include foreign policy analysis, political economy, security relations, and domestic institutions. His research has been published in *Politics and Religion*, *Political Studies Review*, and the *Asian Journal of Comparative Politics*, as well as through chapters in edited volumes.

Alicia Pastor y Camarasa is a Postdoctoral Researcher at the Swiss Graduate School of Public Administration at the University of Lausanne. She holds a Ph.D. in Law from the University of Louvain and an LL.M in Transnational Law from King's College London. She was a 2018 Belgian American Educational Foundation Fellow at the University of Massachusetts Amherst. Her doctoral research explored the transnational dimension of constitution-making, and she is preparing a manuscript set for publication with Routledge in 2024. Her current research area centres on democratic governance, drawing on comparative constitutional law, empirical approaches to law, and legal theory. With a socio-legal approach to public law, her work aims to answer legal questions using empirical analysis, grounded in qualitative methodologies from the social sciences. Alicia has practical experience in transitional justice and governance, previously working in the New Zealand Ministry of Justice on issues surrounding the reconciliation process between the indigenous Māori and the British Crown. She has also worked in a variety of international organisations and NGOs on topics such as human rights, gender, and governance.

Maria Popova is an Associate Professor of Political Science at McGill University. She held the Jean Monnet Chair "Europe and the Rule of Law" in 2017–2021. Her work explores judicial politics in the post-Communist region. Dr. Popova's book, *Politicized Justice in Emerging Democracies* (Cambridge University Press, 2012), won the American Association for Ukrainian Studies prize for best book in the fields of Ukrainian history, politics, language, literature, and culture. Her recent work has focused on judicial reform and court chair elections in Ukraine, the politics of corruption prosecutions in Eastern Europe, and courts and informal politics in Bulgaria.

Kirk A. Randazzo is a Professor of Political Science at the University of South Carolina and currently Chair of the Department of Political Science (since 2019). He received his Ph.D. in Political Science in 2003 from Michigan State University; an MA in International Studies from the University of South Carolina in 1997; and a BA in Music from the University of South Carolina in 1994. Prior to joining the Department of Political Science at the University of South Carolina in 2008, he taught at the University of Kentucky from 2003–2008. From 2013–2016, Randazzo served as the Director of the Carolina Leadership Initiative and continues to serve (since 2017) as the Director of Leadership Studies. His primary research and teaching interests involve law and judicial politics. He has published several books, including *Checking the Courts: Law, Ideology, and Contingent Discretion* (with Richard W. Waterman) in 2014, and *Defenders of Liberty or Champions of Security? Federal Courts, the Hierarchy of Justice, and U.S. Foreign Policy* in 2010, both published by SUNY Press. He has published numerous articles in journals such as the *American Journal of Political Science*, the *Journal of Politics*, and *Political Research Quarterly*. He serves on the editorial boards of Routledge Press Law and Court series, the *Justice System Journal*, and *Research and Politics*, and was the Chair of the Law and Courts Section of the American Political Science Association from 2019–2020.

Rebecca A. Reid is an Associate Professor in the Department of Political Science and Public Administration at the University of Texas at El Paso. She received her Ph.D. in Political Science from the University of South Carolina in 2015. Her research interests include judicial politics, comparative courts, international law, human rights, indigenous law, gender, and diversification and inclusion. More specifically, she examines how courts and judges make decisions, the impact of these decisions on the rule of law and human rights, and the development and interaction of laws across international and domestic spheres.

Michael Romano is an Associate Professor in the Political Science Department at Shenandoah University. He received his Ph.D. in political science from Western Michigan University in 2014. His primary area of research is how elites—specifically judges in both the federal and state courts in the United States—communicate with various audiences to affect policy goals, political outcomes, and forge a representational link with these audiences to maintain legitimacy. His work has been published in *Justice System Journal*, *Social Science Quarterly*, and *PS: Political Science & Politics*. His book, *Creating the Law: State Supreme Court Opinions and the Effect of Audiences*, with Todd A. Curry, was released by Routledge Press in 2019.

Maoz Rosenthal is a Senior Lecturer in the Lauder School of Government, Diplomacy, and Strategy at Reichman University (IDC, Herzliya). Dr. Rosenthal is a Tel-Aviv University Political Science Department graduate and a former visiting scholar at SUNY Binghamton University's Political Science Department. He studies the interaction between strategy and structure in a variety of political arenas, with a focus on the Israeli case. Recent publications include: "Estimating the 'Legislators in Robes': Measuring Judges' Political Preferences", published in *Justice System Journal*; "Introducing a New Dataset: The Israeli Policy Agendas Project", in *Israel Studies Review* (2022); and "Judicial Review in a Defective Democracy", published in the *Journal of Law and Courts* (2021).

Christine Rothmayr Allison (D.Phil. University of Zurich) is a Professor in the Department of Political Science at the University of Montreal. Her main fields of interest are comparative public policy, focusing on the fields of biotechnology and biomedicine; and courts and politics, in particular, the impact of court decisions on public policy making in North America and Europe. She has published articles in the *European Journal of Political Research*, *Comparative Political Studies*, *West European Politics*, *Regulation & Governance*, *Journal of European Public Policy* and the *Canadian Journal of Political Science*, among others.

Kyle Shen is a Ph.D. candidate at the University of Texas at Austin. His work focuses on the intersections between international law and national constitutional design, with a regional interest in constitution-making in East and Southeast Asia. He holds a J.D. from the University of Texas School of Law. Prior to graduate school, Kyle completed an internship with the Office of the Co-Prosecutor at the United Nations Assistance to the Khmer Rouge Trials in Phnom Penh, Cambodia. His work has also been published in the *Annual Review of Law and Social Science*.

Shai Talmor earned her BA and MA in the Lauder School of Government, Diplomacy, and Strategy at Reichman University (IDC, Herzliya). Her recent publication, "Estimating the 'Legislators in Robes': Measuring Judges' Political Preferences", was published in *Justice System Journal*.

Alexei Trochev is an Associate Professor at Nazarbayev University Department of Political Science and International Relations. He is a co-investigator in the Economic and Social Research Council-funded project, "In the GULAG's Shadow: Producing, Consuming & Perceiving Prisons in the Former Soviet Union."

Jake S. Truscott is a post-doctoral researcher at the Center for C-SPAN Scholarship and Engagement at Purdue University (West Lafayette, Indiana).

Teena Wilhelm, Ph.D, is Associate Professor of Political Science at the University of Georgia. Her authored or co-authored research has appeared in major political science and legal journals, and has been honored by the Southern Political Science Association. Her research has also received support from the National Science Foundation. Wilhelm's research specialties include judicial institutions, state politics, and public land policy.

Harold A. Young is an Associate Professor in the Department of Political Science and Public Management at Austin Peay State University, Tennessee. He earned his Ph.D. in Philosophy (Political Science) from Georgia State University and J.D. (LL.B./C.L.E.) from the University of the West Indies/Norman Manley School of Law. Dr. Young's research interests include the death penalty, American and international perspectives on judicial institutional changes and decision-making. His work is published in several journals and his new book, *The Judicial Committee of the Privy Council and the Caribbean Court of Justice: Navigating Independence and Changing Political Environments*, is now available.

1. Introduction to the *Research Handbook on Law and Political Systems*

Robert M. Howard, Rebecca A. Reid, and Kirk A. Randazzo

How should we think about law and political systems? This is a pertinent question, as political questions inevitably become legal ones. Legal system institutions often issue legal rulings overriding legislation, whether by legislative and executive design, or because of flaws in informal rules that allow courts' opinions to supersede legislation. In essence, courts often act more as a political than legal institution. This is so despite the formal rules, institutional structure, and protections that are supposed to prevent this from occurring. So, how do we begin to analyze the relationships between law and political systems?

One way is to recognize that law and political systems reflect, reinforce, and are mutually constitutive of each other. That is, law is both structured and defined by the political system within which it operates, but law also further structures and defines that very same political system. However, scholarship often treats these systems as independent, often working in parallel but with little interaction. Even the categorization of academic areas of study reflects this assumption of independence, where law-oriented fields are separate from political fields. Part of the reason for this myth of independence between law and politics is to ensure the legitimacy and power of law and courts. For political systems to promote the rule of law and social order, law needs to be perceived as impartial and apolitical, such that rules are fairly and justly enforced. Acknowledging the political aspects of the creation and implementation of law can undermine its perceived impartial nature in a way that can threaten the normative power of law.

Approximately 25 years ago, some scholars answered the call put forward by Tate and Vallinder (1995) to focus explicitly on this intersection, called the "judicialization of politics." While researchers continue to examine the dynamic and interdependent nature of law and politics, we need to remain cognizant that not all laws and legal systems have the same impact on political systems; nor do all political systems have the same impact on law. Scholars may note in the abstract that courts and law perpetuate existing power structures, allocate resources, enforce social order, and set the bounds of the government power; however, little scholarship explicitly evaluates the evolving dialogs between law and politics to offer concrete mechanisms upon which to examine this relationship and its consequences. As such, we need systematic analyses to determine the impact of law on political systems and political systems on law.

This research handbook deals with this very question by examining law and political systems around the world, primarily in the more than quarter-century since the publication of Tate and Vallinder's seminal work (1995). These relationships are informed by legal traditions as well as by histories and cultures that vary across regions and are differentially impacted by various transnational court systems. Political scientists tend to examine information either through country-specific analyses, through comparative analyses, or through the examination of transnational institutions. Our contributors similarly examine the impact of law on politics (and of politics on law) through these lenses.

Some of our contributors provide examples primarily from single jurisdictions, associated with dominant single-party systems and competitive-party systems that affect the way in which constitutions are written, amended, and interpreted. Others examine law and politics through a comparative perspective, illustrating how different political contexts can lead to different uses of law and how courts can respond to these political environments. Finally, some examine transnational courts and influences that emphasize the interconnectedness of the domestic and international through linking legal and political systems across international, regional, and national levels. In all, we present 19 different analyses that we think begin to help us understand the answers to some of our questions about the relationship between law and political systems.

In the first grouping, scholars follow country-specific analyses. Aylin Aydin-Cakir investigates Turkey to generalize about courts and political systems, particularly in more authoritarian regimes that undermine courts, in "Court-curbing through legal reforms or coercion? Evidence from Turkey." She argues that in the past few decades, there has been a worrisome, growing trend in the world whereby elected authoritarian leaders curtail the judiciary's power by legal reforms and coercion mechanisms. The core issue then, is, what are the contextual factors that affect their decision to use different types of court-curbing mechanisms? In reviewing the literature, Aydin-Cakir finds a lack of any sort of theoretical framework from which to assess this issue and uses this chapter to build such a framework to explain the political and social conditions under which the leaders use formal legal reforms and the conditions under which they use coercion mechanisms for court-curbing. Her analysis shows that elected authoritarian leaders usually prefer to use formal legal means to curtail the power of the judiciary. However, she finds that when there is an imminent threat against the government and when the potential for public backlash is low, coercion mechanisms of court-curbing are preferred. The major finding is that the potential of public backlash for attacking the judiciary will be low if the majority of citizens are not capable or willing to punish the government. Low public awareness and transparency affect citizens' capability, and the authoritarian political culture, ingrained networks, and high political polarization influence citizens' willingness, to punish the ruling government.

Todd Curry and Michael Romano examine the changing public perception of the roles and nature of the judiciary as public opinion starts to shift from seeing the judiciary as a legal institution to more of a political one. In "Majoritarians in robes: Judicial representation and the changing nature of judicial audience in the United States," they find that while most citizens feel that judges should remain outside of the "political" system, the reality is very different in that judges are part of representative government. They argue that historical changes to the methods of selection and retention of judges and the regular, voluntary issuance of opinions require us to reevaluate judges as representatives of the public's trust rather than guardians of the law. They claim that changes to institutional structures, specifically to how judges are selected and retained, have an important impact on the link between representative and constituent "audiences."

Tao Dumas and Alexandra Mannix analyze the influence of gender, race, and political affiliation on judicial processes. In their chapter, "Gender, race, and politics in judicial process: Do trial judges' gender, race, and partisanship impact verdicts, appeals, and reversals?", they try to determine how judges' gender, race, and party affiliations interact with state institutional arrangements to shape the judicial process. While the scholarly community overwhelming accepts the notion that judges' ideological preferences and judges' race and gender impact their rulings, less is known about how litigants and attorneys respond to judges' personal attributes. This is a key contribution because very few scholars have examined the response of those in the judicial system to these characteristics. The authors explore whether judges who are minorities on the bench, in terms of their party affiliation, gender, or race, are subject to more judicial scrutiny in the form of appeals and reversals. They compile their own unique data collection comprising 17 years of trial court data in the state of Alabama and resulting appeals court rulings, along with demographic and partisan affiliation data, to test these hypotheses.

Lewis Graham examines judges and politics in the courts of the United Kingdom in "Judges and politics in UK courts." Graham asks the very simple question of whether or not judges are acting political, and if so, how we know or measure that fact. Graham attempts the difficult task of trying to define the line between law and politics. This is a seemingly simple, yet critical and often overlooked, task. As Graham notes, ruling on political legislation is not necessarily acting politically. It is a thoughtful and necessary chapter that forces us to think about the connection between ideology, politics, and judicial rulings.

Returning to the United States, Gbemende Johnson, in her chapter "Government transparency and judicial deference: An outcomes-based overview of Freedom of Information Act litigation in the U.S. Supreme Court," examines the intersection of law and politics through the Freedom of Information Act (FOIA). This law is very relevant and important to the scholarly community as researchers file requests through The FOIA to aid in analyses and examinations of the U.S. government and its bureaucratic agencies. Johnson looks at the U.S. Supreme Court's decision-making in FOIA litigation. The FOIA's purpose is to act as a check on governmental action through private action to obtain information on the government, where the Supreme Court is supposed to act as a referee. Johnson finds that while few FOIA requests result in litigation, the Supreme Court plays a central role in providing guidance to agencies and requesters regarding executive branch autonomy over disclosure decisions and the scope of transparency afforded by the FOIA. Overall, she finds that the U.S. Supreme Court exhibits a substantial degree of deference to agency interpretations of the FOIA, thus potentially exhibiting a bias toward the government in its attempt to keep information hidden.

Maoz Rosenthal and Shai Talmor focus on Israel and its high court for their analysis in "A court of law or a court of judges? The Israeli High Court of justice and the judicialization of politics in Israel." Analyzing the question of politics versus law in judicial decision-making, the authors examine the court's decisions on petitions related to Israel's executive branch during 1995–2017, and then identify the decisions' political context through an examination of the patterns of the judges' decisions. They demonstrate that judicial review in the court varies with political context, is politically moderate, and reflects dynamically changing judicial factions within the court; and they conclude that the court is neither a court of law nor a court of judges, but a court of judicial factions.

Kyle Shen examines the constitutional design of Cambodia in "Planting seeds but bearing different fruit: International peace-building and constitutional design in Cambodia, 1991–1993." He argues that the Paris Agreements and the UN Transitional Authority in Cambodia sought to build liberal democratic constitutionalism in Cambodia after decades of conflict and grave human rights abuses. While the multiparty democracy achieved initial successes during the UN intervention, it did not evolve into a lasting political system. As a result, Cambodian politics is dominated by a single party. Shen analyzes and seeks to explain this discrepancy by arguing that the outcome in Cambodia emerged from a complex and heterogenous response among domestic political factions to international norms and international actors. He finds that constitutional design is the culprit and that reliance on textual language is misplaced. Rather than a uniform process of learning or acculturation, the diffusion of constitutional models through international peacebuilding triggered a multifaceted response among soft- and hard-liner elites, resulting in a text with democratic aspirations on paper yet without political bargains that could sustain those aspirations.

In our final chapter examining specific countries, Jake Truscott and Teena Wilhelm, in "Explaining congressional support for the federal judiciary," note how support for the federal judiciary is tied to decisions made by Congress. Of course, the American separation-of-powers reality is that Congress also depends on the judiciary to reinforce and "constitutionalize" its policymaking. The authors argue that a legislature interested in policy longevity can choose to strategize and support the judiciary in an opportunistic manner, which in turn impacts the judiciary's influence and capacity. The extent to which support is demonstrated over time reflects the institutional development of the federal judiciary itself. Their results find that increases in overall Congressional spending correspond to increases in federal judicial support, economic downturns do not have a significant impact, and interbranch ideological distance does not have a significant impact on Congressional support for the entire judiciary.

Turning to multinational and transnational analyses, we lead with Alexei Trochev and Alisher Juzgenbayev examining Central Asian republics in "Instrumentalization of constitutional law in Central Asia," and their view that there is a lack of scholarly acknowledgment of any sort of judicialization of politics in examining these countries. They argue that for the most part, scholars see these courts as instruments of the governing authorities with little independence and as passive servants or "pawns" of the ruling regime. However, the two stress that courts can be assertive provided certain conditions are met, including a lack of unilateral appointment control by the ruling authority.

Maria Popova and Christine Rothmayr Allison provide a timely and thorough review of politicization of European democratic courts, particularly in Eastern Europe, in "Politicization of courts in European democracies." While stressing that much work needs to be done to fully understand the phenomenon, the authors argue that this empirical analysis is critical for normative reasons. If judicial decisions are not seen as different from political decisions and judges become just another political actor, this can undermine legitimacy and compliance with judicial rulings. Therefore, we need to understand what factors lead to weaponized legalism and what European institutions and actors can do to stop this process.

Alicia Pastor y Camarasa, in "Constitution-making and transnational expertise: Lessons from the 2014 Tunisian Constitution," analyzes the internationalization of constitution-making. As Pastor y Camarasa notes, constitutional scholars often overlook the transnational dimension of constitution-making. Thus, the author explores the transnational dimensions of constitution-making by examining the process of constitutional drafting. Using a case study of the making of the 2014 Tunisian Constitution, she shows the involvement of international actors during constitutional drafting.

Mónica Castillejos-Aragón, in "The battle for judicial independence: Courts functioning as constitutional beacons and political responses in El Salvador," provides a timely examination of judicial behavior and action during the initial stages of the COVID-19 pandemic. She shows how the Constitutional Chamber and Salvadorian magistrates moved very rapidly to address the challenges from the pandemic. The chapter demonstrates how the judicial system was vigilant and acted as a lighthouse keeper by setting up constitutional buoys and markers for the executive and legislators to navigate within constitutional and legal boundaries. The author also shows these institutions are constantly checking and repositioning themselves as needed.

Amanda Driscoll and Martín Gandur examine public support and compliance with high courts in the chapter "Public support and compliance with high courts around the world." The authors start by acknowledging the intrinsic weakness of courts, which, to quote Alexander Hamilton, possess neither the "purse nor the sword," and thus lack enforcement mechanisms. They then argue that public support as a potential mechanism for authority is relatively understudied, yet is critical for any examination of court authority. The difficulty lies in measuring public understanding and compliance with decisions. After a thorough review of the literature on courts and public opinion, the authors argue for a framework to understand this critical issue and suggest avenues for future research to aid the scholarly community and government in establishing compliance with courts' decisions.

Philipp Meyer, in "Open justice at highest courts: A new a venue for comparative research," analyzes one possible solution for compliance – namely openness and transparency at high courts. Meyer argues that openness and transparency, often missing in court proceedings that are often deliberately designed to be secretive, results in the loss of trust and legitimacy for courts. Initially proposing a way to conceptualize and measure trust, the author then uses this measure in a dataset of legal systems in 27 European countries. He then presents evidence for the seemingly well-established assumption that open justice increases public trust, and this includes courts. The author argues that this is the first study to provide empirical results showing that the principle of open justice fosters the public's trust toward legal institutions. Another result demonstrates that the degree of openness and transparency varies greatly between courts and countries. Finally, he asserts that the approach used for this analysis can easily be applied to any court that maintains a website.

Hayley Munir and Syed Rashid Munir, in "Courting dissent: Judicial legitimacy and protests," examine the role of the judiciary in promoting peaceful dissent. The authors argue that if a citizenry views a court as legitimate, the courts can play a remedial role in fostering peaceful dissent and acceptance of government policy. In effect, an independent judiciary is an institutional dispute resolution mechanism that formally addresses contention and resolves disputes. In addition to acting as an institutional check on the legislative and executive branches, judicial institutions that the public hold in high regard allow those in the minority formal opportunities to protect their interests, which would otherwise be impossible through traditional political processes. Using regression analysis on a dataset from 1996 to 2017 for 144 countries, the authors provide support for this hypothesis and find that when perceptions of judicial legitimacy are present, people do not need to resort to protests to express their grievances. Finally, they complement the quantitative analyses with a case study of India.

Valenta Kabo moves beyond the institutional analyses to examine the macro-level phenomena of the relationship between legal pluralism and economic development in the aptly titled "The theoretical and empirical relationship between legal pluralism and economic development." Kabo analyzes the prevalent notion that law and rule of law, in systems where the law is not regime-dominated, positively influence economic development. The theory is that a legal system that enforces rules and prevents arbitrary rulings reinforces and supports economic growth and development. However, using data from 118 developing countries over a 20-year period, a traditional measure of economic development finds little, if any, relationship between law and economic development by the most widely used traditional measure. The author does find a negative relationship between a country with customary-dominant law (as opposed to common law or civil law). The author concludes that nuance is needed in these evaluations before any definitive relationship can be determined.

Finally, we conclude with several chapters on transnational courts. Harold Young examines the legacy of colonialism on Caribbean courts in "The Caribbean Court of Justice: Meeting the challenges of a post-colonial Caribbean." Young examines the creation of the Caribbean Court of Justice (CCJ) as a replacement for the Judicial Committee of the Privy Council (JCPC) located in London, England. The JCPC is a colonial advisory committee to the British monarch on appeals from the British Empire and former colonies, including many Caribbean nations. In response to remove this vestige of colonialism, several Caribbean nations formed the CCJ to allow local control over appeals. Young reviews the JCPC formation with its historical roots in the British Empire and its continuing role in the Caribbean. He then reviews the emergence of the CCJ and its importance to regional integration in the Caribbean community. Finally, he uses comparative analyses to examine the differences in decision-making by these courts for capital punishment cases and cases involving the government as a party. While arguing for the importance of continued movement toward the CCJ, Young notes that some of the largest and most economically developed Caribbean nations, including Jamaica and the Bahamas, and paradoxically Trinidad and Tobago (the home of the CCJ), still use the JCPC.

M.P. Broache examines the International Criminal Court in his chapter, "Law and violence against civilians: Country-level effects of the International Criminal Court." The Court was established by a treaty that was adopted in 1998, and came into existence in July 2002. In many respects, the ICC represents the most ambitious manifestation of the "justice cascade." The Court was established as a permanent tribunal, with broad-based geographic and personal jurisdiction, encompassing the territory and nationals of situations referred by the UN Security Council, and non-states parties can voluntarily accept its jurisdiction. Established to prosecute (war crime) atrocities, the author notes that it is an open question as to whether or not the Court can prevent atrocities. To answer this question, Broache reexamines the effects of the ICC on atrocities, focusing on the impact of the Court's territorial jurisdiction on violence against civilians. Using civilian death data from all countries from 1995 to 2010, the author finds that ICC jurisdiction has had little impact on violence against civilians.

Joshua Boston and Dino Hadzic examine the European Court of Justice (ECJ) in their chapter, "Strategic deference of the European Court of Justice: Economic influences on judicial decision-making." The authors return to the question of compliance with the judiciary, specifically: when is the ECJ likely to rule for or against the government in question, given that it lacks enforcement mechanisms? Marshalling their evidence, the authors argue that ECJ deference is conditioned by members' economic circumstances. That is, European Union policies pertain primarily to trade and regulatory practices, where compliance with adverse ECJ rulings can impose substantial costs if a member's economy is already performing poorly. The results suggest that economic performance constrains ECJ decision-making when the state has lower levels of growth and is most dependent on trade, and thus more likely to not comply with the court's judgment. As the authors conclude, this means the ECJ uses its power very strategically to avoid noncompliance.

We hope that the reader will enjoy these contributions as much as we have. We trust the reader, as we have, will learn a lot about law and political systems. However, there is, of course, no definitive answer to this question of the intersection of law and politics. These enlightening chapters highlight the opportunities for future research and scholarship in these areas. We hope that the legacy from this handbook is that someone continues this challenge with a new volume some 25 years from now.

REFERENCE

Tate, C.N., and T. Vallinder. 1995. *The Global Expansion of Judicial Power*. New York University Press.

2. Court-curbing through legal reforms or coercion?

Evidence from Turkey

Aylin Aydin-Cakir

INTRODUCTION

In the last decade, the world has seen an immense increase in the number of authoritarian regimes. The Freedom in the World Report (2019) asserts that the share of non-free countries increased by 26 percent in the last 13 years, while the percentage of free countries decreased by 44 percent. While during the Cold War most democratic regimes collapsed via military coups or election fraud, especially in the past two decades, democratic erosion came through the gradual destruction of democratic institutions by elected leaders (Bermeo 2016; Levitsky & Ziblatt 2018; Corrales 2018; Haggard & Kaufman 2021; Svolik 2013; Mechkova, Lührmann & Lindberg 2017).

With the rise of authoritarian populism, many scholars have emphasized that the elected authoritarian leaders preferred to use formal legal means to curtail institutions' power instead of directly attacking them. For instance, as soon as Fidesz won the 2010 elections in Hungary, it started to curtail the judicial power by passing a series of constitutional amendments that changed the appointment procedure of the judges of the Hungarian Constitutional Court. Afterward, in 2012, a new constitution came into force that increased the number of constitutional court judges from 11 to 15, changed the appointment procedure of the President of the constitutional court, and decreased the retirement age for ordinary judges from 70 to 62. These mechanisms can be defined as court-packing strategies that aim to fill the higher and lower courts with partisan judges (Scheppele 2011; Bodnar et al. 2017; Pocza, Dobos & Gyulai 2019). Similarly, in Venezuela in 2004, by issuing a new law, the National Assembly increased the Venezuelan Supreme Court's size from 20 to 32 judges (Landau & Dixon 2020).

The general argument is that restructuring the institutions via constitutional amendment, constitutional replacement, or legislation would provide legitimate grounds for the ruling government. Labeling these mechanisms as "constitutional authoritarianism" (Tushnet 2015; Işıksel 2013), "rule by law" (Ginsburg & Moustafa 2008), "abusive constitutionalism" (Landau 2013) or "autocratic legalism" (Scheppele 2018), many scholars tried to explain how authoritarian leaders use laws to curtail the power of democratic institutions. It has been argued that by changing the constitution or issuing specific laws, elected authoritarian leaders can remove the political opposition, weaken or pack the courts, and establish government control over the media and other vital institutions (Landau 2013: 194). As a result, by using legal means, authoritarian leaders try to consolidate power, remain in office, construct a more authoritarian order, and protect their self-interests.

Although the use of legal means as a court-curbing mechanism has been an increasing trend among elected authoritarian leaders, we see that they continue to use coercion at some points.

Removing or threatening to remove judges from office, imprisoning some of them based on false charges, forcing judges into resignation, claiming that judicial decisions are politically motivated, or accusing judges of being corrupt can be presented as some of these coercion mechanisms. For instance, in Ecuador in 2010, by sending a memo to all judges, President Correa explicitly threatened the judiciary. He stated that "...any judge who finds a public works project unconstitutional would be personally liable to the state for 'damage and harm' caused by the lost opportunity to pursue the project" (Landau & Dixon 2020: 1339). Judges have also been threatened in Fiji. In 2006, after the military coup, judges reported that their houses were burnt or vandalized (Landau & Dixon 2020).

Although there are various explanations about how and why elected leaders abuse the legal means or attack the judiciary in the literature, we do not know much about how the contextual factors affect authoritarian leaders' decision to use specific court-curbing mechanisms. In other words, we do not know whether elected authoritarian leaders prefer to use certain types of court-curbing mechanisms only under certain conditions. This chapter aims to provide a theoretical framework to explain when elected authoritarian leaders prefer to use legal reforms and when they prefer to use coercion mechanisms against the judiciary. This study's key assumption is that elected authoritarian leaders are rational actors and will choose the court-curbing mechanisms that would provide higher benefits and incur lower costs. Asserting that each type of mechanism would have different costs and benefits, I suggest that the political and social conditions under which these mechanisms are applied would affect their costs and benefits. Thus, the theoretical framework proposed in this study is developed by presenting the costs and benefits of each court-curbing mechanism and the contextual framework that shapes them.

Using Turkey as a case study, the court-curbing mechanisms used by the AKP (*Adalet ve Kalkınma Partisi*, Justice and Development Party) government and the contextual framework under which these mechanisms were used are critically analyzed. The analysis shows that an elected authoritarian leader usually prefers to use formal legal means to curtail the power of the judiciary; but coercion mechanisms will be preferred when there is an imminent threat against the government and when the potential for public backlash is low. It is argued that the possibility of public backlash for attacking the judiciary will be low if citizens are not willing to punish and capable of punishing the government. While low public awareness and transparency affect citizens' capability, the authoritarian political culture, clientelistic networks, and high political polarization affect citizens' willingness to punish the ruling government.

The chapter starts with a literature review on court-curbing mechanisms and the conditions under which leaders prefer to use them. The next section reviews the mechanisms used by the AKP government to curtail the judiciary's power and independence. After elaborating on the potential costs and benefits, the fourth section presents a theoretical framework that can be used to understand the rationale behind using different court-curbing mechanisms. The study ends by reviewing the implications of the theoretical framework and explaining how the contextual factors affect court-curbing mechanisms.

COURT-CURBING MECHANISMS: LITERATURE REVIEW

In this study, court-curbing is taken as a comprehensive concept that refers to various attempts by the ruling government that aim to curtail the judiciary's power and independence.

Court-curbing can be done through formal and informal means. Formal legal means mostly refer to constitutional reforms or legislation that arranges the higher court judges' appointment and removal procedures, their tenure, salaries, and review power. Regulating judges' rights and duties and specifying the institutional structure in the written constitution are accepted by many scholars as some of the essential protections for judicial independence. These institutional regulations include the specification of the judges' appointment and removal procedures and their tenure and salaries (Feld & Voigt 2003; Ríos-Figueroa 2011; Melton & Ginsburg 2014). If these aspects are regulated in the constitution, any intervention will necessitate a constitutional amendment.

Through constitutional amendments or legislation, an incumbent government can change the appointment and removal procedures of constitutional court judges (Pozas-Loyo & Ríos-Figueroa 2011; Perez-Linan & Castagnola 2016; Brinks & Blass 2013). Suppose that the executive becomes more involved in the appointment and removal of constitutional court judges. In that case, the executive will appoint likeminded judges and remove judges with different political preferences (Ríos-Figueroa 2011). Increasing the number of sitting judges in the constitutional court can be used as another mechanism to create a subservient judiciary. Increasing the number of judges allows politicians to pack the court with friendly judges instead of removing unfriendly ones (Perez-Linan & Castagnola 2016).

The tenure of constitutional court judges is another critical element of judicial independence, and most of the time, it is specified in the constitution. Trying to create a subservient judiciary, the incumbent government may try to reduce the term limit of constitutional court judges and make it renewable so that judges will make decisions in line with the preferences of whoever controls their reappointment (Brinks & Blass 2013). Another mechanism through which an incumbent government can create a weak and dependent judiciary is by weakening the constitutional court's judicial review power's extent and nature. For instance, requiring a supermajority for unconstitutionality might undermine the court's authority (Ríos-Figueroa 2011). On the other hand, limiting the types of cases that the constitutional court can review might be represented as another limitation on its constitutional review power.

Through legal reforms, ruling governments can also restructure the judicial council, which is responsible for appointments, transfers, promotions, and disciplinary proceedings of judges. The government can pack the legal system with partisan judges and prosecutors. Partisan prosecutors can initiate legal cases against any citizen, political party member, media outlet, or institution that criticizes and opposes the incumbent government's policies. And partisan judges can punish the accused suspects. Silencing the opposition and suppressing any potential threat by the judiciary help populist governments shore up public support.

Authoritarian rulers may also use coercion (Gandhi & Przeworski 2006). There are many examples of leaders trying to curtail the judiciary's power via direct attacks. Removing or threatening to remove judges from office, imprisoning some of them based on false charges, forcing judges to resign, claiming that judicial decisions are politically motivated, or accusing judges of being corrupt, biased, or criminals are some of these mechanisms. For instance, under the rule of Evo Morales, between 2017 and 2019, Bolivia's Magistrates Council dismissed almost 100 judges without informing them about the cause of their dismissal (Human Rights Watch 2019). Similarly, to restructure the court that Carlos Menem packed, President Nestor Kirschner in Argentina initiated an impeachment process for the President of the Supreme Court. Yet the impeachment process acted as an implicit threat, and the President of the court, with three more justices, resigned rather than face an impeachment process in 2004 (Merco Press 2004).

As a result, there are various mechanisms through which ruling governments curtail the judiciary's power. But when do elected authoritarian leaders choose to use formal legal reforms, and when do they prefer to use coercion mechanisms to curtail the judiciary's power? Before finding an answer to this question, it is essential to understand why leaders decide to use court-curbing mechanisms in the first place. Many studies provide systematic explanations of why and under which conditions incumbent governments choose to empower the judiciary. However, since it has been assumed that a weak and dependent judiciary is common characteristic of authoritarian regimes, providing a theoretical explanation for the erosion of judicial power did not get much scholarly attention until very recently (e.g., Helmke 2017).

In the judicial politics literature, critical explanations for the relationship between the judiciary and executive are provided by separation-of-powers models and the insurance theory. Separation-of-powers models suggest that the concentration of political power across the branches of government forces judges to behave strategically to avoid having their decisions overturned or to prevent political sanctions. In line with this logic, some scholars designate political fragmentation as a proxy for political competition and assert that the judiciary is more independent when political power is highly fragmented (Chavez 2004; Harvey & Friedman 2006; Ríos-Figueroa 2007; Iaryczower, Spiller & Tommasi 2002). On the other hand, the insurance theory claims that politicians offer independent courts when political competition is intense, and incumbents' expectation of winning future elections is low. This theoretical explanation asserts that an incumbent government that anticipates losing power soon will empower the judiciary to protect its rights and policies once it falls into minority status (Ramseyer 1994; Ginsburg 2003; Finkel 2008; Landes & Posner 1975). Although these two strands of research have successfully explained the establishment and maintenance of judicial independence in advanced democracies, they cannot explain judicial independence's erosion by elected authoritarian leaders.

Although both approaches provide different mechanisms, it would not be wrong to state that separation-of-powers models and the insurance theory suggest that weak governments empower the judiciary. Yet some scholars argue that this might be valid only in the context of advanced democracies and assert that in the context of hybrid and authoritarian regimes, as the executive starts to think that it may lose power, it will try to curtail judicial independence (Popova 2010; Aydin 2013). Similarly, Helmke (2017) argues that presidents try to erode the judiciary's power when they expect to be attacked. Referring to this as offensive strike logic, she asserts that the rulers try to curtail the judiciary's power if they believe that an independent judiciary can cause them harm. When we look at the democratic backsliding literature, we also see that stability of democracy is explained by the "security" argument. O'Donnell and Schmitter (1986) argue that for the endurance of democracy, the incumbent elites must feel secure. Similarly, Levitsky and Ziblatt (2018) assert that only when politicians believe that they will win again and think that being defeated in the election will not bring tragic consequences will they keep democracy alive.

When we look at the judicial politics literature, we see that a few studies explain the conditions under which rulers are more prone to curtail judicial independence. For instance, Helmke (2010) argues that a lack of public support for institutions and concentration of power in the presidency trigger institutional instability. In other words, the government curtails judicial independence when the ruling government is centralized and when the judiciary has low public support (Helmke & Rosenbluth 2009). Regarding the impact of political fragmentation on the government's attacks on the judiciary, the argument is that the opposition's incentives to attack the presidency would increase under the rule of strong presidents. In turn, to prevent these attacks, the president's incentives to control the judiciary would increase (Helmke 2010). Regarding the public support for the judiciary, the argument is that if judges lacked public support, attacking the judiciary would have lower costs for the rulers (Helmke 2010). Vanberg (2005) and Staton (2010) also present public support as an effective enforcement mechanism. Based on this logic, one can argue that if the public has a high level of confidence in the judiciary, the government will not attack the judiciary.

As a result, some studies provide systematic explanations for the causes and conditions under which the ruling elite curtail the judiciary's power. Yet we do not have a unified theoretical explanation for the conditions under which elected leaders choose to use specific court-curbing mechanisms to suppress the judiciary. By looking for an answer to this question, the current study aims to contribute to the judicial politics literature and the democratic backsliding literature that try to explain the elected leaders' attacks on democratic institutions.

COURT-CURBING UNDER THE RULE OF THE AKP GOVERNMENT

In 2010, the AKP government adopted a series of constitutional amendments. Among the 24 articles that were amended, the most controversial ones were those that changed the composition and structure of the High Council of Judges and Prosecutors (*Hakim ve Savcılar Yüksek Kurulu*, HSYK) and the Turkish Constitutional Court (TCC). In Turkey, the HSYK is responsible for judges' and prosecutors' appointments, transfers, promotions, and disciplinary proceedings. Changing the composition of the HSYK and making its structure more pluralistic, representative, and independent from the influence of the government were among the main objectives of the constitutional reforms (Özbudun 2015). In this regard, the power of the Minister of Justice was reduced to the point of a symbolic figure; the members of the judicial council increased from seven to 22; the percentage of members elected by peer judges was increased; and the judicial council was set to have an independent budget (Özbudun 2015).

In 2010, one of the most critical amendments regarding the TCC was increasing the number of sitting judges from 11 to 17. According to the previous arrangement, the President was appointing all TCC judges. According to the new amendment, the Parliament selects three of the 17 judges from among candidates nominated by the Court of Accounts and bar association presidents (Özbudun 2011). Another amendment related to the tenure of the judges. While in the previous system, the retirement age of 65 was indicated as a term limit for the TCC judges, the 2010 amendments set the length of tenure at 12 years. Calculating the average tenure length for all judges that served between 1984 and 2010 in the TCC, a study showed that each judge served for six years and eight months on average (Aydin 2012). In this regard, the amendment appears increase the length of the tenure. Another amendment related to individual applications to the TCC. Individuals whose constitutional rights have been violated by an administrative or judicial decision can bring the case in front of the TCC. Finally, the decisional quorum in party closure cases is set top change from three-fifths to a two-thirds majority to make it harder for the TCC to close down political parties.

The 2010 constitutional amendments that restructured the TCC started certain debates. Some scholars argued that increasing the number of TCC judges would allow the AKP government to appoint judges who share similar preferences with the ruling party, eroding the court's ability and willingness to efficiently control and constrain the executive and legislation (Kalaycıoğlu 2012). On the other hand, other scholars stated that after adopting the constitutional amendments, four alternate judges who were chosen before 2010 were given permanent seats in the court. The Parliament would appoint only two judges from among the candidates nominated by the Court of Accounts. In other words, it has been argued that following the 2010 constitutional amendments, there would not be imminent court-packing by the government (Bali 2010).

During 2013 to 2016, two crucial events considerably affected the AKP's policies toward the judiciary. In December 2013, serious corruption charges against four ministers from the AKP government turned into a big corruption scandal. The AKP's government reacted to these charges by changing the law so that the police would be obliged to inform the executive in advance. The HSYK denounced the AKP's attempt as unconstitutional and argued that this would threaten any investigation's independence and secrecy. Afterward, Prime Minister Recep Tayyip Erdoğan stated that weakening the Minister of Justice's role in the council with the 2010 constitutional amendments was a big mistake. In this regard, in February 2014, the AKP government passed a bill that gave the Minister of Justice almost unlimited authority to reorganize the HSYK (Özbudun 2015).

Second, on 15 July 2016, there was a coup attempt against the AKP government. After the coup attempt, Turkish President Recep Tayyip Erdoğan and the AKP government declared a state of emergency that remained in place until July 2018. Under the state of emergency, Erdoğan passed a decree law that allowed the TCC to dismiss its members with a supposed link to the Gülen movement.[1] As such, two TCC judges were dismissed (Olcay 2017). Starting with the corruption charges and reaching its peak with the coup attempt, the AKP government initiated a severe purge of the judiciary, at the end of which thousands of judges and prosecutors were dismissed from the profession, reassigned, or relocated and were being accused of being followers of Gülen (*Financial Times* 2017).

Under the state of emergency, we witnessed the adoption of the 2017 constitutional reforms and the presidential election on 24 June 2018, at the end of which Recep Tayyip Erdoğan was reelected. In 2017, the AKP had 317 out of 550 seats in Parliament. Although this number was enough to propose the constitutional amendment, it was not enough for its approval. Creating an alliance with the Nationalist Movement Party (*Milliyetçi Hareket Partisi*, MHP), the proposed constitutional amendments were accepted by 339 MPs. Recep Tayyip Erdoğan, who served as Prime Minister under the AKP government, sent the constitutional amendment package for a public referendum. It was accepted by 51.41 percent of the citizens.

With the 2017 constitutional amendments, the number of HSYK members decreased from 22 to 13. Moreover, according to the 2010 amendments, a majority of HSYK members would be chosen by peer judges (18 out of 22). While the President would have appointed four of the HSYK members, the rest would have been appointed by the Parliament. As a result, with the 2017 reforms, all HSYK members would be chosen by political actors (Emrah-Öder 2017).

1 The Gülen movement, led by Islamic cleric Fethullah Gülen since the 1980s, has infiltrated the whole political system and had many followers in the military, police, intelligence, and judiciary (Başaran 2016).

In the new presidential system that was formulated with the 2017 constitution, the presidential and parliamentary elections would be held on the same day. So in this new system, the President's political party would most probably take the majority of seats in the Parliament. As such, the ruling party would appoint all members of the HSYK. This judicial reform presents a significant obstacle to the judges' independence and impartiality that this committee would select. The amendment that regulates the council's structure also states that the council's decisions cannot be appealed, apart from decisions on dismissal from the profession. This provision profoundly endangers the principle of rule of law, judicial independence, and impartiality. Due to this constitutional amendment, it is predicted that the council will have an ideological and political composition (Emrah-Öder 2017).

With the 2017 constitutional amendment, the membership of two military court judges was abolished so that the number of constitutional court judges decreased from 17 to 15. The appointment procedure for judges did not change. While the President would appoint 12 judges, three of them would be appointed by the Parliament. As a result, the President would select the majority of the top-ranking members of the judiciary (Ekim & Kirişçi 2017). If the President's party had the majority of seats in the Parliament, this would significantly erode judicial independence and put the judiciary under the President's influence.

A STRATEGIC MODEL OF COURT-CURBING: THEORETICAL FRAMEWORK

Focusing on the court-curbing mechanisms used by the AKP government, this chapter aims to provide a theoretical framework that can explain the conditions under which elected authoritarian leaders choose to use formal legal reforms or coercion as court-curbing mechanisms. Assuming that elected authoritarian leaders are rational actors, I argue that they would make cost–benefit calculations and decide to curtail the judiciary's power by using the mechanisms that would have higher benefits and lower costs. Asserting that each type of mechanism would have different costs and benefits, I suggest that the political and social conditions under which these mechanisms are applied would affect their costs and benefits. For this reason, to develop a theoretical framework to understand the use of different types of court-curbing tools, it is essential to present the costs and benefits of each court-curbing mechanism and the contextual framework that shapes them.

The Benefits

By restructuring the judiciary, the ultimate aim of elected authoritarian leaders is to create a subservient judiciary. A judiciary that is under the control of the ruling government can provide various benefits to it. First, by closing down the opposition parties, imprisoning their leaders, or cutting the party's budget, a constitutional court that is highly dependent on the incumbent party can weaken the political opposition and help the incumbent government to remain in office (Popova 2010; Aydin 2013). Especially in countries such as Turkey, where the level of trust between the political parties is relatively low, and politicians perceive politics in zero-sum terms (Kalaycıoğlu 1990), a subservient judiciary may empower the ruling party and secure its place. Additionally, a dependent judiciary will abstain from annulling the laws promulgated by the incumbent government. In this way, the incumbent government would secure its reelection by changing any law (i.e., election law) to serve this purpose.

Second, if there is an antagonistic relationship between the judiciary and the ruling party, fear of retribution might push the incumbent party to curtail the judiciary's power. When we look at the Turkish case, it becomes evident that the relationship between the TCC and the AKP is not based on trust or friendship. The TCC has closed many political parties, including pro-Islamist parties such as the National Salvation Party (*Milli Nizam Partisi*, 1971), the Welfare Party (*Refah Partisi*, 1998), and the Virtue Party (*Fazilet Partisi*, 2001) on the grounds that their actions were against the secular principles of the Turkish Republic. The AKP was formulated as a split from the Islamist movement that supported Islamic values in public and political life. As a result, there was an organic tension between the AKP and the TCC from the very beginning.

The first concrete challenge directed by the TCC against the AKP government was in 2007 when the AKP's presidential candidate, Abdullah Gül, had been opposed and brought in front of the TCC by the main opposition party. The TCC declared the first round of the 2007 presidential elections null and void (Tezcur 2009). After the TCC approved the appeal, the AKP proposed a constitutional amendment for the President's direct election by the citizens instead of the Parliament and won the constitutional referendum in 2007 (Kalaycıoğlu 2012). Subsequently, the AKP proposed a constitutional amendment on lifting the ban on wearing a headscarf in public places and was supported by four-fifths of the Parliament. To annul the bill, the main opposition party – the CHP – went to the TCC (*Hürriyet Daily News*, 2012). Based on anti-secularist allegations, the Chief Public Prosecutor of the Court of Appeals (*Yargıtay*) applied to the TCC to close the AKP. In 2008 the TCC decided that lifting the headscarf ban was against the constitution and violated secularism. Although most of the court members voted to ban the AKP, the "qualified majority" (seven out of 11 judges) necessary for a party closure could not be reached. Declaring that the AKP was involved in anti-secular activities, the TCC cut the public funding of the AKP by half (Tezcur 2009). As a result, the challenge directed by the TCC toward the AKP was one of the most important motivations behind the AKP's desire to restructure the judiciary and propose the 2010 constitutional amendments.

Third, a subservient judiciary would help the government secure its power, especially if an imminent threat against its survival emerged. This threat might appear in different forms. In 2013 and 2016, two critical events showed that the AKP government's rule was not secure. First, in December 2013, serious corruption charges connected with the AKP government erupted. Then-Prime Minister Erdoğan defined the whole investigation as a coup attempt organized by the Gülen movement that targeted his government (Oruçoğlu 2015). After 2015 the AKP government declared this movement as a terrorist group and named it FETO (Fethullah Terrorist Organization). Second, on 15 July 2016, there was a coup attempt against the AKP government. After the coup attempt, the AKP government declared a state of emergency. After these incidences, more than 3,000 prosecutors, and judges were arbitrarily dismissed and accused of being FETO members. Two Constitutional Court judges, 109 members of the Court of Cassation, 41 members of the Council of State and five members of the HSYK, and a total of more than 2,000 judges and prosecutors, were detained (International Commission of Jurists, 2016).

The Costs

Although restructuring the judiciary to create a dependent judiciary might give the incumbent government considerable benefits, it would not be without its costs. This chapter asserts that different court-curbing mechanisms would have different levels of cost for the ruling government.

To put it more precisely, I argue that for the ruling government, the costs of court-curbing via legal reforms would be lower compared with the costs of court-curbing via coercion mechanisms.

One should note that legal reforms are not easy procedures. For instance, a constitutional amendment should be approved by the legislature and ratified by the President or the public via referendum. For this reason, a ruling government will try to adopt constitutional reform only if it thinks that there is a chance to pass it from the Parliament. If the number of veto players and their ideological distance from one another increase, the ruling government's ability to change significant laws will decrease (Tsebelis 1999). For this reason, if there is a single-party government that holds the majority of seats in the Parliament, there will be no veto player that can create setbacks in the proposal or approval stages of the process. Under these conditions, the incumbent government will be more willing to restructure the judiciary through legislation or constitutional amendment. However, if there is a coalition government or a high level of fragmentation in the legislature, the ruling party will probably abstain from proposing a constitutional amendment due to the high number of veto players.

After the legislature approves a constitutional amendment bill, it has to be ratified by the President or public referendums. In that case, the President and the electorate appear as important veto players. Suppose that the President is from the same political party that holds the majority of seats in the Parliament. In that case, the public remains the only veto player in the ratification stage. For this reason, the incumbent government would have to consider the preferences of the people before proposing constitutional reform. Another potential backlash may come from the military. Especially in countries with a history of military coups, the military might appear as a powerful institution that can constrain the incumbent government. If the military has a vital role in politics in these political regimes, the incumbent will fear that the army might retaliate or replace it via a military coup. Due to this fear, the incumbent government may not attempt to change the constitution.

In the Turkish case, the military is the most critical institution that could have strongly reacted against the AKP's court-curbing mechanisms. Before 2002, the military was one of the strongest allies of the TCC. Bringing society "to the level of contemporary civilization" and protecting secularism were the common objectives of both institutions. The TCC functioned as an administrative agent of the military in this regard (Shambayati & Kirdiş 2009). However, during its rule, the AKP reduced the military's political influence through various mechanisms. For instance, the AKP changed the structure and power of the National Security Council and delegitimized the military's interventions in politics. More importantly, with the Ergenekon and Balyoz cases, the AKP government criminalized any attempt to intervene in politics, and many military officials were imprisoned (Esen & Gümüşçü 2016). The erosion of the military's power left the judiciary vulnerable to any political intervention.

When the military is not a potential threat to the ruling government, the significant cost that an elected government can face for court-curbing is public backlash. Restructuring the judiciary by changing the constitution that the public has ratified in the national referendum would legitimize the incumbent government's intervention in the judiciary. As such, the potential of public backlash against legal reforms would be lower than the possibility of public backlash against court-curbing via coercion mechanisms. The public backlash may reveal itself in different forms, ranging from elections to street protests and demonstrations. Yet one should note that two conditions should exist for citizens to hold the government accountable for its actions against the judiciary. Citizens should be both capable of punishing and willing to punish the government for its wrongdoings.

For citizens to be capable of punishing the ruling government for court-curbing activities, they have to be informed about its wrongdoings and discern the executive's attempts to interfere in the judiciary. With the power to increase public awareness, media mitigates the government's attacks against the judiciary. If the media is not independent, the public will not be aware of the judicial reforms or their results. When we look at the Turkish case, we see that the AKP government has managed to control the mainstream media. This aspect has eroded media independence and created a bias in the news. Analyzing the change in Turkey's Media Bias Index of V-Dem across years, we see that in 2002 Turkey's Media Bias Index was 3.29, whereas in 2017 it had declined to 1.63. The index measures the media bias against opposition parties and ranges between 0 and 4, with increasing numbers referring to less bias. The change in this index shows the extent to which media independence decreased during the AKP period.

To hold the incumbent government accountable for intervening in the judiciary, the public should first have strong democratic values and give importance to the rule of law and judicial independence. However, when we look at the Turkish case, it is seen that Turkish citizens hold materialistic values and give priority to issues such as security and economic well-being rather than the protection of civil rights, equality, and justice. The World Values Survey (2005–2009), for instance, shows that while in advanced democracies such as Norway and Sweden, only 10 percent of respondents see the prospering of the economy as an essential characteristic of democracy, in Turkey 47 percent of respondents see it as a necessary characteristic of democracy.

Second, high political participation and interest in politics indicate a higher engagement with the political system, a better understanding of political processes, and higher motivation and ability to evaluate the system. However, if the majority of citizens abstain from engaging in unconventional political behavior or criticizing the powerholders' policies, public reaction does not appear as a credible accountability mechanism. When we look at the Turkish case, we see that compared with advanced democracies, Turkish citizens' tendency to participate in lawful protests or demonstrations is relatively low. The World Values Survey (2005–2009) data shows that while the percentages of Turkish respondents who said they would never join a boycott, attend peaceful demonstrations, or sign a petition were 63.9, 62.4, and 52 percent, respectively, the percentages of Swedish respondents were 22, 21, and 5 percent, respectively.

Third, when the incumbent government uses clientelistic strategies to gain individuals' political support, public backlash would not appear as a credible threat. In Turkey, the incumbent governments have been quite effective at taking public support through clientelistic means that include the distribution of individual and collective goods (Sayarı 2011). After the AKP came to power, it allocated favors and goods to AKP supporters. AKP supporters knew that if the AKP government lost power, they would also lose the benefits provided by the AKP (Esen & Gümüşçü 2020). A recent study empirically showed that taking social assistance benefits had a positive impact on Turkish citizens' support for the transition to presidentialism (Özel & Yıldırım 2019). The AKP government could gain votes even from opposition voters in return for benefits. Thus, it would not be wrong to argue that the beneficiaries of social assistance or recipients of individual favors would tolerate the AKP government's anti-democratic policy.

Fourth, the political opposition is quite fragmented in Turkey and does not present a potential alternative to voters. There are three main opposition parties whose coalition is difficult to imagine. One of the key opposition parties is the Republican People's Party (*Cumhuriyet Halk Partisi*, CHP), which represents secularism and opposes Turkey's Islamist political and social forces (Sayarı 2016). The second opposition party is the MHP, which represents Turkish nationalism and strongly opposes Kurdish nationalism. Yet the MHP supported the AKP government in the 2017 referendum[2] and formed the People's Alliance with the AKP government for the 2018 general elections. On the eve of these developments, the internal fragmentation within the MHP became more visible, and in 2017 a new party named the Good Party (*İyi Parti*, İP) was founded as a new opposition party. Turkey's third main opposition party is the People's Democratic Party (*Halkların Demokrasi Partisi*), which resembles the Turkish and Kurdish ethnic cleavage and represents the Kurdish national movement. As a result, the deep fragmentation among the opposition parties does not provide an alternative to the ruling government, decreasing the potential of public backlash against the government's misconduct.

Fifth, in general, restructuring the judiciary and changing the judicial appointment and removal procedures is not an issue that average citizens easily understand. Moreover, some empirical studies have found that partisanship is a powerful factor that prevents citizens from punishing the incumbent government for violating institutional integrity (Mummolo, Peterson & Westwood 2018). Similarly, Clark and Kastellec (2015) suggest that the public is willing to accept some attacks on courts when they approve of the attacker (Clark & Kastellec 2015). In light of these empirical studies, one can suggest that under the rule of a single-party government that holds the majority of the electorate's support, the probability of a massive public backlash against the ruling government for restructuring the judiciary would be relatively low. Going one step further, Svolik (2020) argues that in polarized societies, since the supporters of the incumbent party would hate the challengers, they would not punish the ruling government by voting for a challenger. As a result, political polarization provides the ruling government an opportunity to attack the judiciary and escape any public punishment.

The final and most important condition that would increase the potential for public backlash is high public support for the judiciary. Many scholars have presented public support as an effective enforcement mechanism (Vanberg 2005; Staton 2010; Helmke 2010). The argument is that if judges lack public support, attacking the judiciary would have lower costs for the rulers (Helmke 2010). Based on this logic, one can argue that if the public has a high level of confidence in the judiciary, the government will not attack the judiciary. The World Values Survey data shows that Turkish citizens' confidence in the judiciary is much higher than their confidence in the government and the Parliament. While in 2007, Turkish citizens' confidence in government and Parliament was 1.73[3] and 1.65, respectively, their confidence in the judiciary was 2.02. Although in 2011 public confidence in the judiciary decreased to 1.85, it was still higher than the public confidence in the government and Parliament (Ecevit 2016). As a result, the Turkish case shows us that high levels of public support for the judiciary did not

---

2 With this referendum, the amendment of the 18 articles of the Turkish constitution was ratified. One of the most important aspects of this referendum was adopting the presidential system in Turkey.

3 The data range between 0 (no trust) and 3 (high trust).

prevent the ruling government from curtailing judicial independence. Yet it did affect the types of mechanisms used by the government to suppress the judiciary.

It is possible to claim that the AKP government preferred to restructure the judiciary via constitutional amendments in the first half of its 20-year rule. Using formal legal means increased the legitimacy of the government's policies in the eyes of the people. Yet after the corruption scandal in 2013 and the coup attempt in 2016, the AKP government started to restructure the judiciary via removals, relocations, and imprisonment of judges. By accusing these judges and prosecutors of being FETO terrorist group members, the AKP tried to legitimize its attacks. Going one step further, by declaring a state of emergency between 2016 and 2018, the AKP tried to provide a legal framework for these coercion mechanisms. As Yılmaz (2020) argues, this is an example of strategic legalism that allowed the consolidation of presidential power and the demobilization and suppression of the opposition. As a result, I argue that the mass purges of thousands of judges under the state of emergency rule cannot be presented as an example of a formal legal court-curbing mechanism. They are rather an example of a coercion mechanism legitimized and legalized by declaring a state of emergency.

DISCUSSION AND CONCLUSION

We have witnessed the frequent use of formal legal reforms as a court-curbing mechanism in the past decade. By changing the appointment and removal procedures of high court judges or changing their tenure, elected authoritarian leaders packed the courts with partisan judges. These legal reforms weakened the judicial power to control and constrain the government by eroding judges' impartiality. Yet since the Parliament approves the legislation and public referendums ratify the constitutional amendments, the legal reforms are legitimate. As a result, restructuring the judiciary or curtailing its power via formal legal means would lower the ruling government's costs. As such, the ruling governments that hold the majority in the Parliament will prefer to use these court-curbing mechanisms.

Although using formal legal reforms for court-curbing has lower costs than directly attacking the judiciary, we see that authoritarian leaders may use coercion against the judiciary under certain conditions. In the literature, there are various explanations about how and why elected leaders abuse constitutions to curtail the power of democratic institutions or attack the judiciary. However, we do not know much about the contextual factors that affect leaders' decision to use different court-curbing mechanisms. This chapter aims to provide a theoretical framework to explain the political and social conditions under which elected authoritarian leaders use constitutional reforms and under which conditions they use coercion mechanisms against the judiciary. This chapter argues that elected authoritarian leaders are rational actors and that they choose the court-curbing mechanisms that pertain to lower costs and higher benefits. Asserting that each type of court-curbing mechanism will have different costs and benefits, I suggest that the political and social conditions under which these mechanisms are applied will affect their costs and benefits. Thus, the theoretical framework proposed in this study develops the potential costs and benefits of each court-curbing mechanism and the contextual framework that shapes it. Using Turkey as a case study, the court-curbing mechanisms used by the AKP and the contextual framework under which these mechanisms were used are critically analyzed.

The Turkish case analysis shows that whether the ruling government uses constitutional reforms or direct coercion mechanisms for court-curbing, the benefit for the ruling party is the same: the establishment of a subservient judiciary. Yet the time required to establish a subservient judiciary will differ across different court-curbing mechanisms. Constitutional amendments or the adoption of new constitutions might take months, if not years. After adopting constitutional amendments or issuing legislation, observing the change in the structure of the judiciary or its decisions would take a specific period. However, coercion mechanisms can be used directly and reveal their results in a short period. For instance, trying to empirically show the impact of the 2010 judicial reforms on the TCC decisions, Varol et al. (2017) could not find a significant effect of the 2010 reforms on pro-government decisions, and argued that it might be too soon to detect a substantial change in judicial behavior. Although the 2010 constitutional reforms increased the TCC judges' number from 11 to 17, the AKP government did not immediately fill the new seats. Four out of the six new places were filled by appointing the previous substitute judges as permanent members. On the other hand, with the severe judicial purges in Turkey, we have seen an immediate change in the judiciary's structure and behavior. For this reason, I argue that when there is an imminent threat against the incumbent's survival, the ruling government will prefer to use a coercion mechanism to establish a subservient judiciary.

Despite an imminent threat, as a rational actor, the ruling government will only attack the judiciary when the potential of public backlash is low. First, this study asserts that the possibility of public backlash for attacking the judiciary will be low if most citizens cannot hold the government accountable. Citizens' ability to punish the government for its court-curbing activities depends on public awareness and transparency. Leaders will try to manipulate citizens by using different mechanisms to shape public opinion. To prevent any public backlash, the government will legitimize their court-curbing practices. In this regard, leaders will prefer to blame the judiciary for being inefficient, corrupt, or politicized, and will allege that it needs to be restructured. As we have seen in the Turkish case, after the corruption allegations against the AKP government, President Erdoğan urged a reformation in the judicial system, claiming that a terrorist group had infiltrated the legal system. Based on these claims, thousands of judges were purged (AA News Agency 2017). To shape public opinion, authoritarian leaders will also try to control the media. By establishing partisan media outlets, authoritarian leaders will justify their use of coercion against judges by accusing judges of being terrorists, corrupt, or biased. As Norris and Inglehart (2020) argue, decreasing individuals' trust toward democratic institutions by triggering feelings such as anxiety and fear is one of the most important mechanisms used by populist leaders.

In addition to preventing public awareness, coercion against any opposition curtails public capability to hold the government accountable. As Lührmann and Rooney (2021) argue, a state of emergency provides leaders with an opportunity to weaken all democratic institutions and suppress the opposition and any other constraints. For this reason, declaring a state of emergency and extensive use of coercion mechanisms against any opposition are deployed by authoritarian leaders to prevent any potential public backlash. Accordingly, the Turkish case shows that the incumbent government will try to legitimize its attacks and establish a legal basis by various means.

Second, this study asserts that the potential of public backlash for attacking the judiciary will be low if the majority of citizens are not willing to punish the government. Suppose most citizens do not have liberal democratic values, abstain from engaging in unconventional political behavior, or criticize the powerholders' policies. In that case, public reaction does not appear as a credible accountability mechanism. If the incumbent government uses clientelistic strategies to gain individuals' political support, public backlash will not appear as a credible threat either. Moreover, if there is deep political polarization, the incumbent party's supporters will hate the challengers and not punish the ruling government by voting for a challenger. This condition will also decrease the potential for public backlash against the government's anti-democratic policies.

REFERENCES

AA News Agency. (2017, 18 January) "President Erdogan urges reformed judicial system" Available at: https://www.aa.com.tr/en/politics/president-erdogan-urges-reformed-judicial-system/730087

Aydin, A. (2012) *Strategic Interaction Between Constitutional Courts and Political Actors in Developing Democracies*. Unpublished Ph.D. Dissertation, Sabanci University.

Aydin, A. (2013) "Judicial Independence across Democratic Regimes: Understanding the Varying Impact of Political Competition" *Law & Society Review* 47(1),105–134.

Bali, A. (2010) "Turkey's Referendum: Creating constitutional Checks and Balances" *Foreign Policy* Available at: https://foreignpolicy.com/2010/09/15/turkeys-referendum-creating-constitutional-checks-and-balances

Başaran, E. (2016). "Turkey coup: Who was behind Turkey coup attempt?" *BBC News* (16 July) Available at: https://www.bbc.com/news/world-europe-36815476

Bermeo, N. (2016) "On Democratic Backsliding" *Journal of Democracy* 27(1), 5–19.

Bodnar, E., Gárdos-Orosz, F., and Pozsár-Szentmiklósy, Z. (2017) "Developments in Hungarian Constitutional Law: The Year 2016 in Review" *I-Connect Blog*. Available at: http://www.iconnectblog.com/2017/12/developments-in-hungarian-constitutional-law-the-year-2016-in-review/

Brinks, D. and A. Blass (2013) "Potemkin Courts" Paper Presented at the "Ruling Politics" Conference, University of Chicago, May 3–4.

Chavez, R. (2004). *The Rule of Law in Nascent Democracies: Judicial Politics in Argentina.* Stanford, CA: Stanford University Press.

Clark, T. (2009). "The Separation of Powers, Court Curbing and Judicial Legitimacy" *American Journal of Political Science* 53(4), 971–989.

Clark, T. S. and Kastellec, J. P. (2015) "Source Cues and Public Support for the Supreme Court" *American Politics Research* 43(3), 504–535.

Corrales, J. (2018). *Fixing Democracy: How Power Asymmetries Help Explain Presidential Powers in New Constitutions, Evidence from Latin America.* New York: Oxford University Press.

Ecevit, Y. A. (2016) "Turkey's Judicial Reforms and the Evolution of Public Confidence in the Legal System." In Cengiz Erisen and Paul Kubicek (eds.) *Democratic Consolidation in Turkey: Macro and Micro Challenges,* pp. 65–89 London: Routledge.

Ekim, S. and K. Kirişçi (2017) "The Turkish Constitutional Referendum Explained." Available at: https://www.brookings.edu/blog/order-from-chaos/2017/04/13/the-turkish-constitutional-referendum-explained/

Emrah-Öder, B. (2017) "Turkey's Ultimate Shift to a Presidential System: The Most Recent Constitutional Amendments in Details" *ConstitutionNet*, Available at: http://constitutionnet.org/news/turkeys-ultimate-shift-presidential-system-most-recent-constitutional-amendments-details

Esen, B. and S. Gümüşçü (2016) "Rising Competitive Authoritarianism in Turkey" *Third World Quarterly* 37(9), 1581–1606.

Esen, B. and S. Gümüşçü (2020) "Why Did Turkish Democracy Collapse? A Political Economy Account of AKP's Authoritarianism" *Party Politics* 27, 1075–1091.

Feld, L. P. and S. Voigt (2003) "Economic Growth and Judicial Independence: Cross Country Evidence Using a New Set of Indicators" *European Journal of Political Economy* 19(3), 497–527.

Financial Times (2017) "Turkey Says Purge of jJudiciary Over After Sacking 4000," 26 May. Available at: https://www.ft.com/content/0af6ebc0-421d-11e7-82b6-896b95f30f58

Finkel, J. (2008) *Judicial Reform as Political Insurance: Argentina, Peru, and Mexico in the 1990s*. Notre Dame, IN: University of Notre Dame Press.
Freedom House Report "Freedom in the World 2019: Democracy in Retreat" *Freedom House Report*. Available at: https://freedomhouse.org/report/freedom-world/2019/democracy-retreat
Gandhi, J. and A. Przeworski (2006) "Cooperation, Cooptation and Rebellion Under Dictatorship" *Economics & Politics* 18(1), 1–26.
Ginsburg, T. (2003) *Judicial Review in New Democracies: Constitutional Courts in Asian Cases*. New York: Cambridge University Press.
Ginsburg, T. and T. Moustafa (2008) *Rule by Law: The Politics of Courts in Authoritarian Regimes*. New York: Cambridge University Press.
Haggard, S. and R. Kaufman (2021) *Backsliding: Democratic Regress in the Contemporary World*, New York: Cambridge University Press.
Harvey, A. and B. Friedman (2006) "The Limits of Judicial Independence: Congressional Constraints on the Supreme Court's Constitutional Rulings, 1987–2000" *Legislative Studies Quarterly* 31(4), 533–562.
Helmke, G. (2010) "The Origins of Institutional Crises in Latin America" *American Journal of Political Science* 54(3), 737–750.
Helmke, G. (2017) *Institutions on the Edge: The Origins and Consequences of Inter-Branch Crises in Latin America*. New York: Cambridge University Press.
Helmke, G. and F. Rosenbluth (2009) "Regimes and the Rule of Law: Judicial Independence in Comparative Perspective" *Annual Review of Political Science* 12, 345–366.
Human Rights Watch (2019) "Bolivia: Dozens of Judges Dismissed" *Bolivia Report*. Available at: https://www.hrw.org/news/2019/04/29/bolivia-dozens-judges-arbitrarily-dismissed
Hürriyet Daily News (2012, 29 November). "Turkish Top Court Annuls Headscarf Law." Available at: http://www.hurriyet.com.tr/english/turkey/9107525.asp?gid=231&sz=39508
Iaryczower, M., P. T. Spiller and M. Tommasi (2002) "Judicial Independence in Unstable Environments: Argentina 1935–1998" *American Journal of Political Science* 46(4), 699–716.
International Commission of Jurists (2016) "Turkey: Emergency Measures Have Greatly Damaged the Rule of Law." Available at: https://www.icj.org/turkey-emergency-measures-have-gravely-damaged-the-rule-of-law/
Işıksel, T. (2013) "Between Text and Context: Turkey's Tradition of Authoritarian Constitutionalism" *International Journal of Constitutional Law* 11(3), 702–726.
Kalaycıoğlu, E. (1990) "Cyclical Breakdown, Redesign and Nascent Institutionalization: The Turkish Grand National Assembly." In Liebert, U. and M. Cotta (eds.) *Parliament and Democratic Consolidation in Southern Europe: Greece, Italy, Portugal, Spain and Turkey*. London and New York: Pinter, pp. 184–222.
Kalaycıoğlu, E. (2012) "Kulturkampf in Turkey: The Constitutional Referendum of 12 September 2010" *South European Society and Politics* 17(1), 1–22.
Landau, D. (2013) "Abusive Constitutionalism" *UC Davis Law Review* 47, 189–260. Available at: https://lawreview.law.ucdavis.edu/issues/47/1/articles/47-1_Landau.pdf
Landau, D. and R. Dixon (2020) "Abusive Judicial Review: Courts Against Democracy" *UC Davis Law Review* 53, 1315–1383. Available at: https://lawreview.law.ucdavis.edu/issues/53/3/53-3_Landau_Dixon.pdf
Landes, W. M. and R. A. Posner (1975) "The Independent Judiciary in an Interest-Group Perspective" *Journal of Law and Economics* 18, 875–901.
Levitsky, S. and D. Ziblatt (2018) *How Democracies Die*. New York: Crown.
Lührmann, A. and B. Rooney (2021) "Autocratization by Decree: States of Emergency and Democratic Decline" *Comparative Politics*, https://doi.org/10.5129/001041521X16004520146485
Mechkova, V., A. Lührmann, and S. I. Lindberg (2017) "How Much Democratic Backsliding?" *Journal of Democracy* 28(4), 162–169.
Melton, J. and T. Ginsburg (2014) "Does De Jure Judicial Independence Really Matter?: A Reevaluation of Explanations for Judicial Independence" *Journal of Law and Courts* 2(2), 187–217.
Merco Press. (2004, 2 September) "Supreme Court Justice Resigns in Argentina." Available at: https://en.mercopress.com/2004/09/02/supreme-court-justice-resigns-in-argentina

Mummolo, J., E. Peterson and S. Westwood (2018) "Conditional Party Loyalty." Working Paper. Available at: https://tinyurl.com/y75ysn74

Norris, P. and R. Inglehart (2020) *Cultural Backlash: Trump, Brexit and Authoritarian Populists.* New York: Cambridge University Press.

O'Donnell, G. A. and P. C. Schmitter (1986) *Transitions from Authoritarian Rule. Tentative Conclusions about Uncertain Democracies,* Baltimore, MD: Johns Hopkins University Press.

Olcay, T. (2017) "Firing Bench-Mates: The Human Rights and Rule of Law Implications of the Turkish Constitutional Court's Dismissal of Its Two Members. Case Note." *European Constitutional Law Review* 13(3), 568–581.

Oruçoğlu, B. (2015) "Turkey's political elite is sweeping it all under the rug" *Foreign Policy*. Available at: https://foreignpolicy.com/2015/01/06/why-turkeys-mother-of-all-corruption-scandals-refuses-to-go-away/

Özbudun, E. (2011) "Turkey's Constitutional Reform and the 2010 Constitutional Referendum" *Mediterranean Politics.* Available at: https://www.iemed.org/observatori-en/arees-danalisi/arxius-adjunts/anuari/med.2011/Ozbudun_en.pdf

Özbudun, E. (2015). "Turkey's Judiciary and the Drift Toward Competitive Authoritarianism" *The International Spectator* 50(2), 42–55.

Özel, I. D. and K. Yıldırım (2019) "Political Consequences of Welfare Regimes: Social Assistance and Support for Presidentialism in Turkey" *South European Society and Politics* 24(49), 485–511.

Perez-Linan, A. and A. Castagnola (2016) "Judicial Instability and Endogenous Constitutional Change: Lessons from Latin America" *British Journal of Political Science* 46(2), 395–416.

Pocza, K., G. Dobos and A. Gyulai (2019) "The Hungarian Constitutional Court: A constructive partner in constitutional dialogue." In K. Pocza (ed.) *Constitutional Politics and the Judiciary*. New York: Routledge, pp. 96–124.

Popova, M. (2010) "Political Competition as an Obstacle to Judicial Independence: Evidence from Russia and Ukraine" *Comparative Political Studies* 43(10), 1202–1229.

Pozas-Loyo, A., and J. Ríos-Figueroa (2011) "The Politics of Amendment Processes: Supreme Court Influence in the Design of Judicial Councils" *Texas Law Review* 89(7), 1807–1833.

Ramseyer, M. (1994) "The Puzzling (In)Dependence of Courts: A Comparative Approach" *The Journal of Legal Studies* 23, 721–747.

Ríos-Figueroa, J. (2007) "The Emergence of an Effective Judiciary in Mexico, 1994–2002" *Latin American Politics and Society* 49, 31–57.

Ríos-Figueroa, J. (2011) "Institutions for Constitutional Justice in Latin America." In G. Helmke and J. Ríos Figueroa (eds.) *Courts in Latin America.* Cambridge: Cambridge University Press, pp. 27–54

Sayarı, S. (2011) "Clientelism and Patronage in Turkish Politics and Society." In B. Toprak and F. Birtek (eds.) *Essays in Honor of Şerif Mardin: The Post-Modern Abyss and the New Politics of Islam: Assabiyah Revisited.* İstanbul: İstanbul Bilgi Üniversitesi Yayınları, pp. 81–94.

Sayarı, S. (2016) "Back to a Predominant Party System: The November 2015 Snap Election in Turkey" *South European Society and Politics* 21(2), 263–280.

Scheppele, K. L. (2011) "Hungary's Constitutional Revolution" *The New York Times.* Available at: https://krugman.blogs.nytimes.com/2011/12/19/hungarys-constitutional-revolution/

Scheppele, K. L. (2018) "Autocratic Legalism" *The University of Chicago Law Review* 85, 545–583. Available at: https://lawreview.uchicago.edu/sites/lawreview.uchicago.edu/files/11%20Scheppele_SYMP_Online.pdf

Shambayati, H. and E. Kirdiş (2009) "In Pursuit of 'Contemporary Civilization': Judicial empowerment in Turkey" *Political Research Quarterly* 62(4), 767–780.

Staton, J. K. (2010) *Judicial Power and Strategic Communication in Mexico.* Cambridge: Cambridge University Press.

Svolik, M. (2013) *The Politics of Authoritarian Rule.* New York: Cambridge University Press.

Svolik, M. (2020) "When Polarization Trumps Civic Virtue: Partisan Conflict and the Subversion of Democracy by Incumbents" *Quarterly Journal of Political Science* 15(1), 3–31.

Tezcur, G. M. (2009) "Judicial Activism in Perilous Times: The Turkish Case" *Law & Society Review* 43(2), 305–336.

Tsebelis, G. (1999). "Veto Players and Law Production in Parliamentary Democracies: An Empirical Analysis" *The American Political Science Review* 93(3), 591–608.

Tushnet, M. (2015) "Authoritarian Constitutionalism" *Cornell Law Review* 100(2), 391–461.
Vanberg, G. (2005) *The Politics of Constitutional Review in Germany*. Cambridge: Cambridge University Press.
Varol, O., L. D. Pellegrina and N. Garoupa (2017) "An Empirical Analysis of Judicial Transformation in Turkey" *The American Journal of Comparative Law* 65(1), 187–216.
Yılmaz, Z. (2020) "Erdoğan's Presidential Regime and Strategic Legalism: Turkish Democracy in the Twilight Zone" *Southeast European and Black Sea Studies* 20(2), 265–287.

3. Majoritarians in robes

Judicial representation and the changing nature of judicial audience in the United States

Todd Curry and Michael Romano

In June of 2020, amidst heightened racial tension after the murder of George Floyd and in the middle of a deadly, global pandemic, North Carolina's Chief Justice Cheri Beasley held a press conference. Broadcast over the Internet via social media platforms, the Chief Justice called for accountability in the wake of an explosion of protests over police brutality and racial injustice. But the speech was more than just a statement of concern or an official act of the court. Chief Justice Beasley spoke not just to concerns about the role of the judiciary in adjudicating criminal justice reform; she spoke of her own, deeper, personal concerns over the state of American politics. "I felt compelled to speak,"[1] she said in her opening remarks, highlighting the extraordinary circumstances that plagued not just North Carolina but the United States as a whole, and making claims to the power she had to usher in reform to the judicial system to make it more equitable and fairer.

> In our courts, African-Americans are more harshly treated, more severely punished and more likely to be presumed guilty… We must develop a plan for accountability in our courts. Judges work hard and are committed to serving the public. But even the best judges must be trained to recognize our own biases. We have to be experts not just in the law, but in equity, equity that recognizes the difficult truths about our shared past.[2]

Chief Justice Beasley's remarks spurred other chief justices and state high courts to issue similar statements, with a total of 24 statements made across 52 state high courts. Recognizing that the primary reason for courts to exist is to settle disputes as an unbiased arbiter, we should ask why courts and judges issue statements that recognize the judicial system has intrinsic biases that cut along racial identities. We argue that the answer is implicit in the institutional design of these state courts: They are designed to create representatives.

It has been argued, "the true test of a good government is its aptitude and tendency to produce a good administration."[3] To this end, across the various institutional structures within the United States, we operate under the belief that the entire governmental system is working for the benefit of the people it exists to serve. Ours is a representative system of government,

---

[1] Cheri Beasley, Chief Justice Beasley Addresses the Intersection of Justice and Protests around the State North Carolina Judicial Branch (2020), https://www.nccourts.gov/news/tag/press-release/chief-justice-beasley-addresses-the-intersection-of-justice-and-protests-around-the-state (last visited Sep 9, 2020).

[2] Ibid.

[3] Hamilton, A., Jay, J., Madison, J. and Kessler, C., 1999. *The Federalist Papers*. New York: Signet Classic.

where political actors should exist to serve the interests and demands of the people.[4] However, in our constellation of political institutions, the judiciary exists as one of few institutions designed to be shielded from the public. More specifically, the federal judiciary, which served as a model for most state judiciaries, specifically takes its form to subtract judges from popular pressure. The framers' argument for the inclusion of a judiciary with lengthy tenures was based on the idea that judges would be responsible for patrolling the "borders of the constitution" to ensure that the legislature and the public would remain in check.[5]

As such, the image of judges in the eye of the public conforms most often to the theory of mechanical jurisprudence, wherein judges make choices based on fact and precedent without regard for whether they should "stand for" a particular group or belief. Judges throughout their careers espouse this view as well, from initial appointment until death or personal circumstance causes them to leave the bench. Most notably, Chief Justice John Roberts, in his appointment testimony before the Senate, described the job of judging as acting as an "umpire," assessing whether the ball merely fell within the strike zone or not. For Roberts, the judge only responds to the pitch, and mechanically says ball or strike. Shockingly enough, even within the empirical study of law and courts, where theories articulating the role of ideology and strategy in judicial decision-making abound, few scholars view judges as representatives. Collins and Ringhand come closest to accepting judges as representatives, noting that nominees for the U.S. Supreme Court are only confirmed if they represent the majority's ideas of appropriate jurisprudence.[6]

The simple fact, however, is that no judge simply materializes, whole cloth, onto the bench, draped in black robes with a gavel in hand. The "judges as umpires" theory disguises the fact that judges come to the bench with past histories and life experiences which can affect the way in which they make decisions,[7] and this narrative is often used to obfuscate the concept of "fairness" and "neutrality" as being above the need for adequate representation.[8] The process of *selection* that all judges must go through to receive their commission, while varied across jurisdictions, predicates those judges must represent *something* upon ascending to the bench. Simply put, judges "stand for" something – either descriptively, symbolically, or substantively. For "constituents" of the court, substantive representation is desired of those who select them; judges are tasked with carrying out not only their own goals but the goals of those who put them in office. Coupled with the fact that most judges in the United States face some system of *retention*, and the concept of *judicial representation* gains new strength as judges are not only "authorized" to act, but must also face accountability for their actions. Scholars have devoted much effort to teasing out the specifics of just what judges stand "for," within the political world, examining concepts of symbolism as it pertains to legitimacy,[9] accounta-

---

[4] Dahl, R. A. 1956. *A Preface to Democratic Theory*. Chicago: University of Chicago Press; Pitkin, H. F. 1967. *The Concept of Representation*. Berkeley: University of California Press.

[5] Breyer, S. 2010. *Making Our Democracy Work: A Judge's View*. New York: Vintage Books.

[6] Collins, P. M., Jr. & Ringhand, L. A. 2013. *Supreme Court Confirmation Hearings and Constitutional Change*. New York: Cambridge University Press.

[7] Scherer, N., and Curry, B. 2010. Does Descriptive Race Representation Enhance Institutional Legitimacy? The Case of the US Courts. *Journal of Politics*, 72(1): 90–104.

[8] Kirkpatrick, J. 2020. Fairness has a Face: Neutrality and Descriptive Representation on Courts. *Politics, Groups, and Identities* 8(4): 803–811.

[9] Gibson, J., Lodge, M., and Woodson, B. 2014. Legitimacy, Losing, but Accepting: A Test of Positivity Theory and the Effects of Judicial Symbols. Available at SSRN: https://ssrn.com/abstract=

bility,[10] independence,[11] or engaging directly with the literature on representation by focusing on concepts of audience.[12]

Our focus here is to clearly outline how we may understand judges as representatives from a conceptual level. We emphasize the institutions of selection and retention specifically, and how they provide judges with an outlet for *audience representation* in the United States generally, rather than focusing on the often-divergent views of descriptive vs. substantive representation that often arise in the literature. While the average citizen may not conceive of judges as a defining part of democratic governance, even the late Justice Scalia argued that judges played an important role in meeting the representative promise of electoral democracies.[13] Whereas judges have the potential for passive representation across institutions,[14] judges are constrained from providing active representation depending on the level of public involvement and the availability of outlets for the public to learn about judicial decisions. Systematically, it varies whom the judges are representatives of and how representative they are of the public's will. Despite obfuscating language used when debating the role of the judiciary, we believe that judges are selected as representatives and that their actions on the bench accentuate their role as representatives of the public. Judicial representation is unique as an institution, as it is more greatly constrained by the various methods of selection and retention utilized to populate the courts, especially at the state level. This constraint, we argue, makes it more imperative to understand judicial representation as part of the communicative process of representation, the relaying of a representative's rationale for deciding to the public to form a representative link and maintain accountability, rather than simply focusing on the authorization to act.

2448710; Gibson, J., and Nelson, M. 2014. Can the US Supreme Court Have Too Much Legitimacy? In Bartels, B.J. and Bonneau, C.W. *Making Law and Court Research Relevant: Normative Implications of Empirical Research*. New York: Routledge; Mondak, J. J. 2014. Policy Legitimacy and the Supreme Court: The Sources and Context of Legitimation. *Political Research Quarterly*, 47(3): 675–692; Strothers, L., and Glennon, C. 2021. An Experimental Investigation of the Effect of Supreme Court Justices' Public Rhetoric on Perceptions of Judicial Legitimacy. *Law and Social Inquiry*, 46(2): 435–454.

10 Gibson, J. 2012. Electing Judges: Future Research and the Normative Debate about Judicial Elections. *Judicature*. 96: 223–231; Hanssen, F. A. 2004. Is There a Politically Optimal Level of Judicial Independence? *The American Economic Review* 94: 712–29.

11 Geyh, C.G. 2019. *Who Is To Judge?: Judicial Elections, Judicial Appointments, and the Perennial Debate Over Judicial Selection in America.* Oxford: Oxford University Press; Hanssen, F.A. 2004. Is There a Politically Optimal Level of Judicial Independence? *The American Economic Review* 94: 712–29.

12 Baum, L. 2008. *Judges and Their Audiences: A Perspective on Judicial Behavior*. Princeton: Princeton University Press; Romano, M. K. and Curry, T. A. (2019). *Creating the Law: State Supreme Court Opinions and The Effect of Audiences*. New York: Routledge.

13 *Republican Party of Minnesota v. White.* (2002). 536 U.S. 765.

14 Bonneau, C.W. & Rice, H.M. 2009. Impartial Judges? Race, Institutional Context, and U.S. State Supreme Courts. *State Politics and Policy Quarterly*, 9(4), 381–403.

A FRAMEWORK FOR JUDICIAL REPRESENTATION

Contemporary standards of political representation begin from the basic framework wherein the representative is examined in relation to the constituency they stand for.[15] At the most abstract level, general accounts of representation start with the question of how one actor can be authorized to perform some action in place of another, whether that be legally, politically, or symbolically. The relationship between the two parties can be complex and often convoluted, since representation can take various forms. Political representation, specifically, starts as the formalistic process in which an agent is authorized to perform some action, most often deciding on policy, in the interests of another body. This form of representation is what Mansbridge[16] refers to as "promissory," since agents are held accountable by past agreements. Once we move past this abstract level, much of the theoretical work done on the concept of political representation has attempted to show how one individual (an agent) is held accountable to a population for the decisions they make, as well as the relationship that exists between the agent and her constituents. This allows the formal, minimal model of representation to evolve into more substantive political representation; as agents act on behalf of the people they serve, in a manner ideologically and politically consistent with their constituencies.

Treatments of the concept of representation have varied since Pitkin's[17] examination, often focusing on the assessment of topics such as descriptive representation,[18] institutional justifications for different forms of representation,[19] and behavioral aspects and how representatives may work for and cultivate a link with the constituents they serve.[20] While such assessments

---

15 Mansbridge, J. 2003. Rethinking Representation. *The American Political Science Review*, 97(4), 515–28; Mansbridge, J. 2011. Clarifying the Concept of Representation. *The American Political Science Review*, 105(3), 621–630; Pitkin, H. F. 1967. *The Concept of Representation.* Berkeley: University of California Press; Rehfeld, A. 2009. Representation Rethought: On Trustees, Delegates, and Gyroscopes in the Study of Political Representation and Democracy. *American Political Science Review*, *103*(2), 214–30.

16 Mansbridge, J. 2003. Rethinking Representation. *The American Political Science Review*, *97*(4), 515–28.

17 Pitkin, H.F. 1967. *The Concept of Representation.* Berkeley: University of California Press.

18 Canon, D. T. (1999). *Race, Redistricting, and Representation: The Unintended Consequences of Black Majority Districts.* Chicago: Chicago University Press; Grose, C.R. 2011. *Congress in Black and White: Race and Representation in Washington and at Home.* New York: Cambridge University Press; Grose, C.R., Mangum, M. & Martin, C. 2007 Race, Political Empowerment, and Constituency Service: Descriptive Representation and the Hiring of African-American Congressional Staff. *Polity*, 39(9), 449–478; Sobolewska, M., McKee, R., and Campbell, R. 2018. Explaining Motivation to Represent: How Does Descriptive Representation Lead to Substantive Representation of Racial and Ethnic Minorities? *Western European Politics*, 41(6): 1237–1261; Wolak, J. 2020. Descriptive Representation and the Political Engagement of Women. *Politics and Gender*, 16(2): 339–362; Wolak, J., and Juenke, E.G. 2021. Descriptive Representation and Political Knowledge. *Politics, Groups, and Identities*, 9(1): 129–150.

19 Manin, B. 1997. *Principles of Representative Government.* New York: Cambridge University Press; Rehfeld, A. 2006. Toward a General Theory of Political Representation. *Journal of Politics*, 68(1), 1–21; Rehfeld, A. 2009. Representation Rethought: On Trustees, Delegates, and Gyroscopes in the Study of Political Representation and Democracy. *American Political Science Review*, 103(2), 214–30; Saward, M. 2010. *The Representative Claim.* New York: Oxford University Press.

20 Fenno, R. F. Jr. 1978. *Home Style: House Members and Their Districts.* New York: Longman; Grimmer, J. 2010. A Bayesian Hierarchical Topic Model for Political Texts: Measuring Expressed Agendas in Senate Press Releases. *Political Analysis*, 19(1), 32–47; Grimmer, J, Messing, S. &

vary in their focus, most have only narrowly concentrated on a relationship forged by electoral outcomes without considering "non-traditional" relationships in representation, though more recent scholarship focuses on how political appointees like judges can still meet the substantive definition of a political representative. When examining judges as representatives, scholars often take one of two frameworks that guide their studies. Those interested in the constituent connection between judges and the public tend to focus on the descriptive aspects of representation, recognizing that for some judges the lack of an electoral connection requires that judges find a different way to legitimize the branch and their work.[21] These studies tend to start from the normative foundation recognizing that diversification of the judiciary should lead to greater trust in the branch in the eyes of constituent groups, and will often point to the prolonged efforts (primarily pushed by Democratic administrations and epitomized by Presidents Carter and Clinton's argument that diversification of the federal judiciary is necessary to provide minorities with both descriptive and substantive representation on the federal bench so as to increase the legitimacy of the court in the eyes of Black citizens).[22] Such literature has not only expanded our understanding of representation generally, but has examined more explicitly how judges act as descriptive agents for representation based on gender[23] and race[24] in particular.

A secondary framework for studies of judicial representation focuses less on whether the bench "looks like" various citizen bodies, and more on how judges bring their own life experiences to the bench and make decisions in ways that will substantively improve the lives of the groups they choose to represent. From one perspective, female and minority judges serve as "high profile, substantive representatives"[25] that can work to advance in-group goals while in office through their decisions.[26] While this work has trended toward examining whether and

---

Westwood, S. 2012. How Words and Money Cultivate a Personal Vote: The Effect of Legislator Credit Claiming on Constituent Credit Allocation. *American Political Science Review*, 106 (4), 703–719; Reingold, B., Haynie, K. L. and Widner, K. 2021. *Race, Gender, and Political Representation: Toward a More Intersectional Approach*. Oxford: Oxford University Press.

21 Scherer, N, and Curry, B. 2010. Does Descriptive Race Representation Enhance Institutional Legitimacy?: The Case of the US Courts. *Journal of Politics*, 72(1): 90–104.

22 Scherer, N. 2004. Blacks on the Bench. *Political Science Quarterly*, 119(4): 655–675.

23 Dovi, S. and Luna, F. 2020. Women "Doing" the Judiciary: Rethinking the Justice Argument for Descriptive Representation. *Politics, Groups, and Identities*, 8(4): 790–802; Gleason, S. 2020. Beyond Mere Presence: Gender Norms in Oral Arguments at the US Supreme Court. *Political Research Quarterly*, 73(3): 596–608; Gleason, S., Jones, J. J. and McBean, J. R. 2018. The Role of Gender Norms in Judicial Decision Making at the US Supreme Court: The Case of Male and Female Justices. *American Politics Research*, 47(3): 494–529; Kirkpatrick, J. 2020. Fairness has a Face: Neutrality and Descriptive Representation on Courts. *Politics, Groups, and Identities*, 8(4): 803–811; Badas, A., and Stauffer, K. E. 2017. Someone Like Me: Descriptive Representation and Support for Supreme Court Nominees. *Political Research Quarterly*, 71(1): 127–142.

24 Gleason, S, and Stout, C.T. 2014. Who is Empowering Who?: Exploring the Causal Relationship Between Descriptive Representation and Black Empowerment. *Journal of Black Studies*, 45(7): 635–659; Scherer, N., and Curry, B. 2010. Does Descriptive Race Representation Enhance Institutional Legitimacy?: The Case of the US Courts. *Journal of Politics*, 72(1): 90–104; Scherer, N. 2004. Blacks on the Bench. *Political Science Quarterly*, 119(4): 655–675.

25 Boyd, C.L. 2016. Representation on the Courts? The Effects of Trial Judges' Sex and Race. *Political Research Quarterly*, 69(4): 798.

26 Farhang, S., and Wawro, G. 2004. Institutional Dynamics on the U.S. Court of Appeals: Minority Representation under Panel Decision Making" *Journal of Law, Economics, and Organization*, 20(2): 299–330; Kastellec, J.P. 2013. Racial Diversity and Judicial Influence on Appellate Courts. *American*

how specific, marginalized groups receive greater representation in judicial decision-making when members of the group are on the bench, Kirkpatrick[27] notes that we should understand that all judges, not just those from marginalized communities, represent something when ascending to the bench and deciding on a case.

Courts in the United States have often been described as having an awkward, if not contentious, relationship with the public and other government agencies due to their peculiar role in the policy-making process. In democratic societies, political power rests in the hands of the popular majority and their representatives in government. To affirm that a court in the United States has some power to make policy decisions, the described "countermajoritarian" influence on public policy, is to presume that judges are willing and able to wrest political power away from the majority will in favor of protecting minority rights and providing greater political equality. As a counter, Dahl[28] notes that this argument is unrealistic if we are to believe that courts play an influential role in the American political system. Rather than take power away from the majority, courts most likely follow the dominant policy trends of the lawmaking majorities. For Dahl[29] this is true because we do not select judges in the United States primarily for their "judicial" qualities, but rather based on their attitudes on policy. Thus, "the fact is, then, that the policy views dominant on the Court are never for long out of line with the policy views dominant among the lawmaking majorities of the United States,"[30] stating that even the U.S. Supreme Court can act as a majoritarian institution. Justice Antonin Scalia, a stalwart advocate for judicial restraint, explicitly acknowledges this fact in *Republican Party of Minnesota v. White*,[31] noting that judges are part of the representative system in the United States, rather than outside of it. As Justice Scalia argues, "This complete separation of the judiciary from the enterprise of representative government might have some truth in those countries where judges neither make law themselves nor set aside the laws enacted by the legislature. It is not a true picture of the American system."[32]

To better understand just how a group of seemingly unrepresentative actors like judges may fit within the representative system in the United States, we must focus on how the judiciary is designed to be responsive to various "audiences" when carrying out their duties.[33] Manin[34] first designs the concept of "audience democracy" to distinguish between changes in representative systems that have occurred throughout history. Audience, the "relevant group of people who must recognize a claimant as a representative,"[35] is more significant in modern representative

---

Journal of Political Science, 57(1): 167–183; Pitkin, H.F. 1967. The Concept of Representation. Berkeley: University of California Press.

27 Kirkpatrick, J. 2020. Fairness has a Face: Neutrality and Descriptive Representation on Courts. *Politics, Groups, and Identities*, 8(4): 803–811.

28 Dahl, R.A. (1956). *A Preface to Democratic Theory*. Chicago: University of Chicago Press.

29 Ibid.

30 Ibid, p. 285.

31 *Republican Party of Minnesota v. White*. (2002). 536 U.S. 765.

32 Ibid, p. 784.

33 Baum, L. 2008. *Judges and Their Audiences: A Perspective on Judicial Behavior*. Princeton: Princeton University Press ; Romano, M.K. and Curry, T.A. 2019. *Creating the Law: State Supreme Court Opinions and The Effect of Audiences*. New York: Routledge.

34 Manin, B. 1997. *Principles of Representative Government*. New York: Cambridge University Press.

35 Rehfeld, A. 2006. Toward a General Theory of Political Representation. *Journal of Politics*, *68*(1), 5.

systems due to the reliance of these systems on electoral selection mechanisms to choose representative agents and should go beyond simply assuming an implicit "electorate." By doing so, we can better understand representation more generally, which will allow researchers to make arguments about representation in cases where agents are not chosen through election, such as lobbyists, diplomats, and non-elected judges. Focusing specifically on non-elected judges, the selection process makes explicit that judges are chosen to represent *something*, which is essentially the argument Collins and Ringhand[36] make regarding federal judges. Including state courts makes this representative argument even stronger, as in the absence of life tenure, judges must face reauthorization, which makes audience representation explicit.

According to this account, audiences in representative systems are part of the formal process through which agents are chosen and legitimized by a population. Representatives do not *necessarily* have to be selected through democratic means, which allows for non-democratic representation to exist.[37] Audience is key as it helps us conceptualize the constituency that the representative is standing for. So long as a court's interpretation of the law does not come into conflict with the will of the people, the judicial branch is able to act without issue. However, when conflict does occur, as it often does, the theory of representation requires that judges justify their decisions to the public to satisfy accountability.[38] The act of communicating with the public, clarifying and justifying their decisions, is necessary if we assume an institution is not only political, but also representative. Montanaro[39] notes that self-appointed representatives can in this way provide democratically legitimate forms of representation when they provide a political voice for constituencies affected by political issues. Such representatives are useful in the political arena when they seek to provide a presence for constituencies that may not have the option to select advocates via traditional means of election.[40] Thus, Montanaro[41] outlines an argument through which we should understand representation as being based on the ability of an agent to substantively stand for two kinds of constituencies: the "authorizing" constituency empowered to select representatives, and that thus maintains a level of accountability; and also the "affected" constituency, whose interests a representative is primarily interested in and responsible for legitimating. Judges in the United States, according to these more general accounts, can still be representative agents of their state so long as the audience they make claims to (whether that be the public, elite actors, or an amalgamation of both) recognize the judge as qualified for that position. In these cases, the method of selection is important to keep

---

36 Collins, P.M., Jr. & Ringhand, L.A. 2013. *Supreme Court Confirmation Hearings and Constitutional Change*. New York: Cambridge University Press.

37 Rehfeld, A. 2006. Toward a General Theory of Political Representation. *Journal of Politics*, *68*(1), 1–21.

38 Mansbridge, J. 2011. Clarifying the Concept of Representation. *The American Political Science Review*, *105*(3), 621–630; Rehfeld, A. 2009. Representation Rethought: On Trustees, Delegates, and Gyroscopes in the Study of Political Representation and Democracy. *American Political Science Review*, *103*(2), 214–30.

39 Montanaro, L. 2012. The Democratic Legitimacy of Self-Appointed Representatives. *The Journal of Politics*, *74*(4), 1094–1107.

40 Hirst, P. 1994. *Associative Democracy: New Forms of Economic and Social Governance*. Boston: University of Massachusetts Press; Montanaro, L. 2012. The Democratic Legitimacy of Self-Appointed Representatives. *The Journal of Politics*, *74*(4), 1094–1107.

41 Montanaro, L. 2012. The Democratic Legitimacy of Self-Appointed Representatives. *The Journal of Politics*, *74*(4), 1094–1107.

in mind. Saward[42] argues that representation should be seen as an evolving process in which agents construct claims to an audience about their ability to represent constituents' interests. Representation is evaluated, therefore, based on signals sent by representatives to their constituents about the substantive political activities they engage in, and whether constituents accept these activities as correct.

SELECTION, RETENTION, AND AUDIENCE REPRESENTATION

If judges are representatives, as we claim here, they must meet agreed-upon requirements. These requirements start with the basis of authorization representation and the role of audience as outlined above, which are reaffirmed through the processes of retention. Certainly, to recognize judicial representation, we must identify the methods of selection and retention that vary across the different jurisdictions and levels of the judiciary, but this is only one facet of the representative enterprise. Scholars of representation have focused a great deal of attention on how agents are selected and retained, thus focusing on how to maintain accountability between representative and constituent. The history of the judicial branch in the United States can be traced back as an attempt to balance two sometimes competing imperatives: judicial independence and judicial accountability. Initially, judges were exclusively appointed by elites and given life tenure, prioritizing independence. However, every subsequent alteration made to the methods of selection and retention used within the states increased the accountability of judges in this country, by enshrined term lengths and the need to be retained. The movement of the judicial branch in the United States was toward increased representation.

If we begin with the assumption that courts in the United States act as majoritarian institutions, we may arguably conclude that judging is an act of representation since decisions made can be evaluated by the public and judges can be held accountable to the public will. Representatives, according to Pitkin,[43] act in the interest of the represented and are responsive to their desires. It is not unreasonable to state that the role of the judicial branch is to ensure that there is correspondence between the preferences of citizens and lawmakers with the governing laws of the nation.[44] Even early formulations of the representative claim focus not only on standing for another group, but on the justification the representative supplied their audience to explain their decision-making.[45] The need for justification when deciding is what legitimates a representative's authority to act on the behalf of constituents and ensures that authorized agents remain in step with their audience. Justification is a key component in the transformation of a political actor from passive representative of an audience into an active representative of their wants and desires in the public sphere. For judges to be fully accepted as representatives, therefore, there must not only be an authorization to act on behalf of others and the opportunity for those affected to influence the decision, but also the judges must provide some form of *justification* for their actions. Thus, all U.S. courts are charged with "upholding the Constitution," first, and ensuring that the laws of the nation correspond with the will of the

---

42 Saward, M. (2010). *The Representative Claim.* New York: Oxford University Press.

43 Pitkin, H.F. 1967. *The Concept of Representation.* Berkeley: University of California Press.

44 Collins, P.M., Jr. & Ringhand, L.A. 2013. *Supreme Court Confirmation Hearings and Constitutional Change.* New York: Cambridge University Press.

45 Pitkin, H.F. 1967. *The Concept of Representation.* Berkeley: University of California Press.

people, second. This reasoning is even stronger when focusing on state judicial institutions, where we would assume that political institutions exhibit a higher degree of congruency with citizen preferences than at the federal level.

Primarily through written opinions, the justification step not only provides judges with the ability to explain their decisions to their audience, but also allows them to demonstrate how they are being representative of the audience they are making claims to. This requirement for justification is carried out uniquely in the enterprise of judging, as it provides the authorization constituency with vastly more information than many other types of representatives. More importantly, the opinion not only provides judges with the opportunity not only to passively justify their decisions; especially when the decision made is unpopular among their constituency, judges can actively persuade that their decision was the best choice to resolve a given conflict. Given the requirement for adversarial parties when presenting a case before the judiciary, the language chosen by judges in crafting the opinion is important as judges play an active role in determining not only how policy and law should be interpreted, but how the broader public perceives their views on the law.[46] According to Justice Breyer,[47] the opinion is significant for several reasons, not the least of which is to explain to the public, as well as persuade those reading a judge's opinion. "A strong opinion," says Breyer, "should prove persuasive, making a lasting impression on the minds of those who read it."[48] If this were not expected of the court, if the judiciary was not a representative institution, we would arguably not emphasize the need for judges to write opinions, but rather would only require that they make mechanical decisions by applying laws to facts. Written opinions represent the justification for their action to their constituency.

Because opinions – whether majority, concurrence, or dissent – are written with specific purposes in mind, justices can employ different communication strategies when drafting these opinions to communicate substantive goals to their audiences. When the representative believes their preferred outcome matches neatly with their constituency, they are more likely to employ a strategy of justifying their opinion. A justification strategy will weigh other perceived outcomes and employ a clear rule-based approach to explain why the outcome which the author wishes is the only correct one which could be reached. This justification strategy should be juxtaposed with a persuasive strategy. Persuasion as a communication technique is more likely to be used when the audience constituency would disagree with the position taken by the representative. This strategy relies in part on informational asymmetry between the communicator (judge) and the audience. Information is selectively presented which makes the case for the position which the author takes and requires advocacy on behalf of the author. The author is trying to "sell" their position as correct, as opposed to a justification strategy, where the author is using a rule-based approach and reaching the "obvious" conclusion. Both strategies stem from the representative connection between the judge and their audience. Empirical evidence exists that judges regularly employ these strategies under different contexts[49] and lends evidence to our conjecture that judges view themselves as representatives.

---

[46] Romano, M.K. and Curry, T.A. 2019. *Creating the Law: State Supreme Court Opinions and The Effect of Audiences*. New York: Routledge.

[47] Breyer, S. 2010. *Making Our Democracy Work: A Judge's View*. New York: Vintage Books.

[48] Ibid, p. 43.

[49] Romano, M.K. and Curry, T.A. 2019. *Creating the Law: State Supreme Court Opinions and The Effect of Audiences*. New York: Routledge.

JUDICIAL REPRESENTATION AND AMERICAN POLITICAL DEVELOPMENT

Following the founding of the nation, the various states and the federal government followed the lead of Great Britain in appointing their judges and giving them life tenure. The appointing institution varied depending on the state, but all states that entered the union until 1832 appointed their judges to the Court of Last Resort. The addition of Mississippi to the union in 1832 is seen as a turning point for understanding the political influence of the judiciary, as the state's constitution required judges at every level be popularly elected. Indeed, as populism began to gain momentum within the United States, many states turned to elections to select their state judges. The pace of this change was rapid: by the conclusion of the Civil War, a total of 24 states were using elections as the primary way to select and retain judges. While the federal judiciary has not augmented the life tenure of judges, as of today all but three states that use a form of elite appointment (either gubernatorial or legislative) have instituted some type of judicial term length. In doing so, states have created an explicit check on the judiciary, one designed to ensure that judges remain tacitly representative to the public when making decisions.

Beyond the general tenets of the populist movement, there were at least three other contributing factors which guided states toward partisan elections for judges, and thus toward establishing and refining the representative link between judges and constituencies. First, following some problematic decisions from the United States Supreme Court, including *Marbury v. Madison*[50] and *Dred Scott v. Sandford*,[51] there was a worry that judges, unaccountable to anyone, would begin to overturn laws in ways inconsistent with the wishes of the public. As judicial review began to spread, this concern became more pronounced, and it was thought that making judges accountable to the same constituency that selects the legislatures would help assuage this concern. Second, and certainly related, there developed a concern that appointed judges, with life tenure, was just another example of the problems which arise under the spoils system.[52] These judges, accountable to no one, were seen as wards of the institution or party that was pivotal in their selection. It was thought that by giving them their own constituency, these judges would be independent of the other two branches of government. Lastly, under appointment systems, there was no easy mechanism to remove ineffective judges. While impeachment existed, it proved politically improbable except in the worse cases. By shifting to partisan elections, it transferred this responsibility to the public, and in turn, made the process easier. Ultimately, the shift to partisan elections for judges created an institution far more accountable than existed before, solving many of the perceived problems with an elite appointment system. However, partisan elections did not eliminate all issues within the judiciary, and most certainly, created some of their own.

While the ultimate deciders of who would serve as a judge were the public, they did not get to choose the candidates. And in the absence of a primary system, the political machines dominating politics chose the candidates who ran for judge. Despite the goals of institutional reformers in the move to partisan elections for judges, this did not create a more independent

---

[50] *Marbury v. Madison.* (1803). 5 U.S. 137.

[51] *Dred Scott v. Sandford* (1857). 60 U.S. 393.

[52] Dubois, P.L. 1980. *From Ballot to Bench: Judicial Elections and the Quest for Accountability*. Austin: University of Texas Press.

judiciary. Judges were still thought of as tools of the political machinery. As the Progressive Era firmly took hold, several states chose to remove partisan identification from the ballot, and thus, remove the role of the party in selecting judicial nominees. This relatively small institutional shift, especially during a time where primaries were not widely used, removed the control of the party over the judge. Nonpartisan elections made judges independent of the party, the governor, and the legislature, and wholly accountable to the public.

We understand the audiences for representation by first identifying the method of selection utilized to initially populate the bench, what Montanaro[53] identifies as the "authorization" constituency. Further, we must also recognize the retention mechanism used to maintain accountability after the fact. This system of separating initial authorization from subsequent accountability is unique to the judicial branch; however, it is vital in providing judges an outlet to represent constituencies. All judges may provide a form of passive representation via descriptive characteristics of the individual judge; however, these varied institutions provide judges with the ability to provide a voice to constituents. Therefore, when groups like the American Judicature Society and the American Bar Association argued for blending of different institutional types for selection and retention, they separated authorization and accountability into different institutions. Under a plan initially called "merit selection," judges were to be vetted by a nonpartisan/bipartisan commission which evaluated individuals before forwarding a list of potential judges to the chief executive of the state to make the final nomination. These judges, however, would not be accountable to the governor, but instead the public of the state. However, unlike partisan and nonpartisan elections, judges in this system would be retained in an uncontested election, which amounts to a referendum on retaining a given judge. After the first state adopted this system in 1940, it widely became referred to as the "Missouri Plan." The goal of this system was to shield judges from overt politics while still leaving a method in place for public accountability.

The current landscape of judicial selection in the various states exhibits a wide range of variation, but the patterns that remain are, to a degree, holdovers from the various political movements that occurred while states were admitted to the union. Table 3.1 lists the states and their current method of selection. Despite the myriad selection methods used by the states, our claim of judicial representation is not diminished, just differentiated.

Partisan electoral systems and nonpartisan electoral systems make the claim of judicial representation the clearest. These judges are elected by the public and retained by the public. This provides the public with the explicit authority to make a choice between whom they wish to represent them. These methods of selection and retention share much in common with their legislative counterparts. Also, considering these judges need to justify their decisions not only during their elections, but also in writing following every decision, it may be argued that elected judges more easily meet the qualifications for representatives than other elected officials in the U.S. context.

Appointment systems, while removing the explicit connection to the electorate, simply shift the accountability mechanism for judges to either the legislature or governor of the state. According to Rehfeld,[54] these institutions are the selection agent applying their decision rule

---

53 Montanaro, L. 2012. The Democratic Legitimacy of Self- Appointed Representatives. *The Journal of Politics, 74*(4), 1094–1107.

54 Rehfeld, A. 2006. Toward a General Theory of Political Representation. *Journal of Politics*, *68*(1), 1–21.

Table 3.1 *Selection and retention systems for state courts of last resort, 2020*

Partisan elections	Term length	Nonpartisan elections	Term length	Missouri Plan	Term length	Appointment	Term length	Hybrid elections	Term length
Alabama	6	Arkansas	8	Alaska	10	Connecticut	8	Illinois**	10
Louisiana	10	Georgia	6	Arizona	6	Delaware	12	Michigan***	8
North Carolina	8	Idaho	6	California	12	Hawaii	10	New Mexico**	8
Texas	6	Kentucky	8	Colorado	10	Maine	7	Ohio***	6
	12	Minnesota	6	Florida	6	Massachusetts	Life	Pennsylvania**	10
		Mississippi	8	Indiana	10	New Hampshire	5		
		Montana*	8	Iowa	8	New Jersey	Life		
		Nevada	6	Kansas	6	New York	14		
				Maryland	10	Rhode Island	Life		
		North Dakota	10	Missouri	12	South Carolina	10		
		Oregon	6	Nebraska	6	Vermont	6		
		Washington	6	Oklahoma	6	Virginia	12		
		West Virginia	12	South Dakota	8				
		Wisconsin	10	Tennessee	8				
				Utah	10				
				Wyoming	8				

Notes:
* Retention elections held if incumbent is unopposed.
** Justices are initially chosen in partisan elections but in subsequent terms only stand for retention election.
*** During the general election candidates appear without a party identification on the ballot, but they are initially chosen in a partisan manner (partisan caucus/partisan primary).

to the qualified set of individuals considered to be a judge. The selection agent would not retain a judge of whom the electorate does not approve, because the selection agent is directly responsible to the electorate for *their* retention. As such, these judges' justifications for their actions, in the form of written opinions, are explicitly for two groups: the retention institution (either the governor or legislature) and the public.

States that utilize the Missouri Plan provide us with an interesting query, as they have separate selection and retention mechanisms. The selection agent is divided between two institutions, with bipartisan/nonpartisan commissions determining the list of qualified individuals, which will be delivered to the governor. The governor then chooses one individual on the list to be a judge. Following a short period, usually one to three years, judges are evaluated by the electorate based on their justifications of their decisions. The electorate is asked if they approve or disapprove of the judicial incumbent. While this is not a traditional election, in that the incumbents do not face a challenger, they are evaluated on the adequacy of their decisions alone. This connection to the electorate has proven to have the function of an accountability check, as witnessed by the retention elections in Iowa in 2010, when three judges were removed from office based on a few decisions that were perceived as out of step with the values of the electorate.

The states that remain all utilize modified forms of electoral systems. Illinois, New Mexico, and Pennsylvania also have different methods of selection and retention; however, unlike states which utilize the Missouri Plan, the fundamental institution remains the same. Judges are initially chosen via partisan elections. After winning their initial selection, to keep their seat they need to win an uncontested retention election, identical to those used under the Missouri Plan. Therefore, in these three states, the public remains the only participant in the selection and retention process. Both Michigan and Ohio simply combine parts of partisan and nonpartisan elections, leaving the representative claim clear.

CONCLUSION

Establishing the foundations of judicial authority and legitimacy has always been a difficult task for the federal judiciary. Two puzzles tend to perplex judicial scholars when attempting to establish the authority and legitimacy of the court. First, how can an undemocratic institution be legitimate within a democracy? The legal training required to become a judge tends to ground individuals with the belief that it is the duty of judges to protect minority rights from majority tyranny. This common foundation is claimed as the basis for judges' legitimacy. This question, however, erodes in importance if we recognize judges as representatives. Only a minority of judges in the United States have the benefit of life tenure. While judges may be undemocratically selected when they are appointed or retained by political elites, the implicit claim between the individual or body choosing and their constituency is that the judge represents their interest, and thus the elected officials have authorized them to act in this position, legitimating them to the people. Judges who are elected make this connection with the public more directly, and thus claim their authority and legitimacy stem from the same origins as any other elected official: popular sovereignty.

Considering the variations in the methods of selection and retention used in the United States for judges at all levels, as well as the nature of opinion writing, the claim that judges do not conform to our expectations of a representative is invalid. Judges are initially chosen to represent something, dependent upon the institution; and all judges, even those with life tenure, are approval seeking, especially in their decision-making and opinion writing. Thus, while more modern judicial innovations have made accountability more explicit, this is not a necessary condition to be a political representative.

Still, most judges in the U.S. are selected and/or retained via some form of election. Regardless of how they initially populate the bench, judges who do not have life tenure should behave like strategic actors who represent some constituency to remain in power. Based upon the method by which judges are retained, we should see the institutions incentivize certain behavior.

The second question is generally stated as: How do we enforce or police institutions such as the judiciary when they use their power illegitimately?[55] Judges are paramount in the modern formulation of democracy as the bastions of the rule of law; however, if judges are allowed to make political decisions free from the confines of representation, what stops them from becoming "partisans in robes"? For Peretti,[56] the solution to both questions is easier than legal scholars tend to make it: We simply acknowledge the judiciary is a political institution, and that its members are chosen because they conform to the dominant ideology. Judges, for Peretti, are not quite politicians in robes, but they are chosen because, at a minimum, they conform to the majority's conception of the correct jurisprudence. Furthermore, if judges are selected on this basis, it reduces the likelihood of abuse of power.

At the state level, viewing the judiciary as a political institution is both easier and more obvious, due to the lack of life tenure for judges in 47 states. If judges wield their power in a manner that the selection set would deem illegitimate, they can be removed when their term is up for renewal, much like any representative actor. This accountability function serves to revitalize the representative link between judges and their constituency, while also having the function of reducing the likelihood of abuse of power. Much like any political actor, judges have goals. Minus crafting their legacy, these goals are attainable only while maintaining power in office. If judges are retained by political elites, either the governor or legislature, it is likely they will consider their audience when making decisions, especially on governmental policies.[57] Similarly, if judges are retained through contested elections, they will likely modify their decisions on salient issues to the public.[58] The proponents of retention elections also assume judges will be held accountable by voters,[59] and indeed, when their decisions are out of line with constituency standards, judges are removed, as evidenced by the retention elections in California in 1986 and in Iowa in 2010.

The act of choosing a judge or any representative, whether it is through elite selection or via public contestation, is only one part of the representative process. Beyond these authorization steps, representatives are required to justify their actions to the public to maintain accounta-

---

55 Peretti, T.J. 1999. *In Defense of a Political Court.* Princeton: Princeton University Press.

56 Ibid.

57 Langer, L. 2002. *Judicial Review in State Supreme Courts: A Comparative Study.* Albany: State University of New York Press.

58 Brace, P. & Boyea, B.D. 2008. State Public Opinion, the Death Penalty, and the Practice of Electing Judges. *American Journal of Political Science*, *52*(2), 360–372; Canes-Wrone, B., Clark, T.S. & Kelly, J.P. 2014. Judicial Selection and Death Penalty Decisions. *American Political Science Review*, *108*(1), 23–39.

59 Caufield, R.P. (2009) Reconciling the Judicial Ideal and the Democratic Impulse of Judicial Retention Elections. *Missouri Law Review*, *74*(3), 1–32.

bility between periods of reauthorization. For public officials traditionally viewed as "representatives" of the people, this amounts to regular to semi-regular public statements made via press conferences, releases, speeches, and other events.[60] While these actions are validating in that they are persuasive attempts by a representative to explain their actions to constituents, it is rare for such representatives to definitively stake a position on policy. Judges, on the other hand, are one of the few types of representative that must justify all their binding decisions with written explanations. As Breyer[61] notes, these opinions are not produced for the judge's own benefit, but for the public and for others in the governing system to digest in hopes that they will be seen as adequate justification for their decision. This provides their constituents with the ability to easily identify if their representative is shirking their duty.

What changes when we begin to think of judges as political representatives? Functionally, nothing. We have described the situation not as some ideal type we envision, but as it currently stands. Following in the tradition of the legal realists (who claimed that personal ideology and public policy played a role in decision-making), we claim that judges are, in reality, representatives. Judges must make promises to a constituency. They must also justify their decisions in writing, the majority of which are published. Finally, after a term, many need to be retained, opening the possibility for them to be held accountable for the previous decisions they have made. The power of judges hasn't changed; as Hamilton stated, they still possess neither the purse nor sword, but merely judgment. However, the source of their power has changed. Their legitimacy stems less from their independence, and more from their nature as representatives. This is the reality in the states.

---

[60] Zaller, J.R. 1999. *A Theory of Media Politics: How the Interests of Politicians, Journalists, and Citizens Shape the News*. Draft. http://www.ssnet.ucla.edu/polisci/faculty/zaller/media%20politics%20book%20.pdf

[61] Breyer, S. 2010. *Making Our Democracy Work: A Judge's View*. New York: Vintage Books.

4. Gender, race, and politics in judicial process

Do trial judges' gender, race, and partisanship impact verdicts, appeals, and reversals?

Tao Dumas and Alexandra Mannix

INTRODUCTION

In 2017 Alabama voters elected nine Black women Democratic judges to its district and circuit courts (small claims and general jurisdiction trial courts). This impressive feat is a result of Alabama's practice of electing lower-court judges in partisan, district-based elections. Yet Alabama uses partisan statewide races to elect judges to its appellate bench, resulting in two levels of the judiciary that differ both demographically and politically. In fact, Alabama's judicial electoral scheme results in a trial bench comprising a Democratic majority, despite Republican and conservative domination of politics at the state level. The purpose of this research is to explore the extent to which the institutional design in Alabama impacts how cases move from trial to appeal, which, by consequence, also shapes both judges' careers and outcomes for litigants. In particular, we are interested in whether cases presided over by minority judges (whether racial, gender, partisan, or a combination of traits) receive greater judicial scrutiny in the form of appeals and reversals. We begin by exploring the relevant literature, which suggests at least two possible reasons why minority judges might experience greater scrutiny, and utilize an original dataset to explore the empirical evidence.

This research provides important insights into understudied relationships in judicial politics research. First, we combine theory and data related to trial courts and appellate courts to explore judicial process more fully. Most empirical investigations of courts focus on either appeals or trials, preventing scholars from understanding how trials shape the pool of cases appellate courts review.[1] Part of the explanation for the dearth of scholarship in this area stems from the difficulty in obtaining trial court rulings (especially at the state level) and the resulting lack of readily available data. Here we rely on a novel dataset of 18 years of trial court data in the state of Alabama and any ensuing appeals court rulings. We also gather demographic and partisan identification data for both trial and appellate judges. This new dataset allows us to investigate previously unanswered questions about which cases litigants and attorneys appeal, which decisions' appeals courts reverse, and whether trial judges' partisan and demographic backgrounds influence those outcomes. As such, the research presented here contributes to case selection literature, research focused on appellate court decision-making, and scholarship concerned with the impact of gender and race on judging.

---

[1] See, Barry Friedman, *Taking Law Seriously*, 2 PERSP. ON POL. 261 (2006); Lee Epstein and Gary King, *The Rules of Inference*, 1 U. CHI. L. REV. 1 (2002), arguing for a need to amalgamate legal academic and social science law research to produce more robust theory and empirical analyses.

Extant scholarship provides at least two causal mechanisms that might lead losing litigants to appeal their cases more often when a minority (race, gender, or ideological) judge presides over the trial. First, the literature suggests minority judges might inherently make different decisions than their white, male, ideological majority counterparts, which could lead to different case outcomes, and consequently more appeals and reversals. A second possibility is that litigants view minority judges as less legitimate, which in turn makes losing parties more likely to seek additional adjudication. Priest and Klein[2] first articulated the selection hypothesis which posits that strategic litigants and their attorneys make calculated decisions about which cases to take to trial. According to the theory, easy cases settle during the pre-trial stage, and only the most difficult cases advance, resulting in a 50% success rate for plaintiffs. Priest and Klein predict similar behavior and patterns of outcomes upon appeal. Although support for the 50% success hypothesis remains considerably mixed,[3] most scholars accept the notion that litigants and their attorneys engage in strategic behavior. A second body of scholarship maintains that losing litigants look for ideological signals from the higher court to gauge their future chance of success upon appeal.[4] Taken together, these theories suggest that litigants and their attorneys who lose at trial will make strategic calculations to determine whether an appeal makes sense. As such, trial judges whose courts produce rulings that routinely differ ideologically from those rendered by the appeals courts will likely experience more appeals and more reversals. Similarly, trial judges whose decisions are perceived as less legitimate, due to gender and racial bias or other factors, might also experience more appellate oversight, even if their decisions do not deviate from state norms.

Understanding how a diversifying judicial bench impacts judicial process is important both for the academic study of judicial process and for improving the real-world operation of the courts. Not only can increased descriptive representation on the bench improve public perceptions of fairness and confidence in the legal system,[5] but judges from diverse backgrounds

---

2 George L. Priest and Benjamin Klein, *The Selection of Disputes for Litigation*, 13 JLS 1 (1984).

3 For studies largely finding support for the selection thesis, see Daniel Kessler, Thomas Meites, and Geoffrey Miller, *Explaining Deviations from the Fifty Percent Rule: A Multimodal Approach to the Selection of Cases for Litigation*, 1 JLS 233 (1996); Peter Siegleman and John J. Donohue, III, *The Selection of Employment Discrimination Disputes for Litigation: Using Business Cycle Effects to Test the Priest-Klein Hypothesis*, 24 JLS 427 (1995); Joel Waldfogel, *Reconciling Asymmetric Information and Divergent Expectations Theories of Litigation*, 41 J.L. & Econ. 451 (1998). Conversely, for research rebutting Priest and Klein's assumptions, see William Baxter, The Political Economy of Antitrust (Robert D. Tollison ed., 1980); Theodore Eisenberg, *Testing the Selection Effect: A New Theoretical Framework with Empirical Tests*, 19 JLS 337 (1990); Douglas O. Linder, *Some Doubts Concerning the Selection Hypothesis of George Priest* 37 U. Kan. L. Rev. 319 (1988); Keith N. Hylton, *Asymmetric Information and the Selection of Disputes for Litigation*, 22 JLS 187 (1993). Also see Eric Helland, Daniel M. Klerman, and Yoon-Ho Alex Lee, *Maybe There's No Selection Bias in the Selection of Disputes for Litigation*, 174 JITE 143 (2018), arguing that settled and tried cases are actually very similar.

4 John M. de Figueiredo, *Strategic Plaintiffs and Ideological Judges in Telecommunications Litigation*, 21 J.L. Econ. & Org. 501 (2005); Jeff Yates & Elizabeth Coggins, *The Intersection of Judicial Attitudes and Litigant Selection Theories: Explaining U.S. Supreme Court Decision-Making*, 29 Wash. U. J.L. & Pol'y 847 (2009); Jeff Yates, Damon M. Cann & Bernt D. Boyea, *Judicial Ideology and the Selection of Disputes for the U.S. Supreme Court* 10 JELS 847 (2013).

5 Amber Fricke & Angela Onwuachi-Willig, *Do Female 'Firsts' Still Matter? Why They do for Female Judges of Color*, 5 Mich.St.U.L.Rev. 1529 (2012); Nancy Scherer & Brett Curry, *Does*

might also increase substantive representation for various underrepresented groups and issues.[6] However, if higher courts disproportionately overturn the decisions rendered by trial judges from underrepresented backgrounds, this pattern of reversals could undermine the gains garnered from a diversifying bench. This chapter proceeds by summarizing existing scholarship concerned with the influence of judicial ideology, gender, and race on court outputs and then uses an original data collection of 3,419 trial court verdicts and any subsequent review of those decisions to examine patterns of verdicts, appeals, and reversals across judges' partisan and demographic backgrounds. We find little evidence that verdicts vary by trial judges' backgrounds; however, reversals appear higher for judges of color who are Democrats, especially women of color.

PREVIOUS LITERATURE

Ideology and Judicial Decision-making

If a difference in appeal and reversal rates emerges for trial judges of varying ideological or demographic backgrounds, the literature suggests that one explanation for this could be that minority judges (gender, race, or political minorities) are ideologically different, which results in case outcomes that differ from norms. Patterns of rulings that diverge from the majority of judges in a state could in turn lead to more appellate review and reversals. Although there is ongoing scholarly debate about whether judges' personal characteristics affect their decision-making, judicial ideology represents one of the more commonly cited explanations for their decision-making. A wealth of research shows that judges' liberal or conservative viewpoints shape judges' behavior on both federal[7] and state[8] appellate benches. In fact, judicial ideology appears to exert an independent influence on case outcomes, even after controlling for case selection effects.[9] Moreover, scholarship indicates that women[10] and

---

Descriptive Race Representation Enhance Institutional Legitimacy? The Case of the U.S Courts, 72 J.POL. 90 (2010).

6 See, Gbemende Johnson, *Gender, Diversity, and the United States Judiciary*, 41 SAIS REV.INT. AFFAIRS 61 (2021).

7 Virginia A. Hettinger, Stefanie A. Lindquist, & Wendy L. Martinek, *Comparing Attitudinal and Strategic Accounts of Dissenting Behavior on the H.S. Courts of Appeals*, 48 AJPS 123 (2004); Erin B. Kaheny, Susan Brodie Haire, and Sara C. Benesh, *Change over Tenure: Voting, Variance, and Decision Making on the U.S. Courts of Appeals* 52 AJPS 490 (2008); Glendon Schubert, *The Judicial Mind: Attitudes and Ideologies of Supreme Court Justices*, Northwestern University Press (1965); Jeffery A. Segal & Harold D. Spaeth, *The Supreme Court and the Attitudinal Mode*, Cambridge University Press (2002).

8 Paul Brace, Laura Langer, & Melinda Hall, *Measuring the Preferences of State Court Judges*, 62 J.POL. 387 (2000); Jason H. Windett, Jeffery H. Harden & Matthew E. K. Hall, *Estimating Dynamic Ideal Points for State Supreme Courts*, 23 POL. ANALYSIS 461 (2015).

9 See Yates & Coggins, supra note 3.

10 Christina L. Boyd & Michael J. Nelson, *The Effects of Trial Judge Gender and Public Opinion on Criminal Sentencing Decisions*, 70 VAND. L. REV. 1819 (2017); Brian D. Johnson, *Judges on Trial: A Reexamination of Judicial Race and Gender Effects across Modes of Conviction*, 25 CRIM. JUSTICE POL'Y REV. 159 (2014); Donald R. Songer & Kelly A. Crews-Meyer, *Does Judge Gender Matter? Decision Making in State Supreme Courts*, 81 SOC.SCI.Q. 750 (2000); Fred O. Smith, Gendered Justice: *Do Male and Female Judges Rule Differently on Questions of Gay Rights*, 57 STAN.L.REV. 2087 (2005).

racial and ethnic minority[11] judges tend to possess more liberal viewpoints than their white, male counterparts. Yet despite the overwhelming evidence that ideology matters for judges on appellate benches, scholars often fail to uncover a relationship between judicial ideology and trial judges' decisions.[12] However, if minority trial judges' case outcomes reflect partisan and ideological leanings that differ from those of their majority counterparts or the appeals court, we might expect these cases to receive more judicial oversight.

Gender, Race, and Judging

Beyond ideology, scholars find myriad factors influence judicial behavior, including a judge's age, if they have daughters, and even the results of football games relative to the time they implement sentences.[13] Although a considerable amount of scholarship examines whether judges' demographic backgrounds affect their judging, the traditional underrepresentation of women of color largely produces scholarship examining either race or gender. Scholars looking for gender or racial differences among judges offer several theoretical explanations that support a hypothesis that women and racial minority judges might behave differently on the bench than their majority race and gender colleagues. These theories range from assertions that women and minority judges' unique life experiences related to discrimination[14] shape their decisions in cases regarding related issues to arguments that women and minority judges seek to substantively represent members of their demographic groups on the bench.[15]

Yet researchers seeking evidence of gender or race differences among judges produce mixed findings and inconsistent results depending on the court and the issues examined. However, a substantial body of existing literature supports the assertion that judges' gender or

---

11 Max M. Schanzenbach, *Racial and Sex Disparities in Prison Sentences: The Effect of District-Level Judicial Demographics*, 34 JLS 57 (2005); Pat K. Chew & Robert E. Kelley, *Myth of the Color-Blind Judge: An Empirical Analysis of Racial Harassment Cases*, 86 WASH. U. L. REV. 1117 (2009); Jill D. Weinberg & Laura Beth Nielsen, *Examining Empathy: Discrimination, Experience, and Judicial Decisionmaking*, 85 SO.CAL.L.R. 313 (2012); Christina L. Boyd, *Untangling the Causal Effects of Sex on Judging*, 69 POL.RES.Q. 788 (2016).

12 Christina L. Boyd, *Litigant Status and Trial Court Appeal Mobilization*, 37 L. & POL'Y 295 (2015); Tao L. Dumas & Stacia L. Haynie, *Building an Integrated Model of Trial Court Decision-making: Predicting Plaintiff Success and Awards across Circuits*, 12 ST. POL. & POL'Y Q. 103 (2012); Denise M. Keel, Robert W. Malmsheimer, Donald W. Floyd, & Lianjun Zhang, *An Analysis of Ideological Effects in Published and Unpublished Judicial Opinions*, 6 JELS 213 (2009).

13 See Kenneth L. Manning, Bruce A. Carroll & Robert A. Carp, *Does Age Matter? Judicial Decision Making in Age Discrimination Cases*, 85 SOC.SCI.Q. 1 (2004), finding that a judge's age is a determination of rulings in age discrimination cases; Adam N. Glynn & Maya Sen., *Identifying Judicial Empathy: Does Having Daughters Cause Judges to Rule for Women's Issues?*, 59 AJPS 37 (2015), finding that being a parent of a female child encourages more feminist voting among U.S. Courts of Appeals judges; Ozkan Eren & Naci Mocan, *Emotional Judges and Unlucky Juveniles*, 10 AM. ECON. J. OF APPLIED ECON. 171 (2018), finding that judges who are alumni issue longer juvenile sentences following an unexpected loss by the state's flagship football team.

14 Gerard S. Gryski, C. Elanor Main & William J. Dixon, *Models of High Court Decision Making in Sex Discrimination Cases*, 48 J.POL. 143 (1986); Kathleen Sullivan, *Constitutionalizing Women's Equality*, 90 CLR (2002); Christina L. Boyd, Epstein, Lee & Martin, Andrew D., *Untangling the Causal Effects of Sex on Judging*, 54 AJPS 411 (2010).

15 Sean Farhang & Gregory Wawro, G., *Institutional Dynamics on the U.S. Court of Appeals: Minority Representation under Panel Decision Making*, 20 J.L.ECON.&ORG. 330 (2004); Jonathan P. Kastellec, *Racial Diversity and Judicial Influence on Appellate Courts*, 57 AJPS 167 (2013).

race affects decision-making (at least in certain contexts) at both the trial and appellate levels. The most consistent evidence of gender and race effects on judging comes from the appellate courts. For example, in sex discrimination cases, female judges on the U.S. Courts of Appeals evidence greater support for the party alleging discrimination.[16] Not only that, but female state supreme court judges are also more likely to dissent in women's issue cases.[17]

Turning to studies of race and appellate court behavior, scholars uncover evidence that Black circuit court judges are also more likely to accept criminal defendants' assertions of police misconduct, whereas white judges are significantly more likely to rule against the suppression of incriminating evidence.[18] Additionally, Black Courts of Appeals judges exhibit substantially greater support for affirmative action programs.[19] Furthermore, minority race Courts of Appeals judges are more than twice as likely to rule for liability in Voting Rights Act cases, making race a stronger predictor of judicial decisions than political affiliation.[20] Yet minority judges are less supportive of immigrant claims, regardless of the minority group they belong to.[21] Moreover, in Social Security Administration disability cases across four federal district courts (which are appeals cases, unlike most district court cases), racial minority judges are significantly more likely to rule in favor of disability plaintiffs.[22] Studies of state appellate courts also uncover similar evidence of judge race effects. For example, Bonneau and Rice find African-American judges across all 50 state supreme courts vote for defendants more often in criminal appeals but only in states without intermediate appellate courts, suggesting that race shapes judicial decision-making, along with judges' socialization and experience and institutional arrangements.[23]

What is more, the presence of a female or minority judge on a circuit court panel can have a significant effect on judicial outcomes. When male judges serve on a panel with a female judge, they are significantly more likely to decide for the litigant claiming rights.[24] Furthermore, Williams and Law examine circuit court decisions in immigration cases and uncover evidence that patterns of panel gender effects persist beyond gender-salient cases.[25] Like studies finding panel effects for mixed-sex panels, studies examining interactions between judges of different races uncover similar relationships. White judges were significantly more likely to rule for liability when they were on panels with minority judges in Voting Rights Act cases.[26] Not only

---

16 Christina L. Boyd, Epstein, Lee & Martin, Andrew D., *Untangling the Causal Effects of Sex on Judging*, 54 AJPS 411 (2010); Jennifer L. Peresie, *Female Judges Matter: Gender and Collegial Decisionmaking in The Federal Appellate Courts*, 114 YALE L.J. 1759 (2005).

17 John Szmer, Robert K. Christensen & Erin B. Kaheny, *Gender, Race, and Dissensus on State Supreme Courts*, 96 SOC.SCI.Q. 553 (2015).

18 Nancy Scherer, *Blacks on the Bench*, 119 POL.RES.Q. 655 (2004).

19 Kastellec, supra note 15.

20 Adam B. Cox & Thomas J. Miles, *Judging the Voting Rights Act*, 108 COLUM.L.REV. 1 (2008).

21 Margaret S. Williams & Anna O. Law, *Understanding Judicial Decision Making in Immigration Cases at the U.S. Courts of Appeals*, 33 JUST.SYST.J. 97 (2012).

22 Christina L. Boyd & Adam G. Rutkowski, *Judicial Behavior in Disability Cases: Do Judge Sex and Race Matter?*, 8 POL. GROUPS, & IDENTITIES 834 (2020).

23 Chris W. Bonneau & Heather Marie Rice, H., *Impartial Judges? Race, Institutional Context, and U. S. State Supreme Courts*, 9 ST. POL. & POL'Y Q. 381 (2009).

24 Boyd et al., supra note 16; Farhang & Wawro, supra note 15; Peresie, supra note 16.

25 Williams and Law, supra note 21.

26 Cox & Miles, supra note 20.

that, but the presence of a racial minority judge on a panel nearly guarantees rulings in favor of affirmative action programs cases.[27]

When examining trial courts, several studies find a relationship between gender, race, and verdicts; however, the results are sometimes counterintuitive to expectations, with women and minority judges exhibiting more conservative or punitive behaviors than hypotheses generated from appellate court behavior might predict. For instance, a study of Equal Employment Opportunity Commission (EEOC)-brought cases in federal district courts finds that female judges are more likely to decide in favor of discrimination claimants in sex discrimination cases.[28] Additionally, female U.S. district court judges rule less favorably for personal rights claimants and minority policy positions, are more supportive of economic regulation, and deferred to positions taken by the government.[29] Furthermore, when comparing U.S. district court cases prior to and following the *US v. Booker* 543 US 220 (2005) ruling (which limited judges' ability to issue enhanced sentences under the U.S. Sentencing Guidelines), female judges, particularly those appointed by Republican presidents, were less likely to rule for defendants.[30] Other scholars observe that women judges treat women criminal defendants less harshly than their male counterparts.[31] An examination of President Clinton's district court appointees compares traditional and nontraditional judges' ruling in "women's issue" cases and finds that male judges were in fact more supportive of claims than female judges.[32] Segal suggests that female judges could strategically rule in a manner opposite to what is expected of them in order to alleviate potential criticism. There is also evidence that judges' gender impacts not only how they decide cases, but also the time and manner in which they do so. Female judges in federal district courts appear to settle their cases more frequently and more quickly than their male counterparts.[33]

Nevertheless, scholars disagree as to whether White and Black judges sentence rule similarly. Across 22 federal district courts, Black judges are more likely to grant pretrial release to White defendants without substantial conditions, compared with White judges.[34] Furthermore, Black judges make incarceration decisions more similarly for White and Black offenders than

---

27 Kastellec, supra note 15.

28 Christina L. Boyd, *Representation on The Courts? The Effects of Trial Judges' Sex and Race*, 69 Pol.Res.Q. 788 (2016).

29 Thomas G. Walker & Deborah J. Barrow, *The Diversification of the Federal Bench: Policy and Process Ramifications*, 47 J.Pol. 596 (1985).

30 Lydia Tiede, Robert Carp, R. & Kenneth L. Manning, K., *Judicial Attributes and Sentencing-Deviation Cases: Do Sex, Race, and Politics Matter?*, 31 Just.Syst.J. 249 (2010).

31 See, Christina L. Boyd & Michael J. Nelson, *The Effects of Trial Judge Gender and Public Opinion on Criminal Sentencing Decisions*, 70 Vand.L.Rev. 1819 (2017), finding that in marijuana-related drug cases in Colorado trial courts, female judges sentence female defendants more leniently than male judges. Also see, Ethan D. Boldt, Boyd, Christina L., Carlos, Roberto F. & Matthew E. Baker, *The Effects of Judge Race and Sex on Pretrial Detention Decisions*, 42 Just.Syst.J. 1 (2021), conducting a study of 22 federal district courts and finding that female judges are more likely to set monetary bail for or detain male defendants and less likely for female defendants.

32 Jennifer Segal, *Representative Decision Making on the Federal Bench: Clinton's District Court Appointees*, 53 Pol.Res.Q. 137 (2000).

33 Christina L. Boyd, *She'll Settle It?*, 1 J.L. & Courts 193 (2013).

34 Boldt et al., supra note 31.

White judges.[35] Steffensmeier and Britt[36] find that Black and White judges sentence Black defendants more harshly. Welch et al. observe Black judges to be somewhat more lenient toward Black defendants than Whites, whereas White judges were more equal in their treatment of Black and White defendants.[37] Additionally, a study of EEOC-brought cases in federal trial courts reveals that Black judges were more likely to rule in favor of plaintiffs making race discrimination claims than White judges.[38]

Meanwhile, other research fails to uncover any significant differences between women and minority judges' rulings and those of their White male counterparts. An examination of disability cases in federal district courts produced no evidence that men and women decide their cases differently.[39] Scholars also failed to observe statistically significant evidence that judges' gender impacts the sentence lengths they imposed in felony cases in the Circuit Court of Cook County, Illinois.[40] When examining criminal sentences in state courts, researchers could not discern any sentencing differences between judges of different races.[41] Furthermore, Steffensmeier and Britt find no difference in the way judges of different races weight case and offender information.[42] Moreover, Black judges were no more likely than White judges to support Black claims in racially salient federal district court cases; and Walker and Barrow uncover few policy and process differences between White and Black judges on U.S. district courts.[43]

Since Crenshaw's formative article articulating the effects of intersectional discrimination, scholars have begun studying how women of color's combined experiences of gender and race shape their lives and careers.[44] Unfortunately, the historical underrepresentation of women of color on the courts long forced scholars to study judicial race and gender as separate attributes; however, a growing body of research investigating the combined influences of intersectional identities on judging has emerged with the increased presence of women of color on the bench. Women of color courts of appeals judges are more likely to rule in favor of criminal defendants' claims than judges from any other race-gender category,[45] and Black

---

[35] Darrell Steffensmeier & Chester L. Britt, *Judges' Race and Judicial Decision Making: Do Black Judges Sentence Differently?*, 82 Soc.Sci.Q. 749 (2001); Susan Welch, Michael Combs & John Gruhl, *Do Black Judges Make a Difference?*, 32 AJPS 126 (1988).

[36] *Id.*

[37] Susan Welch, Michael Combs & John Gruhl, *Do Black Judges Make a Difference?*, 32 AJPS 126 (1988).

[38] Christina L. Boyd, *Representation on The Courts? The effects of Trial Judges' Sex and Race*, 69 Pol.Res.Q. 788 (2016).

[39] Boyd & Rutkowski, supra note 22.

[40] David S. Abrams, Marianne Bertrand & Sendhil Mulainathan, *Do Judges Vary in Their Treatment of Race?*, 41 JLS 347 (2012).

[41] Abrams *Id.*; Cassia Spohn, *The Sentencing Decisions of Black and White Judges: Expected and Unexpected Similarities*, 24 L.& Soc'y Rev. 1197 (1990).

[42] Steffensmeier & Britt 2001, supra note 35.

[43] Segal, supra note 30; Walker & Barrow, supra note 29.

[44] Kimberle Crenshaw, *Demarginalizing the Intersection of Race and Sex: A Black Feminist Critique of Antidiscrimination Doctrine, Feminist Theory and Antiracist Politics*, 1989 U. Chi. Legal F. 139 (1989).

[45] Todd A. Collins & Laura P. Moyer, *Gender, Race, and Intersectionality on the Federal Appellate Bench*, 61 Pol.Res.Q. 219 (2008).

women on the circuit courts vote more liberally in gender discrimination cases.[46] Moreover, Black women on state supreme courts exhibit distinct dissenting behavior.[47] Additionally, the opinions produced by more racially and gender-diverse courts include a broader examination of legal issues.[48] These findings are noteworthy, as they suggest that while intersectionality remains understudied, judges belonging to multiple underrepresented groups appear to decide cases differently than their majority race and gender peers. Overall, researchers attempting to ascertain whether judges from underrepresented groups exhibit distinctive behavior on the bench produce substantial evidence indicating that, while the effect of judges' race and gender appears nuanced and contextual, gender and race are salient facets of judicial behavior.

Gender, Race, and Perceptions of Judicial Competence

Research examining judicial decision-making indicates that minority trial judges might behave differently due to their race, gender, ideologies, or a combination of those attributes (at least in certain contexts), which in turn shapes winners and losers before the courts. If the rulings emerging from minority judges' courts differ substantially from their majority race, gender, and ideological peers, we might expect cases from minority judges' courts to be appealed and reversed more often. On the other hand, research also suggests a second causal mechanism that could lead to more review of minority judges' cases. An equally relevant, but less explored, area of research argues that people's perception of judges varies in response to judges' demographic characteristics. Kirkpatrick argues that the ideal of the neutral, impartial judge in the U.S. is psychologically linked with the White, male standard, which in turn confers an expectation of impartiality on White male judges, while raising issues of suspicion and bias for "non-standard" judges.[49] If Kirkpatrick is correct, and minority judges face credibility issues simply because they do not fit the White, male standard, women and judges of color might experience more judicial scrutiny.

Scholarship consistently shows that women, racial, and ethnic minorities experience discrimination in the legal profession[50] and are often perceived as less capable.[51] When surveyed, Black women judges report experiencing disrespect in the courtroom and having their legitimacy questioned by fellow judges, lawyers, and litigants, and report identity-based recusal

---

[46] Susan B. Haire & Laura P. Moyer, Diversity Matters: Judicial Policy Making in the U.S. Courts of Appeals, University of Virginia Press (2015).

[47] John Szmer, Robert K. Christensen & Erin B. Kaheny, *Gender, Race, and Dissensus on State Supreme Courts*, 96 Soc.Sci.Q. 553 (2015).

[48] Susan B. Haire, Laura P. Moyer & Shawn Treier, *Diversity, Deliberation, and Judicial Opinion Writing*, 1 J.L. & Courts 303 (2013).

[49] Jennet Kirkpatrick, *Fairness Has a Face: Neutrality and Descriptive Representation on Courts*, 8 Pol., Groups, & Identities 803 (2020).

[50] Robert L. Nelson, Ioana Sendroui, Ronit Dinovitzer & Meghan Dawe, *Perceiving Discrimination: Race, Gender, and Sexual Orientation in the Legal Workforce*, L.&Soc.Inquiry 1051 (2019); Todd A. Collins, Tao L. Dumas & Laura P. Moyer, *Intersecting Disadvantages: Race, Gender, and Age Discrimination Among Attorneys*, 98 Soc.Sci.Q. 1642 (2017).

[51] Deborah L. Rhode, Women and Leadership: The Trouble with Lawyers, Oxford University Press (2017); Cecilia L. Ridgeway, Kristen Backor, Yan E. Li, Justine E. Tinkler & Kristan G. Erickson, *How Easily Does a Social Difference Become a Status Distinction? Gender Matters*, 74 Am.Soc.Rev. 44 (2009).

requests.[52] Additionally, other research uncovers evidence demonstrating that the public regularly perceives diverse judges as biased and susceptible to ingroup favoritism.[53] When exploring appeals and reversal rates with respect to judges' gender, race, and ideology, it is possible that biased views of minority judges' legitimacy and quality affect the probability that their cases receive appellate scrutiny, regardless of any empirical differences in trial judges' behavior.

Although evaluators seek impartial measures of judicial performance, scholars uncover evidence that race and gender biases impact these measures. One such judicial evaluation measure is the American Bar Association (ABA) ratings for federal judges. ABA ratings are important because they correlate with whether a judicial nominee is confirmed.[54] Prior studies show that traits such as prestige,[55] ABA qualification ratings,[56] and even religious beliefs[57] impact perceptions of judges' quality. Moreover, multiple studies of federal judicial selection observe that female and minority race judicial nominees consistently receive lower ratings than males, even when controlling for their experience and several other relevant factors.[58] Sen, however, observes the noteworthy finding that ABA ratings are not predictive of judges' reversal rates, suggesting that lower ABA ratings are not necessarily associated with poorer performance once on the bench.[59] Although the judicial confirmation process also serves as another measure of judges' perceived quality, research also finds gender and race differences. Female and racial minority candidates for Courts of Appeals are only confirmed after atypically long vacancies, regardless of their qualifications.[60] Studies of other judicial ratings systems produce similar evidence of race and gender bias in supposedly objective rating systems. When surveyed, attorneys in Clark County, Nevada consistently rated female and

---

[52] Taneisha N. Means, *Her Honor: Black Women Judges' Experiences with Disrespect and Recusal Requests in the American Judiciary*, 1554–4788 J.WOMEN.POL.POL'Y 1 (2022).

[53] For a discussion of the debates and evidence regarding judges' attributes and perceived bias, see Allision P. Harris & Maya Sen, *Bias and Judging*, 22 A.REV.POL.S. 241 (2019); Also see, Yoshikuni Ono & Michael A. Zilis, *Do American Perceive Diverse Judges as Inherently Biased?*, 14 POL. GROUPS & IDENTITIES 1 (2021), using an experimental survey design and a nationally representative sample to show that a large portion of the public believe that women and Hispanic judges are biased in favor of women and Hispanics, respectively.

[54] Maya Sen, *Below the bar? Racial and Gender Bias in Judicial Nominations, In Visions in Methodology Conference*, State College, PA. (2012).

[55] David Klein & Darby Morrisroe, *The Prestige and Influence of Individual Judges on the U.S. Courts of Appeals*, 28 JLS 371 (1999).

[56] Royce De Rohan Barondes, *ABA Judicial Ratings as the 'Gold Standard' or Fool's Gold: Federal District Judge Ratings and Reversals, Working Paper*, School of Law, University of Missouri–Columbia (2010).

[57] Andre P. Audette & Christopher L. Weaver, *Faith in the Court: Religious Out-Groups and the Perceived Legitimacy of Judicial Decisions*, 49 L.& SOC'Y REV. 1022 (2015).

[58] Susan Brodie Haire, *Rating the Ratings of the American Bar Association Standing Committee on Federal Judiciary*, 22 JUST.SYST.J. 1 (2001); Sen *id.*; Maya Sen, *How Judicial Qualification Ratings May Disadvantage Minority and Female Candidates*, 2 J.L. & COURTS 33 (2014).

[59] Sen *Id.*

[60] David C. Nixon & David L. Goss, *Confirmation Delay for Vacancies on the Circuit Courts of Appeals*, 29 AM.POL.RESEARCH 246 (2001).

minority race judges' judicial performance significantly lower than their male counterparts, even with all other factors being equal.[61]

Other measurements of perceived judicial quality involve how judges view each other, such as determining opinion assignment and whom to citate in opinions. When deciding which precedents to cite, judges likely reference other judges whom they respect or agree with to strengthen their own opinions. Yet there is an apparent gender gap in citations. A study of federal circuit courts uncovers ingroup favoritism among female and minority judges who cite each other but not among males.[62] In terms of assigning a writer for a majority opinion, the judge making the decision generally prefers a strong opinion that will be upheld; therefore, the judge will likely assign opinion authorship to a colleague whom she/he perceives as capable of writing a strong and respected opinion that will prevent a reversal. However, when male courts of appeals judges assign opinions, they tend to assign published opinions to other male judges and assign women judges more unpublished opinions, suggesting that male opinion assigners perceive women judges as less capable of writing strong opinions.[63] Additionally, White judges were more likely to assign published opinions to other White judges and less likely to assign White judges unpublished opinions.[64]

Another key measurement of judges' perceptions of each other is an appellate judge's decision to overrule a lower court judge. A judge's choice to overturn another's decision is an indication of disagreement, and therefore disapproval. A judge whose decisions are rarely overturned is more likely to be perceived as legitimate by their peers and members of the higher court, as other judges agreed with her, and therefore approved of her rulings. In both federal district and appeals courts, Black judges' decisions were overturned on appeal significantly more than White judges, even after controlling for several relevant qualifications.[65] Taken together, these studies indicate that White judges are more likely to overturn minority judges' decisions, are less likely to cite minority judges' opinions, and are less likely to assign minority judges important opinions to write; all indicating that White, male judges either consciously or unconsciously perceive their non-White and non-male counterparts as less capable.

In addition to studies of elite perception of judicial quality, researchers also investigate how the general public evaluates judges. A study where participants analyzed the legitimacy of judges on the Indiana Supreme Court uncovered two main findings: First, across all levels of education, men had lower levels of diffuse support for judges when the men were told that the chief justice was a woman. Second, women with lower levels of education had significantly increased legitimacy scores when they knew the chief justice was a woman.[66] When under-

---

[61] Rebecca D. Gill, Sylvia R. Lazos & Mallory M. Waters, *Are Judicial Performance Evaluations Fair to Women and Minorities? A Cautionary Tale from Clark County, Nevada*, 45 L.& Soc'y Rev. 731 (2011).

[62] Rachael K. Hinkle & Michael J. Nelson, *The Intergroup Foundations of Policy Influence*, 71 Pol. Res.Q. 729 (2018).

[63] Elizabeth A. Tillman & Rachael K Hinkle, *Of Whites and Men: How Gender and Race Impact Authorship of Published and Unpublished Opinions in the US Courts of Appeals*, 5 Res. & Pol. DOI: https://doi.org/10.1177/2053168018762869 (2018).

[64] Tillman and Hinkle, *Id.*

[65] Maya Sen, *Is Justice Really Blind? Race and Appellate Review in U.S. Courts*, 44 JLS 187 (2015).

[66] Claire Lee, Rorie Solberg, & Eric N. Waltenburg, *See Jane Judge: Descriptive Representation and Diffuse Support for a State Supreme Court*, DOI: 10.1080/21565503.2020.1864651 Pol. Groups, & Identities 1 (2021).

graduate students participated in an experiment where they read fictitious vignettes about judicial decision-making in child custody cases, the judge's gender determined whether the subjects agreed with the ruling; although the gender of the subject conditioned the effect.[67] For instance, when a judge ruled in favor of a female litigant, male respondents were more likely to attribute the decision to external influences, such as gender. In other words, the correspondence between the gender of the successful party and the survey respondent conditions the respondent's agreement with the judge's decision and the perceived legitimacy of that decision. Taken together, research tends to show that women and racial minority judges are evaluated more critically by external audiences and by their fellow judges and may suffer from a lack of perceived ability, even when there is no empirical difference in quality.

Collectively, extant research indicates that minority judges (race, gender, or ideological) might make decisions that differ from those of their majority gender, race, and ideological peers. If the verdicts emanating from these courts differ substantially from the norm, we might expect more appeals and reversals of these cases. However, the considerably mixed findings regarding the relationship between race, gender, and trial court ideology and case outcomes could imply that the constraints of the judicial hierarchy might cause trial judges to make similar decisions, regardless of the trial judges' disposition or preferences. Yet research uncovers considerable evidence that minority, gender and race judges are perceived as less capable and/or legitimate, even when empirical evidence suggests otherwise. If litigants and appeals court judges view minority trial judges as less legitimate, these judges might find themselves subject to greater review and reversal, even if the verdicts rendered in the courts do not deviate from the norm.

DATA AND METHODS

The purpose of this research is to first explore whether verdicts vary across courts based on trial judges' demographic and partisan backgrounds and then to investigate whether race, gender, and partisan minority judges are subject to more appeals and reversals. Studying the judicial process of cases from trial to appeal requires access to both trial court outcomes and appeals court rulings. State trial court data, unlike appeals court data, is not easily accessed using legal research search engines such as Westlaw or LexisNexis, which has consistently limited scholarly study of these courts. Although considerably more is known about state appellate courts, the lack of trial court data limits our understanding of the filtering process that determines which cases these courts adjudicate. The data collection for this study is uniquely useful for studying judicial process in the state courts.[68] We first relied on an original dataset of all case outcomes rendered in Alabama circuit courts, general jurisdiction trial courts, between 2001 and 2018 (3,419 verdicts) using the *Alabama Jury Verdict Reporter*.[69] We then used Westlaw

[67] Michael P. Fix & Gbemende E. Johnson, *Public Perceptions of Gender Bias in the Decisions of Female State Court Judges*, 70 VAND.L.REV. 1845 (2017).

[68] Alabama organizes its general jurisdiction trial courts into 49 circuits, comprising one or more counties. The Supreme Court of Alabama has exclusive jurisdiction over civil cases where the controversy exceeds $50,000. The Court of Civil Appeals serves as the intermediate appellate court and has appellate jurisdiction over cases where the damages do not exceed $50,000.

[69] This is a paid subscription service, used primarily by attorneys, that attempts to report every recorded trial verdict in the state of Alabama each year. We used the reporters to manually code each case. Denise Miller, ed, *The Alabama Jury Verdict Reporter* (2001–2018), 17 vols.

searches to ascertain which cases were appealed and reversed,[70] resulting in 297 appeals (9%) and 75 reversals (2% of all cases and 25% of appealed cases).[71] Finally, we obtained judges' partisan identifications[72] from election archives obtained from the Alabama Secretary of State. Alabama trial courts during the time period comprised judges who were 46% Democrats, 43% Republicans, and 10% non-major party affiliated. We then coded each judge's gender using judges' names for gender cues.[73] Finally, we used Google searches to determine the judges' gender when it was not immediately discernible, and to find each judge's race. Of the judges in our data, 86% are men and 12% are women. In terms of race, Alabama trial judges are 81% White, 7% Black, and 0.5% some other demographic beyond White or Black.

We first seek to understand whether verdicts vary across judges' demographic and partisan backgrounds. Although one may not typically think of civil litigation as a political issue, debates around tort reform evidence a clear ideological dimension. The Republican party maintains a pro-reform stance in the current party platform that views civil courts as largely pro-plaintiff and seeks to limit the size of awards plaintiffs can collect.[74] Meanwhile, trial lawyers who often align themselves with the Democratic party argue that the civil justice system serves an important role in protecting the public from negligence. According to Yeazell, tort reform, framed as an attempt to rein in "frivolous" lawsuits and excessive damages awards, emerged in the late 1970s as a partisan political issue due to significant economic changes, such as a decline in domestic manufacturing and rising healthcare costs.[75] When both parties failed to protect workers and consumers, "Republicans sought to limit civil litigation on the grounds that lawyers and litigation were ruining the country—or at least important swaths of the economy—while Democrats defended litigation and proposed more of it as a solution to one or more problems."[76]

---

[70] We coded any case in the dataset where an appeals court made any ruling on the case, even if the ruling was a denial of *cert* or a dismissal, in published and unpublished decisions. The aim of this measure was to determine, to the extent possible, whether one party sought an appeal. This measure admittedly does not capture cases where an appeal was filed but where the parties eventually settled. This data is unfortunately not available. Like previous scholarship investigating appeals in the federal courts (see Boyd, supra note 11), we include partial reversals in the reversal variable.

[71] Although we were unable to find an estimate of the rate of appeals for state civil trials, 9% seems reasonably consistent with the 10% appeals rate reported for federal courts; see Theodore Eisenberg, *Appeal Rates and Outcomes in Tried and Nontried Cases: Further Exploration of Anti-Plaintiff Appellate Outcomes*, 1 JELS 659 (2004).

[72] We acknowledge that partisan identification and ideology are separate and distinct concepts, and that more nuanced measures of ideology might yield better predictions of judicial behavior (see Brace et al., supra note 6; Adam Bonica & Maya Sen, *Estimating Judicial Ideology* 35 J. of Economic Perspectives 97 (2021); Windett et al., supra note 7). However, we are interested in how external audiences perceive judges, rather than predicting their behavior. As such, party ID serves as the most readily cognizable and available method for nonacademics to approximate a judge's ideological background, especially in a state such as Alabama where all judges run for reelection in partisan races.

[73] We acknowledge that gender is not a variable (see David R. Cox, *Causality: Some Statistical Aspects*, 155 J. Royal Statistical Society, Series A 291 (1992)), and measures of judges' gender identity (as masculine or feminine) would provide a better measure of gender; however, we unfortunately cannot assess judges' gender identities from the data available.

[74] See p. 44 of the 2016 Republican Party Platform (renewed in 2020).

[75] Yeazell, Stephen, Lawsuits in a Market Economy, University of Chicago Press (2018).

[76] Yeazell, 83, *Id.*

The tort reform debate was especially contentious in Alabama following the salient ruling in the fraud and breach of contract case *BMW of North America, Inc v Dole* 646 So.2d 619 (where the Supreme Court of Alabama reduced a jury's $4 million punitive damages award to $2 million, which was later overturned by the Supreme Court of the United States). In the wake of the ruling, the Alabama state legislature ultimately adopted 29 different tort reforms. Additionally, the politics of tort reform directly impacted judicial selection in the state. Alabama utilizes partisan elections to retain judges at all levels of the judiciary, and has possessed a conservative, Republican majority since Carl Rove, a famous Republican political consultant, and pro-business groups actively worked to elect Republican appeals court judges following the *BMW* ruling.[77]

Consequently, the issue of civil litigation is likely salient in Alabama and one where we might reasonably expect judges to possess ideological preferences. Likewise, pro-plaintiff verdicts and larger awards should represent liberal rulings, while defense verdicts and smaller awards reflect more conservative outcomes. As such, we might expect women, racial and ethnic minorities, and Democratic judges to possess more liberal views, which might lead to more pro-plaintiff dispositions. Moreover, if pro-plaintiff verdicts represent liberal outcomes in a state where the appeals courts comprise Republican judges, we might also expect higher appeals and reversal rates for judges with higher percentages of plaintiff wins and larger awards. While a variety of factors likely shape the decision to appeal, the data supports the notion that appeals are largely brought by defendants who lost at trial. Sixty-five percent of appeals were brought by original defendants, which could imply that appellants who were originally aligned with the side typically supported by Republicans (defendants) expect more favorable outcomes from the appeals courts.

Table 4.1 reports case outcomes at trial and on appeal across judges' demographic and partisan backgrounds. The table first reports plaintiff success rates and median and average awards based on the independent variables: judges' race (White or Black),[78] gender (male or female),[79] race and gender (White males and females, compared with racial minority males and females), and party affiliation (Democrat or Republican). We then conduct bivariate regressions for each dependent variable (percent pro-plaintiff verdicts, median and mean awards, and whether the case was appealed or reversed).[80] The data shows that for most judges, the plaintiff success rate is close to 50%, which is consistent with the expectations of Priest and Klein's selection hypothesis.[81] Interestingly, plaintiffs have the least success when a Black judge presided over the case (plaintiffs won only 34% of these cases); however, this effect is not statistically significant. Given that a pro-plaintiff outcome is generally considered liberal (and pro-defendant conservative), this finding is opposite what one might expect. This might support previous studies that find that racial minority and women judges act in ways counter to expectations in

---

[77] For a history of tort reform and judicial selection in Alabama and other states, see Anthony Champagne, *Tort Reform and Judicial Selection*, LOY. L.A. L. REV. 1483 (2005).

[78] Although we coded for other races/ethnicities, there are too few judges belonging to other race/ethnic categories to make meaningful comparisons.

[79] We acknowledge that gender is not binary and that a measure of each judges' gender identity would be more accurate; however, we lack the ability to create such a measure.

[80] For continuous dependent variables (the percent pro-plaintiff verdicts, and median and average awards), we use ordinary least squares regressions. For the dichotomous dependent variables (whether the case was appealed or reversed), we utilize logistic regression.

[81] Priest and Klein, supra note 2.

Table 4.1 *Case outcomes by judges' race, gender, and party ID*

	% Pro-plaintiff	Median award	Average award	% Appealed	% Reversed
White	54%	$35,000	$975,657	8%	2% [–]
Black	34%	$37,500	$1,205,441	10%	3% [+]
Male	51%	$35,000	$1,545,718	8%	2%
Female	52%	$35,000	$491,488	8%	3%
White male	54%	$35,000	$1,015,955	8%	2% [–]
White female	52%	$40,000	$552,951	8%	2%
Racial minority male	38%	$35,000	$2,227,684 [+]	10%	2% [+]
Racial minority female	51%	$28,591 [–]	$386,406	8%	5% [+]
Republican	53%	$30,000	$2,361,430	8%	3% [–]
Democrat	49%	$37,500	$847,987	9%	2% [+]

Note: Symbols in brackets denote the direction of statistically significant effects from bivariate regressions at the 0.05 significance level or higher.

order to avoid negative scrutiny.[82] Yet none of the gender, race, or partisan affiliation variables significantly impact the percent pro-plaintiff verdicts, indicating that verdicts are similar across judges' background characteristics.

Next the table reports the median and average award for each group of judges. First, median awards for all judges are $37,000 or less, indicating that the typical award in civil trials is not especially large. Although median and average awards are largest in courts with Black and Democratic judges, the differences between the awards rendered by courts with Black and White and Democrat and Republican judges is not especially large. Yet the data also shows that successful plaintiffs receive the smallest median and average awards when a non-White woman presided over the trial, and this difference is statistically significant. This is an especially surprising finding, given that this is the opposite of what theory would predict. On the other hand, awards rendered in minority male judges' courts are significantly larger than those of courts with other race/gender combinations of judges. On average, the data indicates that plaintiff success rates and awards are largely similar, regardless of the judges' background. Based on these data, there is little reason to expect differences in appeals and reversals for any demographic or partisan group of judges. While plaintiffs win somewhat less often before racial minority male judges and receive smaller awards when the trial judge is a non-White woman, these outcomes should align with the conversative preferences of the appeals courts in the state.

Yet when we turn to appeals and reversals, the data shows that the appeals rate is only 2% higher for Black judges than for White judges and 1% higher for Democrats than Republicans. Bivariate regression analyses confirm that there is no significant difference between the appeals rate for gender, race, or partisan grouping of judges. However, when we turn to reversals, the data shows interesting differences relating to judges' gender, race, and party affiliation. White judges are significantly less likely to have their cases overturned than minority race judges. Alabama appeals courts reverse male and White judges in only 2% of cases. The data shows female judges experience a 3% reversal rate; however, the effect of judge gender is not significant without the additional consideration of the judge's race. Interestingly, the data indicates that appeals courts reverse the largest percentage of verdicts when a non-White

82 William and Law, supra note 21; Segal, supra note 32.

woman presided over the case, even though these are the cases where plaintiffs experience no apparent advantage in win rates and receive the smallest awards when successful. In fact, the data shows that minority race men and women are overturned significantly more often than their majority race counterparts. Although this finding cannot confirm a causal relationship between a judge's gender and race and appeals courts' rulings, the data reveal patterns of appeals and reversals that are not intuitively related to patterns of verdicts and awards, which support a hypothesis of racial and gender bias.

To more deeply explore the relationship between judges' race, gender, and partisanship, Table 4.2 reports the appeals and reversal rates for White male, White female, racial minority males, and racial minority females, separated by partisan affiliation (Democrat or Republican), and the results of additional bivariate regressions. First the data shows that the appeals rate for judges remains similar across gender, race, and partisan groupings of judges, and we uncover no significant effects for appeals. Alabama appeals courts review 8% of White male judges' cases and reverse them in 2% of cases, regardless of party affiliation. Appeals rates for minority men are also identical, and the reversal rate is similar. For White female judges, the appeals rate doubles when she is a Democrat (10%, as compared with only 5% for Republican women), and while no Republican, White women were reversed, 3% of Democrats were. There are no minority race women who are Republicans in the data, which unfortunately prevents a comparison. However, the appeals rate for non-White women judges is also similar to other judges; yet minority women Democrats are reversed at the highest rate (5%). This is especially interesting, since these are also the judges whose courts evidence no real advantage for plaintiffs and dispense the lowest median and average awards. While we cannot definitively explain what causes this phenomenon, it would appear that minority women attempt to conform to conservative norms but are still more likely to have their rulings appealed and reversed. More information is needed to determine precisely why this happens, but gender and race bias that lead appellate court judges to view minority women as less competent presents one possible explanation. Yet when we turn to reversals, the data once again produces evidence that judges' gender, race, and partisan affiliation predict the likelihood that the appellate court reverses verdicts. The data indicates that appeals courts reverse trial court decisions significantly less often when a Republican man presided over the case, and this effect holds for both White and minority male judges. However, appeals courts reverse cases presided over by minority race men and women who are Democrats significantly more often. Although more information is needed to fully explicate the causal mechanisms, the observed pattern of reversal could support a hypothesis that Alabama appeals courts view judges belonging to both a minority race or ethnic group and the minority party more critically.

Table 4.2 *Appeals and reversals for combinations of judges' race, gender, and party ID*

	Republicans		Democrats	
	Appealed	Reversed	Appealed	Reversed
White male judge	8%	2% [–]	8%	2%
White female judge	5%	0	10%	3%
Racial minority male judge	10%	2% [–]	10%	4% [+]
Racial minority female judge	—	—	9%	5% [+]

Note: Symbols in brackets denote the direction of statistically significant effects from bivariate regressions at the 0.05 significance level or higher.

DISCUSSION

In this research we seek to explore how cases progress from trial to appeal and whether the attributes of the trial judges, relative to the judges who review them, affect the judicial process. We rely on an original data source of trials and appeals and judges' demographic and partisan backgrounds. This new and extensive data collection allows for an exploration of 18 years of trial court data in the state of Alabama and any resulting appeals court rulings. The data collection provides an opportunity to shed light on understudied relationships concerning judicial process. Although the results provide an initial assessment, in only one state can we jointly theorize about trials and appeals and begin to empirically investigate their linkages. Additionally, this research contributes to extant scholarship concerned with case selection, judicial decision-making, and gender and race effects on judging.

Our first goal was to discern whether trial court rulings vary in significant ways across judges' gender, race, and partisan affiliations. The data suggests very little difference in trial outcomes across judges of different races, genders, or partisan affiliations. To the extent that we observe differences in verdicts, the data suggests patterns opposite to what we might intuitively expect. The data shows that pro-plaintiff verdicts, the liberal outcome, occur less frequently in courts presided over by Black and Democratic judges, and the awards winners receive are significantly smaller when the judge is a non-White woman. Segal argues the apparent contradiction in female judges' behavior might stem from women judges' perceptions of themselves as minorities and a deliberate attempt to decide cases in a manner to alleviate potential criticism, rather than in line with personal policy or ideological positions.[83] Although we cannot know for certain what causes the observed pattern between judges' demographics and case outcomes, one possible explanation is that minority judges (gender, race, and partisan identification) in Alabama are cognizant of their minority status and seek to avoid standing out.

Next, we examined patterns of appeals and reversals to discern whether an apparent relationship exists between trial outcomes and appeals. We find that appeals rates are similar across judges' demographic and partisan backgrounds for all judges, which suggests that other factors besides the presiding judge determine the decision to appeal in many cases. Although more research is needed to explain what causes losing parties to appeal these cases, the data presented here does not support the hypothesis that losing parties view their losses as less legitimate, and therefore appeal more frequently, when a minority judge presides over the case. While reversals are similar for all men and White women, reversals show a stronger relationship with the judges' race, gender, and partisan identification. The data indicates that appeals courts reverse cases presided over by minority race women and men who are Democrats far more often than cases presided over by any other combination of race, gender, or partisan identification. Moreover, reversals do not seem to reflect patterns of verdicts. Although successful plaintiffs receive the least compensation, on average, when a minority woman presides over the case, reversal rates for this group of judges are still noticeably higher than for their peers. This finding could suggest that appeals court judges view minority women as less legitimate than other judges. Taken together, the data indicates that judges across gender, race, and party ID experience relatively similar rates of appeals; meanwhile, gender, race, and party ID appear

---

[83] See Segal, supra note 32.

to strongly predict reversals for men and women of color. Our findings also imply that while lawyers' and litigants' appeals choices do not appear to be responses to judges' demographic or partisan backgrounds; appellate court judges' views of their minority lower-court counterparts might reflect biased beliefs about minority judges' ability or decision-making, even though major differences in their verdicts are not overtly apparent in the data.

The results presented here are clearly exploratory; however, they provide several pathways for future research. First, our research indicates that the institutional structure of Alabama courts affects the judicial process by conditioning which cases are reversed by the appellate courts. The institutional design in Alabama, where trial judges retain their seats through partisan, district-based elections, results in a trial bench populated by a sizable number of judges who belong to a minority party, race, gender, or combination of those attributes; however, statewide races for the state's appeals courts create a white, Republican appellate bench. Bonneau and Rice maintain that in addition to judges' race, the overall composition of the bench, the socialization and experience of the judges, and institutional arrangements impact behavior.[84] Our results bolster their argument regarding an interaction between race (as well as gender) and institutions and judicial behavior. The findings uncovered in Alabama should generalize to other states where the public selects trial judges locally and where appellate judges are selected through a statewide election or other selection process. Additionally, the findings here indicate a need for a multi-state study of judicial process. States rely on a variety of institutional arrangements and methods of judicial selection and retention, and often utilize different methods and rules across levels of the judiciary. Comparative state court research examining which cases are appealed and reversed could shed light on the relationship between a variety of combinations of judicial institutions and judicial process. All these features potentially condition trial judges' behavior, litigants' responses to trial verdicts and the decision to appeal, as well as which cases appeals courts reverse. Investigating the relationship between different state institutional arrangements and judicial process presents a fruitful avenue for future study.

Finally, future research should also explore the impact of the patterns uncovered here. Civil trial courts process important cases that impact the lives of everyday citizens. While we uncover some differences in outcomes across judges' demographics, we do not investigate which litigants win and lose in which courts; however, this information is important for understanding trial court decision-making and its impact on the people who access the courts. We also know that trial judges avoid reversals in order to protect their reputations, improve their chances of obtaining a higher office, and minimize their workloads.[85] The observation that women of color experience more reversals than their peers (even though the decisions from their courts actually appear more conservative) could have implications for the advancement of women of color to higher levels of the judiciary. Future research should explore whether patterns of reversals affect which judges ascend to higher courts. Our initial findings suggest that trials, appeals, and reversals are connected, as are judges' partisan and demographic backgrounds. In order to understand judicial process more fully, we must further explore these linkages.

---

84 See Bonneau and Rice, supra note 23.

85 Stephen J. Choi, Mitu Gulati & Eric Posner, *What Do Federal District Judges Want? An Analysis of Publications, Citation, and Reversals*, 28 J.L.Econ.&Org. 518 (2012).

5. Judges and politics in UK courts

Lewis Graham

In recent years in the United Kingdom, there has been something of a growing sentiment, largely (but not exclusively) coming from conservative circles, that judges are straying too far from the law and into the realm of politics. Resistance to the "judicialisation" of political issues is hardly a new phenomenon, but it has recently been taken up not only by commentators,[1] but also by the (Conservative) government.

It is now somewhat common, for example, to hear politicians deriding "activist judges"[2] and "lefty human rights lawyers"[3] who curry their favour. This rhetoric is amplified in the aftermath of an unpopular judicial decision. Responding to an unpopular judgment in relation to Brexit, one minister criticised the "biased" judges for "interfering in politics".[4] The government's legal officers have notably said similar; the Attorney General has accused judges of "exercis[ing] political power" and "trespass[ing] into… political terrain" – her solution was to "take back control" to reverse the "chronic and steady encroachment" of "activist judges".[5]

Framing the judiciary as an institution espousing political values, especially where those values can be framed as being in opposition to the government of the day, or "the will of the people", is doubtless a useful political tool. It can be employed to deflect criticism of government policies,[6] and to bolster support for policies which seek to control or limit the judiciary, particularly with regards executive oversight.

---

1 The most infamous example in recent times is the *Daily Mail*'s "Enemies of the People" headline (*Enemies of the People*, DAILY MAIL, 4 November 2016), which attacked three judges who ruled that the approval of Parliament was required in order to lawfully invoke Article 50 of the Treaty of the European Union, initiating withdrawal from the European Union. Over 1,000 complaints were made against the piece, which described the judges as biased, out of touch and, in one passage, "openly gay".

2 See e.g. Suella Braverman, 671 Parl Deb HC (2020), col. 331: "the explosion of… judicial activism has led to a censoriousness and litigiousness in our society and has distorted questions that ought to remain exclusively political"; Baroness Noakes, 810 Parl Deb HL (2021), col. 324: "we have an activist judiciary, especially… in the Supreme Court"; Lord Blencathra, 809 Parl Deb HL (2021), col. 2098: "I have believed for some time that judicial activism in this country… has gone too far."

3 *Conservative conference: Boris Johnson's attack on 'lefty human rights lawyers' branded shocking by Bar Council* THE INDEPENDENT, 6 October 2020.

4 *Kwasi Kwarteng criticised for biased judges comment*, BBC NEWS (12 September 2019), https://www.bbc.co.uk/news/uk-politics-49670901.

5 Suella Braverman, *People we elect must take back control from people we don't. Who include the judges*. CONSERVATIVE HOME (27 January 2020), https://www.conservativehome.com/platform/2020/01/suella-braverman-people-we-elect-must-take-back-control-from-people-we-dont-who-include-the-judges.html.

6 For example, whilst Home Secretary, Theresa May decried the judges for using human rights laws to protect "violent drug dealer[s]" and "the illegal immigrant who cannot be deported because… he had a pet cat". The latter claim has been debunked: Adam Wagner, *Catgate: another myth used to trash human rights*, THE GUARDIAN, (4 October 2011), https://www.theguardian.com/law/2011/oct/04/theresa-may-wrong-cat-deportation. Such claims are not exclusive to members of the Conservative Party: David Blunkett frequently clashed with senior judges ("airy-fairy libertarians") who declared his national secu-

Further, and paradoxically, it seems that judges are simultaneously viewed as old guard conservatives as well as soft-hearted members of the chattering classes.[7] Conventionally, there has been a perception that senior judges are, first, traditional; second, part of the establishment; third, on the right of the political spectrum.[8] As Stevens put it, "[o]ne suspects most normally voted Tory."[9] However, more recently there has been something of a shift to a vision of the judiciary as a more liberal institution.[10] There is some evidence that they are viewed as "soft" in some areas, such as where human rights are concerned,[11] in immigration cases,[12] or in sentencing matters.[13] In light of successful challenges to the government's Brexit strategy, some media outlets have characterised the judiciary as a whole of holding a pro-EU position.[14] It might be common to hear that judges behave in political ways, but the nature of their political commitments is harder to discern, often depending on who is being asked, and the purposes served by their answer.

With this in mind, this chapter asks the following questions: in the UK context, in what sense, if at all, do judges in UK courts act in a political manner? Is the charge "the judges are doing politics" true? What evidence needs to be marshalled to demonstrate this? And, ultimately, are the above criticisms fair?

---

rity decisions unlawful. Philip Davies MP openly criticised "lily-livered, wet, soft, liberal judges who hand out… unduly lenient sentences" in the House of Commons (458 Parl Deb HC (2012) col. 161).

7 Sir Mark Potter, *Do the Media Influence the Judiciary?* Foundation for Law, Media and Society, (18 August 2011), https://www.fljs.org/sites/www.fljs.org/files/publications/Potter_PB.pdf.

8 Jerold Waltman, The Courts in England in The Political Role of Law Courts in Modern Democracies (Jerold Waltman and Kenneth Holland eds. 1988), 116; Leslie Moran, *In conversation with Lord Justice Etherton: judicial legitimacy, diversity and the representation of judicial authority*, Public Law 662, 668 (2010); Penny Darbyshire, Sitting in Judgment: The Working Lives of Judges, 19–23 (2011).

9 Robert Stevens, The English Judges: Their Role in the Changing Constitution 58 (2002), This is backed up by Waltman, ibid., 117.

10 Adam Gearey, Wayne Morrison and Robert Jago, The Politics of the Common Law 190, 193 (2nd ed. 2013).

11 Lord Dyson, a senior UK judge, has remarked that in human rights cases, the senior judiciary has been seen as a threat to the establishment: Lord Dyson, *Criticising Judges: Fair Game or Off-Limits?* Third Annual Bailii Lecture at 19, https://www.bailii.org/bailii/lecture/03.pdf.

12 David Campbell has claimed that "tribunals and courts hearing asylum and immigration cases have repeatedly refused to give effect to government policies the substance of which they do not favour, and have frustrated the legislative intent of Parliament in order to do so": see David Campbell, *Decency, disobedience and democracy in immigration law,* Public Law 413, 413 (2018).

13 Penny Darbyshire, Sitting in Judgment: The Working Lives of Judges 27–31 (2011); Lord Burnett, *Why accusations that judges have gone soft are unfounded*, Prospect Magazine (22 January 2021), https://www.prospectmagazine.co.uk/magazine/sentencing-criminal-justice-uk-courts.

14 See e.g. Andrew Pierce, *And now here's the next lot lining up to have a go: judges who will rule on Brexit impact*, Daily Mail (7 November 2016). There is some limited support for this view from certain academics; Nicol has criticised the "well to-do" judges with a "class interest in Britain's continued EU membership" for supporting the neoliberal project of "intensified capitalist globalisation": Danny Nicol, *Supreme Court Against the People*, UK Constitutional Law Association Blog (25 September 2019), https://ukconstitutionallaw.org/2019/09/25/danny-nicol-supreme-court-against-the-people/.

JUDGES NEVER ACT POLITICALLY?

The first, and perhaps most common, response to the claim that "judges do politics" is to declare that there is *no* political aspect to judicial decision-making whatsoever. I suggest, however, that this claim is neither useful nor accurate.

Can a judge who rules on the validity of the election of a parliamentarian really be said to have nothing to do with politics?[15] Can the same be said of a judge who decides whether the UK's ban on assisted suicide is lawful,[16] or a judge who leads a political inquiry into historic state violence whilst serving on the UK's highest court?[17] Of course, this sort of political engagement may not necessarily be the target of politicians' ire. But it shows that the answer to the question "Are judges political?" depends on what is meant by the term "political". Defining the term more precisely is necessary to evaluate whether political behaviour might be tolerated or justified, and whether critiques of the kind set out above are sustainable. Although countless definitions are surely possible, below, five of the most cogent and frequently used conceptions of "political" behaviour applicable in the context of the UK judiciary are listed, explained and evaluated in turn. It will be shown that whilst the true picture is far from straightforward, and that there may be merit in *some* of the above critiques, the majority tend to lack the necessary sophistication and nuance to withstand proper scrutiny.

JUDGES ACT POLITICALLY WHEN THEY GO BEYOND APPLYING THE LAW?

The first, and most straightforward, way of framing the issue is that judges act politically whenever they stray across the fixed boundary between law and *some other thing*. It separates political decision-makers who decide what the law is from judicial decision-makers who apply it. The judiciary is equipped to do the latter, but it should keep away from the former; failure to do so is to trespass across a fundamental constitutional boundary.

There is clearly some weight to this idea. Commenting on the role of the judiciary, one senior UK judge once stated, simply, that "the judiciary's job is to apply the laws".[18] This declaratory theory – which gives rise to a kind of "slot machine jurisprudence"[19] – is neat, attractive, and, at least in a Diceyan sense, orthodox.[20]

However, no matter how neat such an idea may be, it is difficult to suggest that it reflects reality. Very few could seriously argue that judges in the UK *only ever* declare what the law is and apply it to the facts before them. Lord Reid, a senior mid-20th-century judge sitting in the UK's highest court, once famously described such a view as a "fairytale".[21]

---

15 Robinson v. Secretary of State for Northern Ireland [2002] UKHL 32 (appeal taken from N. Ir.).

16 R (Nicklinson) v. Ministry of Justice [2014] UKSC 38 (appeal taken from Eng. and Wales).

17 Lord Saville headed the Bloody Sunday Inquiry, which was established in 1998, finished hearing evidence in 2004, and reported in 2010. He served as a judge on the UK's highest court from 1997 to 2010.

18 Lord Phillips, *Terrorism and Human Rights*, 2(2) HIGH COURT QUARTERLY REVIEW 61, 73 (2006).

19 DAVID ROBERTSON, JUDICIAL DISCRETION IN THE HOUSE OF LORDS 19 (1998).

20 AV DICEY, STUDY OF THE LAW OF THE CONSTITUTION (1885).

21 Lord Reid, *The Judge as Lawmaker*, 12(1) SOCIETY OF PUBLIC TEACHERS OF LAW 22 (1972).

Judges are called upon to interpret incommensurable terms in ambiguous pieces of legislation. They are required to exercise discretion in order to determine, for example, what constitutes "a reasonable period",[22] "compelling reasons"[23] or "exceptional public interest".[24] Judges in the UK have responsibility for developing and applying the common law; as another senior judge, Lord Browne-Wilkinson, once said:

> In truth, judges make and change law. The whole of the common law is judge-made and only by judicial change in the law is the common law kept relevant in a changing world.[25]

In developing this body of non-statutory law, judges may find themselves not only free to develop the law absent any legislative constraints but often in fields "awash in the rolling and mucky waters of political power".[26]

As such, most have long since discarded the simple declaratory theory (although some attempt to defend it still).[27] It is a very blunt idea and, despite the allure of simplicity, fails to hold in practice. In the words of Stephen Sedley, the "idealised dualism of law and politics… the latter making for moderation, toleration and compromise, the former doing no more than patrol the boundaries of political reality, is spent."[28] Those that continue to insist on its application must not only demonstrate that this simple idea applies to a complex reality which seems, even on a very cursory assessment, to contradict it,[29] but must contend with the fact that very few people, including the judges themselves, now subscribe to this theory in practice.

However, rubbishing the declaratory theory does not necessarily dispense of the charge that "judges do politics". Many of the better criticisms are more precise, and certainly more grounded in reality.

JUDGES ACT POLITICALLY WHEN THEY REVIEW THE GOVERNMENT'S ACTIONS?

This second conception relies on defining politics according to where it happens: that which is political falls in the domain of the democratically elected body (Parliament), and/or the government drawn from the largest party. These institutions hold a mandate for political action;

---

22 E.g. whilst the government is able to detain illegal immigrants for a period, it must undertake "reasonable expedition" to deport them within a "reasonable period" of time: R (Hardial Singh) v. Governor of Durham Prison [1984] 1 WLR 704; [1983] EWHC 1 (QB) (Eng. and Wales).

23 Human Rights Act 1998, c. 42 §10(2) (UK).

24 E.g. Criminal Justice and Courts Act 2015 c. 2, §84(1)(2B) (UK).

25 Kleinwort Benson Ltd v. Lincoln City Council [1999] 2 AC 349; [1998] UKHL 38 (Lord Browne-Wilkinson) (appeal taken from Eng. and Wales).

26 Allan Hutchinson, *Judges and Politics: An Essay from Canada*, 24 Legal Studies 275, 284 (2004). As Lord Hodge, a senior UK judge, has pointed out, the common law is a very powerful tool not only because it affects such a wide range of topics, but because it applies retrospectively: Lord Hodge, *The scope of judicial law-making in the common law tradition,* 15, https://www.supremecourt.uk/docs/speech-191028.pdf.

27 Alan Beever, *The Declaratory Theory of Law*, 33(3) Oxford Journal of Legal Studies 421 (2013).

28 Stephen Sedley, *A Boundary Where There Is None*, London Review of Books (Sep. 12, 2019).

29 See e.g. Roscoe Pound, *Mechanical Jurisprudence,* 8 Columbia Law Review 605 (1908).

judges, unelected and unaccountable, do not, and should not, interfere in such matters. This conception defines "doing politics" as reviewing (certain) actions of the legislature, or more expansively, the executive. Taken to an extreme, such a conception throws suspicion upon the very idea of judicial review – and perhaps on *public law* as a whole.

It is hard to deny that, defined in such a way, judges do involve themselves in political decisions. But three important points should be borne in mind here.

First, and obviously, the fact that judges might operate in a "political" space does not mean that their actions in that space are themselves politically motivated, or that they are anything other than purely legal in nature. Although the "heads" of judicial review have developed over the years, even the most interventionist grounds of review stop well short of permitting judges to make policy decisions – at least expressly. Judges can prevent ministers from acting on a faulty understanding of the law; from flouting procedural rules; from reneging on their express promises. But they cannot tell ministers what to do, which policies to pursue or which political goals are worthy. As Lord Keith said in 1989, "courts judge the lawfulness not the wisdom of the decision".[30]

Second, judicial review is generally[31] concerned with *secondary* legislation. It is a tool used to challenge rules made by the executive, local authorities and devolved legislatures, as well as policies and procedures of public bodies such as prisons, hospitals and immigration authorities. Owing to the cardinal principle of parliamentary sovereignty, valid Acts of Parliament are off limits to the courts. This means, first, the body with the most democratic legitimacy has powers which are insulated from the courts. It also means that judicial review can be, and frequently is, used to ensure that *secondary* bodies act in compliance with the laws and rules passed by Parliament. Because acts of the executive can be evaluated in a way which acts of the legislature cannot, judicial review, at least in one sense, can act as a means of ensuring that *only* Acts of Parliament, rather than decisions of the government, reign supreme. This picture is not one in which the judiciary usurps the political function, but one where it facilitates the proper political process.

The third point is that even in this space, where judges are permitted to scrutinise *only* the acts of non-sovereign bodies, and only ever on purely *legal* grounds, they are generally cognisant of the political nature of the space in which they operate. They frequently deploy a kind of democratic deference – whilst acknowledging that acts of the executive do not enjoy the same constitutional insulation as primary legislation, they note that government decision-makers in particular hold some degree of democratic legitimacy, even if it is indirect, which affords decision-makers a degree of leeway where appropriate.

Further, even when a judge finds that a decision-maker has acted unlawfully, they exercise a discretion as to whether to invalidate that provision immediately,[32] or to issue some other remedy, including merely issuing a declaration as to the correct legal position.[33] The political

---

30 R. v Secretary of State for Trade and Industry ex p Lonrho Plc [1989] 1 WLR 525 at 536 (Eng. and Wales).

31 There are some exceptions: primary statutes can be assessed and even invalidated where they conflict with (certain) EU laws.

32 This remains the "default" remedy when it comes to unlawful executive action, although courts can issue a prospective-only remedy: see British Academy of Songwriters, Composers and Authors v. Secretary of State for Business, Innovation and Skills [2015] EWHC 2041 (Admin) [15]–[16] & [19] (Eng. and Wales) and see now the Judicial Review and Courts Act 2022 section 1.

33 Supreme Court Act 1981 c. 54, §31 (UK).

ramifications of invalidating an impugned action are frequently borne in mind when judges exercise their remedial discretion.[34]

So yes, in a sense, judges involve themselves in politics when they evaluate the acts of politicians. But they do not necessarily *act politically* when they do so, especially when the three points set out above are borne in mind. Regardless, some are seemingly hostile to even this bare conception of judicial politics.[35]

JUDGES ACT POLITICALLY WHEN THEY ENTER SUBJECT AREAS IN WHICH POLITICAL FIGURES ARE DEEMED TO HAVE PARTICULAR LEGITIMACY OR EXPERTISE?

This conception is similar to that described above, in that it defines "political behaviour" as interference within a site which non-judicial figures are more appropriately qualified to occupy. However, even if it is accepted that judges ought to retain some oversight over the decisions of elected officials (or that a democratic mandate is not, taken alone, sufficient to insulate a decision-maker from judicial oversight), it may be thought that certain decision-makers are uniquely qualified to take certain actions, because of the nature of the subject matter of the decisions they make. In other words, since judges do not possess the necessary skills, expertise or legitimacy to make decisions in certain fields, they should stay out of them. To do otherwise is to act politically.

Is there merit in this critique? On the one hand, it is inevitable that judges will regularly encounter questions which touch on matters of public policy and are asked to consider decisions made by those with particular expertise.[36] However, in addition to *democratic deference*, courts also show deference on grounds of legitimacy and expertise. Dyson MR put it the following way in one case:

> The more the decision which is challenged lies… in relation to issues which the court is ill-equipped to judge, the less likely it is that true abuse of power will be found.[37]

In other words, the court will modify its approach (whether that means applying a weaker standard of scrutiny, applying a higher bar for unlawfulness or simply not questioning the factual propositions of certain bodies) when it considers itself unqualified to evaluate matters itself, especially where it recognises that a party to a case *is* so qualified. This kind of deference permeates the case law. In fact, some have criticised the courts for being *too* deferential to decision-makers in this respect.[38]

---

34 See e.g. R (Tigere) v. Secretary of State for Business, Innovation and Skills [2015] UKSC 57 (appeal taken from Eng. and Wales).

35 Thomas Poole, *The Executive Power Project*, London Review of Books, (2 April 2019).

36 Shimon Shetreet and Wayne McCormack, The Culture of Judicial Independence in a Globalised World 58 (2016).

37 R (Rashid) v. Secretary of State for the Home Department [2005] EWCA Civ 744 [47] (Eng. and Wales).

38 Trevor Allan, *Human rights and judicial review: a critique of due deference* 65 Cambridge Law Journal 671 (2006).

One classic area in which the courts have shown significant deference is in the realm of foreign policy.[39] Two examples are sufficient to demonstrate the general approach. First, in the case of *Abassi*,[40] the Court of Appeal rejected a judicial review application lodged by a British national detained at Guantanamo Bay, seeking an order that the UK government intervene in his situation. Owing to "the width of discretion enjoyed by the executive" in that field,[41] the court found that absent some "extreme case",[42] the court should stay out of matters concerning foreign affairs. On the facts, it found that it had no jurisdiction to compel the government to act, since "the court cannot enter… forbidden areas, including decisions affecting foreign policy."[43]

A more recent example is the high-profile case of *R (Begum) v Special Immigration Appeals Commission*.[44] That case involved British-born Shamima Begum, who, at the age of 15, left the UK to join the terrorist organisation ISIL in Syria. The Home Secretary decided to deprive her of her citizenship as a result. Begum sought to re-enter the UK to challenge that decision before a UK court; permission to re-enter the UK was refused. Begum asked the UK courts to quash the Home Secretary's refusal, on grounds that she had effectively been denied a fair trial as a result. The Supreme Court was heavily deferential to the Home Secretary's evaluation as to the threat Begum posed to the United Kingdom, as well as her own determination of where the balance between national security and Begum's fair trial rights should fall. It held, controversially, that there could be situations where national security considerations could legitimately outweigh an individual's right to a fair hearing. The threat Begum posed was considered serious enough to outweigh her right to a fair trial, and her appeal was postponed indefinitely as a result.

Deference of this kind is not limited to the field of foreign policy. For example, judges have now adopted the view that they will not interfere in decisions involving social security and welfare benefits unless a particular decision is not just wrong but "manifestly without reasonable foundation".[45] The same test has recently been applied to decisions which concern the allocation of economic resources more generally.[46]

---

[39] See R v. Secretary of State for Foreign and Commonwealth Affairs ex p Butt [1999] EWHC 624 (Admin) (Eng. and Wales) and R (Gentle) v Prime Minister [2008] UKHL 20 [8] (appeal taken from Eng. and Wales).

[40] R (Abassi) v Secretary of State for Foreign and Commonwealth Affairs [2002] EWCA Civ 1598 (Eng. and Wales).

[41] *Ibid* [102].

[42] *Ibid* [104].

[43] *Ibid* [106].

[44] [2021] UKSC 7 (appeal taken from Eng. and Wales).

[45] R (MA) v. Secretary of State for Work and Pensions [2016] UKSC 58 (appeal taken from Eng. and Wales); R (DA) v. Secretary of State for Work and Pensions [2019] UKSC 39 (appeal taken from Eng. and Wales) cf. R (SC) v Secretary of State for Work and Pensions [2021] UKSC 26 at paragraphs 157–167.

[46] Langford v. Secretary of State for Defence [2019] EWCA CIv 1271 (Eng. and Wales); R (Drexler) v. Leicestershire County Council [2020] EWCA Civ 502 (Eng. and Wales). See Jeff King, *The Justiciability of Resource Allocation*, 70 Modern Law Review 197 (2007).

Deference has been shown by judges when decisions fall into certain fields, such as those in the "technical sphere"[47] and those which involve "economic and social policy".[48] It has been applied to certain *types* of decisions, such as "military and diplomatic" decisions[49] and the assessment of national security risks.[50] Finally, deference is often shown to certain individuals or bodies who carry legitimacy and expertise by their very nature; courts have taken a hands-off approach when they evaluate the decisions of experts in their field,[51] as well as the decisions of prosecutors[52] and "most decisions taken by the Attorney-General".[53]

The reality is that courts have gone a long way – in some cases perhaps too far – to balance their constitutional duty to ensure that the law is being applied fairly and correctly with respect for the legitimacy and expertise of certain institutions and decision-makers. Some may yet think that courts have not applied enough deference in a certain field or that a certain set of decisions are wrong. This charge requires specific examples backed up with specific evidence; and such a charge is very different from the general criticism that courts willingly trample over the views of expert decision-makers. It is clear that, as a whole, they do not.

JUDGES ACT POLITICALLY WHEN THEY DEAL WITH QUESTIONS WHICH ARE POLITICALLY SENSITIVE, INCLUDING THOSE RELATING TO HUMAN RIGHTS?

A fourth conception suggests that judges act politically when they deal with any issues which are politically sensitive, or are the result of policy choices. Human rights adjudication is perhaps the main offender under this conception. The Human Rights Act 1998 (HRA) empowered judges to evaluate all acts of public bodies, and all legislation, including primary legislation, according to whether they comply with the rights in the European Convention on Human Rights (which are also set out in Schedule 1 of the 1998 Act). Whilst judges cannot invalidate Acts of Parliament using the HRA, they can issue a "declaration of incompatibility" which sends a signal to the legislature that the law is not compatible with human rights.[54] The Act also authorises them to apply a strong, sometimes radical, interpretation of legislation, beyond that which would otherwise be appropriate, in order to render the law rights-compatible.[55]

---

[47] Secretary of State for Environment, Food and Rural Affairs v. Downs [2009] EWCA Civ 664 [76], [114] (Eng. and Wales).

[48] R (Hooper) v. Secretary of State for Work and Pensions [2003] EWCA Civ 813 [63]–[64] (Eng. and Wales).

[49] Chandler v. DPP [1964] AC 763 at 798 (appeal taken from Eng. and Wales).

[50] R (Lord Carlile) v. Secretary of State for the Home Department [2014] UKSC 60 [49] (appeal taken from Eng. and Wales).

[51] E.g. members of the Parole Board when making parole decisions: see R (DSD) v. Secretary of State for Justice [2018] 694 (Admin) [117]–[121] (Eng. and Wales).

[52] R (Corner House Research) v. Serious Fraud Office [2008] UKHL 60 (appeal taken from Eng. and Wales).

[53] Which "are not amenable to judicial review" at all: Bahamas Hotel Maintenance & Allied Workers Union v Bahamas Hotel Catering & Allied Workers Union [2011] UKPC 4 [36] (Lord Walker of Gestingthorpe) (appeal taken from Bahamas).

[54] Human Rights Act 1998 c. 42 §4 (UK).

[55] Human Rights Act 1998 c. 42 §3 (UK).

The HRA clearly gives judges a lot of power; Lord Neuberger, former President of the Supreme Court, has even stated that "the biggest factor in increasing judicial power... has been the Human Rights Act".[56] But the HRA also requires judges to apply standards which are open-structured and arguably incommensurable.

Many of the rights under the Convention are "qualified rights", meaning that they are to be balanced against competing considerations, including the furthering of other rights. Freedom of speech must be balanced against the right to privacy; freedom of religion can be limited to protect the freedoms of others. Further, the court's task is often very political – not just in terms of the content of the laws being challenged – the UK Supreme Court has determined the lawfulness of restrictions on abortion,[57] a ban on euthanasia,[58] and limits on welfare benefits,[59] amongst many other politically and morally contentious areas.

The HRA requires judges to undertake human rights "balancing": they must determine whether purported rights restrictions are undertaken in pursuit of a so-called "legitimate aim", and whether the requirement of "proportionality" is satisfied – that is, whether the actions taken to achieve the aim pursued are the "least intrusive" measures possible.[60] Further, judges must, where appropriate, show a degree of deference to the expertise of the original decision-maker, whilst at the same time ensuring that they evaluate the proportionality question themselves. It all makes for a difficult, and often imprecise, balancing exercise.

Critics allege that these sorts of questions inevitably bring judges into the political decision-making.[61] Indeed, the former Lord Chancellor, Lord Mackay, specifically argued against incorporating the European Convention into domestic law for this reason.[62] So, are these criticisms fair? Again, the devil is in the detail.

The HRA itself was passed by Parliament, meaning that the *organ primarily responsible for making political decisions* authorised the courts to make calls on human rights issues. And even so, Parliament retains the ultimate power over courts in this realm. Declarations relating to secondary legislation can be overturned by a simple legislative Act. Declarations relating to primary legislation are not legally binding.

Further, in human rights cases, judges very often employ *both* kinds of deference outlined above: to democratic legitimacy (especially, but not exclusively, where primary legislation is being considered) as well as to expertise (especially, but not exclusively, where human rights challenges relate to established policy).

The judges do not have an entirely free discretion, either. They are bound to "take into account" the jurisprudence of the European Court of Human Rights in Strasbourg where

---

[56] LORD NEUBERGER AND PETER RIDDELL, THE POWER OF JUDGES 32 (2018).

[57] In Re Northern Ireland Human Rights Commission [2018] UKSC 27 (appeal taken from N. Ir.).

[58] R (Nicklinson) v. Ministry of Justice [2014] UKSC 38 (appeal taken from Eng. and Wales).

[59] R (MA) v. Secretary of State for Work and Pensions [2016] UKSC 58 (appeal taken from Eng. and Wales).

[60] See e.g. Bank Mellat v. HM Treasury (No 2) [2013] UKSC 39 [20] (appeal taken from Eng. and Wales). On proportionality, see Julian Rivers, *Proportionality and Variable Intensity of Review*, 65(1) CAMBRIDGE LAW JOURNAL 174 (2006).

[61] See e.g. JONATHAN SUMPTION, TRIALS OF THE STATE (2019).

[62] ROBERT STEVENS, *THE ENGLISH JUDGES: THEIR ROLE IN THE CHANGING CONSTITUTION* 104 (2002).

relevant.[63] In practice, this generally means that domestic judges will not go further than their European counterparts.[64]

In addition, judges have been very cautious when it comes to imposing remedies for breaches of human rights. Although judges can, for example, render secondary legislation which breaches the HRA invalid, they often refrain from doing so, in light of the political consequences such an action would have. In fact, one study found that in a *majority* of cases where secondary legislation was successfully challenged on human rights grounds, the court chose *not* to quash the offending legislation.[65] This sort of caution is evident across the whole gamut of human rights claims.[66]

Taken together, adjudication relating to policy decisions, and especially those involving human rights claims, may inevitably seem to be political in nature. However, judges are clearly well aware of this and, at least in the field of human rights law, have acted with tactful restraint to ensure the legitimacy of their actions. They are not able to impose their own political choices, being subject to a whole host of conditions, limitations and qualifications, some of which are self-imposed. This is why, when asked whether human rights were "political" in a radio interview, Lady Hale, former President of the Supreme Court, answered: "they are and they aren't."[67]

IS ALL ADJUDICATION POLITICAL?

One final way of defining political decisions is to suggest that all judicial decision-making is inherently political, as all decisions necessarily involve "the authoritative allocation of values".[68] Under this view, "[j]udges in the United Kingdom cannot be politically neutral because they are placed in positions where they are required to make political choices."[69]

Indeed, many areas invite judges to make choices and evaluative judgments, in public as well as private law. On one view, the exercise of this sort of judicial discretion "necessarily

---

63 Lewis Graham, *The Modern Mirror Principle*, Public Law 523 (2021).

64 N v. Secretary of State for the Home Department [2005] UKHL 31 [24]–[25] (appeal taken from Eng. and Wales) cf. R (Keyu) v. Secretary of State for Foreign and Commonwealth Affairs [2015] UKSC 69 [232]–[235] (appeal taken from Eng. and Wales).

65 Joe Tomlinson, Lewis Graham and Alexandra Sinclair, *Does judicial review of delegated legislation under the Human Rights Act 1998 unduly interfere with executive law-making?* UK Constitutional Law Association Blog (Feb. 22, 2021), https://ukconstitutionallaw.org/2021/02/22/joe-tomlinson-lewis-graham-and-alexandra-sinclair-does-judicial-review-of-delegated-legislation-under-the-human-rights-act-1998-unduly-interfere-with-executive-law-making.

66 E.g. in Barnet v. AG and Others [2021] EWHC 1523 (Fam) (Eng. and Wales) the High Court ruled that the national rules in relation to diplomatic immunity did not breach the ECHR, but went on to say that even if they did, a declaration of incompatibility would not be issued because of the perceived difficulties which would stand in the way of the government remedying the problem.

67 Lady Hale, *The Emma Barnett Show,* BBC Radio 5 (June 11, 2019) (radio broadcast).

68 Richard Hodder-Williams, Six Notions of Political and the United States Supreme Court, 22 British Journal of Political Science 1, 2–3 (1992).

69 JAG Griffith, Politics of the Judiciary 336 (5th ed. 1997).

involves political decision-making".[70] This sort of discretion may inevitably be susceptible to the natural variation between individuals.

Further, each individual judge likely brings their own personal inclinations and attitudes to the courtroom with them.[71] As one former Supreme Court judge put it, "[i]t may be surprising, but occasionally we need to remind ourselves that judges are human beings. They respond to problems in different ways."[72] And as Michael Kirby put it, "if judges say they have no sin of personal inclinations… they deceive themselves."[73] Indeed, Benjamin Cardozo once declared that "there is in each of us a stream of tendency, whether you choose to call it philosophy or not, which gives coherence and direction to thought and action. Judges cannot escape that any more than other mortals."[74] As long ago as 1943, Lord Wright, a senior UK judge, opined that "the judge does not approach the case with a blank mind. Subconsciously or consciously, trained mental processes are involved, rules learned in the past function in his mind, his own past experience and his past reading of other cases all combine to lead to a judgment."[75] A judge's inner workings influence their output. If some of these inner workings are ideological or value-laden in nature, does this make their output *political*?

Perhaps judges might be thought to apply legal, rather than political, reasoning. But a subscription to legal realism is not necessary to admit that (at least some) legal reasoning is influenced by certain political presumptions. Some have even suggested that legal and ideological aspects of judicial reasoning cannot be meaningfully distinguished,[76] or that even the most straightforward, "objective" legal decisions ultimately break down into base ideological choices.[77] Even in relatively settled areas of law, where opportunities for development and discretion are limited, certain ideological presumptions and choices may lie beneath the surface (e.g., the value of property, individual liberty, the authority of government), even if they are thought to be uncontroversial or widely accepted.[78]

Is this conception of "judges doing politics" tenable? The thesis can be doubted and is somewhat difficult to test empirically. Further, it is one thing to say that "all judging *can be* political" and another to say that "all judging is *necessarily* political". The above description of judicial behaviour is couched in very general terms, and may not apply straightforwardly

---

70 Leslie Moran, *In conversation with Lord Justice Etherton: judicial legitimacy, diversity and representation of judicial authority*, Public Law 662, 664 (2010).

71 For an exploration of judicial attitudes in the UK context, see Rachel Cahill-O'Callaghan, Values in the Supreme Court: Decisions, Division and Diversity (2020) and Chris Hanretty, A Court of Specialists: Judicial Behaviour in the UK Supreme Court (2020).

72 Lord Dyson, *The Shifting Sands of Statutory Interpretation*, Statute Law Society Lecture, http://www.statutelawsociety.co.uk/wp-content/uploads/2014/01/Sir_John_Dyson.pdf, 3.

73 Michael Kirby, *A Darwinian Reflection on Judicial Values,* in From House of Lords to Supreme Court: Judges, Jurists and the Process of Judging (James Lee ed. 2013).

74 Benjamin Cardozo, The Nature of the Judicial Process 12 (1921).

75 Lord Wright, *Precedents*, 8(2) Cambridge Law Journal 118, 138 (1943). In doing so, he cited, seemingly approvingly, the work of Karl Llewellyn, one of the most famous writers of the American realist tradition.

76 Joshua Fischman and David Law, *What is judicial ideology and how should we measure it?*, 29 Washington University Journal of Law and Policy 133 (2009).

77 Ward Farnsworth, *Signatures of Ideology: The Case of the Supreme Court's Criminal Docket*, 104 Michigan Law Review 67, 71–73 (2005).

78 Duncan Kennedy, *The Political Significance of the Structure of the Law School Curriculum*, 14 Seton Hall Law Review 1, 9–12 (1983).

to the United Kingdom, which places a number of significant limits, formal and informal, upon its judges, limiting the space for personal values to influence judicial decision-making.[79] Parliamentary sovereignty is the most obvious one – no matter how political a judge's actions may be, they can (almost) always be overturned by the legislature.[80] Much of the law is housed in statute – although judges are tasked with interpreting these laws, they cannot ignore their wording or rewrite them completely. The doctrine of precedent requires judges to follow previous judicial decisions absent special circumstances. Suspicious judicial decisions can be overturned on appeal. Less formal constraints, such as the desire to achieve a positive reputation[81] or avoid the censure of colleagues,[82] surely apply too. Some have argued that these constraints eliminate the opportunity for the exercise of personal preferences in the UK context.[83] But even if this is not accepted, it is undoubtedly true that such constraints certainly *limit* such opportunities, sometimes quite significantly.

Overall, it is hard to imagine that the sort of behaviour described here – the translation of internal values into decisions in the exercise of discretion – represents the kind of political behaviour complained of by politicians, as set out at the start of this chapter. The more fundamental point, however, is that if this conception of politics is accepted, and if this is what critics mean when they allege that judges act politically, it becomes hard to imagine any conception of the judicial role without running into the problem of "doing politics". How can judges stop doing something so inherent? Ideological "seepage" is not a judicial phenomenon but a human one.[84] The only way to prevent this sort of judicial behaviour would be to blot out the "humanity" of the judiciary itself.

CONCLUDING THOUGHTS

When the claim is made that judges are "doing politics" or "acting politically", this could relate to any of the five conceptions sketched out above (and, indeed, potentially many others). But each of those five conceptions is different from the others – some radically so. Criticisms

---

79 See e.g. Songer and Lindquist, *Not the Whole Story: The Impact of Justices' Values on Supreme Court Decision Making*, 40(4) American Journal of Political Science 1049 (1996); Gillman, *What's law got to do with it? Judicial behaviouralists test the legal model of judicial decision making*, 26 Law and Social Inquiry 465 (2001); Bailey and Maltzman, The Constrained Court: Law, Politics, and the Decisions Justices Make (2011).

80 EW Thomas, *The Judicial Process* (CUP 2005), 86; Chris Hanretty, *The Decisions and Ideal Points of British Law Lords*, 43(3) British Journal of Political Science 706 (2013).

81 Benjamin Alaire and Andrew Green, Commitment and Cooperation on High Courts (2017), 39–40; Logan Strother, *Case Salience and the Influence of External Constraints on the Supreme Court*, 7(1) Journal of Law and Courts 129 (2019).

82 There is ample evidence that a judge's colleagues can assert significant influence – intentionally or otherwise – on a judge's behaviour: see Harry Edwards, *The Effects of Collegiality on Judicial Decision Making*, 151(5) University of Pennsylvania Law Review 1639 (2003); Jorge Blanes i Vidal and Clare Leaver, *Social Interactions and the Content of Legal Opinions*, 29(1) Journal of Law, Economics and Organization 78 (2013) and more generally, Birne Häcker and Wolfgang Ernst, "Collective Judging in Comparative Perspective" (2020).

83 EW Thomas, The Judicial Process (2005).

84 See Lee Marsons, *Distancing Devices and Their Challenge to Judicial Emotion Realists – So Far, Yet so Near* in Research Handbook on Law and Emotion (eds. Susan Bandes et al, 2021).

relying on certain conceptions of political behaviour may need to be taken seriously, whereas others can be discarded more easily. One problem with claiming that judges are simply behaving politically, and failing to elaborate on exactly what is meant by this, is that *even* if there is some truth to the claim made, this becomes impossible to identify and evaluate owing to the general level at which the argument is made. Whilst the generic charge that judges should not "act politically" is unhelpful, more specific criticism (e.g., that judges are not presently showing enough deference to the authority or expertise of political decision-makers in a certain field) is not only more cogent but is more likely to convince; although, in light of the points made above, such a claim would still require strong, specific evidence to do so.

Further, specification is required so that the claim can be evaluated and responded to properly. The approach of judges to the "problem" of politics differs depending on how political behaviour is construed. In some respects, political behaviour is an absolute barrier to action, completely closing off any possibility of judicial intervention. In others, political considerations moderate or weaken judicial oversight. In yet others, appeals to "politics" do not really limit the judicial reach in a meaningful way.

As has been shown, judges have refused to question legislative mechanisms such as the passage of primary legislation and, but for some narrow exceptions, respect the democratic legitimacy of the legislature by refraining from questioning the legality of that primary legislation. Judges are generally quite hands-off when it comes to reviewing decisions relating to certain fields in which politicians are deemed to have greater expertise, such as foreign affairs and economic policy. They are less reluctant to disavow such challenges when human rights issues are involved, but a degree of deference is often shown in the appropriate circumstances. Otherwise, when it comes to simply reviewing secondary legislation, judges have not generally been receptive to the argument that they should show some great deference just because a policy or a rule has been adopted by the executive, which itself holds political acumen or legitimacy.

In truth, much of the criticism of judges described at the beginning of this chapter relies on the conception of politics which is most difficult to defend: the outdated idea that *judges act politically when they go beyond applying the law*. For the reasons outlined above, this reduces the complex constitutional landscape to a single epithet: sovereignty wins. It is easy to see why it is invoked time and time again: it is an idea which is straightforward, easy to explain, and politically useful. But if it is accurate, it is only accurate *some* of the time, and only superficially so. It is an idea which ignores other cardinal principles embedded in the UK constitution, including the rule of law and the need to do justice. Exactly what each of these principles requires in practice, how they operate in the context of parliamentary sovereignty, and how any tension between them is to be resolved are complicated and controversial questions, but answering them requires moving beyond the simple idea of "judges do law, politicians do politics".

Greater weight may be placed on the need to achieve justice and compliance with the rule of law in some instances (e.g., in judicial review of government actions, or in the context of human rights challenges), whereas respect for sovereignty and the separation of powers may be more important in others (e.g., the great deference shown by judges to national security matters, and the rule that judges cannot question primary legislation more generally).

This is how it should be. Very rarely can big constitutional questions be solved with simple answers (especially if those simple answers sound suspiciously like political soundbites). It is the result of a mature and cosmopolitan understanding of the role of law and courts in the constitutional order. It is not settled, and is open for debate and, potentially, recalibration. But in this space the unfair trump card of "judges doing politics" has very little purchase. We should therefore be very cautious when this attack is invoked, especially if it is employed by those who might seek to benefit from it personally and professionally.

6. Government transparency and judicial deference

An outcomes-based overview of Freedom of Information Act litigation in the U.S. Supreme Court

Gbemende Johnson

INTRODUCTION

The participation of newly installed Supreme Court Justice Amy Coney Barrett brought an unusual amount of media attention to the case of *U.S. Fish and Wildlife Service v. Sierra Club* 592 U. S. ____ (2021), a case involving a Freedom of Information Act (FOIA) dispute. The Sierra Club had previously submitted FOIA requests for records held by bureaus of the Department of Interior and Department of Commerce that were related to a rule promulgated by the Environmental Protection Agency (EPA). The government argued that the withheld documents were drafts that were part of the agencies' deliberative process, and therefore exempt from disclosure under FOIA's Exemption 5. Exemption 5 of the FOIA allows agencies to withhold records considered "pre-decisional," created prior to the "adoption of agency policy," and "deliberative," in that a record "makes recommendations or expresses opinions on legal or policy matters" (Reisch 2017: 1905; Weaver and Jones 1989). The Sierra Club disagreed, arguing that the withheld documents, while labeled drafts, were functionally closer to a final policy assessment, which would not find protection under the FOIA. After a Ninth Circuit panel ordered the agencies to release some of the withheld drafts, the federal government petitioned the U.S. Supreme Court for review. In a seven-to-two majority opinion, authored by Associate Justice Barrett, the Court agreed that the withheld documents were exempt from disclosure under the FOIA. The Supreme Court's ruling in favor of the agencies in *U.S. Fish and Wildlife Service v. Sierra Club* is an example of the deference that the U.S. Supreme Court shows the government in FOIA disputes over withheld documents.

FOIA challenges before the U.S. Supreme Court usually do not attract the same public attention as cases involving the First Amendment or reproductive rights disputes. However, FOIA rulings play an extremely important role in delineating the public's reach into the internal workings of the federal government, and in providing direction to lower courts that adjudicate the vast majority of FOIA disputes. These cases also provide important instructions to federal agencies regarding proper FOIA implementation. In this chapter, I examine Supreme Court decision-making in cases involving Freedom of Information Act disputes. Similar to empirical research on the FOIA in lower federal courts (Johnson 2019a; Mart and Ginsburg 2014; Verkuil 2002), I find a high rate of U.S. Supreme Court deference toward federal agencies in FOIA cases. However, on multiple occasions, Congress has overruled the Supreme Court's executive deference by passing amendments to strengthen the disclosure provisions of the FOIA, and by narrowing the breadth of FOIA exemptions. Below, I discuss key provisions of the FOIA and provide an empirical overview of outcomes in U.S. Supreme Court FOIA litigation, with a discussion of key themes that emerge in these cases.

THE FREEDOM OF INFORMATION ACT

Signed by President Lyndon B. Johnson in 1966 and enacted in 1967, the FOIA facilitates government transparency through proactive disclosures of information, and the disclosure of records upon request (Cuiller 2016; Halstuk and Chamberlin 2006; Johnson 2021; Samahon 2019). Prior to the FOIA, Section 3 of the 1946 Administrative Procedure Act (APA) included a disclosure provision to allow outside access to government records. However, critics argued that the formulation of Section 3, which specified that "matters of official record shall in accordance with published rules be made available to persons *properly and directly concerned* [emphasis added],"[1] provided little guidance regarding who fit within the category of "properly and directly concerned," and could therefore facilitate the withholding of requested information instead of promoting disclosure (Cross 1953: 228). The Administrative Procedure Act also did not offer an explicit remedy for retrieving information that was improperly withheld.[2] Representative John Moss (D-CA), who had previously faced resistance in his own attempts to retrieve information from the federal executive branch, was a key advocate and architect of the 1966 FOIA, which was proposed as an amendment to Section 3 of the APA (Reisch 2017). The Act passed with broad congressional support in the face of significant resistance from federal administrative agencies and President Johnson himself. Congress has amended the FOIA multiple times, most recently in 2016 with the FOIA Improvement Act. One provision of the 2016 amendments requires agencies to publish records that have been requested through the FOIA at least three times to promote proactive disclosure.[3]

The FOIA currently requires agencies to publish rules and "statements of general" policy adopted by agencies in the Federal Register. The FOIA also requires agencies to publish final, concurring, and dissenting opinions arising from agency adjudication. In addition to these proactive disclosures, the FOIA dictates the release of agency records upon request. Recognizing that situations exist where disclosure may be problematic or not in the public interest, Congress included nine exemptions that allow agencies to withhold requested information for reasons ranging from the protection of personnel and medical records to the protection of records related to law enforcement proceedings. Records exempt from disclosure under FOIA include:[4]

- Exemption 1: records "specifically authorized under criteria established by an Executive order to be kept secret in the interest of national defense or foreign policy…"
- Exemption 2: records "related solely to the internal personnel rules and practices of an agency
- Exemption 3: records "specifically exempted from disclosure by statute…"[5]

---

1 Administrative Procedure Act of 1946, Pub. L. No.79-404, 60 Stat. 237 § 3(c).

2 *EPA v. Mink* 410 U.S. 73 (1973).

3 The Freedom of Information Act, 5 U.S.C. § 552(b)(5).

4 *Ibid.*

5 The full text of Exemption 3 protects records "specifically exempted from disclosure by statute (other than § 552b of this title), provided that such statute (A) requires that the matters be withheld from

- Exemption 4: "trade secrets and commercial or financial information obtained from a person and privileged or confidential"
- Exemption 5: "Inter-agency or intra-agency memorandums or letters that would not be available by law to a party other than an agency in litigation with the agency"
- Exemption 6: "Personnel and medical files and similar files the disclosure of which would constitute a clearly unwarranted invasion of personal privacy"
- Exemption 7: "Records of information compiled for law enforcement purposes…"[6]
- Exemption 8: Records that "Contain in or related to the examination, operating, or condition reports prepared by, on behalf of, or for the use of an agency responsible for the regulation or supervision of financial institutions"
- Exemption 9: "Geological and geophysical information and data, including maps, concerns wells."

When records are withheld in whole or in part, requesters can also seek the assistance of the Office of Government Information Services, which can provide mediation assistance. The FOIA also dictates that requesters can file a claim in federal district court to require the disclosure of records that are "improperly" withheld. The FOIA instructs district courts to review agency withholdings *de novo*, which should technically afford a low degree of deference to the agency's withholding decision (Kwoka 2013). Importantly, the FOIA carries a presumption in favor of disclosure and agencies bear the burden of justifying their withholding decisions (Johnson 2019a). Requesters, on the other hand, do not have to provide a reason or justification for why they need the requested information. However, there are instances, particularly where privacy interests are implicated, where federal judges will weigh the benefit to public interest versus the risk to privacy interests that may result from disclosure.[7] Requesters make hundreds of thousands of FOIA requests each fiscal year. The rate of FOIA litigation increased under the Trump administration; however, only a small proportion of requests result in litigation (less than one percent) (Mehta 2018).

Importantly, Congress has amended the FOIA multiple times in direct response to judicial decision-making when courts were seemingly too deferential to executive branch preferences. For example, in *EPA v. Mink* (1973), a suit brought by members of Congress, the Supreme Court reviewed a decision by the D.C. Circuit to require *in camera* review of records withheld

---

the public in such a manner as to leave no discretion on the issue, or (B) establishes particular criteria for withholding or refers to particular types of matter to be withheld."

[6] Exemption 7 is divided into six subsections. Exemption 7 exempts from disclosure: "records or information compiled for law enforcement purposes, but only to the extent that the production of such law enforcement records or information (A) could reasonably be expected to interfere with enforcement proceedings, (B) would deprive a person of a right to a fair trial or an impartial adjudication, (C) could reasonably be expected to constitute an unwarranted invasion of personal privacy, (D) could reasonably be expected to disclose the identity of a confidential source, including a State, local, or foreign agency or authority or any private institution which furnished information on a confidential basis, and, in the case of a record or information compiled by a criminal law enforcement authority in the course of a criminal investigation or by an agency conducting a lawful national security intelligence investigation, information furnished by a confidential source, (E) would disclose techniques and procedures for law enforcement investigations or prosecutions, or would disclose guidelines for law enforcement investigations or prosecutions if such disclosure could reasonably be expected to risk circumvention of the law, or (F) could reasonably be expected to endanger the life or physical safety of any individual."

[7] *National Archives and Records Administration v. Favish* 541 U.S. 157 (2004).

under Exemption 1 and Exemption 5. The D.C. Circuit also ruled that non-exempt components of otherwise classified and protected documents could be disclosed to requesters. In their review of the D.C. Circuit's decision, the Court majority deferred to the government's position and ruled that the FOIA does not authorize judicial *in camera* inspection of withheld records, particularly under Exemption 1, and does not require the release of portions of otherwise classified documents. Although Justice Stewart signed on with the majority, he expressed concern over the reach of Exemption 1 in his concurring opinion, stating:

> it [Congress] has built into the Freedom of Information Act an exemption that provides no means to question an Executive decision to stamp a document "secret," however cynical, myopic, or even corrupt that decision might have been.[8]

A year later, in 1974, Congress amended multiple FOIA provisions, over President Ford's veto, and explicitly authorized *in camera* inspection of withheld documents by federal judges.[9] The 1974 exemptions also required agencies to segregate non-exempt information from records that may fall under one of the exemptions (Halstuk and Chamberlin 2006; Hammitt, Sohbel, and Stedman 2004). Congress also amended the FOIA subsequent to dissatisfaction with a Court ruling that upheld the withholding of records under Exemption 3. In the case of *Federal Aviation Administration v. Robertson* 422 U.S. 255 (1975), the Supreme Court ruled that Exemption 3 protected commercial airline maintenance records from release under Section 1104 of the Federal Aviation Act. Section 1104 of the Federal Aviation Act, which was passed eight years *prior* to the passage of the FOIA, allowed the FAA administration to restrict disclosure records upon receiving an objection from "any person" to the proposed disclosure.[10] In an attempt to reduce agency discretion, and to provide better direction for agencies to follow when invoking Exemption 3, Congress added additional detail to the exemption. In addition to "specifically exempting records from disclosure by statute," Congress added subclauses A and B, which state:

> providing that such statute (A) requires that the matters be withheld from the public in such a manner as to leave no discretion on the issue, or (B) establishes particular criteria for withholding or refers to particular types of matter to be withheld.

The legislative history of the 1976 amendments specifically noted Section 1104 of the 1958 Federal Aviation Act as an example and stated that this section would not allow agencies to withhold records under Exemption 3.[11] The additional specificity in the revised Exemption 3 not only provides additional guidance to agencies as they implement the FOIA, but also seemingly limits judicial discretion (Randazzo, Waterman, and Fix 2011) in deferring to agency withholdings.

---

8 *EPA v. Mink* 410 U.S. 73, 94 (1973) (P. Stewart, concurring).

9 Pub.L.No.93-502, 88 Stat. 1561.

10 *Federal Aviation Administration v. Robertson* 422 U.S. 255 (1975).

11 Government in the Sunshine Act. H. Rep. No. 94-880. March 8, 1976.

FEDERAL AGENCIES AND JUDICIAL OUTCOMES

Scholars have extensively discussed the implementation of the FOIA and the impact of FOIA litigation outcomes (Halstuck, Cramer, and Todd 2014); however, few studies examine FOIA litigation outcomes empirically (Johnson 2019a; Mart and Ginsburg 2014; Perlin 2020; Verkuil 2002). Mart and Ginsburg (2014) and Perlin (2020) both examine lower federal court outcomes in Exemption 1 claims and find that agency applications of Exemption 1 are usually upheld by federal courts. For example, Mart and Ginsburg find that in disputes over Exemption 1, "only 5% of such cases will result in an outright win for a plaintiff" (2014: 728). Johnson (2019a) analyzes deliberative process claims in both the civil discovery and FOIA context and finds that federal district courts are more likely to defer to agency claims of the deliberative process privilege in both contexts. And in an analysis of FOIA litigation between 1990 and 1999, Verkuil finds that FOIA agency decisions are affirmed by district courts at a rate of 90 percent (2002: 713). Although this high rate of deference in lower courts may be surprising given the FOIA's presumption of disclosure and expectation of *de novo* review, it is somewhat reflective of a general trend of judicial deference to executive actors and agencies in court (Humphries and Songer 1999; Sheehan 1992; Yates 1999).

Agency Success in Federal Court

Previous empirical analyses of litigation outcomes involving federal administrative agencies noted win rates for the government as high as 70 percent (Canon and Giles 1972; Crowley 1987; Handberg 1979). And Yates' (1999) analysis of agency litigation before the U.S. Supreme Court between 1953 and 1995 found agency success rates of between 70 and 80 percent. Repeat player experience, resource advantages, preference congruence between judges and agency policy, deference doctrines, and anticipation of executive branch response are a few reasons scholars provide for the success rate of agencies and executive actors in federal court (Black and Owens 2012, 2013; Ducat and Dudley 1989; Epstein and Posner 2018; Galanter 1974; Sheehan 1990, 1992; Smith 2007; Songer, Kuersten, and Kaheny 2000; Yates 2002). For example, in regard to the influence of ideology, multiple studies find that U.S. Supreme Court justices are more likely to vote in favor of agency decisions when those decisions align with judicial preferences (Sheehan 1990; Smith 2007; Yates 1999).

Repeat litigant experience also provides agencies with valuable information to assist in the formulation of effective legal arguments and strategies (Galanter 1974). In terms of Supreme Court litigation, scholars highlight the unique relationship between the Office of the Solicitor General (OSG) and the U.S. Supreme Court (Black and Owens 2012; McQuire 1998; Salokar 1992). Specifically, the Supreme Court is more likely to grant cert when the OSG petitions the Court (compared with non-government petitioners) and the OSG has a higher rate of success compared with non-OSG attorneys. The skill of the attorneys in the OSG's office and selectivity in OSG petitioning behavior are offered as explanations for the high degree of success for the federal government. However, Black and Owens (2013) note that OSG advantages in win rates before the U.S. Supreme Court are present even when controlling for litigant resources and experience differences between OSG and non-OSG attorneys.

Separation of powers considerations also influence the relationship between the Court and the federal executive branch (Collins and Eshbaugh-Soha 2019; Epstein and Knight 1998; Epstein and Posner 2018; Johnson 2019b; Thrower 2017). Specifically, courts must rely on the president and executive agencies to enforce judicial decisions; aggressive judicial monitoring of executive policies could produce resistance in implementation or, depending on the position of Congress, motivate Congress and the president to act together to push back against the Court. These considerations may be particularly acute when presidents are popular and their political capital allows them to afford and survive conflicts with the judiciary (Howell 2003; Yates 1999, 2002).

Scholars have yet to isolate U.S. Supreme Court decision-making in FOIA litigation to discern whether deference patterns in other issue areas translate to transparency disputes. Transparency disputes are unique in that the underlying action of the agency (usually to withhold documents) does not entail a substantive policy decision. The decision to release or withhold requested records encapsulates the issue of executive branch autonomy and the ability to control access to information (Johnson 2019a). And both Democratic and Republican administrations have been accused of eschewing transparency responsibilities and FOIA goals (Johnson 2021; Wagner 2021). Below I provide an overview of outcomes in the Supreme Court involving FOIA disputes. I also discuss key themes that emerge in FOIA litigation before the U.S. Supreme Court. Overall, I find a high rate of deference from the U.S. Supreme Court toward the executive branch's interpretation of the FOIA.

THE SUPREME COURT AND FOIA

Using the Supreme Court database, I identified 32 Supreme Court cases involving a decision on a FOIA provision between 1973 and 2019.[12,13] Each of these cases involved a dispute over requested records; however, many cases address additional legal questions central to whether records are subject to release. In four of the 32 cases, the Court had to address the question of whether the federal entity involved in the litigation qualified as an agency and/or whether the documents under dispute qualified as "agency records." For example, in the case of *Department of Interior v. Klamath Water Users Protective Association* 532 U.S. 1 (2001), the Court unanimously ruled that the Department of Interior's (DOI) application of Exemption 5 (deliberative process privilege) was improper and did not apply to correspondence records between the DOI's Bureau of Reclamation and Klamath Native American Tribes. The DOI applied Exemption 5 to consultation records requested by a non-profit organization. The Supreme Court held that the records related to consultation between the DOI and the Klamath

---

[12] I isolated cases falling under the "privacy" category of the "Issues" variable. The 50040 category of the "Issues" variable includes cases involving the freedom of information and similar state/federal regulations. Isolating disputes within this category produced 49 cases. I then reviewed each case and removed cases that either were adjudicated prior to the passage of the FOIA or did not involve a direct ruling on a provision of the federal Freedom of Information Act. This process resulted in 32 Supreme Court federal FOIA cases. "The Supreme Court Database." Washington University Law. http://scdb.wustl.edu/index.php, accessed March 30, 2021.

[13] This count excludes the case of *Weinberger, Secretary of Defense, et al. v. Catholic Action of Hawaii/Peace Education et al.* 454 U.S. 139 (1981), which involved a dispute over whether the Navy had to develop an environmental impact statement (EIS) under the National Environmental Policy Act of 1969 for a weapon storage construction project. The Court ruled that even if the Navy was required to develop an EIS, a requirement that was not clearly established, the EIS would be protected from disclosure under Exemption 1.

Native American Tribes and were neither inter-agency nor intra-agency records. The Court recognized that some lower courts extended the "agency" category to consultative entities whose function was similar to that of agency "personnel." However, the Court distinguished the position of the Klamath Tribes, noting:

> The Tribes, on the contrary, necessarily communicate with the Bureau with their own, albeit entirely legitimate, interests in mind. While this fact alone distinguishes tribal communications from the consultants' examples recognized by several Courts of Appeals, the distinction is even sharper, in that the Tribes are self-advocates at the expense of others seeking benefits inadequate to satisfy everyone.[14]

In addition to the question of what qualifies as agency records, four cases entailed reverse-FOIA elements. Reverse-FOIA disputes occur when a third party, often a commercial entity, intervenes to prevent the release of agency records. These cases often involve Exemption 4, which protects trade secret and commercial information submitted to an agency. Usually, the third-party entity and the agency disagree about whether the requested records should be released; however, in the case of *Food Marketing Institute v. Argus Leader Media* 588 US_ (2019), discussed later, the third-party entity and agency (the U.S. Department of Agriculture (USDA)) both wanted requested records withheld.

A Pattern of Deference

One feature that is readily apparent when reviewing Supreme Court rulings on the FOIA is the substantially high degree of deference the Court has shown to the federal executive branch. Specifically, the Supreme Court ruled in favor of the government's position in 77 percent of FOIA cases.[15] This FOIA success rate is higher than the post-Reagan rate of success for recent presidential administrations in Supreme Court cases involving the executive branch (Epstein and Posner 2016). However, the executive branch's success rate in the U.S. Supreme Court reflects the findings of judicial deference in FOIA cases in lower federal courts (Verkuil 2002). In addition to scholarly criticism over what some view as excessive deference to agency decision-making in FOIA disputes (Alvarez-Jones 2017; Kwoka 2013), the justices themselves have sometimes registered disapproval at the degree of FOIA deference exhibited by the Court. In his dissent in *John Doe Agency v. John Doe Corporation* 493 U.S. 146 (1989), a six-to-three decision where the Court upheld the use of Exemption 7A, which protects law enforcement records that "could reasonably be expected to interfere with enforcement proceedings," Justice Scalia stated:

---

14 *Department of Interior v. Klamath Water Users Protective Association* 532 U.S. 1, 12 (2001).

15 Figures describing government success and petitioning rates exclude the case of *United States Department of Defense, et al. v. Federal Labor Relations Authority et al.* 510 U.S. 487 (1994), which involves federal agencies as both petitioner and respondent. The Solicitor General joined briefs of the petitioning agencies (Department of Defense, Navy, etc.), which wanted to block the disclosure of requested home addresses of civil service employees requested by union representatives. When the Department of Defense refused to release the requested records, the unions filed a charge of unfair labor practices with the Federal Labor Relations Authority. The Court ruled in favor of the Department of Defense and other petitioner agencies that Exemption 6 and the Privacy Act protected the requested records from release.

> From the prior opinions of this Court, I had thought that at least this much about the Freedom of Information Act was clear: its exemptions were to be "narrowly construed." ... We use the same language again today... but demonstrate by our holding that it is a formula to be recited rather than a principle to be followed.[16]

Selectivity in petitioning the U.S. Supreme Court could also explain the substantially high success rate, because the federal government is more likely to appeal cases where success is expected on the part of the agency. The federal executive branch was the petitioner in approximately 81 percent of U.S. Supreme Court FOIA cases, with the Supreme Court ruling in the government's favor in 76 percent of these cases. However, federal agencies were also overwhelmingly successful in cases where they were the respondent. Albeit a small sample, of the six cases involving a non-federal government petitioner, the U.S. Supreme Court ruled in favor of the federal executive branch position in all but one of these cases, a success rate of 83 percent.

Whether petitioner or respondent, the U.S. Supreme Court provides substantial deference to federal agency interpretations of the FOIA; however, there is an added layer of complexity in the Supreme Court FOIA cases involving non-government petitioners. One of the more recent cases involving a non-government petitioner, *Food Marketing Institute v. Argus Leader Media* 588 US_ (2019), involved the application of Exemption 4. The federal agency that originally withheld the requested documents, the USDA, was not a direct party to the dispute before the Court. Specifically, the Eighth Circuit had ruled that the USDA had inappropriately applied Exemption 4 to withhold store-level data on store proceeds from users of the Supplemental Nutrition Assistance Program (SNAP). The USDA decided not to appeal the ruling. However, the Food Marketing Institute, a grocery retailer trade association, intervened in the dispute and petitioned the U.S. Supreme Court for cert, arguing that the release of the records could result in financial injury given that stores prefer to keep SNAP proceed data confidential from competitors. The Department of Justice filed an amicus brief in support of the Food Marketing Institute. In a six-to-three decision, the U.S. Supreme Court overturned the ruling of the Eighth Circuit and ruled that the USDA did not have to disclose the requested records, as retailers treat the data as private and presume confidentiality when they submit SNAP data to the USDA.

Unanimity

U.S. Supreme Court jurisprudence is marked not only by a high degree of deference but also by a comparatively high rate of unanimity. The Court produced unanimous rulings in FOIA disputes in approximately 60 percent of cases, and an additional 9 percent of cases included only one dissenting vote. This is higher than the unanimity rate of 40 percent during the same period for all U.S Supreme Court cases. Unanimous rulings for and against the government occurred approximately at the same rate, with 58 percent of rulings in favor of the government's position being unanimous and 57 percent of the rulings against the government returning a unanimous opinion. *National Archives and Records Administration v. Favish, et al* 541 U.S. 157 (2004) is a recent example of a unanimous ruling in an FOIA dispute over an agency's use of Exemption 7C. Exemption 7C exempts from disclosure records "compiled for law enforcement purposes..." that "could reasonably be expected to constitute an unwarranted

---

16 *John Doe Agency v. John Doe Corporation* 493 U.S. 146, 160 (1989) (Scalia, dissenting).

invasion of personal privacy."[17] Respondent Allan J. Favish requested death and autopsy photos of White House lawyer Vince Foster, who died by suicide in 1993. While many photos were released to Favish, the National Archives withheld a number of photos under Exemption 7C. Favish argued that because Foster was deceased, there was no applicable privacy interest. However, the Court unanimously ruled that the privacy interest captured in 7C also extended to Foster's surviving relatives and that any public interest benefit gained from the release of the photos did not outweigh the family's privacy interest. The majority stated:

> As a general rule, citizens seeking documents subject to FOIA disclosure are not required to explain why they seek the information. However, when Exemption 7C's privacy concerns are present, the requester must show that the public interest sought to be advanced is a significant one, an interest more specific than having the information for its own sake, and that the information is likely to advance that interest.[18]

Cases by court

EPA v. Mink 410 U.S. 73 (1973) was the first FOIA case heard by the U.S. Supreme Court, after previously denying cert in other FOIA disputes (Mink 1974: 8). Of the 32 FOIA cases in this discussion, the Burger Court adjudicated the majority of FOIA cases, issuing decisions in 19 cases between the 1973 and 1984 Court terms. The higher proportion of cases during the Burger Court is understandable given that agencies and requesters were still navigating the relatively new provisions of the FOIA. The Burger Court ruled against the government's position in two out of 19 cases. Interestingly, one of those adverse rulings involved the Court ordering an agency *not* to release records to a requester. In the case of *Consumer Product Safety Commission et al. v. GTE Sylvania, Inc.* 447 U.S. 102 (1980), consumer groups requested accident report records submitted by the petitioner television manufacturer Sylvania. The Consumer Product Safety Commission agreed to release the reports, finding that the reports did not fall within any of the nine FOIA exemptions; however, Sylvania filed suit in district court to prevent the release of the reports, arguing that their release was prohibited by provisions under the Consumer Product Safety Act and the Trade Secrets Act. In a unanimous ruling, the Supreme Court agreed with Sylvania, ruling that the Consumer Product Safety Act restricted the release of the records, thereby making FOIA Exemption 3, which protects information specifically exempted by statute, applicable.

The Rehnquist Court issued decisions in ten FOIA cases between the 1987 and 2003 Court terms, ruling against the government's position on two occasions. For the Rehnquist Court, one of the rulings against the government involved the question of what constitutes an agency record eligible for disclosure under the FOIA. Whether something meets the threshold of an agency record is a central aspect of whether the Court can provide a remedy. Specifically, if one were to make a request for a record to an entity that does not qualify as an agency under the FOIA (i.e., Congress, federal judiciary, the Executive Office of the President), the record would not qualify for release. Similarly, a request to a qualifying agency for information that does not constitute a "record" would also not qualify for disclosure under the FOIA. In *United States Department of Justice v. Tax Analysts* 492 U.S. 136 (1989), Tax Analysts, an organization that published a newsletter with summaries of tax court decisions, requested judicial

---

17 5 U.S.C. § 552(b)(5).

18 *National Archives and Records Administration v. Favish,* 541 U.S. 157, 170 (2004).

opinions and orders from tax cases received by the Tax Division, a bureau of the Department of Justice. The Tax Division refused to provide the requested information, arguing that they were not agency records, as the opinions and orders did not originate in the Tax Division but rather originated in federal courts, which are not agencies. The Tax Division also argued that the district opinion and orders were not "improperly withheld" given that they are publicly available elsewhere. Building from previous FOIA decisions, the Court explained that a "pre-requisite" to qualifying as an agency record is that the agency in question created or obtained the requested material. In addition, "the agency must be in control of the requested materials" when the FOIA request is made.[19] In an eight-to-one opinion, the Court ruled that the tax court opinions in possession of the Tax Division were in fact agency records, and that they were improperly withheld from requesters.

The Roberts Court took up three FOIA cases between the 2011 and 2018 Court terms, and, akin to the Burger and Rehnquist courts, ruled against the federal government's position in two cases.[20] Interestingly, the case where the Court deferred to an agency's FOIA interpretation involved a dispute where the government preferred to release the requested records (a reverse-FOIA issue). In other high-profile rulings, the Roberts Court faced extensive criticism for seemingly extending constitutional freedom of speech[21] and religious protections[22] to corporations. However, in *Federal Communications Commission v. AT&T* 562 U.S. 397 (2011), a unanimous Roberts Court declined to extend personal privacy protections found in Exemption 7C to corporations. Specifically, a communication trade association organization requested records related to a Federal Communications Commission (FCC) investigation of whether AT&T had overcharged the government during its work for a government-funded education program. The FCC claimed Exemption 4 and Exemption 7C over documents related specifically to individuals who were a part of the investigation, but intended to release records that related to AT&T as a corporate entity. AT&T sued to prevent the release of records, arguing for a broad interpretation of the term "personal" under Exemption 7C to include corporations. The Court analyzed the term "personal" in "ordinary" usage, dictionary definitions, and statutory construction, and found little support for AT&T's argument :

> "Personal" in the phrase "personal privacy" conveys more than just "of a person." It suggests a type of privacy evocative of human concerns—not the sort usually associated with an entity like, say, AT&T.[23]

Chief Justice John Roberts ended the majority opinion by stating he trusted that AT&T would not take the decision "personally."[24] Judicial deference to the federal government's position in the FOIA usually results in information being withheld; however, deference in reverse-FOIA disputes can lead to greater transparency if the agency prefers to release the requested records.

---

[19] 492 U.S. 136, 16 (1989).

[20] The Roberts Court did review additional transparency cases that did not involve a direct ruling on the FOIA. For example, the case of *McBurney v. Young* 569 U.S. 221 (2013) involved a dispute over a state FOIA law.

[21] *Citizens United v. Federal Election Commission* 558 U.S. 310 (2010).

[22] *Burwell v. Hobby Lobby* 573 U.S. 682 (2014).

[23] *Federal Communications Commission v. AT&T* 562 U.S. 397, 406 (2011).

[24] 562 U.S. 397, 410 (2011).

While the Roberts Court showed less deference to federal agency FOIA interpretations between the 2011 and 2018 terms, the Court's 2021 ruling in *U.S. Fish and Wildlife Service v. Sierra Club* over the application of the deliberative process privilege noted in the introduction is more reminiscent of the traditional Supreme Court posture in FOIA disputes over withheld documents. Interestingly, Exemption 5's deliberative process privilege has recently faced scrutiny as agencies have been accused of improperly overusing the privilege, thus reducing government transparency.[25] In 2016, Congress passed the FOIA Improvement Act, which explicitly restricted the reach of the deliberative process privilege. Specifically, in the context of the FOIA, the privilege no longer applies to "records created 25 years or more before the date on which the records were requested."[26] The decision in *U.S. Fish & Wildlife* does not affect the deliberative process privilege time limit put in place by the recent FOIA amendments; however, it represents Supreme Court deference to a privilege that recently had its reach restricted by Congress.

CONCLUSION

While the vast majority of FOIA requests do not result in litigation, the FOIA judicial decisions that do emerge, particularly those that reach the U.S. Supreme Court, have important implications for the thousands of individuals and organizations that make FOIA requests each year. Although the FOIA carries a presumption of disclosure, the Supreme Court has exhibited substantial deference to agency interpretations of the FOIA since its inception. This deference exists whether the government is the petitioner or respondent and across presidential administrations.

While this analysis provides an assessment of the win/loss rate for the federal government in FOIA disputes, several questions remain. Particularly, how does individual justice ideology and background influence outcomes in FOIA cases? While a pro-disclosure outcome could be considered a liberal decision, the disclosure decision by an agency does not neatly align along the liberal–conservative spectrum akin to substantive policy decisions such as environmental policy, health care, and education regulations. Could the unique nature of transparency disputes influence the high rate of unanimous decisions in Supreme Court FOIA decisions?

Similarly, from a separation of powers perspective, presidential administrations of both parties are likely to take similar stances in disputes over documents. For example, in a recent FOIA dispute, many observers expressed shock and surprise when the Biden administration Department of Justice decided to appeal a ruling by D.C. District Judge Amy Berman Jackson that required the release of a Trump administration Department of Justice Office of Legal Counsel memo and related documents. The memo concerned the Mueller investigation into Russian interference in the 2016 presidential election and explained why President Trump should not be charged with obstruction of justice (Barrett and Zapotosky 2021). The Department of Justice claimed the deliberative process and attorney–client privileges of Exemption 5 to restrict the release of memo and other documents requested through the

[25] Brief for the Reporters Committee for Freedom of the Press and 28 Media Organizations at 5, *U.S. Fish and Wildlife Service v. Sierra Club*, 592 U.S. (2021) (No. 19–547).

[26] 5 U.S.C. § 552(b)(5).

FOIA.[27] The policy differences between President Trump and President Biden are vast. However, when viewed from the perspective of executive branch autonomy over internal information, the decision of the Biden administration Department of Justice to defend the right of the DOJ to withhold information *when the agency sees fit* is comprehensible and does not require agreement on the substance of the documents in question. Perhaps the unique alignment of preferences across administrations to control the release of requested records also contributes to judicial deference and unanimity in FOIA disputes.

Finally, while the FOIA is the public's main vehicle for access to government records, a number of other federal transparency laws exist to promote visibility and access to government activity (e.g., the Federal Advisory Committee Act). Additional analyses should entail an examination of judicial decision-making on multiple government transparency tools to gain a comprehensive understanding of U.S. Supreme Court transparency jurisprudence and whether deference varies according to legal context.

REFERENCES

Alvarez-Jones, Stephanie. 2017. "Too Big to FOIA: How Agencies Avoid Compliance with the Freedom of Information Act." *Cardozo L. Rev.* 39: 1055.

Baron, Kevin M. 2021. "Informal and Private: Bargaining and Veto Threats over the Freedom of Information Act." *Congress & the Presidency* 49(2): 165–199.

Barrett, Devlin and Matt Zapotosky. 2021. "Justice Dept. Releases Part of Internal Memo on not Charging Trump in Russia Probe." May 25, 2021. *The Washington Post* https://www.washingtonpost.com/national-security/justice-department-memo-mueller-trump/2021/05/24/50b0f580-b432-11eb-a980-a60af976ed44_story.html, accessed May 28, 2021.

Black, Ryan C., and Ryan J. Owens. 2013. "A Built-in Advantage: The Office of the Solicitor General and the US Supreme Court." *Political Research Quarterly* 66(2): 454–466.

Black, Ryan C., and Ryan J. Owens. 2012. *The Solicitor General and the United States Supreme Court: Executive Branch Influence and Judicial Decisions*. Cambridge University Press.

Canon, Bradley C. and Michael Giles. 1972. "Recurring Litigants: Federal Agencies Before the Supreme Court." *Western Political Quarterly* 25: 183–191.

Collins Jr, Paul M. and Matthew Eshbaugh-Soha. 2019. *The President and the Supreme Court: Going Public on Judicial Decisions from Washington to Trump*. Cambridge University Press.

Cross, Harold L. 1953. *People's Right to Know: Legal Access to Public Records and Proceedings*. Columbia University Press.

Crowley, Donald W. 1987. "Judicial Review of Administrative Agencies: Does the Type of Agency Matter?" *Western Political Quarterly* 40(2): 265–283.

Cuillier, David. 2016. "The People's Right to Know: Comparing Harold L. Cross' Pre-FOIA World to Post-FOIA Today." *Communication Law and Policy* 21(4): 433–463.

Ducat, C.R. and R.L. Dudley. 1989. "Federal District Judges and Presidential Power during the Postwar Era." *The Journal of Politics* 51(1): 98–118.

Epstein, Lee and Eric A. Posner. 2018. "The Decline of Supreme Court Deference to the President." *U. Pa. L. Rev.* 166: 829.

Epstein, Lee and Eric A. Posner. 2016. "Supreme Court justices' loyalty to the President." *The Journal of Legal Studies* 45(2): 401–436.

Epstein, Lee and Jack Knight. 1998. *The Choices Justices Make*. Sage Publishing

Galanter, Marc. 1974. "Why the Haves Come out Ahead: Speculations on the Limits of Legal Change." *Law & Soc'y Rev.* 95.

27 *Citizens for Responsibility & Ethics in Wash. v. United States* DOJ, 2021 U.S. Dist. LEXIS 83948 (D.C.).

Halstuk, Martin E., Benjamin W. Cramer and Michael D. Todd. 2014. "Tipping the Scales: How the U.S. Supreme Court Eviscerated Freedom of Information in Favor of Privacy." In *Transparency 2.0: Digital Data and Privacy in a Wired World*. Edited by Charles N. Davis and David Cuillier. Peter Lang.

Halstuk, Martin E. and Bill F. Chamberlin. 2006. "The Freedom of Information Act 1966–2006: A retrospective on the rise of privacy protection over the public interest in knowing what the government's up to." *Communication Law and Policy* 11(4): 511–564.

Hammitt, Harry A., David L. Sobel and Tiffany A. Stedman (eds.). 2004. *Litigation Under the Federal Open Government Laws*. EPIC Publications.

Handberg, R., 1979. "The Supreme Court and Administrative Agencies: 1965–1978." *Journal of Contemporary Law* 6: 161–176.

Howell, William G. 2003. *Power Without Persuasion: The politics of direct presidential action*. Princeton University Press.

Humphries, Martha Anne and Donald R. Songer. 1999. "Law and Politics in Judicial Oversight of Federal Administrative Agencies." *The Journal of Politics* 61(1): 207–220.

Johnson, Gbemende. 2021. "The Law: Government Transparency and Public Access." *Presidential Studies Quarterly* 51(3): 705–724.

Johnson, Gbemende E. 2019a. "Adjudicating Executive Privilege: Federal Administrative Agencies and Deliberative Process Privilege Claims in US District Courts." *Law & Society Review* 53(3): 823–850.

Johnson, Gbemende. 2019b. "Degrees of Separation: Judicial–Executive Relations in the US and Latin America." In *Research Handbook on Law and Courts*. Edward Elgar Publishing.

Kreimer, Seth F. 2007. "The Freedom of Information Act and the Ecology of Transparency." *U. Pa. J. Const. L.* 10: 1011.

Kwoka, Margaret B. 2013. "Deferring to secrecy." *BCL Rev.* 54: 185.

Mart, Susan Nevelow and Tom Ginsburg. 2014. "[Dis-]Informing the People's Discretion: Judicial Deference Under the National Security Exemption of the Freedom of Information Act." *Admin. L. Rev.* 66: 725.

McGuire, K.T. 1998. "Explaining Executive Success in the US Supreme Court." *Political Research Quarterly* 51(2): 505–526.

Mehta, Christine. 2018. "Annual Report: FOIA Lawsuits Reach Record Highs in FY 2018." *The FOIA Project*, November 12. http://foiaproject.org/2018/11/12/annual-report-foia-lawsuits-reach-record-highs-in-fy-2018/, accessed January 5, 2021.

Mink, Patsy T. 1974. "The Mink Case: Restoring the Freedom of Information Act." *Pepp. L. Rev.* 2(1): 8–27.

Perlin, Paulina. 2020. "Defense and Deference: Empirically Assessing Judicial Review of Freedom of Information Act's National Security Exemption." *Harv. Nat'l Sec. J.* 11: 257.

Pozen, David E. 2016. "Freedom of Information Beyond the Freedom of Information Act." *U. Pa. L. Rev.*: 1097.

Randazzo, Kirk A., Richard W. Waterman, and Michael P. Fix. 2011. "State Supreme Courts and the Effects of Statutory Constraint: A Test of the Model of Contingent Discretion." *Political Research Quarterly* 64(4): 779–789.

Reisch, Zachary D. 2017. "The FOIA Improvement Act: Using a Requested Record's Age to Restrict Exemption 5's Deliberative Process Privilege." *BUL Rev.* 97: 1893.

Salokar, Rebecca Mae. 1992. *The Solicitor General: The politics of law*. Temple University Press.

Samahon, Tuan N. 2019. "Fifty Years of FOIA in Operation, 1967–2017." *Vill. L. Rev.* 63: 855.

Sheehan, Reginald S. 1992. "Federal Agencies and the Supreme Court: An Analysis of Litigation Outcomes, 1953–1988." *American Politics Quarterly* 20(4): 478–500.

Sheehan, Reginald S.1990. "Administrative Agencies and the Court: A Reexamination of the Impact of Agency Type on Decisional Outcomes." *Western Political Quarterly* 43(4): 875–885.

Smith, Joseph L. 2007. "Presidents, Justices, and Deference to Administrative Action." *The Journal of Law, Economics, & Organization* 23(2): 346–364.

Songer, Donald R., Ashlyn Kuersten and Erin Kaheny. 2000. "Why the Haves don't Always Come Out Ahead: Repeat Players Meet Amici Curiae for the Disadvantaged." *Political Research Quarterly* 53(3): 537–556.

Thrower, Sharece. 2017. "The President, the Court, and Policy Implementation." *Presidential Studies Quarterly* 47(1): 122–145.
Verkuil, Paul R. 2002. "An Outcomes Analysis of Scope of Review Standards." *Wm. & Mary L. Rev.* 44: 679.
Wagner, A. Jay. 2021. "Pandering, Priority or Political Weapon: Presidencies, Political Parties & the Freedom of Information Act." *Communication Law and Policy* 26(1): 53–102.
Weaver, R.L. and J.T. Jones. 1989. "The Deliberative Process Privilege." *Mo. L. Rev.* 54: 279–321.
Yates, Jeff. 2002. *Popular Justice: Presidential Prestige and Executive Success in the Supreme Court.* SUNY Press.
Yates, Jeff. 1999. "Presidential Bureaucratic Power and Supreme Court Justice Voting." *Political Behavior* 21(4): 349–366.

7. A court of law or a court of judges?

The Israeli High Court of Justice and the judicialization of politics in Israel

Maoz Rosenthal and Shai Talmor

INTRODUCTION

Judges develop an authoritative legal system of judicial review through their interpretations of law, precedents and doctrines.[1] The consensus of the court when reviewing a case signals that the legal system it develops is not an outcome of individual judges' whims, but an outcome of a thoughtful collective process, which should be accepted as the implementation of the rule of law.[2] In the Israeli Supreme Court (ISC), judges have explicitly expressed concerns that their judicial review is regarded as an individual effort rather than reflecting a legal system. These concerns relate to the lack of consensus and cohesiveness in the judicial review as mirroring "…a law of judges rather than a law of court."[3,4] These concerns have been repeatedly expressed over the years when judges viewed their colleagues as deviating from existing precedents in their judicial review, thereby creating dissensus on the panel and breaking from past decisions.[5] Thus, ISC judges use this term when they wish to signal that their decisions are an outcome of a cohesive interpretation of the law, rather than a decision made by an individual judge's impulse that can be altered when this judge is no longer on the court.[6] Potentially, this issue is particularly sensitive for the court and the rule of law when the context of this discussion turns to cases that relate to core social values that are politically contested, the so-called "political questions."

When courts review cases that relate to such issues and rule against the executive and the legislative branches, some claim that they are judicializing politics.[7] The judicialization of politics is a process in which courts with constitutional and administrative review powers become

---

1 Frank B. Cross, James F. II Spriggs, Timothy R. Johnson & Paul J. Wahlbeck, Citations in the U.S. Supreme Court: An Empirical Study of Their Use and Significance, 2010 U. Ill. L. Rev. 489 (2010).

2 Lee Epstein, Jeffrey A. Segal & Harold J. Spaeth, The Norm of Consensus on the U.S. Supreme Court, 45 Am. J. Poli. Sci. 362, 364 (2001); Ran Hirschl, Towards Juristocracy: The Origins and Consequences of the New Constitutionalism (Harvard 2004).

3 *Balan v. Litvinski*. 1961. 15 PD (Supreme Court of Israel), 71.

4 The Hebrew expression is: "*Ba'it shel mishpat ve'lo ba'it shel shoftim*." Its literal translation is: "A house of doing justice (*mishpat*) and not a house of judges."

5 HCJ 967/16. Elbasset v. West Bank Chief Commander. 2016 (High Court of Justice); HCJ 1125/16 Hamed Mer'i v. West Bank Commander. 2016. (High Court of Justice).

6 HCJ 781/15 Itai Arad-Pinkas v. The Committee for the Approval of Agreements for Surrogacy. 2017, 36. (High Court of Justice).

7 Ran Hirschl, The Judicialization of Mega-Politics and the Rise of Political Courts, An. Rev. Pol. Sci 93–118 (2008).

veto players with enhanced agenda-setting powers.[8] One of the key features of the judicialization of politics is judicial activism,[9] manifested in judges striking down the executive branch's decisions.[10] The way activist judicial review corresponds with the extent of the judicialization of politics has clear effects on the legitimacy of the courts' decisions.[11] Being able to pinpoint the source of the judicialization of politics is a major task in understanding this phenomenon, which is one of the hallmarks of democratization and embedded democracies.[12]

One source of the judicialization of politics could be a cohesive court seeking to implement its vision, which manifests political core values through legal policymaking.[13] The judicialization of politics could also stem from the practices of individual judges on the court, pursuing their personal ideological and policy preferences.[14] We use the Israeli case to examine *whether the judicialization of politics is an outcome of a collective effort of courts, or an outcome of the purposeful action of specific judges who consistently pursue the implementation of their desired political ideologies.*

In the context of political questions that the ISC reviews, especially as a High Court of Justice (HCJ), and its willingness to rule against the executive and legislative branches on these matters, the issue of legitimacy becomes crucial. Such decisions raise both scholarly and public criticism regarding the HCJ's behavior,[15] charging it as acting as a branch of the liberal political parties.[16] The case of Israel's HCJ includes variations in its activism and judicial independence that take place in a dynamic political environment.[17] As such, it constitutes a rich

---

[8] Georg Vanberg, Judicialization and the Political Executive, in *The Oxford Handbook of Political Executives*, 566–587 (Rudy B Andeweg et al. 2020).

[9] Hirschl, supra note 7.

[10] Margit Cohn & Momrdechai Kremnitzer, Judicial Activism: A Multidimensional Model, 18 CAN. J. L. & Jurisprudence 333 (2005); Frank B. Cross & Stefanie A. Lindquist, The Scientific Study of Judicial Activism, 91 MINN. L. REV. 1752 (2007).

[11] Hirschl, supra note 7.

[12] Steven Levitsky and Daniel Ziblatt, *How Democracies Die* (2018); Neal C. Tate, *The Global Expansion of Judicial Power* (1995); Georg Vanberg, Establishing and Maintaining Judicial Independence, in *The Oxford Handbook of Law and Politics*, 99–118 (Gregory A Caldeira, Keith E Whittington, and Daniel R. Keleman 2008).

[13] Ran Hirschl, The Socio-Political Origins of Israel's Juristocracy, 16 *Constellations*. 476, 492. Assaf Meydani, *The Anatomy of Human Rights in Israel: Constitutional Rhetoric and State Practice* (2014).

[14] Lawrence Baum, *Judges and Their Audiences: A Perspective on Judicial Behavior* (2009). Eileen Braman, Reasoning on the Threshold: Testing the Separability of Preferences in Legal Decision Making,68 *The Journal of Politics* 308, 321(2006). Lee Epstein and Jack Knight. Reconsidering Judicial Preferences. 16 ANN. REV. OF POLI. SCI. 11, 31 (2013). Lidquist and Cross, supra note 10. Jeffery A. Segal, Judicial Behavior, In *The Oxford Handbook of Law and Politics*, 19–33 (Gregory A Caldeira, Keith E Whittington, and Daniel R. Keleman 2008). Jeffrey A. Segal and Harold J Spaeth, 2002. *The Supreme Court and the Attitudinal Model Revisited* (2002). Donald R. Songer, The Dog That Did Not Bark: Debunking the Myths Surrounding the Attitudinal Model of Supreme Court Decision Making. 33 JUST. SYS. JOUR. 340–62 (2012).

[15] Hirschl, supra note 13.

[16] Simcha Simcha. 2020. *The Bagaz Party* (2020) Hebrew.

[17] Yoav Dotan, Judicial Activism in IHCJ. in *Judicial Activism: For and Against, The Role of the High Court of Justice in Israeli Society*, 5–65 (Ruth Gavison and Mordechai Kremnitzer eds. 2000). (Hebrew). Maoz Rosenthal, Gad Barzilai, and Assaf Meydani, Judicial Review in a Defective Democracy Judicial Nominations and Judicial Review in Constitutional Courts, 9 *Jour. of Law and Courts*. 9 137, 57 (2021).

case study whose relevance potentially goes beyond its particular setting.[18] In our empirical analysis we find that HCJ decisions vary between judges on cases with political implications. However, HCJ judges cluster around particular policy positions, showing faction-like behavior. Therefore, they reflect not a court of "judges" or of "law," but a court of judicial factions.

JUDICIAL ACTIVISM: BETWEEN A COLLECTIVE AND A PERSONAL EFFORT

We begin our analysis of the judicialization of politics and its source by focusing on activist judicial review. We highlight one aspect of judicial activism in which judicial review nullifies or amends government decisions or parliamentary legislation.[19] When judges review cases that can be considered "political questions," they potentially go beyond the purview of a restrained judicial review and follow their ideological preferences.[20] Some claim that judicial review is a legal analysis of the cases the court reviews that happens to have some correlation with those cases' political context.[21] Clearly, many court cases have political and ideological ramifications, with judges using different strategies to handle such cases.[22] If judges are unaware of their decisions' political implications and review cases based only on legal analysis, ideological preferences and judicial review should not even correlate, not to mention have a clear causal relationship with each other. Let us offer a null hypothesis to guide our analysis:

H_0: *There should be no consistency in judicial decisions on cases related to political or ideological matters.*

To what extent do judges consider the political or ideological contexts of the petitions they review? Either the judges are aware of these contexts and this awareness has a direct effect on their judicial review, or they are cognizant of the political consequences related to the case but rely solely on legal tools to review it. In the first instance, judges review cases as a direct outcome of their own policy preferences and their desire to implement these preferences.[23] In

---

18 John Gerring, What Is a Case Study And What Is It Good For?, 98 Am. Pol. Sci. Rev. 341, 54 (2004).

19 Cohn and Kremnitzer, supra note 10; Lindquist and Cross, supra note 10; Rosenthal, Barzilai, and Meydani, supra note 17.

20 Hirschl, supra note 7.

21 Michael A. Bailey and Forrest Maltzman. 2008. Does Legal Doctrine Matter? Unpacking Law and Policy Preferences on the U.S. Supreme Court. 102 Am. Pol. Sci. Rev. 369–84 (2008). Daniel B. Rodriguez 2008. Administrative Law, in *The Oxford Handbook of Law and Politics*, 340–59 (Gregory A. Caldeira, Keith E. Whittington, and Daniel R. Keleman 2008).

22 Bernard Grofman and Timothy J Brazill, Identifying the Median Justice on the Supreme Court through Multidimensional Scaling: Analysis of 'Natural Courts' 1953–1991. 112 Pub. Cho. 55–79 (2002). Menachem Hofnung, Policy-Making by Out-of-Court Settlements: Palestinian Informers at the Israeli High Court of Justice, 273–87, in *The Legal Process and the Promise of Justice: Studies Inspired by the Work of Malcolm Feeley* (Rosan Greenspan, Hadar Aviram, and Jonathan Simon eds. 2019). Keren Weinshall, Udi Sommer, and Ya'acov Ritov, Ideological Influences on Governance and Regulation: The Comparative Case of Supreme Courts.12 Reg. & Gov. 334–52 (2018).

23 Lee Epstein and Jack Knight. 1998. *The Choices Justices Make*. Washington DC: CQ Press. Maxwell L. Stearns, 2002. *Constitutional Process: A Social Choice Analysis of Supreme Court Decision Making*. Ann Arbor: University of Michigan Press.

the second instance, the judges might be aware of the political or ideological context in which they act, but conduct a legal analysis of the case. Over time, their approach might cohere within itself but would not cohere with different ideological contexts.[24]

To demonstrate how judicial awareness of political or ideological judicial contexts works in the Israeli case, let us consider a case reviewed by Israel's HCJ: *Gaza Beach Regional Council et al. v. Israel's Knesset et al. 2005*. In this court case, a group of Israeli settlers living on the Gaza Strip faced forced evacuation in the wake of the Israeli government's decision to dismantle all Israeli settlements in the Gaza Strip and the northern part of the West Bank and evict their residents. These residents petitioned the HCJ to annul the decision.[25] The court's majority partially accepted the petition, yet maintained the constitutionality of the petitioners' pending eviction from the Gaza Strip.[26] In his dissenting minority opinion, Judge Edmond Levi placed a high value on the emotions and rights of those being evicted, and essentially declared that he was taking their side and writing his opinion from that standpoint. In his ruling, he accepted a principle the majority rejected: the court's right to intervene in the government's foreign policy decisions. He did so while taking a position associated with Israel's right wing according to which Jews should have the right to inhabit all parts of Israel-Palestine.[27]

Judges might also intervene in matters of political controversy (a political question) but would base their argument on legal analysis that relates to law, precedent and doctrine, without revealing their political affinities in their opinion. An illustration of that type of judicial review is a decision made by the HCJ to accept conversions to Judaism made by religious movements that either are private or do not belong to the Jewish Orthodox establishment.[28] Following a set of HCJ decisions on that matter, in 2005 a wave of petitions were made seeking the HCJ's agreement to accept such conversions as legitimate for purposes of citizenship registration by non-Orthodox religious communities residing in Israel. From the petitions' submission and acceptance for review, the state asked for and received continuous postponements of the HCJ's decisions so that it could develop a policy and pass legislation to support it. For 15 years the HCJ abided by the state's demands for postponements due to the highly charged political nature of this issue.[29] At the end of 2020 the HCJ decided not to grant the government more time and indicated that it needed to make a final decision. The majority decision and the minority dissent recognized and related to the political implications of any decision they would make on that matter. However, both also declared that they closely followed the precedents set by previous decisions on that matter, fearing again becoming "a court of judges and not a court of law."[30] The decision had clear political implications. It ruled against the wishes of the ultra-Orthodox parties and effectively legislated on a matter that the Israeli parliament (or Knesset) refrained from deciding on. The dissenting judge in this case who wanted to give

---

24 Braman, supra note 14.

25 *Gaza Beach Regional Council et. al. v. Israel's Knesset et. al.* 2005. 59(2) PD (High Court of Justice) [hereinafter *Gaza Beach*].

26 Suzie Navot, Israel – The Israeli Withdrawal from Gaza – A Constitutional Perspective, 12 Eur. Pub. L. 17 (2006).: 17–34. Hillel Sommer and Guy Seidman. 2006. The Israeli Supreme Court and the Disengagement. *MishPat Ve'Mimshal* 9(2): 579–618.

27 Gaza Beach, supra note 24, 269–78.

28 Natalia Dahan et al v. The Minister of Interior Affairs. 2021. (High Court of Justice) [hereinafter *Dahan*].

29 *Dahan*, supra note 28.

30 *Dahan*, supra note 28, 16.

the government another extension was Judge Noam Solberg, a religious Jew who lives on the West Bank and favors the Israeli religious right.[31] In his opinion, Solberg made it clear that he understood the full scale of the decision's public and political implications. He agreed with the majority's legal analysis but disputed its result.[32]

Hence, a legal analysis of Solberg's decision could refute the claim that his decision was ideological. However, the decision related to a political and ideological issue to which all of the judges alluded. Furthermore, Solberg's dissent coincided with the preferred policy position of Israel's religious right, whose political leaders criticized the HCJ's majority decision.[33] Thus, even when the judges' decision does not rely on direct political argumentation, they do understand the political situation, and the results of their legal analysis do not take them too far from where their political preferences would lead. Therefore, we can offer a competing hypothesis to our null hypothesis:

H_1: Judges' decisions are consistent with the political or ideological context of cases related to political or ideological matters.

Hence, we have two competing hypotheses for the source of the judicialization of politics. Still, we are left with the question of whether the convergence in judicial review would reflect the court's spirit,[34] or the manner in which individual judges reason on issues of a political or ideological nature.[35] As we noted above, beyond mere judicial awareness of the political or ideological contexts, the issue of the source of a judicial review that coheres with these contexts relates to the court's legitimacy. A court that consistently and coherently develops a legal system through the use of law, precedent and doctrine would gain more public legitimacy.[36] Clearly, on matters that pertain to politically charged cases, this issue would matter more because courts rely on public legitimacy to avoid maneuvers by the executive branch to curb the court's powers.[37,38] As we noted above, this issue is indeed a key topic for HCJ judges. Thus, we offer the following two hypotheses:

H_{1a} ("a court of law"): The judicialization of politics is an outcome of court activities, reflected in consistency in court rulings on matters pertaining to political or ideological issues.

---

31 Briner, Josh. 2012. "Who Is the News Supreme Court Judge Noam Solberg?" *Walla News*. https://news.walla.co.il/item/1880037 (April 21, 2021).

32 *Dahan*, supra note 28, 16–30.

33 Chen Maanit. 2021. HCJ Determined: The State should Accept non-Orthodox Conversion. Globes. https://www.globes.co.il/news/article.aspx?did=1001362496 (March 6th 2022).

34 Hirschl, supra note 13.

35 Weinshall, Sommer, and Ritov, supra note 22.

36 Daniel A. Farber, The Rule of Law and the Law of Precedents, 90 Minn. L. Rev. 1173 (2006). Guy Harpaz, The European Court of Justice and its relations with the European Court of Human Rights: The quest for enhanced reliance, coherence and legitimacy, (2009), 46, *Common Market Law Review*, Issue 1, pp. 105–141.

37 Assaf Meydani & Shlomo Mizrahi, The Relationship Between the Supreme Court and Parliament in Light of the Theory of Moves: The Case of Israel, 22 Rationality & Soc'y 55, 71 (2010).

38 This review is a shorter version of the review appearing in Maoz Rosenthal & Shai Talmor, Estimating the "Legislators in Robes": Measuring Judges' Political Preferences, 43, *Justice Syst. J.*, 1 (2022).

H_{1b} ("a court of judges"): The judicialization of politics is an outcome of particular judges' activities, reflected in individual-level variance between judges on matters pertaining to political or ideological issues.

Thus, our empirical analysis involves verifying that there is meaningful variance in judicial review when the petitions the judges review relate to political or ideological issues. Furthermore, after revealing such a variance, our next step is to examine whether that variance goes beyond the court level to the individual judges' level.

RESEARCH CONTEXT: ISRAEL'S HIGH COURT OF JUSTICE

The ISC serves as a court of last resort in the Israeli court system. The Supreme Court handles appeals on decisions related to a wide variety of topics by lower courts in Israel's legal system.[39] The court comprises 15 judges and two senior clerks (*Rasham*), and is headed by a president, who is one of the ISC judges nominated by seniority. In petitions against the government's decisions and activities on either administrative or constitutional matters that might have broad implications, the Supreme Court serves as a first and final instance and is referred to as the HCJ.[40] Between 2011 and 2018, 46% of the cases the court heard were in its capacity as the HCJ.[41] No other legal procedure the ISC serves was as frequent as this one. A person or a group who regards an executive activity or a decision as possibly harmful either to the petitioner or to some more significant collective need can petition the HCJ for an injunction, which could eventually become permanent. Petitioners must prove that they have the right of standing before the court and that their petition is justiciable.[42] If accepted for review, a panel of three judges reviews the petition.[43] This panel makes a final decision regarding the petition to abolish the injunction or make it permanent. In rare cases of major public importance there will be an extended odd-numbered panel of judges.[44]

The authority granted to the HCJ implies that it can annul Knesset legislation and government decisions, based on a demand to do so by citizens who have standing before the court. Yet that possibility is not self-evident. In 1969, in the *Bergman* case,[45] the HCJ declared that Israel's Basic Laws – a set of laws that function in place of a constitution – give it the right to annul legislation.[46] Later, the HCJ maintained and expanded its constitutional powers gradually over primary and secondary legislation, as well as over government decisions. It did so

39 Vered Deshse. 2019. *Israel's Legal System*. Tel Aviv: Nevo (Hebrew): 398–400.

40 Dotan, supra note 17.

41 Weinshall Keren, Lee Epstein & Andy Worms. The Israeli Supreme Court Database, 2018 version URL: http://iscd.huji.ac.il

42 Deshe, supra note 39, 439.

43 Procedures in the High Court of Justice Regulations, 5744 1984, articles 16–18. https://www.nevo.co.il/law_html/law01/055_063.htm#Seif5 (Hebrew).

44 Margit Cohn. 2019. Judicial Deference to the Administration in Israel. In *Deference to the Administration in Judicial Review*, ed. Guobin Zhu. Springer, 231–69.

45 HCJ 98/69 Bergman v. Minister of Fin. and State Comptroller 23(1) PD 693 [1969]. [hereinafter Bergman]

46 Gary J. Jacobsohn, and Yaniv Roznai. 2020. Constitutional Revolution. Yale University Press., 192–193.

by using both Israel's Basic Laws and the 1948 Israeli Declaration of Independence, which includes a commitment to uphold human and civil liberties.[47]

During the early 1980s, the HCJ determined that it would review government decisions based on their reasonableness. Decisions had to be reasonable, unbiased, and non-arbitrary.[48] Should the court decide that the government made an unreasonable decision, it would annul the decision.[49] The HCJ expanded its use of the reasonableness doctrine in scrutinizing government decisions by examining both the decision-making process of the and the considerations it included.[50] This move potentially allowed judges to veto government decisions and make alternatives based on the judges' considerations of a reasonable decision-making process. The court went on to determine the range of reasonableness, setting limits on government decision-making processes.[51] Furthermore, the court expanded its justiciability doctrine, thereby allowing it to review various issues that used to be included in the space of non-justiciable decisions.[52] This expansion meant that potentially every decision (and eventually laws) could be reviewed by the court.[53] Moreover, the court also offered standing rights not only to petitioners directly harmed by government decisions, but also to public petitioners who were able to identify some collective level of rights infringement by government activities.[54]

In 1992 two Basic Laws were passed by the Knesset: *Human Dignity and Freedom* and *Freedom of Occupation.* The latter was amended to include an override clause and finally approved in 1994. These laws created a constitutional structure that potentially limited the Knesset's legislative powers not only due to procedural matters (as implied by the *Bergman* case) but also in substance. The Knesset could face judicial review to ensure the civil and human rights embedded in these two laws. The laws did provide the possibility of legislation infringing on these rights, but only for a worthy purpose and in a proportional manner. Without being able to prove proportionality and worthiness, a law could be annulled by the court. That legal interpretation became a political fact after the Israeli Supreme Court made this point very clearly in the *United Mizrahi Bank v. Migdal Cooperative Village* case.[55] Furthermore, the court extended the proportionality doctrine stemming from reasonableness and embedded in the 1992–1994 Basic Laws to various cases that related not only to constitutional but also to administrative review.[56] Hence, now all of the executive's decisions needed to comply with reasonableness and proportionality, expanding the HCJ powers to act as a veto player in the government's handling of day-to-day activities.[57] We now turn to present the methodology we used here, especially the way we associated judicial review with political ideologies.

---

47 Jacobsohn and Roznai, supra note 46, at 193–94.

48 Yellow Pages Ltd. v. the Broadcasting Authority. 1980. PD 35(1) HCJ (High Court of Justice).

49 Rivka Weill. The Strategic Common Law Court of Aharon Barak and its Aftermath: On Judicially-Led Constitutional Revolutions and Democratic Backsliding *The Law & Ethics of Human Rights*, vol. 14, no. 2, 2020, pp. 227–272.

50 Cohn, supra note 44.

51 Weill, supra note 49.

52 Weill, supra note 49.

53 Weill, supra note 49.

54 Cohn, supra note 44.

55 Jacobsohn and Roznai, supra note 46, at 194–200.

56 Cohn, supra note 44.

57 Yoav Dotan. 2014. *Lawyering for the Rule of Law: Government Lawyers and the Rise of Judicial Power in Israel*. New-York: Cambridge University Press.

DATA, VARIABLES AND MODEL

For this analysis we used the Israel High Court of Justice Executive Branch Merits Decisions (IHCJE) dataset.[58] This dataset comprises data collected from several sources, mainly from the Israeli legal database Nevo. It includes all court decisions that received certiorari and were accepted on merit by the HCJ during the period from *United Bank Hamizrahi LTD v. Migdal Cooperative Village, 1995* until December 2017. The decisions in this dataset relate to petitions submitted to the HCJ, with the prime minister, a particular minister or a junior minister being one of the parties against whom the petition was filed. This dataset allows us to observe judges making mindful decisions with clear policy implications.[59] It splits 2,960 court decisions into 9,806 judicial decisions made by individual judges. This dataset's unit of analysis is a Supreme Court judge sitting on an HCJ panel reviewing petitions against the political branch within the executive.

Variables[60]

Judges' decisions

On each petition, judges decide whether to reject, partially accept or fully accept petitions against the government as expressed in the HCJ's case transcripts. Based on these definitions, we modeled our dependent variable as an ordinal variable, with each value representing a qualitatively different level of judicial review. Rejection received the lowest value (1), partial acceptance the middle value (2) and acceptance of the petition the highest value (3).

Political petitions and ideological contexts

One particularly comprehensive effort for coding the ideological aspects of political decisions is that of the Manifesto Research on Political Representation (MARPOR) project, previously known as the Manifestos Research Group and the Comparative Manifestos Project.[61] The coders who are trained by MARPOR need to examine any quasi-sentence in the manifesto and associate it with seven ideological "domains," with a varying number of domain categories.[62] While some criticize this research tool,[63] this coding scheme is widely used for the study of political ideologies in political institutions.[64]

MARPOR's ideological domains include the state and its preference for power in international relations, democracy and human rights; state governance; government intervention in the markets; the extent to which the welfare state needs to be expanded; the state's commitment to national ethos; and the willingness to support the weaker parts of society. According to MARPOR's assumptions regarding political identities, the left places a high value on social

---

58 Rosenthal, Barzilai, and Meydani, supra note 17.

59 Rosenthal, Barzilai, and Meydani, supra note 17.

60 We used the same set of procedures thoroughly described in Rosenthal and Talmor, supra note 38, yet we have also changed some of our procedures to calculate the judges' preferences and intra-court factions.

61 Further details on the project are here: https://manifesto-project.wzb.eu/information/documents/information. Viewed April 18, 2021.

62 Rosenthal and Talmor, supra note 38.

63 Rosenthal and Talmor, supra note 38.

64 Rosenthal and Talmor, supra note 38.

welfare policies and economic equality combined with an appeasing foreign policy. The right emphasizes individual freedom manifested in national collectives having a unique tradition, and favors strong leadership with the state operating within an anarchic global system. Finally, the center values stability and dignity, emphasizes non-corrupt yet effective governance and respects tradition. In addition, the political center takes a cautious approach to reforms and supports the right to individual property, even at the cost of harming social equality.[65]

The usage of MARPOR's scheme is based on coding done by coders trained by the MARPOR staff and follows MARPOR's regulations. When analyzing party manifestos, each coder divides a political text into quasi-sentences, and decides whether it has a political quality. Then, the coder associates these sentences with the domains and issues from MARPOR's scheme. In a political text there are right, left and center types of quasi-sentences. The assessment of a political text's aggregated right–left policy positions (RILE) is calculated by subtracting the number of left-wing quasi-sentences from the number of right-wing quasi-sentences, divided by all of the left-, center and right-wing quasi-sentences and multiplied by 100. The closer the score is to (+100), the more right-wing is the party's orientation. A score of 0 reflects a centrist orientation. The closer the score is to (–100), the more left-wing is the party's orientation.[66]

To evaluate judge' political preferences, we assume that the petition's context and details as well as the judges' decisions are the main indicators for the analysis. Thus, the petition is the quasi-sentence: it relates to a main topic that can have a political interpretation, which can be defined in left-right terms. Viewed this way, judges' rulings on a variety of petitions then become the judges' "manifesto," which we can use to evaluate their political position.[67] Our main line of inquiry here would be to examine the way the judges sitting on the HCJ since 1995 made decisions on petitions in a manner that allows analysts to discern them based on the MARPOR coding scheme and the RILE aggregation method.

ANALYSIS AND RESULTS[68]

The first step we took was to ascertain the proportion of petitions related to MARPOR topics that received an on-merits decision. Table 7.1 lists the basic distributions of the judges' decisions on topics that accounted for more than 1% of the HCJ's merits decisions.

As Table 7.1 illustrates, in the IHCJE dataset, more than 50% of our cases are not ideologically connected with either left-wing or right-wing political positions. The rest of the cases deal with issues of human rights and freedoms, then national identity issues, market regulation and the way democracy should be handled.[69] Our next step was to focus on the petitions that the judges accepted. Taking this step reduced our dataset significantly, as on most occasions the HCJ tends to reject petitions against the executive.[70] In order not to determine ideological

---

65 Rosenthal and Talmor, supra note 38.

66 Rosenthal and Talmor, supra note 38.

67 Please see Rosenthal and Talmor, supra note 38 for the detailed coding process.

68 Please note that unlike Rosenthal and Talmor supra note 38, here we show the descriptive statistics of the judges' decisions and not the case-level-data.

69 Rosenthal, Barzilai, and Meydani, supra note 17.

70 Maoz Rosenthal. 2019. Is the IHCJ a Unitary Player: An Invitation to Discuss the IHCJ as a Public Institution. *ICON-S-IL Blog*. https://israeliconstitutionalism.wordpress.com/2019/06/26 (September 17, 2019).

Table 7.1 *Distribution of policy topics*

MARPOR Code	*Policy Domain*	*Policy Issue*	*Left–Right Emphasis**	*Freq.*	*%*
504	Welfare and Quality of Life	Welfare State Expansion	Left	158	1.61%
201.1	Freedom and Democracy	Freedom	Right	161	1.64%
401	Economics	Free Market Economy	Right	162	1.65%
304	Political System	Political Corruption	Other	261	2.66%
503	Welfare and Quality of Life	Equality: Positive	Other	310	3.16%
602.2	Fabric of Society	Immigration: Positive	Other	339	3.46%
604	Fabric of Society	Traditional Morality: Negative	Other	342	3.49%
601.1	Fabric of Society	National Way of Life: Positive	Right	354	3.61%
602.1	Fabric of Society	National Way of Life: Negative	Other	728	7.42%
201.2	Freedom and Democracy	Human Rights	Other	866	8.83%
303	Political System	Governmental and Administrative Efficiency	Other	1085	11.06%
0	Non-Political	Non-Political	-----	4274	43.59%

Note: * Based on: https://manifestoproject.wzb.eu/down/papers/budge_right-left-scale.pdf.

positions from a very few decisions, we took the largest number of petitions a particular judge accepted (Judge Beinish with 102 accepted petitions) and removed from the data judges who accepted less than 10% of that number.

We organized Table 7.2 with selected MARPOR categories in columns. The first column contains political petitions, and the last two columns are topics that relate to specific Israeli issues: petitions regarding the Israeli settlements in the West Bank and Gaza Strip, and the tension between state and religion. These two topics are the crux of Israeli politics, essentially defining right and left in Israeli politics.[71] Of these, we have the decisions of judges regarding petitions supporting the expansion of Israeli settlements in the 1967 occupied territories and those negating the continuation of the influence of Jewish religious institutions on Israeli public life.

Each column ranks the judges in accordance with the frequency of their support for petitions related to the topics in the column. The judges in the lower-ranked rows are those who accepted the least number of petitions supporting the topic the column relates to.[72] The

[71] Asher Arian, and Michal Shamir. 2008. A Decade Later, the World Had Changed, the Cleavage Structure Remained: Israel 1996–2006. *Party Politics* 14(6): 685–705. Gideon Doron. 2005. Right as Opposed to Wrong as Opposed to Left: The Spatial Location of "Right Parties" on the Israeli Political Map." *Israel Studies* 10(3): 29–53.

[72] Following Grofman and Brazil, supra note 22, we also used Multidimensional Scaling (MDS) to rank-order the judges on each separate dimension. The results were identical to the frequency-based ordering.

Table 7.2 *Judges' support patterns across dimensions*

Political Ideology Petitions	*Human Rights and Democracy Positive*	*Political System*	*National Way of Life Negative (against settlements)*	*Traditional Morality Negative (sep. of state and religion)*
Shtrasburg Cohen, Tova	Metza, Eliyahu	Grunis, Asher	Engelrad, Itzhak	Engelrad, Itzhak
Engelrad, Itzhak	Shtrasburg Cohen, Tova	Hendel, Neal	Tirkel, Yaakov	Arbel, Edna
Tirkel, Yaakov	Engelrad, Itzhak	Shtrasburg Cohen, Tova	Zamir, Itzhak	Prukchia, Ayala
Or, Theodor	Melzer, Hanan	Rivlin, Eliezer	Arbel, Edna	Tirkel, Yaakov
Zamir, Itzhak	Or, Theodor	Amit, Itzhak	Prukchia, Ayala	Zamir, Itzhak
Amit, Itzhak	Tirkel, Yaakov	Melzer, Hanan	Danziger, Yoram	Levi, Edmond
Melzer, Hanan	Zamir, Itzhak	Zamir, Itzhak	Levi, Edmond	Danziger, Yoram
Danziger, Yoram	Dorner, Dalia	Barak, Aharon	Or, Theodor	Grunis, Asher
Fogelman, Uzi	Heshin, Mishael	Or, Theodor	Shtrasburg Cohen, Tova	Or, Theodor
Hendel, Neal	Rubinstein, Elyakim	Prukchia, Ayala	Rivlin, Eliezer	Rivlin, Eliezer
Grunis, Asher	Amit, Itzhak	Engelrad, Itzhak	Fogelman, Uzi	Shtrasburg Cohen, Tova
Metza, Eliyahu	Arbel, Edna	Fogelman, Uzi	Grunis, Asher	Amit, Itzhak
Rivlin, Eliezer	Fogelman, Uzi	Hayut, Ester	Amit, Itzhak	Dorner, Dalia
Arbel, Edna	Barak, Aharon	Danziger, Yoram	Metza, Eliyahu	Fogelman, Uzi
Prukchia, Ayala	Danziger, Yoram	Heshin, Mishael	Barak, Aharon	Jubran, Salim
Rubinstein, Elyakim	Grunis, Asher	Naor, Miryam	Hendel, Neal	Metza, Eliyahu
Levi, Edmond	Hendel, Neal	Metza, Eliyahu	Jubran, Salim	Barak, Aharon
Naor, Miryam	Jubran, Salim	Tirkel, Yaakov	Melzer, Hanan	Rubinstein, Elyakim
Barak, Aharon	Prukchia, Ayala	Arbel, Edna	Hayut, Ester	Hendel, Neal
Hayut, Ester	Rivlin, Eliezer	Dorner, Dalia	Rubinstein, Elyakim	Melzer, Hanan
Jubran, Salim	Beinish, Dorit	Jubran, Salim	Naor, Miryam	Beinish, Dorit
Dorner, Dalia	Hayut, Ester	Beinish, Dorit	Dorner, Dalia	Hayut, Ester
Heshin, Mishael	Levi, Edmond	Levi, Edmond	Beinish, Dorit	Heshin, Mishael
Beinish, Dorit	Naor, Miryam	Rubinstein, Elyakim	Heshin, Mishael	Naor, Miryam

next step that MARPOR's scale allows us to take is to use the RILE formula and apply it to the HCJ's judicial decision-making. To do so, we aggregated the RILE scale for each judge based on the rates at which the judge fully accepted petitions on the various policy issues that received values on the right–left MARPOR scale.

$$\textit{Judge RILE} = \frac{\begin{bmatrix} (\textit{Judge's acceptance of a right wing petition}) - \\ (\textit{Judge's acceptance of a left wing petition}) \end{bmatrix}}{\textit{all political petitions the judge accepted: right, center, left}} * 100$$

Our formula included several components. The more accepting a judge was of right-wing petitions, the higher his or her positive RILE score and vice versa. The results appear in Figure 7.1.

As Figure 7.1 indicates, in the HCJ the results range between Judge Barak, a well-known and long-standing President of the Israeli Supreme Court with a RILE score of (–12), and Judge Engelard with a RILE score of (+33.3). The descriptive statistics for the HCJ judges' RILE score indicate a mean score of (5.50) and a median of (5.0), with a standard deviation of 10.6. The upper quartile begins with (10.31) and the lower quartile begins with (–4.18). Comparing these results with data taken from MARPOR's dataset of party manifestos, the HCJ judges' overall scores are like those associated with Israel's centrist parties. An example of an Israeli party that conforms with MARPOR's definition as centrist would be *Yesh Atid* with (–6.048) in 2013 and then (–15.106) in 2015. This outcome is different from the public

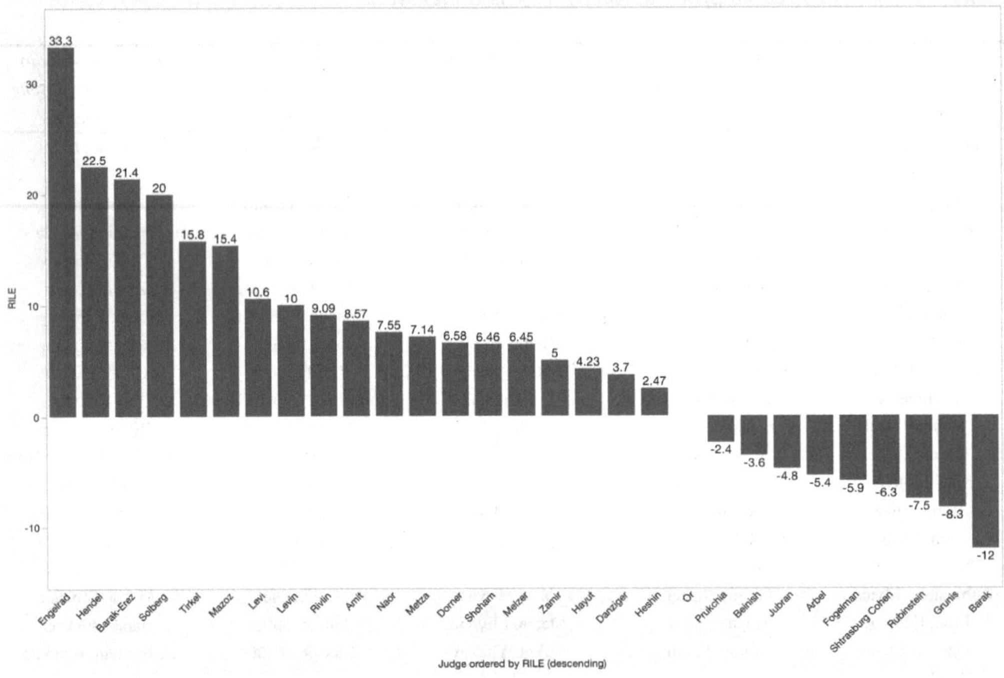

Figure 7.1 *The HCJ's judges' right–left RILE scores*

perception of the HCJ, especially among Israel's right-wing groups, that the court functions as a branch of the left-wing political parties.[73]

In terms of our hypotheses, there is consistency with respect to political and ideologically contextualized petitions. Hence, H_0 can be discarded and H_1 is more correct. In terms of hypotheses H_{1b} (consistency between topics on an individual level) vs. H_{1a} (consistency on a court level), H_{1b} seems to reflect the reality about the variance between judges. Thus, our results verify the "court of judges" hypothesis: individual judges react differently and consistently to petitions that have a political or ideological context. However, exploring that outcome in greater depth leads to insights that go beyond the court of law/court of judges dichotomy.

If we divide the distribution of the judges' RILE scores into quartiles, the lowest quartile stretches between (–12) and (–4.18), from President Barak to Judge Jubran. The second quartile stretches between (–4.18) and (5.55), from President Beinish to Judge Zamir. The third quartile stretches from Judge Meltzer (10.31) to Judge Levin and then to (33.33) from Judge Levi to Judge Engelrad. Most of this variance is quite moderate, with (0.611) skewness and (0.293) kurtosis. Hence, this distribution includes rather close values. This closeness is especially clear within the quartiles, implying that the difference *within* the groups is less than that *between* the groups. Indeed, using JMP Pro 15 to analyze a one-way analysis of variance between these groups produces a 52.561*** outcome, showing that there is a significant vari-

[73] Just one example among many: https://www.timesofisrael.com/justice-minister-high-court-no-longer-a-branch-of-left-wing-meretz-party/ viewed April 2020.

ance *between* rather than *within* these groups. Thus, our analysis goes beyond the court of law/court of judges dichotomy and offers an alternative option: a court of factions. We should note that not all of these judges served at the same time on the HCJ. Thus, our analysis goes beyond the court of judges/court of law dichotomy and offers an alternative option: a court of factions.

We should note that not all these judges served simultaneously on the HCJ. Thus, the fact that each time one of them was sitting on a panel representing that set of preferences maintains this pluralism of factions throughout the period we studied. Thus, the HCJ included judges with different ideological positions, whereas, throughout the studied period, the court included a set of judges with varied ideological positions. That variance repeatedly included judges with ideological positions that create a set of factions: several judges with similar positions who are different from the other judges on the court simultaneously. Over the years, with judges stepping into their term in court, they became a part of these judicial factions.

CONCLUDING DISCUSSION: A COURT OF JUDICIAL FACTIONS?

Our coding and analysis show that variances in judges' decision-making are far from random when it comes to political or ideological cases. Moreover, these variances indicate that individual judges vary in how they see such cases. However, a deeper exploration of our results using MARPOR coding and its RILE measure reveals that judges' decisions converge into *judicial factions*. Furthermore, the divergence between HCJ judges' positions does not favor either Israeli political extreme. Hence, in the Israeli case, the law works in factions that are not substantially different from one another and are generally consistent with a centrist policy position.

Thus, here the source of the judicialization of politics is not an individual judge but judicial factions. These factions do not take over the court at any particular time. Over time, there are judges from the different factions we identified as being part of the same composition of judges. Hence, while the court sets judicial policy and promotes it, it does so with various voices within it. The way these factions interpret and sustain the law is based on an ongoing conversation within the different parts of the Israeli polity represented on the court. This finding, which locates judicial factions as the driving force of the court's interpretation of political questions, relates to an ongoing debate within Israeli politics as a whole and the study of judicial politics in Israel. Some critics of the court claim that the HCJ functions as a left-wing political party.[74] However, based on a systematic, quantitative study, our analysis shows that the HCJ is not one party; nor is it a left-wing party. Politically, the HCJ functions as a collection of moderate parties deliberating on issues with political significance, with no one politically identified clear hand dominating this process.

Some more general lessons that can be taken from our analysis could relate to our method. Future studies could use it to examine the question we posed here in a variety of settings to assess judicial preferences, even when the nomination process is not overtly partisan and does not provide clear indications of the judges' political ideology. In terms of its essence, this chapter offers a way to think about courts as developing their legal analyses of political realities based on judicial factions formed within the court, rather than thinking about the

---

[74] Simcha Rotman. 2019. *The Bagaz Party*. Jerusalem: Sela-Meir Pub. (Hebrew).

court as a unitary player or a set of separate individuals.[75] Hence, the path for further analysis of the judicialization of politics in democracies that we provide is to go beyond the analysis of individual judges' behavior[76] or the courts' behavior.[77] An alternative approach is to examine how competing factions within the court set the terms for the judicialization of politics, either blocking or promoting it.

---

[75] Rosenthal, supra note 70.

[76] Eileen Braman. 2009. *Law, Politics, and Perception: How Policy Preferences Influence Legal Reasoning*. Charlottesville, University of Virginia Press. Epstein, Lee, William M Landes, and Richard A Posner. 2011. Why (and When) Judges Dissent: A Theoretical and Empirical Analysis. *Journal of Legal Analysis* 3(1): 101–37. Weinshall, Sommer, and Ritov, supra note 22.

[77] Hirschl, supra note 7; Meydani and Mizrahi, supra note 37.

8. Planting seeds but bearing different fruit

International peace-building and constitutional design in Cambodia, 1991–1993

Kyle Shen

The moment of constitutional design is an encounter between domestic and international politics. Particularly with the development of human rights in constitutional texts since the mid-20th century, constitution-making responds to the exigencies of local politics, but also to transnational legal standards of constitutionalism, incorporating discourses regarding rights, democracy, and the rule of law. The encounter between the international and the local is particularly salient in post-conflict settings, where peace processes often include transnational actors acting as peacekeepers and peacebuilders, and even transnational agreements establishing a blueprint for post-conflict and post-colonial constitutions.[1]

The dominant theory connecting international politics to domestic constitution-making is diffusion, in which foreign and international legal sources provide models that local actors adopt based on domestic contexts.[2] Within the diffusion literature there exist a number of mechanisms for explaining why foreign models percolate into domestic contexts, often described as competition, coercion, learning, and acculturation.[3] Though they vary widely, all of these mechanisms describe different motivations for local elites to respond in some way to transnational models of constitutional design.

This literature provides a wealth of evidence that diffusion is deeply intertwined with the practice of constitution-making throughout the world. Furthermore, it emphasizes the agency of local actors in selecting foreign mechanisms.[4] The emphasis on local actors in this process

---

1 Vijayashi Sripati, *UN Constitutional Assistance Projects in Comprehensive Peace Missions: An Inventory 1989–2011*, 19 International Peacekeeping 93 (2012). International and regional organizations also have developed their own documents discussing legal standards for constitution making. See, e.g., Venice Commission, *Rule of Law Checklist*, Council of Europe Study No. 711/2013 (March 17, 2016); U.N. Office of the High Commissioner for Human Rights, *Human Rights and Constitution Making*, U.N. Doc HR/PUB/17/5 (2018).

2 Benedikt Goderis & Mila Versteeg, *The diffusion of constitutional rights*, 39 Int'l Rev. L. & Econ. 1 (2014); Zach Elkins et al., *Getting to Rights: Treaty Ratification, Constitutional Convergence, and Human Rights Practice*, 54 Harv. Int'l L.J. 61 (2013); Zach Elkins et al., The Endurance of National Constitutions (2009). David Law & Mila Versteeg, *Sham Constitutions*, 101 Calif. L. Rev. 864 (2013).

3 Respectively, these mechanisms involve signaling friendly attitudes to potentially friendly foreign actors, responding to external pressure, adopting models observed to have some success elsewhere, and buying into transnational norms of constitution-making. Goderis & Versteeg, *supra* note 2. Goderis & Versteeg expand on Goodman & Jinks's tripartite framework of coercion, persuasion, and acculturation. Ryan Goodman & Derek Jinks, Socializing States: Promoting Human Rights Through International Law (2014).

4 Although not expressly about constitutional design, these theories are echoed in the discussions of domestic rights-based advocacy found in Beth Simmons, Mobilizing for Human Rights (2009)

seems especially significant given that, among the four mechanisms described above, there appears to be the least evidence in favor of theories of external pressure or coercion from foreign powers,[5] and more in favor of learning[6] and acculturation.[7]

However, where much of the diffusion literature suggests an optimistic tone for local adoption and implementation of external models, the track record of global constitutionalism reflects a more mixed picture.[8] Certainly, there are notable success stories of institutional development and strong implementation of rights-based constitutionalism.[9] While the diffusion story is one of local elites adopting constitutional norms which include commitments to rights and democracy, many hybrid and autocratic regimes also engage in these practices, with more mixed records of institutional development and compliance.

This chapter asks for a closer examination between the process of diffusion and the institutional outcomes in less-than-ideal contexts for rights-based constitutionalism, and whether the process of diffusion may have a role in explaining constitutional weakness, particularly in post-conflict regimes. Using the Cambodian Constitution of 1993 as a demonstrative case, this chapter examines the complex and iterative engagements among international and domestic actors – in this case the United Nations Transitional Authority in Cambodia, a legion of foreign diplomats, and four separate domestic political factions.

The scale of the intervention and the gravity of this moment in history offer an opportunity to examine the role of international influences on constitution-making, particularly in post-conflict settings. Over the course of three years and two major U.N. missions to Cambodia in the early 1990s, the United Nations and its donors spent over US$1.6 billion (approximately US$3 billion in current US dollars) in a nation whose average annual gross

---

and MARGARET KECK & KATHRYN SIKKINK, ACTIVISTS BEYOND BORDERS: ADVOCACY NETWORKS IN INTERNATIONAL POLITICS (1998), both positing the significant of local activists seeking out foreign norms or advocacy networks that augment domestic efforts.

[5] GOODMAN & JINKS, *supra* note 3.

[6] Law & Versteeg, *supra* note 2.

[7] GOODMAN & JINKS, *supra* note 3.

[8] Summary statistics using the Comparative Constitutions Project's (CCP) data on national constitutions and Polity scores for democracy are illustrative. The CCP data contains constitutional texts starting from 1789 to the modern day. Polity scores for democracy range from 10 to –10, and contain three conceptual regime types: democracy, autocracy, and anocracy. Examining Polity scores corresponding to the year of constitutional adoption, 174 countries (38.5%), countries scored less than –6 on the Polity scale, denoting an autocracy. 186 countries (41.2%) scored between –5 and 5, denoting anocracy. Since the post-WWII renaissance of constitutional drafting, there are 331 constitutions in the dataset, 131 of which (39.6%) had a corresponding country score for autocracy, while 104 (31.4%) were scored as hybrid regimes or anocracies. Although the connection between de jure and de facto institutions is not always clear cut, the summary statistics show that most constitutions in the world are not written under the ideal conditions of democratic rule of law, despite the close theoretical association between constitutionalism and liberal democracy. Zachary Elkins & Tom Ginsburg, *Characteristics of National Constitutions, Version 3.0*, COMPARATIVE CONSTITUTIONS PROJECT (May 20, 2021), comparativeconstitutionsproject.org; Monty G. Marshal et al., *Polity IV Project: Political Regime Characteristics and Transitions, 1800–2018*, available at https://govdata360.worldbank.org/indicators/h6906d31b.

[9] Daniel M. Brinks & Varun Gauri, *The Law's Majestic Equality? The Distributive Impact of Judicializing Social and Economic Rights*, 12 PERSPECTIVES ON POLITICS 375 (2014); William Forbath, *Cultural Transformation, Deep Institutional Reform, and ESR Practice: South Africa's Treatment Action Campaign, in* STONES OF HOPE: HOW AFRICAN ACTIVISTS RECLAIM HUMAN RIGHTS TO CHALLENGE GLOBAL POVERTY 51(Lucie E. White & Jeremy Perelman, eds., 2010); GARY J. JACOBSOHN, WHEEL OF LAW (2009).

domestic product at the time hovered around US$2.5 billion. This coordinated effort saw substantial involvement not only by the U.N. Security Council and the U.N. Secretary-General and his staff, but also the coordination of numerous diplomatic efforts by global and regional powers, including Australia, China, Indonesia, Japan, and the United States.

It also involved the development of linkages between the Cambodian people and the U.N. staff. Beginning in 1992, U.N. troops, diplomats, and other staff would arrive in Cambodia to work on projects ranging from education and promotion of elections and voting to building infrastructure, resettling refugees, and using their military presence to discourage any lingering armed conflicts in the country. As the U.N. staff arrived, they sought to coordinate with Cambodians to build a government framed around principles of human rights and liberal democracy, tailored to the needs of Cambodian society, which had endured decades of conflict and authoritarian rule.

The constitution that emerged from this process makes strong written commitments to these principles.[10] Yet, in practice, the international framing for the goals of the peace process and the constitution saw clashing goals among both local and international factions. The international intervention introduced a balance of power among the domestic factions which held the constitutional coalition together during the time leading up to and during the drafting of the constitution. However, the intervention also put a thumb on the proverbial scale of the balance of power. This involvement distorted the reality of political contestation on the ground, thus generating a pluralistic text with liberal democratic commitments de jure, but one lacking the de facto political commitments to preserve these textual commitments.

1. CONSTITUTIONAL WEAKNESS AND DIFFUSION

Imbalances of power at the international level shape the way that norms take root once they are translated into domestic constitutions. As a site where international and domestic actors engage in politics, international factors are not only a source of possible constitutional models, the construction of which is left to political conditions within a country. In addition to this role, the engagement among international and domestic political actors is a critical antecedent[11] to the political engagement among domestic political actors during the drafting stage of the constitution and afterwards, the outcomes of which will frame the development of local institutions, and especially constitutions.

The incorporation of international politics as a critical antecedent for domestic constitutional design is of particular relevance for understanding constitutions in hybrid or autocratic regimes. In this literature, constitutions in nondemocracies typically are understood as weak

---

10 Taing Ratana, *Pluralist Constitution in Cambodia*, in PLURALIST CONSTITUTIONS IN SOUTHEAST ASIA 169 (Jaclyn Neo & Bui Ngoc Son, eds., 2019); Sok Socheat, *Institution Protection of Basic Human Rights in Cambodia, in* CAMBODIAN CONSTITUTIONAL LAW 357 (Hor Peng et al., eds., 2016).

11 Dan Slater & Erica Simmons, *Informative Regress: Critical Antecedents in Comparative Politics*, 43 COMPARATIVE POLITICAL STUDIES 886 (2010).

institutions.[12] These constitutions serve three possible roles: window-dressing, billboarding, and blueprints.[13]

Each of these categories describes a separate way in which the constitution responds to elite politics. These types are not mutually exclusive, as a single constitution may be developed with many purposes in mind.

In the case of billboards, the constitution is a signal by local elites to international observers, especially potential economic partners. This variety is most notably described in Moustafa's case study of the Egyptian Supreme Court, which was promoted as a business-friendly institution to encourage confidence among foreign investors that their investments would remain unencumbered by expropriation.[14]

Window-dressing constitutions also signify preemptive reactions to international pressure, but to potential political pressures to conform the text to a set of norms, including the inclusion of human rights. The North Korean constitution is an example, where there are almost no opportunities for political contestation, yet nonetheless it contains a number of rights provisions.[15]

Both billboard and window-dressing constitutions often fail to convince their target audiences that these constitutions are earnest attempts to develop the rule of law. The Egyptian experiment in judicial independence collapsed once the Supreme Court began ruling in favor of critics of President Mubarak's rule; while few would suggest that a North Korean citizen would find much success invoking the constitution's rights guarantees, beginning with Article 64's "genuine democratic rights and liberties as well as the material and cultural well-being of all its citizens." That these constitutions often do not work as window-dressing or as billboards, despite persisting as such, suggests some other explanation for why these constitutions take the time to create weak institutions on purpose.

Finally, blueprint constitutions reflect the most locally oriented category of authoritarian constitutions, as a way to organize elite politics within a country. The construction of autocratic legislatures described in Gandhi (2010) reflects this form of constitutional politics. These texts help authoritarian parties structure elite politics such that outcomes continue to favor ruling authoritarians over the manifestation of opposition groups.

In each of these roles, the constitution conveys a message that benefits elites rather than constraining their power; an understanding of constitutionalism that contradicts classical definitions of constitutions that have shaped studies in comparative constitutional theory today.[16]

---

[12] Borrowing the definition from Brinks, Levitsky, & Murillo, a weak institution is one which fails to meaningfully shift political outcomes away from the pre-existing preferences of institutional actors. This may occur either where an institution is conservative and does not introduce ambitious institutional goals, or where an institution fails to secure compliance, whether from lack of enforcement or capacity. Daniel M. Brinks et al., Understanding Institutional Weakness (2019).

[13] Tom Ginsburg & Alberto Simpser, *Introduction, in* Constitutions in Authoritarian Regimes 6 (Tom Ginsburg & Alberto Simpser, eds., 2014).

[14] Tamir Moustafa, *Law and Resistance in Authoritarian States: The Judicialization of Politics in Egypt, in* Rule by Law: The Politics of Courts in Authoritarian Regimes (Tom Ginsburg & Tamir Moustafa eds., 2008).

[15] Constitution of North Korea 1972, amended 2019, Chapter V: Fundamental Rights and Duties of Citizens.

[16] Albert H.Y. Chen, *The achievement of constitutionalism in Asia: moving beyond 'constitutions without constitutionalism', in* Constitutionalism in Asia in the Early Twenty-First Century 1 (Albert H.Y. Chen ed. 2015); Walter Murphy, Constitutional Democracy: Creating and

Where classical theories of constitutionalism consider rule of law and, more recently, human rights and supporting institutions like judicial independence as the *sine qua non* of a viable constitutional order, constitutions in nondemocracies often display little regard for this theoretical understanding in practice, aside from window-dressing with low rates of compliance.

Challenging the association between the rule of law and constitutionalism, some recent scholarship suggests that constitutions may be understood better as institutions for ordering power and maintaining a balance of power among elite factions.[17] This scholarship relies on interrogations of the conditions facing different elite groups at the moment of constitutional origin. The design of the constitution is a political arrangement entrenching a system of politics best suited for the balance of power at the time of origin. There is little normative content to this process. Rather, to the extent that the constitution favors political openness and democratic institutions like a strong judiciary, it is more likely to take place where no one power can secure a significant advantage at origin, thus incentivizing all actors to leave an open door that will provide for their future inclusion in politics.[18] In this reading, the rule of law is not so much an essential normative component of constitutionalism, but rather the outcome of a need for political insurance when no one faction is able to guarantee that it can secure power for the long term.

If constitutionalism largely is an outcome of political negotiations at a critical moment, there exists a wider space in which one can understand constitutions in nondemocracies. Extant scholarship often considers constitutions in nondemocracies as a deviant subtype of constitutionalism.[19] This typology, though often used as a descriptive tool, risks understanding nondemocratic constitutions as weak institutions a priori. Autocrats have little reason to design institutions which lead them away from their desired policy preference, and therefore any constitutional language that would contradict this preference must be either unambitious or low in compliance.

Yet some evidence suggests that autocratic constitutions are designed with various goals in mind, not merely domination of politics using elite institutions. In cases where they are tools for facilitating rule by law,[20] there are a variety of ways in which constitutions go about achieving this goal, depending on the circumstances on the ground. This variation suggests that authoritarian constitutions are not merely texts intended to justify and exert the state's power, but also include some normative content, such as the rule of law; or perhaps other norms, such as reflecting populist or cultural values. The story of the Egyptian Supreme Court, for example, is one case of an autocrat tying his hands by building an independent court to promote credible commitment for foreign investment.[21] Scheppelle's concept of "constitutional malice" describes cases where constitutions written during democratic backsliding expressly distinguish their designs from extant constitutional models, in order to build domes-

---

MAINTAINING A JUST POLITICAL ORDER (2007); Karl Lowenstein, *Constitutions and Constitutional Law in the West and in the East*, 30 THE INDIAN JOURNAL OF POLITICAL SCIENCE 203 (1969); Giovanni Sartori, CONSTITUTIONALISM: A PRELIMINARY DISCUSSION, 56 *APSR* 853 (1962).

17 DANIEL M. BRINKS & ABBY BLASS, THE DNA OF CONSTITUTIONAL JUSTICE IN LATIN AMERICA (2018).

18 Ibid.; TOM GINSBURG, JUDICIAL REVIEW IN NEW DEMOCRACIES (2003).

19 Chen 2015, *supra* note 16.

20 TOM GINSBURG & TAMIR MOUSTAFA, RULE BY LAW: THE POLITICS OF COURTS IN AUTHORITARIAN REGIMES (2008).

21 Moustafa, *supra* note 14.

tic institutions that chart a different path from most liberal democratic constitutionalism. She uses this concept to describe the nationalist and populist turn in Hungarian constitutionalism, for example.[22] Furthermore, even nondemocratic constitutions have reflected attempts to build constitutions that express the local social, cultural, or political context.[23]

These studies show that a large variety of constitutional models can exist, even in nondemocratic settings. This variation in constructing nondemocratic constitutions, relying also on the argument that constitutions are mechanisms for organizing elite politics, therefore pushes back against treating these texts as deviant subtypes of rule-of-law constitutionalism, hollow shells of the stronger constitutions that restrain state power in democracies. Instead of assuming institutional weakness a priori, one might ask how these constitutions are constructed, what factors might influence this process, and if one might expect extant theories of constitutional design to apply equally in these contexts.

To be clear, this literature on constitutions in nondemocracies shows little evidence for optimism that rule-of-law constitutionalism will flourish in nondemocratic contexts. Given the proliferation of rights language in constitutions,[24] these texts likely include superficial references to rights and liberal democratic norms such as judicial independence, but the distinction between law in text and in practice surely will be significant. However, the literature on weak institutions and constitutional design, and extant studies of nondemocratic constitutions converge to suggest that the weakness of nondemocratic constitutions is constructed from the political conditions at the origin of these institutions.

The peace process in Cambodia and the story of its constitution as a part of that process offer an ideal case study for illustrating the engagement among international and political actors during a moment of peacebuilding and constitutional design. Furthermore, while the prospect of growing liberal democratic constitutionalism is a daunting notion for any post-conflict setting, the ambitions of its architects, as preserved in archival records and periodicals from the time, and the material investment of the U.N. intervention were designed to give the Cambodian constitution the most favorable conditions to last for the long term. It hoped to do so by balancing the interests of the four major political factions in Cambodia at the time; although, as will be seen, this balance of power rested in part on the political role of foreign and U.N. diplomats. Because of this distortion in political conditions during the peace process, the negotiated peace that emerged addressed a different political reality in the country after the U.N. left the country.

Before engaging in the case study, one comment must be noted: that the use of "weak institution" in this chapter takes up an extant concept in the comparative study of political institutions.[25] This concept offers significant descriptive and analytical value for explaining the political development of the Cambodian constitution and helps map this case study onto a broader set of literature. It is not used as a normative judgment. Indeed, one goal of this chapter is to do the opposite. It argues that constitutions, even those in nondemocracies, evolve from the consequences, both intended and unintended, of the political conditions at their origin.

---

[22] Kim Scheppele, *Autocratic Legalism*, 85 U. CHI. L. REV. 545 (2018).

[23] NATHAN BROWN, CONSTITUTIONS IN A NONCONSTITUTIONAL WORLD: ARAB BASIC LAWS AND THE PROSPECTS FOR ACCOUNTABLE GOVERNMENT (2012).

[24] David Law & Mila Versteeg, *supra* note 2; ZACH ELKINS ET AL., *supra* note 2.

[25] BRINKS ET AL. 2019, *supra* note 12; Steven Levitsky & María Victoria Murillo, *Variation in Institutional Strength*, 12 ANN. REV. POL. SCI. 115 (2009).

The Cambodian case is an ideal case to understand both Cambodian history since 1993 and the role of international politics in constitutional design in nondemocratic regimes – a category which makes up a supermajority of constitutions in the world.[26] In order to study constitutions as a descriptive matter, let alone to seek out the explanations for how constitutional models diffuse and take root, a better understanding of these texts is necessary.

2. PEACEBUILDING AND CONSTITUTION-MAKING IN CAMBODIA

2.1 Introducing the Four Cambodian Factions

Negotiated in the summer and ratified in the early autumn of 1993, the current constitution of Cambodia was drafted by a Constituent Assembly elected by a United Nations-supervised popular vote and saw negotiations largely among three political parties that were key players in the civil war of the 1980s and the subsequent peace process that culminated in the Paris Peace Agreements in 1991.[27] These three parties were the Cambodian People's Party (CPP),[28] the Buddhist Liberal Democratic Party (BLDP),[29] and the National United Front for an Independent, Neutral and Peaceful Cambodia (FUNCINPEC).[30] A fourth party also played an essential role in the peace process but was not represented among the Constituent Assembly. Despite its influential role in the peace process, the Khmer Rouge (Democratic Party of Kampuchea, DPK)[31] boycotted the Constituent Assembly elections and fielded no candidates.[32]

Representing four different visions for the country, and each of these four major factions in Cambodia would leave its mark in some way on the shape of the peace process. The State

---

26 See discussion of CCP and Polity IV data, footnote 8.

27 A fourth party, MOLINAKA, received one seat among the 120 members of the Constituent Assembly, but largely played a minimal role during negotiations. Andrea Hamilton, *Molinaka Looks to Play a Swinging Role*, Phnom Penh Post (June 15–July 1, 1993), at 5.

28 Best described as a hardline post-communist Soviet party, this party held power over most of the state of Cambodia.

29 Led by former Prime Minister Son Sann, this group was best characterized as in favor of a democratic Khmer nationalism and anti-Communist, although the latter was not a hard ideological position. When operating as a military faction and not a political party, the BLDP, then known as the Khmer People's National Liberation Front, opposed the CPP most vigorously, which led them to coordinate at times with the Maoist Khmer Rouge.

30 Second to the CPP, the FUNCINPEC was the largest military and political force in the country. Founded by King Sihanouk as an opposition movement to the CPP and its backing by the Vietnamese government, this was not only the largest source of political resistance to the CPP, but also was the channel for King Sihanouk, who had ruled the country from 1955–1970 and continued to hold reverence among many Cambodian people since that time, to regain a foothold in Cambodian politics.

31 This was the same party that infamously ruled Cambodia from 1975–1979 and oversaw the mass displacement and deaths and killings of much of the country's population. A party with roots in Maoist ideology, its ideological stances were nationalistic. After their defeat during the Vietnamese invasion of Cambodia in 1979, the Khmer Rouge remained a relevant military and political force. They held the seat of Cambodia at the U.N. General Assembly until 1990. Ramses Amer, *The United Nations and Kampuchea: The issue of representation and its implications*, 22 Bulletin of Concerned Asian Scholars 52 (1990).

32 Nate Thayer, *Interview with Khieu Samphan*, Phnom Penh Post (Nov. 6 – 19, 1992), at 5.

of Cambodia, headed by the CPP, maintained power as a holdover from its leadership under the Vietnamese-backed regime in the 1980s. The CPP, through its control of the organs of the Cambodian state, sought to maintain its dominant role no matter the political outcome. Hun Sen, head of government throughout the 1980s and, since 1998, the long-sitting prime minister of Cambodia, held the reins over the CPP and over much of the state apparatus. Both a hardline party and the institutionally and militarily most established faction, it had the most to lose by ceding power to other factions as a part of the peace process.

The DPK were the other hardline faction. Responsible for forced deurbanization, forced labor, and killings on a countrywide scale during their rule over Cambodia from 1975–1979, they were defeated by a Vietnamese occupying force in 1979 and exiled largely to the western provinces of Cambodia. Yet this party nonetheless remained a major military and political force in the country well into the 1990s. The party continued to represent Cambodia at the U.N. General Assembly until 1990.[33] Throughout the peace process and during the U.T. Transitional Authority in Cambodia's (UNTAC) presence in country, the DPK consistently took a harsh nationalist stance, arguing that Vietnamese troops and ethnic Vietnamese civilians had infiltrated the country, enabled by foreign intervention and by the Vietnam-friendly CPP.[34] Though they were in no position to take control of the entire state, they were able to disrupt the elections and the peacekeeping process by threats to, and in many cases, killings and abductions of, Cambodians and in some cases of U.N. officials.[35] Khieu Samphan, the second in command over the Khmer Rouge during the 1975–1979 reign of terror and later, was the most prominent figure from this party.

Though the boundary lines of opposition were not always clear, there also are two soft-line parties that exhibited some more favorable attitudes to foreign intervention. At a military disadvantage to the CPP and lacking the presence in government that the CPP held, these parties stood to gain the most from a pluralist post-conflict government. The major opposition faction, FUNCINPEC, was a royalist party backing King Norodom Sihanouk. Sihanouk was a key player in orchestrating the initial peace talks to end the civil war, working as a mediator among the Cambodian factions throughout the peace process and even after the arrival of the UN.[36] Seeking to resume his status as head of state regardless of the outcome of the constitutional process, Sihanouk would step down from leadership of FUNCINPEC prior to the elections, replaced by one of his sons, Prince Ranariddh.

The fourth and final faction, while small, would be a lynchpin in the peace process. The BLDP, led by long-time civil servant Son Sann, held little influence on its own. However, since both the royalist FUNCINPEC and the state of Cambodia fell just short of holding a majority of seats in the Constituent Assembly, the BLDP's support was essential to establish a majority coalition. Furthermore, the BLDP leadership would play a significant role in the drafting process, as both BLDP leader Son Sann and his son, Son Soubert, held leadership

---

[33] Suellen Ratliff, *UN Representation Disputes: A Case Study of Cambodia and a New Accreditation Proposal for the Twenty-First Century*, 87 CALIF. L. REV. 1207 (1999).

[34] Nate Thayer, *Interview with Khieu Samphan*, PHNOM PENH POST (Nov. 6–19, 1992), at 5.

[35] Ker Muntith, *DPK Robs UN Peace-Keepers*, PHNOM PENH POST (March 12–25, 1993), at 4; Kevin Barrington, *DPK Slay Bulgarian Hosts of Peace Dinner*, PHNOM PENH POST (April 9–22, 1993), at 3.

[36] BENNY WIDYONO, DANCING IN THE SHADOWS: SIHANOUK, THE KHMER ROUGE, AND THE UNITED NATIONS IN CAMBODIA (2008).

positions in the Constituent Assembly. Nevertheless, it provided some of the strongest voices for democracy and human rights among the four factions.

Framed here as soft- and hardliners based on their attitudes toward foreign intervention, these four parties would react in different ways to the peace process and to the word of the Constituent Assembly largely based on their attitudes and their stake in the future of Cambodia's constitutional government.

2.2 The Path from Negotiation to Constitutional Ratification

With the domestic stage of actors set, a brief timeline will sketch the events before proceeding into a more thorough discussion. As the timeline and discussion will show, international actors were an essential component to the peace process, yet the Cambodian factions were the key movers in the process, even stymieing progress to the frustration of foreign diplomats. These reactions by the four factions to the international actors illustrate how the process of peace-building and translation of international norms of liberal democracy and constitutionalism are not only processes where norms travel from international to local venues, but also venues for contestation and negotiation among domestic parties, often with drastically divergent aspirations and incentives to react, depending on their stakes in the post-conflict government.

The Constituent Assembly held sovereignty over the drafting process; the blueprint for the constitution originated in an international treaty, from the Paris Agreements in 1991.[37] A decade-long effort[38] of fits and starts at peacemaking had culminated in a rapid succession of international meetings with the Cambodian factions and a host of foreign diplomats from Australia, China, France, Japan, Indonesia, the United States, Vietnam, and numerous other states from the Association of South East Asian Nations and the United Nations.

By the late 1980s and early 1990s, on the agenda for these meetings not only was how to broker a peace among the four major political factions within Cambodia, but also the plans for rebuilding Cambodia, including the development of a Cambodian constitution enshrining liberal democracy and the rule of law.[39]

The goals of the peace process were fourfold:[40]

1. maintaining a ceasefire and ending the conflict among the four factions to the Cambodian civil war;
2. refugee resettlement;
3. withdrawal of the remaining remnants of the Vietnamese occupying forces in Cambodia since 1979 invasion; and

---

[37] Final Act of the Paris Conference on Cambodia Annex 5, Oct. 23, 1991, U.N. Doc. A/46/608 (1991).

[38] As early as 1981, the U.N. General Assembly had issued a report concerning a peacebuilding process in Cambodia. Convening an international conference of U.N. member states and Cambodian political factions, the meeting resulted in a report and declaration that emphasized, among other things, free elections under U.N. supervision. The report did not mention the need for a new constitution. U.N. General Assembly, Report of the International Conference on Kampuchea, U.N. Doc. A/CONF.109/5 (July 17, 1981).

[39] Final Act of the Paris Conference on Cambodia Annex 5, Oct. 23, 1991, U.N. Doc. A/46/608 (1991).

[40] Ibid.; Kenneth Berry, Cambodia: From Red to Blue (1997), 11.

4. rebuilding Cambodian political institutions with a special regard for human rights and liberal democratic governance through free and fair elections.

This last goal saw extensive elaboration in Annex 5, describing the norms for Cambodia's future post-conflict constitution. This annex, along with the rest of the Paris Agreement, met with the approval of all four parties and received signatures from representatives of each party, along with the foreign states involved in the negotiation.

Once signed, the issue of implementing the agreement came to the fore, ultimately leading to two missions organized by the United Nations, the second of which became the most important: UNTAC.[41] Using the Paris Agreements as a mandate, UNTAC's work with respect to the constitution culminated in a country-wide effort to educate voters and organize an election to decide the members of the Constituent Assembly who would draft the new text. As later sections will show, UNTAC's work on the constitution did not end here, as it lent material and subject-matter assistance to the Constituent Assembly during its work.

Immediate reactions to the election and to the constitution gave cause for optimism. Both the U.N. and independent observers concluded that the elections were largely free and fair,[42] despite some reports of voter intimidation by the CPP,[43] threats against polling stations from the Khmer Rouge, and attacks on U.N. election volunteers and FUNCINPEC and BLDP party offices in the weeks leading up to the election.[44] Two attempts to contest the election by Hun Sen, the leader of the CPP, and by Norodom Chakrapong, a son of the King and half-brother to FUNCINPEC leader Ranariddh but a CPP stalwart, quickly subsided.[45] Once the dust settled, the royalist opposition FUNCINPEC held 58 of 120 seats, the incumbent CPP held 51, the BLDP ten, and a fourth minor party, MOLINAKA, one.[46]

In addition to considering the mandate for liberal democratic constitutionalism set out in the Paris Agreement, the Constituent Assembly looked to previous constitutions for guidance,[47]

---

[41] The first, the U.N. Mission Advance Mission in Cambodia, (UNAMIC) largely provided military advisors and conducted surveys in preparation for the larger and subsequent intervention from UNTAC.

[42] William Shawcross, Cambodia's New Deal (1994), 20–23; Amnesty International, Kingdom of Cambodia: Human rights and the new constitution, (1994), 3; U.N. Security Council, Resolution 835, U.N. Doc. S/RES/835 (1993).

[43] William Shawcross 1994, *supra* note 42, at 21; Sara Colm, *Factions, UNTAC Debate Electoral Law*, Phnom Penh Post (July 10, 1992), 1–4 (reporting armed harassment by police against FUNCINPEC staff and an armed late-night raid against a regional party headquarters).

[44] Kevin Barrington, *KR Open Bloody Anti-Poll Campaign*, Phnom Penh Post (May 7–20, 1993) (discussing attacks by Khmer Rouge guerillas on poll workers); Kevin Barrington, *Tragedy Throws Polls into Question*, Phnom Penh Post (April 23–May 6, 1993) (reporting the execution of a U.N. volunteer and his Cambodian interpreter); M.P. Nunan, *Direct Attack on UNTAC*, Phnom Penh Post (Jan. 29 – Feb. 11, 1993) (describing an artillery barrage that killed two Cambodian women working as UNTAC electoral workers); Nate Thayer, *Sihanouk Slams Political Violence: Presidential Election in the Cards*, Phnom Penh Post (Jan. 15–28, 1993) (describing an assault on FUNCINPEC workers by people in military vehicles).

[45] Widyono, *supra* note 36, at 128–129.

[46] Phnom Penh Post, *Distribution of Seats in the Constituent Assembly*, Phnom Penh Post (June 18–July 1, 1993).

[47] *Attachment to Letter from UNTAC Political Adviser Karim to UNTAC Head Akashi*, U.N. Archives Folder S-0794-0001-0003-00002 (Aug. 5, 1993), at 70–78.

as well as to UN[48] and independent foreign experts.[49] While the process itself faced obstacles, even in some cases lacking adequate office furniture and stationery and relying on the U.N. for material support,[50] these obstacles did not prevent the Assembly from engaging in an intense debate over how to organize the distribution of power in post-war Cambodia. One key debate on human rights found particular contention, where FUNCINPEC and BLDP members urged for the constitution to create an independent ombudsman or commission to protect human rights, and the CPP sought to prevent the constitutionalization of such a body, effectively filibustering the debate until the matter was dropped.[51]

With no party in obvious control of the Constituent Assembly and a dedicated engagement in the drafting process, one might expect that the Cambodian Constitution would have succeeded in fulfilling the Paris Agreement's aspirations for installing a liberal democracy based on human rights and the rule of law. However, some hints of instability of the constitution's political arrangement emerged as soon as a year after the constitution's promulgation. The guarantee of a liberal democracy met another significant challenge in 1997, when a military coup toppled the multi-party balance of power between FUNCINPEC and the CPP.[52]

Numerous foreign commentators have described the institutional weakness of the constitution. One year after ratification, a detailed report by long-time Cambodia reporter William Shawcross noted the deepening of political fractures between the three parties, as well as fissures within the parties.[53] Although holding a plurality in the Constituent Assembly-turned-National Assembly, and a potential majority coalition if coordinating with the CLDP, FUNCINPEC had taken a back seat in governance compared with the second place CPP.[54] Although none would expect a post-conflict society to fix all social and political ails through a brief transition period, this evaluation of the political institutions, which were a major component of the Paris Agreements and of UNTAC's mission, suggests a wide gap between institutional aspirations and political realities, only one year after the Constituent Assembly approved of those institutions.

In the decades since then, Cambodia has not seen a strengthening of the multiparty liberal democracy that was central to its constitutional aspirations in 1993.[55] The country consistently

---

48 *Meeting with Dr. Ing Keith, Vice President of the Constituent Assembly*, U.N. Archives Folder S-0794-001-004-00001 UC (July 27, 1993), at 67.

49 Stephen Marks, *The Process of Creating a New Constitution in Cambodia*, *in* Framing the State in Times of Transition: Case Studies in Constitution-Making 207 (Laurel E. Miller & Louis Aucoin, eds., 2010), 227.

50 *Urgent Request for Vehicles and Mobile Phones for the Support of the Constituent Assembly Secretariat, Memorandum from Constituent Assembly Senior Administrative Assistant Sam Borin to UNTAC Electoral Component Director Reginald Austin*, U.N. Archives Folder S-0794-0001-0005-00002 (June 27, 1993), at 23; *Creation of the Secretariat of the Constitutional Assembly, Memorandum from Kawakami to Akashi*, U.N. Archives Folder S-0794-0001-0005-00003 (May 20, 1993), at 64.

51 *Constituent Assembly Debate of Draft Constitution for Cambodia*, U.N. Archives Folder S-0794-001-002-00001 (Sept. 15, 1993), at 10–11.

52 Kingdom of Cambodia Office of the Council of Ministers, White Paper: The Defence of Young Democracy in Cambodia: The 1998 Election & Its Aftermath (1998).

53 Shawcross 1994, *supra* note 42, at 93–93.

54 Ibid.

55 Marks (2010), *supra* note 49, at 242–244.

receives categorization as a hybrid regime,[56] and since a Supreme Court judgment in 2017, the country's largest opposition party to the CPP has been outlawed.[57] Even Gareth Evans, one of the principal negotiators of the peace process, has since decried the trajectory of Cambodia's political institutions.[58]

The single-party dominance of politics that exists in modern-day Cambodia is a far cry from what was envisioned in 1993, at least on paper. For all of the efforts by the Cambodian factions, international organizations, and foreign diplomats, the aspirations of the text did not translate into political reality. The remainder of this section will focus on drawing out that history and the major actors from that time, using the political origins of the constitution to explain why there is such a wide gap between aspiration and implementation.

3. DECODING THE OUTCOME: WHY DID LIBERAL DEMOCRACY FALTER IN THE CAMBODIAN CONSTITUTION?

3.1 The Legal Framework of the Paris Agreements

The 1991 Paris Agreements[59] establish the normative framework of the international intervention in the Cambodian peace process. It is the source of the promise for building a liberal democratic Cambodia. Both the procedure and the basic principles of the constitution as established in Annexes 3 and 5 of the Paris Agreements call attention to the protection of human rights, particularly given Cambodia's recent history of human rights violations.[60] Both the process of creating the constitution and the constitution itself were to prevent a return to what existed in Cambodia prior to the peace process.

Annex 5 in particular envisions that the constitution will contain principles of liberal democracy and modern human rights law. It was to protect rights consistent with contemporary international human rights law as well as promote the norms of a pluralist liberal democracy, with an independent judiciary.[61]

At the same time, the terms of Annex 5 took care to consider Cambodia's history of conflict as well as its colonial history. This constitution was meant to be as much a reflection of Cambodia's particular context as it was an attempt to create a new democratic arrangement.

---

56 See, e.g., STEVEN LEVITSKY & LUCAN WAY, COMPETITIVE AUTHORITARIANISM (2010), at Appendix I.

57 Prak Chan Thul & Amy Sawitta Lefevre, *Cambodia's main opposition party dissolved by Supreme Court*, REUTERS (Nov. 16, 2017), available at https://www.reuters.com/article/us-cambodia-politics-idUSKBN1DG1BO.

58 Gareth Evans, *Cambodia's Violent Peace*, PHNOM PENH POST (Feb. 28, 2014), available at https://www.phnompenhpost.com/analysis-and-op-ed/cambodia%E2%80%99s-violent-peace.

59 Final Act of the Paris Conference on Cambodia, U.N. Doc. A/46/608 (1991), at art. 6.

60 Final Act of the Paris Conference on Cambodia, Annexes 3, 5, U.N. Doc. A/46/608 (1991).

61 "Cambodia's tragic recent history requires special measures to ensure protection of human rights. Therefore, the constitution will contain a declaration of fundamental right…" Final Act of the Paris Conference on Cambodia, Annex 5, U.N. Doc. A/46/608 (1991), arts. 2. Other parts of Annex 5 make express reference that "Cambodia will follow a system of liberal democracy, on the basis of pluralism… An independent judicial will be established to enforce the rights provided under the constitution." Ibid., 4–5.

Not only does it make express mention of human rights as a response to Cambodia's recent history of mass violence, but it also makes reference to Cambodian sovereignty, independence, and national unity.[62] These references were particularly salient to Cambodian history, which experienced an erosion of its national borders in the period leading to and during colonization, as well as to longstanding disputes with Vietnam over its eastern border.[63]

Far from a story of foreign imposition of international norms, Annex 5 was a prescription for Cambodia's political situation, negotiated and signed by each of the four parties as well as the other states party to the Paris Agreement. While the political reality, and the implementation of these agreements, as we have seen, were far from the prescribed reality, the contents of Annex 5 nonetheless show a moment where the meeting of international and domestic actors created at least some degree of commitment to liberal democratic constitutionalism.

3.2 Divergent Responses to Implementing the Paris Agreements

By the time UNTAC arrived, the cohesive message set forth by the Paris Agreements had given way to a far more complicated reality. On the Cambodian side, the unified front offered by King Norodom Sihanouk in the Paris Conference, necessary for negotiating a cohesive agreement proved a poor reflection of the political situation in Cambodia. Each faction had committed to peace during the Paris Agreements, not only through signing the treaty but also in press releases, public statements, and private communication. Even the DPK, the most xenophobic of the hardline factions, embraced the prospect of U.N. intervention with gusto.[64] The Paris Agreements and their promises of rights and liberal democracy framed the agenda for the work to be carried out by UNTAC in coordination with the four factions.

Yet while Paris had brought the parties together, cracks reappeared as the focus turned from negotiating the plan to implementation. However, the DPK would eventually disengage from the peace process, arguing that UNTAC was failing to create a neutral political environment, favoring or excusing noncompliance by the CPP, and therefore not faithfully implementing the Paris Agreements.[65] Broadcasting their discontent over party-sponsored radio, the DPK would

---

62 Final Act of the Paris Conference on Cambodia, Annex 5, U.N. Doc. A/46/608 (1991), at art. 3.

63 Yan Vandeluxe, *The Historical Development of Cambodia's Constitutions, in* CAMBODIAN CONSTITUTIONAL LAW 137 (Hor Peng et al., eds., 2016) at 64.

64 Khieu Samphan, one of the leaders of the Khmer Rouge, communicated to the other three factions emphasizing the importance of the UNTAC presence toward fully realizing the goals of the Paris Agreements, including elections. "*À la présente réunion comme lors de celle du ler avril dernier, la partie Kampuchea Democratique se sent vivement encouragee par le developpement progressif de l'application des accords de paris, en particulier en apprenant l'arrivee de nouvelles forces de maintien de la paix dans la troisieme semaine de ce mois, totalisant 4000 personnes. Ils seront certainement les bienvenus, nous exprimons notre profonde reconnaissance a S.E. Akashi pour le rapport qu'il vient de nous presenter.*" Khieu Samphan, Statement to the Supreme National Council, Point of Order of the Day (April 6, 1992), *in* Cambodian National Archives Box 690, Database 6174. On the same day Khieu Samphan also argued that a full implementation of the Paris Agreements' guarantees of full rights to all Cambodians and free and fair elections, as well as 100% demilitarization, were essential to the peace process. Khieu Samphan, Statement to the Supreme National Council, Point of Order of the Day #2 (April 6, 1992), *in* Cambodian National Archives Box 690, Database 6174.

65 "*En effet, comment peut-on creer un environnement politique neutre, indispensable a la tenue des elections generales et equitables, si l'APRONUC ne procede pas au controle direct, effectif et efficace des 5 domaines dont plus particulierement celui de la securite et de la police secrete du regime de*

allege that UNTAC was building a puppet government for the Vietnamese government, led by members of the CCP, FUNCINPEC, and the BLDP.[66] These disputes over UNTAC's implementation of the Paris Agreements eventually led to more contentious confrontations between UNTAC troops and the DPK and eventually to attacks on UNTAC troops and civilian staff.[67] Furthermore, as the date of the election approached, the DPK faction became increasingly hostile to UNTAC efforts, denying UNTAC staff access to DPK territory, even where the head of the UNTAC mission and special representative of the U.N. Secretary-General, Akashi Yasushi, personally arrived to negotiate with the group.[68] By March, two months prior to the election, the DPK had announced that it would refuse to participate in elections and threatened to attack polling places. These threats turned into physical assaults on UNTAC staff.[69] One U.N. electoral volunteer was killed.[70]

In the midst of the Khmer Rouge withdrawal and hostility, both FUNCINPEC and BLDP offices also suffered attacks. FUNCINPEC and BLDP party offices reported harassment from men in State of Cambodia (CPP) military uniforms, with the BLDP reporting 21 instances of lethal violence perpetrated against their offices.[71]

Leaders from both parties also wrote to UNTAC leadership over concern that the CPP was engaging in political violence and using its control over the government to discourage support for opposition parties, and that UNTAC had done too little in preventing political violence that would help opposition parties compete with the incumbent CPP.[72] This concern for political violence accompanied more systemic resistance[73] by the CPP to demilitarization and the replacement of its administrative staff by UN-trained workers, both UNTAC mandates under the Paris Agreements.[74] While the DPK response to frustrations over imbalances of power was to quit the process, FUNCINPEC and the BLDP continued to participate, working with UNTAC despite ongoing concerns about attacks and future prospects of faithfully implementing the Paris Agreements.

While the norms of the Paris Agreements established the baseline for the peace process, the factions' different interpretations of implementation would lead to a divergence in responses

---

Phnom Penh" Khieu Samphan, Telegram to UNTAC head Akashi, (Dec. 6, 1992), *in* Cambodia National Archives Box 689, Database 6098.

66 Voice of the Grande Union Nationale du Cambodge (Khmer Rouge-sponsored radio) (Dec. 7, 1992), *in* Cambodia National Archives Box 689, Database 6098.

67 Kevin Barrington, *KR Open Bloody Anti-Poll Campaign*, PHNOM PENH POST (May 7–20, 1993).

68 This particular encounter holds symbolic weight for UNTAC's mission as a whole. The Khmer Rouge remnant had blocked a path with a small bamboo barricade. UNTAC staff and armed forces were unable to negotiate entry past this barricade, and, not wanting to escalate the situation, turned back. A single piece of bamboo had stymied the progress of the U.N. in Northwest Cambodia. *Fear and Hope in Cambodia* (1993), directed by Isabella Abric and William Shawcross.

69 Ken Stier, *Helicopter Potshots Shoot Down UNTAC Mobility*, PHNOM PENH POST (Nov. 20, 1992).

70 U.N. Volunteers, *In Memory of Atsuhito Nakata*, (April 8, 2013), https://www.unv.org/News/memory-Atsuhito-Nakata.

71 Sara Colm, *Voters Continue to Sign Up Despite Violence*, PHNOM PENH POST (Nov. 20–Dec. 3, 1992).

72 Sihanouk, Letter to Akashi (Jan. 3, 1993), *in* Cambodia National Archives Box 689, Database 6096; Son Sann (leader of the BLDP) to UNTAC head Akashi, (Dec. 21, 1992), *in* Cambodia National Archives Box 689, Database 6096.

73 Berry 1997, *supra* note 40, at 275.

74 Final Act of the Paris Conference on Cambodia, Annex 2, U.N. Doc. A/46/608 (1991), art. 3–5; Final Act of the Paris Conference on Cambodia, Annex 1, U.N. Doc. A/46/608 (1991), section B.

by the softliners, FUNCINPEC and the BLDP, and the hardliners, CPP and DPK. These divergences would have consequences for the constitution and the peace process. While the softliners complied and demobilized their military, putting faith in the peace process, the hardliners resisted compliance. This discrepancy in arms has some symbolic significance in capturing the political dynamics among the factions and their engagement with the U.N., but would also have material consequences. As one observer noted after the election, "The winner has no armed forces, and the loser has the army."[75]

3.2.1 Post-election clouds

Despite these concerns over the implementation of the Paris Agreements, the election unfolded peacefully. FUNCINPEC had won a commanding presence in the Constituent Assembly, with the pro-democracy BLDP and MOLINAKA likely to join its coalition. Almost immediately, the CPP filed a report alleging election irregularities, despite the U.N.'s conclusion of a free and fair election. Citing these alleged irregularities, the CPP refused to accept the results of the election, demanding that the CPP be granted an equal share of power in the Constituent Assembly and in the interim government.[76] Sihanouk, seeking to maintain the fragile bargain of peace, acceded to these demands.[77] Although members of the royal family and supporters within FUNCINPEC protested Sihanouk's decision and the state involved in the peace process expressed concern surrounding the rejection of the election outcome to adopt a CPP and FUNCINPEC joint government, there was little choice.[78]

The peace-making efforts by the U.N. had hampered its goals at state-building. Defanging only the groups that were willing to cooperate, UNTAC had left the hardliners in a strong position to force their way into continued power. Although they won at the polls, the royalist and pro-democracy camps were left unable to enforce the outcome of the election. This would not be the last time that the CPP leveraged its strength to overcome the liberal democratic goals of the Cambodian constitutional experiment.

Despite their intervention to expand representation at the constituent assembly, the CPP largely did not resist the constitution-making process. The constitution that emerged in late 1993 advances the guiding principles stated in the Paris Agreements. For example, the constitution includes not only a chapter with rights provisions,[79] a standard section among modern constitutions regardless of regime type,[80] but also commitments to the liberal democratic characteristics of the constitution, based on its unamendability provisions, prohibiting amendment to the constitution during a state of emergency and any amendment that would "[affect] the liberal multi-party democracy system and the constitutional monarchy regime."[81] This is a text that not only reflects the emergence of rights as an essential component to the rule of law, but also incorporates procedural protections of democracy.

Notably, however, the constitution does not include a dedicated independent body charged with enforcing human rights such as a human rights commission or ombudsman. Despite the

75 Nate Thayer, *Split Emerges in Core Group*, PHNOM PENH POST (June 18–July 1, 1993).
76 Widyono 2008, *supra* note 36, at 124.
77 Ibid., 124–25.
78 Ibid.
79 Constitution of Cambodia (1993, amended 2018), at chap. 3.
80 ELKINS ET AL. 2013, supra note 2.
81 Constitution of Cambodia (1993, amended 2018), at art. 153.

urging of UNTAC staff and by local rights organizations, the Constituent Assembly declined to introduce such an organization in the constitution.[82]

The terms of the Paris Agreements set the foundations for a liberal text that sought to address some of the most salient social and political issues in Cambodia at the time. On paper, this resulting text fulfilled many of the institution-building aspirations of the UNTAC mission and the Paris Accords.

It would not, however, stand the test of time. The weakness introduced by the U.N.'s unequally applied peace process would reverberate beyond the constitutional moment, making the CPP's post-election coup a part of the constitutional framework beyond 1993.

Four years later, the joint CPP–FUNCINPEC government collapsed, and open conflict took place in the capital city.[83] This time, FUNCINPEC, no longer operating under the cover of UNTAC election observers and peacekeepers, could not withstand the CPP's efforts. At the end of the three-month conflict, FUNCINPEC leaders were forced to flee the country and the party lost in the next round of elections to the CPP in 1998. In 1999, the CPP-dominated National Assembly promulgated amendments that would establish the Senate, a separate house of the legislature that would be elected largely by local communal representatives, not general election. Local commune leaders were largely CPP supporters, thus almost ensuring that opposition parties would be unable to form a majority coalition government or take over both houses of the legislature.

After all of the efforts in 1993 by both UNTAC and Cambodian officials to establish a liberal democratic constitutional polity, by 1999 the practical framework of constitutional governance had altered the textual framework to set Cambodia on a path toward electoral authoritarianism: government legitimized by elections, but with no real possibility of electoral opposition. Instead of a story of diffusing norms, the process toward building constitutionalism in Cambodia was more like a poker game. The softliner parties played a straightforward game, coordinating faithfully with UNTAC. The hardliner CPP, less inclined to cooperate, leaned hard into its bluff, complying with the normative conditions of constitutionalism mandated by Paris but resisting UNTAC just enough to hold on to power. The bet paid off for the CPP, although it also set the stage for the institutional weakness of the constitution.

4. ANTECEDENT CONDITIONS AND ALTERNATIVE EXPLANATIONS

In the story provided so far, the intervention of international actors was a necessary component of the peace process and was essential for organizing elections for the Constituent Assembly. However, it also distorted the political reality in Cambodia, where the two softliner parties, FUNCINPEC and BLDP, benefited from the international engagement, receiving cover from international actors that enforced an even political playing field. The hardliner parties, the DPK and the CPP, either became sidelined when acting too hardline (DPK) or curbed their hardline tendencies during the peace process (CPP), while resisting enough that they were able to keep doors open for future military and political contestation.

---

82 *Constituent Assembly Plenary on the Constitution*, U.N. Archives Folder S-0794-0001-0002-00001 (Sept. 16, 1993).

83 Widyono 2008, *supra* note 36, at 240–48.

While all factions signed up to the norms written into the Paris Agreements, the responses to intervention created discrepancies in the political reality of the constitution. The Cambodian factions held both sincere and cynical commitments to liberal democratic constitutionalism, and thus responded differently to efforts to adopt these norms. This mixture of commitments accompanied a lopsided implementation of other political and military components of the peace process among the factions. This imbalance created conditions which appeared to create a liberal democratic constitution at the time, yet which quickly would reveal themselves as an unsustainable balance of power among the factions.

Beyond this political story of uneven diffusion and implementation of international norms as an explanation for institution weakness, a few competing explanations may also be present that would explain the discrepancy between the aspirations of the Cambodian constitution and its implementation. The most significant is the counterfactual: that the current conditions in Cambodia would have been little changed regardless of the international intervention. Other possible explanations may stem from low capacity in post-conflict societies, cultural antagonism to newly introduced liberal democratic institutions, and local cynicism toward international demands by authoritarians seeking a rubber stamp of approval.

4.1 Cambodia's Political Institutions without Paris and UNTAC

In some ways, the before and after images of UNTAC and the constitutional process look similar. The CPP governed Cambodia through the 1980s, ceded power to UNTAC and shared power with FUNCINPEC for a brief period in the 1990s, and has ruled Cambodian politics since 1998. The actors have largely remained the same, with Hun Sen as head of government. The international efforts to introduce liberal democracy as part of the peace process are largely null because any constitutional process, with or without international intervention, would have come to the same result due to the conditions on the ground pre-dating the peace process.

This counterfactual is attractive because of the circular path that seemed to occur in Cambodia during the 1990s. The challenge of peacebuilding in this context was so overwhelming that any foreign intervention would have been able to do little to alter the political and material conditions on the ground.

Two specific explanations in this counterfactual analysis might come from lack of state capacity,[84] and from autocratic consolidation following long periods of instability and contentious politics.[85] After all, Cambodia's modern history of civil war, mass crimes against humanity, and a mass exodus saw a dramatic decline in its population. Prior to the DPK, the country had experienced instability from U.S. bombings, the spillover of the conflict in Vietnam into its eastern provinces, and a coup by a right-wing military regime that deposed its constitutional monarchy. After 1979, Vietnamese forces occupied much of Cambodia, while the Khmer Rouge maintained some strongholds in more remote provinces, maintaining an ongoing low-level conflict in the country into the 1990s. The country had few resources to rebuild itself, let alone a thriving democratic government.

---

[84] Jessica Fortin, *Is there a Necessary Condition for Democracy? The Role of State Capacity in Postcommunist Countries*, 45 Comp. Pol. Stud. 903 (2012).

[85] Dan Slater, Ordering States: Contentious Politics and Authoritarian Leviathans in Southeast Asia (2010).

Even after the most traumatic period under the Khmer Rouge, the Cambodian state relied on Vietnamese advisors and the Vietnamese military backing. In this environment, few opportunities existed for a locally driven reconstruction of the Cambodian state, or for the development of individuals or organizations with the capacity to rebuild Cambodia. Attempts at reconstructing Cambodia were designed more to glorify the Vietnamese-backed government than to build sustainable institutions.[86] Pay for civil servants did not provide a livable wage, fostering corruption and building a civil service advanced on connections to the CPP rather than merit.[87] Given these conditions prior to the transitional period, the low capacity of the Cambodian state and of actors within the state offer one plausible argument for the institutional weakness of the constitution. The destruction of the Cambodian government in the 1970s, followed by the frustrated reconstruction of the 1980s, provided a foundation of shifting sand upon which the transitional government built its constitution.

While the effects of low state capacity and prior political instability cannot be ignored, these factors also contributed to the single-party political outcomes through Cambodia's institutional development. Since the question here focuses on the design and institutional weakness of Cambodia's constitution, the question is not only about the de facto outcomes, but also the discrepancies between the constitution de facto and de jure.

With respect to the constitution, the story of low state capacity and political instability cannot be addressed without the role of international actors in bringing the four factions to the negotiating table and setting the normative framework for the constitution.[88] Due to the highly contingent and fraught relations among the four factions, the foreign parties were necessary for holding the peace together. Had the CPP been destined to take power based on its standing prior to the peace process, it had little incentive to come to the table, as it sat in Phnom Penh and held the reins over government.

Low capacity may have plagued the Cambodian state during and after the transitional period, but not for a lack of effort by international actors and by the U.N. Recall that Annex 1 of the Paris Agreements included in UNTAC's mandate that it would replace the current administrative staff in Cambodia with U.N.-trained staff. Cognizant of the challenges that lack of capacity could pose, this administrative replacement and training would have helped develop a professional civil service. This aspect of the UNTAC mandate was firmly stymied by the CPP, the mass professionalization of the civil service did not occur, and the CPP held a firm control over most critical organs of the government.[89] Thus, even this lack of capacity remains in the chain of causation connecting international intervention to institutional weakness, through the successful local resistance by domestic actors against foreign leverage.

The story of modern Cambodia cannot be told without this period of international intervention. Relating diffusion to political outcomes like institutional weakness helps build a stronger understanding of why Paris and UNTAC fell short, and also helps build the Cambodian case into a broader theoretical understanding of institutional development in post-conflict societies.

---

[86] Rachel Hughes, *Dutiful Tourism: Encountering Cambodian Genocide*, 49 Asia Pac. Viewpoint 318 (2008), 318–30; William Shawcross, Quality of Mercy (1979).

[87] Widyono 2008, *supra* note 36, at 148; Ben Davies, *Complaints Rack Up Against the SOC*, Phnom Penh Post (Dec. 18–31, 1992).

[88] Widyono 2008, *supra* note 36, at 33–35.

[89] Shawcross 1994, *supra* note 42, at 13.

4.2 External Pressure and Cultural Unfamiliarity

If not lack of capacity, perhaps UNTAC was simply forcing concepts that were too foreign to local contexts, thus preventing the constitution from taking root.[90] After all, the election in 1993 was hailed as the first in Cambodian history, and the constitution was assumed by many observers, along with many Cambodians, to be the first of its kind in Cambodian history.[91] As such, the novelty of liberal democratic institutions suggests a possibility that local politics might reject them as a valid venue through which to conduct politics.[92]

Two points suggest that local custom and external pressure should not provide a barrier to the institutional strength of the constitution in this case. First, the Cambodian constitution features numerous characteristics which seek to address the specific history and needs of the country. Second, the Constituent Assembly negotiations show that the design process took time to evaluate foreign models, but did not feel pressure to kowtow to any one model. The rejection of the liberal democratic aspects of the constitution do not result from a cultural aversion to western values writ large.

This argument does not discount the manifestation of local culture and history in constitutions. As constitutional ethnographers have documented in numerous examples, local culture and history establish fundamental aspects of a constitutional text, defining its evolution throughout its subsequent practice.[93] The Cambodian case exhibits its unique context, reflecting the effect of Buddhism and Cambodia's unique history of territorial disputes with rival kingdoms and later neighboring states and manifesting itself throughout the 1993 constitution. Articles 43 and 68 of the constitution make express reference to Buddhism as the state religion and impose a duty on the state to "propagate and promote the Pali schools and the Buddhist education."[94] Commenting on this duty, the Constitutional Council affirmed in 2009 that these articles committed the state to support various aspects of Buddhist culture, including education as well as major ceremonies and holidays.[95] Some experts of Cambodian constitutionalism suggest that the incorporation of international norms into the Cambodian constitution, such as human rights, required a mediation of rights through the language of Buddhism.[96] According to this perspective, the impact of Buddhism in this context was to act as the local translator of universal norms to local contexts.

These local effects suggest that the Cambodian constitution featured at least some local tailoring to Cambodia's specific context, evidence that the drafters took steps to ensure that the document would not be seen as a foreign imposition but rather a document tailored to local needs.

---

[90] Though in different contexts, previous examinations of constitutionalism and Asian culture have shown that culture, while influential for certain aspects of design, is not solely determinative of the design features of a constitution. See, e.g., GINSBURG (2003).

[91] The 1993 constitution is the sixth constitution of Cambodia, succeeding documents adopted in 1947, 1972, 1976, 1981, and 1989.

[92] Raoul Jennar, *Monarchy or Republic?*, PHNOM PENH POST (June 18–July 1, 1993).

[93] JACOBSOHN, CONSTITUTIONAL IDENTITY (2009); Kim Scheppele, *Constitutional Ethnography, An Introduction*, 38 LAW & SOC'Y. REV. 389 (2004).

[94] Constitution of Cambodia (1993), at arts. 43, 68.

[95] Constitutional Council of Cambodia, Case 169/008/2009 (Dec. 23, 2009).

[96] Kong Phallack, *Freedom of Religion in Cambodia*, *in* CAMBODIAN CONSTITUTIONAL LAW 389 (Hor Peng et al. eds., 2016).

Additionally, records from the Constituent Assembly proceedings suggest little external pressure. While foreign consultants were present and the assembly considered foreign models, most evidence suggests a deliberative process. On the question of judicial review, the Constituent Assembly debated a memorandum weighing three separate models from different jurisdictions, with in-depth discussion regarding ex post and ex ante review, strong and weak systems of judicial review, specialized constitutional courts, and critiques over the judicialization of politics, especially in the American context.[97]

As alluded to above, one source of concern among the FUNCINPEC and BLDP softliners, as well as among UNTAC officials, was the lack of a dedicated and independent human rights body. Also of concern was the lack of express adoption of a law of non-retroactive punishment, a core tenet of international human rights law. These issues become so concerning that UNTAC head Akashi Yasushi wrote directly to the Vice-President of the Constituent Assembly on two occasions regarding the matter.[98] Although Cambodia did sign and ratify a slew of human rights treaties around this time, and the Cambodian constitution features a section dedicated to protecting human rights, the Constituent Assembly did not adopt either of these suggestions. The modern Cambodian constitution mentions neither the prohibition of non-retroactive punishment nor an independent human rights body.

5. CONCLUSION

The Cambodian constitution was drafted as part of a transnational project for rebuilding Cambodia as a liberal democracy after decades of conflict. Despite all of the resources plunged into this effort, the text is a weak institution, promising liberal democracy and pluralism but delivering a single-party regime.

International actors were an essential factor in this process, bringing the Cambodian factions to the negotiating table, developing the normative framework for the constitution, and implementing the peace process that culminated in the election and the Constituent Assembly in 1993. However, this process also triggered heterogenous responses to the international intervention among the different Cambodian factions. These heterogenous responses saw softliners embracing the peace process and hardliners either resisting or committing more cynically.

This uneven response to the peace process established a system that rested on the strong, but temporary, institutions of the U.N.: the peacekeepers and the electoral staff. Once these were no longer a part of the political framework, the institutions that had been built by that framework began to falter, and the actors who had successfully held onto power during the intervention were able to overwhelm those who had chosen to give up power based on good-faith dealings with the U.N. This interaction between foreign and a diverse set of domestic actors helps explain the discrepancy between the text of the constitution and its implementation. Furthermore, once the institutional weakness was solidified at this critical juncture, the weak-

[97] *Attachment to Letter from UNTAC Political Adviser Karim to UNTAC head Akashi*, U.N. Archives Folder S-0794-0001-0003-00002 (Aug. 5, 1993), 70–78.

[98] *Letter from Akashi to Ing*, U.N. Archives Folder S-0794-0001-0002-00001 (Sept. 5, 1993), 40–42; *Additional Observations on the Draft Constitution for Cambodia (Letter from Akashi to Ing Kieth)*, U.N. Archives Folder S-0794-0001-0002-00002 (Aug. 26, 1993), 57.

ness resonated in the history that followed, leading to the modern day where only one party, the CPP, can feasibly hold influence in national government.

Although not offering an exhaustive explanation for the political development of Cambodia's modern institutions, this case study has traced the impacts of international actors on institutional design and an attempt at democratic transition in a post-conflict setting. By explaining this understudied, but highly relevant, case, this chapter hopes to generate further discussion and theorization about the roles that international actors play and the often unintended consequences they can have on institutional design and institutional weakness in post-conflict settings.

BIBLIOGRAPHY

Amer, Ramses. 1990. "The United Nations and Kampuchea: The Issue of Representation and its Implications." *Bulletin of Concerned Asian Scholars* 22(3): 52–60.

Amnesty International. 1994. *Kingdom of Cambodia: Human Rights and the New Constitution.*

Berry, Kenneth. 1997. *Cambodia: From Red to Blue.*

Brinks, Daniel M. and Abby Blass. 2018. *The DNA of Constitutional Justice in Latin America.*

Brinks, Daniel M. and Varun Gauri. 2014. "The Law's Majestic Equality? The Distributive Impact of Judicializing Social and Economic Rights," *Perspectives on Politics* 12(2): 375–393.

Brinks, Daniel M., Steven Levitsky, and Maria Victoria Murillo. 2019. *Understanding Institutional Weakness.*

Brown, Nathan. 2012. *Constitutions in a Nonconstitutional World: Arab Basic Laws and the Prospects for Accountable Government.*

Chen, Albert H.Y. 2015. "The Achievement of Constitutionalism in Asia: Moving Beyond 'Constitutions Without Constitutionalism.'" In *Constitutionalism in Asia in the Early Twenty-First Century.* Edited by Albert H.Y. Chen.

Constitution of Cambodia (1993, amended 2018).

Constitution of North Korea (1972, amended 2019).

Elkins, Zachary and Tom Ginsburg. 2021 "Characteristics of National Constitutions, Version 3.0." Comparative Constitutions Project. Available at comparativeconstitutionsproject.org

Elkins, Zachary, Tom Ginsburg, and Beth Simmons. 2013. "Getting to Rights: Treaty Ratification, Constitutional Convergence, and Human Rights Practice," *Harvard Int'l L. Rev.* 54(1): 61–96.

Elkins, Zachary, Tom Ginsburg, and James Melton. 2009. *The Endurance of National Constitutions.*

Final Act of the Paris Conference on Cambodia, Annex 5, U.N. Doc. A/46/608 (1991).

Forbath, William. 2010. "Cultural Transformation, Deep Institutional Reform, and ESR Practice: South Africa's Treatment Action Campaign." In *Stones of Hope: How African Activists Reclaim Human Rights to Challenge Global Poverty.* Edited by Lucie E. White and Jeremy Perelman.

Fortin, Jessica. 2012. "Is there a Necessary Condition for Democracy? The Role of State Capacity in Postcommunist Countries." *Comparative Political Studies* 45(7): 903–930.

Ginsburg, Tom. 2003. *Judicial Review in New Democracies.*

Ginsburg, Tom and Alberto Simpser. 2014. "Introduction." In *Constitutions in Authoritarian Regimes.* Edited by Tom Ginsburg and Alberto Simpser.

Goderis, Benedikt and Mila Versteeg. 2014. "The Diffusion of Constitutional Rights." *International Review of Law and Economics* 39: 1–19.

Goodman, Ryan and Derek Jinks. 2014. *Socializing States: Promoting Human Rights Through International Law.*

Hughes, Rachel. 2008. "Dutiful Tourism: Encountering Cambodian Genocide," *Asia Pacific Viewpoint* 49: 318–330.

Jacobsohn, Gary J. 2003. *The Wheel of Law.*

Jacobsohn, Gary J. 2010. *Constitutional Identity.*

Keck, Margaret and Kathryn Sikkink. 1998. *Activists Beyond Borders: Advocacy Networks in International Politics.*

Kingdom of Cambodia Office of the Council of Ministers. 1998. *White Paper: The Defence of Young Democracy in Cambodia: The 1998 Election & Its Aftermath.*
Law, David and Mila Versteeg. 2013. "Sham Constitutions." *California Law Review* 101(4): 863–952.
Levitsky, Steven and Maria Victoria Murillo. 2009. "Variation in Institutional Strength." *Annual Review of Political Science* 12: 115–133
Levitsky, Steven and Lucan Way. 2010. *Competitive Authoritarianism.*
Lowenstein, Karl. 1969. "Constitutions and Constitutional Law in the West and in the East," *The Indian Journal of Political Science* 30(3): 203–48.
Marks, Stephen. 2010. "The Process of Creating a New Constitution in Cambodia." In *Framing the State in Times of Transition: Case Studies in Constitution-Making.* Edited by Laurel E. Miller with Louis Aucoin.
Moustafa, Tamir. 2008. "Law and Resistance in Authoritarian States: The Judicialization of Politics in Egypt." In *Rule by Law: The Politics of Courts in Authoritarian Regimes.* Edited by Tom Ginsburg and Tamir Moustafa.
Murphy, Walter. 2007. *Constitutional Democracy: Creating and Maintaining a Just Political Order.*
Phallack, Kong. 2012. "Freedom of Religion in Cambodia." In *Cambodian Constitutional Law.* Edited by Hor Peng, Kong Phallack, and Jörg Menzel.
Ratana, Taing. 2019. "Pluralist Constitution in Cambodia." In *Pluralist Constitution in Southeast Asia.* Edited by Jaclyn Neo and Bui Ngoc Son.
Ratliff, Suellen. 1999. "UN Representation Disputes: A Case Study of Cambodia and a New Accreditation Proposal for the Twenty-First Century," *California Law Review* 87(5): 1207–1264.
Sartori, Giovanni. 1962. "Constitutionalism: A Preliminary Discussion," *American Political Science Review* 56(4): 853–64.
Scheppele, Kim L. 2004. "Constitutional Ethnography, An Introduction." *Law & Society Review* 38: 389–406.
Scheppele, Kim L. 2018. "Autocratic Legalism". *University of Chicago Law Review* 85(2): 545–584.
Shawcross, William. 1979. *Quality of Mercy.*
Shawcross, William. 1994. *Cambodia's New Deal.*
Simmons, Beth. 2009. *Mobilizing for Human Rights.*
Sripati, Vijayashi. 2012. "UN Constitutional Assistance Projects in Comprehensive Peace Missions: An Inventory 1989–2011," *International Peacekeeping* 19(1): 93–113.
Slater, Dan. 2010. *Ordering States: Contentious Politics and Authoritarian Leviathans in Southeast Asia.*
Slater, Dan and Erica Simmons. 2010. "Informative Regress: Critical Antecedents in Comparative Politics." *Comparative Political Studies* 43(7): 886–917.
Sok Socheat. 2019. "Institution Protection of Basic Human Rights in Cambodia." In *Cambodian Constitutional Law.* Edited by Hor Peng, Kong Phallack, and Jörg Menzel.
UN General Assembly, Report of the International Conference on Kampuchea, U.N. Doc. A/CONF.109/5 (July 17, 1981).
UN Office of the High Commissioner for Human Rights, "Human Rights and Constitution Making," U.N. Doc HR/PUB/17/5 (2018).
UN Security Council, Resolution 835, U.N. Doc. S/RES/835 (1993) Venice Commission. Rule of Law Checklist. Council of Europe Study No. 711/2013 (March 17, 2016).
Vandeluxe, Yan. 2016. "The Historical Development of Cambodia's Constitutions." In *Cambodian Constitutional Law.* Edited by Hor Peng, Kong Phallack, and Jörg Menzel.
Widyono, Benny. 2008. *Dancing in the Shadows: Sihanouk, the Khmer Rouge, and the United Nations in Cambodia.*

Primary Sources and News Articles

"Additional Observations on the Draft Constitution for Cambodia (Letter from Akashi to Ing Kieth)," S-0794-0001-0002-00002 (Aug. 26, 1993), 57; "Letter from Akashi to Ing," S-0794-0001-0002-00001 (Sept. 5, 1993), 40–42.
"Attachment to Letter from UNTAC Political Adviser Karim to UNTAC Head Akashi," U.N. Archives Folder S-0794-0001-0003-00002 (Aug. 5, 1993), 70–78.

"Constituent Assembly Debate of Draft Constitution for Cambodia," U.N. Archives Folder S-0794-001-002-00001 (Sept. 15, 1993), 10–11.
"Constituent Assembly Plenary on the Constitution," U.N. Archives Folder S-0794-0001-0002-00001 (Sept. 16, 1993).
"Creation of the Secretariat of the Constitutional Assembly, Memorandum from Kawakami to Akashi," U.N. Archives Folder S-0794-0001-0005-00003 (May 20, 1993), 64.
"Distribution of Seats in the Constituent Assembly," *Phnom Penh Post* (June 18–July 1, 1993).
"Meeting with Dr. Ing Kieth, Vice President of the Constituent Assembly, U.N. Archives Folder S-0794-001-004-00001 UC (July 27, 1993), 67.
"Urgent Request for Vehicles and Mobile Phones for the Support of the Constituent Assembly Secretariat, Memorandum from Constituent Assembly Senior Administrative Assistant Sam Borin to UNTAC Electoral Component Director Reginald Austin," U.N. Archives Folder S-0794-0001-0005-00002 (June 27, 1993), 23.
Barrington, Kevin. April 9–22, 1993. "DPK Slay Bulgarian Hosts of Peace Dinner." *Phnom Penh Post.*
Barrington, Kevin. April 23–May 6, 1993. "Tragedy Throws Polls into Question." *Phnom Penh Post.*
Barrington, Kevin. May 7–20, 1993. "[Khmer Rouge] Open Bloody Anti-Poll Campaign." *Phnom Penh Post.*
Chan Thul, Prak and Amy Sawitta Lefevre. Nov. 16, 2017. "Cambodia's Main Opposition Party Dissolved by Supreme Court." *Reuters*. Available at https://www.reuters.com/article/us-cambodia-politics-idUSKBN1DG1BO.
Colm, Sara. July 10, 1992. "Factions, UNTAC Debate Electoral Law." *Phnom Penh Post.*
Colm, Sara. Nov. 20–Dec. 3, 1992. "Voters Continue to Sign Up Despite Violence," *Phnom Penh Post.*
Davies, Ben. Dec 18–31, 1992. "Complaints Rack Up Against the SOC." *Phnom Penh Post.*
Evans, Gareth. Feb. 28, 2014. "Cambodia's Violent Peace." *Phnom Penh Post*. Available at https://www.phnompenhpost.com/analysis-and-op-ed/cambodia%E2%80%99s-violent-peace.
Gandhi, Jennifer. 2010. *Political Institutions Under Dictatorship*. Cambridge University Press.
Hamilton, Andrea. June 15–July 1, 1993. "Molinaka Looks to Play a Swinging Role." *Phnom Penh Post.*
Jennar, Raoul. June 18–July 1, 1993. "Monarchy or Republic?" *Phnom Penh Post.*
Muntith, Ker. March 12–25, 1993. "DPK Robs UN Peace-Keepers," *Phnom Penh Post.*
Nunan, M.P. Jan. 29–Feb. 11, 1993. "Direct Attack on UNTAC." *Phnom Penh Post.*
Samphan, Khieu. April 6, 1992. Statement to the Supreme National Council, Point of Order of the Day. Cambodian National Archives Box 690, Database 6174.
Samphan, Khieu. April 6, 1992. Statement to the Supreme National Council, Point of Order of the Day #2. Cambodian National Archives Box 690, Database 6174.
Samphan, Khieu. Telegram to UNTAC head Akashi, (Dec. 6, 1992), Cambodia National Archives Box 689, Database 6098.
Sann, Son to Yasushi Akashi, (Dec. 21, 1992), Cambodia National Archives Box 689, Database 6096.
Sihanouk, Norodoum. Jan. 3, 1993. Letter to Akashi, Cambodia National Archives Box 689, Database 6096.
Stier, Ken. Nov. 20, 1992. "Helicopter Potshots Shoot Down UNTAC Mobility," *Phnom Penh Post.*
Thayer, Nate. Nov. 6–19, 1992. Interview with Khieu Samphan, *Phnom Penh Post.*
Thayer, Nate. Jan. 15–28, 1993. "Sihanouk Slams Political Violence: Presidential Election in the Cards." *Phnom Penh Post.*
Thayer, Nate. June 18–July 1, 1993. "Split Emerges in Core Group." *Phnom Penh Post.*
UN Volunteers. April 8, 2013. "In Memory of Atsuhito Nakata." Available at https://www.unv.org/News/memory-Atsuhito-Nakata.
Voice of the Grande Union Nationale du Cambodge. Dec. 7, 1992. Cambodia National Archives Box 689, Database 6098.

9. Explaining congressional support for the federal judiciary

Jake S. Truscott and Teena Wilhelm

INTRODUCTION

An independent judiciary it is not an empirical reality in the American political system, in part because the federal judiciary is tied to decisions made by Congress. Of course, the American separation-of-powers reality is that Congress also depends on the judiciary to reinforce and "constitutionalize" its policymaking. Given this, a legislature interested in policy longevity can choose to strategize and support the judiciary in an opportunistic manner. The degree to which Congress chooses strategies that support the judiciary impacts the institution's influence and capacity. The extent to which support is demonstrated over time reflects the institutional development of the federal judiciary itself.

Over time, the federal judiciary has undoubtedly undergone institutional transformation. McGuire (2004) keenly noted, "an observer today would scarcely recognize the U.S. Supreme Court of the 19th century. With little prestige, modest power, a meager caseload, and no permanent courtroom, it was a bench on which few were anxious to serve" (p. 128). McGuire's observation translates to the entirety of Article III courts. Since the period preceding the Civil War, the population of Article III judgeships ballooned from only 51 authorized federal judgeships in 1855 to 850 in 2015 – a number that more than doubled between 1940 and 1970 alone. In the same period, the total number of Article III courts also grew exponentially, from 37 in 1855 to 108 by 2015. These expansions of institutional structure coincided with the evolution of judicial prestige itself. The era of self-taught lawyers or aspiring politicians serving as federal judges has given way entirely to career judges with expert legal training.

The transition to the modern federal judiciary is not explained by a singular congressional policy event. Prior research helps us understand the historical progression, albeit with a focus primarily on the U.S. Supreme Court. In particular, McGuire (2004) saw the Court's institutional development as rooted in a set of exogeneous political factors that helped facilitate *differentiation*, *durability*, and *autonomy* for the institution. By creating a dynamic index that measured institutional change over time, he mapped the historical trajectory of Supreme Court institutional development and observed the long-term implications for Supreme Court power.

This conceptualization of institutional development is a valuable framework as we expand the inquiry beyond the Supreme Court. Specifically, we are interested in the long-term record of action taken by Congress to support the institutional development of the entire federal judiciary. Our analysis indicates a long-term trend of congressional support that appears more stable than what scholars have found specific to the Supreme Court (McGuire, 2004; Ura and Wohlfarth, 2010). To this end, we find that economic and political conditions can motivate or deter congressional support to varying degrees. Overall, our analysis explores the dynamic between Congress and the federal judiciary and the evolving conditions of that relationship.

CAUSES OF CONGRESSIONAL SUPPORT FOR THE SUPREME COURT

The U.S. Constitution provides no direct guidance concerning the size, structure, or jurisdictional scope of the federal court system beyond the assertion that "the judicial power of the United States shall be vested in one Supreme Court." Instead, the founders provided Congress with the power to "ordain and establish inferior courts" and regulate the jurisdictional scope of the Supreme Court. Likewise, the judicial branch is dependent upon Congress to fund America's legal system – which broadly includes both the salaries of judges and the ancillary costs needed to promote and maintain every Article III body. This dependence on Congress has promoted a recurring principal–agent problem. Further, the judicial branch must compete with the countless other agencies, institutions, and programs across the federal government. Generally speaking, the support that Congress can provide the judiciary is grouped into financial and institutional considerations. Also generally speaking, scholars have found that the proclivity of Congress to provide support has been mixed over time. What seems to factor into the congressional calculus are factors related to the political relationship between the branches, as well as economic considerations.

What we know about the impact of interbranch relations on congressional support comes primarily from analyses of Congress's relationship with the Supreme Court. Scholars have operationalized this relationship in several ways, including interbranch ideological differences and congressional reaction to Supreme Court decision-making. The impact of ideological differences has, not surprisingly, been shown to constrain congressional support for the federal judiciary. In other words, when Congress collectively views the Supreme Court as more favorable to its preferred policy outcomes, research finds that support for the judiciary is more likely. For example, Vining, Wilhelm, and Hughes (2019) found requests made by the Chief Justice for federal judicial improvements were more likely to be granted by Congress when legislative-judicial ideological distance was smaller.

Scholars have also considered interbranch relations in light of Supreme Court decision-making, and congressional reaction to it. Toma (1991) found that Supreme Court decision-making that runs counter to congressional preferences impacted the degree of their willingness to support the institution. She offered an anecdote from the Warren Court to illustrate how Congress employs tools like budget appropriations to punish the Supreme Court for decision-making that they view as antagonistic: "In response to the liberal Court of the 1960s, a less liberal Congress passed the 1964 Government Employees Salary Reform Act that increased the annual salaries of members of Congress and of federal judges, except Supreme Court justices, by $7,500. The justices of the Supreme Court received increases of only $4,500" (p. 135). That congressional support is impacted by Supreme Court decision-making is echoed in Barnes's (2004) work on congressional overrides and Clark's (2009) investigation of court-curbing legislation as well.

Evidence by McGuire (2004) seemed to stand to the contrary, at least in terms of longitudinal impact. In his research, Supreme Court decision-making is a surrogate measure for judicial power. His analysis reveals that long-term institutionalization of the Supreme Court is not impacted by Supreme Court decisions. In other words, the Court's long-term institutional capacity is not increased when the Supreme Court exercises power. Importantly, institutional support does not appear to be hindered by Supreme Court power either. McGuire concludes, notably, that the institutional development of the Supreme Court can itself lead to increases in the Court's use of power, but not the other way around.

Beyond the politics of interbranch relations, other conditions have been found to mediate congressional support as well. Ura and Wohlfarth (2010) found that public support serves as a reference point for congressional decisions about the judiciary. Namely, even when controlling for the ideological separation between the Court and Congress, they find that "congressional support for the Supreme Court is a function of public opinion about Congress as well as public opinion about the Supreme Court" (p. 953). Clark's (2009) analysis of court-curbing legislation echoes this finding as well.

EXPLAINING CONGRESSIONAL SUPPORT FOR THE FEDERAL JUDICIARY

Prior research suggests that interbranch relations, economic conditions, and public support all might factor into congressional decisions to support the Supreme Court as an institution. We expect that congressional considerations for the entire federal judiciary are similarly motivated. Importantly, we expect that congressional support is tied to political and economic trends throughout history. Here we identify specific factors that may explain historical support for the federal judiciary. Given that our analysis covers 220 years (1796–2015), we examine those conditions that can be operationalized for the entire time period.

Economic Considerations

We consider that economic conditions should impact congressional support for several reasons. Most important is that the overall health of the American economy acts as a gatekeeper for federal spending. When economic health is proficient, the necessity to curtail or adjust spending preferences for Congress is less likely. Alternatively, when the nation's economic health is relatively poor, the federal government may naturally respond by reducing unnecessary expenditures. This can have an impact on the judiciary, which lobbies for appropriations like any other federal office, agency, or department.

We measure economic conditions in two ways. First, we include a dichotomous variable that indicates whether the economy is experiencing a downturn in a given year. Downturns are defined as periods where the nominal gross domestic product (GDP) in a given year is less than the previous year. Once a downturn is indicated, it remains until the nominal GDP rebounds and surpasses the prior maximum.[1] Of the 220 years in our dataset, economic conditions are classified as being in a downturn for 75 non-consecutive years. Our second economic indicator is the overall spending of the federal government. We base this measure on expenditure receipts.[2]

---

[1] For example, the aggregated nominal GDP in 1841 was $1.62 million. However, it was reduced in the following year ($1.57 million in 1842). Until the nominal GDP surpassed $1.62 million, the economy was measured as being in a downturn (=1).

[2] Federal spending data was retrieved from: https://www.usgovernmentspending.com/

Political Considerations

Like economic conditions, political considerations undoubtedly factor into congressional decisions for judicial support. As discussed, prior scholarship confirms this in very direct ways related to the Supreme Court. Based on this research, we posit that interbranch political conditions should temper congressional willingness to support institutional development within the entire federal judiciary as well. We consider the congressional–judicial interbranch relationship to be represented in two ways: ideological distance and judicial decision-making.

Measuring interbranch ideological distance over time presents an interesting obstacle for our research. Specifically, illustrating the full judiciary's political or ideological composition is difficult, and even more so over the course of the last two centuries. Given this, we frame the ideological preferences of the judiciary as a reflection of the Supreme Court rather than the entire judiciary. The Supreme Court, though not the entire judiciary, acts as its primary representative. Further, prior literature has routinely reinforced that the primary source of interbranch perceptions toward the judiciary stems from evaluations of the Supreme Court (e.g., Toma, 1991; Walker and Barrow, 1985). Even if political conditions in the lower federal courts do not completely match those in the Supreme Court, support from Congress is nonetheless bound to the Supreme Court as its proxy.

To gauge interbranch political conditions, we use a spatial assessment of the interbranch relationship. Specifically, we use two measures rooted in the Poole-Rosenthal (1985) NOMINATE methodology. These represent the average first-dimensional score for both chambers of Congress during a given year, as well as the average of the Supreme Court.[3] The scores for the Court were determined by assigning the justices with the scores of the president who appointed them. While alternative scaling methodologies exist, a comparison using NOMINATE is the only one that allows for measurement for the entirety of our dataset. To gauge ideological distance, we measure the absolute value of the distance separating the means of the Court and Congress on a discrete NOMINATE scale. Scores greater than absolute (0) represent lesser degrees of congruity.

Our measure of judicial decision-making is a composite index. We are interested in how expansive decision-making (McGuire's "power" variable) shown by the Supreme Court impacts levels of congressional support for the entire judiciary. To model this consideration, our index components include: (1) the number of times the Supreme Court declares acts of Congress unconstitutional in a given year; (2) the number of times the Supreme Court rules against an official, agency, or department of the federal government in a given year; and (3) a measure of landmark decision-making from the Court. After factor analysis, our resulting composite score returned only one principal axis with an eigenvalue greater than 1.[4,5] Figure 9.1 illustrates this variable over time.

---

[3] First-dimension NOMINATE scores were retrieved from Voteview: Congressional Roll-Call Votes Database. Retrievable at: https://voteview.com/

[4] The data for components one and two was sourced from the Spaeth et al. Supreme Court database, retrievable at: http:// Supremecourtdatabase .org. For landmark decision data, we relied on the Legal Information Institute's (Cornell Law School) List of Historic Supreme Court Decisions, retrievable at: https://www.law.cornell.edu/supct/cases/name.htm

[5] The first principal component returned an eigenvalue of 2.01, accounting for 68% of the common variance.

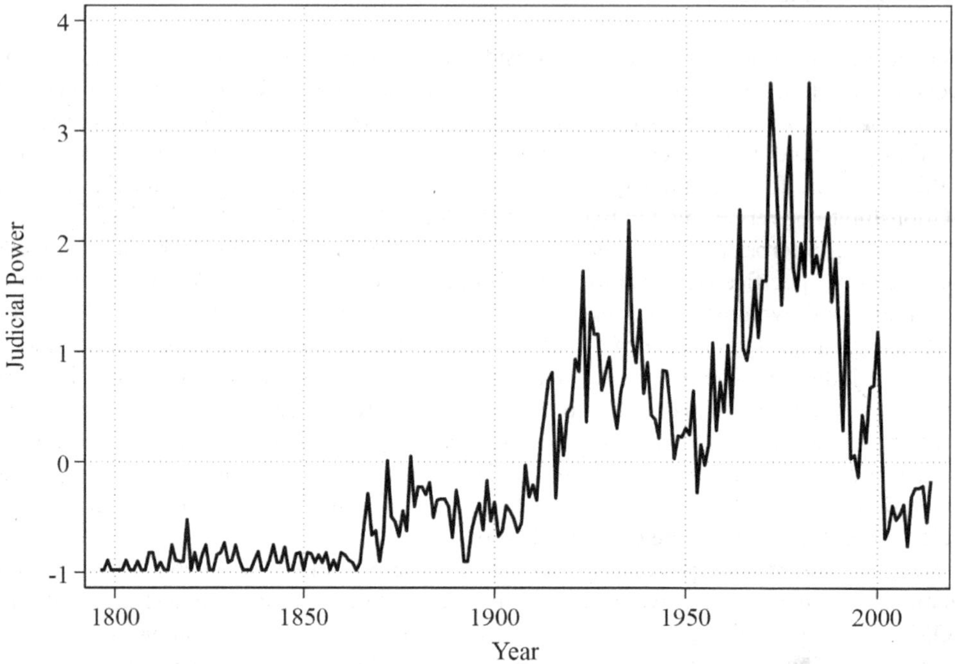

Figure 9.1 *Index of judicial power, 1796–2015*

Notably, prior literature suggests that judicial workload and public opinion should factor into congressional decisions related to the federal judiciary. Unfortunately, we do not have a way to measure such considerations for the entire federal judiciary for the entire time period of our analyses. For this reason, these factors are not included in our analyses.

OPERATIONALIZING CONGRESSIONAL SUPPORT FOR THE JUDICIARY

To understand the institutional development of the federal judiciary, as facilitated by congressional support over time, we consider foundational work by McGuire (2004), which was subsequently augmented by Ura and Wohlfarth (2010). McGuire operationalized congressional support for the Supreme Court over time as an aggregated index, derived from principal factor analysis of underlying indicators. McGuire's index measures the Supreme Court's ability (over time) to *differentiate* as a distinct political institution; demonstrate *durability* in adapting to change; and exhibit *autonomy* in decision-making. In this research, we consider factors that promote differentiation, durability, and autonomy for the entirety of the federal judiciary.

Durability

The durability of the federal judiciary is reflected in its ability to adapt to change through institutional growth. Factors such as long-term financial stability and workload (institutional) capacity provide a framework for durability of the judiciary. Much of this is accomplished, of course, by impactful legislation passed by Congress (de Figueiredo et al., 2000; McGuire, 2004). In the case of the Supreme Court, McGuire (2004) specifically considered durability relative to the role of law clerks and pay scales for Supreme Court justices. Ura and Wohlfarth (2010) expanded this to include Supreme Court appropriations more generally. Logically, as Congress increases allocations of financial and institutional resources to the court, it indicates support for the institutional output.

We agree that these factors reflect durability. As such, we first incorporate law clerk support for the entire judiciary. This indicator reflects historical milestones that expand support for law clerks in the federal courts. Beginning in 1864 when the first federal law clerks were hired, we identify congressional developments that financially and institutionally incorporate (and expand) law clerk support within the judiciary. Next, we expand McGuire's (2004) metric of Supreme Court salary information to include annual changes in salaries for all federal judges. We also incorporate the total sum of appropriations allocated to the federal judiciary in a given year (Holt, 2012),[6] similar to the index update by Ura and Wohlfarth (2010). Finally, we consider one additional factor: the total number of authorized Article III courts and judgeships in a given year. This additional component indicates the degree of congressional response for emerging institutional need (e.g., Hughes, Vining, and Wilhlem, 2017). It also indicates support for the entire judiciary by way of authorized institutional expansion.

Differentiation

Components of differentiation are those that promote a "clear boundary [line] that mark [the institution's] distinctiveness" (McGuire, 2004, p. 130). That is, these factors indicate the judiciary's clearly defined and specialized role. McGuire (2004) measured differentiation by the extent to which veterans within the judiciary were recruited to serve in positions of power and influence. More specifically, he measured the average service of Supreme Court justices in lower Article III courts prior to appointment. By his logic, more judicial experience for members of the judiciary corresponds to an increase in collective institutional understanding and respect. Accordingly, our analysis includes a similar indicator for the average years of judicial service on the federal bench in any given year.[7]

Autonomy

Autonomy of the judiciary is indicated when the institution exercises decision-making at its own discretion. McGuire (2004) framed autonomy as a reflection of the Supreme Court's

---

[6] Itemized budget allocations for the federal judiciary for 1796–2010 were sourced from the Federal Judicial Center (Holt, 2012). 2010–2015 were sourced from the American Bar Association's annual reports on federal court funding.

[7] Notably, our average judicial service indicator pertains only to Supreme Court justices, as data on the entire federal judiciary is not available for every year in our dataset.

ability to set its own agenda. He correctly identified how, over much of American political history, the federal courts were governed by statutory jurisdictional requirements. As jurisdictional requirements have subsided over time, the progression from rights of appeal to an agenda dictated more by the discretion of federal judges represents an increase in institutional autonomy. This is particularly telling at the highest level, which promotes a residual effect on the operations and decision-making of the lower federal courts.

Like McGuire, we incorporate considerations of agenda control into our index. Similar to that research, we measure this as congressional action over time that gives more agenda control to federal judges. We also include a variable to indicate change in the jurisdictional scope of the federal judiciary as a whole. Importantly, this variable is operationalized to indicate expansion as well as contraction of jurisdiction for all Article III courts.

Our index also incorporates McGuire's (2004) measure for the length of the Supreme Court rulebook. This includes requirements, procedures, and other provisions that guide the operations. While McGuire thought this reflected durability for the judiciary, we see it as providing a natural fit for autonomous decision-making. The extent that the judiciary formalizes its rules and procedures represents an important illustration of autonomy. Autonomous decisions on procedure that impact the Supreme Court can also impact operations of the lower federal courts.

We incorporate a final indicator for autonomy, not included in prior research. Specifically, we measure any major change in judicial administration, whether arising from legislation or internal decisions from within the judiciary. Over time, the administration of the federal courts has moved away from dependence on the Departments of Interior, Treasury, or Justice to handle most of its day-to-day operations. We measure this change as an additive total of legislation or other events that have changed the administrative structure of Article III courts.

Constructing a Dynamic Index of Judicial Institutionalization

Each of these indicators illustrates some aspect in the evolution of the institutional capacity of the federal judiciary. Like prior research, we maintain that each individual component is best understood as necessary, but not sufficient. Instead, the composite index of all these factors best illustrates our underlying concept (Berry and Feldman, 1985; McGuire, 2004). Like prior research, we construct our index using factor analysis. This analysis resulted in two principal axes with an eigenvalue greater than 1.0, collectively accounting for some 94% of the cumulative variance. Notably, most variables load substantially on the first principal axis.[8]

As McGuire (2004) notes, "the correlations between these variables may simply be an artifact of a mutual trend, and because of that, any one of the variables could be quite exogenous to any underlying dimension of institutional change" (p. 133). In other words, even if the components in the index appear to be collectively cointegrated, correlation is still possible. Given that each individual component represents an independent, non-stationary time series, we performed a set of robustness checks to ensure that the individual measures reflect a single dimension. These results can be found in the Appendix. Once satisfied that the individual components reflected the evolving trends expressed by the latent dimension, we constructed our

---

8 Specifically, the first principal axis presented an eigenvalue of 8.33 and accounted for 83.4% of the cumulative variance. The second principal axis presented an eigenvalue of 1.15 and accounted for 11.58% of the cumulative variance.

final index using scores from the first principal axis. Figure 9.2 represents the graphed barometric evolution of the institutional development of the federal judiciary. Figure 9.3 represents our index in comparison with the Supreme Court index developed by McGuire (2004), and Figure 9.4 represents our index in comparison with the Ura and Wohlfarth (2010) modified Supreme Court index. Figure 9.5 represents the comparison of all three.

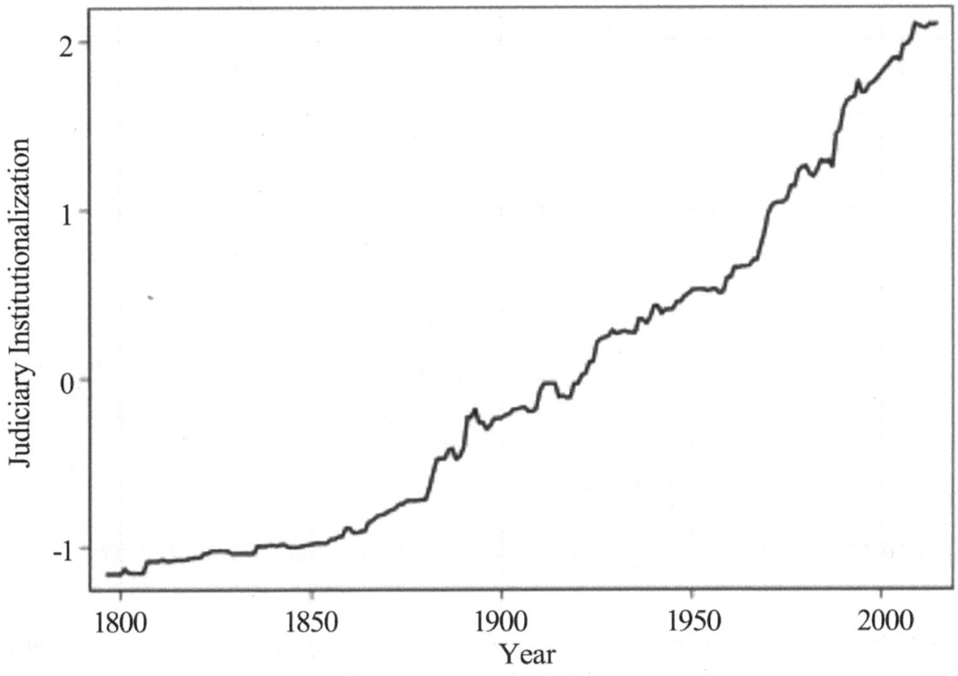

Figure 9.2 *Institutionalization of the federal judiciary, 1796–2015*

In comparison with prior developed indices specific to the Supreme Court, there is a similar variance between all measures.[9] This is not entirely surprising. Many milestones in the history of the federal judiciary happen in a top–down fashion. Moreover, most financial and institutional changes that occur at the Supreme Court are followed (or mirrored) by changes to the entire branch. For example, decisions to increase the salaries of federal judges are hardly exclusive to Supreme Court justices; nor are legislative decisions that change legal jurisdictions or administrative structures. By adjusting the scope of measurement, many components incorporated into prior analyses appear to be sufficiently replicable for an analysis of the entire judiciary. Still, while there does exist a similar variance, our full judiciary measure appears more stable over time than Supreme Court specific measures, as the comparative graphs in Figures 9.2, 9.3, and 9.4 illustrate.

9 Specifically, 0.96 with McGuire (2004) and 0.91 with Ura and Wohlfarth (2010).

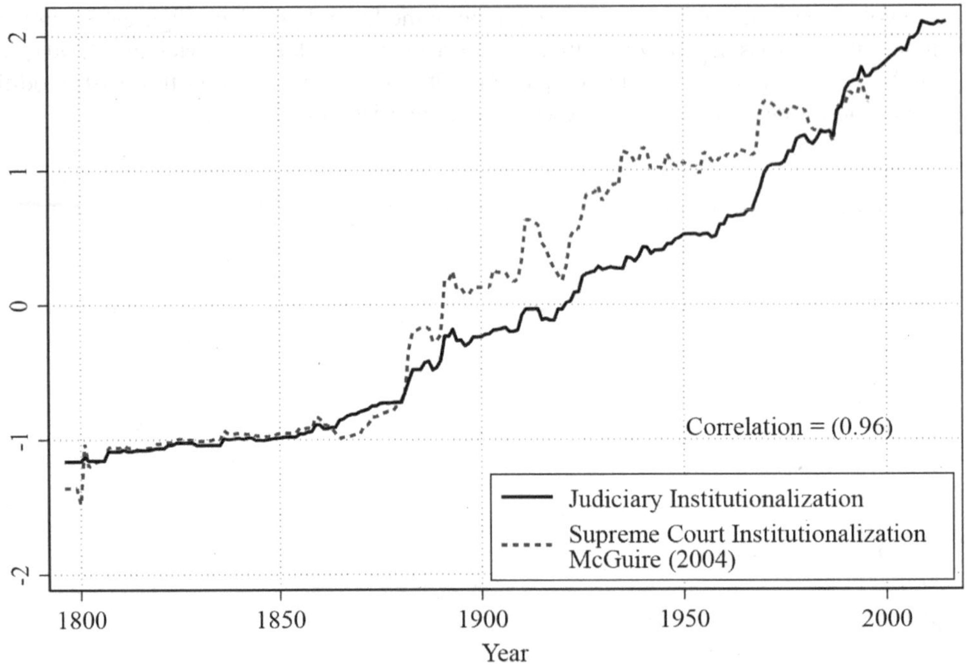

Figure 9.3 *Federal judiciary index compared with Supreme Court index (McGuire, 2004)*

One explanation could be related to the data itself. Institutional changes that impact the broader Article III court system are more regular and frequent across time than those specific to the Supreme Court. For example, while the population of the Supreme Court changed periodically throughout the nineteenth century, it has remained stagnant at nine since 1869. Alternatively, the number of federal district court judges has grown routinely until the early 2000s. Further, the broader set of Article III judgeships and courts rarely decreases. Moreover, while financial support can vary from year to year, the institutional side of congressional support for the judiciary is more additive in nature, as support is rarely decreased for the entire judiciary.

Another possible explanation, of course, is that the comparative stability of our measure means that the historical record of congressional support for the institutional development of the judicial branch is not as fragile as that for the Supreme Court. Given that the Supreme Court is constantly subject to scrutiny, as the most visible judicial body, this is not necessarily surprising. In fact, the more stable graph for the entire federal judiciary suggests that factors related to Supreme Court institutional support may *not* impact the lower federal courts. In effect, the economic and political conditions that impact support for the Supreme Court may not reflect the whole picture. Our longitudinal analysis explores this further.

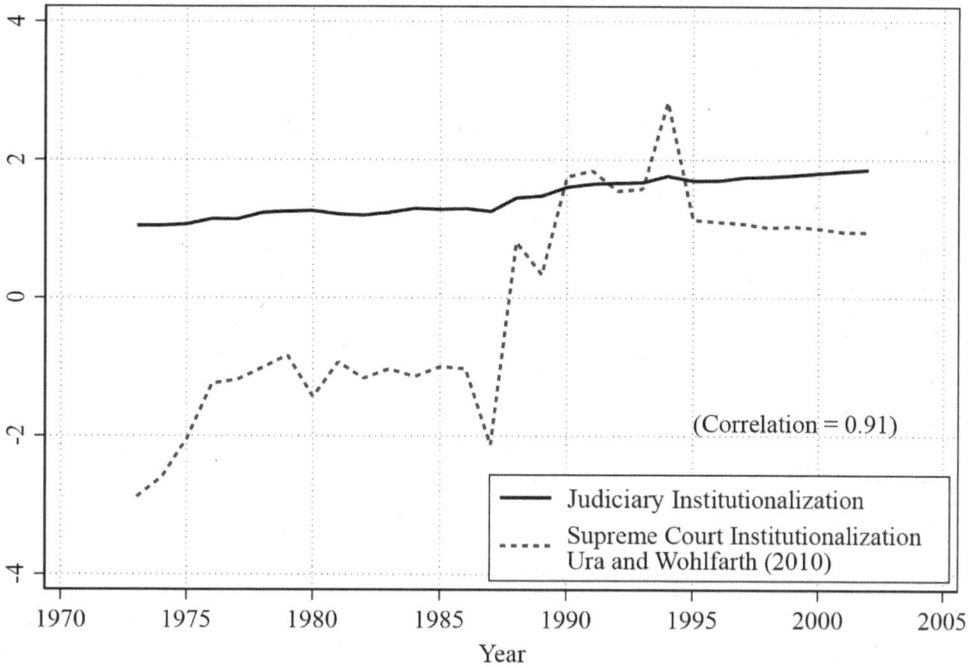

Figure 9.4 *Federal judiciary index compared with Supreme Court index (Ura and Wohlfarth, 2010)*

MODEL AND RESULTS

We constructed a model to consider factors that influence support by Congress for the federal judiciary over time. To model changes in longitudinal congressional support, we use an autoregressive distributed lag (ARDL) framework. We chose ARDL for three primary reasons. First, an illustration of the dependent variable's autocorrelative functions highlights that judicial institutionalization follows a meaningful trend of autoregressive parameters but offers little evidence of moving average parameters.[10] This indicated that a model focusing on moving average parameters was likely unnecessary. Second, ARDL provided a framework to include lagged values of our dependent variable, since current and future values of the dependent variable are very likely reflective of prior values. Finally, ARDL allows us to model current values of the dependent variable as a response to prior values of explanatory variables, which is how we expect congressional decisions regarding support to be structured. Specifically, we expect lagged values in $year_{(t-2)}$ to be the most indicative period. For example, Congress appropriates funds to the judiciary for FY2010 with legislation passed in 2009 (i.e., $year_{(t-1)}$). We expect that Congress, in 2009, considers conditions of the year prior (2008 $year_{(t-2)}$). Employing an ARDL

[10] A graphic illustration of the autocorrelative and partial-autocorrelative functions can be found in the Appendix (Figure 9A.1).

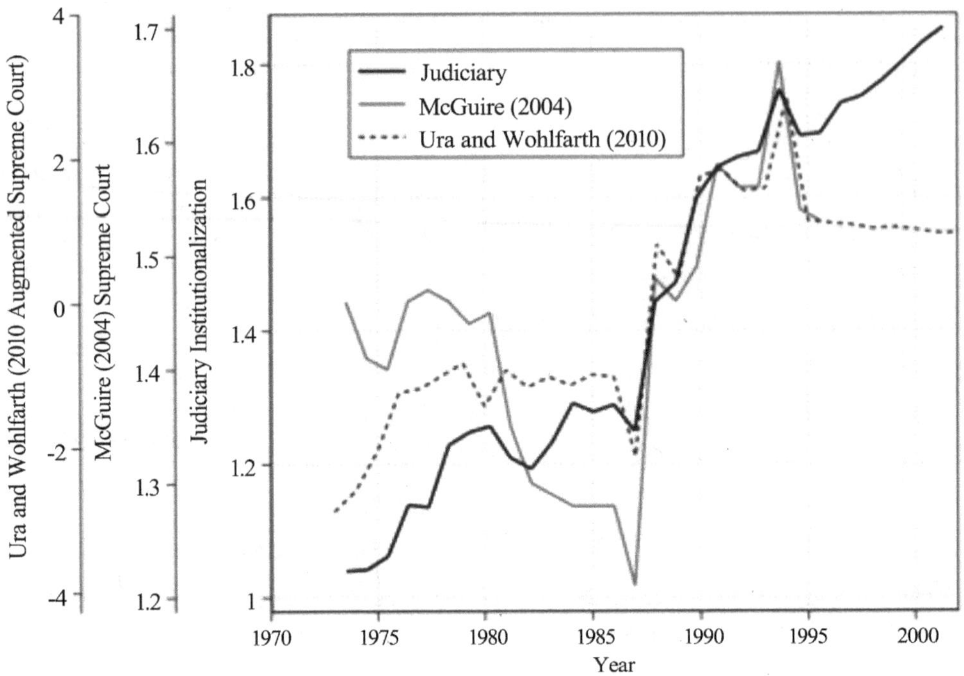

Figure 9.5 *Federal judiciary index compared with Supreme Court indexes of institutionalization (McGuire, 2004; Ura and Wohlfarth, 2010)*

approach allows us to consider these lagged terms as explanatory variables for institutionalization in the contemporary period.

Table 9.1 displays our model results, illustrating the effects of our covariates on congressional support for the federal judiciary. Of note, we provide estimates for both our index of federal judicial support and the Supreme Court-specific support index from McGuire (2004).

Table 9.1 *Effects of political and economic conditions on judicial institutionalization*

		Judiciary			Supreme Court		
Years of Observation		(1796–2015)			(1796–1996)		
	Lag(t-*i*)	Coef.	SE	Sig.	Coef.	SE	Sig.
Index (DV)	2	0.936	(0.02)	***	0.878	(0.03)	***
Economic Downturn (=1)	2	−0.031	(0.02)		0.016	(0.01)	
Federal Spending (Trillions, USD)	2	0.087	(0.03)	*	0.002	(0.03)	
Ideological Distance	2	−0.065	(0.10)		−0.213	(0.08)	*
Judicial Power	2	0.066	(0.01)	***	0.011	(0.01)	
Year(t)	2	0.002	(0.00)	*	0.002	(0.00)	***
Constant		−3.89	(1.79)	*	−4.24	(1.11)	***

Notes:
*0.05, **0.01, ***0.001 at a 95% confidence interval.
The *Index (DV)* variable indicates that each model's respective dependent variable is being incorporated as a lagged term.

In terms of economic factors, economic downturns do not appear to have a significant impact on congressional support for the federal judiciary, while overall federal spending does. Specifically, we find that an increase in the overall spending rate of the federal government is significantly related to congressional support for the federal judiciary. This is not surprising considering that two of the major components found within our index – the total judicial budget and Article III judge salaries – are monetary appropriations. It stands to reason that longitudinal increases in overall federal spending would coincide with increases in their budgetary support for the judiciary too. We were, however, surprised to find that this did not translate to the Supreme Court. Although McGuire's (2004) only budgetary variable was total expenditures per justice (i.e., the justices' salaries), we expected that any positive trends for federal spending for the entire judiciary – which included the Supreme Court – would likely be reflected in support for the Supreme Court.

Why do the results for financial support seem to differ between the federal judiciary and the Supreme Court considered alone? One idea is that the Supreme Court may more likely be subject to interbranch obstacles than the other Article III courts. Considering how prevalent the Supreme Court is in the public eye, the decisions of the Court invite greater congressional scrutiny. Consequently, the difference in our results may suggest other mediating factors. A natural place to look for these factors is within the political environment.

In terms of political conditions, we also find differences in the impact of congressional–judicial ideological distance on the congressional support indexes. Specifically, ideological distance does not have a statistically significant impact on congressional support for the entire judiciary but is negative and significant for the Supreme Court. In other words, increases in the ideological distance separating the Supreme Court from Congress correspond with a decrease in congressional support for the Supreme Court, but do not appear to impact congressional support for the broader judiciary. This result, in some ways, reinforces the findings of prior literature that emphasize the significance of interbranch relationships in the separation-of-powers system for the Supreme Court (e.g., Clark, 2009; Toma, 1991; Walker and Barrow, 1985).

Figure 9.6 offers an illustration of the marginal effects of ideological distance on expected congressional support toward the Supreme Court. Specifically, we find that increases in the ideological distance separating the Court and Congress correspond with a decrease in congressional support across all values of separation. It is worth noting that we have no expectation that the Supreme Court's politics reflects all judicial politics found in the lower federal courts, which may further explain the differences in results between the two indexes.

Our second variable reflecting political conditions is a measure of expansive decision-making by the Supreme Court (labeled *Judicial Power*). Once again, we find differences between our two congressional support indexes. Our results indicate a significant and positive effect for the entire judiciary, but this does not extend to the measure of the Supreme Court. Substantively, this means that we find a higher level of congressional support when the Supreme Court exercises more judicial authority. This is both interesting and unexpected, considering that it does not translate to the Supreme Court, whose exertions of judicial power serve as the foundation of the measure.

We consider that these results may be more corollary than causal. The primary components that constitute our measure – landmark decisions, declarations of unconstitutionality, and anti-government decision-making – each represent Supreme Court authority in the modern era, of which none was particularly prominent in the early history of the federal courts. Our results likely illustrate that the longitudinal evolution of judicial power trends alongside the

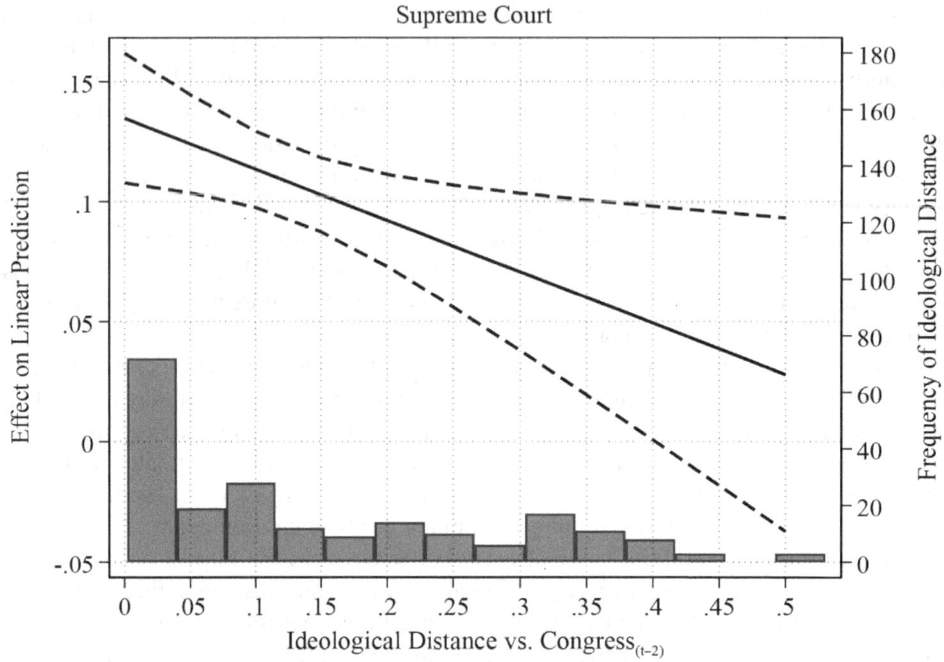

Figure 9.6 *Marginal effects of lagged ideological distance$_{(t-2)}$ on congressional support*

institutional development of the federal judiciary. In other words, as the judiciary's institutional capacity has grown over time, so too has the ability of the Court to employ expansive decision-making. This presumption is reaffirmed in the prior literature. Specifically, McGuire (2004) found that the long-term growth of the Supreme Court's power was caused by its institutionalization – a result that is not upheld when the causal hypothesis is flipped.

CONCLUDING THOUGHTS

In this research, we analyze longitudinal congressional support for the federal judicial branch. In comparison with similar studies done on the Supreme Court (McGuire, 2004; Ura and Wohlfarth, 2010), support for the entire judiciary exhibits a more stable trend over time. Our analysis of this trend reveals that the entire federal judiciary has been less impacted by economic conditions and interbranch relations than the Supreme Court. Thus, the relative stability that is visible in our graphed index, in comparison with that of the Supreme Court, is likely a real thing.

We analyze congressional support as a function of economic and political conditions. Our results for the impact of economic conditions perform generally as expected. We find that increases in overall congressional spending correspond to increases in federal judicial support, and economic downturns do not have a significant impact. Both results suggest relative stability in our index. The impact of political conditions is somewhat mixed. Interbranch ideological distance does not have a significant impact on congressional support for the entire judiciary, while expansive decision-making by the Supreme Court is both significant and positive. This seems to contrast with prior research that suggests expansive judicial decisions can often deter congressional willingness to support the judiciary. We speculate that this finding is measurement related. Moreover, we believe expansive decision-making is likely a response to congressional support, rather than the opposite.

In future research, we hope to shift our focus to the consequences of institutional development, rather than the causes. We believe that the extent that one institution has leverage over the other requires further investigation. The separation of powers ensures that Congress holds the keys to the financial and institutional stability of the Article III courts, but this has not prevented the judiciary from assuming power on its own. Investigating the dynamic of legislative–judicial relations can help us understand the consequences of this relationship across American history.

REFERENCES

Barnes, J. (2004). *Overruled?: Legislative Overrides, Pluralism, and Contemporary Court-Congress Relations*. Stanford University Press.

Berry, W. D. & Feldman, S. (1985). *The Multiple Regression model: A Review*. In *Multiple Regression in Practice* (pp. 10–18). SAGE Publications, Inc., https://www.doi.org/10.4135/9781412985208

Clark, T.S. (2009). The Separation of Powers, Court Curbing, and Judicial Legitimacy. *American Journal of Political Science, 53*(4): 971–989.

de Figueiredo, J., Gryski, G., Tiller, E., & Zuk, G. (2000). Congress and the political expansion of the U.S. districts courts. *American Law and Economics Review, 2*(1): 107–125. doi:10.1093/aler/2.1.107

Holt, D.S. (2012). Federal Judicial Appropriations, 1792 to 2010. [Dataset] Federal Judicial Center. https://www.fjc.gov/content/federal-judiciary-appropriations-1792-2010-0

Hughes, D.A., Vining, R.L., Jr. and Wilhelm, T. (2017). The Politics of the U.S. Federal Judiciary's Requests for Institutional Reform. *Social Science Quarterly, 98*: 1277–1295. doi:10.1111/ssqu.12378

McGuire, K. (2004, updated 2007). The Institutionalization of the U.S. Supreme Court. *Political Analysis, 12*(2): 128–142. Retrieved June 22, 2021, from http://www.jstor.org/stable/25791761

Poole, K., & Rosenthal, H. (1985). A Spatial Model for Legislative Roll Call Analysis. *American Journal of Political Science, 29*(2): 357–384. doi:10.2307/2111172

Toma, E. (1991). Congressional influence and the Supreme Court: The budget as signaling device. *Journal of Legal Studies, 20*(1): 131–146.

Ura, J.D., & Wohlfarth, P.C. (2010). "An Appeal to the People": Public Opinion and Congressional Support for the Supreme Court. *The Journal of Politics, 72*(4): 939–956.

U.S. Const. art. III, § 1.

Vining Jr, R. L., Wilhelm, T., & Hughes, D. A. (2019). The Chief Justice as Effective Administrative Leader: The Impact of Policy Scope and Interbranch Relations. *Social Science Quarterly, 100*(4): 1358–1368. doi:10.1111/ssqu.12637

Walker, T. G., & Barrow, D. J. (1985). Funding the federal judiciary: The congressional connection. *Judicature, 69*(1): 43–50.

APPENDIX 9A

Table 9A.1 Granger causality tests of judicial institutionalization index and its indicators

Indicator	*F*	*Prob > F*
Total Judiciary Budget	1.03	0.348
Article III Judge Salaries	0.14	0.866
Agenda Control (SCOTUS)	3.71	0.022
Total Authorized Judgeships	0.52	0.587
Total Article III Courts	0.46	0.622
Role of Law Clerks	0.05	0.951
Jurisdiction Change Events	1.07	0.335
Administration Change Events	0.37	0.683
Federal Judicial Experience (SCOTUS)	4.25	0.015
Rules Length (SCOTUS)	1.62	0.189

Note: Our *Granger-Causality* procedure was derived from McGuire (2004, p. 133–134) and represents a variation of the Engle-Granger two-step method.

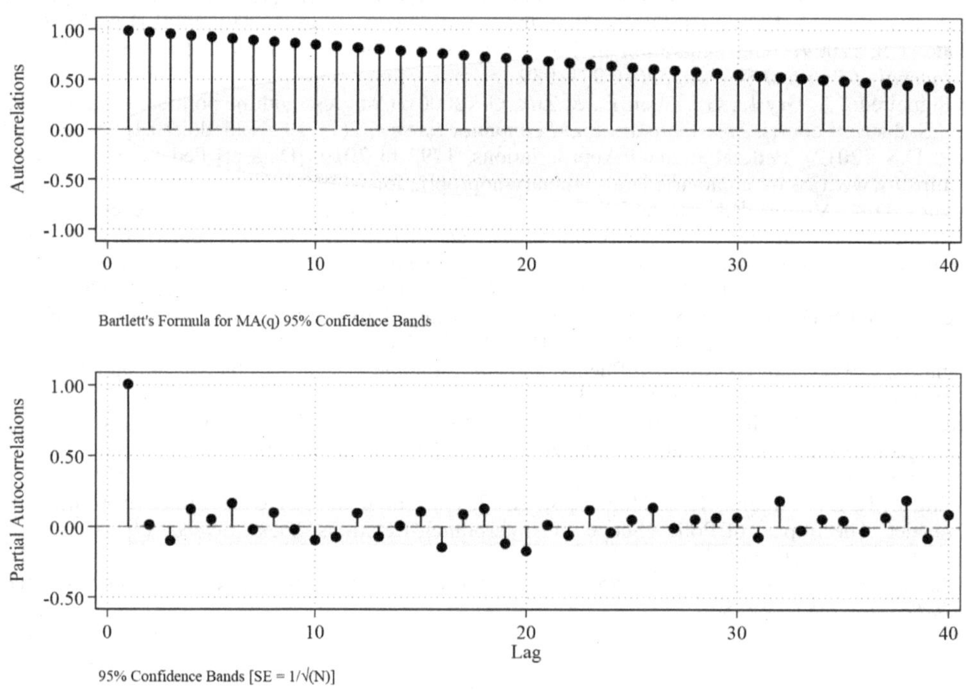

Figure 9A.1 Autocorrelative and partial-autocorrelative functions of judicial institutionalization

Federal judiciary institutionalization (measure of congressional support) index components

Total judiciary budget – Itemized funds allocated to the federal judiciary in each fiscal year (Millions, Adjusted to 2018 USD). Source: https:// www .fjc .gov/ content/ federal -judiciary -appropriations-1792–2010–0

Note: 2011–2015 data were sourced from the American Bar Association's reports on appropriations requests to the federal judiciary.

Article III Judge Salaries – Total of all Article III judge salaries per year. Sources:

1. https://www.fjc.gov/history/judges/judicial-salaries-us-district-court-judges
2. https://www.fjc.gov/history/judges/judicial-salaries-u.s.-circuit-court-judges-1801–1891
3. https://www.fjc.gov/history/judges/judicial-salaries-us-court-appeals-judges
4. https://www.fjc.gov/history/judges/judicial-salaries-supreme-court-justices

Agenda Control (adapted from McGuire 2004) – Measures the ability of the Supreme Court to manage its own docket.

0. Initial baseline (*lack of*) agenda control – *[1796] to 1890*
1. Passage of Circuit Court of Appeals Act of 1891 (which provided limited discretionary review via the writ of certiorari) – *1891 to 1924*
2. Passage of the Judiciary Act of 1925 (which expanded certiorari power) – *1925 to 1988*
3. Passage of the Act to Improve the Administration of Justice (which moved to eliminate mandatory appeals requirements) – *1988 to [2015]*

Total Authorized Judgeships – Total number of (statutorily) authorized Article III judgeships in a given year. Source: https://www.uscourts.gov/judges-judgeships/authorized-judgeships
Total Article III Courts – Total number of (statutorily) authorized Article III courts in a given year. Source: https://www.fjc.gov/history/timeline/8276
Law Clerks – Adapted from McGuire's (2004) original measurement to reflect the entire judiciary. Source: https://www.fjc.gov/history/administration/court-officers-and-staff-law-clerks

0. Initial baseline of no law clerks in the federal judiciary – *1796 to 1863*
1. Judge (and later Associate Justice) Horace Gray hires (and personally pays) a personal assistant to aid with his legal duties. – *1864 to 1885*
2. Congress heeds advice of Attorney General to fund a single stenographer for each Supreme Court justice "to assist in such clerical work as might be assigned to him." – *1886 to 1918*
3. Congress begins to provide funds to pay for legally trained assistants, dubbed "law clerks" – *1919 to 1929*
4. Congress expands funding to allow each Circuit Court judge to hire a single law clerk – *1930 to 1935*
5. Congress again expands funding to allow District Courts to hire law clerks as a measure of necessity, which was prescribed by the Senior Circuit Judge – *1936 to 1958*
6. Congress authorized judges to hire "necessary" law clerks subject to the limits of their chambers' staff budgets and establishes a minimum law clerk salary – *1959 to 2015*

Jurisdiction Change Events – Legislation and other events that expanded (+1) or diminished (−1) the jurisdiction of Article III Courts. Source: https://www.fjc.gov/history/timeline/8271
Administration Change Events – Total legislation or other events that changed the administrative structure of Article III courts. Source: https://www.fjc.gov/history/timeline/8286

> Note: Events that placed greater administrative responsibility on the judiciary were coded as (+1), while those that reshuffled administrative control to other actors were coded as neutral (0).

Federal Judicial Experience –The average number of years of service of all Supreme Court justices on the federal bench, prior to being elevated to the Supreme Court. Source: Adapted from McGuire (2004).
Rules Length –Measured as the total length (in pages) of the *Rules of the Supreme Court of the United States*. Source: Adapted from McGuire (2004).

Table 9A.2 *Index component comparison summary (Truscott and Wilhelm, 2021; McGuire, 2004; Ura and Wohlfarth, 2010)*

Area	Component	Truscott and Wilhelm (2021)	McGuire (2004)	Ura and Wohlfarth (2010)
Years of Analysis		1796–2015	1796–1996	1973–2002
Monetary ($$)	Total Judiciary Budget	✓		
	Article III Judge Salaries	✓		
	Expenditures Per Justice		✓	✓
	SCOTUS Appropriations			✓
	Appropriations to AO			✓
Institutional	Docket Control (SCOTUS)	✓	✓	✓
	Jurisdiction Change Events	✓		
	Administration Change Events	✓		
	Law Clerks	✓	✓	
	Federal Judicial Experience (SCOTUS)	✓	✓	✓
	SCOTUS Rulebook Length	✓	✓	✓
	Authorized Article III Judgeships	✓		
	Authorized Article III Courts	✓		
	Circuit Riding (SCOTUS)		✓	
	Location of Supreme Court		✓	

10. Instrumentalization of constitutional law in Central Asia

Alexei Trochev and Alisher Juzgenbayev

INTRODUCTION

Constitutional law and politics in five Central Asian countries – Kazakhstan, Kyrgyzstan, Tajikistan, Turkmenistan, and Uzbekistan – have been a terra incognita in comparative constitutional studies. A few scholars have analyzed formal constitutional texts (see, e.g., Gönenç, 2002; Kachkeev, 2012a; Newton, 2017) and emphasized the lack of the rule of tradition and conservation of Soviet legacies as obstacles to democratization and constitutionalism in this part of the world. More recently, scholars have explored the interplay between formal and informal domination of authoritarian presidents as patrons-in-chief (Hale, 2015), who, in turn, build personalist (Stykow, 2019), neopatrimonial (Laruelle, 2012; Isaacs, 2014; Izquierdo-Brichs and Serra-Massansalvador, 2021) and globally connected kleptocratic (Cooley and Heathershaw, 2017; Magyar and Madlovics, 2020) regimes and govern through coercion, cooptation and corruption. However, we still know very little about constitution-making and constitution-breaking in these countries. Indeed, as Table 10.1 shows, Central Asia's "dictators without borders" (Cooley and Heathershaw, 2017) invest significant efforts in making and remaking constitutions and constitutional courts, even if constitutions and constitutional courts are solely meant to be façades for disguising their personalist regimes and barricades for preventing the judicialization of high-level politics.

Indeed, we know little about the degree of judicialization of politics in these countries. Scholars view judges in these countries as passive servants or "pawns" of the ruling regime (Mazmanyan, 2015), explore the institutional dependence of the judiciary on the patron-in-chief (Kachkeev, 2012b), and examine regime-sponsored violence against human rights activists (Hug, 2020; Hug, 2021a; Hug, 2021b), who could activate the judicialization of human rights disputes. Yet by examining the absence of judicialized politics in the context of the formal empowerment of constitutional courts in Central Asia, we can better understand how necessary conditions of the judicialization work. Moreover, as Table 10.2 shows, there is a lot of variation among Central Asian constitutional courts in terms of their willingness to strike down laws and regulations as unconstitutional. This shows that similar abuses of human rights, similar socioeconomic conditions, and similar neopatrimonial regimes, which arose from common Soviet pasts and legal cultures, may result in both passive and assertive constitutional courts. Moreover, by exploring the differing trajectories of judicialization of high-level politics in Kazakhstan and Kyrgyzstan – each having two constitutional review tribunals in the past 30 years – we can identify key factors which stymied and/or enabled the willingness of constitutional courts to have an autonomous say in national politics.

We argue that outcomes of judicialized politics depend on the nature of the process of judicialization and on the political salience of issues brought to constitutional courts. We focus on separation-of-powers disputes because they directly concern the distribution of political

Table 10.1 Constitutional amendments in post-Soviet Central Asia

	1991–1995	1995–2000	2000–2005	2005–2010	2010–2015	2015–2021
Kazakhstan	**1993** Constitution ratified; **1995** current presidentialist Constitution ratified after referendum	**1998** Presidential age limit eliminated; term increased to 7 years	–	**2007** "First president" status established, eliminating term limits; term reduced to 5 years	-	**2017** Parliament's power increased; "Security Council" established with Nazarbayev as its head
Kyrgyzstan	**1993** Constitution ratified; **1994** Bicameral parliament established; constitutional referendum procedure enacted	**1996** Presidential powers in appointment and dissolution expanded; **1998** Private property enshrined	**2001** Kyrgyz language established as state language, Russian as official, with guarantees to minority languages; **2003** President's term limits abolished	**2006** Two new drafts introduced; **2007** Constitutional Court suspended previous constitution and enacted the 1993 constitution; **2007** Presidentialist constitution ratified in the referendum	**2010** New semi-parliamentary constitution introduced with one-term limit for president	**2016** Supremacy of international agreements suspended; prime minister's power expanded; **2021** Presidentialist constitution adopted; constitutional court reorganized
Uzbekistan			**2003** Bicameral parliament established; presidential term increased		**2011** President's term limit reduced; prime minister's power expanded; **2014** Cabinet and parliament's power increased	**2017** Supreme Court and constitutional court reorganized; **2018** Local government reorganized; **2019** Parliament's assent required for members of the cabinet
Tajikistan						**2016** President's term limits abolished; minimum age for presidential candidates reduced to 30

Table 10.2 Proportion of "activist rulings" by constitutional tribunals in Central Asia

	Number of decisions that invalidate the legislative or executive provision	The proportion of decisions invalidating a legislative provision
Kazakhstan (2013–2019)	25	45%
Kyrgyzstan (1996–2019)	29	33%
Tajikistan (1996–2019)	7	16%
Uzbekistan (1995–2019)*	6	18%

Notes:
This includes only decisions in which the constitutionality of the provision was under question; the questions of constitutional interpretation are omitted from this summary due to difficulty in classifying these interpretations as "activist."
* The majority of decisions in which tribunals recommend amendments to the legislative bills before promulgation are not considered as invalidation.
Sources: Juzgenbayev, 2019a; Juzgenbayev, 2019b, Ismatov, 2020; Nazarova, 2021.

Table 10.3 Clientelist structure and appointment procedure of constitutional tribunals in Central Asian countries

Constitutional tribunal and its years of operation	Do competing patron–client pyramids exist?	Who nominates the judges of the constitutional tribunal?	Who confirms the nominations of the judges of the constitutional tribunal?	Do constitutional tribunals make "activist" rulings?
Kazakhstani Constitutional Court 1992–1995	Yes	President with Presidium of Parliament	Parliament	Yes
Kazakhstani Constitutional Council 1996–2021	No, since 2004	President: 2 members + chairperson; Upper Chamber of Parliament: 2 members; Lower Chamber of Parliament: 2 members	–	Yes, until 2004
Kyrgyzstani Constitutional Court 1995–2010	No	President	Parliament	No
Kyrgyzstani Constitutional Chamber 2013–2020	Yes	Council on Selection of Judges with President	Parliament	Yes
Tajikistani Constitutional Court 1996–2021	No, since 1998	President	Upper Chamber of Parliament	Yes, until 1998
Uzbekistani Constitutional Court 1996–2021	No	President	Upper Chamber of Parliament	No

power in the context of constitutions, which are written with and for specific persons in mind, and in the context of concrete relationships between judges and politicians. We argue that constitutional courts tend to be assertive when (1) they operate in the context of competing patron–client pyramids, and (2) patrons-in-chief do not unilaterally control appointments to the bench of these tribunals (Table 10.3).

Judges of newly created constitutional courts have agency – they make the decision rules for the newly created courts and shape the ways in which these courts choose to decide or not decide cases. This explains the initial short-term assertiveness of the Kazakhstani Constitutional Court

(KCCt) (1992–1995) and the Tajikistani Constitutional Court (1996–1997); and the sustained assertiveness of the Kyrgyzstani Constitutional Chamber (KyrCCh) of the Supreme Court (2013–2020). However, once presidents consolidated their personalist regimes, eliminated rival patron–client pyramids and gained full control over judicial appointments, constitutional courts lost their assertiveness and switched to offering services to the patrons-in-chief, like approving the constitutionality of constitutional amendments which presidents had sponsored, extending the incumbent's terms of office, and dismissing all cases which could threaten their patrons. In exchange for this instrumentalization of constitutional review, constitutional courts gained more powers, and their judges enjoyed higher salaries, perks, and generous retirement benefits, as well as memberships in prestigious international judicial organizations (see Table 10.4).

Table 10.4 *Engagement of the Central Asian constitutional courts in international legal community*

	Membership in the Association of Asian Constitutional Courts and equivalent institutions	Membership in the European Commission for Democracy through Law "Venice Commission"	Hosted meetings with the European Commission for Democracy through Law "Venice Commission"	Opinions of the European Commission for Democracy through Law "Venice Commission"
Kazakhstan	Yes, since 2013	Yes, since 2012	29	9
Kyrgyzstan	Yes, since 2015	Yes, since 2004	46	32
Tajikistan	Yes, since 2011	No	6	3
Turkmenistan	No	No	2	0
Uzbekistan	Yes, since 2010	No	8	3

As a result, the Kazakhstani Constitutional Council (KCCl) resembles an office of presidential administration; while its Tajikistani and Uzbekistani counterparts work more like redundant part-time interpreters of statutes and occasional enforcers of authoritarian rule by law. These judge-made roles indicate both variation and oscillation in the range between a "sidelined" court and a "regime ally" court (see Figure 10.1), to use the typology of constitutional courts which have low autonomy from political leaders (Brinks and Blass, 2017). This judge-made repertoire holds little prospect for the judicialization of politics in Central Asia outside Kyrgyzstan, a country in which the KyrCCh managed to cultivate a nascent support structure in the legal community beyond the confines of the president's patronal network.

To show variation in the mechanisms of instrumentalization of constitutional law and politics in Central Asia, we first distinguish it from the genuine judicialization of politics as a set of processes and relationships (Dressel et al., 2017) which enable or prevent the assertiveness of judges in deciding politically important cases. Next, we explore how six Central Asian constitutional courts handled separation-of-powers disputes. We conclude by summarizing several lessons learned from studying constitutional law and politics in authoritarian personalist patron–client regimes.

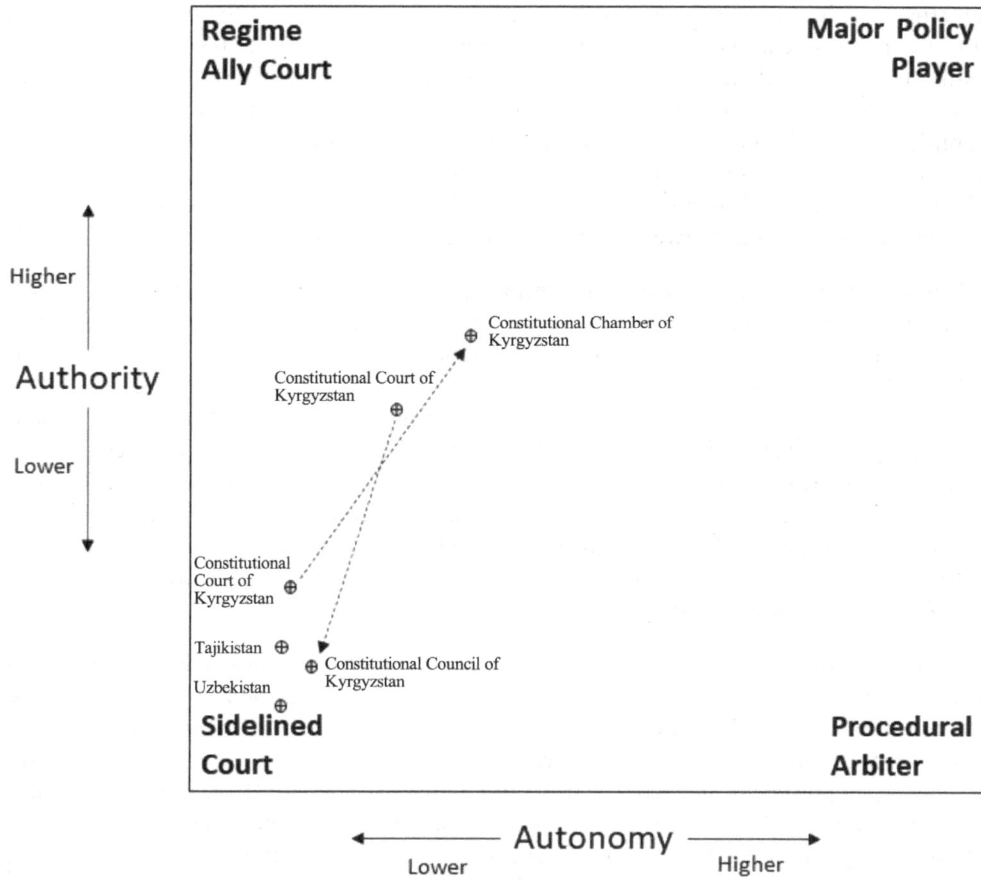

Figure 10.1 *Central Asian constitutional courts as "regime allies" and "sidelined" courts*

OUTCOMES OF JUDICIALIZED POLITICS

Scholars of comparative courts have come a long way since first discussing the descriptive and normative implications of judicialization of politics in Western liberal democracies (Tate and Vallinder, 1995; Hirschl, 2006), and, more recently, in fragile democracies as well as autocracies around the globe (see, e.g., Sieder et al., 2005; Ellett, 2013; Dressel, 2014). Mazmanyan (2015) applied the concept of judicialization to post-Soviet politics and argued that despite the formal empowerment of the high courts in the post-Soviet countries to rule on political issues of the day, these tribunals depend on politicians and act as mere pawns in the hands of the ruling regime. According to him, while many, if not most, of the high courts in the post-Soviet countries did rule on questions of utmost political importance, due to a constellation of factors, these tribunals were unable to truly become political actors that have an independent effect on policy outcomes. These high courts were "regime allies," in the words of Brinks and Blass (2017: 303) – courts which are closely tied to the rulers so that they endorse and promote the preferences of the rulers and serve as tools to impose and legitimize the particular vision of constitutional justice of whoever is in power (Brinks and Blass, 2017: 303).

Still, descriptive judicialization, as a concept, suffers from imprecision in that it is unclear as to *what counts* as the genuine judicialization of politics. How is the genuine judicialization of politics different from the instrumentalization of high courts by powerful executives? What does it precisely mean for judiciaries to be *involved* in politics? We seek to advance this line of inquiry and argue that there are three distinct observable *outcomes* of judicialized politics as the product of relations between politicians, judges and other actors (Dressel et al., 2017):

1. Delegation of formal authority to determine policy outcome on politically salient issues to formally independent tribunals, be they constitutional commissions, councils, or courts. Courts as "regime allies" have broader jurisdiction than the "sidelined" courts (Brinks and Blass 2017).
2. Expectations among the political actors that such issues can be resolved within these tribunals *qua* legal institutions and via the process of *legal reasoning*. Such expectations are stronger for "regime ally" courts than for "sidelined" courts (Brinks and Blass, 2017).
3. The ability of such tribunals to make independent determinations on policy outcomes of disputes on these politically salient issues. Neither "regime ally" courts nor "sidelined" courts have such ability, as both types of tribunals have low autonomy from dominant political actors (Brinks and Blass, 2017).

We recognize, first, that judicialization is a *process*; yet we are agnostic with respect to the causes and the precise conditions that, through the process of judicialization, give rise to the outcomes of judicialized politics. Judicialization may be a direct result of (1) the need for a third-party dispute resolver (Stone Sweet, 2000); (2) a conscious decision on the part of the ruler to empower an independent tribunal (Moustafa, 2003); (3) the attempts of judges themselves to expand their own power (judicialization from *within*; Steytler, 1993); or (4) a combination of these factors. Scholars have also identified conditions which indirectly may facilitate or stymie the judicialization of politics, such as political competition and electoral uncertainty (Ginsburg, 2003; Popova, 2012; Ramseyer, 1994); public opinion (Helmke, 2017; Staton, 2010); formal rules of autonomy and authority (Brinks and Blass, 2017); social support structures (Epp, 1998; Landau, 2018); and attitudes and norms held by judges and political actors (Hilbink, 2012). Regardless, if the process of genuine judicialization of politics is present, we argue that we should necessarily observe these three outcomes. Positioning outcomes of judicialization at the center of our inquiry allows us to more precisely describe the state and dynamics of constitutional law and politics in Central Asia and carefully test theories that best predict conditions that give rise to judicialized politics.

Second, we consider judicialization to be *issue-specific*. This is not to say that judicialization in one area of law does not affect or change actors' perceptions or judicial behavior in other areas of law, and scholars have found abundant evidence of the opposite (Moustafa, 2003). Focusing on *specific* issues matches nicely with the scholarly understanding of patron–client relationships, which are organized around the repeated personalized exchanges of *concrete* rewards and expectations (Hale, 2015) between patron-president and client-judges. Moreover, we focus on judicialization as being issue-specific because it may allow for a more fine-grained exploration of the issue areas in which judicialization has occurred and those in which it hasn't. If a "regime ally" type of constitutional court (Brinks and Blass, 2017) has been able to build a niche within which its decisions supplement (and even overrule) legislative and executive lawmaking, we need to explain why and how judges asserted their power (or how patrons allowed them to assert it) in some issue areas but not in others. For example, "regime ally" courts may exercise autonomy in deciding certain disputes between the central and local levels of government and contribute to genuine judicialization, while not exercising autonomy in handling disputes which concern the prerogatives of the patron-in-chief. In contrast, a "sidelined" constitutional review tribunal (Brinks and Blass, 2017) is unable to build a niche in which it can exercise autonomy and assert its power.

Third, the outcomes of this judicial assertiveness have to deal with *politically salient* issues. These are issues which have important effects on the distribution of the material, coercive, symbolic power of both rulers and a sizable segment of the population. For example, courts deal with politically salient issues when they examine constitutional amendments, allow impeachment of presidents, cancel election results, define religious and gender identity (or mega-politics, to use Hirschl's term), and rule on other core regime and societal interests. According to Svolik (2012), formal institutions like constitutional courts in autocracies may help to share power between the autocrat and the ruling elites by clarifying the procedures of power-sharing, delineating the scope of authority of each key office-holder and enabling the monitoring by the ruling elite of the autocrat's compliance with their promises. In this chapter, we focus on politically salient issues in which constitutional tribunals are supposed to be involved: conflicts over the distribution of political power. There are further distinct types of issues within this broad area, such as electoral politics and executive powers, and so on. Patrons-in-chief can benefit both from disallowing high courts from deciding certain political disputes and from inviting high courts to decide on politically salient issues and "notarize" decisions of the patrons-in-chief. Therefore, both "sidelined" courts and "regime ally" courts (Brinks and Blass, 2017) can decide politically salient issues, but these decisions always favor the core interests of the patrons-in-chief. In this sense, the courts are instrumentalized to preserve the power of the patron-in-chief through shifting expectations about the rigidity of constitutional text and shifting blame for unpopular decisions in the eyes of domestic and international audiences.

To explore the dynamics of the judicialization of politics in authoritarian patron–client regimes, we focus on the decisions of six constitutional tribunals in Kazakhstan, Kyrgyzstan, Tajikistan and Uzbekistan (Turkmenistan did not create a constitutional review tribunal) in the past three decades (see Table 10.5). We demonstrate distinct mechanisms and relationships that drive or prevent judicialization in separation-of-powers disputes in Central Asia. This allows us to shed light on judicial politics in authoritarian clientelist regimes – an understudied topic in the studies of comparative courts.

CENTRAL ASIAN CONSTITUTIONAL TRIBUNALS AND MEGA-POLITICS: INSTRUMENTALIZATION INSTEAD OF GENUINE JUDICIALIZATION

When constitutional courts allocate political power, they do so in distinct ways. These tribunals can directly expand or shrink the powers of branches of government and other state agencies by engaging in constitutional interpretation; they can determine electoral outcomes by declaring the election winner or by striking down certain restrictions on the activities of political parties and political leaders; or they can decide on the constitutionality of referenda

Table 10.5 *Design and period of operation of the constitutional tribunals in Central Asia, 1991–2021*

	Established in constitution	Law on CC adopted	Start – End of CC's operation	Number of CC members	Term limits of CC members	Is dissenting opinion published?	Constitutional complaint
Kazakhstan Constitutional Court	Dec-91	Jun-92	Jul-92 – Oct-95	11	10 years	Yes	Yes
Kazakhstan Constitutional Council	Aug-95	Dec-95	Feb-96 – present	7	6 years	No	No
Kyrgyzstan Constitutional Court	Dec-90	Dec-93	Sep-95 – Apr-10	9	15 years	No	No, since 2003
Kyrgyzstan Constitutional Chamber	Jun-10	Jun-11	Sep-13 – present	11	7 years	Yes	Yes
Tajikistan Constitutional Court	Nov-94	Nov-95 Jul-14	Jan-96 – present	7	5 years; since 2003, 10 years	Yes	Yes, since Mar-08
Uzbekistan Constitutional Court	Dec-92	Aug-95 May-17 Apr-21	Jan-96 – present	7	5 years	No	Yes, since Apr-21

and constitutional amendments. Yet the 1993 constitutional crisis in Russia, in which President Yeltsin shelved the opposition-dominated Parliament and nearly abolished the Constitutional Court for allowing his impeachment, sent a clear signal to Central Asian presidents and potential and actual constitutional court judges that presidents can seriously punish (with impunity) recalcitrant judges for meddling in high-level political disputes. However strong this warning signal was, we still observe differing trajectories of instrumentalization of constitutional review mechanisms instead of judicialization of high politics in Central Asia. Both in Kazakhstan in the 1990s and in Kyrgyzstan, politicians tried to use constitutional courts to win their heavyweight political disputes, and the constitutional tribunals often ruled on such issues; even though, on questions of utmost political significance to the executive, the tribunals failed to have an independent effect on political outcomes. We thus observe how patronal presidents instrumentalized constitutional courts instead of allowing genuine judicialization of high-level politics and instead of cultivating authoritarian constitutionalism (García and Frankenberg, 2019). In contrast, in Uzbekistan and Tajikistan post-1997, constitutional courts were not allowed to distribute political power on their own. Instead, these tribunals marginally assisted patrons-in-chief in enshrining their patronal status, recommending legislative changes and inching toward the rule by law.

CONSTITUTIONAL REVIEW IN KAZAKHSTAN: TOWARD GREATER INSTRUMENTALIZATION

Instrumentalization of constitutional review in Kazakhstan has significantly grown from what it was in the early 1990s because the ruling regime devoured its own "pawn," the constitutional court, and transformed it from a "regime ally" tribunal to a "sidelined" quasi-judicial Constitutional Council. Kazakhstan's first constitutional review tribunal, the 11-member KCCt, was elected for a ten-year-term in July 1992 under the heavily amended Soviet-era constitution and in the context of competing patron–client networks and formal parliamentary supremacy. This tribunal consisted of law professors and government lawyers and was modelled on the First Russian Constitutional Court (Trochev, 2008). But at that time, as in Russia, politicians at all levels in Kazakhstan had no idea what to do with decisions of the constitutional court. As in Russia, the KCCt was led by a legal philosopher, chairman Murat Baimakhanov. He saw the court's mission as educating both politicians and ordinary people about the supremacy of the Constitution. Shortly after election, he together with two other judges spent several weeks at the Russian Constitutional Court, learning from members of the seven-month-old tribunal and its activist chairman Valerii Zorkin, as well as attending public hearings in the famous case of Boris Yeltsin's ban of the Communist Party (Udartsev, 2003). Having returned from Moscow, chairman Baimakhanov announced to his colleagues that they had to be critical thinkers and to protect the Constitution from abuses by government officials (Udartsev, 2003). Indeed, in the three years of its short life, his court issued a total of 15 decisions on the merits, thus averaging five decisions per year. To the displeasure of top politicians, in the 15 decisions on the merits, his court declared unconstitutional statutes, decrees of President Nazarbayev (something unimaginable in today's Kazakhstan), and Cabinet edicts, on top of uncovering various secret legal acts, including one secret constitutional amendment (Baishev, 1994; Udartsev, 2003). As a result of this rapid judicial assertiveness, at the end of 1992, the drafters of the new post-Soviet constitution tried to abolish the KCCt by merging it with the Supreme Court. They were inspired by the model of the US Supreme Court, the model that was advocated by Boris Yeltsin's legal advisors for Russia at the time. Chairman Baimakhanov managed to mobilize the mass media and a broad pro-KCCt coalition in the Parliament, which, in January 1993 preserved both the tribunal in the 1993 constitution and its sitting judges on its bench. According to one journalist, the "fate of the Constitutional Court was able to consolidate society" (Udartsev, 2003). The KCCt was preserved as a compromise between a strong parliament and a strong president. Article 131 of the 1993 constitution codified this compromise. It granted the president and the parliament speaker a unilateral power to veto the KCCt's decision, but it also enabled the court to overrule this "veto" by two-thirds majority, or by a vote of eight (out of 11) judges.

The KCCt used this power in March 1995 in its most famous case, the *Kvyatkovskaya* decision. The Court issued this decision at the request of a journalist, Tatyana Kvyatkovskaya, who had run in the 1994 parliamentary elections and lost to the deputy mayor of the capital city by a very slim margin. She and other election-losers sued local election commissions but to no avail. Her lawyers then asked the KCCt to overturn the election procedures in her district, which were set by the Central Election Commission, and subsequently asked the court to cancel nationwide election results as outcomes of unconstitutional election procedures. After a year of hearings and deliberations, in March 1995, the Constitutional Court agreed with Kvyatkovskaya's arguments. The KCCt judges boldly blamed the Central Election

Commission for gerrymandering, violating the constitutional principle of "one person – one vote" in several electoral districts and violating the rights of electoral candidates; announced that these violations were massive, systemic and "programmed" throughout the country; and declared the elected parliament as unconstitutional (Kazakhstani Constitutional Court decision of March 6, 1995). Both President Nazarbayev, who had been frustrated with parliamentary opposition and faced threats of parliamentary investigations, and enraged Parliamentary Speaker Kekilbayev vetoed this decision, but the KCCt overruled their vetoes. Western election observers also identified massive electoral irregularities and applauded the KCCt's surprising assertiveness. The US Ambassador to Kazakhstan, William Courtney, declared that this unexpected decision was "a democratic victory," that all Kazakhstani citizens could be proud of this lesson in democracy, and that the USA had "a reason to be proud of Kazakhstan" (Laumulin, 2000; Amandykova and Malinovskyi, 2012). The Organization for Security and Cooperation in Europe (OSCE) Office for Democratic Institutions and Human Rights, a European election observation mission, awarded the KCCt a medal "For Courage" in June 1995 (Amandykova and Malinovskyi, 2012).

Indeed, this judge-ordered cancellation of the vote was the first in post-Soviet politics, several years prior to the colored revolutions in Georgia, Ukraine, and Kyrgyzstan – mass street protests over fraudulent election results which had been annulled by the supreme courts in these three countries (Trochev, 2013). Indeed, Toktogazieva (2019: 201) argued that by annulling the entirety of the election results, the KCCt grabbed the power to annul nationwide election results beyond those set for the tribunal in the constitution and beyond redressing harm shown by the complaint. What looked like a genuine judicialization of high-level politics turned out to be an instrumentalization of constitutional law. Independent election observers – both Western and domestic – have not recognized a single election in Kazakhstan as "free and fair" since then.

President Nazarbayev, having received an additional clarification from the court about the legal effects of the cancellation of the vote results (Kazakhstani Constitutional Court decision of March 11, 1995), quickly dissolved the Parliament in March 1995 and regained his power – granted by the previous Parliament – to adopt law-making decrees. He also quickly approved the proposal – coming from his hand-picked and extra-constitutional Assembly of Peoples of Kazakhstan (created five days before the KCCt decision) – "to hold a nationwide referendum at the end of April 1995 to extend his presidential powers until 2000 and do without presidential elections in 1995" (Laumulin, 2000), and authorized the drafting of the new constitution, to be ratified by another referendum scheduled for the end of summer of 1995. The enraged MPs suspended the activities of the KCCt, and some MPs accused its judges of colluding with the president. The MPs had a point, because the justice minister on several occasions publicly accused Chairman Baimukhanov of being dependent on the executive and having informal meetings with Nazarbayev's legal advisors (Shaikenova, 2002). When MPs refused to exit the building of the Parliament, Nazarbayev suspended the supply of water, power, and telephone to the parliament building. To his credit, he learned not to use tanks, like Boris Yeltsin did in his confrontation with the opposition-dominated parliament in Moscow in 1993 (Trochev, 2008). Nazarbayev also scolded those MPs who had accused the KCCt of facilitating the transition to the dictatorship and promised to keep the court in the new draft constitution.

But, to the surprise of KCCt justices who had published a letter critiquing the draft of the constitution, Nazarbayev's draft presented for the approval of voters in August 1995 did not keep their court. Instead, it established a French-style, seven-member Constitutional

Council, not a part of the judiciary, with limited powers and less insulation yet with the president's power of veto of its decisions. Over 89% of voters approved both the extension of Nazarbayev's term in office until 1999 and his super-presidential constitution (Nurumov and Vashchanka, 2016: 156), as a result of which the KCCt was liquidated, and Nazarbayev laid off its judges in October 1995. Four of them served terms of different lengths on the bench of the KCCl between 1996 and 2021, while others retained important positions and yet others returned to teaching in the law schools (Juzgenbayev, 2019b).

Under the 1995 constitution, the KCCl consists of seven members: two members were appointed by each of the president, the senate (upper-chamber) chair, and the Majilis (lower-chamber) chair. The president appoints the chairman of the KCCl unilaterally, and interestingly, Nazarbayev has not appointed law professors to this position any longer (Juzgenbayev, 2019b). He seemed to prefer appointing his loyal clients from the executive branch on the bench. Though the KCCl was no longer a court, it still retained authority to review the constitutionality of legal acts before their promulgation by the president and draft international agreements; to offer interpretations of the constitution; and, on referrals of the courts, to review legal acts for their compliance with the constitutionally protected human rights guarantees (Article 72 of the 1995 constitution). Importantly, neither individuals nor individual MPs had standing before the KCCl, and the Council lacked the power to open cases on its own initiative.

Yet the KCCl did not become the president's "personal bureau" until Nazarbayev's complete takeover of parliament in 2004. It showed some autonomy when adjudicating disputes between the executive and the still vocal parliament between 1996 and 2003, when Nazarbayev's regime was not fully consolidated, and when parliament speakers had open political ambitions. The KCCl decided that the prime minister lacked the power to request a confidence vote in parliament to pass a law on more than one bill (Kazakhstani Constitutional Council decision of 12 March 1999), and that the cabinet lacked the power to denounce any international agreements because the constitution allocated this power only to the legislature (Kazakhstani Constitutional Council decision of 26 December 2000). At the same time, the KCCl also ruled in favor of the executive, by stating that any bill proposed by MPs that would require an increase or decrease in budgetary spending needed to be approved by the cabinet before it could be placed on the legislative agenda (Kazakhstani Constitutional Council decision of 28 June 1997). It sought some, albeit imperfect, balance between the policy goals of the executive and the calls for accountability and power-sharing coming from important factions in the legislature (see Table 10.6).

Table 10.6 Separation-of-power cases in the Kazakhstani Constitutional Council, by petitioner, 1996–2019

	Number of referrals (1996–2004)	Number of interpretations favorable to petitioner/legislation declared unconstitutional (1996–2004)	Number of referrals (2005–2019)	Number of interpretations favorable to petitioner/legislation declared unconstitutional (2005–2019)
Legislature	18	5	6	4
Prime Minister	10	8	5	3
President	9	6	2	0

Source: Juzgenbayev, 2019b.

In the early 2000s, in the crucial period of the move away from democracy, and the growing elite awareness that the president might back away from sharing power, the KCCl permitted Nazarbayev to run for a third term in the presidential election (Kazakhstani Constitutional Council decision of 20 June 2000). It found that the "term limits did not apply to the person who was elected in accordance with the Constitution of 1995." As we show below, both Kyrgyzstani and Tajikistani constitutional courts did the same. In November 2001, the level of political uncertainty increased when several members of the elite who had been disgruntled with the president's policies publicly announced the creation of the "Democratic Choice of Kazakhstan," an organized movement that questioned the foundations of Nazarbayev's rule (Junisbai, 2010; Junisbai and Junisbai, 2005). Nazarbayev's ruling party expelled one of the opposition leaders from its ranks, and the KCCl decided that the expulsion constituted grounds for him no longer being a member of parliament (Kazakhstani Constitutional Council decision of 17 May 2001). Even though this decision conflicted with the Council's own precedent (Kazakhstani Constitutional Council decision of 23 May 1997) and was sharply criticized in the media and in the legal community, it showed the KCCl's use of constitutional law as a weapon against any client who betrayed the patron-in-chief.

However, after the consolidation of Nazarbayev's rule in the second half of the 2000s, the KCCl's adjudicative function became less important (see Table 10.6). On average, the Council issued 3.2 decisions per year. The Council became slightly more active in 2018 when Nazarbayev – by that time with the constitutionally enshrined status of "Father of the Nation" – used it to get a constitutional stamp of approval for his carefully orchestrated resignation in March 2019 and the transfer of some of his authority to his successor, a former diplomat and a former prime minister, Kassym-Zhomart Tokayev (Caron, 2020). After his resignation from the presidency, Nazarbayev retained a seat on the KCCl and even participated, in January 2020, in one hearing on the constitutionality of the eviction of multi-child households from state-provided housing. That hearing did not involve any dispute but demonstrated that the KCCl and Nazarbayev had strong ties and highlighted Nazarbayev's care for the housing of large families as a true Father of the Nation. The KCCl declared the eviction procedure unconstitutional (Kazakhstani Constitutional Council decision of 21 January 2020). As of June 2021, this decision has not been implemented. In the first two years of Tokayev's presidency, the KCCl upheld Tokayev's initiative for joining the Optional Protocol II to the International Covenant for Civil and Political Rights, which allowed Kazakhstan to join the abolition of the death penalty without actually deleting capital punishment from the constitutional text (Kazakhstani Constitutional Council decision of 15 December 2020). And, to the displeasure of most elite attorneys, the KCCl also declared constitutional the law on the bar, which subordinated attorneys to the Justice Ministry, led by a member of Nazarbayev's clan (Kazakhstani Constitutional Council decision of 4 June 2021). In short, for over a decade, the KCCl has been the president's legal assistant, notarizing significant constitutional changes; or a sidelined court that is much more irrelevant to politics than its predecessor, the KCCt.

KYRGYZSTAN'S CONSTITUTIONAL REVIEW: ASSERTING POWER AND LIMITING INSTRUMENTALIZATION

Among Central Asian states, Kyrgyzstan's constitutional politics have been unusual. The country's first president, Askar Akayev, branded his regime as an "island of democracy" and the "Switzerland of Central Asia" in the early 1990s (Anderson, 1999). Yet the country went through several overhauls of constitutional order and several overthrown presidents, including Akayev, in the context of semi-competitive – thanks to the recalcitrant parliament – politics, in which the Kyrgyzstani Constitutional Court (KyrCCt) played a highly visible role as an ally of the ruling regimes until its abolition in 2010. The nine-member KyrCCt was led by a charismatic chairman, Cholpon Baekova, a member of Akayev's clan and a former procurator-general, who was respected by international experts for her pro-democracy views (Collins, 2006: 229). Baekova's court began functioning in September 1995, even though it had been created in 1990; its enabling legislation was adopted only in May 1993 together with the adoption of the constitution. The legislative–presidential standoffs in Kyrgyzstan, including the forced "self-dissolution" of parliament in 1994 by pro-Akayev MPs (Cummings, 2012: 60–76) and repeated parliamentary rejections of Baekova's nomination (Collins, 2006: 229), delayed the activation of the constitutional court.

However, having learned from Boris Yeltsin's suspension of the Russian Constitutional Court – revenge for giving the green light to his (unsuccessful) impeachment in the fall of 1993 – the KyrCCt displayed extreme loyalty to President Akayev, who, in turn, redesigned constitutions and attempted to shape constitutional decision-making through separation-of-powers cases – both to enhance his ruling status. Right before his re-election in December 1995, Akayev had decided to enhance his unilateral presidential powers via constitutional referendum. As he could not do so through the recalcitrant parliament, he asked the recently activated KyrCCt for an advisory opinion. In November 1995, the KyrCCt granted Akayev's wishes and declared them constitutional (Kyrgyzstani Constitutional Court decision of November 9, 1995) without offering any analysis of the proposed expansion of presidential prerogatives (Toktogazieva, 2019: 210–211). In December 1995, the KyrCCt both approved Akayev's changes to the referendum process (Collins, 2006: 230) and certified the electoral victory of Akayev, who had received 72% of the vote in the pre-term elections, for another five-year term, and declared that his first term in office had begun in October 1991 (Kyrgyzstani Constitutional Court decision of December 28, 1995). In July 1998, the KyrCCt overruled this declaration and declared that Akayev's first term in office had begun in December 1995 because his prior term had started before the introduction of the 1993 constitution and, therefore, did not count (Kyrgyzstani Constitutional Court decision of July 13, 1998). The court issued this decision at the request of anti-Akayev MPs, who had feared that he would run for a third term in 2000, contrary to Article 43 of the constitution, which set a two-term limit for the holder of the president's office. Akayev's opponents ridiculed this KyrCCt decision as a sign of the blatant subservience of the tribunal. Indeed, "from 1995 through 1998, the Court issued twenty-four rulings that served primarily to approve executive decrees" (Collins, 2006: 230).

Akayev did run for a third term and won the 2000 elections, which Western election observers declared unfree and unfair, with 74% of the vote. During his re-election campaign, Akayev created a Kyrgyz language exam for presidential candidates in order to target his main opponent, who had weak Kyrgyz, and the KyrCCt nixed the challenge from opposition MPs against the constitutionality of this language exam. Until the fall of 2004, the KyrCCt continued to display extreme loyalty to an increasingly unpopular – at home and abroad – Akayev while gaining power to overrule the decisions of other high courts. In September 2004, when Kurmanbek Bakiev, Akayev's former prime minister, formed the People's Movement of Kyrgyzstan, a loose opposition network (Hale, 2015: 197), a group of anti-Akayev MPs asked the court to declare whether he had the right to run in the 2005 elections. This time, Baekova's court nixed their lawsuit. The KyrCCt argued that this issue was being considered in the parliament at the time, and, therefore, could not be the subject of constitutional review (Toktogazieva, 2019: 217). Shortly after that, the US ambassador announced that Akayev should not run again in 2005.

The nationwide protests over the two rounds of rigged parliamentary elections in February and March 2005, in which the party led by Akayev's daughter seemed to have won, and the cascading defections from Akayev's inner circle led to the "Tulip Revolution," his ouster from the office and his escape to Moscow. At this tense moment the Supreme Court canceled the results of the vote (Trochev, 2013), while the KyrCCt chairwoman, Baekova, claimed that her tribunal was the only constitutional organ. She formalized the peaceful transfer of power by the outgoing parliament to the acting president and prime minister Bakiev, who won elections in July 2005 with 89% of the vote. A series of compromises in 2005 and 2006 – prepared with Baekova's assistance – resulted in constitutional changes that decreased the power of President Bakiev, who has been increasingly governing through cooptation and intimidation of his opponents (Huskey and Iskakova, 2010). Baekova's court, however, in September 2007, at the request of pro-Bakiev MPs, declared the entire text of these compromises null and reverted the constitution back to the super-presidentialist constitution of 2003, which had been written for Akayev (Toktogazieva, 2019: 225), and which Bakiev wanted to restore (Kyrgyzstani Constitutional Court decision of September 14, 2007). The Venice Commission announced that it was "highly unusual, if not unprecedented" to declare the full text of a constitution in force unconstitutional. The parliament rebelled, voted no confidence in the KyrCCt, removed three judges from its bench and accused the court of a de facto coup d'état. Baekova complained to Bakiev about this political interference in the operation of her court. Bakiev dissolved the recalcitrant parliament in October 2007, accusing it of causing a crisis in relations with the KyrCCt and scheduled new elections in December 2007. Baekova quit the bench, won a parliamentary seat on the ticket of Bakiev's party in the fraudulent 2007 parliamentary elections, and became the vice-speaker of the parliament, as Bakiev wanted to strengthen his hold on the parliament. He won the rigged elections in 2009 and used the KyrCCt to approve yet another round of constitutional amendments, which would regulate the transfer of power to his successor, probably his son, by his hand-picked assembly, bypassing the parliament. In January 2010, the KyrCCt again granted his wish and declared Bakiev's constitutional amendments constitutional (Toktogazieva, 2019: 227–229). This was the last decision of the KyrCCt (Kyrgyzstani Constitutional Court decision of January 21, 2010) because in April 2010, street protesters stormed government buildings and forced Bakiev to flee to Belarus, and the interim government dissolved the KyrCCt on April 12, 2010, for helping to concentrate power in the same hands, under both Akayev and Bakiev, and for leading to the violent ouster of the "anti-people regime of Bakiev" (Toktogazieva, 2019: 231). In short, the KyrCCt has been a clear "regime ally" that imposed one autocratic constitutional vision, first of Akayev and then of Bakiev (Dzhurayev et al., 2015: 272).

The April Revolution of 2010 brought about a new constitution of Kyrgyzstan, which 92% of voters approved in the referendum in June 2010. The 2010 constitution set a ten-year moratorium on constitutional changes in order to prevent presidential election-winners from changing constitutional texts as they saw fit. It placed the president firmly in the executive branch and not above all three branches of government, as previous constitutions had done. It created a semi-parliamentary system with a strong 120-member parliament, in which no party could have more than 65 seats and the opposition would control two key parliamentary committees, and which would select a prime minister in charge of a relatively autonomous cabinet, which, in turn, would be a product of a coalition of parties represented in parliament. It also created an 11-member Constitutional Chamber of the Supreme Court (KyrCCh), a tribunal with broad *a priori* and *a posteriori*, abstract and concrete constitutional review powers, except the power to review election results. Importantly, the 2010 constitution introduced an open selection process for the KyrCCh judgeships, a process that limited the domination of a single patron in forming the Chamber. The president nominates the KyrCCh judges for approval by the parliament from a list of nominees drawn up by the separate Judicial Selection Council, a nine-member body elected by the parliament with no formal input from the president. The parliamentary majority, the parliamentary opposition and the Council of Judges would each select three candidates for the Judicial Selection Council. As a result of a highly competitive selection process, the parliament managed to elect the first two judges, a law professor and a private attorney, for life to the bench of the KyrCCh in 2011. And then, in the summer of 2013, the parliament elected seven more KyrCCh judges, all of them being former procurators, judges and government lawyers, for a once-renewable seven-year term.

The KyrCCh issued its first decision in September 2013. In its first two years of operations, the KyrCCh issued 50 decisions (Dzhurayev et al., 2015), averaging 25 a year, a number which is several times greater than the rest of the constitutional courts covered in this chapter. In January 2014, amid a lively public debate and President Atambayev's highly advertised campaign against high-level corruption, the KyrCCh – at the request of a judge who had been charged with bribery – declared that the Procurator-General's office (led by the parliament's appointee) could not delegate the investigation of such cases to other relevant institutions, such as the State Committee for National Security (led by the president's appointee), Atambayev's right hand in his anti-corruption campaign (Kyrgyzstani Constitutional Chamber decision of January 13, 2014). The majority opinion interpreted the vague separation-of-powers principle and reasoned that according to Article 104 of the constitution, the special role, status and competence of the procuracy were necessary for its independence during the criminal investigation and prosecution, and no other law enforcement agency had the same independent status. The lone dissenting judge, Mamyrov, argued that the KyrCCh should have both declared the delegation of investigative powers constitutional and ordered the parliament to clarify the criteria of exceptionality of cases in which such delegation was permitted. The practical effect of this decision was that all anti-corruption investigations had to be transferred to the procuracy. President Atambayev and his supporters in parliament and in the cabinet slammed the KyrCCh's decision for creating chaos in combating corruption and punishing senior officials of the *ancien* regime, and the Chamber caved in to this criticism. Having endured two weeks of Atambayev's condemnations of its "shortcomings," the KyrCCh issued a "clarification," in which it declared that its decision did not have retroactive effect, which meant that all ongoing investigations of high-level corruption by the National Security Committee could continue (Dzhurayev et al., 2015). In response, an emboldened Atambayev continued to criticize the KyrCCh, had one of his outspoken critics expelled from the bench and another one reprimanded in May 2015 (Putz, 2015); managed to have the loyal judge, Mamyrov, elected by his peers to chair the KyrCCh in July 2016; and used his supporters in parliament to introduce a set of numerous constitutional amendments in September 2016 and to request the approval of these amendments in the KyrCCh. One of these amendments concerned Article 104 of the constitution. It excluded criminal investigations of government officials from the purview of the procuracy, which, in effect, overrode the January 2014 KyrCCh decision analyzed above. This time the Chamber approved – by a majority opinion – all constitutional amendments, which reminded many observers of the approach taken by the KyrCCh under previous presidents (Toktogazieva, 2019: 238). The lone dissenting judge, Oskonbayev, who had been reprimanded in 2015, argued that the 2010 constitution had a ten-year moratorium on constitutional amendments, and, therefore, the introduction of these amendments in 2016 violated this moratorium and was unconstitutional (Kyrgyzstani Constitutional Chamber decision of October 11, 2016).

This turnaround of the KyrCCh was a sign that the president had tamed the constitutional review tribunal (Toktogazieva, 2019), while the opposition called Atambayev's successful constitutional referendum an attempt to usurp power. In the wake of the referendum, Atambayev often used law and courts to punish his opponents. He did not run for office again in the highly contested 2017 presidential elections. Instead, Atambayev openly promoted his prime minister, Jeenbekov, hoping that he would still be able to govern behind the scenes. Jeenbekov won with 55% of the vote, which Western election observers generally described as fair. President Jeenbekov successfully used his formal powers to consolidate the patronal network around him, fired Atambayev's appointees, launched his own anti-corruption campaign targeting them, and ultimately authorized the criminal investigation of his anointer. In the fall of 2018, a well-known human rights activist asked the KyrCCh to declare unconstitutional – as violating both the constitutional principle of equality of all before the law and court and the principle of imminence of punishment for crimes – the provisions of the 2003 Law on the Guarantees of President, adopted to protect the first president, Akayev, which guaranteed blanket immunity for former presidents. The KyrCCh agreed that the contested provision of blanket immunity was unconstitutional. The Chamber ruled that this immunity had to be limited and that the procedure for lifting the immunity of ex-presidents had to be legislated. The Chamber also boldly ordered the parliament to design this procedure, which had to be similar to the one lifting the immunity for incumbent presidents (Kyrgyzstani Constitutional Chamber decision of October 3, 2018). Some MPs criticized this boldness as abuse of the Chamber's power, forcing the KyrCCh to issue two press releases with a plea to the parliament to respect constitutional procedures. In essence, the Chamber succeeded in compelling the parliament to handle the fight between Jeenbekov and Atambayev according to its orders (Toktogazieva, 2019: 123). In May 2019, the parliament enacted the required amendments for lifting the immunity of former presidents by copying Russia's model. But the parliament included a clause – applied retroactively starting from 2007 – that immunities and guarantees for former presidents who continue their involvement in politics or return to government service would be waived. This clause clearly targeted Atambayev, who had remained as leader of his political party (Huskey, 2019). In June 2019, the parliament applied this clause retroactively to Atambayev and declared that he had lost his status as former president. Around the same time, parliament elected a new judge, Karybek Duysheev, to the KyrCCh. He was then quickly elected by the Chamber's judges to be its new chairperson, replacing the previous chair, Judge Mamyrov, whose term had expired. Duysheev was thought to be well connected to President Jeenbekov because the former had previously served as an advisor to the president's brother and a former speaker of the parliament (Juzgenbayev, 2019d). Atambayev's supporters complained to the KyrCCh that the waiver of the immunity clause and its retroactive effect as well as the actual lifting of his immunity violated the constitution. He refused to be interrogated in the criminal case of corruption and usurpation of power against him, triggering a bloody raid by special forces and his eventual arrest (Juzgenbayev, 2019c). The Chamber disagreed with Atambayev's arguments and sided with Jeenbekov's lawyers and the parliament (Kyrgyzstani Constitutional Chamber decision of October 24, 2019). In a unanimous decision, the KyrCCh declared almost all changes to the 2003 law constitutional. The Chamber repeated that immunity for former presidents was not absolute, that the waiver of immunity was a proportional measure to protect national security and public order, and that the argument about retroactive effect was moot because the waiver did not impose any new duty or aggravated responsibility on the former president. But the KyrCCh declared unconstitutional the unilateral power of the incumbent president to remove all guarantees and protections of the former president, because the constitution did not establish this power. In effect, the Chamber allowed the arrest of Atambayev and his criminal prosecution to proceed (Juzgenbayev, 2019d), the outcome desired by President Jeenbekov.

In short, the KyrCCh continued to play the role of a "regime ally" court, similar to its predecessor, imposing the constitutional vision first of President Atambayev and then of President Jeenbekov. President Zhaparov, who came to power as a result of Jeenbekov's ouster, had his own version of the constitution (or *Khanstitution* as Zhaparov's opposition called it, in reference to the *khans* who had ruled Central Asia prior to Russia's conquest (Putz 2020)) approved in the April 2021 referendum. This constitution established a standalone constitutional court staffed through the procedure dominated by the president. Therefore, in line with our argument, the new tribunal is not likely to become assertive when the patron-in-chief strengthens his grip over judicial appointments.

TAJIKISTAN'S CONSTITUTIONAL COURT: STRONG ON PAPER, SIDELINED IN PRACTICE

The lack of judicialized high-level politics in Tajikistan may appear puzzling because this country had numerous conditions which are often cited as facilitating the judicialization of conflicts over the distribution of power. The November 1994 constitution that established a constitutional court was adopted in the context of political uncertainty: highly contested presidential elections in which the winner got 60% of the vote amid a bloody civil war. First, justices of the constitutional court were appointed at the end of 1995, and the court heard its first case in March 1996, a year after parliamentary elections in which the president's party won a mere five seats. The justices did not have to begin their work from scratch. They could draw on the jurisprudence of the Constitutional Supervision Committee, a quasi-judicial body established in 1990 and led by an activist law professor, who, in turn, advocated for the establishment of a full-blown constitutional court (Imomov, 1992). Moreover, until 2014, the justices of the constitutional court could initiate judicial review themselves. The five-year-long civil war – the bloodiest conflict in the post-Soviet space – ended in 1997 with a UN-brokered power-sharing agreement. This would also invite peaceful and possibly judge-made clarification of its terms. The government's top priority was to build and maintain peace, and the constitutional court could contribute to maintaining social peace. Moreover, Tajikistan is divided along regional, religious, ethnic, and linguistic lines (Heathershaw, 2009; Thibault, 2018), which is believed to be a judicialization-friendly context. Finally, the ruling patronal network led by President Emomali Rakhmon since 1994 is considered to be weaker than that of President Nazarbayev in Kazakhstan, even though both individuals carry the constitutionally protected title of "Leader of the Nation." Indeed, between 2008 and 2018, the ruling regime faced several serious challenges: military confrontation in the city of Khorog on the border with Afghanistan in 2012; the announcement of the creation of a new political party by a former minister of industry and a member of the president's patronal network in 2013; the defection of the commander of the elite police forces to ISIS in 2015; and violence against opposition leaders and the suppression of the Islamic Renaissance Party of Tajikistan – the only officially registered Islamic political party in post-Soviet countries – in the 2015 parliamentary election campaign.

However, the Tajikistan Constitutional Court has been inactive in terms of defining the separation of powers, a principle established in Article 9 of the 1994 constitution. The court only issued four decisions – all declaring the contested laws unconstitutional – between 1996 and 1997, a period when a peace agreement had yet to be implemented, the strong presidential powers had yet to be established in the constitution, and the recently elected president had yet to build his personalist patronal regime (Nazarova, 2021). Still, this limited output of the court outraged the Majlisi Oli (parliament). The parliament was especially upset at one particular constitutional court case in 1997 challenging provisions of the Constitutional Law on the Majlisi Oli, which allowed for the chairman of the Majlisi Oli to be removed from office by a super-majority of two-thirds of the members, as opposed to the simple majority specified in the constitution. The constitutional court ruled that the contested law had to be amended to comply with the constitution (American Bar Association, 2008: 27). But in December 1997, the parliament, using its power to interpret the constitution, voided this and another decision of the constitutional court in which the court invalidated provisions of two constitutional laws (Nazarova, 2021). President Rakhmon did nothing to defend the court and restrain the parliament. He benefited from this judicial–legislative rivalry, which, according to the former chairman of the Constitutional Supervision Committee (Imomov, 1998), created fertile ground for concentrating power in his hands and building a personalist authoritarian regime. Indeed, neither President Rakhmon nor the cabinet filed cases with the constitutional court, which, in turn, did not decide a single case in 1998–2000, 2002, or 2003. All in all, between 1996 and 2018, the Tajikistan Constitutional Court issued 53 decisions on the merits, averaging 2.3 decisions per year. Between 2008 and 2018, the tribunal dealt with only five cases raising separation-of-powers issues; and in only one of these cases did it declare the contested legal act – a directive of the Ministry of Transport – unconstitutional.

Yet the Tajikistan Constitutional Court played a role like that played by the KyrCCt and the KCCl. It legitimized constitutional amendments which enhanced the ruling status of presidents. In June 2014, the Tajikistani parliament adopted a new Law on the Constitutional Court, which justices helped to draft. The Venice Commission, in its opinion of June 13–14, 2014 on this draft law, noted, "it is a coherent text, which will provide a firm basis for an effective work of the Constitutional Court" (Nazarova, 2021). Among other things, this law extended the tenure of judges to ten years and granted the court new powers to review the constitutionality of draft laws and draft constitutional amendments, which are supposed to be voted on in referenda. And on February 4, 2016, the court heard a case brought by the lower chamber of parliament on whether the 40 proposed constitutional amendments – presented as one package to be adopted in a nationwide referendum – complied with the constitution of Tajikistan. The most significant amendments gave Emomali Rakhmon, the Leader of the Nation, a lifetime presidency; lowered the eligibility age for presidential candidates (supposedly to allow Rakhmon's son – Rustami Emomali – to run for office in 2020), MPs and judges (including constitutional court justices); and banned faith-based political parties (with the clear target being the Islamic Renaissance Party of Tajikistan). Nobody was surprised when the constitutional court approved these regime-sponsored amendments by concluding that they:

> encapsulate the process of political and social democratization of Tajik society, strengthening of legal protections of individuals, and represent a continuation of politico-social, legal and judicial reforms in the country. They are aimed at betterment of the Constitution, and are in compliance with worldwide practice of constitutional amendments and with values and basic principles of the Constitution of the Republic of Tajikistan (Nazarova, 2021).

In sum, the personalist patronal regime that runs Tajikistan through the concentration of power in the hands of the president's extended family (Cooley and Heathershaw, 2017) seems to need the constitutional court only as an assistant for drafting legal cover and a notary for constitutionalizing decisions made within this family. The Tajikistan Constitutional Court, then, is a "sidelined court" that is irrelevant to politics, to use the terminology of Brinks and Blass (2017). The president appears to control the fate of both the tribunal and its members. As Stykow (2017) puts it, in:

> the politically more closed regimes, such as Tajikistan's, ... elite networks are integrated into comprehensive, nationwide "power pyramids," which are led by presidents who enjoy the privilege of an often constitutionally granted status of the "Leader of the Nation." They rely on a carefully calibrated mix of patronage and oppression vis-à-vis the elite and are eager to maintain a high level of popularity among their citizens.

The president granted the tribunal increasing powers, allowed constitutional complaints in 2008, and offered longer-tenure guarantees in exchange for personal loyalty; while justices know what is expected of them and enjoy generous perks of pre-retirement tenure on the bench. The court maintains the element of "the facade of Western patterned legal arrangements" (Abdullaev, 2004: 8; Toktogazieva, 2019: 151), which hides a family-run regime with no interest in the judicialization of high-level politics and with no commitment to share power with the governing coalition (cf. Svolik, 2012).

UZBEKISTAN: STABLE SIDELINED CONSTITUTIONAL COURT

In contrast to the cases described above, the lack of judicialized high-level politics in Uzbekistan is much easier to explain. There, the former Communist Party leader Islam Karimov ruthlessly ruled the country until his death in 2016 (Cooley and Heathershaw, 2017), despite the constitutionally prescribed limit of two five-year presidential terms. Karimov held a tight grip on the constitution-making process, personally drafted constitutional clauses and had his version of the constitution adopted in December 1992 (Ismatov, 2021). This made Uzbekistan the first post-Soviet republic to adopt a new constitution in the wake of the break-up of the Soviet Union. Articles 107–109 of the constitution set up the constitutional court, which would consist of "political and legal experts" elected by the legislature for a once-renewable term of five years. In stark contrast to the speedy adoption of the constitution, Karimov was in no rush to activate the constitutional court. The Karimov-controlled legislature adopted the Constitutional Court Act in May 1993, then adopted another Constitutional Court Act in August 1995. The 1995 Act granted broad powers to the court yet denied it the power to handle constitutional complaints. The legislature then elected five justices of the court – all Karimov's nominees, including two law professors – in December 1995. It took justices another six months to develop the court's procedures, and the court began accepting cases in January 1996. Two more justices were elected in 1998, after an OSCE-sponsored study tour for sitting justices in Paris (Saidov, 2000).

Like in Tajikistan (until 2014), the seven-member constitutional court could initiate judicial review on its own initiative if at least three justices agreed that the contested act merited judicial review. Between 1996 and 2001, the chief justice boasted that the Uzbekistani Constitutional Court had received some 2,000 petitions from firms and citizens and reviewed some 2,000 legal acts of central and local government bodies, including President Karimov's decrees (Eshonov, 2001). But Uzbek lawyers and lower court judges interviewed in the spring of 2002 could not cite a single "decision that had arguably been made against the interests of the executive power," with several lawyers calling the constitutional court "a 'dead' organization" (American Bar Association, 2003: 11). Moreover, according to Ismatov (2020), the court handled even fewer cases than its Tajikistani equivalent – 33 – between 1996 and 2019, averaging 1.4 cases a year. According to two scholars (Brezhnev, 2020; Ismatov, 2020), the constitutional court justices initiated by themselves the judicial review of contested laws and regulations in most of these cases. The texts of all the court's decisions are not publicly available on the court's website. Judging by the texts of several decisions available, the court helped the patron-in-chief to rein in recalcitrant ministers and provincial governors. The court reviewed the compliance of cabinet edicts with President Karimov's decrees and the compliance of provincial governors' regulations with the statutes, a role that had been played by the procuracy in the Soviet Union. In contrast to decisions of the KCCl and the KyrCCh, decisions of the Uzbekistani Constitutional Court are short and consist of quotes from the laws and regulations instead of judicial reasoning and interpretation of constitutional rules (Ismatov, 2020). In fact, the content of Uzbekistani Constitutional Court decisions is very similar to the statements of the procuracy, the government agency – inherited from the Russian Empire and the Soviet Union – that supervises the legality of central and local administration (Smith, 1978). This duplication of procuratorial functions makes this tribunal redundant and indicates that Uzbekistani presidents do not use the constitutional courts for the purpose of sharing power with the ruling elite (cf. Svolik, 2012).

In contrast to other Central Asian constitutional courts, the Uzbekistani court did not play a formal part in any highly symbolic or crucial issues for the president, such as confirming constitutional amendments or extending the presidential term limits. As one journalist wrote at the time of Karimov's unexpected death in 2016, Karimov and his key clients ignored the constitution when "it was deemed inconvenient for the head of the state or contradicted his interests or those of groups providing him support, including corrupt officials, the heads of the security services, organized crime, and regional clans" (Taksanov, 2016).

As with the KCCl and the Tajikistani Constitutional Court, President Karimov's highly coercive and highly corrupt regime (Markowitz, 2017) controlled both individual justices and the fate of the tribunal. Meanwhile, justices knew that he expected their court to play a marginal role in politics, and they did not want to be recalcitrant. His key lieutenants led the court and received perks while serving as chief justices. The first chief justice who led the court between 1995 and 2002 was Karimov's right hand in the legislature and one of the co-authors of the 1995 Constitutional Court Act. His successor between 2002 and 2004 served as procurator-general and oversaw criminal prosecutions of Karimov's opponents prior to joining the bench. The current chief justice has already served as chief justice between 2004 and 2005 and then was appointed to lead the Central Elections Commission between 2005 and 2021. Like other Central Asian patronal presidents, who were confident in the utmost loyalty of constitutional court justices, Karimov gradually expanded the powers of the constitutional court (Mukhamedjanov, 2019). He even allowed the tribunal to become the founding member of the Association of Asian Constitutional Courts and Equivalent Institutions in 2010, which shows that he considered the constitutional court to be important in propagating his constitutional wisdom to external audiences.

Karimov's successor, former Prime Minister Shavkat Mirziyoev, elected in 2016, was keen to modernize the redundant constitutional court. To show his capacity to keep justices under control, President Mirziyoev had one former justice, who had previously served as the procurator-general between 2000 and 2015, imprisoned for ten years for corruption. In April 2021, Mirziyoev signed the new Constitutional Court Act, which enlarged the size of the court from seven to nine justices, removed the power of the court to initiate judicial review on its own initiative, and granted citizens and firms the right to file constitutional complaints. Yet there does not seem to be either demand for or supply of judicialization of high-level politics. In short, the Uzbekistani Constitutional Court, like the one in Tajikistan, is a façade tribunal (Toktogazieva, 2019: 161) or a "sidelined court" that is irrelevant to politics (Brinks and Blass, 2017), with no ability or willingness to distribute political power.

ANALYSIS: DIFFERING TRAJECTORIES OF INSTRUMENTALIZATION OF CONSTITUTIONAL LAW AND POLITICS IN CENTRAL ASIA

Existing research on authoritarian regimes suggests that formal institutions can play a crucial role in elite power-sharing. They may increase coordination among the elites by creating clear procedures of power-sharing, delineating the scope of authority of each key office-holder and enabling the monitoring by the ruling elite of the autocrats' compliance with their promises (Svolik, 2012). Yet our analysis shows that Central Asia's constitutional review tribunals performed these functions only in Kazakhstan until the early 2000s and in the post-2010 Kyrgyzstan. The KCCt in the early 1990s and its successor, the KCCl (only until the early 2000s), served as "information clearing-houses" and mediators between the executive and legislative branches of government and reinforced the power-sharing norm among the elites under Nazarbayev. When the KCCl interpreted the vague provisions of the newly enacted constitution, at the request of the ambitious parliamentary leaders and of the president, to set clear expectations and scopes of authority to which each faction of the elite was entitled, it restrained unnecessary cascades of rebellion against the president that had resulted from the elite perception of the power grab on the part of the president's faction.

There are, of course, clear limits as to the extent to which these institutions can serve as meaningful checks on a would-be autocrat's desire to accumulate power. Scholars argue that formal institutions and constitutional texts, like term limits, can serve as crucial focal points at which factions within the elites can coordinate against the autocrat, thereby creating a self-reinforcing norm of exit and power rotation (Fearon, 2011; Svolik, 2012). In contrast, we find that breaking and making constitutions and bypassing term limits became pet projects of Central Asian patrons-in-chief, who controlled constitutional tribunals through formal and informal means and gained favorable judge-made interpretations of these reforms. In this sense, we argue that formal institutions *per se* do not serve a regime-stabilizing function. Rather than ensuring credible commitment, constitutional tribunals can redistribute power and threaten the power-sharing function of other institutions. While the Kyrgyzstani Constitution of 2010 could, in theory, have stabilized the regime by ensuring power-sharing among different elite groups, it failed to do so. Several pro-president amendments to its structure, coupled with the inability of the KyrCCh to thwart these amendments, ultimately produced destabilizing effects that led to the arrest of the former president by his hand-picked successor in 2019; to the ouster of this successor in October 2020; and to the instrumentalization of the constitutional law. Indeed, as Figure 10.2 shows, in regimes like the post-2010 Kyrgyzstan, where presidents as patrons-in-chief do not control judicial appointments and face stronger judicial constraints, they tend to interfere with the assertive judiciary more in order to tame the courts.

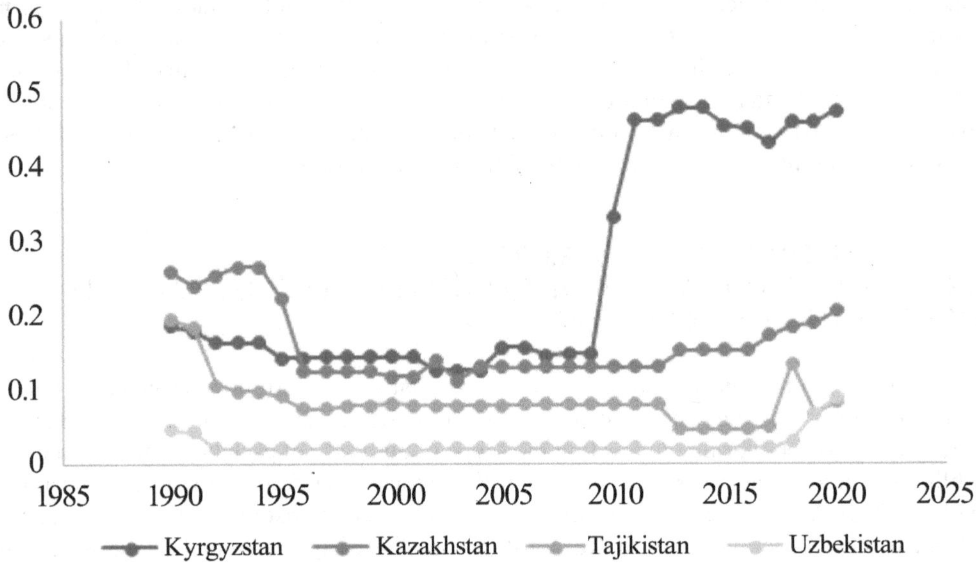

Source: Coppedge et al., 2021.

Figure 10.2 Judicial constraints on executive index

We find little support for the strategic insurance approach, which posits that greater electoral competition and political uncertainty lead to more formal insulation of constitutional courts and the judicialization of politics (see Table 10.7). Neither Kazakhstani competitive politics in the mid-1990s nor the post-civil-war power-sharing in Tajikistan in the same period nor six Kyrgyzstani presidents in the last 30 years made constitutional courts more insulated and independent. To the contrary, presidents (and parliaments in Kyrgyzstan) demanded from these tribunals greater care for their short-term power needs. Central Asian constitutional review tribunals behaved with a remarkable degree of deference to the presidents and oscillated between the "regime ally" and sidelined types of courts (Brinks and Blass, 2017). These tribunals further entrenched these presidents' hold on power yet did not expand their own actual judicial power – either cautiously or through landmark decisions.

Table 10.7 Political context and activism of constitutional courts in Central Asia

	Political competition at the time of activation	Share of academics and private lawyers at the time of activation	Jurisdiction and access	International support	Judicial activism in separation-of-powers cases	Average annual caseload
Kazakhstan Constitutional Court	High	High	Broad	Low	Yes	5 cases
Kazakhstan Constitutional Council	Low	Low	Limited	Moderate	Yes, until 2003	3.2 cases
Kyrgyzstan Constitutional Court	Moderate	Low	Broad	Low	No	7 cases
Kyrgyzstan Constitutional Chamber	High	High	Broad	High	Yes	25 cases
Tajikistan Constitutional Court	Moderate	Low	Broad	Low	No	2.3 cases
Uzbekistan Constitutional Court	Low	Medium	Limited	Low	No	1.4 cases

What factors then explain the outcome of judicial deference to the presidents? We stress three key mutually reinforcing conditions. First, the legacy of the Soviet Union produced regimes with strong executives in Central Asian countries. Even Kyrgyzstan's relatively strong parliament – between 2010 and 2020 – still delegated many powers to the president. Conformity with the wishes of a paternalistic leader who is ultimately responsible for guaranteeing order and social peace, through the use of force if needed, remains a strong social norm, especially with government employees (Ismatov, 2021). In short, judges defer because they do so habitually: they learned to defer in the past, and they also learned from the 1993 Russian constitutional crisis that displays of recalcitrance do not end well.

Second, this strong norm of deference to the strong ruler gains material and symbolic support from patron–client politics in Central Asia, which has become well established in the late Soviet era (Gleason, 1997). This type of politics is a social equilibrium, where "individuals organize their political and economic pursuits primarily around the personalized exchange of concrete rewards and punishments, and not primarily around abstract, impersonal principles such as ideological belief or categorizations that include many people one has not actually met in person" (Hale, 2015: 20). Such equilibrium facilitates greater instrumentalization of constitutional courts because it creates the *capacity* on the part of the presidents as patrons to have leverage over individual members of constitutional courts. Patronal presidents need political "frontmen" serving on the bench of constitutional courts – persons who would be politicians-in-robes "by Western standards" yet who "are indeed, informally, deprived of their autonomy in patronal autocracy and are de facto degraded to mere executors of the chief patron's will" (Magyar and Madlovics, 2020: 617). Because in patronalized politics, judicial recruitment and security of tenure are often shaped by expectations of the rewards and loyalties individual judges can bring to patrons, the autonomy of the judiciary from the executive is limited. This limitation is the result of both the self-selection of individuals with little abstract commitment to impartial justice and the capacity of the executive to punish disloyal judges, formally or informally.

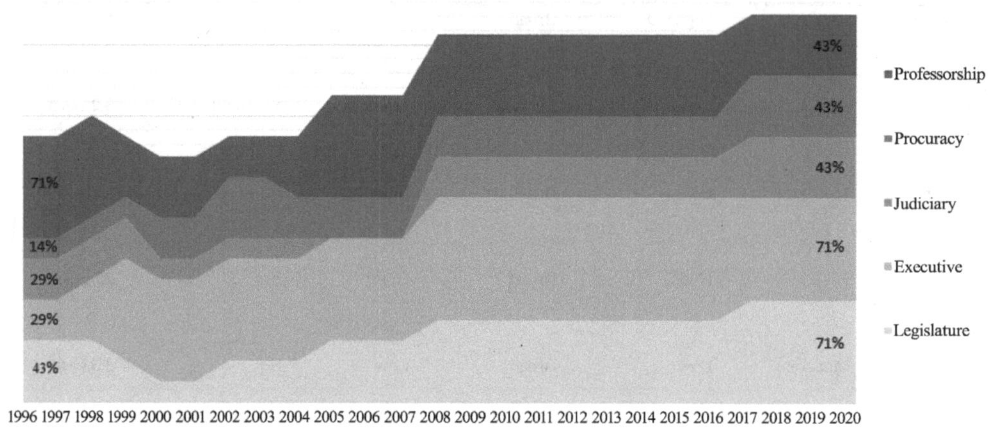

Figure 10.3 *Professional backgrounds of members of the Kazakhstani Constitutional Council*

Consider the dynamics of recruitment in the KCCl, in which President Nazarbayev kept several justices from the previously abolished constitutional court who were loyal to him. As Figure 10.3 shows, the proportion of members who had prior work experience in the executive branch dramatically increased – from 29% to 71% – between 1996 and 2020. In the same period, the share of legal scholars among the Council's members – those who might have support in the legal community outside Nazarbayev's patronal network – also decreased from 71% to 43%. This explains why the new presidents in countries like Ukraine, even after a major turnover in power, only infrequently purge judiciaries upon reaching office (Gomza, 2019), but rather co-opt them using material rewards in exchange for loyalty. It also explains why formerly loyal judges often pledge loyalty to the new patron-in-chief, like Chairwoman Baekova did in 2015 in Bishkek and the Uzbekistani Constitutional Court judges did in 2017; and why the KyrCCh authorized the arrest of former President Atambayev after the new president, Atambayev's protege, came to office and quickly amassed significant powers (Juzgenbayev, 2019c). These informal and personal exchanges of material rewards-for-loyalty explain the unwillingness of constitutional court judges to hold their patrons accountable despite broad jurisdictional rules and formal guarantees of judicial independence. Individual judges of these tribunals gain no material or reputational benefit for asserting judicial power and do not desire to risk their generous retirement benefits granted for long-term loyalty to the patron-in-chief.

Third, patronal presidents are authoritarian leaders who concentrate power in their own hands and instrumentalize constitutional review. They prefer tamed constitutional courts because they *desire* to control them as well as other government organs as institutions. If constitutions were mere façades, we would not expect recurring conflicts over the content of their texts and the extreme attention with which presidents of Central Asian states personally oversee the drafting and interpretation of constitutional texts (Nurumov and Vashchanka, 2016; Ismatov, 2021).

Patronalist regimes are built around the expectations of the power of particular elite networks, and the meaning of constitutional texts is important to control because constitutional rules serve as *signals* about which clientelist networks are expected to maintain and enlarge their share of material resources (Hale, 2015). Ruling coalitions are consistently affected by collective action problems in their efforts to defect from the ruling figure, leaving aspects of constitutions, such as term limits, and efforts to change constitutions that might serve as one of the few focal points for coordination against the ruler. Hale's (2011, 2015) careful comparative studies of post-Soviet constitutions demonstrate how contingent institutional and individual choices led to divergent effects for rulers' hold on power. Due to constitutions' important implications for elite power distribution and the potential unintended effects thereof, the constitutional tribunals are particularly crucial for would-be autocrats to control. Such control introduces a level of flexibility over constitutional meaning, especially because these tribunals' individual acts bypass the costly and often risky mobilization efforts of the parliamentary supermajority or referenda (except for Kyrgyzstan) taking place. The small size of these tribunals and their isolation make them easier to control by patrons-in-chief through appointments, budgets, and administrative support.

Taken together, and supported by patronage-based equilibrium and Soviet-era understandings, the combination of presidential cooptation, control and coercion (sometimes through the threat of releasing compromising information (Markowitz, 2017; Magyar and Madlovics, 2020: 307)) of the individual constitutional court judges and constitutional courts as institutions leads to constitutional tribunals performing as "regime allies" or sidelined courts, which distribute power in favor of presidents and play other non-judicial roles which legitimate both tribunals and their patrons. On paper, constitutional tribunals may gain more powers and become more accessible; yet this does not, by itself, translate into greater judicial power or promote the judicialization of distribution of power because formal and informal relations in which judges are embedded facilitate their instrumentalization by the powers that be.

CONCLUSION

Our analysis of constitutional separation of powers in four Central Asian countries shows a great deal of dynamism. But this dynamism is a product of the ambitions of powerful presidents as patrons-in-chief who aspire to rule unilaterally, and not a product of power-sharing bargains between presidents and the ruling elites legalized by constitutional review tribunals. Just as constitutions have been pet projects of Central Asian presidents, so have the constitutional courts in those countries been of presidents' legal advisors who persuaded their patrons-in-chief of the usefulness of constitutional review tribunals in building a modern personalist autocracy. In the countries we have analyzed, constitutions, the laws on constitutional courts and the decisions of those courts are written with the core interests of specific persons in mind. These legal texts are products of the instrumentalization of constitutional review, not of the judicialization of high-level politics and not of cautious judicial empowerment. Patronal presidents who control both constitutional courts and individual judges through corruption, cooptation and coercion (witness the abolition of the constitutional courts in Kazakhstan and Kyrgyzstan) have their autocratic initiatives approved by the constitutional courts. In exchange for favorable judgments, constitutional court judges enjoy large salaries and paid trips to meetings of prestigious judicial associations in foreign capitals, and do not seek to expand the actual power of their tribunals. Thus, Central Asian constitutional courts fall into the category of non-cases (cases in which judicial empowerment did not occur) in the studies of judicial empowerment in authoritarian regimes (Moustafa, 2014). We have shown that the absence of actual judicial empowerment is the result of institutional design (personalist autocracy); formal and informal patron–client exchange of concrete benefits and sanctions between presidents and judges; and learning on the part of judges that recalcitrance – on the bench and off-bench – carries more costs than benefits. As a result, constitutional tribunals in Kazakhstan, Kyrgyzstan, Tajikistan, and Uzbekistan play redundant roles of legal advisors, notaries and law enforcement monitors for presidents instead of holding them accountable.

REFERENCES

Abdullayev, K. (2004). Current Local Government Policy Situation in Tajikistan. In Luigi De Martino, ed. *Tajikistan at a Crossroad: Politics of Decentralization*, pp. 7–15. Cimera Publications. https://www.files.ethz.ch/isn/48312/SR%204%20Tajikistan%20Crossroad%20Eng.pdf

Amandykova, S., and Malinovskyi, V. (2012). The Constitutional Court and the Constitutional Council of the Republic of Kazakhstan: A Comparative Analysis. European Commission for Democracy through Law (Venice Commission). https://www.venice.coe.int/webforms/documents/?pdf=CDL-JU(2012)022-e

American Bar Association. (2002). *Judicial Reform Index for Uzbekistan*. Washington: American Bar Association.

American Bar Association. (2003). *Judicial Reform Index for Kyrgyzstan*. Washington: American Bar Association.

American Bar Association. (2004). *Judicial Reform Index for Kazakhstan*. Washington: American Bar Association.

American Bar Association. (2008). *Judicial Reform Index for Tajikistan*. Washington: American Bar Association.

Anderson, J. (1999). *Kyrgyzstan: Central Asia's Island of Democracy?* Routledge.

Baishev, Zh. (1994). *Sudebnaia zashchita Konstitutsii*. Almaty: Zheti zhargy.

Brinks, D. M., and Blass, A. (2017). Rethinking judicial empowerment: The new foundations of constitutional justice. *International Journal of Constitutional Law*, *15*(2), 296–331. https://doi.org/10.1093/icon/mox045

Caron, J.-F. (ed.). (2020). *Understanding Kazakhstan's 2019 Political Transition*. Palgrave Macmillan.

Collins, K. (2006). *Clan Politics and Regime Transition in Central Asia*. Cambridge University Press.

Cooley, A. A., and Heathershaw, J. (2017). *Dictators Without Borders: Power and Money in Central Asia*. Yale University Press.

Coppedge, M. et al. (2021). V-Dem [Country–Year/Country–Date] Dataset v11.1. *Varieties of Democracy Project*. https://doi.org/10.23696/vdemds21

Cummings, S. (2012). *Understanding Central Asia: Politics and Contested Transformations*. Routledge.

Dressel, B. (ed.). (2014). *The Judicialization of Politics in Asia*. Routledge.

Dressel, B., Sanchez-Urribarri, R., and Stroh, A. (2017). The informal dimension of judicial politics: a relational perspective. *Annual Review of Law and Social Science*, *13*, 413–430.

Dzhurayev, E., Toktogazieva, S., Esenkulova, B., and Baetov, A. (2015). The Law and Politics of Keeping a Constitutional Order: Kyrgyzstan's Cautionary Story. *Hague Journal on the Rule of Law*, *7*(2), 263–282. https://doi.org/10.1007/s40803–015–0013–7

Ellett, R. (2013). *Pathways to Judicial Power in Transitional States: Perspectives from African Courts*. Routledge.

Epp, C. R. (1998). *The Rights Revolution: Lawyers, Activists, and Supreme Courts in Comparative Perspective*. University of Chicago Press.

Eshonov, B. (2001). Independence and Effectiveness of the Decisions of the Constitutional Court of the Republic of Uzbekistan. *Konstitutsionnoe pravosudie*. No. 3. https://www.concourt.am/armenian/con_right/3.13–2001/uzbekistan.htm

Fearon, J. D. (2011). Self-Enforcing Democracy. *The Quarterly Journal of Economics*, *126*(4), 1661–1708. https://doi.org/10/bqdfmm

García, H. A., and Frankenberg, G. (eds.). (2019). *Authoritarian Constitutionalism*. Edward Elgar Publishing.

Ginsburg, T. (2003). *Judicial Review in New Democracies: Constitutional Courts in Asian Cases*. Cambridge University Press. https://doi.org/10.1017/CBO9780511511189

Ginsburg, T., and Moustafa, T. (eds.). (2008). *Rule by Law: The Politics of Courts in Authoritarian Regimes*. Cambridge University Press.

Gleason, G. (1997). *The Central Asian States: Discovering Independence*. Boulder: Westview.

Gomza, I. (2019). The Complex Politicization of Notorious Ukrainian Court. *PONARS Eurasia Memo*, *629*, 6.

Gönenç, L. (2002). *Prospects for Constitutionalism in Post-Communist Countries* (Vol. 50). Martinus Nijhoff Publishers.

Hale, H. E. (2011). Formal Constitutions in Informal Politics: Institutions and Democratization in Post-Soviet Eurasia. *World Politics*, *63*(4), 581–617. https://doi.org/10.1017/S0043887111000189

Hale, H. E. (2015). *Patronal Politics*. Cambridge University Press.

Heathershaw, J. (2009). *Post-conflict Tajikistan: the Politics of Peacebuilding and the Emergence of Legitimate Order*. Routledge.

Helmke, G. (2017). *Institutions on the Edge: The Origins and Consequences of Inter-Branch Crises in Latin America*. Cambridge University Press. https://doi.org/10.1017/9781139031738

Herron, E. S., and Randazzo, K. A. (2003). The Relationship Between Independence and Judicial Review in Post-Communist Courts. *The Journal of Politics*, *65*(2), 422–438. https://doi.org/10/gh2kpf

Hilbink, L. (2012). The Origins of Positive Judicial Independence. *World Politics*, *64*(4), 587–621. https://doi.org/10.1017/S0043887112000160

Hirschl, R. (2006). The Judicialization of Mega-Politics and the Rise of Political Courts. *Fordham Law Review*, *75*(2), 721–754.

Hug, A. (ed.). (2020). *Spotlight on Uzbekistan*. The Foreign Policy Centre. https://fpc.org.uk/wp-content/uploads/2020/07/Spotlight-on-Uzbekistan.pdf

Hug, A. (ed.). (2021a). *Retreating Rights: Examining the Pressure on Human Rights in Kyrgyzstan*. The Foreign Policy Centre. https://fpc.org.uk/wp-content/uploads/2021/03/Retreating-Rights-Examining-the-pressure-on-human-rights-in-Kyrgyzstan.pdf

Hug, A. (ed.). (2021b). *Retreating Rights: Examining the Pressure on Human Rights in Tajikistan*. The Foreign Policy Centre. https://fpc.org.uk/wp-content/uploads/2021/05/Retreating-Rights-Tajikistan-Publication-May-2021.pdf

Huskey, E. (2019). Kyrgyzstan Weakens Legal and Social Guarantees for Ex-Presidents amid Continuing Confrontation Between the Current and Former President. *Presidential Power*. May 20. https://presidential-power.net/?p=9590

Huskey, E., and Iskakova, G. (2010). The barriers to intra-opposition cooperation in the post-communist world: evidence from Kyrgyzstan. *Post-Soviet Affairs*, 26(3), 228–262.

Imomov, A. (1992). Constitutional Review: Human Rights and Freedoms. *Izvestiia Akademii nauk Respubliki Tadzhikistan. Seriia: filosofiia i pravovedenie*. No. 2. https://www.ca-c.org/datarus/st_11_imomov.shtml

Imomov, A. (1998). On Problems of Interpretation of the Constitution and Laws of Tajikistan. *Tsentralnaia Aziia*. No. 13. https://www.ca-c.org/journal/13–1998/st_06_imomov.shtml

Isaacs, R. (2014). Neopatrimonialism and beyond: reassessing the formal and informal in the study of Central Asian politics. *Contemporary Politics*, *20*(2), 229–245.

Ismatov, A. (2020). The Constitutional Judiciary and its Role in the Democratization Process in post-Soviet Central Asia. The Constitutional Court in Uzbekistan. *Nagoya University Asian Law Bulletin*, (5), 5–20.

Ismatov, A. (2021). Konstitutsionnye prava cheloveka v Uzbekistane: pozitivizm, traditsionalizm i ostorozhnyi razvorot v storonu mezhdunarodno-pravovykh standartov. *Sravnitel'noe konstitutsionnoe obozrenie*. no. 2(141), 94–130. https://academia.ilpp.ru/product/konstitutsionne-prava-tcheloveka-v-uzbekistane-pozitivizm-traditsionalizm-i-ostorozhny-razvorot-v-storonu-mezhdunarodno-pravovh-standartov/

Izquierdo-Brichs, F., and Serra-Massansalvador, F. (2021). *Political Regimes and Neopatrimonialism in Central Asia*. Palgrave Macmillan.

Junisbai, B. (2010). A tale of two Kazakhstans: Sources of political cleavage and conflict in the post-Soviet period. *Europe-Asia Studies*, *62*(2), 235–269.

Junisbai, B., and Junisbai, A. (2005). The Democratic Choice of Kazakhstan: A Case Study in Economic Liberalization, Intraelite Cleavage, and Political Opposition. *Demokratizatsiya*, *13*(3), 373–392.

Juzgenbayev, A. (2019a). *Decisions and Biographies of Judges of the Constitutional Chamber of the Supreme Court of Kyrgyz Republic* [Data set]. https://doi.org/10.7910/DVN/3F9TLI

Juzgenbayev, A (2019b). *Constitutional Council of the Republic of Kazakhstan: Decisions, Budget, Members* [Data set], https://doi.org/10.7910/DVN/L4SSOU

Juzgenbayev, A. (2019c). Ex-President Arrested in Kyrgyzstan: Constitutional Tribunal in Central Asia in the Center of High Politics. *Int'l J. Const. L. Blog*. Aug. 22, 2019, at: http://www.iconnectblog.com/2019/08/ex-president-arrested-in-kyrgyzstan:-constitutional-tribunal-in-central-asia-in-the-center-of-high-politics

Juzgenbayev, A. (2019d). Constitutional Tribunal in Kyrgyzstan Decides Against the Former President, Clearing the Way for His Prosecution. *Int'l J. Const. L. Blog*, Nov. 5, 2019, http://www.iconnectblog.com/2019/11/constitutional-tribunal-in-kyrgyzstan-decides-against-the-former-president,-clearing-the-way-for-his-prosecution

Kachkeev, M. (2012a). *Zentralasien: zwischen Rechtsstaat, Religion und sowjetischer Tradition* (Vol. 17). BWV Verlag.

Kachkeev, M. (2012b). Judicial Independence in Kyrgyzstan and Kazakhstan: A Legislative Overview. In *Judicial Independence in Transition* (pp. 1255–1275). Springer.

Kazakhstani Constitutional Council decision of 23 May 1997. (1998). *Bulletin of the Constitutional Council of the Republic of Kazakhstan*. https://adilet.zan.kz/rus/docs/S970000012_/

Kazakhstani Constitutional Council decision of 23 June 1997. (1998). *Bulletin of the Constitutional Council of the Republic of Kazakhstan*. https://adilet.zan.kz/rus/docs/S970000014_

Kazakhstani Constitutional Council decision of 12 March 1999. (2000). *Bulletin of the Constitutional Council of the Republic of Kazakhstan*. https://adilet.zan.kz/rus/docs/S990000003_

Kazakhstani Constitutional Council decision of 20 June 2000. (2001). *Bulletin of the Constitutional Council of the Republic of Kazakhstan*. http://old.ksrk.gov.kz/rus/resheniya/?cid=11&rid=146

Kazakhstani Constitutional Council decision of 26 December 2000. (2001). *Kazakhstanskaia pravda*. January 6. https://adilet.zan.kz/rus/docs/S000000022_

Kazakhstani Constitutional Council decision of 17 May 2001. (2001). *Kazakhstanskaia pravda*. June 30. https://adilet.zan.kz/rus/docs/S010000007_/

Kazakhstani Constitutional Council decision of 21 January 2020. (2020). *Kazakhstanskaia pravda*. January 28. https://adilet.zan.kz/rus/docs/S2000000001

Kazakhstani Constitutional Council decision of 15 December 2020. (2020). *Kazakhstanskaia pravda*. December 22. https://adilet.zan.kz/rus/docs/S2000000004

Kazakhstani Constitutional Council decision of 4 June 2021. (2021). *The Reference Control Bank of the RLA RK in Electronic Form*. June 14. https://adilet.zan.kz/rus/docs/S2100000001

Kazakhstani Constitutional Court decision of March 6, 1995. (1995). *Kazakhstanskaia pravda*. March 16.

Kazakhstani Constitutional Court decision of March 11, 1995. (1995). *Kazakhstanskaia pravda*. March 16.

Kyrgyzstani Constitutional Chamber decision of January 13, 2014. (2014). http://constpalata.kg/wp-content/uploads/2014/01/RESHENIE-po-delu-Abdy-kaly-kova.pdf

Kyrgyzstani Constitutional Chamber decision of October 11, 2016. (2016). http://constpalata.kg/wp-content/uploads/2016/10/SDPK-rusk.1.pdf

Kyrgyzstani Constitutional Chamber decision of October 3, 2018. (2018). http://constpalata.kg/wp-content/uploads/2018/10/Toktakunova-N.A.-resh.pdf

Kyrgyzstani Constitutional Chamber decision of October 24, 2019. (2019). http://constpalata.kg/wp-content/uploads/2019/10/resh-Kasy-mbekov-N-A-i-dr-poslednij-12–05ch-25–10–2019.pdf

Kyrgyzstani Constitutional Court decision of November 9, 1995. (1995). http://cbd.minjust.gov.kg/act/view/ru-ru/52496

Kyrgyzstani Constitutional Court decision of December 28, 1995. (1995). http://cbd.minjust.gov.kg/act/view/ru-ru/52499

Kyrgyzstani Constitutional Court decision of July 13, 1998. (1998). http://cbd.minjust.gov.kg/act/view/ru-ru/52542

Kyrgyzstani Constitutional Court decision of September 14, 2007. (2007). https://online.zakon.kz/Document/?doc_id=30334977

Kyrgyzstani Constitutional Court decision of January 21, 2010. (2010). http://cbd.minjust.gov.kg/act/view/ru-ru/320044/10

Landau, D. (2018). Courts and support structures: beyond the classic narrative. In Erin F. Delaney and Rosalind Dixon, eds., *Comparative Judicial Review*. Edward Elgar Publishing, 226–243. https://doi.org/10.4337/9781788110600.00020.

Laruelle, M. (2012). Discussing neopatrimonialism and patronal presidentialism in the Central Asian context. *Demokratizatsiya*, *20*(4), 301.

Laumulin, M. (2000). Kazakhstan and the West: Relations during the 1990s in Retrospect. *Central Asian and the Caucasus*, (3). https://www.ca-c.org/online/2000/journal_eng/eng02_2000/05.laum.shtml

Magyar, B., and Madlovics, B. (2020). *The Anatomy of Post-Communist Regimes: A Conceptual Framework*. Central University Press.

Markowitz, L. (2017). Beyond Kompromat: Coercion, Corruption, and Deterred Defection in Uzbekistan. *Comparative Politics*, 50:1, 103–121.

Mazmanyan, A. (2015). Judicialization of politics: The post-Soviet way. *International Journal of Constitutional Law*, *13*(1), 200–218. https://doi.org/10.1093/icon/mov003

Moustafa, T. (2003). Law versus the State: The Judicialization of Politics in Egypt. *Law & Social Inquiry*, *28*(4), 883–930. https://doi.org/10/cqx8zk

Moustafa, T. (2014). Law and courts in authoritarian regimes. *Annual Review of Law and Social Science*, *10*, 281–299.

Mukhamedjanov, A. (2019). Formation, Development and Improvement of the Constitutional Justice in the Republic of Uzbekistan in the Modern Conditions of the Society. *KLRI Journal of Law and Legislation*, 9(1), 199–246. https://www.klri.re.kr:9443/handle/2017.oak/8948

Nazarova, D. (2021). *Vicious circle of patronalism: constitutional court power in Kazakhstan, Kyrgyzstan and Tajikistan* (Doctoral dissertation, Rutgers University-School of Graduate Studies).

Newton, S. (2017). *The Constitutional Systems of the Independent Central Asian States: A Contextual Analysis*. Hart Publishing.

Nurumov, D., and Vashchanka, V. (2016). Constitutional Development of Independent Kazakhstan. In R. Elgie and S. Moestrup (eds.), *Semi-Presidentialism in the Caucasus and Central Asia* (pp. 143–172). Palgrave Macmillan UK. https://doi.org/10.1057/978–1-137–38781–3_6

Olcott, M. B. (2010). *Kazakhstan: Unfulfilled Promise*. Carnegie Endowment.

Popova, M. (2012). *Politicized Justice in Emerging Democracies: A Study of Courts in Russia and Ukraine*. Cambridge University Press.

Putz, C. (2015). Kyrgyz Judge Removed, Another Reprimanded. *Diplomat*. June 27. https://thediplomat.com/2015/06/kyrgyz-judge-removed-another-reprimanded

Putz, C. (2020). What's in Kyrgyzstan's Proposed "Khanstitution"? *Diplomat*. November 20. https://thediplomat.com/2020/11/whats-in-kyrgyzstans-proposed-khanstitution/

Ramseyer, J. M. (1994). The Puzzling (In)Dependence of Courts: A Comparative Approach. *The Journal of Legal Studies*, *23*(2), 721–747. https://doi.org/10.1086/467943

Saidov, A. (2000). Country Study: Uzbekistan. *The United Nations Development Programme Human Development Report*. Unpublished ms. http://hdr.undp.org/en/content/country-study-uzbekistan

Shaikenova, L. (2002). *Podvizhnik prava: Pamiati Nagashbaia Shaikenova*. Vol. 2. Astana, Foliant.

Shapiro, Martin. (1986). *Courts: A Comparative and Political Analysis*. University of Chicago Press
Sieder, R., Schjolden, L., and Angell, A. (eds.). (2005). *The Judicialization of Politics in Latin America*. Palgrave Macmillan US. https://doi.org/10.1007/978-1-137-10887-6
Smith. G. (1978). *The Soviet Procuracy and the Supervision of Administration*. Sijthoff & Noordhoff
Staton, J. K. (2010). *Judicial Power and Strategic Communication in Mexico*. Cambridge University Press.
Steytler, N. (1993). The Judicialization of Namibian Politics. *South African Journal on Human Rights*, *9*(4), 477–499. https://doi.org/10/gh7brq
Stone Sweet, A. (2000). *Governing with Judges: Constitutional Politics in Europe*. Oxford University Press.
Stykow, P. (2017). Tajikistan – Preparing a Succession in Power or Coping with a Severe Regime Crisis? *Presidential Power*. November 7. http://presidential-power.net/?p=7175
Stykow, P. (2019). The devil in the details: constitutional regime types in post-Soviet Eurasia. *Post-Soviet Affairs*, *35*(2), 122–139.
Svolik, M. W. (2012). *The Politics of Authoritarian Rule*. Cambridge University Press.
Tajikistani Constitutional Court decision of December 8, 2009 http://www.codices.coe.int/NXT/gateway.dll/CODICES/precis/eng/asi/tjk/tjk-2009-y-001
Tajikistani Constitutional Court decision of May 22, 2018, http://constcourt.tj/ru/tainotho/o-p-r-e-d-e-l-e-n-i-e-ob-otkaze-v-vozbuzhdenii-konstituczionnogo-sudoproizvodstva-po-hodatajstvu-grazhdanina-dzhuraeva-s/
Taksanov, A. (2016). Post-Karimov Uzbekistan: Palace Coups, Mutinies, or Elections? *CABAR.Asia*. September 2. https://cabar.asia/en/alisher-taksanov-post-karimov-uzbekistan-palace-coups-mutinies-or-elections-2
Tate, C. N., and Vallinder, T. (1995). *The Global Expansion of Judicial Power*. New York University Press
Thibault. H. (2018). *Transforming Tajikistan: State-building and Islam in Post-Soviet Central Asia*. Bloomsbury Publishing.
Toktogazieva, S. (2019). *Constitutional Review in Transition: Central Asian Constitutional Courts in Comparative Perspective*. Doctoral dissertation, Central European University.
Trochev, A. (2008). *Judging Russia: The Role of the Russian Constitutional Court in Russian Politics, 1991–2006*. Cambridge University Press.
Trochev, A. (2013). Fragmentation? Defection? Legitimacy? Explaining judicial roles in post-Communist "colored revolutions". In D. Kapiszewski, G. Silverstein, and R. Kagan (eds.), *Consequential Courts: Judicial Roles in Global Perspective* (Comparative Constitutional Law and Policy, pp. 67–92). Cambridge: Cambridge University Press. doi:10.1017/CBO9781139207843.004
Udartsev, S. (2003). Uchenyi, pedagog, gosudarstvennyi i obshchestvennyi deiatel' (k 70-letiiu akademika M. T. Baimakhanova). *Pravovaia reforma v Kazakhstane*. no. 3, 145–156. https://online.zakon.kz/Document/?doc_id=30012936
Uzbekistani Constitutional Court decision of July 5, 2000 https://lex.uz/ru/docs/1252666
Uzbekistani Constitutional Court decision of August 9, 2001, https://lex.uz/ru/docs/1253420
Uzbekistani Constitutional Court decision of November 14, 2018, https://lex.uz/ru/docs/4622936
Uzbekistani Constitutional Court decision of October 18, 2019, https://lex.uz/ru/docs/4623565

11. Politicization of courts in European democracies

Maria Popova and Christine Rothmayr Allison

INTRODUCTION

Politicization of the courts is a broad term, which can describe diverse phenomena. A starting point is the recognition that courts are political actors, whose decisions reflect, further, and affect political processes despite guarantees of institutional independence and individual autonomy for courts and their judges. Politicization of the courts can thus refer to increased public debate surrounding judicial decisions and actions. This type of politicization raises few concerns about the legitimacy of the judiciary or the foundations of the rule of law, which courts are meant to guarantee and is, in fact, the norm in constitutional democracies, although variations in its intensity exist. In Europe, scholars have long discussed the political role of national constitutional and ordinary judiciaries. At the supranational EU level, scholars have documented the political impact of court decisions on European integration and from the good-faith, "federalist" ambition of the European Court of Justice (ECJ).[1] Another conceptualization of the term politicization emerges when we seek to describe the domination of the political branches over institutionally feeble and behaviourally deferential (or outright subservient) courts. Politicization defined either as the movement towards or as the outcome of politically dependent courts implies that the rule of law is compromised, and constitutionalism is under threat. The thinly veiled abuse of the courts and the legal process as an instrument of repression is *de rigueur* with incumbents in consolidated autocracies and wannabe autocrats in still competitive authoritarian regimes.[2]

[1] See for example Antoine Vauchez, L'Union par le droit. L'invention d'un programme institutionnel pour l'Europe, Presses de Sciences Po (2013); Anne-Marie Burley & Walter Mattli, Europe Before the Court: A Political Theory of Legal Integration, 47 INTERNATIONAL ORGANIZATION 41–76 (1993); Renaud Dehousse, The European Court of Justice: the Politics of Judicial Integration (St. Martin's Press 1998).

[2] Maria Popova, Why Doesn't the Bulgarian Judiciary Prosecute Corruption?, 59 PROBLEMS OF POST-COMMUNISM 35–49 (2012); Maria Popova, Putin-Style "Rule of Law" & the Prospects for Change, 146 DAEDALUS 64–75 (2017); Wojciech Sadurski, Constitutional Crisis in Poland, in Constitutional Democracy in Crisis 257–275 (Mark A. Graber, Sanford Levinson, & Mark Tushnet eds., 2018); Kim Lane Sheppele, Autocratic Legalism, 85 THE UNIVERSITY OF CHICAGO LAW REVIEW 545–584 (2012); Alexei Trochev, Judging Russia: the role of the constitutional court in Russian politics 1990–2006 (Cambridge University Press ed. 2008); Miklós Bánkuti, Gábor Halmai & Kim Lane Scheppele, Hungary's Illiberal Turn: Disabling the Constitution, 23 JOURNAL OF DEMOCRACY 138–146 (2012).

POLITICIZATION OF THE COURTS THROUGH WEAPONIZED LEGALISM

In this chapter, we discuss a third conceptualization of politicization of the courts, which could be conceived as a mid-point on the spectrum between a politically relevant, powerful, and activist judiciary in a liberal democratic setting and a politically subservient judiciary in an autocratic setting. We limit the scope of our discussion to non-authoritarian settings, i.e., democracies and hybrid regimes, where a minimal rule of law threshold is met in so far as even the most powerful political actors hold no monopolized formal or informal control over the courts and, as a result, are occasionally (or often) constrained by judicial decisions. In these settings, a trend towards politicization involves the mobilization of the law by political actors to achieve ideological and/or instrumental political goals. While the instigator of politicization is often the incumbent government that is pursuing an ideological agenda and trying to retain power, other political actors (the opposition, interest groups, or even the courts themselves) can also pursue a politicization agenda to maximize political gains. Politicization is especially consequential to the rule of law and to the body politic when it is perceived not only by direct participants in the legal process (litigants, public prosecution, judges, etc), but by the wider political community. If political competitors and the electorate come to believe that the courts are politicized, public trust in the courts, their legitimacy, and eventually compliance with their decisions all suffer erosion and decline. Thus, understanding the politicization process is essential to monitoring rule of law resilience or backsliding. Figure 11.1 illustrates these three dimensions of the politicization of courts as a starting point of our conceptual discussion.

Dimension 1 What is the purpose of politicization?

- Ideological vs Instrumental

Dimension 2 Who is the agent of politicization?

- Political branches vs Courts themselves

Dimension 3 Who talks about politicization?

- Only legal actors (courts, litigants) vs Society at large

Figure 11.1 Three dimensions of politicization

The first dimension involves political actors seeking to influence the courts' decision-making to achieve different political goals. At one end of the spectrum, we have actors pursuing purely ideological goals. In this area, it is tough to discern politicization from the normal functioning of the constitutional process, i.e., litigants seeking to convince the courts to apply, steer or make law in their preferred ideological direction. Politicization would entail simply increasing attention, monitoring, and debate over court decisions. At the other end of the spectrum, we have actors mobilizing the law to achieve purely instrumental goals, such as undermining their political opponents, protecting or boosting their political partners/allies, or utilizing court decisions that go in their favour to signal strength and power. We call this politicization of the legal process in bad faith, the weaponization of law. To maximize their chances of success in court, weaponizers deploy a set of strategies aimed at influencing the courts and their decisions. These strategies can be reactive or proactive, *ad hoc* or systematic, formal or informal, and we describe them later in the chapter. If weaponization becomes a dominant strategy of political competition, frequently used by actors across the political spectrum, we can talk about the rise of a weaponized legalism regime. When the regime becomes obvious to the wider political community, rather than remaining noticeable only to the actors directly involved in the legal process, it eventually undermines the rule of law by eroding public trust in the courts and the legal process. Thus, we need to pay close attention to the signs of weaponized legalism.

Weaponizing the law is distinct from the use of the courts for political repression, which autocrats regularly engage in. It is also distinct from aggressive, inventive, good-faith efforts to mobilize the law strategically to one's benefit, which has been the norm in the era of judicialized politics in many consolidated democracies. This politicization is related to, but conceptually distinct from, *de jure* or *de facto* judicial independence as it can be high when courts are sufficiently independent, but act as a partisan actor, which either reliably sides with a given political party or switches allegiances, often in pursuit of its own corporate interests. Independent courts become politicized when they prioritize political considerations over legal interpretation in their decision-making.

One manifestation of weaponized legalism is the politicization of judicial careers and frequent judicial reform measures. Judicial appointments, promotions, demotions, and discipline provoke heated political fights. Politicians who expect to wage legal attacks against opponents or to have to fend them off pay close attention to who sits on the bench. Incumbents perennially push judicial restructuring as they try to gain influence over the courts or try to close channels of influence opened by their predecessors. Another manifestation is high volumes of litigation involving important political actors in different legal issue areas. An explosion of corruption prosecutions is particularly likely. In many countries, political corruption and its mechanisms have been in place for decades, so a greater volume of anti-corruption prosecutions shows that political adversaries have started using criminal law to fight their battles, rather than that law enforcement has discovered effective ways to uncover and prosecute corruption. Finally, due to the high levels of litigation involving political actors, weaponized legalism is characterized by extensive media coverage of the courts. Public discourse on the courts does not assume that cases are filed or decided in good faith, but rather that they serve as instruments in a political fight. The media bounces around competing conspiracies about who has managed to weaponize the law in each case.

When, in 2016, the Polish parliament adopted legislation that would allow the executive to reappoint all members of the Supreme Court, the governing party Law and Justice (PiS), argued it was delivering on its election promise to fix the Polish judiciary. Critics countered that the *real reason* the government sought to pack the Supreme Court with loyalists was to orchestrate the overturn of the abuse of power conviction of Kaczinski's close ally and to facilitate the prosecution of PiS's arch enemy, former Prime Minister Donald Tusk. When, in 2017, Hungary's parliament amended its higher education law to require foreign universities to have physical campuses in their home countries, Orban's government claimed it sought to prevent diploma mills from defrauding Hungarian students. Hungary's opposition, Orban's critics abroad, the EU, and the Council of Europe all insinuated that the *real* purpose of the amendment, dubbed Lex CEU, was to attack Orban's perceived political enemy George Soros by legally harassing "his" Central European University.

If the conspiracy theories were confined to a tiny portion of the most ardent supporters of the "victims" or the fiercest critics of the "perpetrators", they would not deserve much attention. But claims that the legal process has been harnessed by incumbents who seek to get a leg up in political competition are, in fact, the dominant interpretations of the cases just described. When the weaponization of law becomes or is perceived to have become a common political strategy, we can talk about the emergence of a new legal regime – weaponized legalism.

The weaponization of law is the mobilization of the law in bad faith to gain a power benefit and improve one's position in the political competition arena in the short term. We use the term bad faith loosely, rather than in the strict legal sense, to describe inauthentic behaviour within the legal process. A case is brought in bad faith when the litigant does not seek the law's application to enforce its spirit, but to draw political gain. For example, all states regulate protest to balance the rights to freedom of assembly and expression against property rights and the state's responsibility to guarantee law and order. But when protestors are prosecuted under these laws with the overarching goal of harassing them and reducing their willingness to participate in future protest, the law is weaponized to weaken political opponents.

Weaponization straddles the fine line between using the law aggressively and abusing it. Savvy political actors could find opportunities to weaponize without violating the letter of the law. The result is a legally sound case pursued in bad faith. But often, weaponization involves varying levels of abuse of the law. At the level of law enforcement, abuse can range from fabricating individual cases from whole cloth, through selective/biased enforcement to deliberate procedural violations or legal overreach. Weaponizers usually try to disguise the abuse of law to avoid public backlash or the triggering of institutional accountability mechanisms. At the level of law enforcement, they deny fabricating evidence or engaging in actions in bad faith and claim to be sticking to their best and sincere interpretation of the facts and the law. At the level of law-making, weaponizers tend to disguise their true intentions either by cloaking actions in ideological garb or by claiming that the new law makes only technical or trivial changes and minor improvements to pre-existing law.

The law can be weaponized to achieve different goals within the arena of political competition. When used offensively, a weaponized legal act undermines political opponents or competitors. When used defensively, a weaponized legal act deflects attacks by opponents and helps the weaponizers themselves or their allies. When used as a PR tool, weaponized legal acts can bolster the perpetrator's position in the competition process by showcasing their strength or facilitating their political grandstanding.

Any type of law – criminal, administrative, public, or civil – can be weaponized. Corruption, tax evasion, and protest violence prosecutions can be an effective weapon against political opponents. Defamation cases, electoral registration cases, party registration, and financing cases, even sanitation and fire code compliance cases, can also be weaponized to hurt political opponents or help allies. Weaponization can take place when laws are drafted and when they are applied in individual cases. Political actors, whether in government or in opposition, as well as judicial actors, can weaponize the law for their own benefit. Weaponization can also affect different stages of the legal process, from law-making, through bringing cases to court, to court decisions. At the level of law-making, weaponization involves passing laws targeting individual political actors, which is a violation of rule of law principles.

In a weaponized legal regime, political competitors (seem to) reach regularly for the law to undermine their opponents, strengthen themselves and their allies, or advertise their power. "Seem to" is in parentheses, because proving bad faith and inauthentic behaviour is a tall order. Political actors regularly go to great lengths to disguise their motives for taking specific actions and are especially loath to appear power-hungry and instrumental. It is difficult, maybe impossible, to uncover direct evidence of the weaponizer's intentions.

But more importantly, "seem to" also refers to the perception, by the public and/or by other political actors, that the law is mobilized in the service of political competition. Actual and perceived weaponization might not completely overlap. Weaponization may take place in practice without being perceived, i.e., the weaponizer manages to (ab)use the law but no one notices. Like the sound of the proverbial tree falling in the forest, the effects of such weaponization are questionable. This disjuncture may happen in regimes where the judiciary has high legitimacy. Political actors and the public give the benefit of the doubt that the legal process has unfolded in good faith. For example, gerrymandering rarely garners significant attention in the US. Its victims sometimes go to court to challenge particularly egregious redistricting, but the controversy often makes only the local news and the subsequent court decisions are taken at face value. Only marginal voices raise concern about potential weaponization of court cases. This faith in the judiciary's output is curious. In many states, the judges who get to hear lawsuits against a party majority's gerrymandering bill have been appointed by that same majority or run in judicial elections as candidates from the same party. Slate's "If It Happened There…" column on the issue practically writes itself. Unnoticed weaponization undermines the fairness of the democratic process but may not affect the legitimacy or public trust in democratic institutions.

Alternatively, weaponization may seem to be happening, when, in fact, it is not. Maybe PiS truly do want to make the Polish judiciary more efficient. Those questions are not likely to be ever resolved with smoking-gun direct evidence. When the explanation that attributes the outcome to the weaponization of law has more traction, the truth becomes a moot point. If most actors perceive that weaponization has taken place, they will adapt their future behaviour to this perception.

In countries with vibrant political competition, weaponized legalism manifests as politicization of judicial careers and frequent judicial reform measures. Judicial appointments, promotions, demotions, and discipline provoke heated political fights. Politicians who expect to wage legal attacks against opponents or to have to fend them off pay close attention to who sits on the bench. Incumbents perennially push judicial restructuring as they try to gain influence over the courts or try to close channels of influence opened by their predecessors.

Whether the judiciary is independent or not, weaponized legalism entails high volumes of litigation involving important political actors in different legal issue areas. An explosion of corruption prosecutions is a particularly useful gauge of the rise of weaponized legalism. In many countries, political corruption is a stable feature of how politics works, and its mechanisms have been in place for decades. A rise in anti-corruption prosecutions seems more of an indication that political adversaries or competitors are attempting to use criminal law to fight their battles than a result of law enforcement suddenly discovering effective ways to uncover and prosecute corrupt activities.

Due to the high levels of litigation involving political actors, weaponized legalism goes hand in hand with an explosion of media coverage of the courts. Moreover, public discourse on the courts does not assume that cases are filed or decided in good faith, but rather that they serve as instruments in a political fight. The media bounces around competing conspiracies about who has managed to weaponize the law in each case.

Proximate, but Distinct Terms

Is weaponized legalism simply another term for the absence of *de facto* judicial independence from politicians? Weaponizers of law may prefer dependent courts if they could get them. However, the weaponization of law is a separate and broader phenomenon from judicial subservience. Savvy weaponizers can mobilize the law for political gain without having to rely on a pocket judge to deliver the decision they want. They may build strong cases in bad faith or with fabricated evidence. Or they may frame their losses in court as the weaponization of law by their opponents. If they manage to make that narrative the dominant interpretation of any litigation they are involved in, weaponized legalism rises, regardless of what an independent judiciary does.

Weaponized legalism can also emerge in countries with powerful and independent judiciaries when the weaponizer is the judiciary itself. In Italy and (perhaps increasingly) in France, judges have been accused of weaponizing the law against leading politicians. Silvio Berlusconi and Nicolas Sarkozy have faced a barrage of corruption-related criminal investigations; Berlusconi has stood trial and has received several convictions, and Sarkozy is heading to trial soon. Berlusconi and Sarkozy (and many of their supporters) claim that ideologically hostile, but independent, judges are out to get them and are (ab)using criminal law in bad faith. If this explanation is correct or if it becomes the dominant narrative, we have the offensive weaponization of law by an independent judiciary.

Weaponized legalism is also distinct from autocratic legalism, a term recently proposed to describe the increased (ab)use of the law by budding authoritarians like Orban, Chavez, Putin, and Erdogan.[3] The terms capture some of the same practices. However, weaponized legalism recognizes that these practices can creep into high-functioning democracies. Scheppele recognizes that some attempts at establishing authoritarian regimes by mobilizing the law might fail. Ecuador's Correa, for example, did not manage to use the law to extend his presidential term and eventually had to cede power. Poland's opposition and civil society may eventually thwart PiS's current campaign to erode judicial independence and media pluralism.[4] Autocratic legalism rests on the teleological assumption that weaponizers' ultimate goal is always authoritarian consolidation. But some political actors engaging in weaponization may have limited, short-term goals of (ab)using the law for immediate political gain. They may lack authoritarian ambition either because they are ideologically committed to democracy or because they recognize their power limitations. Labelling the (ab)use of law for political gain in Orban's Hungary autocratic legalism increases the chances of ignoring signs of similar practices in other seemingly consolidated democracies. Weaponized legalism allows us to see the (ab)use of law for political competition purposes in more descriptive, normatively neutral terms. Assessing its normative and empirical consequences is a separate task.

---

3 Javier Corrales, The Authoritarian Resurgence: Autocratic Legalism in Venezuela, 26 Journal of Democracy, 37–51 (2015); Kim Lane Sheppele, Autocratic Legalism, 85 The University of Chicago Law Review 545–584 (2012); Gabor Halmai, The Case of Hungary, in M. Graber, S. Levinson, M. Tushnet (eds.), Constitutional Democracy in Crisis? (OUP, 2018) 243–253.

4 Scheppele (n 3) 555–556.

STRATEGIES FOR POLITICIZATION

So far, our discussion has focused on what politicization is, who pursues it and towards what goals. We now turn to the question of how weaponizers seek to politicize the courts to reap the benefits of decisions in line with their preferences and political goals. We classify several types of strategies.

The first type are *ad hoc reactive* strategies that focus on individual court cases and respond to actions/steps taken by the courts. The goal of these strategies is to curb or minimize the effects of court decisions that the weaponizers could not prevent or pre-empt. Such strategies include: (1) verbal attacks on the court or individual judges in the context of the case; (2) attempts to discredit the decision/court by branding the process or the outcome political, rather than legal; (3) non-compliance or partial compliance to undermine the legitimacy of the courts. Throughout his term, US President Trump used all these strategies to minimize the political damage from any legal ruling that didn't go his way and to burnish his image as a "deep state" fighter, which was a big part of his electoral appeal. Trump started using this strategy early, as a presidential candidate in 2016, when he excoriated a judge of Mexican descent who had ruled against him in a class-action lawsuit filed by Trump University students. He called Judge Curiel a "hater" and claimed in several interviews that the judge could not be impartial in any case involving Trump due to his political opposition to Trump's plan to build a wall on the Mexican border.[5] Once elected, President Trump escalated the use of this strategy and used it so frequently that federal judges uncharacteristically started speaking out to defend themselves. In 2019, US District Court judge Paul Friedman summarized Trump's relationship with the judiciary this way:

> We are witnessing a chief executive who criticizes virtually every judicial decision that doesn't go his way and denigrates judges who rule against him, sometimes in very personal terms. … He seems to view the courts and the justice system as obstacles to be attacked and undermined, not as a co-equal branch to be respected even when he disagrees with its decisions.[6]

The second type of strategies are *ad hoc proactive* strategies, which again focus on individual court cases, but also involve attempts to interfere in the judicial decision-making process to accomplish a politically favourable result or prevent a politically costly result. One example of such strategy is behind-the-scenes communication with judges presiding over politically relevant cases in a purported attempt to provide the judge with relevant facts/context, which may "help" the judge reach the best decision. This covert strategy rarely surfaces, unless there is a whistle-blower. Another *ad hoc proactive* strategy involves steps to discredit a judge who may take politically adverse decisions on the bench. For example, in Poland, a Deputy Justice Minister had to resign after investigative journalists revealed evidence that he had planted

---

[5] Trump's attacks on Judge Curiel are still jarring to read | CNN Politics, CNN, February 27, 2018, https://www.cnn.com/2018/02/27/politics/judge-curiel-trump-border-wall/index.html (last visited Mar 31, 2022).

[6] Federal judge slams Trump's attacks on judiciary, The Hill, November 7, 2019, https://thehill.com/regulation/court-battles/469499-federal-judge-slams-trumps-attacks-on-judiciary/ (last visited Mar 31, 2022).

media stories with rumours about the personal life of judges critical of the government's judicial reforms.[7]

The occasional use of these strategies is par for the course in any competitive democratic regime with judicialized politics, so individual examples could be isolated scandals about mis-judgement by overzealous political actors. However, sharp and steady escalation of the use of these strategies, which could easily be documented in the US under Trump or in Poland under PiS, signals the rise of weaponized legalism.

A third type of strategies are *systematic formal* strategies, which attempt to alter the institutional structure of the courts with the goal of reducing the *de jure* independence of the judiciary. Formal backlash against the courts can include: (1) court-packing strategies through reappointment, tenure, judicial selection reforms (e.g., Polish reforms); (2) reduction of the courts' budget or their ability to control it; (3) shrinking the jurisdictional power of the courts (e.g., Orban's attack on the Constitutional Court); (4) creating brand new courts to allow incumbent to select the entire judicial corps; (5) removing judges' functional immunity from prosecution, etc.

A final set of strategies are *systematic informal* strategies, which seek to reduce the *de facto* independence of the judiciary by signalling that politicians seek to consistently maximize their preferences in the judicial decision-making process. This informal backlash against the courts can include: (1) orchestrating the promotion of political allies within the judiciary and the demotion of political enemies; and (2) systematically trying to create an environment and discussion in the media which paints the courts as weak, illegitimate, corrupt, or out of touch with the population.

EXPLANATIONS FOR POLITICIZATION

This section explores how we might understand and explain the shift from *ad hoc* reactions with limited impact on the courts to systematic formal and informal strategies and under what circumstances these systematic strategies accumulate to the weaponization of law that potentially threatens the rule of law and results in democratic backsliding. There are three leading explanations of the creeping politicization of the courts that seems to be brewing throughout Europe. The first explanation points the finger at the judicialization of national and international politics trend that saw the creation of powerful and independent judiciaries throughout post-World War II Europe (and beyond). However, while judiciaries have become more powerful throughout Europe, systematic formal or informal strategies to reduce their *de facto* and *de jure* independence and power vary significantly in intensity and success. This varied response to a fairly constant trend raises the question of whether other factors trigger systematic politicization strategies against the backdrop of generally greater independence. The second type of explanation points to mistrust in judicial institutions, a lack or decline of popular support for the courts, which can be the result of populist strategies, judicial corruption, or a more generalized dissatisfaction with government for its failure to address urgent issues. Low trust might enhance the weaponization of the law, as courts are already perceived

7 Polish deputy minister resigns over judge trolling scandal | SaltWire, https://www.saltwire.com/halifax/news/polish-deputy-minister-resigns-over-judge-trolling-scandal-343092/ (last visited Mar 31, 2022).

as being in the service of specific political interests. The broader populist wave provides a third explanation. The judiciary as a guardian of liberal democracy is at odds with populist ideology. Populists interpret the counter-majoritarian effects of judicial decisions on crucial political debates[8] as a usurpation of power by judicial elites with no political mandate. These explanations are not necessarily competing, but as we argue and as Voeten[9] has shown about the backlash against international courts, populism may be the principal trigger for shifting from *ad hoc* attacks on courts to the weaponization of law with detrimental effects to the rule of law and democracy.

Reversing or Limiting the Judicialization

From this perspective, the counter-majoritarian difficulty, i.e., the fact that judges take crucial political decisions, even though they do not have a democratic political mandate, is finally catching up to the juristocracy.[10] Judicialization, understood as the greater *de facto* and *de jure* independence of the judiciary, has increased the power of judicial bodies in national and international politics, in particular through rights protection. The adoption of constitutional rules that delegate more power to independent courts to invalidate legislation and governmental decisions or to create more legal opportunities by adopting new rights in the form of a charter or bill of rights has contributed to empowering judiciaries around the globe. Such institutional changes often go along with changing values and behaviour of various political actors. The literature on judicialization points to complex interactions of citizens demanding better rights protection and more justice, politicians delegating politically costly issues to courts and judges acting more independently and assertively. Several authors have argued that this process of empowerment is necessarily linked to the politicization of courts. Hirschl called this phenomenon the "inevitable flip side of judicialization".[11]

Judicialization is used as an umbrella term for various phenomena.[12] Although a general global trend, within it there is considerable variation across countries, policy issues, and over time. The literature on legal mobilization has documented extensively the variation across time and space in soliciting courts for different policy issues.[13] There is also considerable

---

8 See for example Carlo Guarnieri, Judicial Independence in Europe: Threat or Resource for Democracy?, 49 REPRESENTATION 347–359 (2013); Daniel Abebe & Tom Ginsburg, The Dejudicialization of International Politics?, 63 INTERNATIONAL STUDIES QUARTERLY 521–530 (2019); Alec Stone Sweet, Governing with Judges: Constitutional Politics in Europe (Oxford ed. 2000); Ran Hirschl, The Judicialization of Politics, in Oxford Handbook of Law and Politics 119–141 (Keith E. Whittington, Daniel R. Kelemen, & Gregory A. Caldeira eds., Oxford ed. 2011).

9 Erik Voeten, Populism and Backlashes against International Courts, 18 PERSPECTIVES ON POLITICS 407–422 (2020).

10 Guarnieri (n 8), Abebe & Ginsburg (n 8), Stone Sweet (n 8), Hirschl (n 8).

11 Ran Hirschl, *Towards Juristocracy: The Origins and Consequences of the New Constitutionalism* (Harvard University Press 2007) 254.

12 Jacques Commaille & Laurence Dumoulin, Heurs et malheurs de la légalité dans les sociétés contemporaines. une sociologie politique de la "judiciarisation", 59 L'ANNEE SOCIOLOGIQUE 63–107 (2009); Christine Rothmayr Allison, Juges et politiques publiques, in Steve Jacob & Nathalie Shiffino, *Politiques publiques. Fondements et prospectives pour l'analyse pour l'action publique* (Larcier 2021) 679–716.

13 Charles R. Epp, The Rights Revolution. Lawyers, Activists, and Supreme Courts in Comparative Perspective (University of Chicago Press 1998); Chris Hilson, New social movements: the role of legal opportunity: 9 JOURNAL OF EUROPEAN PUBLIC POLICY 238–255 (2011); Lisa Vanhala, Legal

variation across space; and sometimes even if you build it, they do not come, or at least not in the predicted numbers or issue areas. Demand for law does not flow automatically from the introduction of specific judicial institutions.[14] The literature on the implementation of court decisions and court impact studies has found ample evidence that multiple variables influence the actual outcome of court decisions in terms of policy or even social change.[15] Governments have different options to address unwelcome court decisions, going from override to partial or no-compliance in specific cases. They have the power to mitigate court impact to reduce the discrepancy between their political objectives and judicial policymaking without engaging in *ad hoc* or systematic strategies of politicization. To understand under what circumstances judicialization can explain different politicization strategies, we need to be more specific about potential triggers and political situations favouring *ad hoc* or systematic attacks on courts by political actors.[16]

Hirschl suggests that decisions that touch on mega-politics, i.e., that address fundamental political issues for a polity and trigger "substantive moral dilemmas or watershed political quandaries that the entire nation faces,"[17] are particularly conducive to backlash. Voeten also points to decisions that touch the core of political identity when he seeks to explain backlash against international courts.[18] It has been suggested that governments compare costs and benefits of powerful courts from a strategic point of view. Delegating power to courts might be understood as a rational strategy to preserve power[19] or at least to secure that future elections and governments are played by democratic rules as future insurance.[20] On the flipside, if judicial decisions considerably threaten the likelihood of governing elites to come into power again, for example because they threaten core elements of electoral programmes or promises, or fundamental issues for a polity, we might observe politicization strategies. The example of Spain and Italy might serve to illustrate such situations in the context of established democracies: the case of Spain illustrates how independence movements and intergovernmental tensions threatening central governments can lead to systematic politicization strategies such as delaying the nomination of judges and weaponizing recusal rules to neutralize judges with ideological unfavourable orientation.[21] In the case of Italy, we can also observe a weaponi-

Mobilization under Neo-corporatist Governance: Environmental NGOs before the Conseil d'Etat in France, 1975–2010, 4 Journal of Law and Courts 103–130 (2016); Lisa Conant et al., Mobilizing European law, 25 Journal of European Public Policy 1376–1389 (2018). Christine Rothmayr Allison & Audrey L'Espérance, Regulating Assisted Reproduction in Canada, Switzerland, and the USA: Comparing the Judicialization of Policy-Making, 19 Journal of Comparative Policy Analysis: Research and Practice 262–276 (2017).

[14] Kathryn Hendley, Rewriting the rules of the game in Russia: the neglected issue of the demand for law, 8 E. Eur. Const. Rev. 89–95 (1999); Katharina Pistor, The Supply and Demand for Law: Comment on Hendley, 8 East European Constitutional Review 105–108 (1999).

[15] Rosenberg, Gerald N., The Hollow Hope: Can Courts bring about social change? (University of Chicago Press Second edition) (2008).

[16] Erik Voeten, Public Opinion and the Legitimacy of International Courts, 14 Theoretical Enquiries in Law 411–436 (2013).

[17] Hirschl (n 11) 257

[18] Voeten (n 9).

[19] Hirschl (n 11).

[20] Tom Ginsburg, Judicial Review in New Democracies: Constitutional Courts in Asian Cases (Cambridge University Press 2003).

[21] Jean-Baptiste Harguindéguy, Gonzalo Sola Rodríguez & José Cruz Díaz, Between justice and politics: the role of the Spanish Constitutional Court in the state of autonomies, 8 Territory, Politics, Governance (2020) 231–35.

zation of law. As the judiciary has threatened the future of political elites through targeting corrupt practices, "…Berlusconi's judicial problems have exacerbated a state of permanent tension between the political and judicial branches of the State",[22] with recurring verbal attacks and threats through reform attempts while accusing courts to be political. Another symptom of politicization is the power of courts to decide "issues of elections, referenda, executive impeachment, and lawfulness of political parties in addition to their core function".[23] Courts throughout Europe (Spain, Austria, Romania, Bulgaria, Ukraine, etc) have recently been called to adjudicate central political questions of this kind, which carries enormous potential for politicization. A misstep by the court can easily trigger politicization strategies which in turn might lead to further court decisions and so on, leading down the path of weaponizing the law. Finally, the strategic calculus may incentivize incumbents to systematically pressure and ultimately politicize the courts when the short-term benefits of a dependent judiciary outweigh the potential long-term benefits of an independent and powerful court. This strategic pressure mechanism is often at work in new, unconsolidated democracies where, due to low party system institutionalization and electoral volatility, incumbents' time horizons tend to be shorter.[24]

In terms of verbal attacks against international courts and threats to exit international agreements, Voeten points to cumulative implementation costs.[25] Issues of national sovereignty and self-determination are part of such cost and benefit calculations. Politicization strategies can be observed because of the possible empowering effects of their decisions on national courts (e.g., the European Court of Human Rights (ECtHR) and Russia) or because their decisions limit the capacity to implement nationally preferred solutions (e.g., ECtHR and the United Kingdom with respect to prisoner voting).

In short, there is no doubt that judicialization attracts more attention to the courts and therefore also closer scrutiny. While specific circumstances or explanations for backlash likely vary, the empowerment of courts is a precondition for their politicization in democratic systems. Yet it is important to remember that delegating mega-political decisions to courts can also be intentional and advantageous for ruling elites. The blame for difficult decisions can be deflected to the courts and hence reduce electoral costs.[26] To better understand under what conditions *ad hoc* verbal attacks might turn to systematic formal or informal strategies resulting in weaponized legalism, we need to turn to further variables. Low trust in the courts might provide a particularly fertile environment for politicization strategies resulting in weaponized legalism.

---

22 Alberto Vannucci, The Controversial Legacy of 'Mani Pulite': A Critical Analysis of Italian Corruption and Anti-Corruption Policies, 1 BULLETIN OF ITALIAN POLITICS (2009) 234.

23 Mary L. Volcansek, Judicialization of Politics or Politicization of the Courts in New Democracies?, in Christine Landfried ed., Judicial Power: How Constitutional Courts Affect Political Transformations 66–81 (CUP 2019) 70.

24 Maria Popova, Political Competition as an Obstacle to Judicial Independence: Evidence From Russia and Ukraine, 43 COMPARATIVE POLITICAL STUDIES 1202–1229 (2010); Maria Popova, Why Doesn't the Bulgarian Judiciary Prosecute Corruption?, 59 PROBLEMS OF POST-COMMUNISM 35–49 (2012).

25 Voeten (n 9) 409.

26 Hirschl (n 8).

Low Trust in Courts and Social Networks

In the context of *ad hoc* strategies of politicization, low trust in the judiciary might foster an environment in which political leaders can develop systematic strategies to curb the judiciary's independence and power without being punished by their electorate and in which there will be little resistance from other actors than the courts themselves. To put it in the language of the cost–benefit strategic calculus, low trust in the courts significantly lowers the costs of politicizing the courts for incumbents.[27] In addition, in a low-trust environment, any resistance by the courts might be interpreted as an attempt on their side to weaponize the law for their political struggles or for partnering up with political interests.

In post-communist countries, we observe persistently low trust in political institutions over the last decades. Trust is lower than in established democracies, but trust also fluctuates more over time and there are some differences across countries. The lower trust levels and decreases have been attributed to the Communist legacy since courts were inconsequential weak actors in the communist institutional hierarchy or to the post-Communist high levels of state capture and corruption. As the institution tasked with exposing state capture and corruption, courts have taken a significant reputational hit due to their inability to curb political corruption and are consistently among the least trusted institutions.[28] Constitutional courts, in particular, have been undermined by populists and their reservoir of political trust and legitimacy was not significant enough to make the populist attack prohibitively costly.[29] On the other hand, the EU has devoted significant political efforts and resources to judicial reforms in the region, especially through the CVM mechanism in Bulgaria and Romania.[30] Considerable differences across countries and over time remain.[31]

The literature on trust in the judiciary shows that such trust is strongly correlated with democratic stability and the trust in other political institutions.[32] The strongest predictor of trust in courts in European countries is trust in parliament, as Garupa et al. show.[33] *De jure*, but in particular *de facto*, independence explains variation in trust in courts across European countries.[34] Because of the legitimacy issue that is specific to non-majoritarian institutions

[27] Popova (n 24).

[28] Maria Popova, Can a leopard change its spots? Strategic behavior versus professional role conception during Ukraine's 2014 court chair elections, 42 Law & Policy 365–381 (2020).

[29] Bojan Bugarič & Tom Ginsburg, The Assault on Postcommunist Courts, 27 Journal of Democracy 69–82 (2016).

[30] Aneta B. Spendzharova & Milada Anna Vachudova, Catching Up? Consolidating Liberal Democracy in Bulgaria and Romania after EU Accession, 35 West European Politics 39–58 (2012); Ramona Coman, Quo Vadis Judicial Reforms? The Quest for Judicial Independence in Central and Eastern Europe, 66 Europe-Asia Studies 892–924 (2014).

[31] Gergõ Závecz, Post-communist Societies of Central and Eastern Europe, Handbook on political trust. (Edward Elgar Publishing 2017).

[32] James L. Gibson, Miguel M. Pereira & Jeffrey Ziegler, Updating Supreme Court Legitimacy: Testing the "Rule, Learn, Update" Model of Political Communication, 45 American Politics Research 980–1002 (2017); Michael A. Hansen, Trust in the System? Factors that Impact Citizens' View of Courts in the United Kingdom, 98 Social Science Quarterly 1503–1517 (2017).

[33] Nuno Garoupa & Pedro C. Magalhães, Public trust in the European legal systems: independence, accountability and awareness, 44 West European Politics 690–713 (2021).

[34] Marc Bühlmann & Ruth Kunz, Confidence in the Judiciary: Comparing the Independence and Legitimacy of Judicial Systems, 34 West European Politics 317–345 (2011).

that lack any power to implement their decisions and hence depend on the collaboration of the other branches for their decisions to have any impact, trust is a particularly precious resource for the judiciary.[35]

Low trust in courts might be favourable to politicization strategies and specifically weaponized legalism for several reasons. Systematic politicization strategies likely reinforce the perception of a dependent judiciary in low-trust environments, while where courts are perceived as independent, they are better shielded from the impact of *ad hoc* politicization strategies. Long-standing democracies seem to have more safeguards against politicization strategies succeeding. Nelson and Gibson, with respect to Trump's attacks on the courts, point to the fact that the credibility of the source of the attacks is important, but also the fact that judges are not perceived as being just another type of politician, e.g., that they are not prioritizing political considerations over legal interpretation in their decision-making, is important for legitimacy.[36] Volkansek argues similarly that in new democracies "governing institutions lack long-standing traditions and democratically sustaining precedents",[37] which increases the chances for politicization strategies to succeed. Various political actors will be less likely to defend the *de jure* independence of courts if they are perceived as having little legitimacy.

Strong civil societies that support courts and take initiatives against politicization strategies provide crucial counterweight.[38] Strong civil societies take time to build, which renders new democracies potentially more vulnerable to the successful politicization of courts. Trust might translate into protest when there are attempts to subordinate courts, as was the case in Poland, and such protest can help to protect the judiciary's independence.[39] Older democracies compared with newer seem to have a greater "reservoir of public support and legitimacy that deters disgruntled politicians".[40] Finally, public relations offensives and transparency measures have been used by courts themselves to increase public trust, as for example in the case of the Supreme Court of the United Kingdom.[41] In other words, the highest courts actively manage their own image to positively influence popular trust in the judiciary.[42] The Slovak Constitutional Court, for example, after a controversial nomination process increased transparency through streaming hearings of potential candidates.[43] Such public relations strategies might also contribute to increasing the confidence in the judiciary and render them less vulnerable to politicization attempts.

---

[35] Garoupa et Magalhães (n 33): 690; James L. Gibson & Michael J. Nelson, Reconsidering Positivity Theory: What Roles do Politicization, Ideological Disagreement, and Legal Realism Play in Shaping U.S. Supreme Court Legitimacy?, 14 Journal of Empirical Legal Studies 592–617 (2017).

[36] Michael J. Nelson & James L. Gibson, How Does Hyperpoliticized Rhetoric Affect the US Supreme Court's Legitimacy?, 81 The Journal of Politics 1512–1516 (2019).

[37] Volkansek (n 23) 73.

[38] Andrew Arato, Populism, Constitutional Courts, and Civil Society, in Christine Landfried ed., Judicial Power: How Constitutional Courts Affect Political Transformations 318–341 (CUP 2019). 335.

[39] Volkansek (n 23) 70.

[40] Volkansek (n 23) 80.

[41] David Kosar & Katarina Sipulova, How to Fight Court-Packing?, 6 Constitutional Studies (2020) 2020: 154.

[42] Philipp Meyer, Judicial public relations: Determinants of press release publication by constitutional courts, 40 POLITICS 477–493 (2020).

[43] Kosar and Sipulova (n 41) 154.

In environments of particularly tense confrontation between the judiciary and political incumbents, Trochev and Ellett[44] argue that judges could use various informal strategies to try to shield themselves from politicization attempts. These strategies range from informal negotiations (e.g., Russia)[45] and mobilization of informal networks out of the sight of the public, to public relations strategies of various kinds (e.g., Romania or Germany),[46] including seeking support from actors on the international level or even more drastic measures such as going on strike (e.g., Ukraine and Romania).[47] The basic idea behind their argument is that judicial power is socially constructed, and judges take an active role in this process through their networks, actions and interactions off the bench in order to mobilize allies, which is not without risk,[48] and whether these strategies are successful needs to be further investigated. Judges might be able to protect themselves against politicization if they succeed to mobilize powerful allies nationally or internationally;[49] however, such networks are no guarantee for success and might even have a negative impact. As Della Porta has argued for the Italian case: "Institutional resources, informal contacts and the professional culture have all played a role in the development of strategies of collusion between corrupt politicians and judges, as well as in the repression of corruption."[50] Hence, off-bench networks and mobilization might provide some remedy against the weaponization of courts, but they might also contribute to further politicization.

While low-trust environments are auspicious for weaponized legalism to emerge, politicization strategies must be in the interest of powerful actors to succeed. A third and more powerful explanation focuses on the values and world views put forth by the new populist movements and policy objectives that pursue illiberal visions of democracy.

Rise of Populism

The rise of populist parties in Europe over the last two decades is well documented by the increased percentage of votes that populist parties have obtained, especially during the last decade, and their formation of governments or participation in government coalitions.[51] There are numerous definitions of what constitutes populism. For the analysis of backlash against courts, and other counter-majoritarian institutions, Cas Mudde's definition seems particularly pertinent:

> [Populism is] an ideology that considers society to be ultimately separated into two homogeneous and antagonistic groups, "the pure people" versus "the corrupt elite", and which argues that politics should be an expression of the volonté générale (general will) of the people.[52]

---

[44] Alexei Trochev & Rachel Ellett, Judges and Their Allies: Rethinking Judicial Autonomy through the Prism of Off-Bench Resistance, 2 Journal of Law and Courts 67–91 (2014).

[45] Trochev and Ellett (n 44) 72.

[46] Trochev and Ellett (n 44) 75–76.

[47] Trochev and Ellett (n 44) 77.

[48] Trochev and Ellett (n 44) 71.

[49] Trochev and Ellett (n 44) 78–80.

[50] Donatella Della Porta, A judges' revolution? Political corruption and the judiciary in Italy, 39 European Journal of Political Research (2001) 18.

[51] Milada Anna Vachudova, Populism, Democracy, and Party System Change in Europe, 24 Annual Review of Political Science 471–498 (2021).

[52] Cas Mudde, The Populist Zeitgeist, 39 Government and Opposition 541–563 (2004) 543.

Systematic empirical analysis of the relation between populist governments and backlash against the national judiciary is yet to come. Voeten and colleagues have analysed the link between populist governments and backlash against international courts through exiting international treaties.[53] Voeten argues that backlash against international courts is often preceded by attacking national courts or the two simultaneously,[54] and some of his findings are therefore relevant for both national and international judiciaries. He argues: "Strong populist movements or populist presidents make it more likely that governments opt for challenging the authority of courts over alternative strategies such as acceptance, non-compliance, or avoidance."[55] Because of their counter-majoritarian and international character, international courts "fail to reflect the vox populi".[56] He shows that two issues seem to trigger backlash in particular: international court judgments that constrain domestically popular redistribution initiatives regarding land, property and resources, and decisions that protect the rights of unpopular minorities. On the national level as well, populist governments might go against decisions from counter-majoritarian institutions that protect the liberal character of democracy for ideological reasons. Such court decisions might also offer a good opportunity for agenda-setting and strengthening the populist movement in view of further electoral gains and support for policy change in particular with regard to the protection of minority rights. As Voeten points out: "International courts will sometimes come down with rulings that populists can use to mobilize support. Opposing these court rulings can be a source of popularity for leaders who rely on populist mobilization."[57]

For ideological reasons, populist governments attack not just specific rulings, but the entire formal institutional structure of the judiciary. The impetus is both ideological and instrumental. As Grzymala-Busse argues about Hungary's Fidesz and Poland's PiS, governing populists despise the courts because they see them as "the creatures of corrupt elite deals and exploitation, rather than as autonomous institutions of democratic accountability and legal constraint".[58] As a counter-majoritarian institution, the judiciary is representative of the problem with ruling elites not respecting the preferences of the population according to the populist movement. Courts are depicted as allies of liberal elites to protect liberal policies against the will of the majority.[59] In the case of Italy, under Berlusconi, Vannucci has argued in the same vein: "The constantly asserted need for a reform of the administration of justice to reduce the allegedly arbitrary power of judges, who it is claimed are politically biased and without any electoral legitimation, has become the central issue on the political agenda."[60]

There are ideological reasons that weaponized legalism is more likely to form under populist governments. Over the last half a century, the judiciaries have considerably contributed to the expansion of rights protection and to the strengthening of liberal democracy, and hence they

---

53 Voeten (n 9); Øyvind Stiansen & Erik Voeten, Backlash and Judicial Restraint: Evidence from the European Court of Human Rights, 64 International Studies Quarterly 770–784 (2020).

54 Voeten (n 9) 145.

55 Voeten (n 9) 408.

56 Voeten (n 9) 411.

57 Voeten (n 9) 411.

58 Anna Grzymala-Busse, How Populists Rule: The Consequences for Democratic Governance, 51 POLITY 707–717 (2019) 709.

59 Voeten (n 9) 408, 411; Cas Mudde & Cristóbal Rovira Kaltwasser, Populism: A Very Short Introduction (OUP 2017), 116–118.

60 Vannucci (n 22) 234.

are likely at odds with populist governments' often illiberal ideological agenda. Furthermore, as political newcomers, populists have relatively little experience in successful legal mobilization and might also lack the networks traditional parties had built to strategically mobilize the law to further their political agendas. Weaponizing the law promises a relatively rapid and – in low-trust environments, as discussed earlier – electorally not costly strategy to curb the courts' power and independence and obtain a jurisprudence better aligned with their own political views. The leader of Poland's PiS, Kaczynski, has admitted as much by justifying targeting the courts with the need to prevent them from undermining the PiS political agenda.[61]

In short, politicization strategies may vary according to the political context. Mainstream parties in established democracies tend to opt for *ad hoc* public criticism of the judiciary. As Stiansen and Voeten documented,[62] *ad hoc* public criticism of the ECtHR has been widely expressed by established, liberal democracies, including Switzerland, Belgium, Sweden, Denmark, Italy, the UK and others. By contrast, populist parties, especially those governing in new democracies, tend to reach for systematic formal politicization strategies that seek to undermine and restructure (or outright subordinate) the judiciary.

The politicization of courts and weaponized legalism at the national level might also have an impact on the politization of the ECJ. As Blauberger and Kelemen point out, "There is a risk, however, that in seeking to depoliticize conflicts over fundamental values by pushing them into the courts, these approaches might end up heavily politicizing the European and national judiciaries and thus undermining their legitimacy and authority."[63] At the same time, Kelemen discusses whether a number of court-curbing measures identified in the US literature could be reasonably employed against the ECJ, namely (a) "legislative or constitutional override", (b) "resource punishment", (c) "jurisdictional stripping", (d) "court packing", (e) "judicial selection and reappointment" and (f) "public opinion". The first four court-curbing mechanisms are difficult to implement for institutional reasons because of the challenges involved in amending EU treaties. In a brief analysis, he points out that controversial decisions seem not to influence the rather stable trust in the ECJ, which is considerably higher compared with other institutions.[64] The judicial appointment process and the internal organization of the courts also contribute to the "strong political foundations"[65] of the court and don't lend themselves well to court-curbing strategies.

While the success of initiating a backlash against the ECJ through court-curbing mechanisms might be unlikely or very limited, it will need systematic empirical research to better understand under what conditions weaponized legalism on the national level succeeds and to what extent we can actually observe a sort of "spillover" effect on the ECJ and also the ECTHR.[66]

---

[61] Grzymala-Busse (n 58) 711.

[62] Stiansen and Voeten (n 53) 779.

[63] Michael Blauberger & R. Daniel Kelemen, Can courts rescue national democracy? Judicial safeguards against democratic backsliding in the EU, 24 JOURNAL OF EUROPEAN PUBLIC POLICY (2017) 331.

[64] R. Daniel Kelemen, The political foundations of judicial independence in the European Union, 19 JOURNAL OF EUROPEAN PUBLIC POLICY (2012) 45–50.

[65] Kelemen (n 64) 54.

[66] Stiansen and Voeten (n 53).

CONCLUSION

Politicization takes various forms, as discussed above, and its consequences vary not only depending on the types of strategies used, but also in terms of the ideological background, power and credibility of the weaponizer. Populist leaders might be more likely to turn to politicization strategies, but we need more research to test this hypothesis. Established democracies are less prone to going down the weaponized legalism path and their judiciaries are more resilient in the face of politicization pressure from weaponizers due to higher levels of trust in courts. However, court decisions addressing core issues of the polity and its identity might trigger politicization strategies in older democracies as well. In addition, the populist wave in the wake of Trump, Johnson (UK) and Salvini (Italy) is unlikely to crest soon, so judiciaries in established democracies are not safe from politicization either. *Ad hoc* attacks on courts don't automatically and necessarily lead to weaponized legalism, but they create auspicious ground for its emergence. Weaponized legalism is a specific style of politics that might be facilitated in certain political and institutional contexts, but that needs actors that initiate strategies of politicization and others that contribute to fuel such strategies. Courts and judges play an active part in these processes too. There is little research on how judiciaries react towards politicization and under what circumstances their reaction counters such strategies successfully, or to the contrary participate in weaponized legalism. Stiansen and Voeten demonstrate that criticism by established democracies has had an impact on decisions rendered by the ECtHR with rulings becoming more restrained, which goes along with nominating judges exerting more restraint. However, this change is more modest.[67] Moreover, investment tribunals have adopted the margin of appreciation doctrine and have become more predisposed towards states after withdrawals from the Convention on the Settlement of Investment Disputes between States and Nationals of Other States or investment agreements.[68] How judicial bodies respond to increased scrutiny is a promising area for future research and should be enlarged to include overt and covert politicization strategies.

Weaponized legalism contributes to undermining the rule of law and the legitimacy of judicial institutions. Judicial decisions are no longer perceived to be any different from political decisions and judges become just another political actor, which further undermines their legitimacy and the compliance with judicial rulings. The longer such strategies stay in place, the more difficult it will become to reverse the process of democratic backsliding that we currently observe in the European context. It is therefore crucial to better understand what factors favour the shift towards weaponized legalism and to what extent European institutions and actors successfully contribute to breaking this path.

---

67 Stiansen and Voeten (n 53) 777.

68 Malcolm Langford & Daniel Behn, Managing Backlash: The Evolving Investment Treaty Arbitrator?, 29 European Journal of International Law 551–580 (2018).

12. Constitution-making and transnational expertise: lessons from the 2014 Tunisian Constitution

Alicia Pastor y Camarasa

INTRODUCTION

Tunisia adopted a new Constitution in July 2022, signalling the deep crisis of governance that Tunisia, once the great hope of democratisation in the Middle East and North Africa (MENA) region, now faces.[1] Ten years after the adoption of a new constitution in 2014, which was hailed internationally as a resounding success,[2] the country is facing serious social, economic, and political problems. The 2022 Constitution follows years of a dire economic situation, where several key institutions that were enshrined in the new Constitution, such as the constitutional court and independent constitutional bodies, had not been implemented.[3]

Constitutions adopted in a context of democratic transition contain a variety of normative ideals. When implemented, a constitution fails to deliver on its expansive set of promises, the democratic project becomes at risk. Constitution-making is conceived traditionally as the epitome of exercising popular sovereignty, through the constituent power. The reality on the ground is far more multifaceted and complex. The process of making constitutions has been pervaded by transnational influences. For instance, the first Constitution of the Arab World, the 1861 Tunisian Constitution, was imposed on the Bey of Tunis, Muhammad III as-Sadiq, by British and French diplomats.[4]

Today, the transnational dimension of constitution-making is less obvious, but no less persistent. Cheryl Saunders has recently noted that foreign advising is *the* defining marker of constitution-making in the twenty-first century.[5] New constitutions are often developed by a body that represents the people, in the form of a national constituent assembly. However, in recent cases of constitution-making, several external actors, that is, actors whose intervention

1 Nouri Mzid et Kamel Baklouti, "Une nouvelle Constitution tunisienne dans un contexte de crise" (2023) 1 *Revue de droit comparé du travail et de la sécurité sociale* 188–191.

2 Editorial, "Tunisia's Remarkable Achievement" New York Times (28 January 2014); UNSG, Statement attributable to the Spokesperson for the Secretary-General on the adoption of Tunisia's New Constitution (United Nations 26 January 2014).

3 Camille Lafrance, "Blocage de la Cour Constitutionnelle en Tunisie: 'les modernistes sont perdants'" *Jeune Afrique* (12 October 2018); Mohammed Haddad, "En Tunisie, le parlementarisme en crise" *Le Monde* (2 October 2019).

4 Theresa Liane Womble, "Early Constitutionalism in Tunisia, 1857–1864: Reform and revolt" (PhD dissertation, Princeton University, 1997) 27; Mezri Bdira, Relations internationales et sous-développement. La Tunisie 1857–1864 (Uppsala, Acta Universitatis Upsaliensis 1978) 27–28.

5 Cheryl Saunders, 'Constitution-Making in the 21st century' (2012) *International Review of Law* 1, 3.

transcends national borders,[6] were present during the drafting stage, providing comparative expertise to constitution-makers; these external bodies include organisations such as the the United Nations Development Programme (UNDP), the International Institute for Democracy and Electoral Assistance (International IDEA), and the European Commission for Democracy through Law, commonly known as the Venice Commission.[7]

While there has indeed been scholarly interest in constitution-making, in particular in the context of democratization,[8] there has been little empirical analysis of how it unfolds in situ.[9] Legal scholars have tended to consider that the provision of expertise in constitution-making is marginal, and hence not worthy of in-depth examination.[10] The literature on constitution-making interested in the transnational dimension is driven by normative concerns rather than descriptive ones.[11] This chapter aims to contribute to filling this gap.

This chapter argues that studying the transnational dimension of constitution-making is an important element of understanding how political systems are built. Drawing on discussions on the political dimension of expertise in legal reforms, the chapter describes how this translates to constitution-making, providing a more accurate and comprehensive picture of the transnational dimension of constitution-making, with an empirically driven account of foreign expert involvement. This chapter uses the case study of the 2014 Tunisian constitution to shed light on the transnational dimension of constitution-making.

To understand the dynamics of practices surrounding constitution-making, Tunisia represents an illustrative case because of its geopolitical location, as well as being a recent case of constitutional drafting. Tunisia triggered the so-called Arab Spring and the latest wave of democratisation in the MENA region, which has remained understudied by democratisation studies. Tunisia's constitution is also one of the most recent cases of constitution-making in the context of democratisation. The presence of transnational actors during constitution-making is a trend that has been acknowledged incidentally in other recent instances of constitution-making, such as South Sudan, Nepal and even Bolivia, where the process was branded by local leaders as immune to foreign involvement. If the scope of the

---

6 Roger Cotterrell, 'What is Transnational Law?' (2012) 37 *Law & Social Inquiry* 500, 501.

7 See Maartje De Visser, "A Critical Assessment of the Role of the Venice Commission in Processes of Domestic Constitutional Reform" (2015) 63 *The American Journal of Comparative Law*, 963; Quentin Deforge, "Une expertise internationale sans 'bonnes pratiques': Soutenir la professionnalisation du travail parlementaire dans la Tunisie d'après 2011" (2019), 127 *Critique internationale*, 299–302; Vijayashri Sripati, *Constitution-Making under UN Auspices: Fostering Dependency in Sovereign Lands*, (Oxford, Oxford University Press, 2020); Joseph Geng Akech, "Re-thinking Approaches to the International Constitutional Assistance in South Sudan" (2022) *The Sudd Institute Policy Briefs*.

8 David Law, "Constitutions" in Peter Cane and Herbert Kritzer (eds), *The Oxford Handbook of Empirical Legal Research*, (Oxford University Press 2010) 379.

9 See for instance Gregory Shaffer, Tom Ginsburg and Terence Halliday (eds), Constitution-Making and Transnational Legal Order (Cambridge University Press 2019); Ngoc Son Bui, "Contextualizing the Global Constitution-Making Process: the Case of Vietnam" (2016) 64 *The American Journal of Comparative Law*, 931.

10 Andrew Arato, "Constitution-Making" in Anthony Lang and Antje Wiener (eds), *Handbook on Global Constitutionalism* (Cheltenham, UK, Edward Elgar Publishing 2017), 285; Philipp Dann and Zaid Al-Ali, "The Internationalized Pouvoir Constituant-Constitution-Making under External Influence in Iraq, Sudan and East Timor" (2006) 10 *Max Planck Yearbook of United Nations Law* 423, 429.

11 Jon Elster, "Forces and Mechanisms in the Constitution-Making Process" (1995) 45 *Duke Law Journal*, 362.

external actors' involvement varies according to different contexts, Tunisia, by its geopolitical location, provides useful insights for a common trend.

To study the transnational dimension of constitution-making, data collected includes institutional documentation published by external actors, such as project and annual reports, as well as website publications. Another resource used to furnish an account of the intricacies of the process were the memoirs of three National Constituent Assembly (NCA) representatives. Twenty-three semi-structured interviews, conducted in French and/or English, were carried out with internal and external actors to complement the other data, lasting between 11 and 70 minutes. The interviews were conducted in person during fieldwork in Tunisia (February–April 2018) and during a research stay in the United States, while others were conducted over Skype (October 2018–February 2019). The snowball method was used to identify the sample.

This chapter analyses the involvement of external actors in Tunisia during the constitution-making process, which has received only anecdotal attention.[12] The provision of transnational expertise is a key feature that underpins the creation of new political systems and which tends to be elided by constitutional scholars beyond sparse references to the 'provision of expertise' and 'best practices'; there have not been descriptions of what this expertise entails *in concreto*.[13] It also contributes to constitutional scholarship by challenging idealised visions of the theory of constituent power, which underpins most of the literature. More generally, for a literature that has a normative focus, increasing our understanding at the descriptive level allows us to build fertile ground to discuss how constitution-making processes ought to be. Further, this chapter focuses on constitution-making, an area whose transnational element has only been sparsely studied by political scientists. Finally, describing this process is also helpful for future constitution-makers, who can better understand the political motivations of foreign expertise. It also allows constitution-makers to have a better grasp of how constitutional norms are actually created and may give them a better shot at achieving their normative goals.

Several caveats are in order before beginning. First, this chapter does not aim to assess the actual impact and influence of external actors on the constitution-making process, and how foreign expertise affected the final constitution. Instead, the goal is more descriptive, showing *how* constitutional expertise is provided by external actors, and shedding light on the political dimension. Second, the political dimension discussed in this chapter relates to external actors. There is also a political dimension of the provision of expertise on the domestic side as domestic actors can use expertise provided by external actors to achieve their own political goals. External actors also provided other types of support such as financial support or logistical and institutional support, through capacity-building or funding to cover human resources

---

[12] See Corrina Mullin, "Tunisia's Revolution and the domestic-international nexus" in Larbi Sadiki (ed), *Routledge Handbook of the Arab Spring: Rethinking Democratization*, (New York, Routledge, 2014); Esther Sigillo, "Beyond The Myth of the Tunisian Exception: the Open-Ended Tale of a Fragile Democratization" in Loretta Dell'Aguzzo and Diodato Emidio (eds), *The 'State' of Pivot States in South Eastern Mediterranean: Turkey, Egypt, Israel, and Tunisia After the Arab Spring*, (Perugia, Perugia Stranieri University Press, 2016) 111.

[13] See Tom Ginsburg, "Constitutional Advice and Transnational Legal Order" in Gregory Shaffer, Terence C. Halliday and Tom Ginsburg (eds), *Constitution-Making and Transnational Legal Order*, (Cambridge, Cambridge University Press, 2019); Sara Kendall, "'Constitutional Technicity': Displacing Politics through Expert Knowledge" (2015) 11 *Law, Culture and the Humanities*, 363–377.

necessary for day-to-day operations of the NCA, including parliamentary assistants.[14] This is beyond the scope of our inquiry. Finally, it should be emphasised that this chapter does not make an evaluative claim regarding the political dimension of expertise, but simply aims to examine this understudied aspect of constitution-making through the lens of the development enterprise.

This chapter first briefly highlights what constitutes the analytical lens of this chapter: the political dimension of the provision of expertise in other areas of political reform (1) before introducing the external actors involved in the drafting of the 2014 Tunisian Constitution (2). The chapter then moves to examine the provision of expertise during the drafting of the 2014 Tunisian constitution (3).

1. THE POLITICS OF TRANSNATIONAL LEGAL EXPERTISE IN POLITICAL LEGAL REFORMS

The topic of expertise has sparked scholarly discussions related to other areas of legal reforms that affect the political arena. These scholars put forward a simple thesis: expertise is political and has political consequences.[15] In the words of David Kennedy, 'experts act politically when they distribute resources among groups and individuals'.[16] The knowledge upon which expertise is based lies consciously or not against a particular 'background of common sense' about how the world is and ought to be.[17] This 'background of common sense' is political, as it dictates in universal terms what is actually a contested interpretation of reality, 'point[ing] to the hidden contestations and political nature of the expertise'.[18] Kennedy explains:

> The work of legal and policy experts is all about struggle, a form of struggle in which the saying and the doing blend into one another, the knowing is partial, the universal up for debate, while the technical, the ideological and the partisan are everywhere linked together.[19]

In other areas of legal reforms arising in the context of transition, such as peace-building, transitional justice or elections, there is an increasing volume of critical scholarship that sheds light on the fact that the provision of expertise by international actors is deeply political. Chandra

---

[14] See Alicia Pastor y Camarasa, "Demystifying How Constitutions Are Made – External Actors' Modes of Actions in the 2014 Tunisian Constitution" (2022) *Michigan Journal of Law and Society*, 51–112.

[15] See James Ferguson, *The Anti-Politics Machine: 'Development', Depoliticization and Bureaucratic Power in Lesotho* (London, Routledge, 1990); Raphaëlle Parizet, *Les paradoxes du développement: sociologie politique des dispositifs de normalisation des populations indiennes au Mexique* (Paris, Dalloz, 2015); Lucile Maertens and Raphaëlle Parizet, "'On ne fait pas de politique!' Les pratiques de dépolitisation au PNUD et au PNUE" (2017), 41 *Critique internationale*, 41.

[16] David Kennedy, "The 'Rule of Law', Political Choices, and Development Common Sense" in David M Trubek and Alvaro Santos (eds), *The New Law and Economic Development: a Critical Appraisal* (Cambridge, Cambridge University Press, 2006) 95.

[17] David Kennedy, *A World of Struggle: How Power, Law, and Expertise Shape Global Political Economy* (Princeton, Princeton University Press, 2018) 89.

[18] Briony Jones, "The Performance and Persistence of Transitional Justice and its Ways of Knowing Atrocity" (2020), 1 *Cooperation and Conflict*, 7.

[19] David Kennedy (2018), supra n 17 at 3.

Sriram has pointed out how post-conflict strategies resulting in institutional reform, including 'rewriting constitutions', involve struggles for power.[20] In this sense, expertise that is provided in these situations is neither neutral nor apolitical. Similarly, Dustin Sharp has observed that in transitional justice reform, 'the international assistance offered in such a context is projected as apolitical and technocratic, yet it carries heavy implications for the distribution of power (political, legal, social, etc.) in the post-conflict context'.[21] Finally, in the field of elections and parliament-building, Quentin Deforge has shown how international actors crafted and built a technocratic expertise.[22] Deforge's research highlights in detail how building a depoliticised technical expertise is the fruit of political struggle that is itself embedded in politics. However, in the area of constitution-making, there is very little work that centres on the political dimension of expertise.

Understanding the political dimension of expertise can help us to understand the full extent of its consequences. Indeed, the kind of expertise that is valued as legitimate is produced by a particular network of experts, which carries a vision of what is possible; for example, of which questions should be addressed in transitional justice,[23] or the specific political model most accommodating to peace-building. This means that if experts are treated as legitimate by international actors, other types of knowledge, holding a different vision on what is possible, are disregarded.[24] As Briony Jones notes, examining transitional justice, the politics of knowledge affects what is 'imagine[d] to be possible in policy and practice'.[25] It is important to bear in mind that the expertise provided by external actors carries its own epistemic limitations, which results in practical consequences. In the field of transitional justice, scholars have criticised the Western-centric conception of the legalistic state-led institutional approach set forth by international actors, as well as the impact that their involvement can have on any given process.[26] Patricia Lundy and Mark McGovern call into question the purported apolitical nature of international actors, pointing out how international assistance always carries with it deeply political implications.[27] For instance, deciding who counts as a 'victim' and what kind of reparations are in order are both fundamentally political questions. In contexts of peace-building, when a peace agreement is reached it often enshrines the distribution of power among different actors; and in the field of elections, providing advice on a particular type of electoral system obviously results in political consequences as it determines who can access and exercise political power.

---

[20] Chandra Lekha Sriram, "Justice as Peace? Liberal Peacebuilding and Strategies of Transitional Justice" (2007) 21 *Global Society*, 588.

[21] Dustin Sharp, "Addressing Dilemmas of the Global and the Local in Transitional Justice" (2014) 29 *Emory International Law Review*, 82.

[22] See Quentin Deforge, "La fabrique transnationale du politique. Une sociologie historique du champ réformateur de la 'gouvernance'" (1961–2019) (PhD dissertation), Université Paris-Dauphine 20 December 2019) 27.

[23] Briony Jones, supra n 18 at 9.

[24] Séverine Autesserre, *Peaceland: Conflict Resolution and the Everyday Politics of International Intervention* (Cambridge, Cambridge University Press, 2014) 70–90.

[25] Briony Jones, supra n 18 at 2.

[26] Rosemary Nagy, "Transitional Justice as global project: Critical reflections" (2008) 29 *Third World Quarterly*, 275.

[27] Patricia Lundy and Mark McGovern, "Whose justice? Rethinking Transitional Justice from the Bottom up" (2008) 35 *Journal of Law and Society*, 265.

2. INTRODUCING THE EXTERNAL ACTORS: DRAFTING THE 2014 TUNISIAN CONSTITUTION

On 17 December 2010, Mohamed Bouazizi immolated himself following the confiscation of his wares and the humiliation he suffered from the police. This ignited the dignity revolution, whose motto was '*Work! Freedom! National dignity!*'. Following the popular mass protests, the first reaction from the authorities was to call to modify the existing constitution. During the first phase of the transition that began with the sudden departure of Ben Ali, the authorities were taken by surprise and argued for the maintenance of the 1959 constitution. On 17 January 2011, the Committee of Political Reform ('the Committee') was founded and was immediately tasked with studying how to modify the constitution. Half of its members belonged to the Faculty of Juridical, Political and Social Sciences, of Tunis, which has been politically affiliated to a more secular understanding of the law. As Yadh Ben Achour, its president, writes in his memoirs, the Committee was tasked with reforming the constitution from a 'purely legal and technical perspective as well as revising the legal framework that defined the domestic political field'. Protestors called for the drafting of a new constitution. On 3 March 2011, the interim president, Fouad Mebazaa, called for the election of a national constituent assembly.

External actors were present from the first moments of the Tunisian revolution, and were welcomed by the Tunisian authorities. National political actors were surprised by the popular upheaval, to the point that national officials were willing to consider international and regional expertise on the numerous questions that had to be decided during the early period. The first part of the transition was characterised by the ratification of several human rights treaties in the early days of the revolution. It was marked by 'a certain feverishness'; as the former Secretary General of the Government in 2011 recalled, 'we wanted to show that Tunisia would break radically with its past.'

External actors either opened an office in Tunis, or shifted the focus of their work. On one side, some external actors had offices in Tunis for several decades and, at the time of the revolution, shifted their focus from economic issues or purely judicial reform to broader projects of democratic transition. Several German political foundations had been established in Tunisia for several decades, including the Friedrich Ebert Foundation, the Konrad Adenauer Foundation, the Friedrich Naumann Foundation, and the Hans Seidel Foundation. They shifted from economic issues to areas related to democratic transitions. Similarly, the presence of the UNDP in Tunisia can be traced back to 1987; prior to 2011, the UNDP centred its work on issues surrounding development, such as the Millennium Development Goals. On the other side, several external actors established offices in Tunis in late 2011 and early 2012. These include Berlin-based international non-government organisation Democracy Reporting International, the National Democratic Institute, and the Carter Center.

After the elections of the NCA on 23 October 2011, a shift in political power took place. Secular-minded politicians who had led the first part of the transition passed over the command to the Islamist party Ennahda, which won 41% of the seats and took the lead at the governmental level as well as at the NCA. Following the election, a coalition government emerged between Ennahda, Ettakatol, and the Congress for the Republic (Ettakatol and the Congress for the Republic lie on the centre-left of the political spectrum). They divided three high positions of power: Ettakatol took the presidency of the NCA (Mustapha Ben Jafâar), in December 2011; representatives of the NCA elected Moncef Marzouki as President of the Republic (Moncef Marzouki); and Hamadi Jebali became the Head of Government.

A deep polarisation between the 'moderates' and the 'Islamists' took place throughout the constitution-making process, which has been widely noted in the literature on the constitution-making process. This polarisation pervaded every step of the process: in every decision that had to be made in the different constituent committees tasked with drafting different chapters of the constitution, ranging from the status of religion, the choice of a political regime, to the choice of which constitutional bodies to enshrine. The crisis exploded in 2013, when the political assassinations of Chokri Belaïd (6 February 2013) and Mohamed Brahmi (25 July 2013) left Tunisia on the brink of chaos. The work of the NCA was suspended on 6 August 2013 and recommenced a month later. The military coup that took place in Egypt in July 2013 was understood by national actors to be a triggering event that pushed Ennahda to compromise. Formed during the summer of 2013, the Quartet composed of four civil society Tunisian associations (the Tunisian General Labor Union; the Tunisian Human Rights League; the Tunisian Order of Lawyers; and the Tunisian Union of Industry, Trade and Handicrafts) managed to rebuild dialogue between the antagonistic parties. The constitution was adopted on 26 January 2014.

3. UNPACKING THE PROVISION OF TRANSNATIONAL EXPERTISE DURING THE DRAFTING OF THE 2014 TUNISIAN CONSTITUTION

This section examines the political dimension of the expertise provided by external actors. To go beyond the internal perspective of external actors, which are often taken at face value by the literature, this section draws on cues from scholarship concerning the political dimension of expertise within the context of the development enterprise. Insights from other areas of legal reform – ranging from international human rights to peace-building, and transitional justice – point to the fact that expertise is inherently political, and *depoliticising* expertise has *political* consequences.

A central aspect of external actor involvement in the constitutional drafting stage was the provision of expertise to Tunisian constitution-makers. In a UNDP report, its involvement in the Tunisian constitution-making process is presented as 'resolv[ing] certain *technical* details (relating to various constitutional, legal and regulatory texts) to facilitate ending the political impasse that the country witnessed between July and December 2013'.[28] International IDEA explains that it provided expertise on issues such as 'system of government, fundamental rights, decentralisation', as well as producing 'a series of in-depth reports on each of these issues, which were made widely available to civil society and to members of the Constituent Assembly'.[29]

This section describes the provision of expertise by external actors during the constitutional drafting stage of the Tunisian constitution. It first highlights how external actors conceive of their expertise as neutral and apolitical (3.1), before examining transnational constitutional expertise more closely and exposing its political dimension (3.2).

---

[28] UNDP. Project of Support to Constitution-Building, Parliamentary Development and National Dialogue in Tunisia. Activity Report: May 2012 – September 2014. UNDP (2014), 9.

[29] International IDEA, *A Record of Actions* 2013 (2014) 18.

3.1 Providing 'Neutral' and 'Technical' Expertise

Throughout the constitution-making process in Tunisia, external actors – both non-governmental organisations and INGOs alike – were adamant that the expertise they provided was apolitical and neutral. The UNDP employee working in Tunisia highlights how 'there was no real imposition in terms of content'.[30] 'Political neutrality' is one of the guiding principles of the Max Planck Foundation: 'only when partners are convinced that the Foundation is not following a political agenda, can it successfully provide sustainable and lasting support.'[31] Across the board, external actors conceived of their involvement as apolitical and technical. The NCA legal adviser stressed that the UNDP 'cared about neutrality [...] the provided financial, logistical support [...] but in terms of advice no[thing]'.[32] This is in contrast with the constitutional expertise provided by Tunisian scholars, which was stamped as *political*.

Expertise provided by local experts was seen as tainted, as this is evidenced both by external actors and Tunisian actors. For instance, the UNDP employee noted how 'constitutional scholars were people that labelled themselves as progressives [secularist strand]'.[33] Tunisian actors similarly conceived of Tunisian expertise as political; this is evidenced by the debate surrounding local expertise during the drafting stage that was one of the manifestations of the polarisation that existed throughout the constitution-making process, with Ennahda on one side, and the 'secular' moderates on the other. Local expertise was thus treated as politically loaded, with constitutional experts belonging to one side or the other[34] – as the NCA legal adviser noted, regarding constitutional experts 'as the choice reflects the political affinities of those who chose them'.[35]

Throughout Tunisia's democratic transition, the constitutional scholars that belonged to the Faculty of Legal, Political and Social Sciences of Tunis ('Faculty'), which was politically oriented towards the moderates, were involved, particularly in the early stages. The Commission for Political Reform, which was set up in January 2011 to amend the 1959 constitution, was composed of 12 experts, and six of those were from the Faculty: Professors Laghmani, Horchani, Chekir, Sarsar, Ghrairi, and the Commission's President, Professor Yadh Ben Achour.[36] The results of the NCA giving Ennahda the upper hand led to questioning the political affiliations of these experts involved in the early days of the transition.

---

30 Interview, UNDP employee, 20 December 2018: "Y'a pas vraiment d'imposition en terme de contenu". [My own translation]

31 Max Planck Foundation for International Peace and the Rule of Law "Guiding Principles" http://www.mpfpr.de/foundation/foundation/guiding-Principles/ (accessed 10 February 2022).

32 Interview, legal adviser at the NCA, 13 mars 2018: "Ils avaient le souci de la neutralité, [...] ils ont fourni un véritable soutien financier, logistique, [...] Mais sur le plan du conseil non, sur le plan du conseil non". [My own translation].

33 Interview, UNDP employee, 20 December 2018: "la plupart des constitutionalistes étaient clairement des gens qui se disaient progressistes.". [My own translation].

34 Selma Mabrouk, *Le Bras De Fer, 2011–2014.* Tunis: Arabesques, 2018, 127.

35 Interview, legal adviser at the NCA, 13 mars 2018: "certains experts, n'ont pas eu d'impact, bien que le choix [des experts] reflète les affinités politiques de ceux qui les ont choisis". [My own translation].

36 See "La Commission Supérieure Pour La Réforme Politique." Portail de la Présidence du Gouvernement, 28 January 2011, accessed 26 July 2018, http://www.pm.gov.tn/pm/actualites/actualite.php?lang=fr&id=2087.

During the constitutional drafting phase, 'expertise' was a central issue that divided the Islamists and secularists. NCA representative Selma Mabrouk recalled that the Committee on Rights and Freedoms hosted hearings in July 2012 with representatives of the *Association des Femmes Démocrates*, which politically leans towards the secular, which were obstructed by Ennahda.[37] Mabrouk also notes other instances where polarisation hindered the quality of the debate.[38]

The relationship that existed between Tunisian constitutional experts and a political party, or at least a commitment to either Islamist or secularist thought, meant that their expertise was branded as 'political' by NCA representatives. In contrast, external actors were treated as politically neutral, given that they did not have specific ties to any Tunisian political party, and that they provided advice to *all* political groups represented in the NCA. An employee of Democracy Reporting International (DRI) insisted that they offered expertise to all political parties 'in an equitable matter', and that the constitutional drafting process was sovereign.[39]

3.2 Content of Transnational Expertise

A closer look at the content of transnational expertise reveals its political dimension. Whether it is by raising awareness (3.2.1) or commenting or constitutional drafts (3.2.2), external actors' involvement deals ultimately with the sharing of power among political actors, and thus has political consequences, as the first section of this chapter highlighted.

3.2.1 Raising awareness

The provision of expertise from external experts can first be characterised as 'raising awareness' on the range of options available to constitution-makers. As the Max Planck Institute explains its involvement in Tunisia: 'The aim of the project is, first and foremost, to educate the members of the Constituent Assembly on important constitutional topics and raise awareness about the far-reaching decisions they will make when developing the new constitution.'[40] This facet of expertise manifested early on, when constitution-makers were still at the discussion stage. A UNDP employee highlighted how the provision of expertise manifested by showing different options of what existed in other legal systems, raising awareness on the different options available to them:

> Only on points where they came to ask us. Here we're blocked, can you tell us what are the options that exists? [...] The idea is that if there is support on the content, [...] it is to explain what exists everywhere, what are the options possible that can be integrated.[41]

---

37 Selma Mabrouk, supra n 34 at 127.

38 Selma Mabrouk, supra n 34 at 154.

39 Interview, former employee of DRI, 21 February 2018.

40 Max Planck Institute, *Ten Years of Global Knowledge Transfer* 2002–2012 (2012) 100.

41 Interview, UNDP employee, 20 December 2018: "uniquement sur les points où ils sont venus vraiment nous demander, voilà là on bloque, est-ce que vous pouvez nous dire quelles sont les options qui existent, [...] Donc en fait l'idée, si y'a un appui au niveau du contenu, c'est surtout un appui, c'est pour expliquer ce qui existe partout, les options qui sont possibles, qui peuvent s'intégrer avec le reste des articles et voilà, après c'est eux qui choisissent". [My own translation].

Similarly, DRI highlighted its role in providing this expertise. An employee of DRI explained that as constitution-makers had no knowledge on constitutional issues, the role of DRI's expert was 'to explain, how a modification in the executive, legislature or judiciary could impact the general shape of the state'.[42] He also explains what his day-to-day activities at the NCA headquarters were: parliamentarians would ask him what DRI could do under each theme and, often in a time period as short as two hours, he would deliver expertise to various NCA representatives. As he recounted, the minimum was to 'deliver a comparative chart with no commentary, without annotation, on, for instance, the constitutional court in Poland, or South Africa'.[43] Finally he notes how certain topics were central to DRI's agenda, such as the division of powers, 'so we must clearly generate their interest for that'.[44] Finally, the expert sent by Max Planck explained how:

> As an expert in comparative constitutional law I also talked a bit on international law, as international law in contemporary constitution-making takes a more important role each day, and how each country has to define its role in the international community, in the regional context.[45]

3.2.2 Commenting on constitutional drafts

External actors also shared comparative knowledge through commenting on various constitutional drafts in Tunisia. Several external actors published specifically on Tunisia covering many areas related to constitutional drafting, including a general overview of the pros and cons of different options. The Center for Constitutional Transitions, in collaboration with International IDEA, published a series of recommendations on the final draft of the Tunisian constitution, released in June 2013; these recommendations addressed the judiciary,[46] decentralisation,[47] human rights,[48] system of government,[49] good governance and corruption,[50] and the security force.[51] The final section of these documents contained specific recommendations regarding the draft of the Tunisian constitution. DRI also released advisory documents

---

[42] Interview, former employee of DRI, 21 February 2018: "C'était plutôt expliquer par exemple, je crois que c'était son exercice favori, ce qu'une modification dans le pouvoir d'un des exécutif, législatif, judiciaire, comment ça pouvait impacter the general shape of the State". [My own translation].

[43] Interview, former employee of DRI, 21 February 2018.

[44] Interview, former employee of DRI, 21 February 2018: "Puis y'avait d'autres thématiques qui entraient dans l'agenda DRI, la répartition des pouvoirs entrait clairement dans l'agenda DRI donc il fallait clairement éveiller leur intérêt pour ça". [My own translation].

[45] Interview, Max Planck Institute expert, 19 November 2018.

[46] Tom Ginsburg, *The Tunisian Judicial Sector: Analysis and Recommendations*. International IDEA & Center for Constitutional Transitions (June 2013).

[47] Jörg Fedtke, Tunisian Constitutional Reform and Decentralization: Reactions to the Draft Constitution of the Republic of Tunisia, International IDEA & Center for Constitutional Transitions (June 2013).

[48] International IDEA & Center for Constitutional Transitions, Tunisian Constitutional Reform and Fundamental Rights: Reactions to the Draft Constitution of the Republic of Tunisia (June 2013).

[49] International IDEA, Semi-Presidentialism as a Form of Government: Lessons for Tunisia.

[50] International IDEA, Preventing and Combatting Corruption: Good Governance and Constitutional Law in Tunisia.

[51] International IDEA, Security Forces Reform for Tunisia.

regarding constitutional review,[52] rights of the opposition,[53] restrictions of human rights,[54] and semi-presidentialism.[55]

More specifically, external actors also commented on the constitutional drafts either during hearings at the NCA or during workshops held in Tunis and abroad. For instance, the Max Planck expert also noted how his hearing at the NCA unfolded:

> You start by giving an assessment of the details draft and then you engage in questions concerning the general outline as well of details concerning the draft, which is before you. That was what happened in June 2012. It's close to the text and the discussion they are having in the Assembly as possible not providing any academic lectures on point that are not or only loosely related of what is relevant to the members of the constituent assembly.[56]

Regardless of where the provision of expertise took place, as International IDEA states in its 2013 Annual Report, its advising for Tunisia began with a 'comparative analysis of diverse constitutional experience', with their experts commenting on constitutional drafts, and 'mak[ing] recommendations based on the lessons learnt of their own constitutional experience'.[57]

Expert advising translated in commenting on the exact wording of specific provisions or the overall coherence of the constitutional text. The expert working for the UNDP noted how when reading a draft, 'I would tell myself, it is well written, it is not well written. It should be corrected, it should be improved.'[58] He recalls, for instance:

> You are given a chapter titled 'the judiciary', which for the legal expert holds a specific meaning, and you note that in this chapter on the judiciary, a constitutional court is included. And no, this does not work, it should not be the judiciary, it must be the judicial authority or it must be jurisdiction.[59]

Expertise also manifested in highlighting potential problems that the constitutional draft did not foresee. Concerning the rules governing the organisation of the Constitutional Court, the Venice Commission stated that, 'the procedures to be followed before it, and the guarantees enjoyed by its members shall be specified in law: these provisions should be set out in an institutional law and not an ordinary law'.[60] Experts also pointed out lacunae in the constitutional

---

[52] DRI, Center for Constitutional Transitions, *Constitutional Review in New Democracies* (September 2013).

[53] DRI, Constitutional Rights of the Opposition (February 2013).

[54] DRI, Lawful Restrictions on Civil and Political Rights (October 2012).

[55] DRI, Systems of Government: Semi Presidential Models (June 2012).

[56] Interview, Max Planck Institute expert, 19 November 2018.

[57] UNDP – International IDEA, Conférence sur les expériences constitutionnelles. Afrique du Sud – France – Canada – Egypt – Jordanie – Kenya – Maroc – Allemagne – Iraq – Etats Unis – Inde. Note conceptuelle (10–11–12 May 2013) 2.

[58] Interview, UNDP expert, 30 April 2021: "Moi je lis les textes, je me dis c'est bien écrit, c'est pas bien écrit. Il faudrait corriger, il faudrait améliorer". [My own translation]

[59] Interview, UNDP expert, 30 April 2021: "Et par exemple pour vous donner un exemple précis on vous donne un chapitre qui s'intitule le pouvoir judiciaire, ce qui pour le juriste a tout de même un sens précis, et vous constaterez que dans ce chapitre le pouvoir judiciaire, on prévoit une cour constitutionnelle. Et non ça ne va pas, il faut ne faut pas mettre le pouvoir judiciaire à savoir il faut mettre pouvoir juridictionnel ou bien il faut mettre les juridictions". [My own translation]

[60] Venice Commission, Observation on the Final Draft Constitution of the Republic of Tunisia (Venice Commission, 11–12 October 2013) 31.

draft. Regarding semi-presidentialism, Sujit Choudhry, Director of the Center of Constitutional Transition, lamented the 'absence of mechanisms by which the government can be called to account before the legislature – such as questions, questions period, interpellations'.[61] Other gaps in the constitution were pointed out, such as the tenure of judges, where Ginsburg noted that 'consideration should be given to defining a judicial term, or a mandatory retirement age'.[62]

Experts not only identified gaps, but they also suggested how to fill them. On the limitation of rights clause (Article 49 of the constitution), Fedtke claimed that the constitutional draft 'in its current form does not provide much guidance as far as these issues are concerned. International experience strongly suggests that the text should at least identify procedures and criteria for the valid limitation of fundamental rights'.[63] In the opinion of the Venice Commission, Slavica Banić, Finola Flanagan, Michael Frendo, Wilhelmina Thomassen and Ben Vermeulen commented:

> The solution currently contained in the draft Constitution is unsatisfactory since the presence of a specific clause only for certain rights is inexplicable and confusing…to reword the second sentence of Article 48 in general terms, removing the reference to certain legitimate aims. As a result, Article 48 would set out the general principles, the application of which is governed in a specific way for each right.[64]

Similar suggestions were made with regard to the anti-discrimination clause, with Banić et al. from the Venice Commission noting that 'Article 20 makes no reference to the specific and different forms of discrimination, namely discrimination on the grounds of sex, race, colour, language, religion, political opinion, national or social origin, membership of a national minority, wealth, birth or any other status';[65] regarding parliamentary immunity, they urged that it should be perpetual, 'under the terms of Article 67, parliamentary immunity relating to parliamentary duties (opinions and votes) applies only during a member's term of office. We believe that it should be perpetual and final, as for example in France and Belgium.'[66]

Finally, experts also suggested that particular institutions or rights were included in the constitution, which were not initially contemplated by Tunisian constitution-makers. In order to foster the independence of the judiciary, Ginsburg suggested to 'consider designating a Prosecutor General in the Constitution'.[67] Experts from International IDEA and the Venice Commission suggested to enshrine fundamental rights surrounding detention in the constitution.[68] The expert working for the UNDP noted an important gap in the structure of the constitution itself: there were no transitional provisions. As he recalls, 'there was no final provision on how we go from the Bourguiba Republic to the Mazourki Republic. The legal expert must

---

61 International IDEA & Center for Constitutional Transitions, *Semi-Presidentialism as a Form of Government: Lessons for Tunisia* (June 2013) 18.

62 Tom Ginsburg, supra n 46 at 5.

63 Jörg Fedtke, supra n 47 at 3.

64 Observation on the Final Draft Constitution of the Republic of Tunisia (Venice Commission, 11–12 October 2013) 12.

65 Slavica Banić et al., Observation on the Final Draft Constitution of the Republic of Tunisia (Venice Commission, 11–12 October 2013) 13.

66 Slavica Banić et al., supra n 65 at 19.

67 Tom Ginsburg, supra n 46 at 9.

68 Jörg Fedtke, supra n 47 at 10; Slavica Banić et al., supra n 65 at 14.

think about that, about the transitional, final provisions. Here I wrote and I claim the writing of the chapter on this topic.'[69]

To formulate these recommendations, experts often rely on 'international standards' and 'best practices'. An expert working for DRI explains how he presented 'an analysis of the Draft of the Constitution compared to standards applicable in constitutional comparative law'.[70] Similarly, Fedtke, an expert working for International IDEA, noted on the topic of limitation clauses that 'proportionality is, by international standards, arguably the single most important factor when it comes to the limitation of fundamental rights'.[71] With regard to freedom of assembly, Banić et al. mentioned that 'it should be pointed out in relation to this Article that there is a need to add the principle of proportionality and necessity in a democratic society and to comply with international standards in relation to the permitted restrictions'.[72] They added, concerning rights limitations, that the 'legitimate aims referred to in Article 48 (protection of the rights of others, public security, national defence and public health) are not all applicable to all rights, and other legitimate aims are recognised by international standards'.[73] On the topic of anti-discrimination law, they recommended that 'the text of Article 20 be harmonised with international instruments'.[74] Finally, with regard to constitutional amendments, Fedtke noted that, 'the substantial limitations envisioned by Art. 136 (declaring that amendments may not prejudice certain enumerated principles and guaranteed fundamental rights and freedoms) seem, by international standards, too restrictive'.[75] These examples of expertise provided on the draft constitution highlight the deeply political dimension, which external actors obfuscate behind technocratic projections of their expertise.

CONCLUSION

This chapter has explored the transnational dimension of constitution-making through a case study of the making of the 2014 Tunisian Constitution, focusing on the political dimension of expertise. Because Tunisia is a typical case of external actor involvement in constitution-making, an examination of its constitution-making process can provide important insights for other similar cases. The chapter first discussed the political dimension of expertise in other areas of political reform before introducing the external actors that were present in Tunisia. It then described what constitutional expertise actually involved, from the perspective of external actors via interviews and institutional documentation. The chapter highlighted how expertise provided by local experts was conceived as political, while constitutional expertise provided by external actors was seen as apolitical and technical. Finally, it classified the

---

69 Interview, UNDP expert, 30 April 2021: "Il n'y a aucune disposition finale sur comment passe-t-on de la République Bourguiba à la Républiques Mazourki. Le hapit doit penser à ça, aux dispositions transitoires, dispositions finales. Voilà, j'ai écrit je revendique la rédaction du hapiter sur ce sujet". [My own translation]

70 Expert working for DRI, Mission reporting on the participation of civil society & political parties to the constitutional making process in Tunisia – June 2013 (Undated (accessed January 2021)).

71 Jörg Fedtke, supra n 47 at 7.

72 Slavica Banić et al., supra n 65 at 17.

73 Slavica Banić et al., supra n 65 at 12.

74 Slavica Banić et al., supra n 65 at 13.

75 Jörg Fedtke, supra n 47 at 9.

content of constitutional expertise, distinguishing between awareness-raising for local actors and direct engagement on constitutional drafts.

Against the backdrop of the experts' own understanding of their activity as "neutral" and "technical", this chapter has endeavoured to describe the political dimension of constitutional expertise. This does not per se invalidate the content of the expertise provided, but it brings important attention to the political dimension of constitution-making by the different actors involved in the process – constitution-makers, social movements and the experts themselves.

The political dimension of expertise emphasises another normative implication, which is that relying on "best practices" and comparative knowledge results in a prioritisation of replication over innovation in constitution-making, ignoring the vast literature and practical manifestations of democratic innovation that have emerged recently.[76] This once again points to the fact that the legal phenomenon of constitution-making remains a black box that warrants further exploration, particularly if we are concerned with the associated normative ideals of legitimacy, sovereignty and democratic participation.

[76] See Hélène Landemore, "Open Democracy: Reinventing Popular Rule for the Twenty-First Century" (Princeton, Princeton University Press, 2020).

13. The battle for judicial independence

Courts functioning as constitutional beacons and political responses in El Salvador

Mónica Castillejos-Aragón

INTRODUCTION

The COVID-19 pandemic unleashed public confrontations between the executive power and the magistrates of the Supreme Court of Justice in El Salvador. The magistrates curbed the executive's efforts to dismantle the rule of law and overt violations of human rights, while adopting measures during the pandemic, including forced confinement for those who did not comply with quarantine. In February 2021, a new Legislative Assembly was elected, and President Nayib Bukele's political party acquired an overwhelming majority. Following this political shift, the Salvadoran president encouraged and defended the vote of the deputies to enforce Article 186 of the Salvadoran Constitution, which contemplates that the Legislative Assembly is empowered to dismiss the magistrates "for specific causes, previously established by law." The Court's packing was approved by an absolute majority (64 of 84 voted in favor, including all the deputies of President Bukele's party and other allies), on the grounds that the magistrates had acted against the constitution, prioritizing particular interests over the health and life of the population. Despite such political clashes, the case of El Salvador offers a new model of judicial behavior, and judicial responses to political threats to judicial independence.

Even in democratic nations, the executive power narrows civil liberties in times of emergency, including personal mobility, the writ of habeas corpus, and mechanisms to access justice systems. Literature in this field suggests that courts function poorly as guardians of liberty in times of crisis. To support the account of such weak judicial behavior during crisis, scholarly research has offered various persuasive reasons. A strain of research claims that courts are ineffective guardians of liberty when the public is clamoring for immediate security (Cole 2003). In times of emergency, the executive becomes unfettered and, for strategic reasons, both judges and legislators delegate a massive amount of power to the executive. The focus of literature on emergencies suggests that courts often evaluate the validity of crisis policies only after the emergency has passed. Judges remain silent and acquiescent to the executive's policies (Cole 2003). In fact, Vermeule and Posner (2008) suggest that during emergencies the executive is "unbound" and it becomes inherently difficult for judges to review the executive measures because information is often asymmetric in comparison with the executive (Posner 2020).

A second strain of research argues that judges do not rule against the government on emergency policies, concerned that their credibility and legitimacy might be tested and that it could trigger the executive's defiance of the court's decision. Socio-legal scholarship also claims that courts are deferential to the executive policies because judicial decision-making is a process. Judicial decisions require a statement of reasons that would bind future cases and would limit the power of the judiciary with future emergencies. Therefore, judges become highly deferential to the executive's will (Cole 2003).

From a political science perspective, scholars claim that courts will only challenge powerful actors in defense of rights and rule of law principles if the formal political context allows them to act. Judges become more assertive when there is political fragmentation (Botero 2018). However, as Hilbink (2012) observes, "something other than political fragmentation is needed to explain assertive judicial behavior."

Does the Salvadoran case teach scholars anything new about the causes, trajectory, and judicial outcomes to explain when and how courts check on elected officials? The recent behavior of the Constitutional Chamber of the Supreme Court in El Salvador challenges those propositions and suggests a different account to understand and assess judicial behavior in times of emergency. Until recently, President Nayib Bukele had governed with a parliamentary minority, which unleashed a permanent confrontation with members of the Legislative Assembly, and with the magistrates of the Supreme Court – the highest tribunal in El Salvador.

Amid the constitutional crisis caused by the presidential policies and management of the pandemic, President Nayib Bukele announced his unwillingness to comply with the Constitutional Chamber's decisions, which had ordered a stop to abusive actions and overt violations of constitutional rights while implementing his executive's measures to contain the COVID-19 pandemic. President Bukele, an avid user of social media, said he would not abide by a resolution that ordered him to murder Salvadoran citizens, which was not the judgment mandate, but to abide by the principles recognized in the Constitution of El Salvador. The Constitutional Chamber's resolution at no time ordered him to suspend the quarantine, but rather the magistrates provided clear guidelines for the executive and legislative to mend abuses reported by citizens (Melendez 2020).

Despite such persistent political hostility and harassment, Salvadoran magistrates exercised their authority, proving – as Hilbink, and Kapiszewski and Taylor suggest – that political fragmentation is neither necessary nor sufficient for judges to assert their power and demonstrate judicial independence (Kapiszewski and Taylor 2008). Rather, additional variables have reinvigorated the Chamber's institutional response *vis-à-vis* highly contested measures imposed by President Bukele to contain the spread of COVID-19.

This chapter describes how recent judicial developments in El Salvador offer a unique model for understanding the role of courts during emergencies. This piece argues that, like a beacon, in uncertain times, the Constitutional Chamber has cast its bright light for the executive and legislative powers to see and follow the meaning of the constitution. The Constitutional Chamber has exercised its power, making active use of the capacity for action conferred on the magistrates in the 1989 constitution, and it has served as institutional check on both the executive's and the legislature's measures. The Constitutional Chamber has assertively protected and enforced rights enshrined in the constitution.

This chapter also describes the novel behavior of the Constitutional Chamber and how Salvadoran magistrates have moved swiftly to address unique challenges resulting from the COVID-19 pandemic, to ensure the judiciary remains vigilant – as a light keeper, setting up constitutional buoys and markers for the executive and legislators to navigate within legitimate constitutional limits, and constantly checking and repositioning them as needed.

With this insight in mind, this chapter explores broader questions about when and how courts check on the elected branches. Featuring hyper-presidential systems and a tradition of judicial dependence, the expectation is that courts will be neither willing nor able to challenge the elected branches of government, but the intriguing question becomes the central configuration of conditions under which judges will dare to act.

To understand the unique and new role of the Constitutional Chamber as a constitutional beacon, the organization of this chapter proceeds as follows. The first section provides a historical overview of the country's political struggle to consolidate the rule of law after the critical years of civil war. The second section describes the process of creation of the Constitutional Chamber in 1989 as well the struggle to establish an independent and autonomous judiciary in El Salvador. The third section describes the executive power response to the COVID-19 pandemic. Finally, the fourth section provides my account of the rise in power and assertiveness of the Constitutional Chamber in El Salvador and its response against President Bukele's extraordinary measures to contain the pandemic.

1. INSTITUTIONALIZATION OF THE ADMINISTRATION OF JUSTICE

The civil war in El Salvador lasted over a decade and cost more than 70,000 Salvadoran lives. Prior to the eruption of the conflict, El Salvador had gone unnoticed from the international panorama. As David Mason (1999) notes, the war brought El Salvador to the attention of academics, activists, policymakers, and the public in general. Even though the United Nations called for major reforms of the judicial and electoral systems, the peace agreements' approach on the role of the judiciary was limited. Several factors triggered such governmental silence. There was a shallow debate resulting in the parties' inability to propose solutions beyond political reproach and public recriminations but also the indifference of judicial operators undermined any efforts to build an independent judicial power in the country (Villacencia Terreros 1996).

The United Nations played a role not just as a mediator in negotiations but as a neutral third party overseeing the implementation of the peace accords, and quickly shifted the discussions from the political arena to the need for human rights monitoring (Mason 1999). The UN Mission, or ONUSAL, carried out an active role in advancing a progressive human rights agenda and protection through the administration of justice system. ONUSAL denounced judicial misconduct practices by local authorities and advanced a series of technical assistance proposals. However, as the process becoming more political led to the early withdrawal of the UN Mission, and decreased its operational capacity and leverage, making it impossible to continue with the active role of monitoring the functioning of the justice system and thus became a mere observer. In the following years, there was an increase in citizens' distrust of the judicial system (Villacencia Terreros 1996).

Although some progress was achieved following the signing of the 1996 peace agreement, a set of reforms introduced to reorganize the judiciary remained insufficient. After 1996, there was no further reflection on the function and nature of the Supreme Court. The institutional apparatus remained fragile, including a weak composition of the National Council of the Judiciary, and the lack of financial independence limited progress to restore the judiciary (Villacencia Terreros 1996). The Supreme Court of the civil war years maintained the *status quo*. The former president of the Supreme Court, Magistrate Mauricio Gutiérrez Castro, held an unhealthy amount of power and became a major obstacle to institutional reform. Magistrate Gutiérrez also interfered in judicial proceedings and influenced the outcome instituted in

1990 to prosecute members of the military for their participation in the infamous *El Mozote* Massacre (Jackson and O'Shaughnessey 1999) Since the outset, the Supreme Court displayed hostility toward the implementation of the peace accords and to the UN recommendations that promoted constitutional reform aimed at the restructuring of and appointment of new magistrates to the Supreme Court of El Salvador. As Jackson and O'Shaughnessy describe, impunity for human rights abuses reflected broader problems for the judiciary, and those judges responsible for handling cases of enforced disappearances, massacres or extrajudicial killings were often killed or threatened (Jackson and O'Shaughnessey 1999).

Thus, judicial reform became a high priority in El Salvador, a country where militarism had harsh consequences for the civilian population, and where the judiciary was especially fragile and corrupt. Similar to other nations in Central America, the judiciary in El Salvador was not deemed an independent branch of government, characterized by its institutional weakness and reflected in a lack of resources, ill-trained personnel, low salaries, and lack of transparency in the decision-making process. As Seider (1996) claims, "throughout the civil war the judicial system consummately failed to challenge the impunity of the military, which refused to submit to the rule of law." After an intense partisan debate, it was in mid-1994 when the Legislative Assembly appointed new magistrates according to the process enshrined in the constitutional reforms advocated as part of the peace process. Magistrates were selected based on professional merits and were less partisan (Villacencia Terreros 1996). The newly appointed magistrates took stock of the various challenges of the administration of justice recognized by both the Truth Commission (Betancour, Figueredo Planchart and Buergenthal 1992–1993) and the UN Mission, including modernizing the judicial system, investigating serious violations of human rights committed during the war, addressing the problem of prisons overcrowded with pretrial detainees, eradicating corruption, training judicial officials, backlogs, delays in delivering justice, and ending impunity (Popkin 2000).

2. POST-CIVIL WAR ERA: THE CREATION OF THE CONSTITUTIONAL CHAMBER

Democratization theorists have only just begun to recognize the importance of the rule of law. The case of El Salvador shows that justice and security reform are central variables for consolidating democracy. Judicial reform laid the groundwork for improving justice institutions that enhance professional standards and judicial independence from the executive power. However, despite significant progress, the justice system continued to be politicized, slow, and held in low regard (Jackson and O'Shaughnessy 1999).

Following the historic Chapultepec Peace Accords in 1992, there was a lingering perception in El Salvador that peace did not equal justice. Despite significant progress, the country's post-civil war struggle to establish fully independent and credible institutions, capable of providing justice to all its people, is well documented. After the peace accords, human rights violations continued. The judiciary lacked independence and failed to investigate and try cases of serious human rights violations. Existing problems withing the judiciary hindered efforts to establish and strengthen the rule of law, including entrenched corruption and institutional inefficiency (Popkin 2000). Public opinion revealed dissatisfaction with progress in reforming the administration of justice.

Emergencies are not new in El Salvador, but the Supreme Court role remained passive and subservient to the executive power. The civil war led to multiple restrictions on civil liberties. The notable resolution of the armed conflict (1979–1992) has been properly praised, but the process of building the rule of law has remained a work in progress in El Salvador. An independent justice system is a necessary component of a democracy. And a justice system capable of protecting rights and remedying wrongs regardless of the power of those responsible has never existed in El Salvador. The widespread rule of law violations reflected the lack of judicial independence.

The creation of the Constitutional Chamber in 1983 represented a crucial step toward the consolidation of democracy, to ensure constitutional supremacy and to safeguard the functioning of institutions against arbitrary power. During the drafting process of the 1984 constitution, a Legislative Commission (1983) considered creating an intermediate system between the creation of a special court not dependent on judicial power and the power of the Supreme Court to review constitutional processes. Such an intermediate system resulted in creating a fourth chamber with jurisdiction to exclusively review constitutional process, such as amparo writs, habeas corpus, and unconstitutionality legal recourses. The Constitutional Chamber is presided over by the president of the Supreme Court.

At the outset, the Constitutional Chamber has operated as a neutral decision-making body and has defined the powers and competencies of public power, avoiding the predominance of any of them as well as the protection of fundamental rights. The Constitutional Chamber is the sole body within the judicial structure, empowered to preserve the principle of separation of powers; to safeguard the democratic principle against abuses by the majority; and to protect fundamental rights, as a guarantee for the development of a true democratic debate (*Inconstitucionalidad* 7–12–2013).

From its creation until 2010, the Constitutional Chamber became subject of a more ideological debate rather than a legal one. Judicial outcomes have been closely scrutinized, mainly because of the number of opinions that have significantly altered the electoral system and reduced the political parties' quota when appointing public officials (Santamaría Alvarenga 2016). However, their role as a guarantor of the fundamental rights enshrined in the constitution was not visible until recent years. The idea of the Constitutional Chamber as a court to promote the consolidation of democracy presented a major challenge and, if achieved, a key progress for justices to build upon.

In 2020, the Chamber became committed to functioning as a court for democracy. Magistrates of the Constitutional Chamber became more responsive to societal demands as part of a strategy to build much-needed legitimacy and challenged the executive's responses to the pandemic when undermining the rights and liberties enshrined in the constitution.

3. EXECUTIVE RESPONSE TO THE COVID-19 PANDEMIC

On March 11, 2020, President Nayib Bukele defied El Salvador's status as a constitutional democracy, causing an unprecedented crisis. Amid the COVID-19 outbreak, President Bukele proposed a series of controversial decrees to limit the spread of the virus among the population. Since their adoption, President Bukele has embarked on an open-ended and seemingly Olympian confrontation with both the Legislative Assembly and the Constitutional Chamber over what he deems an internal power struggle between them, rather than a constitutional controversy. The executive has issued over 87 administrative regulations, including decrees, accords, and ministerial resolutions, imposing highly controversial policies that have affected the lives of thousands of Salvadorans. Three days after the World Health Organization's pandemic declaration, with no known cases in the country, the president took the extreme measure of announcing a collective quarantine – considered by many a *de facto* exception regime with serious implications for people's rights and liberties.

At the outset, Bekele's fast response was, in fact, praised by the international press, especially for the short-term positive impact of such restrictions *vis-à-vis* the number of cases reported in the country. Yet the content and scope of those decrees tell a different story. A *de facto* regime was institutionalized through Decree 594, which allegedly incorporated the "Temporary Restriction of Concrete Constitutional Rights Law to Handle the COVID-19 Pandemic" into the legal system. Even though the law did not formally declare the existence of an exception regime, in practice it restricted and violated rights and freedoms, including the freedom of movement and due process of law rights. Decree 594 was in effect for 60 days and, 15 days after its expiration, its contents had been replicated in Decree 611, with slight variations. Decree 611 included the "Regulation for Isolation, Quarantine, Observation and Surveillance Law," which officially established an exception regime in the country.

Also, under public health pretenses, Nayib Bukele used the military as public security agents and gave the police *carte blanche* to commit a series of human rights violations. Since then, hundreds of Salvadorans have been illegally arrested and detained in overcrowded quarantine centers ("*centros de contención*") with proven unsanitary conditions. Citizens who did not previously present any symptoms tested positive after spending days in such illegal detention, all in clear violation of their due process rights. These measures resulted in higher infection rates and the deaths of some detainees. People were arrested for not wearing a mask – even though the country's supply had run short – or for walking to grocery stores or pharmacies. Both the military and the police became "quasi-medical professionals" empowered to determine who was infected or not, without any scientific basis. Videos have circulated showing police officers beating elderly citizens for violating quarantine measures. Other videos have shown police officers forcing a group of men to walk in line down the street, with their hands on their heads, and shouting, "I don't have to leave my house!"

In April 2020, President Bukele, an avid user of social media, posted a series of shocking photos from a prison, displaying hundreds of gang members sitting on the ground, closely against each other, wearing only underwear and a few face masks. Rival gang members were relocated and commingled in overcrowded cells during the pandemic. President Bukele ordered this measure after more than 20 people were killed in the country and his intelligence office suggested, without an official investigation, that the orders had come from jailed gang leaders. Bukele built a rhetorical discourse that labeled those opposing his measures to control the pandemic as "enemies" of the state. COVID-19 presented the most viable excuse to exercise control over the other branches of government.

His actions have been compared to those implemented during the armed conflict. They have also unleashed fears concerning the remilitarization of the country, as well as causing social distress at the possible return to the years of siege and human rights violations that profoundly marked the history of El Salvador. Police and military members have become, again, "pseudo" judges authorized to assess who is arrested and transferred to detention centers. President Bukele's unfamiliarity with the history of his own country has led him to obliterate years of negotiation and reforms to consolidate the rule of law in El Salvador. It seems that time has erased his memory of the civil war days.

4. THE CONSTITUTIONAL CHAMBER AS CONSTITUTIONAL BEACON

By 2002, judicial reforms had achieved significant progress in promoting formal judicial institutionalism but not in public opinion and legitimacy. As Jackson and O'Shaughnessy (1999) conclude, "the image of the judiciary did not improve in the years immediately following the war." In 1994, only one-fifth of respondents reported an increase in confidence in judicial institutions. In the following years, citizens' perception did not improve. The judiciary was still considered corrupt, dishonest, and dependent on elected officials. Even though judicial reforms produced positive effects on case management and sentencing rates, such impact did not contribute to increase the Supreme Court's legitimacy. Even years after the peace accords, the judiciary remained weak, inefficient, and prone to corruption. The Supreme Court's challenge in subsequent years was to legitimize the institution and set the stage for the Constitutional Chamber to position itself as an independent and autonomous institution capable of protecting the constitution and the rights recognized in it.

As described above, there are numerous reasons and much evidence to support the claim that courts perform poorly during emergencies, particularly during the COVID-19 crisis. However, when assessing what role constitutional judges in El Salvador have played in framing the options available to the executive power, we could, then, offer a less pessimistic account. Contrary to the conventional wisdom, the Constitutional Chamber of El Salvador has played a major role in functioning as a guiding beacon to President Bukele's executive actions to manage the pandemic and advocated for a better interinstitutional dialog among branches of government on this matter.

With these insights in mind, the Constitutional Chamber has determined the scope of legislative power in limiting, suspending, and declaring an exception regime. Second, it formulated an alternative process to expedite the legislative process to declare an exception regime. Third, the magistrates relaxed the standing rules for citizens to have better and swifter access to the Supreme Court during the crisis. Fourth, the Chamber established monitoring and enforcement mechanisms for judicial compliance and actively appointed executing judges to monitor compliance.

4.1 Limitation of Rights, Suspension of Rights, and Exception Regimes

On June 8, 2020, the Chamber issued a landmark decision, *inconstitucionalidad 21–2020*, which struck down a legislative decree that had suspended fundamental rights and liberties aimed at controlling the pandemic. The Constitutional Chamber established important constraints on the exercise of emergency power and restricted the scope of what is acceptable for future emergencies. The magistrates assessed the validity of the emergency measures implemented by President Bukele and the Legislative Assembly, and they gave reasons in a formal manner to set precedential authority for future emergencies.

Since March 2020, plaintiffs had filed various lawsuits challenging the constitutionality of Decree 594 and the Chamber admitted the cases. While the Court was still processing each lawsuit, the decree lost force and expired. To avoid judicial review, the Legislative Assembly issued Decree 611. This new decree officially established a collective quarantine order. The question answered by the Chamber was whether the case would become moot if the decree under analysis lost validity. The Chamber, however, circumvented this legislative tactic by using the "doctrine of transfer of constitutional control" as a judicial remedy to review the content of the now expired Decree 594, considering the language adopted in Decree 611. This doctrine prevents "fraud on the Constitution." It would preclude the legislature from repealing a normative body and transferring its content to a newly enacted body to avoid judicial review. The Chamber has previously held that such legislative practice is fraudulent (*Inconstitucionalidad 3–85*; *Inconstitucionalidad 94–2007* and *Inconstitucionalidad 115–2007*). Contrary to what the constitution provides, both decrees were approved by the Legislative Assembly at the request of President Bukele, without technical-scientific based or legal support to justify such approval.

Upon losing its validity, the Chamber examined whether the contents of Decree 611 were identical to the contents of the expired decree. The magistrates concluded that the decrees were, in fact, alike. According to the legal system of El Salvador, the Legislative Assembly is the body responsible for issuing a state of emergency at the request of the president. The Legislative Assembly, nonetheless, needs to provide evidence that there is a major risk or danger, often supported by reports, including those issued by the Public Health Ministry. According to the constitution, the assembly should take those reports into consideration when making the declaration. Exceptionally, a state of emergency may be decreed by the president, but only when the assembly is unable to hold sessions. If the president requests a declaration of the state of emergency, the Legislative Assembly is responsible for holding a session to discuss the request. President Bukele used the temporary recess of the Legislative Assembly to authorize unconstitutional decrees. The Constitutional Chamber struck them down as unconstitutional.

To support their decision, the Constitutional Chamber magistrates distinguished between a limitation and a suspension of rights during emergency times. The Chamber noted that, even though both are matters reserved to the legislature, they present major differences in terms of voting. The suspension of rights, for example, is an exceptional mechanism that requires a qualified majority of congressional votes, whereas the limitation of fundamental rights involves a simple majority. The limitation of rights also operates in both ordinary and exceptional times, and the general rule is the free exercise of individual rights and the exception the limitation of those rights. The Chamber has ruled those fundamental rights are not absolute, and the Legislative Assembly could limit those rights and requires a simple majority to impose such limitation.

Conversely, in the case of a suspension of rights resulting from an exception regime, there are certain rights that citizens are forbidden to exercise. The Chamber held that rights are suspended when citizens are unable to exercise them, and the public authority will set up the standards under which citizens could exceptionally exercise those rights. Under the suspension of rights scenario, the exception is the permission to exercise one's rights.

To assess President Bukele's collective policies, the Chamber also drew a distinction between individual and collective suspension. The first one is regulated in Article 66 of the constitution and applies to specific cases of individual quarantine. In this case, the constitution mandates the administration of medical attention, even without consent to avoid infection. Conversely, the Chamber held that, under Article 29 of the constitution, a collective suspension applies to a group of unidentified people and can be decreed in all or part of the country. The magistrates, however, said that a collective suspension could only be decreed in an exceptional regime. Article 29 recognizes some cases of atypical situations that can place the constitution at risk, including catastrophes, epidemics, wars, invasions, rebellion, sedition, or other calamities that affect public order. Given that a pandemic places the constitution at risk, the Chamber determined that an exception regime would be justified in El Salvador, but this is not an unlimited power. On the question of whether a domiciliary quarantine should be interpreted as a limitation or suspension of rights, the Chamber concluded that home quarantines are suspensions of freedom of movement and can only be decreed by the Legislative Assembly or the Council of Ministers for their members to declare an exception regime, and not by the president.

4.1.1 Declaration of state of emergency

At the request of the executive, the Legislative Assembly declares states of emergency in part or throughout the country. If the Legislative Assembly is not in session, the President is competent to directly declare it. The Constitutional Chamber, in the landmark decision *Inconstitucionalidad 63–2020*, interpreted that the expression "is not meeting" should not be understood as "not currently in session or is not in session," as the president had suggested, but instead as an impediment arising from *force majeure* or from unforeseeable circumstances that make it impossible for the members of the Legislative Assembly to meet in an official session.

Therefore, the magistrates of the Constitutional Chamber held the President of the Republic was not empowered to declare a state of emergency solely because the Legislative Assembly was not in session, but only when its members are unable to meet. The magistrates also determined that, if the president requests a state of emergency declaration, the Legislative Assembly has the duty to meet urgently, without further formalities than those contained in the presidential request. Thus, the Chamber concluded that the main effect of a state of emergency declaration is to empower the president to enact executive decrees to control a situation that, in normal circumstances, could only be regulated by a piece of legislation passed by the Legislative Assembly. The Constitutional Chamber also established that a decree which declares a state of emergency can neither establish a collective quarantine measure nor restrict the right of mobility. The Chamber also reasoned that those rights and liberties cannot be limited via legislative decree. Because the shelter-in-place policy was a collective measure that suspended the rights of all people, it was deemed unconstitutional. The Chamber struck down Decree 594 and extended the effects to Decree 611 as unconstitutional, unleashing a hostile reaction from President Bukele, who attempted to defy the decision.

4.2 Alternative Process for Exception Regimes

Amid the pandemic, the Chamber has also functioned as an arbiter between the Legislative Assembly and the executive during the process of adoption of appropriate legislation to regulate the emergency according to the constitutional mandates. Given the clash between President Bukele and members of the Legislative Assembly over the authority of declaring an exception regime, the Constitutional Chamber, in an innovative statement, suggested to both the executive and legislative powers an alternative legislative process to regulate an exception regime and its intervening authorities. If approved, this would be a parallel process to the ordinary method of law creation. Under this process, both the Legislative Assembly and the

Council of Ministers would be competent authorities to present legislative initiatives during an exception regime. Because of the exceptional circumstances, the interinstitutional dialog stage would be omitted, but the voting session would remain public, and the president could still veto the initiative. This proposal aimed to delimit competences, expedite the legislative process, and adopt a less formalistic approach that has hampered the work of the Legislative Assembly to regulate the COVID-19 pandemic.

4.3 Lessening Habeas Corpus Procedural Rules

Immediately after adopting Decrees 594 and 611, the police in El Salvador arbitrarily arrested hundreds of citizens in compliance with the restrictions imposed by the executive to prevent the transmission of COVID-19. President Nayib Bukele encouraged the excessive use of force and execution of the measures ordered by his government. Public safety agents committed serious abuses of power. As mentioned earlier, hundreds of detainees were held in overcrowded and unsanitary quarantine centers, and people died after not receiving adequate medical care. Hundreds of citizens filed habeas corpus petitions challenging both the police and military's unlawful detentions.

On March 22, 2020, for example, a group of women filed a habeas corpus petition before the Supreme Court. The plaintiffs stated they were circulating in an urban area, making purchases in the local market to provide themselves with food and medicines, when they were suddenly apprehended by agents of the National Civil Police. The plaintiffs were held in police facilities, without clear legal grounds for their detention. The plaintiffs argued the detention violated their constitutional rights to liberty and physical integrity. The novel feature of this case is that the habeas corpus petition was filed via email to the Constitutional Chamber – even though Article 41 of the Constitutional Procedural Law establishes that a petition for habeas corpus should be filed "[…] directly to the Secretary of the Constitutional Chamber of the Supreme Court or the Secretariat of any of the Chambers of Second Instance that do not reside in the capital or by letter or telegram […]." The general rule, then, requires the party to present the recourse in person at any of the judicial offices or by letter or telegram (*Habeas Corpus* 148–2020).

The Chamber also noted that while email was not contemplated in the procedural rules, on February 17, 2020, in deciding *Inconstitucionalidad 10–2020*, the Chamber also argued that the law cannot be isolated from reality, and must conform to it to avoid its ineffectiveness or insufficiency. The Court also recognized that although the Legislative Assembly and the executive power had issued decrees to contain the COVID-19 pandemic, establishing a mandatory home quarantine, the Constitutional Chamber continued operating as guarantor of fundamental rights, understanding that in times of crisis, the constitution continues to be the instrument for protection against any state act that violates rights.

The Court also underlined that, due to the measures decreed, people attempting to file habeas corpus petitions would not be able to do so directly to the Secretariat of the Supreme Court or by letter or telegram. Hence, the restriction of free movement should not represent an obstacle to the effective protection of people's fundamental rights and to monitoring the constitutionality of any act of government that may be subject to such control. Since June 2020, citizens flocked to a more accessible Supreme Court, particularly when magistrates gave early signals of being rights oriented and more open to hear their demands, especially those filed via email.

Finally, the Chamber, in fact, clarified that home quarantine was mandatory, but forcefully argued those arrests made for not complying with the collective quarantine were illegal if there was no formal law which provided for them. President Bukele dedicated several tweets to minimizing the authority of the country's highest constitutional court and claimed the Constitutional Chamber did not have the power to implement or overrule sanitary measures.

4.4 Judicial Enforcement and the Executing Judge

Over the past decades substantial attention has been paid to the process by which Supreme Court decisions are implemented. Generally, when courts lay down rules which conflict with the constitution, the personnel of executive agencies must decide whether and how they will alter their policies to conform to the Court's rules (Baum 1976). However, El Salvador's legal system provides an alternative institution, the executing judge or *juez ejecutor*, as an alternative model for the enforcement of judicial opinions related to arbitrary detentions.

The right against arbitrary detention is protected by the writ of habeas corpus in El Salvador. Every person has the right to file a habeas corpus mechanism before the Supreme Court for a petitioner who does not reside in San Salvador, when any authority or individual illegally restricts their freedom. The protection offered by this remedy is made effective by means of the writ of exhibition of the person (*auto de exhibición de personas*), and it can be invoked in situations of prison, confinement, custody, or restriction that is not authorized by law. The order is requested in writing and the petition is presented directly to the Court by letter or telegram from the person whose freedom is restricted or from any other person. The petition must state, if possible, the kind of confinement, prison, or restriction suffered by the victim, the place of confinement and the custodial person; and must request that the order of personal exhibition be decreed by the Supreme Court.

During the COVID-19 pandemic, the executing judge has played a relevant function in monitoring the situation of detained citizens under the custody of an authority other than judicial in the so-called *centros de contención*. The executing judge has reported back and requested the Supreme Court to order illegal detentions to end. Also, in case of disobedience to an order to appear before the court, the so-called executing judge has to inform the Court to seek sanctions for failure to obey the court order, such as giving notice (*auto de certificación*) to the Office of the Attorney General for them to initiate a criminal investigation for contempt. The Constitutional Chamber has asserted its power and ordered further criminal investigations for executive authorities reluctant to comply with the Chamber's mandates (*Habeas Corpus* 210–2020)

CONCLUSION

Since March 2020, the Constitutional Chamber has played a visible incremental role in monitoring the executive's response to the pandemic, balancing public health measures *vis-à-vis* fundamental rights. Since June 2020, the Chamber has vigorously asserted its role as constitutional judge and has played various guiding constitutional roles. It has utilized the writ of habeas corpus as the primary mechanism to question and strike down unconstitutional measures implemented by the Bukele administration. It has also promoted better access to justice, by relaxing procedural rules for people to challenge extreme measures to contain the pandemic and departed from formalistic procedures to expedite processing times of cases. Judges have utilized novel judicial remedies (*auto de exhibición* and *juez ejecutor*) to protect citizens against arbitrary arrest and have expanded the scope of constitutional interpretation to protect fundamental rights and liberties. Like a beacon, the Constitutional Chamber has outlined some actions and general objectives for the executive and legislative powers to pursue. The Chamber has asserted its judicial authority and have actively monitored executive compliance with its judicial opinions through a combination of different institutional mechanisms, as described in this chapter.

REFERENCES

Baum, Lawrence. 1976. "Implementation of Judicial Decisions." *American Politics Quarterly* 86–114.

Betancour, Belisario, Reinaldo Figueredo Planchart, and Thomas Buergenthal. 1992–1993. *De la locura a la esperanza : la guerra de 12 años en El Salvador : informe de la Comisión de la Verdad para El Salvador*. San Salvador: United Nations. https://digitallibrary.un.org/record/183599?ln=en.

Botero, Sandra. 2018. "Agents of Neoliberalism? High Courts, Legal Preferences, and Rights in Latin America." In *Latin America since the Left Turn*, by Tulia Falleti G and Parrado A. Emilio, 214–234. Pennsylvania: University of Pennsylvania Press.

Cole, David. 2003. "Judging the Next Emergency: Judicial Review and Individual Rights in Times of Crisis." *Michigan Law Review* 2565–2595.

Commission for the Study of the Proposed Constitution. 1983. *Legislative Report*. San Salvador: Legislative Palace.

Hilbink, Lisa. 2012. "The Origins of Positive Judicial Independence." *World Politics* 587–621.

Inconstitucionalidad. 2013. 7–12 (Sala de lo Constitucional de la Corte Suprema de Justicia, December 16).

Jackson, D.W, and L. Nuzzi O'Shaughnessy. 1999. "Protecting Human Rights: The Legitimacy of Judicial Systems Reforms in El Salvador." *Bulletin of Latin American Research* 403–421.

Kapiszewski, Diana, and Matthew Taylor. 2008. "Doing Justice to Courts? Studying Judicial Politics in Latin America." *American Political Science Association* 741–767.

Mason, David. 1999. "The Civil War in El Salvador: A Retrospective Analysis." *Latin American Research Review* 179–196.

Melendez, Salvador. 2020. "Bukele Anunica Desacato al Fallo Judicial que le Ordena Parar Abusos en la Cuarentena." *Revista Factum*, April 15.

Popkin, Margaret. 2000. *Peace with Justice: Obstacles to Building the Rule of Law in El Salvador*. Pennsylvania: Pennsylvania State University Press.

Posner, Eric. 2020. "The Executive Unbound, Pandemic Edition." *Lawfare Blog*. March 23. https://www.lawfareblog.com/executive-unbound-pandemic-edition.

Santamaría Alvarenga, William Ernesto. 2016. "Sentencias de la Sala de lo Constitucional: ¿Ciudanización de la Democracia?" *Anuario de Derecho Constitucional Latinoamericano* 271–296.

Seider, Rachel. 1996. *Central America: Fragile Transition*. New York: St Martin's Press.

Vermeule, Adrian, and Eric Posner. 2008. *"Emergencies and Democratic Failure"*. John M. Olin Program in Law and Economics Working Paper, Chicago: University of Chicago Law School.

Villacencia Terreros, Felipe. 1996. "Proceso de Paz y Administración de Justicia en El Salvador." *Jueces por la Democracia* 91–95.

14. Public support and compliance with high courts around the world[1]

Amanda Driscoll and Martín Gandur

INTRODUCTION

In the *Federalist 78*, Hamilton famously claimed that courts have neither the powers to coerce nor the tools to incentivize compliance.[2] Consequentially, the effectiveness of judicial decisions hinges on incumbents' willingness to obey them—to comply—a willingness which is neither automatic nor ensured. This axiom of constitutional theory has attracted the attention of researchers interested in the empirical study of law. In light of high courts' intrinsic weakness, when might we expect compliance and how exactly courts build an independent base of authority are questions of central import. One prominent answer emphasizes the public: courts can increase their autonomy and authority by fostering widespread support from the public, who might regard the separation of powers and judicial independence as a desirable and intrinsic democratic value. With sufficiently high levels of public support for high courts, citizens will punish political actors who contravene such values, either by attacking high courts or by ignoring them completely. In this way, courts can strategically grow and wield their public support as both a protective mechanism against political attacks, and a guarantee of judicial independence.

As Georg Vanberg describes:

> If the integrity of the judiciary and respect for its decisions are values that a sufficient number of citizens are willing to defend by withdrawing support from policy makers who attack judicial independence, policy makers are likely to conclude that disciplining the court or resisting unwelcome decisions is not worth the potential costs of a public backlash. Public support provides a shield for judicial independence.[3]

Whereas the extent to which court decisions are implemented is a dimension of the concept of judicial independence as judicial power,[4] compliance is central to our understanding of judicial institutions in comparative perspective.[5] In this chapter, we take stock of the theoretical and

1 The authors acknowledge Marielena Dias for her excellent research assistance.

2 ALEXANDER HAMILTON, JAMES MADISON, AND JOHN JAY, THE FEDERALIST PAPERS (1961).

3 Georg Vanberg, *Constitutional Courts in Comparative Perspective: A Theoretical Assessment*, 18 ANNUAL REVIEW OF POLITICAL SCIENCE 167, 176–77 (2015).

4 Julio Ríos-Figueroa and Jeffrey K. Staton, *An Evaluation of Cross-National Measures of Judicial Independence*, 30 THE JOURNAL OF LAW, ECONOMICS, & ORGANIZATION 104 (2014).

5 Diana Kapiszewski and Matthew M. Taylor, *Doing Courts Justice? Studying Judicial Politics in Latin America*, 6 PERSPECTIVES ON POLITICS 741 (2008).

empirical literature of public support for courts and the public's intolerance of incumbent noncompliance with judicial orders.[6]

This chapter proceeds as follows. In the next section, we summarize two prominent theoretical models of judicial independence, and describe their logical consequences for public attitudes regarding noncompliance. Turning our review to the empirical literature on public support for courts, we find infrequent instances where public evaluation of noncompliance is systematically considered apart from related concepts (such as diffuse support or judicial legitimacy), even when viable survey instruments exist to measure this key quantity of interest; and only rarely do researchers systematically consider the behavioral implications the legitimacy theory implies. We then shift our attention to the scholarly literature on compliance with judicial decisions, and review the various empirical challenges this problem invites when taking seriously its conceptualization and measurement. We then elaborate what these challenges imply for public awareness, comprehension, and evaluation of (non)compliance. We conclude by outlining several opportunities for future research.

PUBLIC SUPPORT FOR COURTS AND THE PROBLEM OF COMPLIANCE

Public support for judicial institutions is widely seen as a key explanation of judicial power, influence, and independence.[7] Acknowledging the intrinsic weakness of judicial institutions

---

[6] We prioritize compliance as it refers to incumbents' (executives, legislative actors, and governments) adherence to judicial orders (*see* Diana Kapiszewski and Matthew M. Taylor, *Compliance: Conceptualizing, Measuring, and Explaining Adherence to Judicial Rulings*, 38 LAW & SOCIAL INQUIRY 803 (2013)). We herein acknowledge the contributions of scholars concerned with states' compliance with international tribunals (*see* Courtney Hillebrecht, *The Power of Human Rights Tribunals: Compliance with the European Court of Human Rights and Domestic Policy Change*, 20 EUROPEAN JOURNAL OF INTERNATIONAL RELATIONS 1100 (2014)), and courts' responsiveness to higher court orders within a judicial hierarchy (*see* James F. Spriggs, *Explaining Federal Bureaucratic Compliance with Supreme Court Opinions*, 50 POLITICAL RESEARCH QUARTERLY 567 (1997); BRADLEY CANON AND CHARLES JOHNSON, JUDICIAL POLICIES: IMPLEMENTATION AND IMPACT (1999); Alexandra V. Huneeus, *Courts Resisting Courts: Lessons from the Inter-American Court's Struggle to Enforce Human Rights*, 44 CORNELL INTERNATIONAL LAW JOURNAL 493 (2011)). We set aside the question of citizens' compliance with the law (c.f. TOM R. TYLER, WHY PEOPLE OBEY THE LAW (2006); James L. Gibson, *Understandings of Justice: Institutional Legitimacy, Procedural Justice, and Political Tolerance*, 23 LAW AND SOCIETY REVIEW 469 (1989)) or the public's support for the rule of law more broadly (see AMANDA DRISCOLL, JAY N. KREHBIEL AND MICHAEL J. NELSON. PUBLIC SUPPORT FOR THE RULE OF LAW: PERSONAL CONVICTIONS AND INSTITUTIONAL CONSTRAINTS. Under Contract at Cambridge University Press (Comparative Constitutional Law and Policy Series).

[7] *See* Georg Vanberg, *Legislative-Judicial Relations: A Game-Theoretic Approach to Constitutional Review*, 45 AMERICAN JOURNAL OF POLITICAL SCIENCE 346 (2001) [hereinafter Vanberg, *Legislative-Judicial Relations*]; GEORG VANBERG, THE POLITICS OF CONSTITUTIONAL REVIEW IN GERMANY (2005) [hereinafter VANBERG, POLITICS OF CONSTITUTIONAL REVIEW]; Georg Vanberg, *Establishing and Maintaining Judicial Independence*, *in* OXFORD HANDBOOK OF LAW AND POLITICS 99 (Gregory A. Caldeira, R. Daniel Kelemen, and Keith E. Whittington eds., 2008) [hereinafter Vanberg, *Establishing and Maintaining Judicial Independence*]; Matthew C. Stephenson, *Court of Public Opinion: Government Accountability and Judicial Independence*, 20 JOURNAL OF LAW, ECONOMICS, AND ORGANIZATION 379 (2004); Jeffrey K. Staton, *Constitutional Review and the Selective Promotion of Case Results*, 50 AMERICAN JOURNAL OF POLITICAL SCIENCE 98 (2006) [hereinafter Staton, *Constitutional*

and their lack of either the "purse" or the "sword" to induce compliance, a devoted public may act as a force that compels incumbent respect. Faced with widespread public backlash and the promise of electoral retribution at the ballot box, incumbents will refrain from undermining high court authority, and instead conform to judicial dictates. Thus, the presence of a sufficiently broad cross-section of public support is a key parameter in many theoretical models,[8] a fact which has fostered a vibrant and compelling research agenda into the determinants of public support for judicial institutions.[9] Here, we review two prominent models of judicial

---

Review]; JEFFREY K. STATON, JUDICIAL POWER AND STRATEGIC COMMUNICATION IN MEXICO (2010) [hereinafter STATON, JUDICIAL POWER]; Gretchen Helmke, *Public Support and Judicial Crises in Latin America*, 13 UNIVERSITY OF PENNSYLVANIA JOURNAL OF CONSTITUTIONAL LAW 397 (2010). Without fully revisiting the issue here, we acknowledge the important conceptual distinctions between judicial power, impact, influence, authority, accountability, and independence (c.f. Vanberg, *Establishing and Maintaining Judicial Independence*; Kapiszewski and Taylor, *supra* note 5; Tom S. Clark and Jeffrey K. Staton, *Challenges and Opportunities in Judicial Independence Research*, 21 LAW & COURTS NEWSLETTER 10 (2011); Daniel M. Brinks and Abby Blass, *Rethinking Judicial Empowerment: The New Foundations of Constitutional Justice*, 15 INTERNATIONAL JOURNAL OF CONSTITUTIONAL LAW 296 (2017)).

8 *See* Vanberg, *Legislative-Judicial Relations*, *supra* note 7; VANBERG, POLITICS OF CONSTITUTIONAL REVIEW, *supra* note 7; Staton, *Constitutional Review*, *supra* note 7; STATON, JUDICIAL POWER, *supra* note 7; Tom S. Clark, *The Separation of Powers, Court Curbing, and Judicial Legitimacy*, 53 AMERICAN JOURNAL OF POLITICAL SCIENCE 971 (2009); Clifford J. Carrubba, *A Model of the Endogenous Development of Judicial Institutions in Federal and International Systems*, 71 THE JOURNAL OF POLITICS 55 (2009); Jay N. Krehbiel, *The Politics of Judicial Procedures: The Role of Public Oral Hearings in the German Constitutional Court*, 60 AMERICAN JOURNAL OF POLITICAL SCIENCE 990 (2016); James R. Rogers and Joseph Daniel Ura, *A Majoritarian Basis for Judicial Countermajoritarianism*, 32 JOURNAL OF THEORETICAL POLITICS 435 (2020); JEFFREY K. STATON, CHRISTOPHER REENOCK, AND JORDAN HOLSINGER, CAN COURTS BE BULWARKS OF DEMOCRACY? JUDGES AND THE POLITICS OF PRUDENCE (2022).

9 *See* Barry R. Weingast, *The Political Foundations of Democracy and the Rule of Law*, 91 AMERICAN POLITICAL SCIENCE REVIEW 245 (1997); Gregory A. Caldeira and James L. Gibson, *The Etiology of Public Support for the Supreme Court*, 36 AMERICAN JOURNAL OF POLITICAL SCIENCE 635 (1992); James L. Gibson, Gregory A. Caldeira, and Vanessa A. Baird, *On the Legitimacy of National High Courts*, 92 AMERICAN POLITICAL SCIENCE REVIEW 343 (1998); James L. Gibson and Gregory A. Caldeira, *The Legitimacy of Transnational Legal Institutions: Compliance, Support, and the European Court of Justice*, 39 AMERICAN JOURNAL OF POLITICAL SCIENCE 459 (1995) [hereinafter GIBSON AND CALDEIRA, *Legitimacy of Transnational Legal Institutions*]; JAMES L. GIBSON AND GREGORY A. CALDEIRA, *CITIZENS, COURTS, AND CONFIRMATIONS: POSITIVITY THEORY AND THE JUDGMENTS OF THE AMERICAN PEOPLE* (2009) [hereinafter Gibson and Caldeira, CITIZENS, COURTS AND CONFIRMATIONS]; Carrubba, *supra* note 8; Brandon L. Bartels and Christopher D. Johnston, *On the Ideological Foundations of Supreme Court Legitimacy in the American Public*, 57 AMERICAN JOURNAL OF POLITICAL SCIENCE 184 (2013); Dino P. Christenson and David M. Glick, *Chief Justice Roberts's Health Care Decision Disrobed: The Microfoundations of the Supreme Court's Legitimacy*, 59 AMERICAN JOURNAL OF POLITICAL SCIENCE 403 (2015); Amanda Driscoll and Michael J. Nelson, *There is No Legitimacy Crisis: Support for Judicial Institutions in Modern Latin America*, 12 REVISTA DE LA SOCIEDAD ARGENTINA DE ANÁLISIS POLÍTICO 361 (2018) [hereinafter Driscoll and Nelson, *No Legitimacy Crisis*]; Amanda Driscoll and Michael J. Nelson, *The Costs of Court Curbing: Evidence from the United States*, 85 JOURNAL OF POLITICS 609 (2023). [hereinafter Driscoll and Nelson, Court Curbing]; Amanda Driscoll and Michael J. Nelson, *Accountability for Court Packing*, THE JOURNAL OF LAW & COURTS 1 (2023) [hereinafter Nelson and Driscoll, Accountability]; Miles T. Armaly, *Extra-Judicial Actor Induced Change in Supreme Court Legitimacy*, 71 POLITICAL RESEARCH QUARTERLY 600 (2018); Jay N. Krehbiel, *Do Voters Punish Noncompliance with High Courts? A Cross-National Analysis*, 41 POLITICS 156 (2021).

independence, noting the differences in their logical implications for public concern for noncompliance.

Courts May Enhance Cooperation: Compliance and Instrumentalism

The public is absent from many theoretical accounts concerning the establishment of independent courts, but emerges as a critical actor in the maintenance of judicial independence.[10] Two exceptions are theoretical models that theorize independent judicial review as a solution to cooperative dilemmas, and models that theorize judicial independence as a solution to a coordination problem. In a standard cooperation game, all players stand to benefit from cooperative outcomes, but each faces incentives to unilaterally defect. Courts are established to help disputing parties solve this problem, by imposing costs for noncooperation, enforcing the rules of a predetermined agreement, and acting as the independent arbiter in regulatory disputes.[11]

Examples of this logic are advanced by Carrubba and Stephenson, who explicitly derive the consequences this cooperative model of judicial review for public evaluation of incumbent noncompliance, wherein public monitoring endogenously determines judicial influence.[12] In both cases, the public has the opportunity to punish incumbents for ignoring the court and defecting from the cooperative outcome, but might also *reward* the incumbent for defection and noncompliance with judicial edicts. The public's regard for judicial orders is rooted in their support for the substantive policy at stake—their beliefs that there are benefits derived from regulatory cooperation, and that the incumbent is acting in the public's best interests by either adhering to or defying the agreement and judicial rules. Public expectations regarding compliance are at heart connected to instrumental considerations, and the public's support of substantive policy outcomes. As Carrubba describes:

> Publics are backing the court because doing so protects their policy interests, not because they come to believe in the intrinsic value of the supremacy of the rule of law, or of judicial institutions. Thus, while the rise of public support for judicial institutions looks like socialization, in fact it is purely instrumental.[13]

---

[10] *See* Vanberg, *Establishing and Maintaining Judicial Independence*, *supra* note 7. Indeed, how the public comes to value court authority such that incumbent compliance is a tangible concern is a question open for future exploration (c.f. Seymour M. Lipset, *Some Social Requisites of Democracy: Economic Development and Political Legitimacy*, 53 American Political Science Review 69 (1959); David Easton, A Systems Analysis of Political Life (1965); Michael J. Nelson and Patrick D. Tucker, *The Stability and Durability of the US Supreme Court's Legitimacy*, 83 The Journal of Politics 767 (2021).

[11] *See* Weingast, *supra* note 9; Douglass C. North, William Summerhill, and Barry R. Weingast, *Order, Disorder, and Economic Change: Latin America versus North America*, *in* Governing for Prosperity 17 (Bruce Bueno de Mesquita and Hilton L. Root eds., 2000); Christopher Reenock, Jeffrey K. Staton, and Marius Radean, *Legal Institutions and Democratic Survival*, 75 The Journal of Politics 491 (2013).

[12] *See* Clifford J. Carrubba, *Courts and Compliance in International Regulatory Regimes*, 67 The Journal of Politics 669 (2005); Carrubba, *supra* note 8; Stephenson, *supra* note 6.

[13] Carrubba, *supra* note 8, at 66. That the public's attitudes about noncompliance are informed by instrumental considerations allows for considerable influence of various elites. This is a point to which we return below.

This conjecture—that public support for judicial institutions is informed by instrumental concerns—has been borne out in a host of related empirical applications.[14] In recent and innovative work, Bartels and Johnston distinguish between subjective (perceived) and objective (measured) disagreement with judicial opinions, and find that professed institutional legitimacy declines as individuals' perceived disagreement with the court increases.[15] The authors contend that even a single decision that is perceived to contravene one's own preferences has the effect of undermining individual-level ascriptions of institutional legitimacy to the court.[16] Christenson and Glick later substantiate this dynamic in a real-world context, examining how highly salient and controversial judicial decisions impact willingness to ascribe institutional legitimacy.[17] They consider public support for the U.S. Supreme Court before and after the Supreme Court's ruling regarding the constitutionality of the Affordable Care Act (ACA),[18] to discern the decision's impact on individual evaluations of the high court's legitimacy. Christenson and Glick report that disagreement with the case outcome yielded a decline in institutional legitimacy, further corroborating the claim that subjective evaluations of judicial output might determine public support, and therefore inform the public's attitudes about compliance.[19]

Courts May Enhance Coordination: Compliance as a Democratic Value

A related theoretical account of public support for compliance instead treats judicial authority as a solution to a *coordination* problem between citizens, whose collective interest lies in restraining a constitutionally transgressive executive or state authority. Under this account, judicial and constitutional review may alert the public to instances of executive overreach, when the actions of incumbents push the boundaries of their legitimate and constitutional authority. This understanding of the rule of law and judicial review presumes a pre-existing, albeit fragile, public "consensus" regarding the appropriate bounds of state authority and

---

[14] Much literature on public support for judicial institutions differentiates between specific support (performance satisfaction) and diffuse support (institutional commitment or legitimacy) (c.f. Easton, *supra* note 10; James L. Gibson and Michael J. Nelson, *Is the US Supreme Court's Legitimacy Grounded in Performance Satisfaction and Ideology?*, 59 American Journal of Political Science 162 (2015)). Compliance is tightly intertwined with the latter, and while some research acknowledges conceptual distinction, most of the literature herein described does not directly interrogate public attitudes regarding compliance apart from diffuse support (c.f. David Easton, *A Re-Assessment of the Concept of Political Support*, 5 British Journal of Political Science 435 (1975)).

[15] Bartels and Johnston, *supra* note 9.

[16] Gibson and Nelson refute this account, arguing that performance evaluation is fundamentally different from institutional legitimacy, and show that policy disagreements result in a substantively unimportant decline in institutional legitimacy (Gibson and Nelson, *supra* note 14, at 169; *see also* James L. Gibson and Michael J. Nelson, *Reconsidering Positivity Theory: What Roles Do Politicization, Ideological Disagreement, and Legal Realism Play in Shaping US Supreme Court Legitimacy?*, 14 Journal of Empirical Legal Studies 592 (2017)).

[17] Christenson and Glick, *supra* note 9.

[18] In *The National Federation of Independent Businesses v. Sebelius*, 567 US 519 (2012), the United States Supreme Court upheld the constitutionality of the ACA, ruling that the individual mandate to purchase minimum health insurance was a valid exercise of congressional power.

[19] Contrary to Christenson and Glick, the panel study of Nelson and Tucker, *supra* note 10, found minimal variance in individuals' diffuse support for courts, even in the face of controversial decisions regarding same-sex marriage and the ACA.

appropriate norms of executive behaviors. Courts and constitutional magistrates may help to uphold constitutional order and preserve this public consensus by alerting the public that active oversight and public accountability are both warranted and required.

Weingast is mum on the mechanisms by which this public consensus emerges, but this theoretical model has direct implications for the foundations of public exaltation of judicial compliance.[20] If it is the case that judicial review provides a focal point for coordinated public action against an executive that pushes the boundaries of public trust, the public's interest in judicial compliance traverses commitments to other political causes, and supersedes individuals' commitments to substantive policy commitments. Rather than stemming from citizens' instrumental concerns, this assumes that the public's policing of incumbent noncompliance emerges from a concern for the common good, in the hopes of upholding executive constraint by the rule of law.

This logic intersects with previous research which casts support for judicial institutions (albeit not compliance *per se*) as one part of a portfolio of democratic values.[21] Recent empirical scrutiny of this claim has been scant and unsystematic, a fact which is surprising given that citizens' attitudes regarding democracy and democratic institutions are often recognized to be a key determinant of institutional support. Mondak and Smithey contend that this values-based commitment to the court explains why public support is both high and stable for the U.S. Supreme Court,[22] and Gibson and Nelson identify democratic values as the "best" predictor of institutional support.[23] Likewise, both Bartels and Johnston and Christenson and Glick show that democratic values have some explanatory power in their analyses as well.[24]

OPPORTUNITIES FOR EMPIRICAL EVALUATIONS OF PUBLIC ATTITUDES REGARDING COMPLIANCE

From our review of the empirical record, the relative explanatory power of either of the above theoretical accounts (much less any alternatives) points to some distinct opportunities for future empirical research.[25] We believe this is the case for at least three reasons.

---

[20] Weingast, *supra* note 9. Driscoll, Krehbiel and Nelson, supra note 1. *See also* Barry R. Weingast, *A Postscript to 'Political Foundations of Democracy and the Rule of Law, in* DEMOCRACY AND THE RULE OF LAW 109 (Adam Przeworski and José María Maravall eds., 2003).

[21] *See* EASTON, *supra* note 10; GABRIEL A. ALMOND AND SIDNEY VERBA, THE CIVIC CULTURE: POLITICAL ATTITUDES AND DEMOCRACY IN FIVE NATIONS (1963); Jeffery J. Mondak and Shannon Ishiyama Smithey, *The Dynamics of Public Support for the Supreme Court*, 59 THE JOURNAL OF POLITICS 1114 (1997).

[22] Mondak and Smithey, *supra* note 21.

[23] Gibson and Nelson, *supra* note 14.

[24] *See* Bartels and Johnston, *supra* note 9; Christenson and Glick, *supra* note 9. This general consensus aside, the items these authors use to measure democratic values vary across contexts and applications. Bartels and Johnston, *supra* note 9, and Christenson and Glick, *supra* note 9, equate measures of trust with democratic values, while Gibson and Nelson, *supra* note 14, use a "direct" measure of democratic values (support for the rule of law, political tolerance, and support for liberty versus order).

[25] Recent research into public support for the rule of law has begun to fill this gap, but many opportunities for further investigation remain. For example, Driscoll, Krehbiel, and Nelson scrutinize the extent to which self-reported compliance and willingness to tolerate incumbent noncompliance are rooted in instrumental considerations, democratic values, or expediency concerns (*see* Amanda Driscoll, Jay N.

First, only infrequently are public attitudes regarding compliance measured directly, and rarely are they empirically differentiated from related concepts and measures.[26] Second, where available data exist to differentiate among these related concepts, they are only infrequently the subject of direct empirical scrutiny. Third, only rarely have researchers addressed the behavioral mechanism legitimacy theory would imply, to explore whether the public's voting or collective behavior is shaped by a concern for noncompliance. We address each of these opportunities in more detail below. We conclude that although the literature on public support for judicial institutions has witnessed a renaissance of late, questions about public attitudes regarding compliance have not been prominently featured.

Compliance and Diffuse Support: Related Concepts or a Consequence?

Public attitudes regarding compliance are tightly entwined with attitudes regarding institutional legitimacy.[27] Many are satisfied to view behavioral or professed support for compliance as a logical consequence of institutional legitimacy,[28] conceiving of voluntary compliance as evidence of a legitimate authority. Legitimate institutions are those whose decisions spontaneously garner widespread adherence, and so these two concepts may well be regarded as coterminous in some applications.

Others take issue with this charge, insisting that institutional legitimacy and compliance are conceptually distinct and empirically differentiable.[29] In his now-famous treatise on the concept of institutional support, Easton acknowledges that compliance may well also exist in the face of coercion, wherein adherence to formal rules occurs in the absence of legitimate authority, as is the case in authoritarian regimes.[30] Conversely, the public may view an institution as legitimate, but defy its orders in any case, such as the case of conscientious objectors

---

Krehbiel, and Michael J. Nelson, *COVID-19, Crises and Support for the Rule of Law* (National Science Foundation Grants SES-2027653, SES-2027664 & SES-2027671, 2020), www.crisesandtheruleoflaw.com.

[26] *See* Gibson, *supra* note 6; Caldeira and Gibson, *supra* note 9; Gibson and Caldeira, *Legitimacy of Transnational Legal Institutions*, *supra* note 9; Georg Vanberg, *Establishing Judicial Independence in West Germany: The Impact of Opinion Leadership and the Separation of Powers*, 32 Comparative Politics 333 (2000); Jeffrey K. Staton, *Judicial Policy Implementation in Mexico City and Mérida*, 37 Comparative Politics 41 (2004).

[27] We use the terms institutional legitimacy, diffuse support, and institutional commitment interchangeably. Easton distinguished diffuse support as a "reservoir of support" for political institutions (Easton, *supra* note 10), an unwillingness to tolerate changes to its fundamental structure (Caldeira and Gibson, *supra* note 9), and an institutional commitment that persists even in the face of unfavorable opinions. This is distinct, per Easton's account, from specific support, which is rooted in short-term evaluations of institutional outputs.

[28] For example, in Vanberg's work, public support for courts—either specific or diffuse—drives citizens' backlash against defiant incumbents (i.e., the public punishes noncompliance *because* they support courts) (Vanberg, Politics of Constitutional Review, *supra* note 7, at 49–53). In this way, judicial legitimacy informs publics' (in)tolerance for noncompliance.

[29] *See* Easton, *supra* note 10; Easton, *supra* note 14; Walter F. Murphy and Joseph Tanenhaus, *Public Opinion and the United States Supreme Court: Mapping of Some Prerequisites for Court Legitimation of Regime Changes*, 2 Law & Society Review 357 (1968); Gibson, *supra* note 6; Gibson and Caldeira, *Legitimacy of Transnational Legal Institutions*, *supra* note 9; Vanberg, *supra* note 26; Staton, *supra* note 26.

[30] Easton, *supra* note 14.

in times of conscriptions of war. In this vein, some scholars have explored the extent to which legitimate institutions are more or less able to spur voluntary compliance, using diffuse support as a predictor for intended compliance or acceptance of unpopular rulings.[31]

Compliance-related Questions on Surveys around the World

Table 14.1 displays court-related questions that appear on survey instruments in international surveys that cover the major regions of the world.[32] The most common court-related questions by far are those that relate to trust or confidence in the high court, courts, the judiciary or judicial system, or the legal system.[33] Less common are questions of diffuse support,[34] which gauge the public's willingness to support fundamental changes to judicial institutions.[35]

Somewhat surprisingly, in light of researchers' tendency to use diffuse support as a proxy for intolerance for noncompliance, questions that tap into public attitudes regarding compliance are *more* common than those that could be used to measure diffuse support in cross-national surveys. Indeed, questions addressing citizens' evaluation of incumbent compliance were included in multiple waves of both the Afro and Americas Barometer surveys, questions which cover both the practical and normative aspects of incumbent compliance. Yet despite these items being available in nationally representative samples in multiple countries, across multiple years, only infrequently have they been the subject of published empirical work, and then used as an indicator of a variety of different concepts. Levi, Sacks, and Tyler, for example, employ the 2005 AfroBarometer question "The courts have the right to make decisions that people always have to abide by," and report that citizens" perceptions of their trustworthiness

---

[31] *See* Gibson and Caldeira, *Legitimacy of Transnational Legal Institutions*, *supra* note 9.

[32] Our review of survey instruments included all of the regional barometer surveys, as well as the LatinoBarometer, the World Values Survey, the European Values Survey, and EuroStat, from 1992–2018. Surveys were not reported here if there were no questions concerning incumbent compliance or institutional commitment included on the survey instruments. A graduate research assistant compiled all court/judiciary-related questions, differentiating between compliance, diffuse support, trust/confidence, performance evaluation, and related public attitudes. We prioritize the reporting of instances where questions were asked in multiple countries, setting aside questions that were only asked in a single country. We do not report the full results of this data collection effort here, but additional information is available upon request.

[33] Some use confidence or trust as a measure of institutional legitimacy or diffuse support (*see* Gretchen Helmke, *The Origins of Institutional Crises in Latin America*, 54 American Journal of Political Science 737 (2010)). However, Gibson, Caldeira, and Spence show that these measures are more closely related to performance evaluation, or Easton's concept of specific support (James L. Gibson, Gregory A. Caldeira, and Lester Kenyatta Spence, *Measuring Attitudes Toward the United States Supreme Court*, 47 American Journal of Political Science 354 (2003)), and do not reflect an enduring institutional commitment (*see* James L. Gibson, Judges, Elections, and the American Mass Public: The Effects of Judicial Campaigns on the Legitimacy of Courts (2012)).

[34] *See* Caldeira and Gibson, *supra* note 9; Gibson and Caldeira, *Legitimacy of Transnational Legal Institutions*, *supra* note 9; Gibson, Caldeira, and Baird, *supra* note 9; Gibson, Caldeira, and Spence, *supra* note 33; Driscoll and Nelson, *No Legitimacy Crisis*, *supra* note 9.

[35] Also, the 2008, 2010, 2012, and 2019 AmericasBarometer surveys contain a single item that measures diffuse support for judicial institutions, while the 2021 survey instruments of eight Latin American countries contain measures of awareness, specific support, and two questions that relate to diffuse support (*see* Amanda Driscoll and Michael J. Nelson, *Judicial Legitimacy in Comparative Perspective/JLAW Project: Judicial Legitimacy Around the World* (National Science Foundation grants SES-1920977, SES-1920915 & SES-2025927, 2019), www.jlawproject.com.

of government, assessment of administrative competence, and procedural justice are associated with citizens' acceptance of court authority.[36] In his study of Zimbabwe, Krönke analyzes responses to two 2017 AfroBarometer questions—relating to whether incumbents *should* comply and *do* comply with judicial orders—which the author takes as a measure of citizens' perceptions of the rule of law.[37] Krönke concludes that "popular assessment of the courts is ... driven by whether the judiciary is perceived as limiting the abuse of power by the president and subjecting officials to the rule of law."[38] Few scholars have analyzed the compliance questions from the Americas Barometer, but when they do they have not been used to directly address questions of noncompliance. Instead, these items have been taken as indicators of the "necessity" of judges and the rule of law,[39] an index of preferences for presidential power,[40] and as part of a measure of diffuse support.[41]

The research of Carlin et al. stands out as one of the few that interrogates public attitudes regarding adherence to judicial orders, while also taking seriously questions of compliance we elaborate below.[42] Their research on the Colombian Constitutional Court offers a systematic approach to measuring noncompliance with judicial orders, a process which is transparent and replicable, and could credibly be reproduced in other judicial contexts and courts. Having estimated the overall rate of noncompliance with *tutela* decisions,[43] the authors then fielded a nationally representative survey in which they publicized this estimated rate of noncompliance, to evaluate both the public's acceptance of noncompliance, as well as their willingness to pay some cost to shame incumbents for their failure to adhere to judicial orders. They report that a wide majority of respondents viewed noncompliance with legal obligations as unacceptable, with a critical mass willing to pay a cost to publicize the rate of noncompliance with *tutela* claims. This paper represents one of the only efforts to systematically and transparently evaluate noncompliance with national court orders, providing a template for a replicable process by which this might be possible in other contexts. More importantly for the ongoing discussion, the authors query public attitudes regarding incumbent noncompliance to address an aspect of public opinion that has long been the subject of scholarly assumptions, but has only rarely been addressed in a systematic way.

---

[36] Margaret Levi, Audrey Sacks, and Tom Tyler, *Conceptualizing Legitimacy, Measuring Legitimating Beliefs*, 53 AMERICAN BEHAVIORAL SCIENTIST 354, 361, 364–67 (2009). *See also* Margaret Levi, Tom R. Tyler, and Audrey Sacks, *The Reasons for Compliance with Law*, *in* UNDERSTANDING SOCIAL ACTION, PROMOTING HUMAN RIGHTS 70 (Ryan Goodman, Derek Jinks, and Andrew K. Woods eds., 2012).

[37] Matthias Krönke, *Bounded Autonomy: What Limits Zimbabweans' Trust in their Courts and Electoral Commission?*, 52 AFROBAROMETER POLICY PAPER 1 (2018).

[38] Krönke, *supra* note 37, at 12.

[39] Juan Carlos Donoso, *Justice and Democracy: The Rule of Law in the Americas*, *in* CHALLENGES TO DEMOCRACY IN LATIN AMERICA AND THE CARIBBEAN: EVIDENCE FROM THE AMERICASBAROMETER 2006-07 277 (Mitchell A. Seligson ed., 2008).

[40] Ryan Salzman and Adam Ramsey, *Judging the Judiciary: Understanding Public Confidence in Latin American Courts*, 55 LATIN AMERICAN POLITICS AND SOCIETY 73, 90 (2013).

[41] Lee Demetrius Walker, *A Multi-Level Explanation of Mass Support for the Judiciary*, 37 JUSTICE SYSTEM JOURNAL 194, 202 (2016).

[42] Ryan E. Carlin, Mariana Castrellón, Varun Gauri, Isabel C. Jaramillo Sierra, and Jeffrey K. Staton, *Public Reactions to Noncompliance with Judicial Orders*, 116 AMERICAN POLITICAL SCIENCE REVIEW 265 (2022).

[43] This process revealed that a wide majority of the Court's orders were followed, but roughly 30% of the judicial orders were ignored or otherwise not adhered to.

Testing the Assumption: Are There Electoral Costs to Noncompliance?

Influential accounts of interbranch judicial behavior construct their models around the notion that, as long as citizens believe in the legitimacy of judicial institutions, voters will punish leaders' noncompliance with court rulings—or will at least become a credible threat of electoral backlash.[44] However, such claim has scarcely been the object of empirical scrutiny[45]—let alone the *mechanism* by which diffuse judicial support informs citizens' assessment of defiant public officials. Yet testing this assumption is far from being a trivial enterprise: Why might the public—whose interests are likely more aligned with incumbents by virtue of the electoral connection—use their vote at the ballot box to punish the government for failing to adhere to judicial rulings?

Recent research addresses this theoretical linchpin, and demonstrates that while the public often professes broad support for judicial institutions and an unwillingness to support changes thereto, concern for incumbent interference with judicial institutions only marginally informs vote choice, relative to other policy concerns.[46] Driscoll and Nelson evaluate voters' calculus via conjoint experiment, comparing the relative influence of court-curbing proposals, candidates' partisanship, and their policy positions on questions like gun control, LGBTQ protections, and abortion policy, based on a nationally representative sample of U.S. adults.[47] Although they find a consistent and high level of diffuse support for the Supreme Court, and open objections to candidates' attempts to change this revered institution, these considerations have a very small influence on vote choice, especially compared with partisanship or more salient and divisive policy concerns.[48] Driscoll and Nelson also evaluate the electoral cost of court-curbing through a series of vignette experiments, where respondents are randomly assigned to treatments that describe efforts to limit or enhance judicial power or influence.[49] As with the conjoint experiment, the public's willingness to punish incumbents for efforts to undermine judicial institutions is muted relative to other concerns. Admittedly, these authors do not directly interrogate questions of compliance, leaving open an obvious opportunity for future research.

---

44 Vanberg, *Legislative-Judicial Relations*, *supra* note 7; Vanberg, Politics of Constitutional Review, *supra* note 7; Staton, Constitutional Review, *supra* note 7; Staton, Judicial Power, *supra* note 7; Carrubba, *supra* note 8; Helmke, *supra* note 7; Krehbiel, *supra* note 8; Staton, Reenock, and Holsinger, *supra* note 8.

45 A notable exception is Krehbiel, *supra* note 9.

46 Armaly, *supra* note 9.

47 Driscoll and Nelson, Court Curbing, *supra* note 9. Nelson and Driscoll, Accountability, *supra* note 9.

48 This dynamic holds even when partisanship is held constant, and when respondents were asked to evaluate co-partisan candidates in a hypothetical primary contest.

49 Driscoll and Nelson, Court Curbing, *supra* note 9. These experiments were included on nationally representative surveys in Argentina, Bolivia, Chile, Costa Rica, Guatemala, Nicaragua, Panama, Paraguay, Poland, Hungary, and the United States (*see* Driscoll and Nelson, *supra* note 35; Amanda Driscoll and Michael J. Nelson, *Spotlight on Support for Reducing Judicial Power in the Americas*, *in* Pulse of Democracy 90 (Noam Lupu, Mariana Rodríguez, and Elizabeth J. Zechmeister eds., 2021)). This represents the first cross-national survey of diffuse support for judicial institutions in more than a quarter-century (*see* Gibson and Caldeira, *Legitimacy of Transnational Legal Institutions*, *supra* note 9; Gibson, Caldeira, and Baird, *supra* note 9; Driscoll and Nelson, *No Legitimacy Crisis*, *supra* note 9).

Table 14.1 *Court-related questions on cross-national survey instruments*

Concept	Question	Afro Barometer	Americas Barometer	Asia Barometer	Euro Barometer
Compliance	If judges frequently hinder the work of our presidents, they should be ignored.		2006		
	Even when judges sometimes hinder the work of our presidents, their decisions should always be obeyed.		2006		
	When the Supreme Court/ Constitutional Tribunal hinders the work of our government, it should not be paid attention to by our Presidents/Prime Minister.		2008, 2010		
	The courts have the right to make decisions that people always have to abide by.	2002, 2003, 2005, 2006, 2008, 2009, 2011–2013, 2014, 2015, 2016–2018			
	Since the President was elected to lead the country, he should not be bound by laws or court decisions that he thinks are wrong.	2005, 2006, 2008, 2009, 2011–2013, 2014, 2015, 2016–2018			
	The President/Prime Minister must always obey the laws and the courts, even if he thinks they are wrong.	2005, 2006, 2008, 2009, 2011–2013, 2014, 2015, 2016–2018			
Diffuse Support	If the national high court started making decisions that most people disagree with, it might be better to do away with the court altogether.		2021		1992–1993
	Do you believe that when the country is facing very difficult times, it is justifiable for the President of the country to dissolve the national high court and govern without it?		2010, 2012, 2014, 2019	2012	
	Do you think that sometimes there can be sufficient grounds to dissolve the Supreme Court of Justice, or do you think that there can never be sufficient grounds to do so?		2006, 2008		
	The Supreme Court/Constitutional Tribunal should have less power to decide on controversial issues.		2021		

In sum, the empirical record that addresses the question of compliance in comparative perspective is admittedly quite mixed. Considerable progress has been made of late in the study of public support for courts, bringing to bear experimental methods,[50] quasi-experimental research designs,[51] and new cross-national samples and panel surveys.[52] This has revitalized our understanding of public support for judicial institutions, both in the United States and abroad. Still, public attitudes regarding compliance are rarely featured,[53] even when survey questions exist whereby critical hypotheses relating to public attitudes might be systematically scrutinized, or these opinions are differentiated from related measures and concepts. Finally, there is much we have yet to understand regarding the behavioral aspect of public intolerance for noncompliance. Although Carlin et al.'s research suggests many Colombian voters would be willing to pay a small cost to enhance compliance with judicial orders—an encouraging finding indeed[54]—the research of Driscoll and Nelson suggests that the electoral connection might be too blunt an instrument to fully incentivize incumbent compliance.[55]

In what follows, we turn to the scholarly literature that addresses compliance, to infer how that corpus of research might inform this discussion regarding public attitudes on the matter.

COMPLIANCE AND PUBLIC ATTITUDE FORMATION

Whereas compliance is central to our understanding of judicial power, influence, and independence, a vibrant and dynamic stream of research addresses the concept and empirical measure of adherence and defiance of judicial orders. Notably, this research is almost entirely divorced from the research on public support for judicial institutions and public evaluation of compliance we summarize above.[56] Here, we address why these two research questions have evolved entirely apart from one another, and identify at least five facets of noncompliance that would seem to be preconditions for public attitude formation.

The Five "Ws" of Compliance

Even a cursory review of the literature on compliance makes evident the challenge to public attitude formation regarding noncompliance.[57] Endemic to any empirical evaluation of compli-

---

50 Bartels and Johnston, *supra* note 9; Armaly, *supra* note 9; Driscoll and Nelson, Court Curbing, *supra* note 9.

51 Christenson and Glick, *supra* note 9.

52 Driscoll and Nelson, *No Legitimacy Crisis*, *supra* note 9; Driscoll and Nelson, *supra* note 35; Driscoll and Nelson, *supra* note 49; Driscoll, Krehbiel, and Nelson, *supra* note 25; Nelson and Tucker (n 10).

53 Driscoll, Krehbiel, and Nelson, *supra* note 25.

54 Carlin et al., *supra* note 42.

55 Driscoll and Nelson, Court Curbing, *supra* note 9.

56 Carlin et al., *supra* note 42, are the one exception to this rule, whose research takes seriously the insights from *both* of the aforementioned literatures.

57 Our review is not exhaustive, but we point interested readers to other scholars who provide excellent and comprehensive critiques of the conceptualization and measurement of compliance (*see* Kapiszewski and Taylor, *supra* note 6; Alexandra V. Huneeus, *Compliance with International Court Judgments and Decisions*, *in* THE OXFORD HANDBOOK OF INTERNATIONAL ADJUDICATION 437 (Cesare Romano, Karen Alter, and Yuval Shany eds., 2014); Courtney Hillebrecht, *Rethinking Compliance: The Challenges and Prospects of Measuring Compliance with International Human Rights Tribunals*, 1 JOURNAL OF HUMAN RIGHTS PRACTICE 362 (2009)).

ance are what we dub the *five "Ws"* of judicial orders: the "who", "what", "when", "where", and "why" of compliance. Scholars who endeavor to measure compliance empirically must grapple with each of these facets of adherence or defiance, among others, each of which implies a nuanced path for how implementation of judicial orders might occur. We briefly address each of the five "Ws" of judicial orders, before turning to the implications for how compliance or defiance might be publicly observed, or how public attitudes regarding compliance might be formed in light of these challenges.

To fully evaluate compliance in practice, one must minimally answer the following five questions:

- *"Who" does the judicial order implicate?* The first consideration when evaluating compliance hinges on determining *who* is to comply with a court order. Monitoring compliance is broadly thought to involve a comparison between a court's decision and the actions taken by those targeted in the ruling,[58] yet there are many instances in which it is unclear whose (in)actions "count." The source of this ambiguity can stem either from the scope or reach of the judicial decision (*erga omnes* or *inter partes*), but also depends on the context of the decision, especially when judicial orders implicate the actions of several parties. Even when judicial orders center on a single target, institutional actors with different levels of responsibilities, such as the executive power and its agencies, complicate this consideration.[59] Identifying (non)compliant actors is all the more challenging when courts order different actors to carry out the same action.[60]
- *"What" actions does the judicial order require?* A second consideration concerns the question of *what actions* are required for full compliance, and which acts constitute proper implementation of a judicial order. Researchers tracking compliance of international tribunals often disaggregate judicial decisions to the specific orders *within* each court ruling; Hillebretch,[61] Staton and Romero,[62] and Basch et al.[63] consider whether the states complied with each "remedy" in a given judicial order, leaving open the possibility that they do not achieve full compliance at the level of the decision. This approach allows for a continuum of possible responses to a court's order—with most responses landing somewhere in between full compliance and overt noncompliance.[64] As Hawkins and Jacoby suggest,

---

58 *See* Kapiszewski and Taylor, *supra* note 6; Huneeus, *supra* note 57.

59 A related complication occurs when a judicial order implicates behavior of collective institutional bodies. Whether the defiance of a single individual renders an institutional response noncompliant, or whether compliance instead hinges on the behavior of a median member or person in leadership, are both critical questions to which there is no universal answer.

60 For example, consider the *Mendoza* decision by the Argentinean Supreme Court (*Mendoza c/ Estado Nacional*, 331:1622 (2008)), which resolved jurisdictional responsibilities for environmental rehabilitation for the highly polluted Matanza-Riachuelo River. The Supreme Court ordered national, state, and municipal governments to submit an integrated plan for remediating the ecological damage, and to prevent future contamination (*see* Sandra Botero, *Judges, Litigants, and the Politics of Rights Enforcement in Argentina*, 50 Comparative Politics 169 (2018)).

61 *See* Hillebrecht, *supra* note 6.

62 Jeffrey K. Staton and Alexia Romero, *Rational Remedies: The Role of Opinion Clarity in the Inter-American Human Rights System*, 63 International Studies Quarterly 477 (2019).

63 Fernando Basch, Leonardo Filippini, Ana Laya, and Mariano Nino, *The Effectiveness of the Inter-American System of Human Rights Protection: A Quantitative Approach to its Functioning and Compliance with Its Decisions*, 7 SUR-International Journal on Human Rights 9 (2010).

64 *See* Huneeus, *supra* note 57; Kapiszewski and Taylor, *supra* note 6.

partial compliance—states responding to some, but not all, directives in an order—is the modal response.[65] Beyond international tribunals, most empirical research into the question of judicial compliance allows for this nuanced, nondichotomous view.[66]

- *By "when" must said actions be instigated, performed, or completed?* A third consideration interrogates *when* state actors must adhere to an order. Some judicial orders specify a deadline to completion; still others leave the question of time to implementation ambiguous, or even up to the discretion of the incumbent government actor.[67] This has led some researchers to explicitly conceptualize and measure compliance temporally,[68] with others incorporating measures of time or delay in their analyses of compliance.[69]
- *"Where" might implementation be performed or observed?* A fourth consideration concerns where and how compliance is observed. In the direct approach to answering this question, and having answered the "who", "what", and "when" questions above, researchers evaluate activities undertaken by a variety of public actors in response to judi-

---

[65] Darren Hawkins and Wade Jacoby, *Partial Compliance: A Comparison of the European and Inter-American Courts of Human Rights*, 6 Journal of International Law & International Relations 35 (2010). The authors report that partial compliance with the Inter-American Court of Human Rights varies only minimally by state, while compliance varies a bit more by nature of the right violated only with respect to European Court of Human Rights decisions.

[66] *See* Spriggs, *supra* note 6; Canon and Johnson, *supra* note 6; Hillebrecht, *supra* note 6; Hawkins and Jacoby, *supra* note 65; Nikolay Vasev, Karsten Vrangbæk, and Filip Křepelka, *The End of Eastern Territoriality? CJEU Compliance in the New Member States*, 15 Comparative European Politics 459 (2017); Michael Blauberger, *With Luxembourg in mind... The Remaking of National Policies in the Face of ECJ Jurisprudence*, 19 Journal of European Public Policy 109 (2012); Lisa J. Conant, Justice Contained: Law and Politics in the European Union (2002). Nevertheless, even some overt challenges to judicial orders are difficult to classify – for example, when Congress overrides the legal interpretation made by a court (*see* James Meernik and Joseph Ignagni, *Judicial Review and Coordinate Construction of the Constitution*, 41 American Journal of Political Science 447 (1997); Conant, *supra*; Vanberg, *Legislative-Judicial Relations*, *supra* note 7, at 374 n.1), or when political actors attempt (Meernik and Ignagni, *supra*) or threaten (Clifford J. Carrubba, Matthew Gabel, and Charles Hankla, *Judicial Behavior under Political Constraints: Evidence from the European Court of Justice*, 102 American Political Science Review 435 (2008)) to defy judicial decisions. The former is legally permissible; the latter is insufficient—lacking actual resistance to behavioral change—to constitute an instance of official noncompliance.

[67] Consider the U.S. Supreme Court's decision in the landmark case *Brown v. Board of Education II*, 349 US 294 (1955), in which the Justices ordered public schools to dismantle racial segregation "with all deliberate speed."

[68] *See* Staton, Judicial Power, *supra* note 7; Varun Gauri, Jeffrey K. Staton, and Jorge Vargas-Cullell, *The Costa Rican Supreme Court's Compliance Monitoring System*, 77 The Journal of Politics 774 (2015); Börzel, Tanja A., Tobias Hofmann, and Diana Panke, *Caving in or Sitting it Out? Longitudinal Patterns of Non-Compliance in the European Union*, 19 Journal of European Public Policy 454 (2012).

[69] *See* Hawkins and Jacoby, *supra* note 65; Basch et al., *supra* note 63. For instance, Staton shows that there is "massive variance" in the time Mexican public authorities take to comply with orders from the Mexican Supreme Court, and that orders involving the transfer of money also involve the longest delays (Staton, Judicial Power, *supra* note 7). Importantly, monitoring increases responsiveness: in their study of the Costa Rican Constitutional Chamber, Gauri, Staton, and Cullell report that the introduction of a compliance monitoring system reduced the average time of compliance by approximately two months (Gauri, Staton, and Cullell, *supra* note 68, at 784).

cial orders. Some have tracked legislative responses,[70] while others have looked at court ruling implementation via federal or state agency decisions within the executive branch of government.[71] Compliance within the judicial hierarchy has also been considered in the comparative and international courts literature.[72]

Where direct observation is unfeasible, indirect approaches instead center on expert or public evaluation of incumbents' behaviors. One prominent example is the strategy taken by the Varieties of Democracy dataset, which queries country experts on the extent to which government complies with "important" judicial orders the government disagrees with; expert scores are then aggregated to create a country-year rating of the level of compliance.[73] Others focus on interviewing the parties involved in judicial cases (litigants or claimants, as well as public officials) about whether the court judgment was implemented.[74]

- *"Why" are judicial orders adhered to?* A final consideration involves evaluating *why* compliance is ultimately observed, and *whether* it is the result of a judicial order.[75] Here, scholars distinguish between impact, effectiveness, and compliance. Canon and Johnson conceptualize impact as "the general reactions and changes (or lack thereof) that follow a judicial decision;"[76] Kapiszewski and Taylor suggest that judicial impact is broader than compliance, as the former refers to the effects of court decisions beyond the actions that directly result from the rulings.[77] Furthermore, work in the international courts literature

---

70 *See* Vanberg, *Legislative-Judicial Relations*, *supra* note 7; Vanberg, Politics of Constitutional Review, *supra* note 7; Canon and Johnson, *supra* note 6.

71 Spriggs, for example, tracks bureaucratic compliance with the U.S. Supreme Court, analyzing 229 rulings and agencies' subsequent actions to determine "whether, and to what extent, agencies complied with the legal rules underpinning the Court's decision" (Spriggs, *supra* note 6, at 574–75).

72 Canon and Johnson examine the so-called "interpreting population," which "responds to the policy decisions of a higher court by refining the policy it has announced" (Canon and Johnson, *supra* note 6, at 18). Trochev analyzes the Russian "war of courts" between the Constitutional Court, on one hand, and the Supreme Court and lower courts on the other (Alexei Trochev, Judging Russia: The Role of the Constitutional Court in Russian Politics 1990–2006, 202–03, 292–294 (2008)). Huneeus examines the extent to which national courts comply with decisions of the Inter-American Court of Human Rights (Huneeus, *supra* note 6).

73 *See* Daniel Pemstein, Kyle L. Marquardt, Eitan Tzelgov, Yi-ting Wang, Juraj Medzihorsky, Joshua Krusell, Farhad Miri, and Johannes von Römer, *The V–Dem Measurement Model: Latent Variable Analysis for Cross-National and Cross-Temporal Expert-Coded Data*, 21 V-Dem Working Paper 1 (2021); Michael Coppedge, John Gerring, Carl Henrik Knutsen, Staffan I. Lindberg, Jan Teorell, David Altman, Michael Bernhard, M. Steven Fish, Adam Glynn, Allen Hicken, Lisa Gastaldi, Haakon Gjerløw, Adam Glynn, Allen Hicken, Anna Lührmann, Seraphine F. Maerz, Kyle L. Marquardt, Kelly McMann, Valeriya Mechkova, Pamela Paxton, Daniel Pemstein, Johannes von Römer, Brigitte Seim, Rachel Sigman, Svend-Erik Skaaning, Jeffrey K. Staton, Aksel Sundtröm, Eitan Tzelgov, Luca Uberti, Yi-ting Wang, Tore Wig, and Daniel Ziblatt, *V-Dem [Country–Year/Country–Date] Dataset v11.1* (Varieties of Democracy (V-Dem) Project, 2021), https://doi.org/10.23696/vdemds21.

74 *See* Robin Creyke and John D. McMillan, *The Operation of Judicial Review in Australia*, *in* Judicial Review and Bureaucratic Impact: International and Interdisciplinary Perspectives 161 (Marc Hertogh and Simon Halliday, eds. 2004); Carlin et al., *supra* note 42; Vasev, Vrangbæk, and Křepelka, *supra* note 66; Conant, *supra* note 66.

75 For a full discussion of causation in the context of compliance, *see* Kapiszewski and Taylor, *supra* note 6, at 22–25; Huneeus, *supra* note 57.

76 Canon and Johnson, *supra* note 6, at 17.

77 Kapiszewski and Taylor, *supra* note 6, at 807. *See also* Botero, *supra* note 60. Conversely, perfect adherence to judicial orders need not imply judicial impact, or independence, but could instead reflect

often distinguishes between compliance and effectiveness.[78] All told, incumbents may behave in ways that are consistent with judicial orders but not because of them; and judicial orders may direct actions that would be completed anyway, even in the absence of judicial orders. These considerations must be weighed to fully evaluate (non)compliance.

The ongoing discussion of the *five "Ws"* of compliance underscores an important point: even under the best of circumstances, with straightforward judicial orders and the most meticulous of observers, the public monitoring of compliance (much less forming an opinion about it) is far from straightforward. The five questions raised above are the minimum that must be addressed. Once those are answered—as the scholars above will no doubt attest—monitoring compliance is both time- and resource-intensive. This implies that our assumptions about public attitude formation regarding compliance are tremendously fragile, hinging on a complex constellation of considerations including public awareness, comprehension, and sophistication. If we take these concerns about what counts as adherence, compliance, or defiance, it then becomes clear what a high bar we have set for public opinion formation. This requires citizens to be attentive to the nuances of both court rulings (the *who*, *what*, and *when*) and incumbent compliance (the *when*, *how*, and *why*) in order to fully supervise this negotiation.[79] More importantly, these varied complications also highlight two central conduits through which public opinions about compliance might be formed: the problem of monitoring, and the question of strategy.

The Problem of Monitoring

The *problem of monitoring* refers to the fact that it is unlikely the public would come to observe noncompliance on their own. The very nature of the social contract between the rulers and the ruled implies the delegation of policymaking responsibility—principal–agent relationships that are riddled with information asymmetry and incomplete information under the clearest of representational circumstances. As to the considerations of compliance laid plain above, how the public monitors or becomes aware of noncompliance is of utmost theoretical import, because it is unlikely to happen spontaneously, without critical information being provided by external monitors.

Most national high courts and many international tribunals do not directly monitor the implementation of their rulings, or if they do this information is not readily publicized. Consequentially, even the most interested parties cannot rely on courts to provide information

---

the decisions of a fully co-opted court, or one whose decisions align perfectly with the preferences of the actors it would otherwise seek to constrain.

78 While some authors explicitly discuss this distinction (*see* Hawkins and Jacoby, *supra* note 65; Staton and Romero, *supra* note 62), others treat compliance, impact, and effectiveness coterminously (*see* Blauberger, *supra* note 66; Vasev, Vrangbæk, and Křepelka, *supra* note 66).

79 Consider what the above framework would imply for the public to fully comprehend compliance. Citizens not only need to observe instances of noncompliance with rulings (the *where*), but then also isolate *who* the court deems responsible for behavioral change, *what* exactly the ruling requires of each targeted actor (and how they might do so); consider and judge the fairness of any delay that might occur in the process; and discern the underlying motives for complying (the *why*). All are preconditions for coordinated action, such as withdrawing support from incumbents for this act of noncompliance (*see* Weingast, *supra* note 9). If this is challenging for researchers devoted to the question, this process of discernment would seem insurmountable to the common observer of modern politics.

on compliance with judicial decisions.[80] Monitoring systems, when they exist, are often indirect: noncompliance is observed after a new claim has been initiated by litigants, in response to a judicial order that has gone unfulfilled.[81] Monitoring noncompliance via litigation implies that noncompliance is likely underreported, as we only observe it when the litigants are sufficiently aggrieved to launch a formal complaint, and sufficiently resource-rich to pursue a legal remedy.[82]

If not courts, who might otherwise be involved in the monitoring process, and sound the alarm to alert the public to noncompliance? Indeed, which actors face incentives to monitor, and have the resources to do so, as well as the resources to publicize it? Here, existing research is instructive, if incomplete. Vanberg suggests that opposition parties and organized groups have both the incentives and resources to increase public awareness.[83] The former—motivated by policy concerns or obtaining political gains—may take advantage of their institutional environment (i.e., through legislative debates, public hearings, or the influence of legislative agenda) in order to police and publicize incumbent noncompliance. Likewise, organized groups in civil society—interested in the implementation of an issue decided by the court—can provide financial resources to monitoring compliance and employ their media connections to call attention to legislative evasions.[84] Others emphasize the role of civil society organizations. For instance, in Staton, Reenock, and Holsinger's model, a robust civil society plays the role of triggering the noncompliance alarm, since it can credibly mobilize organizations interested in seeing court decisions enforced (i.e., bar associations or human rights organizations).[85]

---

80 *See* Kapiszewski and Taylor, *supra* note 6; VANBERG, POLITICS OF CONSTITUTIONAL REVIEW, *supra* note 7; STATON, JUDICIAL POWER, *supra* note 7; Gauri, Staton, and Cullell, *supra* note 68; Carlin et al., *supra* note 42. Most courts lack not only the resources, but also the incentives to monitor: STATON, REENOCK, AND HOLSINGER, *supra* note 8, and Gauri, Staton, and Cullell, *supra* note 68, note that courts and judges must have some minimal tolerance for noncompliance, or they would only ever rule in such a way that they could expect perfect adherence.

81 *See* Carlin et al., *supra* note 42; Gauri, Staton, and Cullell, *supra* note 68. Among the few courts that do rely on some sort of direct monitoring systems are the Costa Rican Constitutional Chamber since 2009 (Gauri, Staton, and Cullell, *supra* note 68), the 1995–2005 Russian Constitutional Court (TROCHEV, *supra* note 72, Ch. 7), the Inter-American Court of Human Rights, the European Court of Human Rights, and the Court of Justice of the European Union.

82 *See* Gauri, Staton, and Cullell, *supra* note 68. These stipulations would also imply complaints might be more likely in certain types of claims and cases, a fact that would endogenously inform both incumbents' likelihood of compliance and the shape and content of court orders.

83 VANBERG, POLITICS OF CONSTITUTIONAL REVIEW, *supra* note 7, at 46–47, 102–103.

84 Vanberg also considers the role of alternative governmental coalitions (other than the one whose laws are subject to judicial scrutiny) in increasing transparency (VANBERG, POLITICS OF CONSTITUTIONAL REVIEW, *supra* note 7, at 103). Note that the media, opposition, and third-party monitors have a different role in Krehbiel's model, where they can punish noncompliance, but not necessarily increase the public awareness of governmental defiance (Jay N. Krehbiel, *Public Awareness and the Behavior of Unpopular Courts*, 51 BRITISH JOURNAL OF POLITICAL SCIENCE 1601 (2021)).

85 STATON, REENOCK, AND HOLSINGER, *supra* note 8. *See also* ADAM CHILTON AND MILA VERSTEEG, HOW CONSTITUTIONAL RIGHTS MATTER (2020); CHARLES R. EPP, THE RIGHTS REVOLUTION: LAWYERS, ACTIVISTS, AND SUPREME COURTS IN COMPARATIVE PERSPECTIVE (1998); THOMAS M. KECK, JUDICIAL POLITICS IN POLARIZED TIMES (2014). In a similar approach, Botero argues that civil society and watchdog agencies can increase monitoring of judicial decisions (and thus incumbent accountability), but only when they have been "activated" by courts through the creation of institutional "collaborative oversight arenas" under judicial control (i.e., follow-up committees, public hearings, and information requests)

The problem of monitoring, thus, has implications for both the study of monitors, and the study of attitude formation. With respect to the monitors, some important theoretical and empirical questions emerge. How and why do courts decide to monitor compliance; and when they do so, how and why do courts decide to publicize (non)compliance? More broadly, how do courts and judicial actors weigh the pros and cons of transparency of any aspect of their work, and when is transparency strategically deployed? The theoretical work by Staton[86] and Krehbiel[87] is instructive and lays plain opportunities for empirical research that systematically tracks courts' communication with the public or some segment of civil society via decisions, press releases, public appearances, or related public-facing activities, as well as the institutional tools courts can employ to monitor, and increase awareness of, noncompliance.[88] As to third-party monitors, how and why might organizations identify judicial orders and compliance as *the* relevant nexus for their public advocacy and activism? For any public monitor, be they courts or otherwise, what efforts do they make to build credibility with the public, fostering trust as a reputable source of information?

As to the question of opinion formation, recent judicial politics research acknowledges the role of partisanship in public evaluation of courts, and is increasingly interested in the role of elite cues that have been shown to shape public attitudes toward judicial decisions and institutions.[89] This new research runs counter, in part, to a well-established body of scholarship that emphasizes the role of socialization and exposure to judicial symbols as instrumental for fostering diffuse support for courts.[90] Digging deeper into these dynamics—how the public weighs cues from incumbents, courts or third-party monitors regarding compliance—is of central import for understanding how the public comes to value compliance, and what spurs public action in the face of incumbent defiance of judicial orders.

The Question of Strategy

No less important, but related to monitoring, is the question of *strategy*, which can implicate judicial behavior, incumbent behavior, or the behaviors of third-party monitors. The possibility that public support for noncompliance is rooted in instrumental considerations allows for the hypothesis that the public will take cues from elite behavior, a caveat that is well represented in the research reviewed here. Scholars have long acknowledged that political sophisticates and opinion leaders hold opinions about courts that are different from the general public,[91] and it is

---

(Botero, *supra* note 60). Note, however, that Botero's mechanism presupposes courts' willingness to increase public awareness, regardless of the incentives by third-party monitors.

86 Staton, *Constitutional Review*, *supra* note 7; STATON, JUDICIAL POWER, *supra* note 7.

87 Krehbiel, *supra* note 8.

88 *See also* Botero, *supra* note 60.

89 *See* Driscoll and Nelson, Court Curbing, *supra* note 9; Gibson and Nelson, *supra* note 16; Tom S. Clark and Jonathan P. Kastellec, *Source Cues and Public Support for the Supreme Court*, 43 AMERICAN POLITICS RESEARCH 504 (2015).

90 *See* EASTON, *supra* note 10; GIBSON AND CALDEIRA, CITIZENS, COURTS, AND CONFIRMATIONS, *supra* note 9; James L. Gibson, Milton Lodge, and Benjamin Woodson, *Losing, but Accepting: Legitimacy, Positivity Theory, and the Symbols of Judicial Authority*, 48 LAW & SOCIETY REVIEW 837 (2014).

91 *See* Tanenhaus and Murphy, *supra* note 29; Caldeira and Gibson, *supra* note 9.

well understood that the public "follows the lead" of political elites.[92] In the realm of judicial politics and interbranch relations, the models of Carrubba and Stephenson allow the public's opinion to be swayed by elite behaviors, taking cues from incumbents about the relative value and benefit of judicial decision-making.[93] Staton and Vanberg describe this dynamic:

> noncompliance by a policy maker today may begin to undermine the general perception that court decisions must be respected, and thus induce more and more noncompliance as citizens and political elites become less likely to react when policy makers fail to adhere to judicial rulings. Once defying decisions becomes a "normal" part of politics, judges lose influence as policy makers are no longer expected to heed rulings they dislike.[94]

That incumbents may inform citizens' assessment of the value of judicial institutions[95] implies that strategic elites can benefit from increasing public awareness of defiant behavior. This logic is consistent with the claim that leaders may advance court-curbing proposals so as to rally a base of electoral support,[96] and to stake out their claim on substantive issues. These may or may not be earnest attempts at meaningful reforms, but rather efforts to rally a base of electoral support, or to signal to interested constituents the seriousness of their commitment to a given cause. Likewise, high-profile shows of noncompliance with judicial orders—"attempts"[97] or "threats"[98] of defiance—is yet another way incumbents' public noncompliance may advance their electoral or political ambitions.[99] All of this research turns the conventional wisdom on its head: if public awareness of judicial disobedience is uniformly disadvantageous to incumbents, we should not observe leaders publicizing instances of their own noncompliance. Yet noncompliance is not only observed, but broadly publicized, suggesting that the high-profile defiance is a valuable end unto itself.

---

92 GABRIEL S. LENZ, FOLLOW THE LEADER? HOW VOTERS RESPOND TO POLITICIANS' POLICIES AND PERFORMANCE (2012).

93 Carrubba, *supra* note 8; Stephenson, *supra* note 6.

94 Jeffrey K. Staton and Georg Vanberg, *The Value of Vagueness: Delegation, Defiance, and Judicial Opinions*, 52 AMERICAN JOURNAL OF POLITICAL SCIENCE 504, 507 (2008).

95 Carrubba, *supra* note 8.

96 *See* TOM S. CLARK, THE LIMITS OF JUDICIAL INDEPENDENCE (2010).

97 *See* Meernik and Ignagni, *supra* note 66.

98 *See* Carrubba, Gabel, and Hankla, *supra* note 66.

99 *See* CLARK, *supra* note 92. Consider the so-called "Southern Manifesto" signed by 96 U.S. senators and Representatives opposed to the *Brown v. Board of Education*, 347 US 483 (1954) decision issued by the U.S. Supreme Court. The document stated that "we pledge ourselves to use all lawful means to bring about a reversal of this decision which is contrary to the Constitution and to prevent the use of force in its implementation" (cited by CANON AND JOHNSON, *supra* note 6 78–79). Also, more recent examples from daily politics suggest that incumbents may find benefits in publicizing court-curbing attempts, even regarding well-respected judiciaries. Consider, for instance, the case of U.S. House members holding a press conference to announce the introduction of a bill to expand the number of seats on the U.S. Supreme Court (*see* Krishnadev Calamur and Nina Totenberg, *Democrats Unveil Long-Shot Plan To Expand Size Of Supreme Court From 9 To 13*, NPR, Apr. 15, 2021, http://www.npr.org/2021/04/15/987723528/democrats-unveil-long-shot-plan-to-expand-size-of-supreme-court-from-9-to-13). Moreover, emergent research shows that an incumbent's court-curbing proposals are met with discontent only among outpartisan citizens (Driscoll and Nelson, Court Curbing, *supra* note 9), building upon the idea that voters follow policy cues from their preferred or elected candidates (*see* Armaly, *supra* note 9; LENZ, *supra* note 92).

However, elite influence is, perhaps fortunately, not a one-way street. If citizens' evaluation of compliance with judicial orders is to be informed by elite behavior—potentially undermining public support for courts by giving the impression that judicial institutions need not be respected[100]—then courts also face incentives to cultivate or protect their public image. Courts can be strategic not only in how they craft opinions to facilitate incumbent compliance or public comprehension,[101] but by their publicizing of decisions or procedures, in a bid to cultivate public support so as to enhance incumbent compliance.[102] A different line of research on judicial behavior shows that judges are attentive to public opinion and interest group constituencies when rendering opinions about controversial topics,[103] and may craft their judicial orders or opinions with more or less specificity so as to enhance the likelihood of compliance, or conversely, increase the chances that noncompliance will go undetected by the public.[104]

Courts may also strategically engage in relations with the media and third-party monitors to gain some control over the content that is reported to the public, with the goal of increasing legitimacy (and thus diffuse support) through the myth of impartiality.[105] Courts that are well regarded by the press can also attempt to take advantage of the media's role as opinion leader to influence the public or signal political leaders about the institution's reputation. For instance, Vanberg's case study of the confrontation between elites and the German Federal Constitutional Court shows that widespread media reactions against incumbents' noncompliance attempts were perceived by the government as a credible threat of public backlash.[106]

That courts, incumbents, and third-party monitors are all critical actors in communicating with the public about (non)compliance—and that said communication may well be strategic to advance or communicate other political interests—imply that these actors, their strategies, and communication ought to be at the center of future research on public attitudes regarding compliance.

OPPORTUNITIES AND AN AGENDA FOR FUTURE RESEARCH

Recent years have witnessed a renaissance in the study of public support for judicial institutions. Scholars have brought new methodological approaches and sources of data to revisit and

---

[100] *See* Carrubba, *supra* note 12; Carrubba, *supra* note 8; Krehbiel, *supra* note 9.

[101] Staton and Vanberg, *supra* note 94.

[102] *See* Staton, Constitutional Review, *supra* note 7; Staton, Judicial Power, *supra* note 7; Krehbiel, *supra* note 8; Botero, *supra* note 60. This strategic transparency is not without potential costs, as enhanced public awareness can undermine courts' legitimacy (Staton, Judicial Power, *supra* note 7), a threat which is more acute when courts lack *ex-ante* public support (Krehbiel, *supra* note 84). Further, while some courts would benefit from publicized decisions where chances of government compliance are high (Staton, Judicial Power, *supra* note 7), in other contexts courts might be better served by increasing public awareness when the likelihood of compliance is comparably *low* (Krehbiel, *supra* note 8).

[103] *See* James A. Stimson, Michael B. MacKuen, and Robert S. Erikson, *Dynamic Representation*, 89 American Political Science Review 543 (1995); Michael J. Nelson, *Responsive Justice? Retention Elections, Prosecutors, and Public Opinion*, 2 Journal of Law and Courts 117 (2014).

[104] *See* Staton and Vanberg, *supra* note 94.

[105] *See* Staton, Judicial Power, *supra* note 7; Gibson, Caldeira, and Spence 2003, *supra* note 33; Gibson, Lodge, and Woodson, *supra* note 90.

[106] Vanberg, *supra* note 26.

revitalize our understanding of judicial legitimacy, and whether and why the public's support may serve as a "shield" to incumbent overreach or stave off interbranch hostilities.[107] Much of this research highlights the partisan foundations of public evaluation of judicial institutions and their decisions;[108] while at the same time it underscores that public veneration of judicial institutions remains both high and relatively stable, both in the United States[109] and abroad.[110]

Yet rarely has the question of public expectations regarding compliance been part of this new wave of research, despite the centrality of compliance for our understanding of comparative judicial power,[111] and despite the public's concern for compliance being prominently featured in many models of judicial power and independence.[112] This is in part a matter of omission—many cross-national or original surveys do not include items that probe expectations regarding incumbent compliance—yet it stands as an open opportunity. We note above that while they are uncommon, compliance-related items do exist on cross-national survey instruments, yet have only been considered by researchers in a handful of cases.[113] This is indeed an opportunity for the taking.

This is also, as we describe above, understandable, in light of the high bar that exists for public knowledge and comprehension of incumbent noncompliance. For the average median voter, to evaluate the *five "Ws"* of compliance we enumerate above is a tall order, and a taller order still to expect them to cast their vote with these considerations in mind.[114] This fact underscores the importance of considering the effects of monitoring and monitoring environments,[115] as well as how strategic elite behaviors interact to inform and shape public opinion surrounding compliance.[116] This also begs the question as to whether the median voter is of prime theoretical import for our concerns regarding judicial compliance.[117]

---

[107] *See* Bartels and Johnston, *supra* note 9; Gibson and Nelson, *supra* note 14; Gibson and Nelson, *supra* note 16; Christenson and Glick, *supra* note 9; Nelson and Tucker, *supra* note 10; Clark, *supra* note 8.

[108] *See* Driscoll and Nelson, Court Curbing, *supra* note 9; Armaly, *supra* note 9; Gibson and Nelson, *supra* note 16; Clark and Kastellec, *supra* note 89.

[109] *See* Gibson, Caldeira, and Baird, *supra* note 9; Mondak and Smithey, *supra* note 21; Gibson and Nelson, *supra* note 16.

[110] *See* Driscoll and Nelson, *No Legitimacy Crisis*, *supra* note 9; Driscoll and Nelson, *supra* note 35; Driscoll and Nelson, *supra* note 49.

[111] Kapiszewski and Taylor, *supra* note 6.

[112] *See* Vanberg, Politics of Constitutional Review, *supra* note 7; Carrubba, *supra* note 8; Staton, Judicial Power, *supra* note 7; Krehbiel, *supra* note 8.

[113] Some of these cases are Levi, Tyler, and Sacks, *supra* note 36; Levi, Sacks, and Tyler, *supra* note 36; Walker, *supra* note 41; Salzman and Ramsey, *supra* note 40; Krönke, *supra* note 37; Donoso, *supra* note 39.

[114] *Cf.* Driscoll and Nelson, Court Curbing, *supra* note 9.

[115] *See* Vanberg, *Legislative-Judicial Relations*, *supra* note 7; Vanberg, Politics of Constitutional Review, *supra* note 7; Krehbiel, *supra* note 8; Staton, Constitutional Review, *supra* note 7; Staton, Judicial Power, *supra* note 7; Botero, *supra* note 60.

[116] *See* Carrubba, *supra* note 8; Krehbiel, *supra* note 9.

[117] Not only is some level of noncompliance to be expected (Staton, Reenock, and Holsinger, *supra* note 8), but judicial authorities may serve constituencies that are far removed from the median voter (*see* Valerie J. Hoekstra and Jeffrey A. Segal, *The Shepherding of Local Public Opinion: The Supreme Court and Lamb's Chapel*, 58 The Journal of Politics 1079 (1996); Lawrence Baum, Judges and their Audiences: A Perspective on Judicial Behavior (2006)). Courts can lack the public support and still be independent, influential and inspire compliance from other key constituencies (e.g., political elites, the legal community, economic interests, etc.) (Vanberg, *supra* note 26).

With data that are readily available, what hypotheses are prime for the testing? Two theoretical models of courts and judicial influence are instructive in this regard, pointing to the possibility that these attitudes either are rooted in instrumental considerations and partisanship,[118] or perhaps are part of a portfolio of democratic values,[119] which manifest in institutional commitment and an unwillingness to tolerate incumbent transgressions.[120] Whereas much of our understanding of these dynamics remains in a theoretical realm, there would seem to be plenty of opportunities for empirical work in this regard, and careful observational analyses of existing data.[121] As to the questions of monitoring and elite strategy, the contextual variance available in existing data—both cross-nationally and over time—would provide interesting leverage on how monitoring or political context might correlate with public attitudes, as one example among many.

Where researchers have the ambition and resources to advance new research designs, there is much to be learned. There are many opportunities for cross-engagement between the literature on public support for courts, the literature on compliance, and the literature on elite behavior and strategic communication.[122] New tools may be brought to bear in the study of public attitudes and evaluation of noncompliance, with attention paid to the influence of source cues and public opinion, as well as the strategic behavior of incumbents, courts, and third-party monitors in their efforts to publicize noncompliance or otherwise cultivate or discourage public attitude formation. Experiments and original survey designs that tap into behavioral manifestation—willingness to bear a cost so as to enhance judicial compliance—will be especially revealing into the question of how public attitudes may incentivize compliance.[123] This will no doubt foster new queries into the question of compliance for many years to come.

---

118 *See* Carrubba, *supra* note 8; Stephenson, *supra* note 6; Bartels and Johnston, *supra* note 9; Christenson and Glick, *supra* note 9.

119 *See* Weingast, *supra* note 9; Mondak and Smithey, *supra* note 21.

120 *See* Easton, *supra* note 10; Easton, *supra* note 14; Gibson and Nelson, *supra* note 14.

121 *Cf.* Gibson and Nelson, *supra* note 14; Krehbiel, *supra* note 9.

122 *Cf.* Carlin et al., *supra* note 42.

123 *See* Gibson and Caldeira, *Legitimacy of Transnational Legal Institutions*, *supra* note 9; Gibson, *supra* note 6; Carlin et al., *supra* note 42; Driscoll and Nelson, Court Curbing, *supra* note 9.

15. Open justice at highest courts

A new avenue for comparative research

Philipp Meyer

INTRODUCTION

Jeremy Bentham once wrote that "publicity is the very soul of justice."[1] These words have become a synonym for the principle of open justice. Nowadays, open justice shapes judiciaries around the world[2] and is associated with three essential claims: (1) courts should conduct their proceedings in public; (2) judicial information should be transparent, open, and accessible—i.e., court decisions should be open for public scrutiny; (3) courts should communicate, promote, and explain decisions to the public.[3] In other words, court cases should be negotiated openly and transparently, court decisions should be explained, and information should be accessible.

Transparency and openness have become watchwords for modern democracies.[4] Especially the trend of open data determines policy initiatives and laws,[5] and is a vital part of the "historic policy movement towards greater transparency, responsiveness, and accountability."[6] Moreover, evolutions in digital information technologies and improvements in computer processing power have led to several additional developments.[7] First, governmental branches can now collect and manage "an unprecedented volume of information and the concept of open government data to proliferate."[8] Second, the public can access a similar volume of informa-

1 Jeremy Bentham, 'Draught for the Organization of Judicial Establishments, Compared with That of the National Assembly, with a Commentary on the Same.' in John Bowring (ed), *The Works of Jeremy Bentham: Published Under the Superintendence of his Executor, John Bowring* (4th edn, William Tait 1843) 316–317.

2 Burkhard Hess and Ana Koprivica Harvey (eds), *Open Justice: The Role of Courts in a Democratic Society* (Nomos 2019).

3 Alberto Alemanno and Oana Stefan, 'Openness at the Court of Justice of the European Union: Toppling a Taboo' (2014) 51 Common Market Law Review 97; Stephan Grimmelikhuijsen and Albert Klijn, 'The Effects of Judicial Transparency on Public Trust: Evidence from a Field Experiment' (2015) 93 Public Administration 995; Burkhard Hess and Ana Koprivica Harvey, 'Open Justice in Modern Societies: What Role for Courts?' in Burkhard Hess and Ana Koprivica Harvey (eds), *Open Justice: The Role of Courts in a Democratic Society* (Nomos 2019).

4 Sarah Moore, 'Towards a Sociology of Institutional Transparency: Openness, Deception and the Problem of Public Trust' (2018) 52 Sociology 416.

5 Mária Žuffová, 'Do FOI Laws and Open Government Data Deliver as Anti-Corruption Policies? Evidence from a Cross-Country Study' (2020) 37 Government Information Quarterly 101480.

6 Gregory Michener and Otavio Ritter, 'Comparing Resistance to Open Data Performance Measurement: Public Education in Brazil and the UK' (2017) 95 Public Administration 4, 4.

7 Henry E Brady, 'The Challenge of Big Data and Data Science' (2019) 22 Annual Review of Political Science 297.

8 Žuffová (n 5) 3.

tion, while citizens' information needs toward governmental branches have increased.[9] Hence, governments provide more information than ever before; and at the same time, the public is more interested than ever in accessing that information.

Transparency is a crucial element of democracies, as it positively impacts the legitimacy of their institutions and the degree of trust citizens have in them. Therefore, trust is the common denominator for legislatures, executives, and judiciaries to increase access to information.[10] However, compared with the other branches of government, trust is of particular importance to the judiciary. Magalhães and Garoupastate that "[c]ompliance with the law, deterrence of cheating behavior, and voluntary collaboration of the public with authorities seem to depend heavily on the supportive attitudes of individual citizens vis-á-vis legal institutions."[11] Public trust and support help courts achieve compliance with their decisions and protect them from governmental challenges.[12] Hence, courts that lack trust are vulnerable to political attacks that challenge and undermine their legitimacy, authority, and independence. As political attacks and mistrust toward courts have become pivotal aspects of recent democratic backsliding processes, it is critical to understand whether and how courts can affect trust.[13]

Courts face obstacles to gaining trust and support because they are unelected institutions.[14] Open justice scholars assume that to gain trust, courts need to "open their doors, enabling the rule of law to be not only transparent and accessible, but open to external scrutiny."[15] However, although this assumption has been echoed several times, it has not yet been tested with empirical data.[16] This chapter aims to address this shortcoming by conceptualizing and

---

[9] Rodrigo Sandoval-Almazan and J Ramon Gil-Garcia, 'Understanding E-Justice and Open Justice Through the Assessment of Judicial Websites: Toward a Conceptual Framework' (2020) 38 Social Science Computer Review 334; Hans J Scholl, 'Digital Government: Looking Back and Ahead on a Fascinating Domain of Research and Practice' (2020) 1 Digital Government: Research and Practice 1; Jonathan Crusoe, Elisabeth Gebka and Karin Ahlin, 'Open Government Data from the Perspective of Information Needs – A Tentative Conceptual Model BT – Electronic Government' in Gabriela Viale Pereira and others (eds) *Electronic Government* (Springer International Publishing 2020).

[10] Žuffová (n 5); Scholl (n 9).

[11] Magalhães, Pedro C, and Nuno Garoupa, 'Judicial Performance and Trust in Legal Systems: Findings from a Decade of Surveys in over 20 European Countries' (2020) 101 Social Science Quarterly 1743, 1743.

[12] James L Gibson and Gregory A Caldeira, *Citizens, Courts, and Confirmations: Positivity Theory and the Judgments of the American People* (Princeton University Press 2009); Georg Vanberg, *The Politics of Constitutional Review in Germany* (CUP 2005).

[13] Hess and Harvey (n 3); Licia Cianetti, James Dawson and Seán Hanley, 'Rethinking "Democratic Backsliding" in Central and Eastern Europe – Looking beyond Hungary and Poland' (2018) 34 East European Politics 243; Magalhães and Garoupa (n 11).

[14] Jenny De Fine Licht and others, 'When Does Transparency Generate Legitimacy? Experimenting on a Context-Bound Relationship' (2014) 27 Governance 111.

[15] Jane Johnston, 'Three Phases of Courts' Publicity: Reconfiguring Bentham's Open Justice in the Twenty-First Century' (2018) 14 International Journal of Law in Context 525, 525.

[16] See e.g., Jason Bosland and Jonathan Gill, 'The Principle of Open Justice and the Judicial Duty to Give Public Reasons' (2014) 38 Melbourne University Law Review 482; Hess and Harvey (n 3); Emma Cunliffe, 'Open Justice: Concepts and Judicial Approaches' (2012) 40 Federal Law Review 385; Sharon Rodrick, 'Achieving the Aims of Open Justice – The Relationship between the Courts, the Media and the Public' (2014) 19 Deakin Law Review 123; Jason Bosland and Judith Townend, 'Open Justice, Transparency and the Media: Representing the Public Interest in the Physical and Virtual Courtroom' (2018) 23 Communications Law 1746; Mila Gasco-Hernandez and Carlos E

measuring open justice and by analyzing whether open justice affects public trust toward the legal system.

This chapter focuses on court websites to measure open justice. Two arguments inform this decision: First, the internet has become the central interface for citizens to receive information and for governmental branches to disseminate information.[17] In the context of courts, scholars found that websites foster public access.[18] Second, the assessment of websites allows adopting the end-user's perspective—i.e., the general public, journalists, etc.—and focusing on whether they can receive relevant information in an open, transparent, and accessible way.[19]

In the following section, open justice will be conceptualized. Subsequently, this conceptualization will be used to construct an index of open justice. Finally, the websites of 27 European highest courts will be assessed, and empirical analysis will be performed to test whether open justice affects public trust toward the legal system. This analysis uses data from the European Social Survey (ESS).[20] Based on ordered logistic regression models, the results show that open justice indeed has a positive impact on citizens' trust in the legal system; however, individual characteristics like citizens' education level seem to moderate this effect.

This chapter contributes to the literature in two ways. First, through the conceptualization and index construction, it establishes open justice as a new avenue for comparative judicial research. Second, it presents first empirical evidence that the degree of openness, accessibility, and transparency at courts influences whether citizens trust legal institutions.

THE CONCEPT OF OPEN JUSTICE

Concepts are the "building blocks of scientific reasoning" and a prerequisite of valid measurements.[21] Scientific concepts contain three core elements: term, intention, and extension.[22] The *term* is the concept's label and its unambiguous referent. The *intension* defines the meaning of a concept by specifying all necessary attributes and aspects that "fill the term with substance. [Moreover,] [t]he intension of a concept should demarcate this concept from other concepts. Otherwise overlaps in meaning will lead to confusion."[23] The *extension* determines a concept's empirical scope and is understood as "the set of class of objects in the world that [the concept] refers to."[24]

How to conceptualize open justice? Referring back to Bentham, open justice is defined as publicity that prevents justice from being delivered behind closed doors. Based on this,

---

Jimenez-Gomez, 'Information and Technology in Open Justice' (2020) 38 Social Science Computer Review 247.

17 Brady (n 7).

18 Michael Parkin and Justin Wedeking, 'Connecting with the Courts: Online Access to State Judicial Systems' (2017) 38 Justice System Journal 22.

19 Ibid.

20 European Social Survey Round 9 ESS, 'Data File Edition 3.1. NSD-Norwegian Centre for Research Data, Norway–Data Archive and Distributor of ESS Data for ESS ERIC'.

21 Dimiter Toshkov, *Research Design in Political Science* (Palgrave Macmillan 2016) 84.

22 Arndt Wonka, 'Concept Specification in Political Science Research' in Thomas Gschwend and Frank Schimmelpfennig (eds), *Research Design in Political Science: How to Practice What They Preach* (Palgrave Macmillan UK 2007).

23 Ibid 42.

24 Toshkov (n 21) 90.

Johnston defines open justice as "fundamental to courts and the judiciary laying open their doors, enabling the rule of law to be not only transparent and accessible, but open to external scrutiny."[25] Accordingly, *accessibility*, *openness*, and *transparency* are the attributes of open justice.[26]

Accessibility is about public access to judicial institutions, which "is a fundamental right and the foundation of any fair and legitimate justice system."[27] It refers to the physical access to courts, which should be equally possible for citizens, businesses, state entities, and nongovernmental organizations; and to access to information about the justice system, laws, constitutional documents, and court decisions. Scholars assume that if citizens can access judicial information, they can "engage with the work of the courts."[28]

Openness is about public scrutiny and the right of citizens to observe the process of justice. It comprises a passive right of citizens to receive information and a proactive institutional duty for courts to communicate this information.[29] Alemanno and Stefan argue that openness helps citizens to assess "whether a certain judgment took into account all the arguments put forward in the case, and whether the law was observed."[30] However, openness has blurred boundaries between accessibility and transparency. For example, Resnik uses the term "openness-as-accessibility,"[31] and Ryder labels the intersection between accessibility and openness "observational justice."[32] Nevertheless, Ryder further argues that the stronger focus on participation distinguishes openness from transparency.[33]

Transparency is about "the idea of seeing *into* activities" of courts[34] and encompasses a moralistic rationale: "Transparency in politics reduces moral hazard problems", and if citizens can monitor political behavior, "politicians have less incentive to pursue policies that are inconsistent with public preferences."[35] Similar arguments are present in the judicial politics literature, where transparency is perceived to be a vital aspect for the assertiveness of judicial review, as it increases certainty and constrains political actions.[36]

---

25 Johnston (n 15) 525.

26 See also Cécile Chainais, 'Open Justice and the Principle of Public Access to Hearings' in Burkhard Hess and Ana Koprivica Harvey (eds), *Open Justice: The Role of Courts in a Democratic Society* (Nomos 2019); Cunliffe (n 16); Hess and Harvey (n 3).

27 Adam R Pah and others, 'How to Build a More Open Justice System' (2020) 369 Science 134, 135.

28 Ibid 136.

29 Alemanno and Stefan (n 3).

30 Ibid 107.

31 Judith Resnik, 'The Functions of Publicity and of Privatization in Courts and Their Replacements (from Jeremy Bentham to #MeToo and Google Spain)', *Open Justice: The Role of Courts in a Democratic Society* (Nomos 2019) 181.

32 Ernest Ryder, 'Securing Open Justice' in Burkhard Hess and Ana Koprivica Harvey (eds), *Open Justice: The Role of Courts in a Democratic Society* (Nomos 2019) 128.

33 Ibid.

34 Resnik (n 31) 180, italics in original.

35 Jeffrey J Harden, Justin H Kirkland and Patrick E Shea, 'Legislative Transparency and Credit Risk' (2021) 46 Legislative Studies Quarterly 189, 189.

36 Jeffrey K Staton, *Judicial Power and Strategic Communication in Mexico* (CUP 2010); Jay Krehbiel, 'Elections, Public Awareness, and the Efficacy of Constitutional Review' (2019) 7 Journal of Law and Courts 53; Jay Krehbiel, 'The Politics of Judicial Procedures: The Role of Public Oral Hearings in the German Constitutional Court' (2016) 60 American Journal of Political Science 990; Vanberg (n 12); Philipp Meyer, 'Explaining Media Coverage on Constitutional Court Decisions in Germany: The Role of Case Characteristics' (2021) 38 Political Communication 426; Philipp Meyer, 'Judicial Public

Consequences and Incentives of Open Justice

From a theoretical point of view, the incentives for judiciaries to adapt the open justice principle are high: (1) judicial trustworthiness, impartiality, neutrality, and accountability increase, as transparency and openness prevent justice from being delivered behind closed doors; (2) judicial reputation increases, as the work of courts can be controlled and, through the presence of the public, legitimized; (3) judicial independence increases, as the public can monitor political actions subsequent to court decisions. In other words, by providing access to transparent information, by:

> openly communicating the debate taking place between the parties, and by clearly justifying its position towards both parties, the courts create the forum for the parties and the public to see and assess whether all considerations were taken into account, whether the law was observed and thus monitor the administration of justice.[37]

Scholars argue that whether courts are trusted and therefore decisive or not depends on the public's understanding of the rule of law, in general, and of the work of courts, in particular.[38] On this account, the relationship between seeing, understanding, and trusting is crucial: When citizens can see that justice is done and can assess whether all reasonable arguments were considered, they will more likely understand how courts function, which, in turn, will increase their trust in the legal system.[39] Indeed, studies have already shown that knowledge about the legal system, in general, and courts, in particular, increases public trust.[40] However, Salzman and Ramsey have found that this connection holds for developed democracies, whereas the reverse is found for developing democracies.[41]

Defined as an evaluation of "whether or not political authorities and institutions are performing according to normative expectations held by the public," trust is a crucial element in democratic political systems. "At the extreme, a lack of trust in governmental institutions undermines the rule of law."[42] Public trust is perceived to influence not only political participation and support, but also compliance with laws and regulations.[43]

Magalhães and Garoupa analyzed whether institutional properties of legal systems affect the level of trust.[44] Their results suggest that performance, independence, and accountability posi-

Relations: Determinants of Press Release Publication by Constitutional Courts' (2020) 40 Politics 477; Philipp Meyer, 'Promoted Media Coverage of Court Decisions: Media Gatekeeping of Court Press Releases and the Role of News Values' (2021) 22 Journalism Studies 723.

37 Hess and Harvey (n 3) 18.

38 Richard Davis, 'Conclusion' in Richard Davis and David Taras (eds), *Justices and Journalists: The Global Perspective* (CUP 2017).

39 Sarah Moore, Alex Clayton and Hector Murphy, 'Seeing Justice Done: Courtroom Filming and the Deceptions of Transparency' [2019] Crime, Media, Culture https://doi.org/10.1177/1741659019883764.

40 Gibson and Caldeira (n 12).

41 Salzman, Ryan, and Adam Ramsey, 'Judging the Judiciary: Understanding Public Confidence in Latin American Courts' (2013) 55 Latin American Politics and Society 73.

42 Miller and Listhaug 1990 cited in Caroline J Tolbert and Karen Mossberger, 'The Effects of E-Government on Trust and Confidence in Government' (2006) 66 Public Administration Review 354, 355.

43 Tolbert and Mossberger (n 42).

44 Magalhães and Garoupa (n 11); Garoupa, Nuno, and Pedro C Magalhães, 'Public Trust in the European Legal Systems: Independence, Accountability and Awareness' (2021) 44 West European Politics 690.

tively shape the public's trust toward the legal system.[45] Other institutional properties seem to be relevant. According to Gibson and Caldeira, the level of trust toward courts is moderated by the court's legal rituals that emphasize impartiality, fairness, and neutrality.[46] However, Magalhães and Garoupa have not controlled for this.[47]

The open justice principle could make a significant contribution to addressing this shortcoming. One of the main objectives of open justice is to avoid justice being rendered in secret. Hence, open justice secures the impartiality and neutrality of courts as it prevents "manipulations of and by judges."[48] Accordingly, courts may seek to increase accessibility, openness, and transparency to increase the public's knowledge about their actions and mitigate mistrust in the judiciary by promoting a neutral and impartial image. This chapter therefore argues that an open judiciary are an institutional property that promotes public trust; and it assumes that the more accessible, open, and transparent a court is, the more it will be trusted by the public. The following section discusses the extension of the concept and its measurement through real-world phenomena.

AN APPROACH TO MEASURING OPEN JUSTICE

Hess and Harvey stress that modern-day open justice needs to be assessed in the light of technological developments.[49] In the current digital era, this encompasses, for example, virtual courtrooms, videoconferencing, live streaming of hearings, audio recording, digital proceedings, online accessible court dockets, and publicly (online) available court decisions.[50]

The approach to measure open justice presented in this chapter focuses on two aspects. First, only national supreme courts and constitutional courts will be considered. They are at the apex of their legal systems, which is why measures of accessibility, openness, and transparency introduced there will most likely trickle down to the lower-level courts. Moreover, these courts control the constitutionality of laws, statutes, and political actions. Hence, for the accountability of democracy, the public must have access to open and transparent information regarding their actions.[51] The question of whether the highest courts have adopted measures to increase open justice is, therefore, of great relevance. Second, only information that is available online on the official court websites will be considered. The reason is that recent studies have shown that court websites enhance "civic engagement, collaboration, and public value cooperation,"[52] and that court websites are an "ideal venue for investigating citizen access,"[53] as they provide information and guarantee availability beyond an actual in-person court visit.

---

45 Magalhães and Garoupa (n 11); Garoupa and Magalhães (n 44).

46 Gibson and Caldeira (n 12).

47 Magalhães and Garoupa (n 11), Garoupa and Magalhães (n 44).

48 Hess and Harvey (n 3) 14.

49 Ibid.

50 Brady (n 7); Chainais (n 26); Moore, Clayton and Murphy (n 39); Gasco-Hernandez and Jimenez-Gomez (n 16).

51 Meyer (n 36).

52 Akemi Takeoka Chatfield and Christopher G Reddick, 'Collaborative Network Governance Framework for Aligning Open Justice and E-Justice Ecosystems for Greater Public Value' (2020) 38 Social Science Computer Review 252, 253.

53 Parkin and Wedeking (n 18) 2.

Judicial Websites and Open Judicial Data

Open government initiatives are found to make active use of innovations in digital computing and information technologies to increase the efficiency of public administration by providing citizens with the possibility "to directly access or request a vast array of detailed public data at the convenience of their own personal devices."[54] These considerations hold for court websites, which provide direct access to open judicial data.[55]

Open judicial data is defined as "data produced or contracted by the judicial branch of the government (or entities controlled by the judicial branch of the government) that anyone can freely access, reuse, and redistribute."[56] Hence, court websites seem to be an ideal venue to measure modern-day open justice.

Evaluating Judicial Websites to Measure Open Justice

Although Parkin and Wedeking and Sandoval-Almazan and Gil-Garcia conclude that judicial websites were barely subject to scientific reasoning, some prior work provides valuable insights.[57]

Parkin and Wedeking assess the websites of all U.S. state supreme courts, focusing on access to judicial systems.[58] They show that courts' administrative capacity and resources explain the degree of (online) access to the courts. Elena and van Schalkwyk analyze whether the open data aspects of accessibility, non-discrimination, sustainability, relevance, and reusability can be detected for online judicial data in seven Latin American countries.[59] They claim that to be classified as open data, judiciaries should publish at least three data types: rulings, statistics on operations, and budget and administrative data.[60] Their results indicate that although the assessed judiciaries publish data and share information, they do not meet the strict requirements to be classified as open data. Sandoval-Almazan and Gil-Garcia assess 32 state court websites in Mexico in 2014 and 2016.[61] Based on four different components—information (e.g., legal foundations, court budgets, court decision full texts), interaction (e.g., web searches), participation (e.g., social media activities), and integration (e.g., links to social media profiles)—they analyzed the availability of information and opportunities for interaction and participation. They show that the assessed websites focus on information dissemination and transparent data disclosure, while tools to promote and enable citizen participation and engagement are seldom used. Finally, Markcović and Gostojić analyze the degree to

---

54 Scholl (n 9) 2.

55 Chatfield and Reddick (n 55); Sandoval-Almazan and Gil-Garcia (n 9); Marko Marković and Stevan Gostojić, 'Open Judicial Data: A Comparative Analysis' (2020) 38 Social Science Computer Review 295; Parkin and Wedeking (n 18).

56 Marković and Gostojić (n 59) 296.

57 Parkin and Wedeking (n 18); Sandoval-Almazan and Gil-Garcia (n 9) 339.

58 Parkin and Wedeking (n 18).

59 Sandra Elena and François van Schalkwyk, 'Open Data for Open Justice in Seven Latin American Countries' in Carlos E Jiménez-Gomez and Mila Gascó-Hernández (eds), *Achieving Open Justice through Citizen Participation and Transparency* (IGI Global 2017).

60 Ibid.

61 Sandoval-Almazan and Gil-Garcia (n 9).

which the websites of ten national judiciaries have adopted open data standards.[62] By assessing whether the websites share information on decisions, case registers, filed document records, and statistical data, they find a similar degree of open data across all judiciaries. Nevertheless, they conclude that "[c]ompared to the quality and quantity of open data sets published by the legislative and executive branches, the quality and quantity of open data sets on the judiciary is [sic] usually the lowest."[63]

These studies have some drawbacks. First, they do not deal with websites of the highest courts. Markcović and Gostojić even explicitly exclude such courts from their study.[64] Second, the presented measurements lack reliability and validity. For example, it is unclear how Sandoval-Almazan and Gil-Garcia have calculated the percentage scores their analysis is based on.[65] Similarly, Markcović and Gostojićuse use a questionnaire that includes numerical values and binary yes/no answers, which results in a final grade per country that is "calculated as an average value of the answers."[66] This chapter aims to address both problems by presenting a parsimonious approach to assess national high court websites.

Measuring Open Justice

The review has shown that to be perceived as open, court websites need to disclose information on the courts, their legal foundation, case statistics, and their docket, budget, and rulings. Moreover, Elena and van Schalkwyk highlighted the importance of integrations to enable barrier-free access; while Markcović and Gostojić emphasized that the data needs to be open, and hence downloadable and reusable.[67] So, to be in accordance with the open justice attributes of *accessibility*, *openness*, and *transparency*, court websites should first provide *transparent information* (i.e., the legal foundation of the court, annual statistics, budget information). Second, information and data should be *open* (i.e., downloadable in a machine-readable format). Third, websites, in general, and their information, in particular, should be *accessible* for every user (i.e., providing text-to-speech options and disclosing information on how to file a complaint to the court).

Table 15.1 summarizes these three points and lists several important aspects.[68] The table presents the foundation to measure open justice. Each aspect can be measured based on a simple question: "Does the website of [court name] contain information on [aspect]?" For example, this aspect is coded with the value 1 if a website contains information regarding a court's rules of procedure, and with the value 0 if a website does not contain this information.[69]

Subsequently, an index can be created that combines all aspects into a single measure of open justice. Indices are "constructed variables"[70] that combine different indicators into one

---

62 Marković and Gostojić (n 59).

63 Ibid 308.

64 Ibid.

65 Sandoval-Almazan and Gil-Garcia (n 9).

66 Ibid 299.

67 Elena and van Schalkwyk (n 64); Marković and Gostojić (n 59).

68 Elena and van Schalkwyk (n 64); Marković and Gostojić (n 59); Sandoval-Almazan and Gil-Garcia (n 9).

69 Parkin and Wedeking (n 18) and Sandoval-Almazan and Gil-Garcia (n 9) adopt similar approaches.

70 Bernhard Miller, 'Making Measures Capture Concepts: Tools for Securing Correspondence between Theoretical Ideas and Observations' in Thomas Gschwend and Frank Schimmelpfennig (eds),

helpful theoretical and empirical measure. Thus, indices have the advantage of reducing complexity and avoiding the arbitrary selection of one indicator over others.[71] Three rules will manage the index construction. First, all aspects have the same impact level (0 or 1) and are summed. Second, all aspects affect the index in the same direction. Third, the sum is divided by the total number of aspects assessed to ensure a continuous range of values between 1 and 0. These rules result in an additive *open justice index* based on 19 unidirectional related values derived from the binary coding of the aspects listed in Table 15.1.[72] Since the rationale for the index components was taken from previous studies, the content validity of the index can be assumed.

Table 15.1 Open justice aspects for high court websites

Transparency of information	*Openness of data*	*Accessibility of services*
Constitutional fundamentals	Web search available	Information on how to file a complaint to the court
Rules of procedure	Open access to information (no registration requirement, free of charge)	Information in foreign languages
Information on judges	Data downloadable in machine-readable formats (e.g., PDF)	Text-to-speech option
Annual statistics		Plain language option
Court docket		Social media activity
Court budget		Social media integration on the court website
News releases		
Court decisions		
Case-related documents		
Video streams of hearings		

INVESTIGATION OF OPEN JUSTICE ON EUROPEAN HIGH COURT WEBSITES

In the following, the websites of 27 European highest courts are assessed to measure the degree of open justice based on the proposed measurement strategy. Table 15.2 lists the selected courts. This case selection matches the countries represented in Round 9 of the ESS, which provides the most comprehensive measure of public trust in the legal system. Moreover, Table 15.2 shows that the selected courts also cover the most dominant legal traditions (civil law, common law, and mixed law) and the two main high court types (specialized constitutional courts and diffuse supreme courts).[73] Hence, this case selection presents an appropriate

Research Design in Political Science: How to Practice What They Preach (Palgrave Macmillan UK 2007) 95.

[71] Miller (n 74).

[72] Open Justice Index $= \frac{x1 + x2 + \ldots x19}{19}$

[73] Jospeh Dainow, 'The Civil Law and the Common Law : Some Points of Comparison' (1966) 15 The American Journal of Comparative Law 419, 424; Lee Epstein, Jack Knight and Olga Shvetsova, 'The Role of Constitutional Courts in Establishment and Maintenance of Democratic Systems of Government' (2001) 35 Law & Society Review 117; Alec Stone Sweet, 'Constitutional Courts and Parliamentary Democracy' (2002) 25 West European Politics 77.

starting point for understanding a more extensive set of cases.[74] Table 15.2 further lists the websites of the courts that were used for the data collection.

Table 15.3 presents the values of the three index components and the aggregated values of the open justice index. The adoption of the open justice principle seems to vary across Europe. However, all websites have implemented aspects that promote open justice, at least to a certain degree. Two points are worth mentioning. First, the websites are found to be focused more on transparency than on openness. For example, all but two courts disclose the full text of rulings (Netherlands and Cyprus) and disseminate annual reports (Cyprus and Poland), while the data of only 14 websites are in a machine-readable and downloadable format. Second, most of the evaluated websites put only a limited focus on accessibility. In the mean, only three out of the six aspects in this category are found on the websites. Further, several courts use social media platforms and linked them on their websites (17 out of 27). While some courts use only one platform, a total of nine courts use more than one platform.[75] Few courts use social media for several purposes like streaming hearings and disclosing information on decisions (e.g., Latvia); however, most use these platforms as just another vessel for disseminating press releases (e.g., Germany). These points are in line with previous studies, which have found that court websites are more focused on information disclosure and transparency than on accessibility, and that press releases are the most crucial tool for courts to disseminate information.[76]

Table 15.2 *Selected European highest courts*

Country	*Legal tradition*	*Name of the court*	*Court type*	*URL*
Austria	CiL	Verfassungsgerichtshof	CC	vfgh.gv.at
Belgium	CiL	Cour d'Arbitrage	CC	const-court.be
Bulgaria	CiL	Konstitutzionen Sud	CC	constcourt.bg
Croatia	CiL	Ustavni Sud Republike Hrvatske	CC	usud.hr
Cyprus	MiL	Ανώτατο Δικαστήριο	SC	supremecourt.gov.cy
Czech Republic	MiL	Ústavny soud	CC	usoud.cz
Denmark	CiL	Højesteret	SC	domstol.dk/hoejesteret
Estonia	CiL	Vabariigi Riigikohus	SC	riigikohus.ee
Finland	CiL	Korkein oikeus	SC	korkeinoikeus.fi
France	CiL	Conseil constitutionnel	CC	conseil-constitutionnel.fr
Germany	CiL	Bundesverfassungsgericht	CC	bundesverfassungsgericht.de
Hungary	CiL	Magyarország Alkotmánybírósága	CC	alkotmanybirosag.hu
Iceland	CiL	Hæstiréttur	SC	haestirettur.is
Ireland	CoL	Supreme Court of Ireland	SC	supremecourt.ie
Italy	CiL	Corte constituzionale	CC	cortecostituzionale.it
Latvia	CiL	Satversmes tiesa	CC	satv.tiesa.gov.lv
Lithuania	CiL	Konstitucinis Teismas	CC	lrkt.lt

[74] Patricio Navia and Julio Ríos-Figueroa, 'The Constitutional Adjudication Mosaic of Latin America' (2005) 38 Comparative Political Studies 189; Tom Ginsburg, *Judicial Review in New Democracies: Constitutional Courts in Asian Cases* (CUP 2003).

[75] For example: Estonia (*Facebook & YouTube*), Czech Republic (*Twitter & YouTube*), France (*Twitter, Facebook & DailyMotion*), Norway (*Twitter, Instagram & LinkedIn)*.

[76] Sandoval-Almazan and Gil-Garcia (n 9); Parkin and Wedeking (n 18); Marković and Gostojić (n 59); Meyer (n 36); Meyer (n 36); David Taras, 'Introduction: Judges and Journalists and the Spaces In Between' in Richard Davis and David Taras (eds), *Justices and Journalists: The Global Perspective* (CUP 2017).

Country	*Legal tradition*	*Name of the court*	*Court type*	*URL*
Netherlands	CiL	Hoge Raad der Nederlanden	CC	hogeraad.nl
Norway	MiL	Høyesterett	SC	https://www.domstol.no/en/Enkelt-domstol/supremecourt/
Poland	CiL	Trybunał Konstytucyjny	CC	trybunal.gov.pl/
Portugal	CiL	Tribunal Constitucional	CC	tribunalconstitucional.pt
Slovakia	CiL	Ústavny súd	CC	ustavnysud.sk
Slovenia	CiL	Ustavno sodišče	CC	us-rs.si
Spain	CiL	Tribunal Constitucional	CC	tribunalconstitucional.es
Sweden	CiL	Hogste Domstolen	SC	domstol.se/hogsta-domstolen
Switzerland	CiL	Bundesgericht	SC	bger.ch
United Kingdom	CoL	The Supreme Court of the United Kingdom	SC	supremecourt.uk

Note: CiL (*civil law*), CoL (*common law*), MiL (*mixed legal system*), CC (*Constitutional Court*), SC (*Supreme Court*). Civil tradition and high court types are coded based on the *CIA World Factbook* (see: www.cia.gov/the-world-factbook).

Table 15.3 Open justice at European high court websites

Country	*Transparency of information*	*Openness of data*	*Accessibility of services*	*Open Justice Index*
Austria	6	3	4	0.68
Belgium	6	3	4	0.68
Bulgaria	7	2	1	0.53
Croatia	7	2	2	0.58
Cyprus	5	2	2	0.47
Czech Republic	7	2	3	0.63
Denmark	5	2	2	0.47
Estonia	4	2	4	0.53
Finland	7	2	4	0.68
France	9	3	3	0.79
Germany	7	3	5	0.79
Hungary	7	2	5	0.74
Iceland	8	2	2	0.63
Ireland	4	3	0	0.37
Italy	7	2	1	0.53
Latvia	9	3	4	0.84
Lithuania	8	2	4	0.74
Netherlands	6	2	3	0.58
Norway	8	3	3	0.74
Poland	5	3	2	0.52
Portugal	5	2	1	0.42
Slovakia	7	2	3	0.68
Slovenia	8	3	4	0.79
Spain	6	3	5	0.74
Sweden	3	3	4	0.53
Switzerland	7	2	3	0.63
United Kingdom	9	3	3	0.79
Mean	6.55	2.44	3	0.62

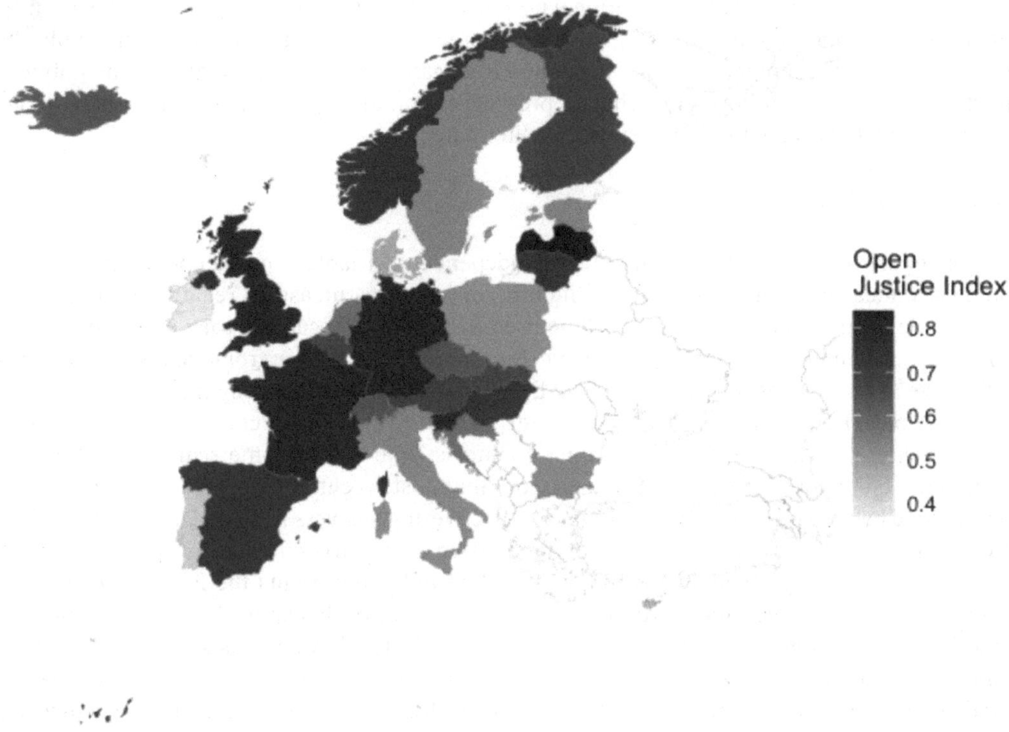

Note: The figure is based on the open justice index values from Table 15.3. Darker shades indicate a higher open justice index value. White shades indicate countries that are not included in the analysis.

Figure 15.1 Open justice in 27 European countries

Figure 15.1 provides a geographic representation of the open justice index. The courts with the highest open justice values (depicted by the dark shades) are Latvia (0.84), France (0.79), Germany (0.79), Slovenia (0.79), and the United Kingdom (0.79); while the lowest open justice values (depicted by the brighter shades) are found for Ireland (0.37), Portugal (0.42), Denmark (0.47), and Cyprus (0.47). For Austria, Croatia, Slovenia, and the United Kingdom, these results align with prior results regarding the degree of open data in these countries presented by Markcović and Gostojić.[77] Overall, these descriptive results show the face validity of the open justice index.

[77] Marković and Gostojić (n 59).

THE INFLUENCE OF OPEN JUSTICE ON PUBLIC TRUST

Open justice is argued to be an institutional property that secures the impartiality and neutrality of courts by making the process of justice accessible, open, and transparent for the public. It is assumed that the more accessible, open, and transparent courts are, the greater the public's trust in them. In what follows, this chapter presents an initial empirical test of this assumption, which is widely accepted in the open justice literature.[78]

Data and Methods

The open justice index will be modeled as an independent variable to predict public trust. Since no unique measurement on trust in the highest courts exists, measures regarding the level of trust in the legal system, in general, will be used as a proxy. To capture trust measures for the 27 European countries listed above, variable *Trust in the legal system* from the ESS is used and will serve as the dependent variable.[79] The ESS is a cross-national survey that covers a multitude of topics. For the trust variable, "each respondent [...] in every country, has been asked to rate the level of trust she deposits in her country's legal system, on a scale of 0 ('No trust at all') to 10 ('A lot of trust')."[80] The data from the most recent ESS Round 9 is used, which was fielded between August 2018 and May 2019, covering answers from 46,276 respondents.[81] Hence, it provides the latest and most comprehensive data of trust in legal systems.

This approach is problematic as the open justice index represents the 2021 status quo of court websites. However, there are two arguments in favor of this approach. First, Magalhães and Garoupa highlighted that the level of public trust in legal systems is stable over the first eight rounds of the ESS.[82] Hence, it is unreasonable to assume that the trust values will change dramatically in future rounds. Second, the *Internet Archive* was used to control whether the court websites have changed since 2018.[83] Only the websites of four courts have changed significantly (France, Estonia, Poland, and the United Kingdom), while for most only marginal or no changes are reported. Nevertheless, the results reported below need to be interpreted cautiously and more as a preliminary test until trust measures are available for 2021.[84]

Besides the open justice index, *legal tradition* and *highest court type* are included to control for differences in legal systems. Both variables are measured according to the information listed in Table 15.2 and coded binary (0 mixed law and civil law/constitutional court, and 1 common law/supreme court). Finally, following Garoupa and Magalhães, two controls for individual-level aspects of each respondent are also included: *Years of education* (measured in years and top coded at 25 years), *Age* (measured in years), and *Gender* (binary).[85] While

---

78 Hess and Harvey (n 3); Johnston (n 15); Cunliffe (n 16); Bosland and Gill (n 16).

79 ESS (n 20).

80 Garoupa and Magalhães (n 44) 8.

81 ESS (n 20).

82 Magalhães and Garoupa (n 11).

83 I used the URLs for each court website listed in Table 15.2 to track website changes via the "Wayback Machine" provided by the *Internet Archive* project: https://web.archive.org/web/changes (accessed May 7, 2021).

84 The results of the regression models remain stable when France, Estonia, Poland, and the United Kingdom are excluded. Results are available upon request.

85 Garoupa and Magalhães (n 44).

formal education is found to influence citizens' trust in courts[86] as it is considered "necessary to acquire the cognitive skills required to develop a greater awareness of the legal system," age and gender are "variables that other studies have found to be correlates of institutional trust."[87] The variables are derived from the ESS data.

Methodologically, an ordered logistic regression model is used to deal with the ordered categorical nature of the dependent variable.[88] Additionally, standard errors clustered by countries are used because the observations in the ESS data are not independent as respondents are clustered in countries. Finally, relative risk ratios and marginal effects are reported to provide a more straightforward interpretation of the model results.

Analysis and Discussion

The results of the ordered logistic regression models are presented in Table 15.4. Model 1 represents the baseline model, Model 2 adds the legal system variables, and Model 3 includes the individual-level variables.

Table 15.4 shows that open justice has a significant positive effect on trust in the legal system. If a website presents transparent, open, and accessible information, public trust increases. The relative risk ratios help to interpret the regression coefficients. For example, for Model 3, the relative risk for open justice is 4.841. *Ceteris paribus*, when the open justice index increases one unit, it is 4.841 times more likely that the respondent has higher trust in the legal system. The effect strength for the open justice index increases when adding the legal system variables (Model 2) and individual-level variables (Model 3). The model fit also increases across the models. Moreover, the reported effects for the system-level and individual-level variables in Models 2 and 3 align with those reported in the studies by Garoupa and Magalhães.[89]

As mentioned above, the ESS questionnaire provides ten answer categories to rate trust in the legal system (0 "No trust at all" to 10 "Complete trust"). To show the effect of open justice on trust within each category, marginal effects for each outcome category are estimated. Figure 15.2 illustrates selected category-specific marginal effects based on Model 3 from Table 15.4. The figure shows that the effects of open justice, court type, and the educational level of respondents have a significant positive impact in the higher trust categories. In contrast, the reverse effects are found for low trust levels.

According to several studies, education, in general, and knowledge of courts, in particular, moderate the influence on trust in the legal system, as education helps individuals develop competencies to process and internalize complex information and to understand how the legal system and the courts function. Magalhães and Garoupa found that trust increases with the respondents' level of education.[90] Benesh and Salzman and Ramsey report similar effects, showing that the more education and knowledge individuals have, the greater their trust in the justice system.[91] According to Moore et al., the relationship between understanding courts and

---

[86] Sara C Benesh, 'Understanding Public Confidence in American Courts' (2006) 68 The Journal of Politics 697.

[87] Garoupa and Magalhães (n 44) 8–9.

[88] As data from only one ESS round is used, multilevel models like those used by Garoupa and Magalhães (n 44) are not feasible.

[89] Ibid; Magalhães and Garoupa (n 11).

[90] Garoupa and Magalhães (n 44).

[91] Benesh (n 93); Salzman and Ramsey (n 41).

Table 15.4 Ordered logistic regression for trust in the legal system (ESS Round 9)

	Dependent variable					
	Trust in the legal system					
	Model 1	Relative risks	Model 2	Relative risks	Model 3	Relative risks
Open justice index	0.549*** (0.066)	1.731	1.680*** (0.069)	5.366	1.577*** (0.070)	4.841
Legal tradition (0 = CiL; 1 = CoL)			–0.835*** (0.031)	0.434	–0.881*** (0.031)	0.414
Highest court type (0 = CC; 1 = SC)			1.310*** (0.021)	3.705	1.281*** (0.021)	3.601
Age					–0.005*** (0.0005)	0.995
Gender (0 = Male; 1 = Female)					–0.160*** (0.017)	0.852
Years of education					0.048*** (0.002)	1.049
Observations / Respondents	45,358		45,358		45,146	
Residual deviance	208,854.74		204,731.94		202,861.25	
AIC	208,876.74		204,757.94		202,893.25	

Notes:
Standard errors clustered by countries in parenthesis. Intercepts are not shown. In Model 1 and 2, 918 observations, and in Model 3, 1,130 observations were deleted due to missingness.
Statistical significance at $^*p<0.1$; $^{**}p<0.05$; $^{***}p<0.01$.

trusting them is strengthened if judiciaries actively promote open justice.[92] Consequently, it can be assumed that education and open justice positively interact with each other and lead to higher levels of trust in the legal system.

This assumption cannot be confirmed. Figure 15.3 illustrates the effect of open justice on trust conditional on respondents' years of education. The figure is based on a fourth model with a corresponding interaction term that is not shown here.[93] The figure shows that greater levels of open justice and education do not automatically lead to more trust in the legal system. This implies that better-educated people are not more likely to be sensitive toward a more open, transparent, and accessible judiciary.

Overall, this preliminary analysis has shown that open justice positively affects trust in legal systems. In this regard, this chapter is the first that provides evidence for this long-stated but never-tested assumption. Nevertheless, the reported results should be considered with caution due to three reasons. First, the open justice index and the chosen measures for public trust do not align temporally. Second, the construction of the open justice index was theory-driven, and its face and content validity seem to hold due to the reported descriptive results, which align with the few existing studies. However, the index's construct validity and criteria validity

[92] Moore, Clayton and Murphy (n 39).
[93] The overall effect of the interaction is statistically insignificant (p = –0.004), while the effects for the variables are similar to those reported in Table 15.4. Results are available upon request.

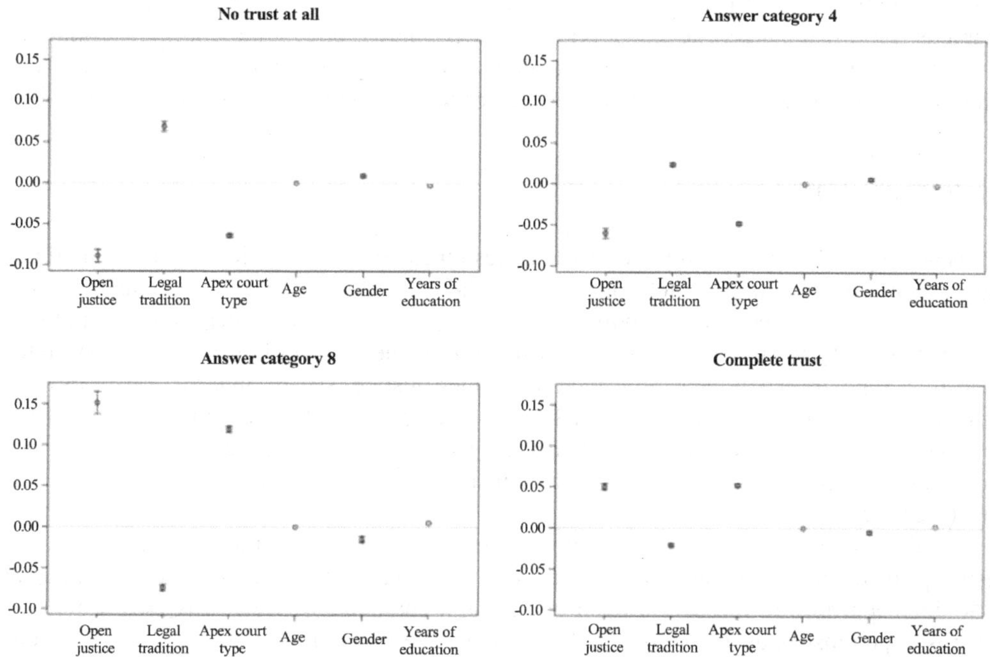

Note: Marginal effects are based on Model 3 (Table 15.4); all other variables are held constant at their means or modes. Whiskers indicate 95% confidence intervals.

Figure 15.2 *Marginal effects on trust in the legal system per selected answer categories*

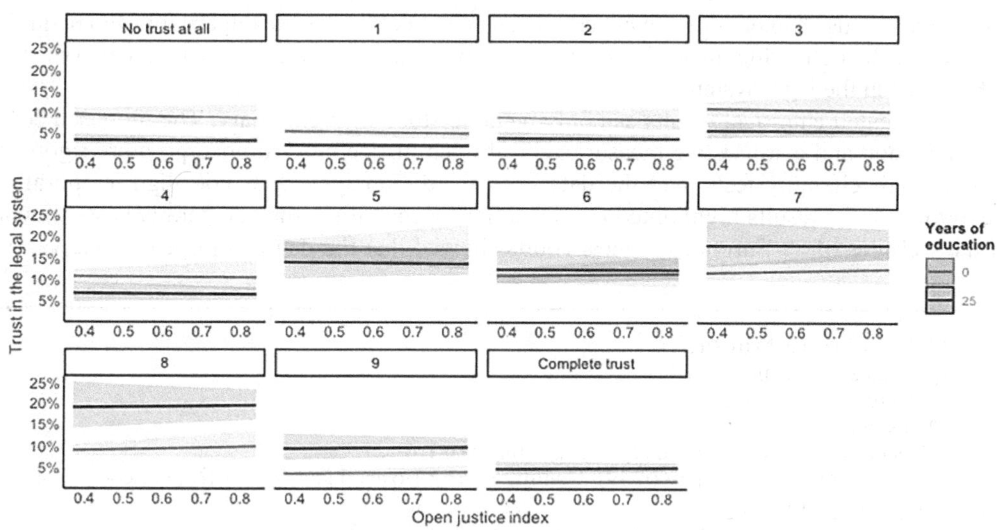

Figure 15.3 *Marginal effects of open justice conditional on years of education*

were not discussed.[94] Third, the analysis has focused on legal system aspects and individual characteristics, while macro-level aspects like the countries' economic power and population size were ignored.[95] As soon as recent data on trust in the legal system is available, these three major drawbacks need to be fixed to test whether the presented results are valid and reliable.

CONCLUSION

Transparency and accountability are prerequisites for liberal democracies to gain and maintain the trust of citizens. This verdict holds for the highest courts, whose assertiveness is conditioned by the transparency of the political environment.[96] These considerations were already anticipated by Bentham, who stated that "[p]ublicity is the very soul of justice."[97] Proceeding from this, scholars developed the principle of open justice, stating that justice needs to be delivered in public, hence, in a way that courts are open, transparent, and accessible. This was accompanied by the assumption that open justice increases public trust in judiciaries.[98] However, although open justice has gained considerable scholarly attention, this assumption has never been tested empirically.[99]

The aims of this chapter were threefold. First, through a conceptualization of the open justice principle and the creation of an open justice index, this chapter sought to present a parsimonious approach to measuring open justice on a comparative scale. Thereby, it aimed to establish open justice as a new avenue for comparative research on judicial politics. Second, as the few existing empirical studies on open justice have focused on ordinary judiciaries, this chapter focused on the highest courts to overcome this shortcoming.[100] Third, by treating open justice as a correlate of public trust in the legal system, this chapter aimed to present a first empirical test of the above-stated assumption.

Previous studies have found that institutional properties like accountability and independence affect the public's trust in the legal system; while others like impartiality and neutrality, for which similar influences on trust and public support have been theoretically argued, were not tested.[101] This chapter argued that because open justice secures the impartiality and neutrality of courts by delivering justice in an accessible, open, and transparent fashion, it also shapes public trust in the legal system.[102]

The presented empirical results can only be understood as preliminary. The proposed conceptualization and comparative measurement of open justice need to undergo more rigorous validity and reliability tests, and the data used for the analysis does not align temporally. Nevertheless, the results highlighted two essential aspects. First, the comparative assessment of the websites of 27 European highest courts showed that the degree of open justice varies

---

94 Miller (n 74); Toshkov (n 21).

95 Garoupa and Magalhães (n 44).

96 Vanberg (n 12); Staton (n 36).

97 Bentham (n 1) 316.

98 Johnston (n 15); Hess and Harvey (n 3); Cunliffe (n 16).

99 Moore, Clayton and Murphy (n 39); Cunliffe (n 16); Bosland and Gill (n 16); Gasco-Hernandez and Jimenez-Gomez (n 16).

100 Marković and Gostojić (n 59); Elena and van Schalkwyk (n 64).

101 Magalhães and Garoupa (n 11).

102 Gibson and Caldeira (n 12).

from country to country, and that the websites consider aspects of transparency to be more important than those of openness and accessibility. This result aligns with previous studies, which have found that court websites primarily focus more on information disclosure and transparency and less on participation.[103] Second, the more open, transparent, and accessible court websites are, the more the public trusts the legal system. Based on data from the ninth round of the ESS, the results show that the odds that citizens rate their trust in the legal system in a higher category increase significantly when the open justice index moves one unit. The effect of open justice seems to be moderated by individual-level aspects like the respondent's education.

This chapter contributes to the literature in several ways. It is the first study to provide empirical evidence for the long-stated but never-tested assumption that the principle of open justice fosters the public's trust in legal institutions. Similarly, by conceptualizing the open justice principle and presenting a parsimonious measurement approach, this chapter shows that the degree of open justice, depicted through court websites, varies between the assessed countries. This measurement approach can be seen as a starting point to measure open justice comparatively across countries and more extended periods. This is particularly the case because the measurement was based on simple coding and index construction rules and focused on court websites. Therefore, this approach can easily be applied to any court that maintains a website.

Finally, more than half (17) of all 27 courts use at least one social media platform for their judicial public relations. This raises the question of whether social media communication can further enhance public trust in courts. Moving forward, future studies should investigate social media activities by courts by, for example, analyzing whether such communication efforts stimulate citizen engagement through legal institutions.[104] Furthermore, the results suggest that open justice influences public trust in the legal system, and that the individual characteristics of the respondents moderate this. To investigate this in more detail, future studies should focus on the relationship between seeing, understanding, and trusting, by, for example, conducting an experimental research design that tests whether the level of trust of participants varies depending on the quality—with regard to transparency, openness, and accessibility—of the information on courts they receive.

REFERENCES

Alemanno A and Stefan O, 'Openness at the Court of Justice of the European Union: Toppling a Taboo' (2014) 51 Common Market Law Review 97.

Benesh SC, 'Understanding Public Confidence in American Courts' (2006) 68 The Journal of Politics 697.

Bentham J, 'Draught for the Organization of Judicial Establishments, Compared with That of the National Assembly, with a Commentary on the Same.' in John Bowring (ed), *The works of Jeremy*

[103] Sandoval-Almazan and Gil-Garcia (n 9); Parkin and Wedeking (n 18); Marković and Gostojić (n 59).

[104] On government Twitter usage see, for example, Nur Siyam, Omar Alqaryouti and Sherief Abdallah, 'Mining Government Tweets to Identify and Predict Citizens Engagement' (2020) 60 Technology in Society 101211.

Bentham: Published under the superintendence of his executor, John Bowring (4th edn, William Tait 1843).

Bosland J and Gill J, 'The Principle of Open Justice and the Judicial Duty to Give Public Reasons' (2014) 38 Melbourne University Law Review 482.

Bosland J and Townend J, 'Open Justice, Transparency and the Media: Representing the Public Interest in the Physical and Virtual Courtroom' (2018) 23 Communications Law 1746.

Brady HE, 'The Challenge of Big Data and Data Science' (2019) 22 Annual Review of Political Science 297.

Chainais C, 'Open Justice and the Principle of Public Access to Hearings' in Burkhard Hess and Ana Koprivica Harvey (eds), *Open Justice: The Role of Courts in a Democratic Society* (Nomos 2019).

Chatfield AT and Reddick CG, 'Collaborative Network Governance Framework for Aligning Open Justice and E-Justice Ecosystems for Greater Public Value' (2020) 38 Social Science Computer Review 252.

Cianetti L, Dawson J and Hanley S, 'Rethinking "Democratic Backsliding" in Central and Eastern Europe – Looking beyond Hungary and Poland' (2018) 34 East European Politics 243.

Crusoe J, Gebka E and Ahlin K, 'Open Government Data from the Perspective of Information Needs – A Tentative Conceptual Model BT – Electronic Government' in Gabriela Viale Pereira and others, (eds) *Electronic Government* (Springer International Publishing 2020).

Cunliffe E, 'Open Justice: Concepts and Judicial Approaches' (2012) 40 Federal Law Review 385.

Dainow J, 'The Civil Law and the Common Law : Some Points of Comparison' (1966) 15 The American Journal of Comparative Law 419.

Davis R, 'Conclusion' in Richard Davis and David Taras (eds), *Justices and Journalists: The Global Perspective* (CUP 2017).

De Fine Licht J and others, 'When Does Transparency Generate Legitimacy? Experimenting on a Context-Bound Relationship' (2014) 27 Governance 111.

Elena S and van Schalkwyk F, 'Open Data for Open Justice in Seven Latin American Countries' in Carlos E Jiménez-Gomez and Mila Gascó-Hernández (eds), *Achieving Open Justice through Citizen Participation and Transparency* (IGI Global 2017).

Epstein L, Knight J and Shvetsova O, 'The Role of Constitutional Courts in Establishment and Maintenance of Democratic Systems of Government' (2001) 35 Law & Society Review 117.

ESS ESSR 9, 'Data File Edition 3.1. NSD-Norwegian Centre for Research Data, Norway–Data Archive and Distributor of ESS Data for ESS ERIC'.

Garoupa N and Magalhães PC, 'Public Trust in the European Legal Systems: Independence, Accountability and Awareness' (2021) 44 West European Politics 690.

Gasco-Hernandez M and Jimenez-Gomez CE, 'Information and Technology in Open Justice' (2020) 38 Social Science Computer Review 247.

Gibson JL and Caldeira GA, *Citizens, Courts, and Confirmations: Positivity Theory and the Judgments of the American People* (Princeton University Press 2009).

Ginsburg T, *Judicial Review in New Democracies: Constitutional Courts in Asian Cases* (CUP 2003).

Grimmelikhuijsen S and Klijn A, 'The Effects of Judicial Transparency on Public Trust: Evidence from a Field Experiment' (2015) 93 Public Administration 995.

Harden JJ, Kirkland JH and Shea PE, 'Legislative Transparency and Credit Risk' (2021) 46 Legislative Studies Quarterly 189.

Hess B and Harvey AK (eds), *Open Justice: The Role of Courts in a Democratic Society* (Nomos 2019).

Hess B and Harvey AK (eds), 'Open Justice in Modern Societies: What Role for Courts?' in Burkhard Hess and Ana Koprivica Harvey (eds), *Open Justice: The Role of Courts in a Democratic Society* (Nomos 2019).

Johnston J, 'Three Phases of Courts' Publicity: Reconfiguring Bentham's Open Justice in the Twenty-First Century' (2018) 14 International Journal of Law in Context 525.

Krehbiel J, 'The Politics of Judicial Procedures: The Role of Public Oral Hearings in the German Constitutional Court' (2016) 60 American Journal of Political Science 990.

Krehbiel J, 'Elections, Public Awareness, and the Efficacy of Constitutional Review' (2019) 7 Journal of Law and Courts 53.

Magalhães PC and Garoupa N, 'Judicial Performance and Trust in Legal Systems: Findings from a Decade of Surveys in over 20 European Countries' (2020) 101 Social Science Quarterly 1743.

Marković M and Gostojić S, 'Open Judicial Data: A Comparative Analysis' (2020) 38 Social Science Computer Review 295.
Meyer P, 'Judicial Public Relations: Determinants of Press Release Publication by Constitutional Courts' (2020) 40 Politics 477.
Meyer P, 'Explaining Media Coverage on Constitutional Court Decisions in Germany: The Role of Case Characteristics' (2021) 38 Political Communication 426.
Meyer P, 'Promoted Media Coverage of Court Decisions: Media Gatekeeping of Court Press Releases and the Role of News Values' (2021) 22 Journalism Studies 723.
Michener G and Ritter O, 'Comparing Resistance to Open Data Performance Measurement: Public Education in Brazil and the UK' (2017) 95 Public Administration 4.
Miller B, 'Making Measures Capture Concepts: Tools for Securing Correspondence between Theoretical Ideas and Observations' in Thomas Gschwend and Frank Schimmelpfennig (eds), *Research Design in Political Science: How to Practice What They Preach* (Palgrave Macmillan UK 2007).
Moore S, 'Towards a Sociology of Institutional Transparency: Openness, Deception and the Problem of Public Trust' (2018) 52 Sociology 416.
Moore S, Clayton A and Murphy H, 'Seeing Justice Done: Courtroom Filming and the Deceptions of Transparency' [2019] Crime, Media, Culture https://doi.org/10.1177/1741659019883764.
Navia P and Ríos-Figueroa J, 'The Constitutional Adjudication Mosaic of Latin America' (2005) 38 Comparative Political Studies 189.
Pah AR and others, 'How to Build a More Open Justice System' (2020) 369 Science 134.
Parkin M and Wedeking J, 'Connecting with the Courts: Online Access to State Judicial Systems' (2017) 38 Justice System Journal 22.
Resnik J, 'The Functions of Publicity and of Privatization in Courts and Their Replacements (from Jeremy Bentham to #MeToo and Google Spain)', *Open Justice: The Role of Courts in a Democratic Society* (Nomos 2019).
Rodrick S, 'Achieving the Aims of Open Justice – The Relationship between the Courts, the Media and the Public' (2014) 19 Deakin Law Review 123.
Ryder SE, 'Securing Open Justice' in Burkhard Hess and Ana Koprivica Harvey (eds), *Open Justice: The Role of Courts in a Democratic Society* (Nomos 2019).
Salzman R and Ramsey A, 'Judging the Judiciary: Understanding Public Confidence in Latin American Courts' (2013) 55 Latin American Politics and Society 73.
Sandoval-Almazan R and Gil-Garcia JR, 'Understanding E-Justice and Open Justice Through the Assessment of Judicial Websites: Toward a Conceptual Framework' (2020) 38 Social Science Computer Review 334.
Scholl HJ, 'Digital Government: Looking Back and Ahead on a Fascinating Domain of Research and Practice' (2020) 1 Digital Government: Research and Practice 1.
Siyam N, Alqaryouti O and Abdallah S, 'Mining Government Tweets to Identify and Predict Citizens Engagement' (2020) 60 Technology in Society 101211.
Staton JK, *Judicial Power and Strategic Communication in Mexico* (CUP 2010).
Stone Sweet A, 'Constitutional Courts and Parliamentary Democracy' (2002) 25 West European Politics 77.
Taras D, 'Introduction: Judges and Journalists and the Spaces In Between' in Richard Davis and David Taras (eds), *Justices and Journalists: The Global Perspective* (CUP 2017).
Tolbert CJ and Mossberger K, 'The Effects of E-Government on Trust and Confidence in Government' (2006) 66 Public Administration Review 354.
Toshkov D, *Research Design in Political Science* (Palgrave Macmillan 2016).
Vanberg G, *The Politics of Constitutional Review in Germany* (CUP 2005).
Wonka A, 'Concept Specification in Political Science Research' in Thomas Gschwend and Frank Schimmelpfennig (eds), *Research Design in Political Science: How to Practice What They Preach* (Palgrave Macmillan UK 2007).
Žuffová M, 'Do FOI Laws and Open Government Data Deliver as Anti-Corruption Policies? Evidence from a Cross-Country Study' (2020) 37 Government Information Quarterly 101480.

16. Courting dissent

Judicial legitimacy and protests

Hayley Munir and Syed Rashid Munir

PROTESTS

Our interest in this chapter is in protests, a specific form of political participation. Protests are an appropriate alternative form of participation on which to focus, as they represent a strategy that minorities can use to protect their interests. In this regard, much of the protest literature is examined through a collective action framework.[1] These scholars show that coordination is critical for the emergence of protests, but they also acknowledge that coordination is not a sufficient condition for protests to occur. Other studies use a different framework and acknowledge that protests are a form of bargaining.[2] Furthermore, the inter-state bargaining literature addresses the role of protests, or resource mobilization, as threats.[3]

It is interesting to note that research has also identified who participates in protests and the purpose of protesting. In this framework, protests exist as a "political resource"[4] which can be used to put pressure on the regime to extract favorable demands. For this reason, it has been argued that protests are used by minorities and those without the financial means to pursue actions to achieve their goals. Protesting is a way for individuals to extract a demand from ruling parties.

Keeping this above dimension of protests in mind, this chapter contributes to the body of literature that focuses on the conditions under which protests occur. Eisinger suggests that conditions for protests are ripe in semi-open systems (i.e., systems that are not deemed repressive or completely open), when conventional methods of achieving goals seem too cumbersome.[5] Research has also shown that transitions and crises provide favorable conditions for protests.[6] For these reasons, minorities in a society can be reasonably expected to resort to protests if the institutional safeguards provided to them do not perform their function.

---

1 Arieh Gavious & Shlomo Mizrahi, *Two-Level Collective Action and Group Identity*, 11 Journal of Theoretical Politics 497 (1999); Rasma Karklins & Roger Petersen, *Decision Calculus of Protesters and Regimes: Eastern Europe 1989*, 55 The Journal of Politics 588 (1993).

2 Carlos Scartascini & Mariano Tommasi, *The Making of Policy: Institutionalized or Not?*, 56 American Journal of Political Science 787 (2012); James Q. Wilson, The Strategy of Protest: *Problems of Negro Civic Action*, 5 The Journal of Conflict Resolution 291 (1961).

3 James D. Fearon, *Signaling Foreign Policy Interests: Tying Hands Versus Sinking Costs*, 41 Journal of Conflict Resolution 68 (1997); Thomas C. Schelling, THE STRATEGY OF CONFLICT, (1960).

4 Michael Lipsky, *Protests as a Political Resource*, 62 American Political Science Review 1144 (1968).

5 Peter K. Eisinger, *The Conditions of Protest Behavior in American Cities*, 67 The American Political Science Review 11 (1973).

6 Charles Tilly and Sidney Tarrow, CONTENTIOUS POLITICS (2015).

It has already been discussed that minorities – due to their disadvantaged positions even in democracies – cannot successfully resort to electoral institutions to make policy demands. In this context, we argue that one particular institutional structure, the judiciary, can provide an avenue for such groups to seek relief. The discussion below will demonstrate how a judiciary that is perceived to be legitimate by the citizenry can provide minorities with an outlet to voice their grievances, and not resort to informal forms of political participation such as protests. In particular, we suggest that judicial legitimacy lowers the likelihood of protests in a society.

JUDICIAL LEGITIMACY

A key element in ensuring regime stability is a government's ability to manage political contention. Scholars agree that an independent judiciary is an institutional dispute resolution mechanism that formally manages political contention.[7] This is the case because judicial institutions give individuals, including those in the minority, a formal opportunity to protect their interests that would otherwise be impossible through traditional political processes. This means that an individual may use litigation to resolve a conflict or to protect their interests.

It is important to remember that not all minorities have the resources to seek out litigation. Even under these circumstances, an independent judiciary plays an important role in curbing societal unrest and managing political contention. This is the case because an independent judiciary also acts as an institutional check on the legislative and executive branches of government. Scholars argue that independent judicial institutions strengthen the credibility of governmental promises to protect individual rights.[8] Most of the literature defines an independent judiciary as an institution with the ability to constrain the executive.[9] Judicial independence could also refer to a court's ability to constrain the legislature. Yet many scholars only focus on the ability of the courts to constrain the executive, as the executive is the political actor most likely to violate individual rights.[10] In this regard, judicial independence is achieved through constitutional and statutory laws giving powers to the judiciary.

However, the mere presence of judicial institutions with de jure judicial independence is not sufficient to protect individual rights or constrain political majorities. A purely structural operationalization of the judiciary fails to consider the possibility that judges have the ability to constrain the executive or the legislature but prefer not to do so. To be clear, while independent judiciaries have the power to check the executive, this does not guarantee that the judges on

---

[7] Charles Tilly, THE POLITICS OF COLLECTIVE VIOLENCE (2003); Lars P. Feld & Stefan Voigt, *Economic Growth and Judicial Independence: Cross-Country Evidence Using a New Set of Indicators*, 49 European Journal of Political Economy 803 (2003).

[8] Lars P. Feld & Stefan Voigt, *Economic Growth and Judicial Independence: Cross-Country Evidence Using a New Set of Indicators*, 49 European Journal of Political Economy 803 (2003); Emilia Justyna Powell & Jeffrey K Staton, *Domestic Judicial Institutions and Human Rights Treaty Violation*, 53 International Studies Quarterly 149 (2009).

[9] Witold J Henisz, *The Institutional Environment for International Business*, In WHAT IS INTERNATIONAL BUSINESS 85 (2004); Gretchen Helmke, COURTS UNDER CONSTRAINTS: JUDGES, GENERALS, AND PRESIDENTS IN ARGENTINA, (2005); Michael G. Findley & Joseph K. Young, *Terrorism, Democracy, and Credible Commitments*, 55 International Studies Quarterly 357 (2011).

[10] Douglass C. North & Barry R. Weingast, *Constitutions and Commitment: The Evolution of Institutions Governing Public Choice in Seventeenth-Century England*, 49 Journal of Economic History 80 (1989).

the bench will exercise this power. In other words, a structural definition of judicial independence does not enable us to identify the actual behavior of judges as independent. This is because what courts have the ability to do and what courts actually do may differ. The leading explanation for the decisions that judges make is attitudes;[11] therefore, unless all judges sitting on a high court have attitudes that favor minority protection, we should not expect them to consistently constrain other political actors to protect minority rights. As noted above, judges may have the ability to protect minorities' rights by constraining the majority but prefer not to do so. To avoid these issues, we focus on the concept of judicial legitimacy.

It must be noted at this point that our argument is not centered on what judges actually do; instead, we are concerned with how individuals in a society perceive the institution. That is, whether the people perceive the court as an impartial institution. Law and courts scholars have yet to agree upon a standard definition of judicial legitimacy. However, the literature is consistent in that scholars focus on the relationship between courts and the public when studying the concept. For example, in a study on international courts, Voeten refers to the concept as public legitimacy, which is defined as "the beliefs among the mass public that an international court has the right to exercise authority in a certain domain." Voeten also notes that legitimacy "depends on trust, which is a coping device for dealing with the freedom of others."[12] Like Voeten, we believe that trust is a critical factor in determining perceptions of legitimacy. When people do not trust their domestic judiciary, they will not perceive the institution as a viable option to seek redress. Nownes and Glennon suggest that legitimacy is determined by perceptions of whether institutions are fair and impartial.[13] Consistent with these scholars, we define judicial legitimacy as the extent to which a public perceives its domestic judiciary to be impartial.

By impartiality, we mean that people do not believe that their domestic judiciary is biased against them, as judicial legitimacy is determined by public perception. The reason that legitimacy is important is connected to the institution's reputation as a countermajoritarian institution. In an analysis on the German Federal Constitutional Court, Vanberg (2004) found that impartiality is key to maintaining public trust.[14] When people believe their domestic courts make impartial decisions, we should observe popular observance of the law in addition to higher levels of trust in the institution. Extant literature has also highlighted the relationship between legitimacy and violence. Tyler contends that institutional legitimacy makes it less likely for people to use extralegal action. This is the case because legitimacy facilitates social order; decisions to comply with or disobey the law are impacted by legitimacy.[15] As Tyler

---

11 C. Neal Tate, *Personal Attribute Models of the Voting Behavior of US Supreme Court Justices: Liberalism in Civil Liberties and Economics Decisions, 1946–1978*, 75 American Political Science Review 355 (1981); Jeffrey A Segal & Albert D. Cover, *Ideological Values and the Votes of US Supreme Court Justices*, 83 American Political Science Review 557 (1989); Jeffrey A. Segal & Harold J Spaeth, The Supreme Court and the Attitudinal Model Revisted (2002); Jeff Yates et al., *Judicial Ideology and the Selection of Disputes for US Supreme Court Adjudication*, 10 Journal of Empirical Legal Studies 847 (2013).

12 Eric Voeten, *Public Opinion and the Legitimacy of International Courts*, 14 Theoretical Inquiries In Law 411 (2013).

13 Anthony J. Nownes & Colin Glennon, *An Experimental Investigation of How Judicial Elections Affect Public Faith in the Judicial System*, 41 Law & Social Inquiry 37 (2016).

14 Georg Vanberg, The Politics of Constitutional Revivew in Germany (2004).

15 Tom R. Tyler, *Legitimacy and Maintenance of Public Order* (2012).

shows, a society that does not perceive its legal system as legitimate is more likely to suffer from extralegal violence.[16]

In this context, people, including minority groups, do not have to agree with every decision that judges make. But it does mean that if they perceive their domestic judiciary as legitimate, they acknowledge the institution's authority and impartiality even when they disagree with specific decisions.[17] The enforcement of judicial decisions has also been linked to judicial legitimacy.[18] As a result, a judiciary viewed with legitimacy is not only trustworthy; it also has its decisions enforced. If other governmental actors do not enforce the decisions that judges make, people will not acknowledge the institution's authority. Thus, the maintenance of legitimacy is crucial to maintain popular observance of the law.[19]

PROTESTS AND JUDICIAL LEGITIMACY

Legal mobilization is the process of identifying grievances and choosing to seek redress.[20] The extent to which political elites insulate themselves from minority pressure in the legislative arena increases the threat of legal mobilization from disgruntled citizens. As noted above, seeking redress is not limited to formal legal processes. People can pursue the protection of their interests in many different ways. Albiston, Edelman, and Milligan created the dispute

---

[16] Tom R. Tyler, Why People Obey the Law: Procedural Justice, Legitimacy, Compliance (1990).

[17] One strand of literature focuses on institutional legitimacy, which is impacted by public support. Support for courts is conceptualized in two ways: specific and diffuse (*see*, for example, Gregory A., Caldeira & James L. Gibson, *The Etiology of Public Support for the Supreme Court*, 36 American Journal of Political Science 635 (1992); Tom R. Tyler & Gregory Mitchell, *Legitimacy and the Empowerment of Discretionary Legal Authority: The United States Supreme Court and Abortion Rights*, 43 Duke Law Journal 703 (1994)). Specific support refers to support for specific institutional decisions. For example, if a court were to rule consistent with audiences' preferences on a case, the audience would have specific support for the court. Diffuse support is a broader concept that refers to support for an institution despite fluctuations in specific support (*see* David Easton, *A Re-Assessment of the Concept of Political Support*, 5 British Journal of Political Science 435 (1975).) For example, an audience may still believe that the judiciary has the authority to hear cases on an issue despite disagreeing with specific decisions in the past. Diffuse support is thought to protect institutional legitimacy even when specific support is low.

[18] Joseph L. Staats, et al., *Measuring Judicial Performance in Latin America*, 47 Latin American Politics and Society 77 (2005).

[19] Brandon L. Bartels & Christopher D. Johnston, *On the Ideological Foundations of Supreme Court Legitimacy in the American Public*, 57 American Journal of Political Science 184 (2013); overwhelming evidence from deterrence literature suggests that threat is not effective at reducing crime *see*, for example, Tom Tyler, *Trust and Legitimacy: Policing in the USA and Europe*, 8 European Journal of Criminology 254 (2011); Joan McCord et al., *Juvenile Crime* (Juvenile Justice, ed. 2001). Therefore, the logic underlying the extant findings and theory put forth here is supported.

[20] Catherine R. Albiston, *Bargaining in the Shadow of Social Institutions: Competing Discourses and Social Change in Workplace Mobilization of Civil Rights*, 39 Law & Society Review 11 (2005); Anna Marshall, *Idle Rights: Employees' Rights Consciousness and the Construction of Sexual Harassment Policies*, 39 Law & Society Review 83 (2005); Laura Beth Nielsen, *The Work of Rights and the Work Rights Do: A Critical Empirical Approach*, in The Blackwell Companion to Law and Society 63 (A. Sarat ed., 2004); Donald Black, *The Mobilization of Law*, 2 Journal of Legal Studies 125 (1973); Laura Beth Nielsen et al., *Individual Justice or Collective Legal Mobilization? Employment Discrimination Litigation in the Post Civil Rights United States*, 7 Journal of Empirical Legal Studies 175 (2010).

tree metaphor to highlight this point.[21] The trunk represents a dispute, and the branches represent the many different ways in which people may protect their interests.[22] These different pathways to resolve disputes can be broken down into two categories: formal and informal pathways. By formal pathways we mean political institutions; and we take informal pathways to mean any non-institutional strategies used to protect interests (e.g., protests, domestic terrorism, mediation).

The discussion in the previous section highlights that judicial legitimacy is associated with several factors that shape the characteristics of informal dispute resolution strategies that mobilized citizens may choose to pursue. In this context, judicial legitimacy facilitates an environment in which people have access to a formal institutional dispute resolution in addition to protection from governmental overreach. When a judiciary is perceived to be legitimate, social order and popular observance of the law are high. This highlights why the legitimacy of judicial institutions is especially important for regime stability. Since judicial legitimacy is associated with trust, impartiality, enforceability, and popular observance of the law, we should observe fewer protests in regimes with high levels of judicial legitimacy.

Hypothesis: High levels of judicial legitimacy are associated with fewer protests.

We also acknowledge that not all protests are alike; some protests are violent and others are not. Thus, we also test for the impact of judiciary legitimacy on violent protests and non-violent protests. The expected relationship when protests are combined and separated by violence is the same nonetheless. In other words, we anticipate the above-stated relationship to be present for non-violent protests and violent protests. This expectation is borne from the fact that judicial legitimacy corresponds with popular observance of the law, which should discourage the number of non-violent protests as well as reduce the efficacy of violent strategies. The following section elaborates on the research design employed to test these expectations.

RESEARCH DESIGN

The unit of analysis is country year, and the time period for the countries in the sample is from 1996 to 2017. The sample includes 144 countries for which data is available. The dependent variable is the number of protests in a country per year taken from the Mass Mobilization dataset.[23] As the dependent variable necessitates a count model, a zero-inflated negative binomial regression is used.[24]

---

21 Catherine R. Albiston et al., *The Dispute Tree and the Legal Forest*, 10 Annual Review of Law and Social Science 105 (2014).

22 The dispute tree was created to replace the dispute pyramid, which did not adequately address the differences between formal and informal pathways in which people resolve disputes *see* Richard E. Miller & Austin Sarat, Grievances, *Claims, and Disputes: Assessing the Adversary Culture*, 15 Law & Society Review 525 (1980).

23 David Clark & Patrick Regan, Mass Mobilization Data Project, Harvard Dataverse (2016). http://www.10.7910/DVN/HTTWYL.

24 A negative binomial regression is used instead of a Poisson since the dispersion parameter test indicates that the data is overdispersed. Due to the abundance of zero values in the dependent variable, a zero-inflated negative binomial regression is being employed to correctly control for such behavior. This model assumes the presence of zeroes in the dependent variable as outcomes of two different pro-

The main independent variable is the Rule of Law Index, and it comes from the World Governance Indicators (WGI) dataset developed by the World Bank.[25] This variable ranges from –2.25 (low) to 2.1 (high) in the sample, and it is used as a proxy for judicial legitimacy. The WGI website indicates that this variable captures the extent to which the citizens in a country have confidence in and abide by the rules of society, and in particular the quality of contract enforcement, property rights, the police, and the courts, as well as the likelihood of crime and violence. Overall, this variable accurately captures whether the people believe the judiciary is an impartial institution. This variable also provides broad coverage in terms of both states and years; and as a robustness check, an additional variable from the extant literature, namely the judicial independence component from the Bertelsmann Transformation Index (BTI), is also employed.[26] This variable ranges from 1 (low) to 10 (high) and is calculated using expert surveys that consider whether the judiciary is free from both unconstitutional intervention and corruption.

We also use several controls. First, as protests in period *t* may be a function of the protests in the period *t-1*, a first-order lag of the dependent variable, i.e., the number of protests in the previous year, is used as a control. This variable is expected to have a positive beta coefficient, as recent experience with protests can be expected to increase the likelihood of protests.

Second, to control for the effect of regime type, the PolityIV scores for each country are used in the dataset as well. This variable comes from the M.G. Marshall, Gurr, and Jaggers dataset and ranges from –10 (autocracies) to +10 (democracies), with middling values reserved for anocracies.[27] As the sample contains both democracies and autocracies, this inclusion is reasonable as both regime types may have vastly different institutional structures that may promote or restrict protests. This variable is expected to have a positive beta coefficient, as democracies routinely allow for the expression of dissent through protests. Additionally, some countries in the sample, such as Qatar, Bahrain, and the UAE, have low PolityIV scores but high scores on the Rule of Law Index. For this reason, autocracies are included in the sample, as public confidence in the judiciary's ability to do its job impartially may be high even in some restrictive regimes.

To control for varying levels of economic development, the natural log of gross domestic product (GDP) per capita is also used. This variable comes from the Penn World Tables and is expected to have a negative beta coefficient; higher levels of economic development can reasonably be expected to decrease the likelihood of protests, as the sustenance and additional material demands of the citizenry may already be satisfied in this case.[28]

---

cesses, and uses a logit model as well as a negative binomial regression model to account for the different processes that may generate the zero values. As a robustness check, the protests variable is also broken down into violent and non-violent protests.

[25] The World Bank, World Governance Indicators (2020). https://datacatalog.worldbank.org/dataset/worldwide-governance-indicators.

[26] Bertelsmann Stiftung, Bertelsmann Transformation Index (2020). https://www.bti-project.org/en/home.html?&cb=00000.

[27] Monty G. Marshall et al., POLITY IV PROJECT: POLITICAL REGIME CHARACTERISTICS AND TRANSITION, 1800–2015, College Park: Center for Systemic Peace (2016). http://www.systemicpeace.org/inscrdata.html.

[28] Robert C. Feenstra et al., *The Next Generation of the Penn World Table*, 105 American Economic Review 105 3150 (2015).

Moreover, other variables controlling for poverty and challenges to human well-being are also employed. Therefore, the percentage of total population living in urban areas is also added to the regression.[29] This variable is expected to have a positive beta coefficient, as urban residents are wealthier and may demand better access to education and other facilities, as well as accountability from the government and protection for their political participation rights.

We also include child mortality to capture the quality of life in a country. This variable measures the number of deaths for children under five years old per 1,000 live births in each country, and is used to proxy the quality of life and healthcare facilities available to the citizenry. This measure robustly accounts for the well-being of the population, and provides an accurate picture of the public services available to the people. This variable comes from the World Bank and is expected to have a positive beta coefficient, as higher mortality rates for children can be expected to generate protests demanding for better living conditions.[30]

To account for the development of new modes of organizing for protests, the total number of telephone lines in a country in a given year (fixed and cellular) is used in the regression to approximate the vehicles available to the population for protest organization. This variable comes from the World Bank and is expected to have a positive beta coefficient, as a higher incidence of connectivity throughout the country may make it easier for the protesters to organize.[31]

Lastly, in a separate variation of the model (Model 1b), additional control variables to control for regional effects are also included. These variables take the form of binary indicators for each region coded by the Correlates of War Project and are included to control for differences in the propensity of different regions to have varying numbers of protests overall.[32] Table 16.1 provides the summary statistics for the variables in the current sample.

RESULTS AND DISCUSSION

This chapter suggests that fewer protests are likely to happen as the judicial legitimacy in a society increases, as the citizenry view an impartial judiciary as a safeguard for their rights and liberties. Table 16.2 provides the estimates from the zero-inflated negative binomial regression model, with the top half of the table providing the results from a negative binomial regression and the bottom half presenting the estimates from a logit regression. As discussed before, this particular model assumes that the abundance of zeroes in the dependent variable could be a result of two different processes. The bottom half of Table 16.2 then presents estimates for the likelihood that a country in the sample belongs to the certain zero protest group, whereas the top half of Table 16.2 predicts the number of protests for the group of countries not in the certain zero group.

---

29 The World Bank, Urban Population (2020). https://data.worldbank.org/indicator/SP.URB.TOTL.IN.ZS.

30 The World Bank, Mortality Rate (2020). https://data.worldbank.org/indicator/SH.DYN.MORT.

31 The regression estimates remain significant in their expected directions when only cellular lines are used in the model; The World Bank, Telephone Subscriptions (2020). https://data.worldbank.org/indicator/IT.MLT.MAIN.

32 Correlates of War Project, State System Membership List, V2016 (2017). http://correlatesofwar.org.

Table 16.1 *Summary statistics for zero-inflated negative binomial regression (1996–2017)*

VARIABLES	Expected Direction	N	Mean	S.D.	Min	Max
Protests		2,668	3.476	6.817	0	143
Years		2,668			1996	2017
Judicial Legitimacy	–	2,668	–0.140	0.972	–2.255	2.100
$Protests_{t-1}$	+	2,668	3.487	6.826	0	143
PolityIV Index	+	2,668	3.806	6.304	–10	10
GDP/Capita (ln)	–	2,668	8.937	1.237	5.408	11.94
Total Phone Lines (fixed & cellular)	+	2,668	6.39×10^6	2.43×10^7	36.67	3.67×10^8
Urban Population (% of total)	+	2,668	56.57	21.84	7.412	100
Child Mortality	+	2,668	45.78	47.12	2.300	265.8

As can be seen, the results from Model 1a in Table 16.2 provide support for the hypothesis that a judiciary viewed as impartial by the people leads to a lower likelihood of protests, as the beta coefficient for judicial legitimacy is positive and significant at conventional levels of statistical significance in the logit part. In the bottom half, where the model is predicting whether a country is in the certain zero groups or not, higher values of judicial legitimacy predict a greater likelihood of a country being in this group. In other words, higher levels of judicial legitimacy result in a country ending up in a certain zero group, i.e., a country is more likely to have no protests statistically. Another way in which the same result can be stated is to see that higher levels of judicial legitimacy lower the likelihood of protests. In isolation, this part of the model bodes well for this chapter's hypothesis; but when seen in conjunction with the results of the negative binomial regression (top half of Table 16.2), the evidence appears even more convincing.

As mentioned previously, the negative binomial regression part in Table 16.2 predicts the number of protests for the group of countries that are not in the certain zero group, i.e., countries that could have had protests. In this part, the beta coefficient for judicial legitimacy is negative and significant at 95% confidence levels. For countries that could have had protests, this negative beta coefficient is predicting a lower incidence of protests if judicial legitimacy is high. This result corresponds well with the central hypothesis of this chapter. It can be reasonably suggested that the citizens in countries with higher levels of judicial legitimacy have more confidence regarding the protection of their civil and sociopolitical rights, and expect the institution of the judiciary to provide safeguards against individual and executive overreach.

The substantive effect from the results in Table 16.2 can be seen in Figure 16.1. Panel (a) in Figure 16.1 plots the predicted number of protests from the negative binomial regression part of Table 16.2 against the actual values of judicial legitimacy in the sample. As can be seen, higher levels of judicial legitimacy do lead to a lower likelihood of protests, and this result is especially informative at extreme values of the main independent variable. Panel (b) in Figure 16.1 plots the predicted number of protests over values of judicial legitimacy for Model 1b, which differs from the previous model in that it contains binary indicators for each region coded by the Correlates of War data, which are expected to account for regional variation in

Table 16.2 Predicted number of protests given judicial legitimacy

EQUATION	VARIABLES	Model 1a	Model 1b
Count Model	$Protests_{t-1}$	0.064***	0.064***
		(0.006)	(0.006)
	Judicial Legitimacy	–0.153**	–0.160**
		(0.072)	(0.072)
	GDP/Capita (ln)	0.135	0.142
		(0.091)	(0.091)
	PolityIV Index	0.014*	0.014*
		(0.009)	(0.008)
	Total Phone Lines (fixed & cellular)	4.77×10^{-9}***	5.10×10^{-9}***
		(0.000)	(0.000)
	Urban Population (% of total)	–0.012***	–0.011***
		(0.003)	(0.003)
	Child Mortality	–0.005**	–0.006**
		(0.002)	(0.002)
	Constant	0.576	0.386
		(0.855)	(0.846)
Logit Model	Judicial Legitimacy	0.763***	0.803***
		(0.201)	(0.205)
	$Protests_{t-1}$	–0.982***	–0.969***
		(0.186)	(0.181)
	Total Phone Lines (fixed & cellular)	-1.94×10^{-7}***	-2.03×10^{-7}***
		(0.000)	(0.000)
	GDP/Capita (ln)	0.517**	0.485**
		(0.229)	(0.232)
	PolityIV Index	–0.096***	–0.098***
		(0.020)	(0.020)
	Urban Population (% of total)	–0.021***	–0.021***
		(0.007)	(0.007)
	Child Mortality	–0.001	–0.000
		(0.005)	(0.006)
	Constant	–3.138	–2.755
		(2.086)	(2.108)
Regional Binary Indicators		NO	YES
$\ln(\alpha)$		0.028	0.024
		(0.074)	(0.071)
	Observations	2,668	2,668

Notes:
*** $p<0.01$, ** $p<0.05$, * $p<0.1$.
Robust standard errors in parentheses.

the number of protests. As can be seen from Figure 16.1, the results also provide evidence to support the hypothesis that higher judicial legitimacy leads to a lower number of protests.

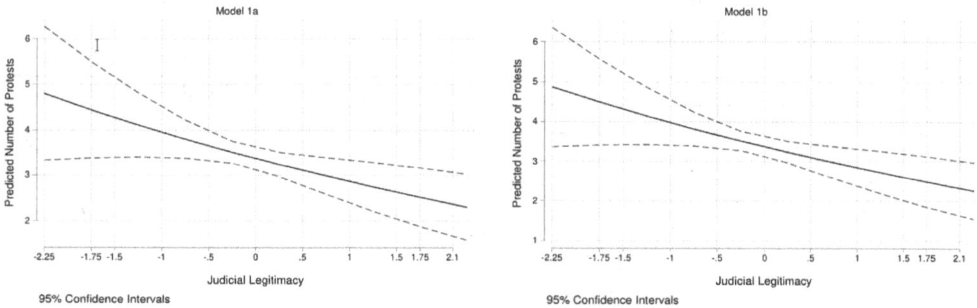

(a) (b)

Figure 16.1 Predicted number of protests given judicial legitimacy

VIOLENT AND NON-VIOLENT PROTESTS

The Mass Mobilization dataset codes – through a binary indicator – whether the protestors engaged in violence during their protest, which allows for another substantive test of the main hypothesis in this chapter.[33] The results in the above section merge violent and non-violent into a single, count variable, and the evidence provided in Table 16.2 demonstrates support for the hypothesis that higher judicial legitimacy leads to lower protests overall. Nonetheless, the total number of protests can still be further divided into violent and non-violent protests to test our hypothesis that high levels of judicial legitimacy correspond with fewer protests.

Violent and non-violent protests are different in that the level of dissatisfaction in the protestors in the former case reaches a point where violent action is considered and executed. Such action can be the outcome of conscious strategy or a response to governmental action, and it may even have psychological and sociopolitical causes at its roots. Nonetheless, these two kinds of protests are interesting for the discussion in this chapter as they provide an opportunity to test precisely how the impact of judicial legitimacy reduces the efficacy of violence. The suggestion is that judicial legitimacy should have an effect on both types of protest.

To examine these relationships, the total number of violent and non-violent protests in a country-year is calculated and two separate variables are created for each category.[34] These variables are subsequently used in zero-inflated negative binomial regressions whose estimates are reported in Table 16.3. Model 2a uses the number of violent protests as the dependent variable, whereas Model 2b uses non-violent protests as the dependent variable.

The results in Table 16.3 provide evidence for the hypothesis that higher levels of judicial legitimacy lead to fewer non-violent protests. It is worth noting that the beta coefficient for judicial legitimacy in Model 2a (violent protests) is positive and significant in the negative binomial part, but its substantive effect (shown in Panel (a) of Figure 16.2) cannot be statistically distinguished. This result is inconsistent with our expectation. One possible explanation

---

[33] David Clark & Patrick Regan, Mass Mobilization Data Project, Harvard Dataverse (2016). http://www.10.7910/DVN/HTTWYL.

[34] The number of violent and non-violent protests adds up to the total number of protests variable used in Table 16.2.

Table 16.3 *Predicted number of protests given judicial legitimacy (violent and non-violent protests)*

EQUATION	VARIABLES	Model 2a	Model 2b
		(Violent)	(Non-violent)
Count Model (Violent Protests)	$Protests_{t-1}$	0.038***	
		(0.007)	
	Judicial Legitimacy	–0.132	
		(0.090)	
	GDP/Capita (ln)	0.130	
		(0.111)	
	PolityIV Index	0.018*	
		(0.010)	
	Total Phone Lines (fixed & cellular)	4.87×10^{-9}***	
		(0.000)	
	Urban Population (% of total)	–0.017***	
		(0.004)	
	Child Mortality	–0.003	
		(0.003)	
	Constant	–0.250	
		(1.048)	
Logit Model	Judicial Legitimacy	0.304	0.146
		(0.230)	(0.390)
	$Protests_{t-1}$	–0.683***	–0.884***
		(0.154)	(0.229)
	Total Phone Lines (fixed & cellular)	-1.30×10^{-7}***	-1.93×10^{-7}***
		(0.000)	(0.000)
	GDP/Capita (ln)	0.907**	1.565**
		(0.358)	(0.640)
	PolityIV Index	–0.040	0.276***
		(0.027)	(0.056)
	Urban Population (% of total)	–0.039***	–0.008
		(0.010)	(0.012)
	Child Mortality	–0.012	0.032***
		(0.010)	(0.009)
	Constant	–4.622	–17.659***
		(3.348)	(5.827)
Count Model (Non-violent Protests)	$Protests_{t-1}$		0.066***
			(0.006)
	Judicial Legitimacy		–0.187**
			(0.074)
	GDP/Capita (ln)		0.178*
			(0.107)
	PolityIV Index		0.031***
			(0.007)
	Total Phone Lines (fixed & cellular)		4.55×10^{-9}***
			(0.000)
	Urban Population (% of total)		–0.011***

EQUATION	VARIABLES	Model 2a	Model 2b
		(Violent)	(Non-violent)
			(0.003)
	Child Mortality		–0.006**
			(0.002)
	Constant		–0.228
			(1.022)
ln(α)		0.265***	0.036
		(0.100)	(0.071)
	Observations	2,668	2,668
	Number of events (non-zero obs.)	956	1,742

Notes:
*** p<0.01, ** p<0.05, * p<0.1.
Robust standard errors in parentheses.

for this finding is that those who view violence as a reasonable means to seek redress of grievances do not view any governmental institution as legitimate. We know that these groups are also in the minority of minority groups and the general trust in courts experienced by some minority groups may not extend to fringe groups. In other words, even in a setting with high levels of judicial legitimacy, we may see violent protests because groups at the fringe cannot be satisfied through institutional safeguards.

On the other hand, the beta coefficient for judicial legitimacy in Model 2b (non-violent protests) is negative and significant in both the logit and the negative binomial part of the model. This result could point to a process whereby more judicial legitimacy cannot completely eradicate non-violent protests, i.e., cannot make a country fall into the certain zero group, but it can still reduce the likelihood of such protests nonetheless. The substantive effect of judicial legitimacy on non-violent protests is shown in Panel (b) of Figure 16.2. As can be seen, higher values of judicial legitimacy lead to a lower statistical likelihood of non-violent protests.

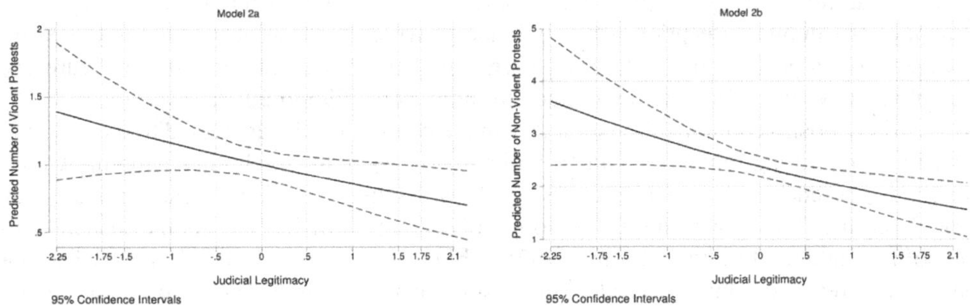

(a) (b)

Figure 16.2 Predicted number of protests given judicial legitimacy (violent and non-violent protests)

INDIA: AN ILLUSTRATION

The results from the empirical analysis support the hypothesis and suggest that as judicial legitimacy increases, protests decrease. This is the case because when citizens view the judiciary as a legitimate institution, it means they see it as an impartial adjudicator through which they can seek formal redress, in addition to trusting that the institution will constrain a repressive executive when necessary. In this section we illustrate how this relationship works by discussing the case of India.

India was established as an independent republic in August 1947 after decades of British colonial rule. It inherited its institutional structures from its colonial history. Besides a system of parliamentary democracy, the 1950 constitution of India also made the country a common law system, with a supreme court at the apex level having judicial review powers. The case of India is useful for our analysis for several reasons. First, India has had a relatively stable democratic government throughout its history with no incidence of military rule. This not only provides a stable baseline for comparison over time, but also helps to show how the mechanism through which citizens protest less in the presence of judicial legitimacy works exclusive of the procedural components regularly found in democracies.

India also has experience with small- and large-scale protest movements whereby citizens demand protection of their rights by expressing dissent. From the 2011 anti-graft protests of Anna Hazare to the recent farmers' protest movement, the Indian citizenry is no stranger to demanding its rights from those in power. The country's democratic setup allows for more freedom of expression than many other countries, but as the example of Western Europe and North American countries shows, the freedom to protest does not necessarily result in actual protests. Therefore, the presence of protests in India is also relevant for the purpose of this illustration. More importantly, however, India is the ideal case to be discussed as an example as despite its relatively stable democratic record – its PolityIV score never changes from 9 throughout the empirical sample – it has nonetheless had stark changes in its judicial legitimacy. This allows for a clear demonstration of the impact of judicial legitimacy on protests in a country, as the following discussion will highlight.

As the research design section noted, the period of analysis is from 1996 to 2017, owing to data availability. During this period, the Indian judiciary underwent changes in its judicial legitimacy. The public perception of the judiciary – which the rule of law variable measures – changed from a positive image to a negative one. This change can be seen in Figure 16.3, which plots the values of judicial legitimacy in India from 1996 to 2017.

The initially positive image of the judiciary in the country can be attributed to the post-1975 period in India, during which the Indian judiciary – especially the Indian Supreme Court – asserted its presence over policy matters. As Das discusses, Indian Prime Minister Indira Ghandi used the Indian Supreme Court to gain legitimacy for her temporary suspension of basic political and civil rights in India in 1975, a blemish which the Indian judiciary has since been trying to remove from its record.[35] As a result, the post-1975 period is noted for the dominance of the Indian judiciary in reviewing legislation and hearing petitions from the citizenry. To achieve this objective, the Indian Supreme Court started interpreting two sections of the

[35] Lalatendu Keshari Das, *Social Movements – Judicial Activism Nexus and Neoliberal Transformation in India: Revisiting Save Chilika Movement*, 67 Sociological Bulletin 84 (2018).

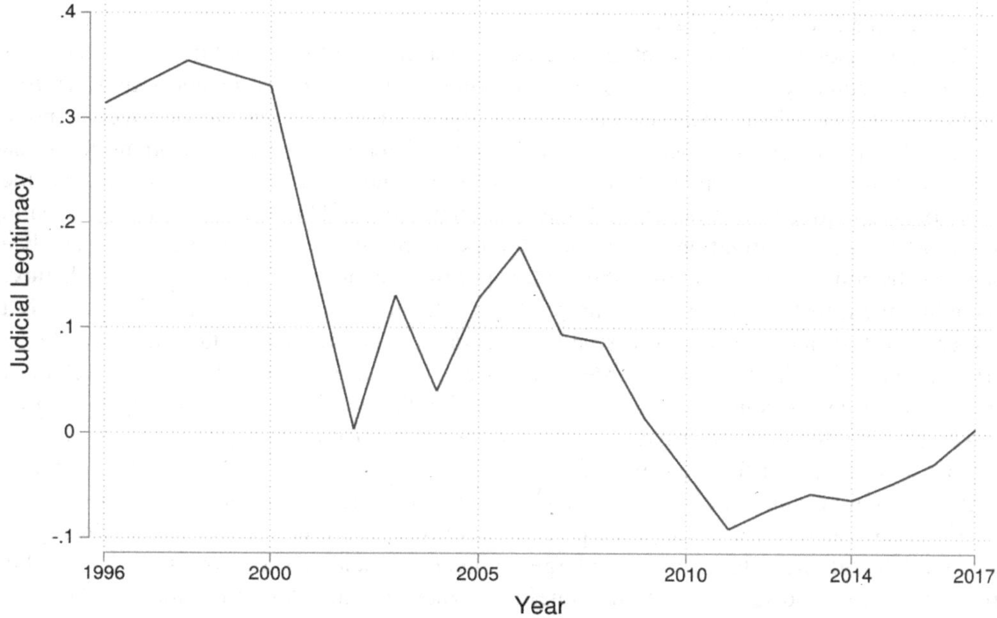

Figure 16.3 *Judicial legitimacy levels in India (1996–2017)*

Indian constitution – the fundamental rights (Articles 14–32) and the directive principles of state policy (36–51) – liberally. Moreover, it started entertaining petitions to add cases to its docket from the general public as well.[36]

During this period and leading up to the first few years of the twenty-first century, the Indian judiciary therefore enjoyed a positive perception among the public. Owing to several reasons discussed here, this perception did not last and eventually changed into a negative one – as shown by the negative score on the judicial legitimacy index. First, the judiciary in recent times has been politicized, due to politicians pressuring judicial institutions to get favorable outcomes. In addition, due to tensions between the executive and the judicial branches of government, administrative inaction has reigned supreme. This has meant that many positions for judges remain vacant, thus adding to the overall inefficiency of the judiciary.[37] According to a report by the Vidhi Centre for Legal Policy, New Delhi, of 8,086 rulings of the Delhi High Court between 2011 and 2015, over 90% experienced a delay of two years or more.[38] It of course did not help that India was undergoing rapid population and economic growth during the start of the new millennium as well, which only added to the aggravations of the newly rich

---

[36] P. N. Bhagwati & C. J. Das, *The Judiciary in India: A Hunger and Thirst for Justice*, 5 NUJS Law Review 171 (2012).

[37] Tanushree Singh & Akash Singh Thakur, *Administration of Justice: Judicial Delays in India*, 65 Indian Journal of Public Administration 885 (2019).

[38] Seetharam N. Khaitan & S. Chandrashekharan, Inefficiency and Judicial Delay: New Insights From the Delhi High Court (2017).

Indian middle class as they could not seek relief from the courts with regard to the protection of their civil and economic rights.

Another reason why the perception of judicial legitimacy in India started to wane is because the Indian judiciary started being seen as corrupt, siding with pro-business and pro-trade lobbies, and also lenient toward executive authority, especially in areas of controversial policy such as labor protections.[39] Moreover, the "pro-poor" reputation that the Indian courts had cultivated for themselves also saw a decline, as more and more cases started being decided in favor of the government or big multinational companies.[40] This fact is especially revealing since public interest litigation (PIL) – a hallmark of the post-1975 Indian courts – has been replaced by concerns for sustaining the modern political economy of the country.[41] Such moves have had the direct impact of reducing public confidence in the judiciary, which is likely to increase protests and dissent expression in the country. The infamous 2000 *Narmada Bachao Andolan* case, in which the court ordered mass evictions of a community for the creation of a dam, serves as an example of this phenomenon.[42] Other similar cases – such as the Chilika Lake case, in which the court gave permission for prawn fishing in a habitat already deteriorated due to industrial fishing – provide evidence of the Indian courts deferring to executive authority in important policy matters, such as climate change and protection of biodiversity.[43]

A result of such degradation in the perception of the Indian judiciary was the growing dissatisfaction with the status quo among large segments of society. The citizens stuck in cyclical poverty already had few avenues for relief, but when the interests of the middle class were threatened due to corrupt politicians and judges, a large-scale protest movement focused on anti-graft and accountability demands started in 2011 under the banner of Anna Hazare. This *India Against Corruption* movement was successful in shoring up domestic support for more transparency as well as an independent judiciary but little has changed since.[44] Additionally, in high-profile cases of rape and sexual assault, the Indian courts have been hesitant in sentenc-

---

[39] Lalatendu Keshari Das, *Social Movements – Judicial Activism Nexus and Neoliberal Transformation in India: Revisiting Save Chilika Movement*, 67 Sociological Bulletin 84 (2018).

[40] Rehan Abeyratne, *Rethinking Judicial Independence in India and Sri Lanka*, 10 Asian Journal of Comparative Law 99 (2015); Lalatendu Keshari Das, *Social Movements – Judicial Activism Nexus and Neoliberal Transformation in India: Revisiting Save Chilika Movement*, 67 Sociological Bulletin 84 (2018).

[41] Modhurima Dasgupta, *Public Interest Litigation for Labour: How the Indian Supreme Court Protects the Rights of India's Most Disadvantaged Workers*, 16 Contemporary South Asia 159 (2008); Payel Rai Chowdhury, *Judicial Activism and Human Rights in India: A Critical Appraisal*, 15 The International Journal of Human Rights 1055 (2010); Anashri Pillay, *Revisiting the Indian Experience of Economic and Social Rights Adjudication: The Need for a Principled Approach to Judicial Activism and Restraint*, International and Comparative Law Quarterly (2014); Lalatendu Keshari Das, *Social Movements – Judicial Activism Nexus and Neoliberal Transformation in India: Revisiting Save Chilika Movement*, 67 Sociological Bulletin 84 (2018).

[42] Anashri Pillay, *Revisiting the Indian Experience of Economic and Social Rights Adjudication: The Need for a Principled Approach to Judicial Activism and Restraint*, International and Comparative Law Quarterly (2014).

[43] Shalini Iyengar et al., *Selectively Assertive: Interventions of India's Supreme Court to Enforce Environmental Laws*, 11 Sustainability 7234 (2019).

[44] Aalok Khandekar & Deepa S. Reddy, *An Indian Summer: Corruption, Class, and the Lokpal Protests*, 15 Journal of Consumer Culture 221 (2015).

ing, which has only furthered their negative perception.[45] Moreover, a 2006 investigation into a homicide case involving a prominent Indian politician's son revealed that the case had been wrongly decided in favor of the perpetrator, resulting in a media campaign which stirred up anger against the Indian courts.[46]

In light of this decline in perceptions of judicial legitimacy in India, the theory suggested in this chapter would predict a higher incidence of protests in the country. As judicial legitimacy has a strong impact on giving the public confidence in institutional protection for their rights, a decline in this characteristic can reasonably be expected to result in more protests and expressions of dissent. Figure 16.3 earlier plotted the decline in perceptions of judicial legitimacy in India from 1996–2017, and Figure 16.4 superimposes the number of protests during the same time period in the country, as reported in the Mass Mobilization dataset.[47]

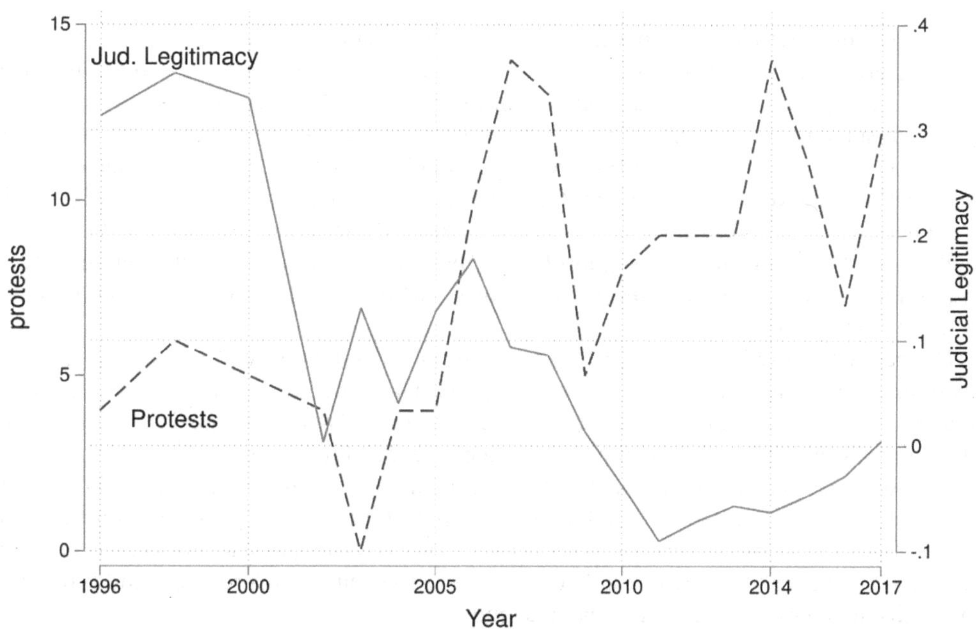

Figure 16.4 Judicial legitimacy and protests in India (1996–2017)

As can be seen, the two variables largely track each other in the opposite, expected direction. During the late 1990s, the perceptions of judicial legitimacy were high; and as can be seen

[45] Meena Menon, A Deep Social Bias Marks the Judiciary's Response to Rape in India, Economic Political Weekly (2020). link.gale.com/apps/doc/A611660129/AONE?u=bingul&sid=AONE&xid=45ba2133.

[46] Srirupa Roy, 2015. *Angry Citizens: Civic Anger and the Politics of Curative Democracy in India*, 23 Global Studies in Culture and Power 362 (2015).

[47] David Clark & Patrick Regan, Mass Mobilization Data Project, Harvard Dataverse (2016). http://www.10.7910/DVN/HTTWYL.

from Figure 16.4, this result corresponds neatly with the central assertion of this chapter. The exact opposite trend can also be seen during 2002–2004, and then more clearly from the year 2006 onwards. During this phase, perceptions about judicial legitimacy were at their lowest during the time period under study, and the number of protests was at its highest. This is precisely the relation that this chapter has suggested between these two variables, as higher confidence in judicial legitimacy is bound to give citizens additional avenues – besides legislation – to get their demands met. In the absence of such avenues, citizens can be reasonably expected to express dissent through protests even in established democracies such as India, as the safeguards provided by the perception of an impartial judiciary are absent in this case.

CONCLUSION

Managing contention is an important factor in regime stability. We know minority groups in a society cannot always turn to their elected officials to protect their interests. In this chapter we argued that a judiciary that the citizenry view as an impartial institution serves as a mechanism to reduce protests. This relationship exists because the perception of an impartial institution gives the citizenry confidence in their ability to seek redress of grievances through adjudication, in addition to giving confidence that the judiciary will check repressive leaders when necessary. As a result, we observe fewer protests when there are high levels of judicial legitimacy. We found empirical support for our hypothesis, and we elaborated on this relationship in the case of violent and non-violent protests while providing an illustration through an in-depth discussion of India.

This research therefore highlights the important role that judicial legitimacy plays in managing political contention. The next step is to identify what other informal means to seek redress of grievances judicial legitimacy impacts (e.g., terrorism). This is an especially important line of inquiry given that leaders amending the independence of the judiciary to secure more executive and legislative power is a fairly common practice (e.g., the "muzzle law" in Poland in 2020 and Mexico's interest in extending the term limit for the sitting Supreme Court President in 2021). Such actions can lead to mistrust in the judiciary, and, as a result, increased societal unrest. This chapter has provided a theoretical basis to examine this relation, and future work can utilize this for other, related research agendas.

17. The theoretical and empirical relationship between legal pluralism and economic development

Valenta Kabo[1]

INTRODUCTION

Law influences economic development. This finding has reverberated in law and economic development literature for decades, and among development organizations, resulted in a clarion call for policies aimed at using the law to achieve economic development. In response, billions of dollars have been spent. For example, over $5.4 billion has been spent since 1996 on judicial reform efforts alone.[2] Despite this exuberance and expenditure, a wistfully familiar cry can also be heard in the literature. Similar to pronouncements about the 1960s law and development movement,[3] some scholars are concerned that the efforts to use law as a tool for development are not producing the desired results.[4]

The findings of some of the current discourse on empirical law and development are based upon singular conceptions of the law that overlook an important empirical reality. Many countries, particularly those that are the targets of development programs, have legal pluralism. Although theoretically, some of the underlying assumptions of the law and development literature are contradictory to the underlying claims of the legal pluralism literature, these two literatures can complement each other and further our understanding of how law impacts development. In this chapter, I present the results of a study of the compatibility of legal pluralism with some development outcomes.

This chapter proceeds as follows. I will provide an overview of the law and development literature, focusing on the rule of law and institutions/governance, as well as an overview of legal pluralism. These overviews are not intended to be comprehensive as such an undertaking is beyond the scope of this chapter. Rather, the purpose of these overviews is to provide a brief conceptual background that will help us understand how pluralism and development are

---

1 I would like to thank Felix Kabo for his thoughtful comments and feedback. All errors made are mine.

2 Matthieu Chemin, *Judicial Efficiency and Firm Productivity: Evidence from a World Database of Judicial Reforms*, 102 Rev. of Econ. and Stat. 1, 49, 49–64 (2020); *Cf* Michael J. Trebilcock & Ronald J. Daniels, Rule of Law Reform and Development: Charting the Fragile Path of Progress, 2 (2009) (noting that since 1990, the World Bank has spent $2.9 billion on rule of law reform.

3 David M. Trubek & Marc Galanter, *Scholars in Self-Estrangement: Some Reflections on the Crisis in Law and Development Studies in the United States*, 1974 Wis. L. Rev. 1062 (1974).

4 Alvaro Santos, *The World Bank's Uses of the "Rule of Law" Promise in Economic Development, in* The New Law and Economic Development: a Critical Appraisal, 253, 254 (David Trubek & Alvaro Santos eds., 2006). See also Kevin E. Davis & Mariana Mota Prado, *Law, Regulation, and Development in* International Development: Ideas, Experience, and Prospects (Bruce Currie-Alder, Ravi Kanbur, David M. Malone & Rohinton Medhora, eds., 2014), 204.

related. This relationship is explored further in the ensuing section, which discusses regression models of the association between legal pluralism and foreign direct investment (FDI). The final section provides some concluding thoughts.

LITERATURE OVERVIEW

Rule of Law

There are two primary ways by which laws are thought to influence development: through the rule of law, and through governance and institutions.[5] The first vehicle, the rule of law, is a concept with universal endorsement[6] and roots in ancient Greek history.[7] Despite this, conceptual clarity remains elusive, and varied definitions of the rule of law abound. While the lack of precision has enhanced the popularity of the term,[8] the rule of law as used in both popular parlance and academic circles can cynically be described as a term whose extension has left it without intension.[9]

Rule of law is sometimes conflated with or used as a synonym for governance measures, including protection of property rights or contract enforcement. However, theoretically, the rule of law is distinct from those concepts[10] and can be defined along both a formal and substantive dimension,[11] as well as along a continuum of the heuristic concepts of thin and thick.[12] Substantive or "thick" definitions of the rule of law are imbued with notions of the rights believed to be concomitant with liberal democracies. Formal, procedural, or "thin" definitions of the rule of law focus on aspects of procedure, and the law's role in coordinating behavior.

---

5 There is also a large literature on legal origins. However, because this literature seeks to trace differences in economic outcomes to legal colonial inheritance or legal families, it has less obvious practical policy implications.

6 *See* Thomas Carothers, *Rule of Law Temptations*, 33 THE FLETCHER F. WORLD AFFS. 1, 49, (2009) (arguing that although "rule of law" has wide consensus, consensus does not always translate into action, and consensus does not always imply agreement about the concept); *see also* Martin Krygier, *The Rule of Law: Pasts, Presents, and Two Possible Futures*, ANN. REV. LAW & SOC. SCI., 200 (2016) (arguing that although the rule of law is cliché and scholars may need to approach it differently, it does engage with some fundamental concepts).

7 Kenneth W. Dam, THE LAW-GROWTH NEXUS: THE RULE OF LAW AND ECONOMIC DEVELOPMENT 13 (2007) (quoting from Plato); *cf* Alvaro Santos, THE WORLD BANK'S USE OF THE "RULE OF LAW" PROMISE IN ECONOMIC DEVELOPMENT 257 (David M. Trubek & Alvaro Santos eds., 2006) (discussing Aristotle).

8 Santos, *supra* note 7 at 257 (discussing the differential uses of the term by the World Bank as the Bank shifted foci); *cf* Carothers, *supra* note 6 (discussing the openness of the term to different ideological and professional interpretations).

9 Trebilcock & Daniels, *supra* note 1 at 12–14.

10 Joseph Raz, *The Rule of Law and Its Virtue*, *in* THE AUTHORITY OF THE LAW: ESSAYS ON LAW AND MORALITY (1979).

11 *See* Brian Z. Tamanaha, *A Concise Guide to the Rule of Law* (St. John's Legal Studies Research Paper, No. 07-0082, 2007).

12 Trebilcock and Daniels, *supra* note 1 at 16–28 (summarizing the literature on "thick" and "thin" definitions, and ultimately arguing for a procedural definition).

At a basic level, "thin" rule of law is the belief that the law applies to all and can usefully be thought of as rule *by* law.[13]

"Thin" rule of law influences economic development primarily by coordinating relationships among economic actors. This can occur in three ways. First, theoretically, the rule of law governs the relationship between different state bodies.[14] For example, relations between executive and judiciary, and importantly, the concept of judicial independence are influenced by the rule of law. Second, the rule of law governs relationships between non-state economic actors within society.[15] Third, the rule of law also governs relationships between those economic actors and the state. Consequently, at a minimum, "thin" versions of the rule of law provide stable expectations for economic actors.

The increase in various types of rights is associated with increasingly "thick" versions of the law and is also thought to encourage economic activities associated with development. For example, in an analysis of human rights, Lorenz Blume and Stefan Voight trace different conceptions of human rights and find that no category of human rights has a negative impact on economic growth.[16] Further, they find that basic human rights, defined as the absence of torture, extrajudicial killings, and disappearances, are related to investment. Some civil and social rights, such as political participation, workers' rights and the absence of censorship, discrimination against women, and restrictions on travel, are related to productivity. These rights associated with "thick" versions of the rule of law are conceptually indistinguishable from the related concept of good governance.

Governance and Institutions

The second vehicle through which law impacts development is governance and institutions. Although the two terms seem now to be used interchangeably, the scholarly beginnings of these ideas are distinct. Veerle van Doeveren summarizes the way the concept of governance, primarily used to mean rules pertaining to governing, spread to multiple disciplines, each with its own definitional perspective and methodology. It began in the 1980s with the concept of "bringing the state back in." This use of the term focused on the process of political decision-making, and like the term "rule of law," became increasingly expansive and empty of agreed-upon meaning. The term "good governance" did not appear until 1989, in a report on sustainable development in sub-Saharan Africa. The use of this term emphasized decision-making guided toward normative ends of efficiency and legitimacy.[17]

Related to the increase in attention on the state, in the 1990s, the work of new institutional economics (NIE) helped to establish a quantitative, empirical connection between government practices and economic outcomes. The work of NIE scholars has its origins in R.H. Coase's *The Problem of Social Cost*, published in 1960.[18] This work was further advanced by Douglas North's conception of the importance of property rights for efficient economic

---

[13] Carothers, *supra* note 6, at 53.

[14] Dam, *supra* note 7 at 15.

[15] *Id.*

[16] Lorenz Blume & Stefan Voigt, *The Economic Effects of Human Rights*, 60 KYKLOS (2007).

[17] Veerle van Doeveren, *Rethinking Good Governance*, 13 PUB. INTEGRITY (2011).

[18] R. H. Coase, *The Problem of Social Cost*, 3 J. OF LAW & ECON. (1960).

organization,[19] and continued with the new growth economics, which began a quantitative literature that further stressed the importance of property rights and contract rights for economic growth.[20] These early works were foundational for a vast and expansive literature that examines the effects of institutions of economic growth.

The World Bank was instrumental in translating this literature into applied policy, and in intertwining governance and institutions. Governance came to be defined as the institutions through which the government exercises authority.[21] Scholars developed indicators that would eventually become the World Governance Indicators (WGIs). The WGIs are/were used by the World Bank and other scholars to measure the quality of governance and institutions. These measures included aggregate measures intended to capture how people in power are selected ("Voice and Accountability" and "Political Instability and Violence"), the capacity of a country to implement policies ("Government Effectiveness and Regulatory Burden") and the respect for law in a country ("Rule of Law" and "Graft").[22] Helped by the availability of these and other indicators, NIE scholarship burgeoned.

Yet, in part because these measures are so broad, "good governance" is not used clearly or consistently. For example, after surveying some common evaluators of good governance, Matt Andrews compiles their common elements, and suggests that if all the components in various measures of governance were used, effective (good) governance might mean the following:

> An effective government is small and limited in its engagement, formalized in mission and process. High-quality personnel devise and implement needed programs and deliver efficient and effective services via participatory processes and disciplined, efficient financial management. Responsiveness to the citizenry's changing needs is high and effected through transparent, decentralized and politically neutral structures; consistently, even during political instability, without impeding (indeed supporting) the private sector.[23]

This represents an obviously impossible standard and highlights the expansiveness of the construct.

Regardless of its conceptual ambiguity, good governance is believed to effect economic development by helping countries to achieve the desired economic outcomes. Simply put, in the current parlance, "[p]oor countries are poor because they have bad governance and the countries that grow or are rich are those that improved their governance."[24] Specifically, the causal mechanism connecting law, governance and economic activity revolves around the structure of incentives. Incentives can be designed to promote behavior which leads to

---

19 Douglas C. North & Robert Paul Thomas, The Rise of the Western World: A New Economic History 1973; Douglas C. North, Institutions, Institutional Change and Economic Performance 1990.

20 *See e.g.*, Robert J. Barrow, *Democracy and Growth*, 1 Journal of Economic Growth, (1996); Christopher Clague, et al., *Property and Contract Rights in Autocracies and Democracies*, 1 J. Econ. Growth (1996); Robert E. Hall & Charles I. Jones, *Why Do Some Countries Produce So Much More Output Per Worker than Others?*, 114 Q. J. Econ. (1999).

21 Daniel Kaufmann, et al., *Governance Matters*, World Bank Policy Research Working Paper (1999).

22 *Id.*

23 Matt Andrews, *The Good Governance Agenda: Beyond Indicators without Theory*, 36 Oxford Dev. Stud. (2008) at 382

24 Jean-Marie Baland, et al., *Governance and Development*, 5 Handbook of Development Economics (2010) at 4958.

economic development. Laws are tools that can be used to structure incentives and activity to promote these goals. It follows that good governance involves using laws to create incentives that lead to investment, productivity, savings, and innovation.[25] In the literature, there are several claims about the relationship between laws and economic development.

Economic actors seek predictability, and assurances that money, capital, or labor put toward an investment will not be arbitrarily lost. Consequently, laws that provide for a basic level of security, and minimize crime and violence, enable actors to engage in economic activity freely. Laws that provide for security of contract enable actors to trade over distance and time in the absence of shared norms.[26] Laws that protect private property create incentives for investments in the property by allowing individuals to reap the benefits of their own efforts.[27] However, laws that govern economic actions among society are not sufficient. Government institutions must be bound by law as well, and the laws that bind them can also play a role in the creation of economic activity. Thus, in addition to encouraging the desired economic activity, laws should adequately constrain the government to guard against expropriation, promote judicial independence,[28] and minimize or eliminate corruption.

Although scholars express some concerns, particularly about causal mechanisms[29] and measurement of key concepts,[30] the majority of quantitative studies find a connection between law, the concept of governance and economic development,[31] as well as broader notions of democracy and growth, or development.[32]

Singularity as a Key Assumption in Law and Economic Development

The assumption underlying many of these models is "singularity." These models rely on a singular system of rules upon which investors can rely, or a singular law to which the state is held accountable. Returning to the discussion on the rule of law, Jørgen Møller and Svend-Erik Skaaning articulated a minimalist definition of the rule of law as a society in which power

---

25 *Id* at 4608, Baland et al. argue that understanding the political economy of a country is necessary to successful change of governance institutions.

26 North, *supra* note 19.

27 HERNANDO DE SOTO, THE MYSTERY OF CAPITAL: WHY CAPITALISM TRIUMPHS IN THE WEST AND FAILS EVERYWHERE ELSE, 2000.

28 Stefan Voigt & Jerg Gutmann, *Turning cheap talk into economic growth: On the relationship between property rights and judicial independence*, 41 J. COMPAR. ECON. (2013).

29 *See e.g.*, Ha-Joon Chang, *Institutions and Economic Development: Theory, Policy and History*, 7 J. INST. ECON. (2011).

30 *See e.g.*, Kevin Davis, *What Can the Rule of Law Variable Tell Us About Rule of Law Reforms*, 26 MICH. J. INT'L. L. (2004); Trebilcock & Daniels, *supra* note 1 at 337; Rohini Pande & Christopher Udry, *Institutions and Development: A View from Below*, *in* ADVANCES IN ECONOMIC AND ECONOMETRICS: THEORY AND APPLICATIONS, NINTH WORLD CONGRESS, 2006; Bo Rothstein & Jan Teorell, *What Is Quality of Government? A Theory of Impartial Government Institutions*, 21 GOVERNANCE (2008); Mila Versteeg & Tom Ginsburg, *Measuring the Rule of Law: A Comparison of Indicators*, 42 L. & SOC. INQUIRY (2017).

31 *See e.g.*, Daron Acemoglu, et al., *Institutions as a Fundamental Cause of Long-Run Growth*, *in* HANDBOOK OF ECONOMIC GROWTH (Philippe Aghion & Steven N. Durlauf eds., 2005); Stephan Haggard, et al., *The Rule of Law and Economic Development*, 11 ANN. REV. POL. SCI. (2008); Pandry and Udry, *supra* note 30.

32 Marco Colagrossi, et al., *Does democracy cause growth? A meta-analysis (of 2000 regressions)*, 61 EUR. J. POL. ECON. (2020).

is exercised by means of positive law.[33] Their second definition of the rule of law, formal legality, refers to laws that are "general, public, prospective, certain, and consistently applied." Conceptually, these definitions would seem to suggest *one* type of law, applying to everyone.

Similarly, other means through which law is theorized to impact development rely on singular conceptions of law. Contract and property rights enforcement, within the broad concepts of good governance and anti-corruption, seem to revolve around a state's enforcement of its own laws. Yet tables found on *Juriglobe* suggest that over 45% of countries could be classified as legally pluralist.[34] Given this, the lack of conception as to how legal pluralism affects economic outcomes obfuscates the findings of the literature for a significant number of countries of the world, many of which are the targets that rely on this literature to improve economic outcomes.

LEGAL PLURALISM

The Concept of Legal Pluralism

Although the definition of legal pluralism is contested,[35] legal pluralism is roughly defined as a single geographic context with multiple systems of law.[36] John Griffiths distinguishes between two types of pluralism. The first is "weak" legal pluralism, which is a state recognition or allowance of different types of law for subsets of the population. The second is "strong" legal pluralism, which is a type of legal pluralism decentered from the state. Multiple legal and normative orders exist in the same space, and their validity and authority are independent of state recognition.[37] Although this distinction is one of the more influential, it has been criticized as not able to neatly fit onto observed realties.

---

33 JØRGEN MØLLER & SVEND-ERIK SKAANING, THE RULE OF LAW, DEFINITIONS, MEASURES, PATTERNS AND CAUSES (2014).

34 University of Ottawa Faculty of Law, *Legal Systems Classification* University of Ottawa, *available at* http://www.juriglobe.ca/eng/.

35 BRIAN Z. TAMANAHA, *LEGAL PLURALISM EXPLAINED : HISTORY, THEORY, CONSEQUENCES* 3 (2021).

36 John Griffiths, *What is Legal Pluralism?*, 18 J. LEGAL PLURALISM & UNOFFICIAL L. (1986); Margaret Davies, *Legal pluralism*, *in* THE OXFORD HANDBOOK OF EMPIRICAL LEGAL RESEARCH (Peter Cane & Herbert M. Kritzer eds., 2010).

37 Griffiths, *supra* note 36. This is not the only conception for legal pluralism. Other scholars have proposed other bases for understanding legal pluralism. For example, William Twining outlines three types of legal pluralism. "Weak" legal pluralism, as described by Griffiths, distinguishes between state legal pluralism (or weak legal pluralism), legal polycentricity (or the use multiple legal sources within the state's system of law), and semi-autonomous legal orders (or multiple sets of legal norms within the same geographical and temporal space). William Twining, *Normative and Legal Pluralism: A Global Perspective*, 20 DUKE J. COMPAR.& INT'L L. 473 (2010). For clarity, many authors have proposed different categorizations of legal pluralism. *See e.g.*, Geoffrey Swenson, *Legal Pluralism in Theory and Practice*, 20 INT'L STUDIES REV. (2018), proposing different legal pluralism archetypes, depending upon the degree of state engagement with the non-state legal system; Gordon R. Woodman, *The Development "Problem" of Legal Pluralism: An Analysis and Steps toward Solutions*, *in* LEGAL PLURALISM AND DEVELOPMENT: SCHOLARS AND PRACTITIONERS IN DIALOGUE (Brian Z. Tamanaha, et al. eds., 2012) offering a descriptive categorization of legal pluralism, and describing the different ways that groups can experience normative or legal pluralism, as a function of ethnicity, economic activity, voluntary opt-in, imposition, or observance of state law; John Griffiths, *Legal Pluralism*, *in* INTERNATIONAL

Legal pluralism as a theory began with descriptive and anthropological accounts in the early 20th century. Some of the earliest studies emerged from colonial interests and the concomitant changes in the societies that these interests commandeered.[38] In their account of the trajectory of the discipline of legal pluralism, Keebet von Benda-Beckmann and Bertram Turner describe its movement away from colonial interests, to dispute processes and social functions of non-state law, and finally to understanding state interactions with normative orders.[39] Thus, while in governance and development literature there was a greater emphasis on the state over time, in legal pluralism studies there was a shift away from state-centrism.

Scholars of legal pluralism propose a paradigm shift where legal pluralism is a fact, and "legal centralism is a myth, an ideal, a claim, an illusion."[40] The fact of legal pluralism is embedded within history. For example, legal pluralism was so quotidian in the early Medieval period that courts would begin their proceedings with the question "*Quale lege vivis* (What is your law)"?[41] It was not until the nation-state emerged that the idea of state-centric law became preeminent.[42] Throughout colonialism, this legal centrism was exported from Europe to locales around the globe.[43] Artificial boundaries in newly claimed territories amalgamated formerly disparate groups and fostered legal polycentricity. Given this history, many legal pluralist scholars are quick to observe that it is state-centric law, not legal pluralism, that is an anomaly.

THEORETICAL CHALLENGES BETWEEN LEGAL PLURALISM AND LAW AS A TOOL FOR ECONOMIC DEVELOPMENT

There are several ways in which the ideas and challenges of legal pluralism described above can impact the assumptions of using law as a tool for development. First, empirically, one of the problems inherent within the concept of legal pluralism is how one defines law. Because legal pluralism explicitly rejects positivism and the notion that law is defined by the state, legal pluralist scholars must confront the normative quagmire of distinguishing law from other social norms. As one earlier work queried, "Where do we stop speaking of law and find ourselves simply describing social life?"[44] Brian Tamanaha states that after decades in pursuit of this question, there is as yet no answer. In his words, "Legal pluralism is a conceptual mess."[45] For those who seek to use law as a tool for development, this question of "What is law?" absent

---

Encyclopedia of the Social & Behavioral Sciences (Neil J. Smelser & Paul B. Baltes eds., 2001); Keebet von Benda-Beckmann & Bertram Turner, *Legal pluralism, social theory, and the state*, 50 J. Legal Pluralism & Unofficial L. (2018) distinguishing between "Juridical legal pluralism" and "Empirical legal pluralism". Juridical legal pluralism is defined as a situation in which a legal system provides different types of rules to different groups. Empirical legal pluralism is a circumstance in which an individual has different and sometimes conflicting expectations for behavior.

[38] Griffiths, *supra* note 37.

[39] von Benda-Beckmann & Turner, *supra* note 37.

[40] Griffiths, *supra* note 37 at 4.

[41] Brian Z. Tamanaha, *supra* note 35 at 24.

[42] von Benda-Beckmann & Turner, *supra* note 37.

[43] Griffiths, *supra* note 37.

[44] Sally Engle Merry, *Legal Pluralism*, 22 L. & Soc. Rev. (1988) at 878.

[45] Tamanaha, *supra*, note 35 at 3.

the state becomes relevant when considering the extent to which a state can use the law to influence economic behavior.

Second, some of the logical conclusions deriving from the idea of the rule of law may be at odds with legal pluralism. Considering the thicker definitions of the rule of law, legal pluralism may be challenging for development given the variety of normative practices that different societies adhere to, and their potential conflict with the standard conceptions of rights that are concomitant with "thick" rule of law. Yet even the thinner conceptions may be at odds with the reality of legal pluralism. At a minimum, in a legal pluralist society, the rule of law entails clarification about which law to adhere to for actors representing the state, who may be themselves governed by multiple norms, as well as for individuals that are governed by the state. Consequently, in legal pluralist society, rule of law entails an agreement about a normative order of law, or at a minimum, a clear agreement about an order of which rules will govern what person in which situation. Consequently, pluralism becomes problematic for the rule of law when "meta-rules" are weak or non-existent.[46]

Yet additionally, following Joseph Raz's conception, if a rule of law means that all are ruled by the law, then several conclusions are warranted: (1) law must be generally applicable to all, (2) it must be known by all (or made public), (3) it must have a clarity that enables people to understand and follow the law, (4) it must not be contradictory, and (5) it must have stability.[47] Legal pluralist countries, particularly if they contain elements of customary law, do not always meet these conditions.

For example, legal pluralism implies that some laws are not generally applicable to all. Some laws apply only to some groups. In legal pluralist societies, all laws are not made public. For example, customary law is thought of as an orally transmitted law. It is a law that is known by participation in a community and not typically accessible by means of a written work.[48] If laws are not made public or accessible to all, then laws may indeed have an internal clarity to their adherents, but not an external clarity that would enable those outside of the tradition to fully understand them.

Legal pluralism may also result in contradictory laws. Groups within the same geographical location may have dictates which conflict with each other. Further, contradictions between state law and non-state law may be particularly problematic. For example, Muna Ndulo notes the conflict between customary traditions and women's rights expressed through state law.[49] Thus, even thin versions of the rule of law may conflict with the reality of legal pluralism. This has significant implications for the promotion of the rule of law as a tool for economic development.

Beyond the rule of law, a third theoretical challenge is that many scholars in the field of legal pluralism operate within a normative framework of advocacy for the fact of legal pluralism, for the acceptance of legal pluralism as a valid form of law, and for the dissolution of state-centric approaches to law. For example, in his seminal article on legal pluralism,

---

[46] Caroline Sage & Michael Woolcock, *Introduction: Legal Pluralism and Development Policy: Scholars and Practitioners in Dialogue*, *in* LEGAL PLURALISM AND DEVELOPMENT: SCHOLARS AND PRACTITIONERS IN DIALOGUE 9 (Brian Z. Tamanaha, et al. eds., 2012).

[47] Raz, *supra* note 10; Santos, *supra* note 8 at 260.

[48] H. PATRICK GLENN, LEGAL TRADITIONS OF THE WORLD: SUSTAINABLE DIVERSITY IN LAW 64–68 (2010).

[49] Muna Ndulo, *African Customary Law, Customs, and Women's Rights*, 18 IND. J. GLOB. LEGAL STUDIES (2011) (arguing for activism and an increased role of the courts in resolving these conflicts).

Griffiths suggests that legal centrism – the idea that law is the sole possession of the state, and is the same for all people – is a normative ideology. One of the goals of some forms of legal pluralism is to challenge this ideology.[50] However, to the extent that this perspective continues, there is an inherent tension between legal pluralism and development.

Development is a necessarily state-centric activity,[51] if only because of the necessity of coordinating activities related to development. States organize resources for the purpose of state-directed goals. It is the state that assumes the goal of development, or movement toward a specific economic outcome. It is the state that organizes its resources around these goals, and it is the state that puts its coercive power toward directives aimed at the manifestation of those goals.[52] This state-centric view does not consider extra-state institutions which may in fact compete with or inhibit this goal.[53]

PRACTICAL CHALLENGES OF LEGAL PLURALISM AND ECONOMIC DEVELOPMENT

In addition to the theoretical challenges that legal pluralism presents to law and development, there are several practical challenges. These challenges not only impact the assumptions of using law as a tool for development, but they are also potentially problematic for policy prescriptions and quantitative empirical analysis.

First, legal pluralism as a fact can conflict with notions of private property. For example, Keebet von Benda-Beckman and Bertram Turner note that one conflict between law and development and pluralism is the notion of property.[54] The promotion of using law as a tool for development inevitably entails certain conceptions of property rights. As noted above, in the governance and institutions literature, property rights and their protection are primary vehicles through which institutions are said to affect development. Property is to be privatized and made marketable, thus providing incentives for investment. Contrarily, in some legal

---

50 Griffiths, *supra* note 37; *cf* Twining, *supra* note 37 at 498–511 (noting that the initial vehemence of legal pluralist scholars was a reaction to a norm that non-state traditions did not merit the assignation "law", suggesting further that legal pluralism is not necessarily antithetical to state-law); von Benda-Beckmann & Turner, supra note 37 at 262 (also noting that the Griffiths article was not a "value judgment" but meant to demonstrate the dominance of state-centrism).

51 *Cf* Woodman, *supra* note 37 at 129 (referencing Twining, and noting that although it is difficult for development policy to avoid state-centrism, this does not necessarily imply that there must be a stronger form of state-centrism).

52 However, this is not to negate the existence of legal pluralism. Legal pluralism, roughly defined, exists regardless of state goals. Further, the fundamental goals of economic development are built upon behavioral change, at the individual level, which when amassed, will have consequences at the national level. For example, a country may have a goal of increasing the rule of law. In this case, individual judges, or administrators or government officials, must be adhering to the law. The collective amalgamation of these individual changes leads to the establishment of new norms which comport with ideas of the rule of law. The difficulty presented by legal pluralism is that individuals may in fact adhere to different "legal" norms, or perhaps the same individual may be governed by multiple, and sometimes conflicting norms. In such cases, the question becomes whether, and to what extent, the state-sponsored legal norms will outweigh or overrule potentially conflicting legal norms.

53 von Benda-Beckman & Turner, *supra* note 37 at 261 (discussing how the interaction of state and non-state legal orders can impact the application of state law).

54 *Id.*

pluralist societies, property, and particularly land, is subject to communal rights. For example, Sandra Joireman describes the existence of communal property rights in sub-Saharan Africa, the creation of customary law under colonialism, and how the rights under such systems vary.[55]

Second, legal pluralism also influences governance notions of a well-functioning judiciary. In governance and institutions parlance, a well-functioning judiciary can serve as a guarantor of protection against expropriation, and can help to protect property rights and enforce contracts. Yet Brian Tamanaha, citing other sources, notes that in some locales, customary law can include up to 90% of a local population.[56] Given that dispute resolution is a significant component of customary traditions, this suggests that in some places, most disputes are resolved outside of state-judicial institutions. Additionally, even when disputes are resolved by a state judiciary, it is sometimes unclear what customary norm should apply, and in some cases, judges are left with little guidance.[57] From the perspective of using law as a tool for development, the existence of competing or overlapping jurisdictions may provide for uncertainty.

Third, law is dynamic. This applies to all law, even state-centric law. However, it is particularly the case with many forms of customary or chthonic traditions that comprise many legal-pluralistic states.[58] Yet law is dynamic not just in terms of its internal meaning and practices. The law is also dynamic regarding its bailiwick. Theoretically, individuals may opt in and out of these laws at various times or may follow a state law in one instance and follow an alternative law in another. Consequently, analyzing these laws means engaging with a fluid construct, which can make it both difficult to understand and difficult to operationalize in an empirical analysis. Further, given the multiplicity of legal traditions and their dynamism, analyzing such traditions on any empirical scale results in necessary but unfortunate generalizations.

Related to the dynamic nature of many non-state legal traditions, customary law is not a closed system. Legal pluralist scholars have noted the interaction of state law with customary law induces changes in the customary traditions.[59] Further, economic development and some of the programs aimed at achieving it can intensify legal pluralism.[60] For example, Marc Galanter describes examples of the threat of using formal courts being used to reinforce indigenous norms.[61] Consequently, the standardized practices aimed at increasing predictability can have the opposite effect. For those investigating development outcomes, it is possible that the presence of programs aimed to increase investment may have long-term consequences which deter them.

The above discussion demonstrates that it is not just significant that legal pluralism exists, but to better understand how pluralism impacts development, it is necessary to understand *how* it exists in a particular context. How does pluralistic law influence economic development?

---

55 Sandra F. Joireman, *Entrapment or Freedom*, *in* THE FUTURE OF AFRICAN CUSTOMARY LAW (Jeanmarie Fenrich et al. eds., 2011).

56 Tamanaha, *supra* note 35 at 14.

57 *See e.g.*, Janine Ubink, *The Quest for Customary Law in African State Courts*, *in* THE FUTURE OF AFRICAN CUSTOMARY LAW (Jeanmarie Fenrich et al. eds., 2011).

58 *See generally*, WERNER F. MENSKI, COMPARATIVE LAW IN A GLOBAL CONTEXT: THE LEGAL SYSTEMS OF ASIA AND AFRICA (2006); Joireman, *supra* note 55; Ubink, *supra* note 57.

59 von Benda-Beckman & Turner, *supra* note 37.

60 Sage & Woolcock, *supra* note 46 at 11.

61 Marc Galanter, *Justice in Many Rooms: Courts, Private Ordering, and Indigenous Law*, 13 J LEGAL PLURALISM & UNOFFICIAL L. (1981) at 24.

Through what mechanisms does development occur in the context of legal pluralist countries? These questions are important, but lack any concrete, empirical resolution. Although scholars have advanced work on quantifying and measuring pluralism,[62] to the author's knowledge, there are no empirical studies which undertake these questions. This chapter takes a modest step forward in answering these questions, using an analysis of the effects of legal pluralism on FDI. Given the importance of investment to economic development in the governance literature described above, and the common use of the institutions literature to understand FDI determinants,[63] understanding investment and legal pluralism is an ideal first step to understanding the ways in which pluralism impacts development.

Foreign Direct Investment

The determinants of FDI are often analyzed in terms of what factors make a country more (or less) attractive to a potential investor. Thus, the FDI determinants literature is a type of cost–benefit analysis. The eclectic ownership, location, internalization (OLI) paradigm outlines the benefits of FDI, while much of the institutional literature outlines the costs. The OLI paradigm defines three types of advantages of FDI to potential investors: internalization advantages, ownership advantages, and location advantages.

The FDI determinants literature focuses on locational advantages. These occur when a firm derives a competitive advantage from something peculiar to the chosen location of its investment. Three such advantages typically comprise this category: natural resource, market, and efficiency advantages. For natural resource advantages, a firm derives a benefit from co-locating with a natural resource necessary to its function. Market advantages derive from investing in a location that has a large market for the firm's products. Finally, efficiency advantages derive from using an input from the investment location that ultimately increases the efficiency of the firm's production. Efficiency advantages typically include factor prices of low labor, capital, or technology costs.[64]

DATA DESCRIPTION

This analysis uses data from 118 developing countries, referred to by the World Bank as low-income, low-middle-income, and high-middle-income countries, from the years 1995–2015. A list of these countries is in Appendix 17A.

The dependent variable is FDI, and the measures of FDI are taken from the United Nations Conference on Trade and Development, and measured stock in millions of US dollars. Given the high presence of skew and kurtosis, for this and the main predictors of FDI, I use a log of the variable.

---

[62] *See e.g.*, Yüksel Sezgin, *Theorizing Formal Pluralism: Quantification of Legal Pluralism for Spatio-Temporal Analysis*, 36 13 J LEGAL PLURALISM & UNOFFICIAL L. (2004).

[63] *See e.g.*, Fathi Ali, et al., *Do Institutions Matter for Foreign Direct Investment?*, 21 OPEN ECONS. REV. (2010); Agnès Bénassy-Quéré, et al., *Institutional Determinants of Foreign Direct Investment*, 30 WORLD ECON. (2007).

[64] John H. Dunning, *The Eclectic (OLI) Paradigm of International Production: Past, Present and Future*, 8 INT'L J. ECON. BUS. (2001).

To operationalize the concept of legal pluralism, I rely on the *Juriglobe* categorization. Juriglobe places countries into one of five legal categories: common law, civil law, customary law, Muslim law and "mixed." The countries placed in the mixed category are further identified by which of the previous four categories the legal system is mixed with. Using this, I use two measures of legal pluralism. The first measure is a variable indicating whether a country has more than one legal family. Second, legal pluralism is measured as whether customary law is predominant. I define a customary-dominant system as whether customary law is the first or second legal influence in a mixed family system.[65]

Several caveats must be stated about using an indicator variable to measure legal pluralism. First, operationalizing legal pluralism in this way does not account for the varieties of customary traditions and how they interact with the state. As was noted above, one of the key considerations for how development efforts may successfully engage with legal pluralism is to be found at a micro level – how different actors in different arenas engage with state law. Second, operationalizing legal pluralism in this way centers the analysis on the state, and employs what Griffiths called "weak pluralism." Third, there are some necessary generalizations which come at the expense of nuance. For example, although South Africa is influenced by customary law, it is not customary-dominant in this analysis because civil and common law are the first two legal influences. Finally, as with any assessment, disagreements as to the categorization of countries will inevitably arise. Nevertheless, this measure does provide valuable information, and represents an initial step toward a larger cross-country empirical analysis.

For control variables, I rely on FDI determinants literature. Although this literature is vast, to achieve parsimony, I use proxies for primarily the theoretical constructs of the location component of the OLI model: markets, natural resources, and efficiency. Market is proxied by *GDP per capita*. The natural resources segment of the locational advantage is proxied by *Total natural resources rents (% of GDP)*. Inflation is used to proxy for efficiency-seeking investment. Although not included in the OLI model, I also control for trade openness. Following previous studies,[66] I proxy for *Trade openness* as a measure of exports plus imports as a percentage of GDP. All these variables are taken from the World Development Indicators.

Finally, I include a rule of law variable. The concept of the rule of law has been operationalized in a variety of ways, most commonly by survey data. A prominent measure comes from the World Bank's WGIs. The WGIs' "rule of law" is a composite measure of 32 sources, including the International Country Risk Guide law and order measure. It is intended to represent perceptions of the confidence that actors have in the law, as well as their own abidance by the law. The measure focuses on contract enforcement, property rights, the judiciary, the

---

[65] Although it is not stated on Juriglobe's website that the order of systems listed is intended to have the independent meaning that I assign it here, this is confirmed by my correspondence with Juriglobe. Further, in my assessment, this type of ordering makes sense. For example, Gabon is listed as "Civil law/ Customary." Other sources confirm that the primary legal system is civil, with influences of customary law.

[66] *See e.g.*, Elizabeth Asiedu, *On the Determinants of Foreign Direct Investment to Developing Countries: Is Africa Different?*, 30 World Dev. (2002); Nathan M. Jensen, *Democratic Governance and Multinational Corporations: Political Regimes and Inflows of Foreign Direct Investment*, 57 Int'l Org. (2003); Mike Pournarakis & Nikos Varsakelis, *Institutions, internationalization and FDI: the case of economies in transition*, 13 Transnat'l Corps. (2004); Glen Biglaiser & Joseph L. Staats, *Finding the "Democratic Advantage" in Sovereign Bond Ratings: The Importance of Strong Courts, Property Rights Protection, and the Rule of Law*, 66 Int'l. Org. (2012).

prevalence of crime and the police.[67] The WGIs represent a "thick" version of the rule of law and are used not only to control for the rule of law in the minimal sense, but also for other incentive factors outside of legal pluralism that may impact investment.

Data Description

For this dataset, legal pluralism is more common than customary-dominant law. There are 66 countries with legal pluralism, and 34 with customary-dominant law. The two variables have a correlation of $r = 0.57$.

Additionally, sub-Saharan Africa has the greatest number of observations for countries for both legal pluralism (520) and customary law (350). The next highest regional observations for these two categories are the Middle East and North Africa, which has 144 observations of legal pluralism; and Latin America, which has 57 observations for customary law.

Table 17.1 provides descriptive statistics by legal pluralism. Values are presented in the log forms used in the regression models. There are almost 300 fewer observations where legal monism is the norm. The minimum values for FDI inflows and stock are lower for countries with legal pluralism, and countries with legal pluralism have lower means on these measures than do countries with legal monism. Countries with legal pluralism also have a lower mean of GDP per capita. Inflation and trade openness are approximately the same in both sets of countries. In countries with legal monism, the mean value of the rule of law is higher. Given the theoretical difficulties between the dominant conceptions of the rule of law and the concept of legal pluralism, the lower mean of pluralist countries on rule of law measures is to be expected.

Table 17.1 Summary statistics for sample, sorted by the presence of legal pluralism

	(1)	(2)	(3)	(4)	(5)	(6)	(7)	(8)	(9)	(10)
	Legal Monism					Legal Pluralism				
VARIABLES	N	mean	sd	min	max	N	mean	sd	min	max
FDI inflows	686	6.266	2.823	−8.871	11.49	905	5.537	2.759	−9.228	11.82
FDI stock	686	8.680	2.132	1.719	13.41	917	7.896	2.301	0.007	14.00
Greenfield number	459	3.158	1.509	0.693	6.392	585	2.534	1.381	0.693	6.884
Rule of law	686	−0.407	0.630	−1.795	1.356	917	−0.517	0.618	−2.130	1.077
GDP per cap	686	8.182	0.824	5.895	9.432	917	7.391	0.976	5.403	9.433
Natural resource rents	686	1.194	0.900	0	4.040	917	1.955	1.071	0	4.418
Trade openness	686	4.384	0.410	2.859	5.192	917	4.197	0.619	0.155	5.744
Inflation	686	1.762	0.926	−1.589	5.787	917	1.754	0.934	−2.950	6.244

Model and Estimation

I model investment as a function of legal pluralism and a number of control variables:

$$investment \sim f(control\ variables + legal\ pluralism)$$

[67] The World Bank Group, World Governance Indicators (The World Bank Group ed., 2021).

I estimate this as

$$FDI\ stock_{it} = GDP\ per\ capita_{it} + Natural\ resource\ rents_{it} + Inflation_{it} + Trade/GDP_{it} + Rule\ of\ law_{it} + legal\ pluralism_{i}$$

The models below are estimated using ordinary least squares (OLS) with Huber-White standard errors. As robustness checks, I also estimate OLS models with alternative measures of investment, as well as OLS models with Newey-West standard errors to control for autocorrelation.

Results

Table 17.2 presents the results of the first set of regression estimations. The first two columns regress the variables on FDI stock, and the latter two use FDI inflows as the dependent variable. The first and third columns present the results when using OLS with Huber-White standard errors, clustered around country. The second and fourth columns present the results when OLS is used with Newey-standard errors to control for autocorrelation. Lags of three years were used for the estimations with Newey-standard errors.

Table 17.2 *Results of OLS models, with Huber-White standard errors, using FDI stock and FDI inflows as dependent variables, and legal pluralism as the key independent variable of interest*

	(1)	(2)	(3)	(4)
VARIABLES	FDI stock	FDI stock	FDI inflows	FDI inflows
GDP per cap	1.330***	1.330***	0.970***	0.970***
	(0.227)	(0.122)	(0.227)	(0.142)
Natural resource rents	0.517***	0.517***	0.277	0.277*
	(0.175)	(0.0958)	(0.223)	(0.143)
Inflation	0.201*	0.201***	0.220*	0.220**
	(0.108)	(0.0765)	(0.111)	(0.0905)
Trade openness	–0.711***	–0.711***	–0.763**	–0.763***
	(0.264)	(0.146)	(0.347)	(0.206)
Rule of law	–0.229	–0.229	0.120	0.120
	(0.335)	(0.181)	(0.354)	(0.221)
Legal pluralism	–0.283	–0.283	–0.306	–0.306
	(0.396)	(0.205)	(0.462)	(0.276)
Constant	–0.147	–0.147	1.005	1.005
	(2.092)	(1.141)	(2.267)	(1.449)
Observations	1,603	1,603	1,591	1,591
R-squared	0.318		0.125	

Notes:
Robust standard errors in parentheses.
*** p<0.01, ** p<0.05, * p<0.1.

Across all models, the variables based on the theoretical model from the location part of the OLI paradigm behave as expected. The *GDP per cap* variable, used to represent market-based location, is a significant predictor across all three models at the 1% level. *Natural resource rents*, used to represent resource-seeking investment, are significant in three of the models. When used to predict FDI stock, they are significant at the 1% level. When used as a predictor for FDI inflows, natural resource rents are significant in the Newey model, and significant at the 10% level in the standard model with Huber-White standard errors. *Inflation*, used to represent efficiency-seeking investment, is significant in all models.

Trade openness is significant, but surprisingly negative across all models. This suggests that for this subset of countries, trade openness is a deterrent rather than a draw. *Rule of law* is not significant in any of the models. This suggests that for these countries, and these years, rule of law, as measured here, does not draw investors.

Legal pluralism is also insignificant across all the models. In other words, the presence of more than one type of legal family within a state neither deters nor draws investment.

Table 17.3 presents the results of regression estimations using an indicator variable for customary-dominant law.

Table 17.3 Results of OLS models, with Huber-White standard errors using FDI stock and FDI inflows as dependent variable, and customary law as the key independent variable of interest

	(1)	(2)	(3)	(4)
VARIABLES	FDI stock	FDI stock	FDI inflows	FDI inflows
GDP per cap	1.076***	1.076***	0.793***	0.793***
	(0.265)	(0.138)	(0.285)	(0.160)
Natural resource rents	0.648***	0.648***	0.366	0.366**
	(0.177)	(0.0974)	(0.223)	(0.144)
Inflation	0.182	0.182**	0.208*	0.208**
	(0.110)	(0.0776)	(0.113)	(0.0921)
Trade openness	–0.719***	–0.719***	–0.764**	–0.764***
	(0.250)	(0.139)	(0.331)	(0.198)
Rule of law	–0.0503	–0.0503	0.234	0.234
	(0.324)	(0.173)	(0.352)	(0.210)
Customary law	–1.134**	–1.134***	–0.884	–0.884**
	(0.554)	(0.281)	(0.629)	(0.348)
Constant	1.933	1.933	2.396	2.396
	(2.256)	(1.204)	(2.527)	(1.506)
Observations	1,603	1,603	1,591	1,591
R-squared	0.346		0.135	

Notes:
Robust standard errors in parentheses.
*** p<0.01, ** p<0.05, * p<0.1.

As with Table 17.2, the first two columns of Table 17.3 use FDI stock as the dependent variable, while the last two use FDI inflows. Further, the second and fourth columns use OLS with Newey-standard errors, while the first and third columns use the Huber-White estimator.

As with the first set of models, here, market-seeking investment, represented by *GDP per capita*, is significant across all models. *Natural resource rents* are positive and significant in all models except for the third model, where the variables are regressed on FDI inflows, using OLS with the Huber-White estimator. *Inflation* is again positive and significant in all models, except the first. *Trade openness* is a negative predictor of FDI, significant across all models. *Rule of law* is again not significant in any of the models.

The indicator for customary-dominant law is negative and significant. In the first two models, where FDI stock is used as the dependent variable, the customary-dominant law variable is significant at the 1% level. In the model where FDI inflows are the dependent variable, customary law is insignificant when not controlling for autocorrelation. The models together suggest that customary law does play a role in investment. Specifically, where customary-dominant law is an indicator variable signaling whether customary law is a prominent feature of the legal system, it may deter investment.

DISCUSSION: LEGAL PLURALISM

The models presented suggest two initial conclusions about legal pluralism. First, the presence of more than one legal family within a state does not necessarily lead to a decrease in investment. These were the results from models 1–4 in Table 17.1, where the legal pluralism variable was negative but not significant. This could be a function of the type of pluralism. The legal pluralism present in the countries in the sample was not only what Griffiths would call the "weak" form of legal pluralism, but the majority of the countries are mixed with either civil law or common law, and in some cases both. This type of pluralism would likely provide for the clear rules and expectations that investors seek.

A second conclusion is that legal pluralism may impact areas not related to investment. If we adhere to some of the arguments made by legal pluralist scholars described above, legal pluralism is not ubiquitous in all situations; nor is it confined to a single categorization. Legal pluralism can govern economic activity, but in some countries, it may be restricted to those areas that are not the concern of outside investors. If this is the case, there may be little reason to expect legal pluralism to impact foreign investment activity.

Customary-dominant Law

The models suggest that customary-dominant systems may deter investment. Specifically, legal systems where customary law is either a primary or secondary influence are negatively correlated with FDI. While this could reflect a correlation between customary-dominant and other factors that influence FDI, one conclusion that may be drawn from this is that customary law may be a type of law that has the most "distance" from other types of legal systems; it may be more qualitatively different. Customary systems, by definition, are oral and relatively inaccessible to outsiders.[68] Consequently, these types of systems provide less certainty and predictability to investors.

Additionally, systems with customary-dominant law may be signaling the presence of additional systems that exist outside of the state system, beyond state-recognized customary traditions. The label "customary law" may obscure multiples of different customary traditions. For example, in Kenya, which has customary law, the government of Kenya estimates 42 different customary groups.[69] In Indonesia, there are hundreds of different groups.[70] If the variable is interpreted in this way, it may suggest that this variable represents, or contains, those circumstances in which the normative order within the state is not clear. In other words,

---

[68] Glenn, *supra* note 47.

[69] Ministry of East Africa Community and Regional Development, *About Kenya* (2019).

[70] *See e.g.*, ZULYANI HIDAYA, A GUIDE TO TRIBES IN INDONESIA: ANTHROPOLOGICAL INSIGHTS FROM THE ARCHIPELAGO (2020).

in the words of Caroline Sage and Michael Woolcock, it may be capturing situations in which there is a lack of meta rules for negotiating different normative orders.[71] In the vernacular of the governance and institutions tradition, either circumstance would produce situations of uncertainty for investors and would detract from investment opportunities in those countries.

General Discussion

As discussed above, there are several underlying causal mechanisms through which institutions affect economic development. First, institutions affect development outcomes by providing stability and reducing uncertainty for investors. Legal pluralism can affect this by providing uncertainty as to which rules are governing. In short, to use North's language, if institutions are "the rules of the game in a society,"[72] legal pluralism means that there are multiple sets of rules for the game. It can be unclear to an outside actor which rules to follow to achieve a desired outcome. This may not only be the case for understanding the boundaries and rights of property, but also for navigating judicial systems which may be subject to different rules.

Yet these results suggest that investment is undeterred by state-controlled or weak legal pluralism; and more broadly, these results suggest that legal pluralism is not wholly incompatible with development goals. However, these results may also be context dependent. They may depend on the type of legal pluaralism and the degree to which it impacts the state legal system. For example, while customary-dominant law had a negative impact on investment, additional robustness checks not discussed above suggested that when the model included an indicator variable for the presence of any customary law, the customary law variable was insignificant. This supports the contention that it is the way that pluralism is manifest in the system that may create uncertainty for investors. A significant limitation is that this study only captures officially recognized non-state law. In addition, it does not capture the interactions between customary and state law at the micro level.

CONCLUSION

This chapter has presented a brief overview of law and economic development and legal pluralism literatures, and explored the connections between them. Both are conceptually murky, and both have normative claims and critics. However, despite their surface contradictions, on some level both represent empirical realities. There is an observed connection between rule of law, institutions, and economic outcomes, even with the assumption that law is a state-centric construct. Legal pluralism also exists as an empirical reality, throughout history and in the current times in many developing and developed countries. For those interested in development outcomes, confronting and reconciling these two facts is a necessity if development outcomes are to move beyond their current state. For scholars, this combination may look like theorizing about ways in which countries that do not mimic the West can also achieve development goals. For practitioners, this may entail broadening current activities to have more participatory development projects. This chapter has shown that theoretically and empirically combining these two fields is possible.

---

[71] Sage & Woolcock, *supra* note 46 at 9.

[72] North, *supra* note 19 at 3.

APPENDIX 17A

Table 17A.1 List of countries used in the regression analysis

Albania	Ecuador	Liberia	Rwanda
Algeria	Egypt, Arab Rep.El Salvador	Libya	Samoa
Angola	Estonia	Lithuania	Serbia
Armenia	Eswatini	Madagascar	Seychelles
Azerbaijan	Ethiopia	Malawi	Sierra Leone
Bangladesh	Fiji	Malaysia	Slovak Republic
Belarus	Gabon Gambia, The	Mali	Solomon Islands
Benin	Georgia	Mauritania	South Africa
Bhutan	Ghana Grenada	Mauritius	Sri Lanka
Bolivia	Guatemala	Mexico	Sudan
Bosnia and Herzegovina	Guinea	Micronesia, Fed. Sts.	Tajikistan
Botswana	Guinea-Bissau	Moldova	Tanzania
Brazil	Guyana	Mongolia	Thailand
Burkina Faso	Haiti	Montenegro	Timor-Leste
Burundi	Honduras	Morocco	Togo
Cabo Verde	Hungary	Mozambique Myanmar	Tonga
Cambodia	India	Namibia Nepal	Tunisia
Cameroon	Indonesia	Nicaragua	Turkey
Chad	Iran, Islamic Rep.	Nigeria	Uganda
Chile	Iraq	Pakistan	Ukraine
China	Jamaica	Palau	Uruguay
Colombia	Jordan	Panama	Vanuatu
Comoros	Kenya	Papua New Guinea	Vietnam
Congo, Dem. Rep.	Kiribati	Paraguay	West Bank and Gaza
Congo, Rep.	Kyrgyz Republic	Peru	Zambia
Costa Rica	Lao PDR	Philippines	Zimbabwe
Cote d'Ivoire	Latvia	Poland	
Croatia	Lebanon	Romania	
Dominica	Lesotho	Russian Federation	

18. The Caribbean Court of Justice

Meeting the challenges of a post-colonial Caribbean

Harold A. Young

INTRODUCTION

In supporting the establishment of the Caribbean Court of Justice (CCJ) for the Commonwealth Caribbean, the former prime minister of St. Lucia, the Honorable Kenny Anthony, states, "No self-respecting nation should allow its sovereignty to be at large" (Anthony 2003). Constitutionally incorporating a judicial institution of a former colonial power as the highest appellate court is arguably an affront to sovereignty. Dr. Anthony is referring to the Judicial Committee of the Privy Council (JCPC) located in London, England, which is a colonial advisory committee to the British monarch on appeals from the British Empire and some former colonies. Dr. Anthony's call is answered with the opening of the CCJ in Port of Spain, Trinidad and Tobago, on April 16, 2005. This chapter will introduce the JCPC with its historical roots in the British Empire and, more specifically, its continuing role in the Caribbean. It then discusses the emergence of the CCJ and its importance to reginal integration in the Caribbean Community (CARICOM). A comparative analysis then looks at two caches of salient court decisions. First, it looks at capital punishment appeals to the JCPC and examines appeals from three of the countries that accede to the CCJ. Second, the JCPC and CCJ decisions where a government is a litigant are compared. Finally, the focus narrows to the justices of the CCJ. Based on written responses from three justices, some insight is gained into how the justices view this new and unique court as it builds respect and credibility with governments, legal practitioners, and the public.

It is necessary to clarify the term "Caribbean," as the meaning depends on vantagepoint and background (Girvan 2001). Terms such as "Caribbean Basin" or "Wider Caribbean" are common and can include countries such as Cuba and the Dominican Republic, former Spanish colonies, and Suriname and Haiti, Dutch and French colonies respectively. When discussing the CCJ, however, I refer to the former British Caribbean (Anglophone), out of which emerged countries sharing "language and identity, geography, history and culture, geopolitical, geo-economics, or organization" (Girvan 2001, 4). In terms of their shared British colonial pass, these countries experienced a median of 207.5 years of British colonial rule (mean 223.5 years), compared with a median of 77 years (mean 93 years) for all other countries in the British Commonwealth (median 87 years and average of 121 years). Primarily, however, I rely for organization on CARICOM, which was originally all the Anglophone countries but now includes other countries in the region (Haiti and Suriname). The Anglophone countries of CARICOM are also members of the British Commonwealth that includes almost all former British colonies.

JUDICIAL COMMITTEE OF THE PRIVY COUNCIL

To understand the real significance of the CCJ, an overview of the JCPC is helpful. The JCPC is a part of the Privy Council, an advisory body to the British monarch in the performance of many ceremonial and substantive functions assigned by the parliament (Privy Council n.d.). Drawing its members from the Privy Council, the JCPC functions like an appellate court and derives its jurisdiction from a custom based on the medieval Curia Regis (the King's Court) or councilors to the king (Merriam-Webster 2015). The JCPC's appellate jurisdiction is based on the theory that the monarch is the ultimate source and distributor of justice. The British government controls appointments, the number and terms of service of the judges, and the fiscal support for the court (Howell 1979; Swinfen 1987). The growth and management of the British Empire from a few scattered outposts to encompassing large parts of North America, the Caribbean, Africa and Asia is not just a military and cultural phenomenon, but a bureaucratic leviathan that included multiple judicial systems with the JCPC at the apex. This court adjudicates civil and criminal appeals from lower court decisions originating in countries, colonies, and other overseas territories. These include the 13 North American colonies that formed the United States in 1776. Colonial appeals did reach the JCPC prior to independence. One count is 265 appeals between 1680 and 1780 (Schlesinger 1913); and Smith (1950) reports 231 between 1696 and 1776. The contribution of the JCPC to the jurisprudence of the colonies and the Empire cannot be overstated and it continues today.

The modern JCPC is a product of British legislative action and practice starting with the Judicial Committee Act 1833 (Howell 1979). First, Law Lords are lawyers unless otherwise specified by the monarch. Second, it establishes procedures and functions that are exercised independently of the monarch, giving the JCPC the power of a court (Burns 1984).

Until 1844, the JCPC had no power to hear appeals without the granting of leave from a colony's court of appeal. The Judicial Committee Act of 1844 (The National Archives n.d.) expands for the right of appeals to all British subjects in overseas territories. Appeals are either by special leave from the JCPC or as a right extended by royal prerogative (Burns 1984; Robert-Wray 1966). Under the Appellate Jurisdiction Act of 1876 (The National Archives n.d.), the Law Lords became the permanent judges of the court. The branches of law on appeal are diverse and important, with fundamental principles being adjudicated (Robert-Wray 1966). Examples include extradition requests; appeals against the death penalty; libel cases involving politicians; eminent domain; personal injury; and issues involving provincial versus federal power. Further, no monarch has ever ignored the advice of the JCPC in any appeal.

Decolonization launches the process of moving a colony to an independent state. During this process, an emerging governing coalition can decide whether the JCPC continues as the final appellate court or replaces it with a domestic final appellate court after independence. With the start of decolonization, the number of jurisdictions declined from 51 in 1946 to just 12 in 2018. After World War II, India won independence in 1947 followed by a plethora of new countries in Africa, Asia, and the Caribbean. With a peak of 119 cases in 1931, the JCPC adjudicated a median of 47 cases (average of 52 appeals per year) from 1932 to 2017 (1,082 cases). Despite the decline, this caseload is not insignificant, considering the U.S. Supreme Court (SCOTUS) allows fewer than 100 appeals per year.

Decolonization notwithstanding, the JCPC is a significant post-colonial bond between the former British colonies and the U.K. For example, Singapore cut ties in 1988, The Gambia in 1996 and New Zealand in 2005. Compared with Asia and Africa, however, the ties are particularly strong in the Caribbean, with all 12 former colonies retaining the JCPC at independence. Today, the court remains the final appellate court for eight of the 12. As of January 1, 2021, four (Barbados, Belize, Dominica and Guyana) countries have acceded to the CCJ.

A COURT IS BORN

Following World War II, efforts at Caribbean integration had a shaky start. There is the short-lived West Indies Federation (1958–1962), which is the first effort at integrating some of the Anglophone Caribbean colonies—Antigua and Barbuda, Barbados, Dominica, Grenada, Jamaica, Montserrat, the then St. Kitts-Nevis-Anguilla, St. Lucia, St. Vincent, and Trinidad and Tobago (CARICOM 2001). A new initiative follows in 1965 with the Agreement of Dickenson Bay (Antigua and Barbuda, Barbados and Guyana) establishing the Caribbean Free Trade Association (CARIFTA) in 1971 (Yakana 2006; Andic, Andic and Dosser 2011). CARIFTA included Antigua and Barbuda, Barbados, Belize, Dominica, Grenada, Guyana, Jamaica, Montserrat, St. Kitts and Nevis, St. Lucia, St. Vincent and the Grenadines, and Trinidad and Tobago. This was replaced by the Treaty of Chaguaramas in 1973, which established the Caribbean Community and Common Market, CARICOM. It was revised in 2001 (Revised Treaty of Chaguaramas 2001) to facilitate the establishment of a single market and economy (CARICOM 2018). The creation of the CCJ is provided for in Article 172, Section 8 of this treaty. The CCJ, therefore, is an irreplaceable part of CARICOM to further integration in the common law and judicial structure and resolve conflicts between countries.

In 2003, Caribbean leaders met in Jamaica to ratify the Agreement Establishing the Caribbean Court of Justice conferring the CCJ both original and appellate jurisdictions. Eight (Barbados, Belize, Dominica, Guyana, Jamaica, St. Lucia, St. Vincent and the Grenadines, and Trinidad and Tobago) of the 14 countries approved the creation of the CCJ.

The CCJ is directly governed by the Agreement Establishing the Caribbean Court of Justice (Caribbean Community Secretariat 2001). The court has jurisdiction to hear cases between states (original jurisdiction) and appeals of decisions of domestic courts within each state (appellate jurisdiction). If requested by the contracting states, the court has the authority under its original jurisdiction to issue advisory opinions interpreting and applying the Treaty of Chaguaramas that establishes CARICOM. The president of the court is joined by not more than nine judges established by Article V of the agreement. Each member serves for a non-renewable term of seven years, or until the age of 72. Judges sit in panels of three or five under the authority and direction of the president or senior judge on panel. There is no requirement that justices hail from a CARICOM or any specific member country. Justices do not represent their country of origin. On retirement, new justices are confirmed by the Regional Judicial and Legal Services Commission (other facets of the court include the Code of Judicial Conduct, the CCJ Trust Fund, administrative staff, a court registry, the court calendar, the court library and the Caribbean Academy for Law & Court Administration). An important aspect of the court is the ability to adjudicate live via the internet, reducing travel to the physical court located in Port of Spain, Trinidad and Tobago. These virtual internet proceedings can be viewed by the public in a courtroom setting in the jurisdictions involved in the case. The importance of this facility cannot be overestimated when one considers the distances between the states. For example, the distance from Belize to Trinidad and Tobago is 1,883 miles (3,030 kilometers).

CHALLENGES

The challenges the CCJ faces in gaining wider acceptance by member states are multifaceted. There are challenges in the spheres of structure, public perception, law and political will. None are mutually exclusive but are presented here as distinctly as possible.

There are two critical structural features attracting attention to the CCJ. The first is the selection of justices and the second is funding for the CCJ. These issues go to the credibility, impartiality, consistency and quality of the court. These are particularly key when compared with the JCPC and in considering whether to accede to the regional court. Yet these are rarely, if ever, widely debated in connection with the JCPC.

Since the Law Lords on the JCPC are members of the highest court of the U.K., the Supreme Court of Judicature, their appointments are completely at the discretion of the British government. Countries that allow appeals to the JCPC have no input, which underpins the view of the JCPC as preferable to a regional court that may be susceptible to regional or domestic politics.

The composition of the body responsible for seating justices on the CCJ reflects a significant effort to minimize bias or individual state interest in the process. Article V (Caribbean Community Secretariat 2001) calls for the establishment of the Regional Judicial and Legal Services Commission with responsibility for seating judges as vacancies arise. *Ex officio* membership is diverse and specifically provides for:

(a) the president, who shall be the Chairman of the Commission;
(b) two persons nominated jointly by the Organisation of the Commonwealth Caribbean Bar Association and the Organisation of Eastern Caribbean States (OECS) Bar Association;
(c) one chairman of the Judicial Services Commission of a Contracting Party selected in rotation in English alphabetical order for a period of three years;
(d) the Chairman of a Public Service Commission of a Contracting Party selected in rotation in reverse English alphabetical order for a period of three years;
(e) two persons from civil society nominated jointly by the Secretary-General of the Community and the Director General of the OECS for a period of three years following consultations with regional non-governmental organisations;
(f) two distinguished jurists nominated jointly by the Dean of the Faculty of Law of the University of the West Indies, the Deans of the Faculties of Law of any of the Contracting Parties, and the Chairman of the Council of Legal Education; and
(g) two persons nominated jointly by the Bar or Law Associations of the Contracting Parties.

In reality, therefore, the selection process for justices of the CCJ is also removed from the member countries who have no direct or official input. The argument, however, is not particularly persuasive for some countries retaining the JCPC. For example, in an interview, the former president of the Bahamian Bar Association, Ruth Bowe Darville, explicitly supports the retention of the JCPC (Rolle 2012). Darville points out that those who advocate the removal of the JCPC are "treading in very dangerous waters": as "litigants who come before us with multimillion-dollar cases … see us as a great financial center, they need assurance that the Privy Council [JCPC] is there" (as cited by Rolle 2012, para. 4). In other words, the JCPC, by virtue of being in England, demonstrates the independence of the judiciary to those with economic interest in the Bahamas. This argument is reminiscent of that used by the sectors of the business community in New Zealand in their public debate leading up to the decision to abolish appeals to the JCPC in 2005 (Kerr 2002).

The second issue is funding for the court. Countries that allow appeals to the JCPC have no direct fiscal responsibility for the court that is funded by the British government. The appellants' (and respondents') costs lie in accessing the court in London (e.g., travel, accommodation, legal counsel, etc.). Article XXVII provides for how countries are to fund the CCJ by writing payment into law. All funds go into a Consolidated Fund (currently U.S.$100 million) administered by a Board of Trustees. The Board of Trustees is also comprised of an array of *ex officio* members representing CARICOM's legal, educational and business elite (Caribbean Court of Justice 2012), namely the Secretary-General (of the Caribbean Community); the Vice-Chancellor of the University of the West Indies; the President of the Insurance Association of the Caribbean; the Chair of the Association of Indigenous Banks of the Caribbean; the President of the Caribbean Institute of Chartered Accountants; the President of the Organisation of Commonwealth Caribbean Bar Associations; the Chair of the Conference of Heads of the Judiciary of Member States of the Caribbean Community; the President of the Caribbean Association of Industry and Commerce; and the President of the Caribbean Congress of Labour. There are also vital protections for the salaries and allowances for the judges during their tenure.

These provisions represent a thoughtful effort to dilute the influence of any single state and detach the membership from direct political influences bolstering the independence of the court. The fact that only four of the 12 states have acceded to the CCJ (appellate jurisdiction) since its inception in 2005 signals the challenges the court faces in establishing itself as a viable alternative to the JCPC.

The challenges for the CCJ are not just structural. The countries face issues of law when attempting to accede to the CCJ. For example, when the countries gain independence, their constitutions include provisions that save the laws enacted by colonial legislatures as existing laws (Ghany 2000). The saved laws include the salient matter of the death penalty for capital crimes. The Commonwealth Caribbean countries are among the 58 countries that retain the death sentence at law, while 140 countries have abolished it by law or de facto by refraining to carry out the sentence (Amnesty International 2016).

The JCPC plays a critical role in changing the course of Caribbean jurisprudence, starting with *Pratt and Morgan v. Attorney General of Jamaica and Other* (1993). On January 15, 1979, the Supreme Court of Jamaica convicted Earl Pratt and Ivan Morgan of murder and sentenced them to death. They remained in prison for 14 years during the appeal process. On three occasions, the authorities read their death warrants and transferred them to the condemned cells immediately adjacent to the gallows. In 1993, Jamaica's final appellate court, the JCPC, heard their appeal. The court concludes that this delay constituted cruel and unusual punishment and commuted the death sentence to life imprisonment. This case is significant in Caribbean jurisprudence as it is the first time the court has explicitly adopted a standard for cruel and unusual punishment based on delays in carrying out the death penalty. The court goes further by setting a threshold of five years on death row, after which execution could be cruel and unusual punishment. The JCPC's preferences are abundantly clear in the Belizean case, *Reyes v. The Queen* (2002). Lord Bingham of Cornwall, in delivering the decision, states, "A generous and purposive interpretation is to be given to constitutional provisions protecting human rights" (26).

Such decisions induce a public backlash in the Caribbean, with the general sentiment being one of support for the death penalty and unhappiness with JCPC decisions on that issue (Anthony 2003). A dispute over capital punishment or judicial imperialism by the region's highest appellate court can also be understood as a response to the overlegalization of governments' human rights commitments (Heifer 2002). Caribbean governments, for their part, see the death penalty as a "vote-winner" with the electorate. The popular majorities support the mandatory death penalty in the belief that it acts as a deterrent to violent crime. Thus, the possibility of its abolition by a panel of Law Lords (judges) thousands of miles away is a highly sensitive political issue. Some death penalty opponents fear that the CCJ will not amount to anything more than a "hangman's court" allowing for countries to carry out the death penalty (Richards 2006).

The public discourse in the Bahamas is exemplary of the bifurcated discussion about acceding to the CCJ. Following the JCPC's decision in *Maxo Tido v. The Queen* (2011) to overturn the death penalty sentence affirmed by the Bahamian Court of Appeals in 2002, a former president of the Bahamian Bar Association, Ruth Bowe Darville, is reported as saying, "I think the question of the death penalty needs to be addressed. I think the country is torn by it because we're in the throes of this crime epidemic as people have labeled it" (as cited by McCartney, June 25, 2011, para. 12). Darville suggests that the issue of the death penalty be addressed through legislation, but with the knowledge that care must be taken not to offend the international community and that any action should be linked to the economic well-being of the Bahamas. Religious leaders are divided. While most Bahamians support the death penalty, the Anglican bishop, the Methodist synod and the Catholic archbishop came out against it (Toote 2013; BahamaCatholic 2009). Most Baptists, however—the single largest denomination in the Bahamas at 40 percent of the population—support the death penalty (Toote 2013).

With few politicians publicly opposing the death penalty (Toote 2013), it is not surprising that the government is cautious. It tries to separately address the issues of the death penalty and any calls to completely abolish appeals to the JCPC. In its Charter of Governance, the Progressive Liberal Party acknowledges that death penalty decisions of the JCPC constrain the state's ability to enforce the death penalty. Instead of calling for the abolition of the JCPC, it pledges to ensure "that all avenues of appeal are exhausted without delay. Cases that are complete and warrant the death penalty shall be deposed of expeditiously...fast-tracked to the Supreme Court to ensure that our laws are no longer reduced to bluffs" (Progressive Liberal Party 2011). This is a pledge to abide by the JCPC precedent set in *Pratt and Morgan v. Attorney General of Jamaica and Other* (1993), which overturned the death penalty sentence on the grounds of undue delay. The then opposition Free National Movement (FNM) makes two main promises in the party's manifesto. First, it promises to reduce delays in the prosecution of criminal cases (Manifesto '07, 4). Second, in a 2014 speech, the Hon. Dr. Hubert A Minnis (then Leader of the Opposition) promises to introduce a bill that would mandate that "an appeal against a sentence of death can only be made to the Bahamas Court of Appeal, and nowhere else" (Minnis 2014, para. 35). Such a constitutional amendment would effectively oust the jurisdiction of the JCPC specifically, but only in death penalty cases. This approach was an effort to recognize voter support for the death penalty, and to retain the JCPC for all other matters to reassure those interested in retaining the JCPC as a hallmark of credibility and independence of the Bahamian judiciary. To date no corresponding bill has been introduced to the Bahamian Parliament.

Other jurisdictions have had other issues. In St. Kitts and Nevis, a 2015 referendum on constitutional changes which included replacing the JCPC with the JCC failed to garner a majority vote. A 2016 referendum in Grenada also failed to win majority support. In the two most populous jurisdictions, Jamaica and Trinidad and Tobago, the issue has been a political football, with political parties promising the change only to renege later, citing various reasons. Then prime minister of Trinidad and Tobago, the Honorable Kamla Persad-Bissessar, explained that the JCPC inspired international confidence in her country that encouraged foreign investors. This vacillation led the former prime minister of Jamaica, the Honorable P.J. Patterson, to remark, "There can be no valid reason why the CCJ cannot be asked by its two most populous member states, who have contributed substantially to its funding, why the CCJ cannot be asked to take responsibility for its final jurisdiction in full" (Fraser n.d.). To date, Jamaica and Trinidad and Tobago have failed to accede to the CCJ.

Considering public and political hostility to the JCPC's death penalty decisions, opponents of the death penalty fear the CCJ will uphold the death penalty and lead to a rash of executions. These fears have not materialized, and the death penalty remains in the laws of all Caribbean countries. This issue is addressed by then prime minister of St. Lucia, the Honorable Dr. Kenny D. Anthony, who, in supporting the establishment of the court, describes stoking these fears as a distraction:

> …what I consider are more salient concerns, namely insulating the Court from political interference and guaranteeing its financial integrity and independence. (Anthony 2003, para 21, 28)

The lower courts in the Caribbean continue to sentence people to death and appeals continue to the JCPC. Figure 18.1 presents the number of appeals and the comparative number when the death penalty was set aside by the court from 1964 to 2014. This review of appeals shows an uptick in death penalty appeals to the JCPC from 1992 to 2002. This accompanies an increase in the number of appeals in which the death penalty was set aside. Even with the declining number of appeals starting in 2002, the comparative number of appeals in which the death penalty is set aside remains high (BBC World News 2007; Caribbean News Now 2004). The decline in appeals is partially attributable to the fact that three states—Barbados, Belize, and Guyana—have replaced the JCPC with the CCJ.

For those states that have acceded to the CCJ, the fears of death penalty opponents have not come to fruition. In *Attorney General, Superintendent of Prisons and Chief Marshal v. Jeffrey Joseph and Lennox Ricardo Boyce* (2006), a death penalty case from Barbados, the court followed the JCPC precedents established in *Pratt and Morgan v. Attorney General of Jamaica and Other* (1993) and *Boyce v. the Queen* (2004). The court upheld the appeal that the mandatory death sentence was unconstitutional. The court noted that Barbados passed a constitutional amendment to further entrench the death penalty but had failed to resolve the contradictions in the case law involving the approximate five-year time lapse in carrying out the death penalty, after which it is no longer mandatory (Pratt and Morgan 1993) and the need for a clemency hearing (*Lewis v. The Attorney General of Barbados* (2000)). Further, in *August and Gabb v. The Queen* (2018), the majority held that the mandatory minimum life sentence as prescribed in section 106 (1) of the Criminal Code of Belize is unconstitutional. To date, the decisions have not visibly mobilized the anti-death penalty supporters nor dampened the calls from those who wish for it to be used more often.

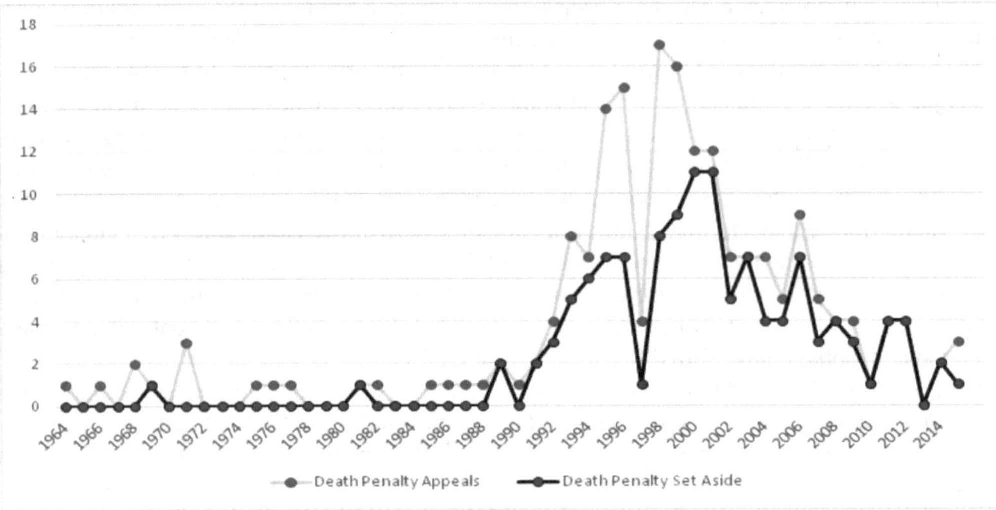

Figure 18.1 *The number of appeals and the comparative number when the death penalty was set aside by the court from 1964 to 2014*

Since the CCJ opened its doors in 2005, however, the court continues to see an increasing number of appeals and a growing docket each year. As countries accede, this regional court is expanding its role as the final judicial adjudicator of intra- and interstate conflicts. A window to how the court approaches this central role in Caribbean jurisprudence is encapsulated in the dissenting opinion of Justice Witt in *August and Gabb v. The Queen* (2018):

> The standard of review must therefore be as broad and liberal as possible and the appellate courts in Belize, both the Court of Appeal and this Court as the final court of appeal, have a duty to be proactive in their handling of appeals against conviction, just as the Legislature intended. We simply cannot afford to follow the conservative and narrow approach of the English courts, lest we create or maintain injustice (75).

There is no denying the judicial experience, quality and prestige credited to the JCPC. Presumptively, the affiliation with the JCPC confers some degree of legitimacy on domestic judicial systems and the colonial legacy persists.

Compared with the centuries behind the JCPC, the 15-year existence of the CCJ is short but not insignificant. As of January 1, 2021, the CCJ has adjudicated almost 200 matters. These decisions impact Caribbean jurisprudence and further entrench regional integration efforts. The court is still working to establish an independent reputation for impartial adjudication. As a concern is government influence, a comparative approach by using appeals in which the government is a party is used. A high level of success by the government may indicate some form of bias in the outcomes. The review includes the nine states with 185 appeals to the JCPC and the three states with 49 fully adjudicated appeals to the CCJ between 2005 (the year the CCJ started hearing appeals) and 2017. It is noted that Dominica acceded to the CCJ in 2018, but there are no recorded appeals for 2018 or 2019. Table 18.2 presents the number of appeals, the percentage favorable to the government, and where the court varied the judgment of the lower court. In this context, a decision is categorized as varied when only a part of the appeal is

Table 18.1 *Number of appeals adjudicated by four states since acceding to the CCJ, and the JCPC for the other nine states between 2005 and 2017*

State	Year Acceded to CCJ	No. of Appeals adjudicated
Barbados	2005 (13 years)	69
Belize	2010 (8 years)	20
Dominica	2016 (1 year)	0
Guyana	2005 (13 years)	69
	Years with JCPC since Independence	
Antigua & Barbuda	37 years	9
Bahamas	45 years	27
Dominica	38 years	4
Grenada	44 years	4
Jamaica	56 years	44
St. Kitts & Nevis	37 years	8
St. Lucia	39 years	5
St. Vincent	39 years	5
Trinidad & Tobago	56 years	74

Table 18.2 *Percentage of appeals won by the government (appellant or appellee) before the JCPC (nine states from 2005 to 2017) and CCJ (three states from 2005 to 2017)*

Country	Court	Total # of Appeals	% in favor of gov't	% varied*
Antigua & Barbuda	JCPC	6	66	0
Bahamas	JCPC	27	44	13
Dominica	JCPC	4	25	0
Grenada	JCPC	4	25	0
Jamaica	JCPC	45	52	16
St. Kitts & Nevis	JCPC	8	75	0
St. Lucia	JCPC	5	60	0
St. Vincent & the Grenadines	JCPC	5	20	
Trinidad & Tobago	JCPC	77	46	14
Barbados	CCJ	28	55	0
Belize	CCJ	10	30	0
Guyana	CCJ	20	65	0

Note: * Part of the appeal is upheld.

upheld. The first nine countries retain appeals to the JCPC and the last three (Barbados, Belize, and Guyana) are appeals to the CCJ.

The analysis reveals that the nine governments are successful at the JCPC in 46 percent of cases on average (median 46; S.D. 19.5), over time. For the three countries with appeals to the CCJ, the governments are, on average, successful 50 percent (median 55; S.D. 18) of the time. This shows a remarkable consistency between the two courts, with no central tendency in favor of the states. In addition, of note is that the governments are the respondent in 98 percent of appeals before the JCPC and 88 percent before the CCJ. This willingness to challenge the state in the highest legal forum is a sign of the trust in the court and that a larger percentage of private litigants access the CCJ than the JCPC. It also reflects the relevance of the judiciary as an avenue checking the legislative and executive branches of government and a trusted arbitrator of private disputes.

The court is not particularly shy in critiquing the government of Belize in *Belize International Services Limited v. The Attorney General of Belize [2020]*. Justice Jamadar states:

> …if the government is permitted to enjoy exemption from its failure to comply with its rule of law obligations… And as well, left unaccounted for they diminish constitutional faith and public trust, and hence democratic legitimacy (368).

With lingering doubts about the independence of the court (Toote 2013; Anthony 2003) partially fueling reticence or lack of political will to accede to the CCJ, this speaks volumes. It exemplifies the court's willingness to speak clearly on the importance of the rule of law, the constitutions of countries and public trust in the justice system in the area of public law.

WHAT DO THE JUSTICES OF THE CCJ SAY?

After 16 years in existence, it is an opportune time to gain some insight into what the current justices think about the CCJ as a new regional judicial institution. Three justices completed key informant written interviews with the guarantee that no specific response would be attributed to any justice by name. The major drawback in using a written questionnaire is the lack of contemporaneous follow-up on responses provided by justices. The justices' responses to the written questionnaire do provide some important insights, not just about the CCJ as an institution, but their awareness that the specter of the JCPC still looms in the Caribbean. This section, therefore, presents some of the salient points made by the justices.

With 400 years of history, the JCPC casts a long shadow over the Caribbean. Colonial ties are deeply entrenched in the fabric of the Caribbean. Decades of political independence have not uprooted centuries of colonial rule. With only four of the 12 former British colonies having replaced the JCPC with the CCJ, the justices suggest that it is a lack of political will impairing expansion of the regional court within the framework of CARICOM. One justice added that a poor job is being done of increasing public awareness of the institutional regime that insulates the court and supports its independence. The long-standing court the public knows little about, but which is seated in London, England, is safer than a new court they also know little about but seated in Port of Spain, Trinidad and Tobago. Without additional and persuasive information, the mediocrity of the local judicial systems the public routinely experiences is projected onto the CCJ. They also acknowledged that members of the court have roles to play in raising its profile domestically and in other common law jurisdictions. The former can be done through public appearances, writing extrajudicially, presentations and readable opinions; the latter can be done by increasing the accessibility of court records for judges and lawyers in all common law jurisdictions. To its credit, the CCJ is making strides on the official website in the latter and many jurisdictions are making courts more available and accessible through electronic platforms such as APEX (electronic filing, case management and court operating system).

The CCJ does not consider itself nor does it intend to be a rubber stamp for any country or class of litigants in the appellate or original jurisdiction. The challenges facing the CCJ are reminiscent of those faced by the newly established SCOTUS under the Constitution of 1789. From the balancing of public and private interests in cases based on the takings clause to marshalling the jealousies and politics between the federal government and states and among states, the SCOTUS continually strives to maintain its authority, independence, and reputation. After 16 years in service to the Caribbean, the parallels with the SCOTUS are not obscure as the CCJ strives to do the same. The single most significant difference is that while the SCOTUS emblazes its authority in *Marbury v. Madison* (1803) in declaring its power of judicial review, every Caribbean constitution specifically entrenches that power to the judiciary.

All the justices interviewed reject that decisions are influenced by the domestic politics of the country where appeals originate. As the court adjudicates in panels, it is possible that there may be no justice from the state from which the appeal originates. While there is no treaty or regulatory requirement for judges to be from any particular country, the seven current justices hail from St. Vincent and the Grenadines, the Netherlands, Jamaica, Belize, Barbados, and two justices from Trinidad and Tobago (Caribbean Court of Justice, n.d.). Only Belize and Barbados that have acceded to the court have justices native to each. This will probably change in the future, but so will the court's processes and traditions.

The court has disposed of 20 matters in its original jurisdiction. In exercising its original jurisdiction, there is a different approach that demonstrates the acknowledged role of the court as a pillar of regional integration and justice. The justices acknowledge their cognizance of regional politics and the role of the court, not just as an adjudicator with original jurisdiction, but also in relation to the goal of regional integration. One justice describes it as follows:

> The role of the Court is not to side with the state or the Community against a non-state litigant, nor is the role of the Court automatically to side with the non-state litigant against a state or the Community. The role of the Court is to advance the goals of the Treaty [Revised Treaty of Chaguaramas 2001] in keeping with the provisions laid out in the Treaty.

Finally, the interviews provide us with a small aperture into the internal processes of the court. The justices communicated the level of collegiality and individualism expected at this level of adjudication. Justice Powel describes the SCOTUS as "nine little law firms" (Peppers 2012, 391). Comparing this with the SCOTUS, we know that the support staff play a major role in the granting of writs of certiorari and which appeals get on the docket (Corley, Ward and Martinek 2016). It is not clear whether the justices and their immediate staff function as "seven little law firms." The responses do indicate, however, the degree to which justices rely on their staff. Responses range from "a great deal" to "little." This could indicate personality differences and the court's volume of work. These answers may change as more countries allow appeals and the caseload increases.

Sitting on panels *en banc*, the justices indicate some preference for unanimity in decisions and, in particular, a united front in decisions in the original jurisdiction. One justice writes:

> In the original jurisdiction we deliver a single judgment or advisory opinion. Part of the reason for this is to send a clear and unambiguous message as to how the treaty should be interpreted and applied...a tension between unanimity and dissent is acknowledged with obvious preference for unanimity but recognizing the dissent can play a very useful role in developing the law in the future.

FUTURE

The subject of judicial dissent presents a very interesting phenomenon worthy of study going forward. Like the SCOTUS, which saw low levels of dissent from 1790 to 1945, there is 91 percent unanimity between 1902 and 1932 followed by a steady decrease to levels below 30 percent (Kelsh 1999). It is reasonable to project that the CCJ may see the same trend over time. A number of factors can contribute to this in the future.

First, as the attraction and influence of the JCPC wane, more countries will accede to the CCJ. This waning is being nudged by the Law Lords (justices) of the JCPC itself. In 2009, Lord Phillips of Worth Matravers, KG, suggests in an interview that hearing appeals in the JCPC is taking up too much time that could be spent adjudicating U.K. appeals to the Supreme Court of Judicature (the same jurists sit on both courts) and that British Commonwealth countries should handle their own appeals (Peel and Croft, September 20, 2009). Coincidentally, Belize and Dominica subsequently stopped appeals to the JCPC. In addition, although multi-issue referendums in St. Kitts and Nevis (2015) and Grenada (2016) failed to gain majority voter support, the issue of their accession to the CCJ is part of the national agenda. It is unclear that the failure is linked to a lack of confidence in the CCJ, or some other constitutional issue on the ballot. The justices, nevertheless, are aware of the possible future surge in appeals as countries accede. As one justice succinctly points out, "Over time, when more states are sending their appeals to the court, I could see the criteria we apply being strengthened somewhat so as to ensure that the Court is not overrun with appeals..." While currently appeals are granted by a "unanimous/consensus vote," the need for a "rule of three" comparable with the "rule of four" in the SCOTUS and a higher threshold for hearing appeals may yet be necessary.

Finally, the CCJ has embraced technology as an indispensable tool for adjudicating cases (original jurisdiction) and appeals (appellate jurisdiction) in the far-flung non-continuous countries of CARICOM. Considering the physical court located on Henry Street, Port of Spain, Trinidad and Tobago is more than 1,400 miles from Nassau, the Bahamas, the advantages of closed circuit and virtual technology are obvious. This also pairs well with the approach to the work of the court, as one justice explains: "It is a service we deliver and that service is often performed with the judges and court staff being very far away from 134 Henry Street...justice is delivered with the same efficiency and effectiveness as if the judges and staff were assembled at 134 Henry Street." This accessibility and dedication to the Caribbean contrast sharply with the JCPC convening physically and almost exclusively in London (4,684 miles from Kingston, Jamaica). Reduced costs and accessibility to the CCJ should underpin an increase in the number of appeals and the diversity and complexity of subject matter. These developments are worthy of study as other regional bodies seek higher levels of integration at law.

SUMMARY

The JCPC is integral to the establishment, expansion and support of the institutions and the common law in the British Empire. Its development contributed greatly to common law jurisprudence, and opinions are still persuasive in many British Commonwealth countries. Simply based on the length of British colonial rule, there is no region of the world where the JCPC is more entrenched than in the Caribbean. All 12 countries constitutionally retain the JCPC as the final appellate court after independence. As of January 1, 2023, eight countries still allow appeals to the JCPC.

While other former colonies establish their own final appellate court, the Caribbean has done the unprecedented in establishing the CCJ as a pillar of regional integration under CARICOM. With original and appellate jurisdictions in independent countries, the only comparable court is the Court of Justice of the European Union. The CCJ appellate jurisdiction is deeper, however, as it is the final court of appeal in all matters for each country that accedes. Because the countries have no voice in who sits in the JCPC and no fiscal obligation to support the court, it is viewed as independent and impartial. In addition, the colonial legacy imbues the immediate perception of superiority over any domestic or regional court. In considering why so few countries accede to the regional court, one justice on the CCJ put it this way: "…the sad truth that for many persons, if you are competing with a British institution, then you are automatically second best." A review of the treaty provisions that set up the CCJ shows that great pains are taken to insulate the selection of the justices from bias, avoid fiscal influence by countries and make the court's decision-making as unconstrained as possible.

Responses by the justices reflect a deep appreciation for the development of "Caribbean jurisprudence" as jurisprudence that takes appropriate account of the Caribbean's socio-historical considerations and place in the common law world. In addition, each notes the responsibility to deliver opinions that further the cause of justice and strengthen the rule of law.

As a new and unique regional court, procedural and substantive issue studies are in their infancy. More research is needed into the domestic environment that either constrains or facilitates accession to the CCJ. As more countries accede, the court will be forced to alter the appeal review process and the threshold or criteria on which to allow appeals. While justices are asked in the written interview about ideology, either the answers are vague or they avoid the question completely. They are probably not the best judges of their own ideological proclivities and preferences! While the literature on judicial ideology in the U.S. continues to be refined and expanded, this is not the case in the Caribbean or even in the other common law jurisdictions. Developing an external ideological measure for CCJ justices is a goal worth pursuing. It is important to build the knowledge base on how the court and Caribbean jurisprudence evolve as justices and societies change over time.

While the CCJ continues to serve four countries and CARICOM, the challenge of gaining full acceptance in the region remains. Paradoxically, as the host to the physical court, Trinidad and Tobago has still not acceded. The largest jurisdiction and the one from which the largest number of appeals originate, Jamaica, has not acceded. Finally, the Bahamas, which has the highest per capita income in the Caribbean (The World Bank 2021), has also not acceded. With these three countries still allowing appeals to the JCPC, the CCJ will continue to struggle to move out of this colonial shadow. Lack of political will and public awareness of the strengths and benefits of the regional court are major contributing factors to the pace of accession to the CCJ. While its existence is not in any immediate danger, there is a long road ahead to exploit its true potential as the center of Caribbean jurisprudence and a major contributor to common law jurisprudence. Ultimately, the goal of increasing Caribbean integration remains a work in progress.

REFERENCES

Amnesty International. (2016). *Death Penalty 2015: Facts and Figures*. https://www.amnesty.org/en/latest/news/2016/04/death-penalty-2015-facts-and-figures/ [13 April 2017].

Andic, Faut, Suphan Andic and Douglas Dosser. (2011). A Theory of Economic Integration for Developing Countries: Illustrated by Caribbean Countries. New York and Oxen: Routledge.

Anthony, Kenny. (2003). The Caribbean Court of Justice: Will it be a Hanging Court? Retrieved from http://archive.stlucia.gov.lc/primeminister/former_prime_ministers/kenny_d_anthony/statements/2003/the_caribbean_court_of_justicc_will_it_be_a_hanging_court_june_28_2003.htm. Accessed August 5, 2015.

BahamaCatholic. (October 25, 2009). Catholic Church Stands Firm against Death Penalty. Retrieved from http://www.bahamacatholic.com/2009/10/catholic-church-remainsresolute-in-its.html. Accessed July 15, 2015.

BBC World News. (2007). Should the Caribbean Abolish the Death Penalty? *BBC World News-Caribbean*. http://www.bbc.co.uk/caribbean/news/story/2007/01/070112_tthanging.shtml [20 June 2017].

Burns, Peter T. (1984). The Judicial Committee of the Privy Council: Constitutional Bulwark or Colonial Remnant? *Otago Law Review*, Vol. 5, pp. 503–522.

Caribbean Community Secretariat. (2001). The Agreement Establishing the CCJ, The Caribbean Court of Justice. http://www.caribbeancourtofjustice.org/wp-content/uploads/2011/09/ccj_agreement.pdf. Accessed March 30, 2018.

Caribbean Court of Justice. (2012). CCJ Trust Fund. http://www.ccj.org/about-the-ccj/ccj-trust-fund. Accessed March 31, 2018.

Caribbean News Now. (2004). *Privy Council to Rule on Caribbean Death Penalty*. http://www.caribbeannewsnow.com/caribnet/2004/03/23/penalty.htm. [20 June 2017].

Caribbean360. (August 25, 2017). CARIBBEAN: Trinidad President urges Region to Dump Privy Council. *St. Lucia News Online*. https://www.stlucianewsonline.com/caribbean-trinidad-president-urges-region-to-dump-privy-council/. [June 3, 2018]

CARICOM. (2001). The West Indies Federation. https://caricom.org/community/the-west-indies-federation/#. Accessed March 30, 2018.

CARICOM. (2018). Who We Are: Pillars of Integration. https://caricom.org/about-caricom/who-we-are. Accessed March 31, 2018. http://www.ccj.org/about-the-ccj/ccj-trust-fund.

CMC. (March 26, 2018). Grenada PM wants to re-open dialogue on CCJ. *St. Lucia News Online*. https://www.stlucianewsonline.com/grenada-pm-wants-to-re-open-dialogue-on-ccj/. [June 3, 2018]

Corley, Pamela C., Artemus Ward, Wendy L. Martinek. (2016). *American Judicial Process: Myth and Reality in Law and Courts*. New York: Routledge.

Fraser, Tony. (n.d.). Jamaica, Trinidad and the CCJ. *Caribbean Intelligence*. Accessed May 11, 2018. https://www.caribbeanintelligence.com/content/jamaica-trinidad-and-ccj.

Ghany, Hamid A. (2000). The Death Penalty, Human Rights and British Law Lords: Judicial Opinion on Delay of Execution in the Commonwealth Caribbean. *International Journal of Human Rights*. Vol. 4, No. 2, pp. 30–43.

Girvan, Norman. (2001). Reinterpreting the Caribbean in New Caribbean Thought: A Reader. Edited by Brian Meeks and Folke Lindahl. Jamaica: University of West Indies Press. https://books.google.com/books?hl=en&lr=&id=mUC4PA7ZedYC&oi=fnd&pg=PR8&dq=related:RLXzRsrj590J:scholar.google.com/&ots=ci2IbELQKL&sig=4KCe9EM4g7yGO7e4b-VMMGHlWqY#v=onepage&q&f=false. Accessed March 30, 2018.

Heifer, Laurence R. (2002). Overlegalizing Human Rights: International Relations Theory and the Commonwealth Caribbean Backlash Against Human Rights Regimes. *Columbia Law Review*. Vol. 102, pp. 1832–1911.

Howell, P.A. (1979). The Judicial Committee of the Privy Council 1833–1876: Its Origins, Structure and Development. New York: Cambridge University Press.

Kelsh, John P. (1999). The Opinion Delivery Practices of the United States Supreme Court 1790–1945, 77 *Wash. U. L. Q.* 137.

Kerr, Roger. (2002). Abolition of Privy Council Major Constitutional Issue, New Zealand Business Round Table, December 10. Retrieved February 3, 2016, from http://www.nzbr.org.nz/documents/releases/releases-2002/abolition_appeals.doc.htm.

Malleson, Kate. (1999). *The Judiciary: The Effects of Expansion and Activism.* Aldershot: Dartmouth Publishing Company, Ltd.

Manifesto '07. (2007). A Matter of Trust. Retrieved from http://www.caribbeanelections.com/eDocs/manifestos/bs/FNM_Manifesto_2007.pdf. Accessed July 10, 2015.

McCartney, Mathew. (2015). Economic Growth and Development: A Comparative Introduction. London: Palgrave.

Merriam-Webster. (2015). *Dictionary*, accessed November 22, 2018. http://www.merriamwebster.com/dictionary/curia%20regis.

Mills, Therese. (2005). *Colonial Power over Death Penalty*. Editor of Newsday. www.bbc.co.uk January 19. Accessed July 10, 2012.

Minnis, Hubert A. (2014). 2014 New Year's Address by Opposition Leader, Hon. Dr. Hubert A. Minnis. Bahamas island info. Retrieved from http://www.bahamaislandsinfo.com/index.php?option=com_content&view=article&id=16777:2014-new-years-address-by-opposition-leader-hon-dr-hubert-minnis&catid=34:Bahamas%20National%20News&Itemid=147. Accessed July 10, 2015.

Peel, Michael and Jabe Croft. (September 20, 2009). Privy Council hampers Supreme Court. *Financial Times*. Retrieved from https://www.ft.com/content/3c5b14a6-a61d-11de-8c92-00144feabdc0.

Peppers, Todd C. (2012). The Modern Clerkship: Justice Ruth Bader Ginsburg and Her Law Clerks. In *Chambers: Stories of Supreme Court Law Clerks and Their Justices*, ed. Todd C. Peppers and Artemus Ward, pp. 391–404. Charlottesville: University of Virginia Press.

Revised Treaty of Chaguaramas Establishing the Caribbean Community Including the CARICOM Single Market and Economy 2001. CARICOM Secretariat. https://caricom.org/documents/4906-revised_treaty-text.pdf. Accessed March 31, 2018.

Richards, Peter. (2006). Death Penalty-Caribbean: When Is It Appropriate to Execute? Available: http://www.ipsnews.net/2006/11/death-penalty-caribbean-when-is-it-appropriate-to-execute/. Accessed August 25, 2017.

Robert-Wray, Kenneth. (1966). Commonwealth and Colonial Law. London: Stevens & Sons.

Rolle, Domek. (June 2012). Abolish the Privy Council, Easier Said than Done. Retrieved from http://www.ilntoday.com/files/2012/06/Abolish-The-Privy-Council-by-D-Rolle.pdf.

Saunders, Adrian. (2010). The Relevance of the Privy Council in Post Independent West Indian Nation States. 2nd Annual Eugene Dupuch Distinguished Lecture. Council of Legal Education. http://www.da-academy.org/uploads/9/2/0/3/92034718/relevance_privycouncil.pdf.

Schlesinger, Arthur Meier. (1913). Colonial Appeals to the Privy Council (pts. 1 & 2), 28 *Pols Ci. Q.* 279, 433.

Smith, Joseph Henry. (1950). *Appeals to The Privy Council from The American Plantations*. New York: Columbia University Press.

Swinfen, David, B. (1987). *Imperial Appeal: The Debate on the Appeal to the Privy Council 1833–1986.* Manchester: Manchester University Press.

The Caribbean Court of Justice. (n.d.). Judges of the CCJ. Retrieved from https://ccj.org/about-the-ccj/judges/

The National Archives. (n.d.). The Appellate Jurisdiction Act 1876. Retrieved from http://www.legislation.gov.uk/ukpga/Vict/39–40/59/contents.

The National Archives. (n.d.). The Judicial Committee Act 1844. Retrieved from http://www.legislation.gov.uk/ukpga/Vict/7–8/69/section/1.

The World Bank. (2021). GDP per Capita (current US dollars) – Latin America and the Caribbean. Retrieved from https://data.worldbank.org/indicator/NY.GDP.PCAP.CD?locations=ZJ

Toote, Michael D. (2013). *Capital Punishment in The Bahamas: The Privy Council Moratorium.* Bloomington, IN: Author House.

Yakana, David. (2006). Employers and Labour-Management Relations: The Guyana Experience in Industrial Relations in the Caribbean Issues and Perspectives. Accessed October 3, 2015, http://www.ilo.org/wcmsp5/groups/public/---americas/---ro-lima/---sro-port_of_spain/documents/publication/wcms_224310.pdf.

Cases

August and Gabb v. The Queen [2018] CCJ 7 (AJ)
Belize International Services Limited v. The Attorney General of Belize. [2020] CCJ 9 (AJ)
Lewis v. Attorney-General of Barbados. (2000). 57 West Indian Reports 275
Marbury v. Madison, 5 U.S. 137
Maxo Tido v. The Queen. 16 U.K. Privy Council (2011).
Pratt and Morgan v. Attorney General of Jamaica and Other. (1993). 43 West Indian Reports 340.
Reyes v. The Queen. (2002). 60 West Indian Reports 26.
The Attorney General, Superintendent of Prisons and Chief Marshal and Jeffrey Joseph and Lennox Ricardo Boyce [2006] CCJ 3 (AJ)

19. Law and violence against civilians

Country-level effects of the International Criminal Court

M.P. Broache

INTRODUCTION

In the past half-century, there has been a substantial increase in prosecutions of individual political and military leaders for atrocity crimes such as genocide, war crimes, crimes against humanity, and other large-scale human rights violations. This "justice cascade" (Sikkink and Kim 2013; Sikkink 2011) has manifested domestically, in both ordinary courts and specially constituted tribunals, and internationally, through the exercise of universal jurisdiction by national courts (Langer 2011); the establishment, by the UN Security Council, of ad hoc tribunals for the former Yugoslavia (1993) and Rwanda (1994); the constitution of hybrid tribunals in Sierra Leone, Cambodia, East Timor, Kosovo, and Lebanon (Raub 2008); and, finally, the establishment of the International Criminal Court (ICC, alternately the Court).

The ICC was established by the Rome Statute, a treaty that was adopted on July 17, 1998, and entered into force on July 1, 2002. In many respects, the ICC represents the most ambitious manifestation of the "justice cascade." Unlike previous international and hybrid courts, which were explicitly temporary, the Court was established as a permanent tribunal, with temporal jurisdiction dating from the Statute's entry into force; furthermore, while not universal, the ICC's geographic and personal jurisdiction is broad-based, encompassing the territory and nationals of all States Parties and situations referred by the UN Security Council, or where non-States Parties voluntarily accept the Court's jurisdiction. Finally, while the Security Council and States Parties may refer situations for investigation, the Statute also established a strong, independent prosecutor, with authority to initiate investigations *proprio motu* in situations involving States Parties.

Human rights activists, practitioners, and scholars have advanced multiple rationales for prosecuting perpetrators of atrocity crimes through the ICC and other institutions, including retribution, restorative justice for victims, and promoting communal reconciliation (Aukerman 2002; Leebaw 2008), *inter alia*. Particularly with respect to the ICC, the Court's supporters have also emphasized the instrumentalist rationale of preventing future atrocities (Cronin-Furman 2013; Drumbl 2004; Vinjamuri 2010). Drawing upon criminological theories, it has been argued that the ICC can deter or otherwise prevent the atrocity crimes under its jurisdiction by increasing costs to perpetrators, incapacitating them, and/or altering underlying norms about the appropriateness of atrocities (Akhavan 2001; Scheffer 1999; Sloane 2010).

However, whether the ICC prevents atrocities is ultimately an empirical question. As scholars of international relations and law have turned their attention to this question since the Court's establishment, a mixed body of evidence has emerged. On the one hand, there is a growing body of evidence based on statistical studies of violence against civilians and human rights repression that the ICC and other judicial interventions have deterrent effects, particularly *vis-à-vis* government actors (Appel 2018; Jo and Simmons 2016; Hillebrecht

2016; McAllister 2020; Meernik 2015; Kim and Sikkink 2010). On the other hand, qualitative evidence from case studies of ICC investigations suggests that the Court's impact on violence is more mixed and conditional (Broache 2016a, 2016b; Kersten 2016; Wegner 2016), and there is also cross-national quantitative evidence indicating that ICC jurisdiction is sometimes associated with *increased* violence against civilians (by rebels, Jo and Simmons 2017).

In light of this mixed evidence, this chapter reexamines the effects of the ICC on atrocities, focusing on the impact of the Court's territorial jurisdiction on violence against civilians. In doing so, this chapter extends previous statistical analyses by incorporating two categories of violence against civilians excluded from previous studies: (1) killings committed by government and non-state actors not otherwise active in international or intrastate armed conflicts, and (2) non-state groups exclusively involved in conflicts with other non-state actors. I combine annual counts of these killings with civilian deaths incorporated in previous studies, including (1) killings by government forces involved in international and intrastate armed conflicts, and (2) killings by non-state groups in active conflict against government forces, to produce annual counts of civilian deaths for all countries of the world for the period 1995–2010. Using these data, I find that ICC jurisdiction has insignificant country-level effects on violence against civilians, after controlling for conflict dynamics and other potential confounding variables; this result holds after accounting for potential endogeneity concerns using a difference-in-differences (DiD) approach.

The remainder of this chapter proceeds as follows: the next section discusses the expectations associated with the establishment of the ICC and elaborates the logic underlying the deterrence hypothesis. The following section reviews previous research addressing the deterrence hypothesis and discusses the limitations of the data used in these studies. The next section introduces the data employed in this study and presents a series of statistical models of the relationship between ICC jurisdiction and violence against civilians at the country level. The final section concludes by discussing the implications of these findings for debates about the ICC and deterrence.

THE ICC AND THE PREVENTION OF ATROCITIES

As the world's first standing international criminal tribunal with broad-based territorial and personal jurisdiction, the establishment of the ICC generated great expectations. For example, after the sixtieth state deposited its ratification of the Rome Statute in April 2002, enabling its entry into force three months later, the director of the International Justice Program at Human Rights Watch, Richard Dicker, hailed the ICC as "potentially the most important human rights institution created in 50 years" (Human Rights Watch 2002). Similarly, the Secretary-General of the UN, Kofi Annan, issued a statement on the date of the Statute's entry into force, calling it "an historic occasion" that "reaffirms the centrality of the rule of law in international relations" (United Nations 2002).

The expectations surrounding the ICC have focused, in large part, on the Court's potential to prevent the atrocity crimes under its jurisdiction. This expectation is explicit in the Preamble to the Rome Statute, which expresses the determination of States Parties "to put an end to impunity for the perpetrators of these crimes and thus to contribute to the prevention of such crimes" (United Nations 1998); and principals of the Court have frequently invoked the language of prevention—for example, in an April 2003 speech shortly after he was elected as the ICC's first prosecutor, Luis Moreno-Ocampo recalled various "horrors" of the twentieth century and expressed hope that the "creation of the International Criminal Court will help us to prevent [those] atrocities from being repeated in the future" (International Criminal Court 2003). Likewise, in a speech shortly after succeeding Moreno-Ocampo as prosecutor in 2012, Fatou Bensouda asserted:

> The true relevance of trials as well as the other activities of the court, will, however, more importantly lie on the fact that by their global impacts, they will contribute to preventing—or prevention of recurring violence (Bensouda 2012).

The claim that prosecutions can contribute to prevention is based largely on the application of criminological models of deterrence to mass atrocities. These models assume that potential perpetrators are rational actors: they will commit crime if, and only if, the expected benefits exceed the expected costs (Becker 1968). In turn, the expected costs of crime are principally a function of the perceived certainty of punishment (Nagin 2013). As such, interventions that increase the subjective probability of punishment are expected to have preventive effects. Applying this logic to the ICC, the Court is expected to generate "prosecutorial deterrence" (Jo and Simmons 2016) by providing a standing mechanism for prosecuting individual leaders who order or condone atrocities; this is expected to increase the subjective probability of punishment, which was hitherto effectively nil (Sikkink and Kim 2013), thereby contributing to the prevention of atrocities at the margins (Gilligan 2006).

While prosecutorial deterrence may operate directly *vis-à-vis* individual perpetrators, it may also contribute to prevention more indirectly by undermining support for leaders facing prosecution. According to this logic, domestic constituents, group members, and external allies may be deterred from supporting such leaders, both because of the stigma of association with accused *genocidaires* or war criminals, and to avoid potential legal liability themselves; this may reduce group capacity to conduct operations and commit atrocities (Wegner 2016, 36–37). Relatedly, the apprehension of individual perpetrators, particularly group leaders, from the battlefield or other positions of power may undermine organizational capacity, cohesion, and morale, reducing the group's ability to perpetrate atrocities (Broache 2016b). In this sense, this logic is broadly consistent with the "incapacitation" mechanism in the criminological literature, through which legal sanctions are posited to reduce crime by removing or otherwise undermining dangerous perpetrators (Piquero and Blumstein 2007).

Beyond the cost–benefit logic of "prosecutorial deterrence" and the related "incapacitation" mechanism, it has also been proposed that prosecutions can prevent atrocities through various social mechanisms. For instance, Kim and Sikkink (2010) argue that, in addition to generating material costs, prosecutions can change social understandings of the appropriateness of atrocities. Similarly, Jo and Simmons (2016) propose a logic of "social deterrence," whereby the ICC is posited to generate extralegal pressures to comply with anti-atrocity norms for groups seeking international recognition; while McAllister (2020) argues that deterrence by international tribunals is more effective *vis-à-vis* belligerents supported by "liberal constituencies" that generate social and political pressure for normative compliance.

Collectively, these mechanisms inform the *deterrence hypothesis*, which can be expressed formally with respect to ICC jurisdiction—the set of "situations" in which the Court can initiate prosecutions per the Rome Statute—as follows:

Atrocities should be less severe in situations under ICC jurisdiction than in situations not under ICC jurisdiction.

Jurisdiction is particularly relevant for deterrence because, while the Court may plausibly generate more general effects in situations beyond its statutorily defined jurisdiction, the ICC is unable to intervene directly in these situations; accordingly, for individuals in situations beyond the Court's jurisdiction, the *ex ante* probability of punishment is significantly lower, if not negligible. Therefore, the ICC's preventive impacts should be stronger in situations under the Court's jurisdiction.

While the Court's principals and supporters have often invoked the deterrence hypothesis, other practitioners and observers have been less optimistic about the Court's preventive powers. For example, some have cautioned that the ICC's treaty-based jurisdiction, which excludes non-States Parties to the Rome Statute (unless referred by the UN Security Council), and its dependence on state cooperation to conduct investigations and enforce arrest warrants, hinder its capacity to deter atrocities (Cronin-Furman 2013; Goldsmith and Krasner 2003; Mendeloff 2018). Indeed, because of jurisdictional limitations, the Court has been unable to intervene in some of the worst cases of alleged atrocities since the Rome Statute entered into force, including Syria, Xinjiang, and Tigray, *inter alia*. Furthermore, the ICC has encountered significant difficulties in executing arrest warrants and securing convictions; as of June 1, 2021, 13 suspects publicly charged by the ICC remained at large, and the Court had returned only four final guilty verdicts for substantive crimes (International Criminal Court 2021a, 2021b, 2021c);[1] moreover, the Court has experienced several high-profile failures due to obstruction or other difficulties in obtaining state cooperation, as in the collapse of the case against Kenyan President Uhuru Kenyatta (Mburu 2018). Beyond the ICC's limited jurisdiction and enforcement powers, other commentators have warned that the Court could unintentionally exacerbate, rather than prevent, atrocities by undermining peace negotiations and/or incentivizing leaders facing prosecution to escalate violence to maintain power (Ku and Nzelibe 2006; Licklider 2008; Snyder and Vinjamuri 2003). Finally, others have argued that the ICC would politicize international justice and, in doing so, undermine, rather than reinforce, anti-atrocity norms (Kissinger 2001).

Ultimately, however, whether the ICC prevents, exacerbates, or has no impact on atrocities is an empirical question. The next section reviews single case and cross-national studies that have examined the ICC's impact on atrocities and related outcomes.

---

1 The ICC has returned final guilty verdicts for substantive crimes (genocide, war crimes, or crimes against humanity) in two situations: DRC—Thomas Lubanga (verdict March 14, 2012, upheld on appeal December 1, 2014), Germain Katanga (verdict March 7, 2014, appeal withdrawn June 25, 2014), and Bosco Ntaganda (verdict July 8, 2019, upheld on appeal March 30, 2021); and Mali—Ahmad Al Faqi Al Mahdi (verdict September 27, 2016, no appeal). Additionally, the Court issued guilty verdicts for Jean-Pierre Bemba (Central African Republic) on March 21, 2016, and Dominic Ongwen (Uganda) on February 4, 2021; however, Bemba's conviction was dismissed on appeal, and Ongwen's case is pending appeal. The Court has additionally returned five final convictions (upheld on appeal March 8, 2018) for "offenses against the administration of justice" that did not involve substantive crimes under the Court's jurisdiction, all relating to the situation in the Central African Republic: Jean-Pierre Bemba, Aimé Kilolo Musamba, Jean-Jacques Mangenda Kabongo, Fidèle Babala Wandu, and Narcisse Arido.

EMPIRICAL LITERATURE REVIEW

The negotiation and entry into force of the Rome Statute sparked a wave of literature focused on the ICC's expected impact on atrocities and other related outcomes. However, in the absence of an empirical record to examine, the initial literature relating to the deterrence hypothesis was mostly theoretical, normative, or outright speculative; moreover, to the extent that studies did incorporate empirical evidence, it was mostly in the form of anecdotes drawn from domestic courts, the *ad hoc* tribunals for Yugoslavia and Rwanda, and hybrid bodies, rather than systematic within-case or cross-case comparative analysis focused on the ICC (Akhavan 2001, 2009; D'Amato 1994; Gilligan 2006; Snyder and Vinjamuri 2003; Wippman 1999). Accordingly, a 2010 review of the empirical literature on transitional justice mechanisms, including the ICC, concluded that the state of knowledge concerning their effects was rather more "faith-based" than "fact-based" (Thoms, Ron, and Paris 2010, 329).

However, as the ICC's membership and caseload have expanded, researchers have conducted more systematic studies testing the deterrence hypothesis. These studies can be broadly grouped into two categories: single case studies, which have focused mostly on the impact of specific ICC actions in situations where the Court has intervened; and cross-national comparative analyses, which have typically used quantitative methods to examine the global impacts of ICC jurisdiction and, in some cases, specific types of ICC actions. Both single case and comparative studies have focused on two outcomes relevant to the deterrence hypothesis: (1) conflict dynamics such as war duration and termination, and (2) the magnitude of atrocities, including violence against civilians and human rights abuses. While the latter set of studies directly tests the deterrence hypothesis, the Court's impact on broader conflict dynamics is also relevant to atrocity prevention, as atrocities are generally more likely and severe during conflict (Straus 2012; Verdeja 2016), and the Court has intervened in multiple cases of ongoing conflict (Kersten 2016; Wegner 2016); accordingly, studies examining the Court's impact on conflict dynamics have also provided important, if indirect, insight into the deterrence hypothesis.

Single Case Study Findings

Single case studies have produced mixed findings concerning the effects of specific ICC actions in situations under investigation. For example, Broache's (2016a, 2016b) analyses of rebel groups in the Democratic Republic of the Congo (DRC)—the location of the Court's first investigation (and, so far, most successful, in terms of total convictions)—suggest the impact of ICC actions on atrocities varies across stages of the legal process; specifically, these analyses indicate that outstanding arrest warrants and associated operations to apprehend suspects triggered increased violence against civilians but that actual arrests were associated with reduced violence, consistent with the incapacitation mechanism.

Case studies of the ICC investigation in northern Uganda, where the Court issued its first arrest warrants in 2005, likewise indicate variation in its impacts. For example, Wegner (2016, 270) finds that the announcements of the ICC investigation and issuance of arrest warrants for five Lord's Resistance Army (LRA) commanders had "partial"—though incomplete— deterrent effects and contributed to the international isolation of the targeted leaders, consistent with the logic of incapacitation. Using time series intervention analysis, Jo, Radtke, and Simmons (2018) similarly find that the ICC investigation contributed to deterrence of civilian killings by the LRA, and the authors also note a strong correlation between the investigation and defections of rank-and-file members, consistent with incapacitation; the authors additionally suggest that ICC action in northern Uganda catalyzed domestic accountability mechanisms and prevented violence by government forces.

However, there is also case study evidence suggesting that the ICC investigation in northern Uganda had more mixed effects. Wegner (2016), for instance, also finds that the investigation and arrest warrants enhanced the internal position of hardline elements in the LRA, triggered some episodes of retaliatory violence, and complicated peace negotiations. Kersten (2016) also finds that the ICC investigation and arrest warrants impacted peace negotiations, although the Court's effects varied across stages of negotiations—initially inducing the LRA to the negotiating table but later complicating the process due to the absence of senior leaders facing ICC arrest warrants.

There is also case study evidence of mixed effects in the two non-State Party situations referred to the ICC by the UN Security Council: Darfur and Libya. In Darfur, Wegner (2016) finds that the ICC investigation and subsequent arrest warrants, including for Sudanese president Omar al-Bashir, mostly failed to generate deterrence, as government forces and allied militia continued to commit various atrocities under the Court's jurisdiction, including attacks against civilian targets involving killing, rape, destruction of property, and looting, *inter alia.* Rodman (2008) similarly finds that the ICC investigation in Darfur failed to deter atrocities, primarily because of the unwillingness of international actors to take enforcement action. While these studies suggest that the ICC failed to prevent further violence in Darfur, Durrsma and Muller (2019) find that the Bashir arrest warrant may have further undermined the security and humanitarian situation, as the government responded by escalating intimidation of peacekeepers and aid workers.

Finally, using intervention analysis of event count data on violence against civilians, Hillebrecht (2016) demonstrates that the announcements of the Security Council referral and the opening of the ICC investigation in Libya were associated with significant reductions in total civilian killings; however, later ICC actions—including the issuance of arrest warrants for Libyan president Muammar al-Qaddafi and two other senior government officials—had mostly insignificant effects on total civilian fatalities. Kersten (2016), meanwhile, finds that the ICC investigation and arrest warrants emboldened rebel forces and weakened incentives to engage in meaningful peace negotiations.

Cross-national Comparative Findings

While single case studies have focused on the impact of discrete ICC actions in specific situations, cross-national comparative studies have examined the effects of the Court's jurisdiction and actions more broadly. Like single case studies, these analyses have focused mostly on two sets of outcomes relevant to deterrence: conflict dynamics, such as war duration and termination; and the magnitude of atrocities under the Court's jurisdiction, including human rights violations and civilian killings. These studies have yielded mixed findings concerning the Court's impact, with variation depending on the actor type and the outcome under analysis. Consistent with the deterrence hypothesis and some case study evidence, these studies consistently find that ICC jurisdiction is associated with reduced atrocities by government actors; however, there is more mixed evidence concerning the ICC's impact on broader conflict dynamics, and data particularities limit the conclusions that can be drawn about the Court's effects on atrocities by non-state actors and in the aggregate.

With respect to conflict dynamics, cross-case quantitative analyses have produced inconsistent findings. On the one hand, Prorok's (2017) analysis of ICC interventions in civil wars indicates that ICC action reduces the likelihood of conflict termination in certain situations; and Krcmaric (2018) finds that international prosecutions disincentivize culpable leaders from fleeing into exile, thereby prolonging conflict. Conversely, Dancy and Wiebelhaus-Brahm (2017) find that criminal trials targeting rebels (including by the ICC) in civil wars are associated with an *increased* likelihood of conflict termination.

Cross-case analyses of the ICC's direct effects on atrocities have focused principally on two outcomes: human rights violations and civilian killings. With respect to human rights violations, Kim and Sikkink (2010) find that both domestic and international prosecutions—including by the ICC in its initial years of operation—are associated with reduced state-level human rights violations. Focusing more specifically on the ICC, Appel (2018) finds that state membership in the Rome Statute is associated with reduced violations of physical integrity rights, while Meernik (2015) similarly finds that state support for the ICC is correlated with lower levels of abuses. Jo and Simmons (2016) report similar results with respect to government violence against civilians, finding that state ratification of the Rome Statute and cross-case ICC actions are associated with reduced civilian killings; however, in a subsequent corrigendum (2017), Jo and Simmons report that ICC jurisdiction under the Rome Statute is associated with *increased* civilian killings by rebel forces.

Studies focusing on the ICC's effects on human rights, including Appel (2018) and Meernik (2015), have used the Cingranelli-Richards (CIRI) Physical Integrity Rights Index, which measures government respect for human rights protections against torture, extrajudicial killings, political imprisonment, and disappearance (Cingranelli and Richards 2010). Combined with Jo and Simmons's (2016) findings concerning civilian killings by government forces, these results suggest that the ICC is an effective deterrent against government atrocities. However, the ICC's impact on atrocities by non-state actors is less clear from these studies, as the CIRI Physic Integrity Index covers only government human rights practices and thus excludes non-state actors;[2] and the findings reported in Jo and Simmons's (2017) corrigendum indicate that the ICC may exacerbate, rather than deter, civilian killings by rebel forces.

Moreover, because of particularities in their source data, a substantial number of actors (primarily, though not exclusively, non-state groups) are omitted from both Jo and Simmons's original (2016) and corrected (2017) analyses. To identify the universe of actors for analysis, Jo and Simmons employ the Uppsala Conflict Data Program (UCDP) Armed Conflict Dataset (ACD);[3] this dataset covers "state-based conflict," defined by the UCDP as involving the use of armed force between two organized groups, at least one of which is the government of an internationally recognized state, which results in at least 25 annual battle deaths (Gleditsch et al. 2002; Pettersson et al. 2021). The authors then use the UCDP One-Sided Violence (OSV) dataset to code group-year observations for violence against civilians; the OSV reports esti-

---

[2] Meernik (2015) additionally uses the Political Terror Scale (Wood and Gibney 2010) and the Major Episodes of Political Violence (Marshall 2019) datasets to measure outcomes. However, neither dataset directly measures violence against civilians or human rights violations by non-state groups.

[3] Other studies relevant to deterrence theory, including Dancy and Wiebelhaus-Brahm (2017), also use this widely employed dataset to identify cases.

mates of intentional killings of civilians by organized groups, with a minimum 25 annual death threshold (Eck and Hultman 2007). However, by using the UCDP ACD to identify the universe of cases, Jo and Simmons—and other studies using this dataset—omit civilian killings, as reported in the UCDP OSV dataset, by groups not simultaneously recorded as active in the ACD in the relevant year; as such, two categories of actors are excluded from analyses that use the ACD to identify the universe of cases: (1) organizations that exclusively perpetrated violence against civilians but were not otherwise active in armed conflict; and (2) groups involved in "non-state conflict," defined by the UCDP as conflict meeting the 25 annual battle-related death threshold where *neither* party is a state government (Sundberg et al. 2012).

This omission is potentially significant for identifying the ICC's impact on violence against civilians and testing deterrence theory. For the period covered in the analysis presented in this chapter, 1995–2010, there are 183 group-years in the UCDP OSV in which the relevant organization was not simultaneously recorded as an active primary belligerent in the dyadic version of the UCDP ACD: this constitutes slightly over one-third (33.64%) of the 544 group-years in the UCDP OSV during this period. Rebel groups account for 143 of the 148 (78.14%) OSV group-years where the organization was not reported as active in the ACD, while governments comprise the remaining 40 group-years (21.86%).[4] In total, there were 46,361 civilian killings in these group-years, amounting to 25.46% of the total civilian killings (182,094) reported in the UCDP OSV during this period; of these killings, 35,466 were attributable to rebel forces (76.50%), with the remainder committed by government actors. The ICC's territorial jurisdiction (through state membership in the Rome Statute, UN Security Council referral, or non-State Party voluntary acceptance) was active in the relevant location for all or part of the given year in 76 OSV group-years not included in the ACD (41.53%); during these group-years, there were 18,103 civilian killings, of which 11,728 (89.07%) were attributable to non-state groups and the remainder to government forces. These include killings by multiple groups whose leaders were subsequently charged by the ICC, including the *Front des Nationalistes et Intégrationnistes* (Germain Katanga), *Force de résistance patriotique d'Ituri* (Mathieu Ngudjolo Chui), and the *Union des Patriotes congolais* (Thomas Lubanga, Bosco Ntaganda) in the DRC and the Janjaweed militia in Darfur, Sudan (Ali Muhammad Ali Abd-Al-Rahman).

Collectively, the omission of broad categories of groups involved in civilian killings from analyses of ICC deterrence suggests, though does not confirm, that estimates of the Court's effects may be biased. The direction of this bias is not *ex ante* clear, although the average number of civilian fatalities in omitted group-years is less (253.34) than included group-years (375.99). In any case, the substantial number of non-state group-years omitted from analyses of ICC deterrence, including organizations whose leaders were subsequently charged by the ICC, raises particular concerns about estimates of the ICC's effects on non-state actors, as well as estimates about the Court's aggregate impacts at the country level. To address this

[4] Jo and Simmons (2016, 2017) include *all* group-years from 1989–2011 for governments recorded as active in the ACD in *any* year during this period; these include government group-years where the government was not recorded as active in the ACD. Accordingly, Jo and Simmons omit only OSV group-years for governments that were not recorded as active in the ACD in any year from 1989–2011. This significantly limits the potential for bias in Jo and Simmons's estimates of ICC deterrence *vis-à-vis* government actors; for the period covered in the analysis presented in this chapter (1995–2010), there are only two OSV government group-years not included in the corresponding period in Jo and Simmons's data: Brazil (2005) and Tanzania (2001).

limitation of previous studies, the next section presents a country-level analysis of the effects of ICC jurisdiction on violence against civilians, including killings by categories of groups excluded from prior analyses.

DATA, ANALYSIS, AND DISCUSSION

In light of the limitations of previous cross-national studies of ICC deterrence, this section reexamines the effects of ICC jurisdiction on violence against civilians using country-level data updated to include civilian killings in the UCDP OSV omitted from previous studies. This allows for a test of the ICC's overall deterrent effects at the country level, including all categories of actors that may perpetrate violence against civilians, per the UCDP OSV: government forces, whether active or inactive in interstate or intrastate armed conflict (UCDP armed conflict); and non-state groups, whether rebel groups engaged in "state-based" conflict versus government forces (UCDP armed conflict), other non-state actors (UCDP non-state conflict), or not active in conflict.[5]

Data Structure

This analysis uses a modified version of the global, country-level, panel data employed in Appel's (2018) study of ICC deterrence.[6] The unit of analysis is the country-year, and the dataset covers 1995–2010; this yields an initial sample of 3,001 observations across 188 countries.[7] This data structure allows for analysis of the effects of variation in ICC jurisdiction both between and within, or across time, units (countries). The time period begins in 1995, when the UN General Assembly convened a committee to consider the establishment of a standing international criminal tribunal, an important first step toward negotiating the Rome Statute (Appel 2018, 18), and ends in 2010; as such, the dataset includes seven full calendar years before the entry into force of the Rome Statute and the activation of the ICC's jurisdiction in 2002 and eight full calendar years in which the Rome Statute was in force (in addition to 2002, in which the Statute was in force for part of the year). Each observation is coded on a series of indicators relevant to ICC deterrence, as described below. Table 19.1 presents descriptive statistics for these variables.

---

5 While groups involved in civilian killings but neither armed nor non-state conflict are included in the UCDP OSV, there is no unique UCDP conflict category for this type of actor.

6 Although this analysis examines violence against civilians, it uses a modified version of Appel's (2018) dataset, rather than Jo and Simmons's (2016, 2017), for two reasons. First, Jo and Simmons use data structured at the group level that are not suitable for aggregate, countrylevel analysis. Second, as noted in the previous section, the Jo and Simmons data exclude multiple categories of actors involved in violence against civilians.

7 The number of observations in the models reported in Table 19.2 is smaller because of the inclusion of lagged variables and missing data for certain country-year observations.

Table 19.1 *Descriptive statistics*

Variable	Mean	Std. Deviation	Minimum	Maximum
Civilian deaths	60.48	703.9	0	32,996
Rome Statute	.30	.46	0	1
Situational jurisdiction	.30	.46	0	1
Ratification	.33	.46	0	1
Democracy	.52	.50	0	1
Democratization	.01	.10	0	1
GDP per capita (log)	8.57	1.29	4.61	11.21
Population (log)	15.43	2.13	9.73	21.01
Independent judiciary	1.09	.80	0	2
Conflict	.17	.38	0	1
Battle deaths (log)	.96	2.22	0	10.80
Conflict termination	.03	.18	0	1
Conflict history	1.55	3.16	0	16
Dissent	.22	.42	0	1

Dependent Variable

The dependent variable, *civilian deaths*, is measured as the best estimate of the total count of civilian fatalities resulting from intentional attacks by all organized groups (government and non-state) on the territory of the relevant state in the given year. This variable was sourced from the UCDP OSV dataset, version 20.1 (Eck and Hultman 2007), version 21.1 (Pettersson et al. 2021), by summing civilian deaths attributable to all actors operating on the territory of the relevant country, including the government of the territorial state, any foreign government forces active in the state, and non-state groups operating in the state. In cases where groups were involved in one-sided violence in multiple countries in the same calendar year, the UCDP Georeferenced Event Dataset, version 21.1 (Pettersson et al. 2021; Sundberg and Melander 2013), was consulted to determine the number of deaths per country; this is relevant for ICC deterrence because of the territorial nature of the Court's jurisdiction.

There are several reasons, both theoretical and practical, for selecting civilian deaths as the dependent variable for this analysis. First, three of the four categories of substantive crimes under the ICC's jurisdiction per the Rome Statute—genocide, crimes against humanity, and war crimes—each include intentional killing of non-combatants as specific offenses; accordingly, civilian deaths provide a useful indicator of the incidence and severity of the types of crimes the Court is intended to prevent (United Nations 1999, Art. 6–8). Second, although the categories of crimes under ICC jurisdiction include a wide range of other acts, including rape, torture, and child soldiering, *inter alia*, there have been more limited cross-national data on these outcomes for the period during which the ICC has been operational, at least until relatively recently (Cohen and Nordås 2014; Haer and Böhmelt 2016). Accordingly, as noted previously, most studies of ICC deterrence have focused on either human rights violations or civilian killings, for which there have been readily available, widely employed datasets, such as CIRI and the UCDP OSV, throughout most of the period of the Court's existence. However, because existing human rights datasets, such as CIRI, focus principally on government human rights practices, these datasets do not allow for analysis of the ICC's effects *vis-à-vis* non-state actors or overall; accordingly, civilian deaths as measured in the UCDP OSV is both a theoretically and practically useful outcome for testing deterrence theory.

Independent Variables

The primary independent variable, *Rome Statute*, is a dichotomous indicator coded 1 if the Statute was in force for the relevant country in any part of the given year. This variable directly measures the ICC's territorial jurisdiction over States Parties, as defined in the Statute. It should be noted that this variable does not measure the Court's personal jurisdiction, which extends to the nationals of States Parties, regardless of the location of the crime. In practice, however, the ICC has relied exclusively on territorial jurisdiction in charging individuals; as of June 1, 2021, the Court had yet to issue a public arrest warrant or summons for a State Party national for crimes allegedly committed on the territory of a non-State Party (International Criminal Court 2021c). More practically, testing the deterrent effects of the ICC's personal jurisdiction would require determining the nationality of all individual perpetrators (and prospective perpetrators) of atrocity crimes—an impractical task given existing data. As such, the analysis in this chapter focuses on the Court's territorial jurisdiction.

Observations are also coded on two alternate measures related to the Court's jurisdiction: the first, *situational jurisdiction*, is a dichotomous measure coded 1 for all country-years where the Court's jurisdiction was active for any part of the year, whether through state membership, UN Security Council referral, or non-State Party voluntary acceptance. The second, *ratification*, is a dichotomous measure coded 1 for all country-years including and after the relevant country ratified (or acceded) to the Rome Statute; this includes country-years before the Rome Statute entered into force for the relevant country, such as for States Parties that ratified the Statute before July 1, 2002, or where there was a lag between joining the Statute and activation of the Court's jurisdiction for the state;[8] for example, Chad deposited its instrument of ratification on November 1, 2006, but the Statute did not enter into force for Chad until January 1, 2007. This variable is intended to capture state commitment to the Court before the formal activation of ICC jurisdiction. All variables relating to ICC jurisdiction are coded based on information from the ICC website (International Criminal Court 2021d).

Control Variables

In addition to the main study variables, each observation is coded on a series of control variables intended to capture other factors that may affect country-level violence against civilians. These variables can be grouped into two broad categories: (1) country-level political, economic, and social structures, and (2) conflict dynamics. Unless otherwise noted, this study uses Appel's (2018) replication data for these variables.

The first category of controls includes measures for various country-level structures linked to violence against civilians, human rights violations, and other forms of atrocities in previous studies (Balcells and Stanton 2021; Krain 2007; Valentino 2014); following Appel (2018), these variables are lagged one year and coded as follows:

1. *Democracy*, a binary indicator coded 1 if the state's Polity regime type score was +6 or greater (Marshall and Gurr 2020).

[8] Article 126.2 of the Rome Statute provides that the Statute "shall enter into force on the first day of the month after the 60th day following the deposit by such State of its instrument of ratification, acceptance, approval or accession" (United Nations 1999).

2. *Democratization*, a dichotomous measure coded 1 if the country experienced a transition to democracy, per the Polity dataset, or more formally, if the country's Polity score increased from less than +6 to +6 or greater (Marshall and Jaggers 2010).
3. *Gross domestic product (GDP) per capita*, the log gross domestic product per capita for the relevant country, sourced from the World Bank (2010) World Development Indicators dataset.
4. *Population*, the log total country population, also sourced from the World Bank (2010).
5. *Independent judiciary*, a three-point ordinal scale indicating the relative independence of the state's courts *vis-à-vis* other domestic actors, including other branches of government and the military (Cingranelli, Richards, and Clay 2014).[9]

The second category of control variables includes country-level indicators of conflict and contestation; these variables are particularly relevant given the strong association between conflict and mass atrocities (Goldsmith et al. 2013; Karstedt 2013; Straus 2012). These variables were coded using the same general criteria as in Appel (2018); however, for variables based on the UCDP ACD, the coding was updated to include non-state conflicts in addition to state-based conflicts. Additionally, because this study focuses on the ICC's territorial jurisdiction, all conflict-related variables were revised to include only violence occurring on the territory of the relevant state; for example, in cases where a government was involved in conflict on a foreign state's territory, the conflict variables were coded for the foreign territorial state, rather than the respective government's home state.

1. *Conflict*, a dichotomous variable coded 1 if state-based or non-state conflict was recorded as active on the territory of the relevant state, per the UCDP ACD version 21.1 (Gleditsch et al. 2002; Pettersson et al. 2021), and Non-State Conflict version 21.1 (Sundberg et al. 2012; Pettersson et al. 2021), datasets.
2. *Battle deaths*, the log total of battle-related deaths that occurred on the state's territory in the respective country-year; this is calculated by summing the "best estimate" of battle deaths in state-based conflicts reported in the UCDP Battle-Related Deaths dataset (Pettersson et al. 2021), version 21.1, and the UCDP Non-State Conflict dataset, version 20.1 (Sundberg et al. 2012; Pettersson et al. 2021).
3. *Conflict termination*, a dichotomous variable coded 1 if the country recorded zero battle-related deaths, inclusive of both state-based and non-state conflict, in the previous year, per the respective UCDP datasets (Gleditsch et al. 2002; Pettersson et al. 2021; Sundberg et al. 2012).
4. *Conflict history*, the cumulative count of years during which any conflict (state-based or non-state) was active on the territory of the state, as of the given country-year, from 1995–2010.
5. *Dissent*, a dichotomous variable coded 1 to record the occurrence of protests, riots, or similar events indicating domestic dissent against the government, per Banks (2010).

---

[9] Appel (2018) describes this variable as dichotomous; however, Appel's replication data and the description of this variable in the CIRI codebook indicate that it is measured as a three-point ordinal scale, with values ranging from 0 (low independence) to 2 (high independence).

Statistical Modeling Strategy and Results

Using the data introduced above, Table 19.2 presents six models of the relationship between ICC jurisdiction and civilian killings. The dependent variable, *civilian deaths*, is an overdispersed event count; as such, all models employ a negative binomial panel estimator (Hilbe 2014). This modeling strategy is also consistent with standard practice in studies using civilian death counts based on the UCDP OSV as the dependent variable (Eck and Hultman 2007; Jo and Simmons 2016, 2017). Models 1–4 employ a random effects negative binomial estimator, while Models 5–6 use a DiD negative binomial estimator.

Models 1–3 include different versions of the main independent variable measuring ICC jurisdiction, respectively *Rome Statute*, *situational jurisdiction*, and *ratification*. Models 4–6 include *Rome Statute* and employ various approaches to correct for potential threats to inference. Models 4 and 6 include a lagged dependent variable to control for correlation within country panels, while Models 5–6 report negative binomial DiD estimates to account for endogeneity concerns arising from the non-random selection of states into ICC membership and jurisdiction (Simmons and Danner 2010; Chapman and Chaudoin 2012; Hashimoto 2020); of particular concern, in this respect, is that states with strong commitment to human rights—and therefore *ex ante* less likely to commit atrocities—may be more likely to join the ICC. The DiD approach to addressing endogeneity accounts for unobserved differences between groups that select into the "treatment" under analysis (in this case, ICC membership and jurisdiction) with "control" groups that do not receive the treatment; specifically, DiD estimates the relative change in outcome (in this case, civilian killings) between the treatment and control groups before and after the administration of the treatment. In including a lagged dependent variable to address serial correlation and using DiD to address endogeneity concerns relating to the ICC's effects on atrocities, this study directly follows Appel (2018).

The results reported in Table 19.2 do not support the deterrence hypothesis. The coefficients for the main independent variable measuring ICC jurisdiction, whether *Rome Statute*, *situational jurisdiction*, or *ratification*, are not statistically significant in any of the six models; accordingly, the null hypothesis that ICC jurisdiction has no effect on country-level civilian killings cannot be rejected. Notably, this result obtains in both the random effects models (1–4) and the DiD models (5–6) that account for possible endogeneity concerns. Furthermore, to the extent that states more strongly committed to human rights and the rule of law—and therefore less likely to commit atrocities—are more likely to self-select into the ICC and similar institutions (Lupu 2013; Meernik 2015; Simmons and Danner 2010), this would imply that failing to account for endogeneity would produce *overestimates* of deterrent effects and significant results for ICC jurisdiction in the random effects models. However, given that even the random effects models produce insignificant results, it can be concluded, with reasonable confidence, that the null findings for ICC jurisdiction are not likely attributable to selection effects resulting from the non-random self-selection of states into ICC membership.

The models in Table 19.2 do not directly test the mechanisms underlying the deterrence hypothesis or provide insight into why ICC jurisdiction does not deter country-level civilian killings. However, there are several plausible explanations for the null findings, in light of previous studies and the structure of the data employed in this analysis. First, given previous statistical findings indicating that ICC jurisdiction and actions deter government civilian killings and human rights violations, the null findings in this study may be attributable to increased violence against civilians by non-state actors offsetting the ICC's deterrent effects *vis-à-vis*

Table 19.2 *Correlates of country-level civilian killings, 1995–2010*

Model	1	2	3	4	5	6
Estimator	Negative Binomial Random Effects				Negative Binomial DiD	
Rome Statute	–.08	—	—	–.02	–.07	–.09
	(.16)			(.16)	(.20)	(.19)
	p=.61			p=.91	p=.71	p=.66
Situational jurisdiction	—	–.00	—	—	—	—
		(.16)				
		p=.99				
Ratification	—	—	–.07	—	—	—
			(.16)			
			p=.67			
Lagged dependent variable	—	—	—	**.00**	—	**.00**
				(.00)		**(.00)**
				p=.00		**p=.00**
Democracy	–.28	–.30	–.28	–.29	–.00	–.01
	(.16)	.16	(.16)	(.16)	(.19)	(.19)
	p=.09	p=.07	p=.09	p=.08	p=.98	p=.97
Democratization	.23	.23	.23	.24	.09	.06
	(.51)	(.51)	(.51)	(.50)	(.51)	(.51)
	p=.66	p=.65	p=.65	p=.64	p=.85	p=.90
GDP per capita (log)	**–.40**	**–.39**	**–.40**	**–.37**	**–.28**	**–.26**
	(.07)	**(.07)**	**(.07)**	**(.07)**	**(.09)**	**(.09)**
	p=.00	**p=.00**	**p=.00**	**p=.00**	**p=.00**	**p=.00**
Population (log)	**.25**	**.25**	**.25**	**.25**	.08	.10
	(.05)	**(.05)**	**(.05)**	**(.05)**	(.07)	(.07)
	p=.00	**p=.00**	**p=.00**	**p=.00**	p=.25	p=.15
Independent judiciary	.15	.15	.15	.16	.03	.06
	(.11)	(.11)	(.11)	(.11)	(.13)	(.13)
	p=.17	p=.16	p=.16	p=.16	p=.84	p=.63
Conflict	.53	.54	.54	.48	.22	.16
	(.30)	(.29)	(.29)	(.30)	(.33)	(.33)
	p=.07	p=.07	p=.07	p=.11	p=.84	p=.63
Battle deaths (log)	**.36**	**.36**	**.36**	**.36**	**.35**	**.35**
	(.04)	**(.04)**	**(.04)**	**(.04)**	**(.04)**	**(.04)**
	p=.00	**p=.00**	**p=.00**	**p=.00**	**p=.00**	**p=.00**
Conflict termination	**1.06**	**1.07**	**1.06**	**1.06**	**.74**	**.68**
	(.31)	**(.31)**	**(.31)**	**(.31)**	**(.32)**	
	p=.00	**p=.00**	**p=.00**	**p=.00**	**p=.02**	**p=.04**
Conflict history	**.05**	**.04**	**.05**	**.04**	**.06**	**.06**
	(.02)	**(.02)**	**(.02)**	**(.02)**	**(.03)**	**(.03)**
	p=.00	**p=.00**	**p=.00**	**p=.01**	**p=.04**	**p=.04**
Dissent	**.87**	**.87**	**.87**	**.83**	**.79**	**.76**
	(.13)	**(.13)**	**(.13)**	**(.13)**	**(.15)**	**(.15)**
	p=.00	**p=.00**	**p=.00**	**p=.00**	**p=.00**	**p=.00**
Observations	2,231	2,231	2,231	2,231	837	837
Log-likelihood	–2,235.07	–2,235.20	–2,235.11	–2,219.20	–1,707.36	–1,700.19
P>Chi-squared	.00	.00	.00	.00	.00	.00

Note: Standard errors in parentheses; variables significant at p<.05 (or less) in **bold**.

governments in an aggregated, country-level analysis. This explanation is broadly consistent with Jo and Simmons's (2017) corrected finding that ICC jurisdiction (in countries that ratified the Rome Statute) is associated with *increased* civilian killings by rebel groups in state-based conflicts and case study evidence suggesting that certain ICC actions may exacerbate non-state violence (Broache 2016a, 2016b; Wegner 2016). To the extent such findings imply that non-state actors are less susceptible to deterrence or more likely to escalate violence in response to the threat of prosecution, the inclusion in this analysis of non-state groups omitted from previous studies (i.e., groups exclusively involved in UCDP non-state conflict or one-sided violence) further suggests that increased killings by non-state actors may have offset reduced violence by government forces associated with ICC jurisdiction.

In addition to the dynamic of offsetting government and non-state violence, it is possible that the null effects in this study may be related to the limited time period analyzed, 1995–2010. While this period allows for comparisons before and after the Rome Statute entered into force in 2002, the years of active ICC jurisdiction in this study represented the Court's first ten years of existence, during which it experienced significant "teething problems" (Cassese 2006); indeed, it was not until March 2006—nearly four years after the Rome Statute entered into force—that the ICC successfully executed its first arrest warrant (for Thomas Lubanga Dyilo), and the ICC did not return its first guilty verdict until March 2012 (also for Lubanga), after the end of the period covered in this study. To the extent that effective deterrence requires potential perpetrators to perceive an increased probability of punishment, the ICC's weak record during this period (especially in light of the significant expectations attached to it) may have undermined deterrence. Relatedly, because the ICC was a new institution during this period, relevant actors may have been uninformed or uncertain about its role and function, leading them to discount the threat of prosecution (Wegner 2016). These dynamics suggest that the ICC could be more effective in deterring atrocities in the future, to the extent that it is successful in securing arrests and convictions, and as relevant actors learn more about the workings of the Court; of course, this also suggests that deterrence could be *less* effective if the Court is unable to build a record of successful prosecutions.

While there are potentially some reasons for optimism about the future effectiveness of ICC deterrence, the results for the control variables in Models 1–6 suggest that the strongest determinants of civilian killings are structural and conflict-related factors that are not directly related to ICC jurisdiction. The coefficients for *GDP per capita* are negative and significant in all six models, indicating that country-level civilian killings decrease as per capita GDP increases; the coefficients for *population* are positive and significant in the random effects models (1–4), indicating that country-level civilian killings are greater in countries with higher populations, although this result does not hold in the DiD models (5–6). With respect to conflict dynamics, the coefficients for *battle deaths*, *conflict history*, and *dissent* are positive and significant in all six models, indicating that these variables—which measure the intensity and duration of ongoing conflict and domestic dissent against the government, respectively—are associated with increased country-level civilian killings. Collectively, and in combination with the findings for ICC jurisdiction, the results for the control variables imply that structural factors, particularly economic conditions (which may also proxy for state capacity, per Hendrix 2010), and underlying conflict dynamics are more important than the threat of prosecution in explaining variation in violence against civilians at the country level. While the ICC might indirectly influence certain conflict dynamics, such as by encouraging participation in peace negotiations (Kersten 2016)—although it could also hinder peace agreements and prolong conflict (Prorok 2017)—these findings suggest that the future prospects for deterrence are rather limited, even if the Court builds a record of successful prosecutions.

CONCLUSION

This chapter has analyzed the country-level effects of ICC jurisdiction on violence against civilians, using data that includes civilian killings by categories of actors omitted from previous statistical studies. *Contra* both the deterrence hypothesis and predictions that the ICC might exacerbate atrocities, the null hypothesis that ICC jurisdiction has no effects on civilian killings cannot be rejected in any of the models presented in this chapter; this result is robust to alternate measures of ICC jurisdiction, inclusion of a lagged dependent variable to correct for serial correlation, and application of a DiD estimator to address concerns about endogeneity.

On the one hand, this finding seems to call into question the growing body of statistical evidence indicating that the ICC can deter atrocities (Appel 2018; Jo and Simmons 2016; Meernik 2015). However, as will be recalled, most of this evidence pertains to government human rights violations or violence against civilians, while the evidence for non-state actors is much more limited, in part due to data particularities, and mixed. In this context, the results of this study do not necessarily challenge or undermine prior research, but rather complement previous studies in two respects. First, this study provides an assessment of the ICC's overall or aggregate impact at the country level, inclusive of all actors—government and non-state—involved in perepetrating violence against civilians, regardless of conflict type. Second, the findings of this study suggest, though do not confirm, that non-state actors may respond to ICC jurisdiction and the threat of prosecution by escalating violence, thereby offsetting any deterrent effects *vis-à-vis* governments.

However, this study does not directly test whether the null finding for ICC jurisdiction is attributable to this dynamic; furthermore, there are several other plausible explanations for the observed result, most notably the limited time period of the study, which focused on the initial years of the Court's operations. This points to the need for further research on deterrence that disaggregates the ICC's effects by actor type and extends the period of analysis to cover the second decade of the Court's operations, as it has begun to build a record of successful prosecutions; relatedly, while this study focused on the impact of the ICC's territorial jurisdiction, future research is also needed to disaggregate the Court's effects at different stages of the legal process, from preliminary examination to sentencing. More broadly, it would be useful to devise and implement tests for the specific mechanisms underlying the deterrence hypothesis in future research, in order to explain why the ICC generates—or, as in the case of this research—fails to generate certain effects; this, in turn, would allow for the development of more nuanced theories concerning the conditions under which the ICC may contribute to the prevention of atrocities.

While future research on deterrence is certainly necessary, this study's findings can inform overall assessments of the Court, particularly with a new prosecutor having assumed office in June 2021. On the one hand, the null effect of ICC jurisdiction on civilian killings suggests that the ICC has failed in one of its core missions, the prevention of atrocities. On the other hand, the null finding suggests that the Court has also not exacerbated atrocities. Given the very real difficulties of deterrence, especially in the case of atrocities where perpetrators may derive substantial material and strategic benefits (Cronin-Furman 2013; Mendeloff 2018), the

ICC's lack of independent enforcement power, and the concerns that the ICC might perversely exacerbate atrocities, the null effect is, at least in some small sense, an accomplishment for the Court; at minimum, it suggests that the ICC has done minimal harm, at least in the aggregate, even if it has not fully lived up to the great expectations that accompanied its establishment.

REFERENCES

Akhavan, Payam. 2001. "Beyond impunity: Can international criminal justice prevent future atrocities?" *American Journal of International Law* 95(1): 7–31.

Akhavan, Payam. 2009. "Are international criminal tribunals a disincentive to peace? Reconciling judicial romanticism with political realism." *Human Rights Quarterly* 31(XX): 624–654.

Amnesty International. 2012. "Landmark ICC verdict over use of child soldiers." https://www.amnesty.org/en/latest/news/2012/03/landmark-icc-verdict-over-use-child- soldiers/ (March 14).

Apel, Robert (2013). "Sanctions, perceptions, and crime: Implications for criminal deterrence." *Journal of Quantitative Criminology* 29: 67–101.

Appel, Benjamin. 2018. "In the shadow of the International Criminal Court? Does the ICC deter human rights violations?" *Journal of Conflict Resolution* 62(1): 3–28.

Aukerman, Miriam J. 2002. "Extraordinary evil, ordinary crime: A framework for understanding transitional justice." *Harvard Human Rights Journal* 15: 39–98.

Balcells, Laia and Jessica A. Stanton. 2021. "Violence against civilians during armed conflict: Moving beyond the macro- and micro-level divide." *Annual Review of Political Science* 24: 45–69.

Banks, Arthur. 2010. Cross-National Time-Series Data Archive. Binghamton, NY: Center for Social Analysis.

Becker, Gary S. 1968. "Crime and punishment: An economic approach." *Journal of Political Economy* 76(2): 169–217.

Bensouda, Fatou. 2012. "The International Criminal Court: A New Approach to International Relations." Council on Foreign Relations (September 21).

Broache, Michael. 2016a. "International prosecutions and atrocities in the Democratic Republic of Congo: A case study of the FDLR." *Journal of the Middle East and Africa* 7(1): 19–38.

Broache, Michael. 2016b. "Irrelevance, instigation, and prevention: The mixed effects of International Criminal Court prosecutions on atrocities in the CNDP/M23 case." *International Journal of Transitional Justice* 10(3): 388–409.

Burke, Jason. 2016. "Jean-Pierre Bemba sentenced to 18 years in prison by International Criminal Court." *The Guardian* (June 21). https://www.theguardian.com/law/2016/jun/21/jean- pierre-bemba-sentenced-to-18-years-in-prison-by-international-criminal-court

Cassese, Antonio. 2006. "Is the ICC still having teething problems?" *Journal of International Criminal Justice* 4(3): 434–441.

Chapman, Terrence, and Stephen Chaudoin. 2012. "Ratification patterns and the International Criminal Court." *International Studies Quarterly* 57(2): 400–409.

Cingranelli, David L. and David L. Richards. 2010. "The Cingranelli and Richards (CIRI) Human Rights Data Project." *Human Rights Quarterly* 32(2): 401–424.

Cingranelli, David L., David L. Richards and K. Chad Clay. 2014. The CIRI Human Rights Dataset: http://www.humanrightsdata.com.

Cohen, Dara Kay and Ragnhild Nordås. 2014. "Sexual violence in armed conflict: Introducing the SVAC dataset, 1989–2009." *Journal of Peace Research* 51(3): 418–428.

Cronin-Furman, Kate. 2013. "Managing expectations: International criminal trials and the prospects for deterrence of mass atrocity." *International Journal of Transitional Justice* 7(3): 434–454.

D'Amato, Anthony. 1994. "Peace vs. Accountability in Bosnia." *American Journal of International Law* 88(3): 500–506.

Dancy, Geoff and Eric Wiebelhaus-Brahm (2017). The impact of criminal prosecutions during intrastate conflict. *Journal of Peace Research* 55(1): 47–56.

Drumbl, Marc A. 2004. "Collective violence and individual punishment: The criminality of mass atrocity." *Northwestern University Law Review* 99: 539–610.

Durrsma, Allard and Tanja R. Muller. 2019. "The ICC indictment against Al-Bashir and its reprucussions for peacekeeping and humanitarian operations." *Third World Quarterly* 40(5): 890–907.
Eck, Kristine and Lisa Hultman. 2007. "One-sided violence against civilians in war: Insights from new fatality data." *Journal of Peace Research* 44(2): 233–246.
Gilligan, Michael J. 2006. "Is enforcement necessary for effectiveness? A model of the international criminal regime." *International Organization* 60(4): 935–967.
Gleditsch, Nils Petter, Peter Wallensteen, Mikael Eriksson, Margareta Sollenberg, and Havard Strand. 2002. "Armed conflict, 1946–2001: A new dataset." *Journal of Peace Research* 39(5): 615–637.
Goldsmith, Benjamin E., Charles R. Butcher, Dimitri Semenovich, and Arcot Sowmya. 2013. "Forecasting the onset of genocide and politicide: Annual out-of-sample forecasts on a global dataset, 1988–2003." *Journal of Peace Research* 50(4): 437–452.
Goldsmith, Jack and Stephen D. Krasner. 2003. "The Limits of Idealism." *Daedalus* 132(1): 47–63.
Haer, Roos and Tobias Böhmelt. 2016. "The impact of child soldiers on rebel groups' fighting capacities." *Conflict Management and Peace Science* 33(2): 153–173.
Hashimoto, Barry. 2020. "Autocratic consent to international law: The case of the International Criminal Court's jurisdiction, 1998–2017." *International Organization* 74(2): 331–362.
Hendrix, Cullen. 2010. "Measuring state capacity: Theoretical and empirical implications for the study of civil conflict." *Journal of Peace Research* 47(3): 273–285.
Hilbe, Joseph M. 2014. *Modeling Count Data*. Cambridge: Cambridge University Press.
Hillebrecht, Courtney. 2016. "The deterrent effects of the International Criminal Court: Evidence from Libya." *International Interactions* 42(4): 616–643.
Human Rights Watch. 2002. "International Criminal Court a Reality: Human Rights Watch Applauds Historic Justice Benchmark" (April 11). https://www.hrw.org/news/2002/04/11/international-criminal-court-reality#
International Criminal Court. 2003. "ICC-Election of the Prosecutor, Statement by Mr. Moreno-Ocampo." Press Release ICC-OTP-20030502-10 (May 2).
International Criminal Court. 2021a. Cases. https://www.icc-cpi.int/cases (last accessed June 15, 2021)
International Criminal Court. 2021b. Defendants. https://www.icc-cpi.int/Pages/defendants- wip.aspx (last accessed June 15, 2021)
International Criminal Court. 2021c. Situations under investigation. https://www.icc- cpi.int/pages/situation.aspx (last accessed June 15, 2021)
International Criminal Court. 2021d. The States Parties to the Rome Statute. https://asp.icc- cpi.int/en_menus/asp/states%20parties/pages/the%20states%20parties%20to%20the%20rom e%20statute.aspx (last accessed June 15, 2021)
Jo, Hyeran and Beth Simmons. 2016. "Can the International Criminal Court deter atrocity?" *International Organization* 70(3): 443–475.
Jo, Hyeran and Beth Simmons. 2017. "Can the International Criminal Court deter atrocity?" CORRIGENDUM. *International Organization* 71(2): 419–421.
Jo, Hyeran, Mitchell Radtke, and Beth A. Simmons. 2018. "Assessing the International Criminal Court." In *The Performance of International Courts and Tribunals*, eds. Andreas Follesdal, Theresa Squatrito, and Geir Ufstein. Cambridge: Cambridge University Press.
Karstedt, Susanne. 2013. "Contextualizing mass atrocity: Moving toward a relational approach." *Annual Review of Law and Social Science* 9: 383–404.
Kersten, Mark. 2016. *Justice in Conflict: The Effects of the International Criminal Court's Interventions on Ending Wars and Building Peace*. Oxford: Oxford University Press.
Kim, Hunjoon and Kathryn Sikkink. 2010. "Explaining the Deterrence Effect of Human Rights Prosecutions for Transitional Countries." *International Studies Quarterly* 54(4): 939–963.
Kissinger, Henry A. 2001. "The pitfalls of universal jurisdiction." *Foreign Affairs* 80(4): 86–96.
Krain, Matthew. 2007. "State-sponsored mass murder: The onset and severity of genocide." *Journal of Conflict Resolution* 41(3): 331–360.
Krcmaric, Daniel. 2018. "Should I stay or should I go? Leaders, exile, and the dilemmas of international justice." *American Journal of Political Science* 62(2): 486–498.
Ku, Julian and Jide Nzelibe. 2006. "Do international criminal tribunals deter or exacerbate humanitarian atrocities?" *Washington University Law Review* 84(4): 777–833.

Langer, Maximo. 2011. “The diplomacy of universal jurisdiction: The political branches and the transnational prosecution of international crimes,” *American Journal of International Law* 105(1): 1–49.
Leebaw, Bronwyn Anne. 2008. “The irreconcilable goals of transitional justice.” *Human Rights Quarterly* 30(1): 95–118.
Licklider, Roy. 2008. “Ethical Advice: Conflict management vs. human rights in ending civil wars.” *Journal of Human Rights* 7(4): 376–387.
Lupu, Yonatan. 2013. “The informative power of treaty commitment: Using the spatial model to address selection effects.” *American Journal of Political Science* 57(4): 912–925.
Marshall, Monty G. 2019. Major Episodes of Political Violence (MEPV) and Conflict Regions, 1946–2018. Center for Systemic Peace (http://www.systemicpeace.org/inscr/MEPVcodebook2018.pdf)
Marshall, Monty G., and Ted Robert Gurr. 2020. *Polity5: Dataset Users' Manual*. Center for Systemic Peace.
Mburu, Daniel M. 2018. “The Lost Kenyan Duel: The Role of Politics in the Collapse of the International Criminal Court Cases against Ruto and Kenyatta.” *International Criminal Law Review* 18(6): 1015–1047.
McAllister, Jacqueline R. 2020. “Deterring wartime atrocities: Hard lessons from the Yugoslav tribunal.” *International Security* 44(3): 84–128.
Mendeloff, David. 2018. “Punish or persuade? The compellence logic of International Criminal Court intervention in cases of ongoing civilian violence.” *International Studies Review* 20(3): 395–421.
Meernik, James. 2015. “The International Criminal Court and the deterrence of human rights atrocities.” *Civil Wars* 17(3): 381–339.
Nagin, Daniel S. 2013. “Deterrence in the Twenty-First Century,” *Crime and Justice* 42(1): 199–263.
Pettersson, Therese, Shawn Davis, Amber Deniz, Garoun Engström, Nanar Hawach, Stina Högbladh, Margareta Sollenberg and Magnus Öberg. 2021. “Organized violence 1989–2020, with a special emphasis on Syria.” *Journal of Peace Research* 58(4): 809–825.
Piquero, Alex R. and Alfred Blumstein. 2007. “Does incapacitation reduce crime?” *Journal of Quantitative Criminology* 23(4): 267–285.
Prorok, Alyssa K (2017). “The (In)compatibility of peace and justice? The International Criminal Court and civil conflict termination.” *International Organization* 71(2): 213–243.
Raub, Lindsey. 2008. “Promoting hybrid tribunals in international criminal justice.” *New York University Journal of International Law and Politics* 41: 1013–1054.
Rodman, Kenneth A. 2008. “Darfur and the limits of legal deterrence.” *Human Rights Quarterly* 30(3): 529–560.
Scheffer, David J. 1999. “The United States and the International Criminal Court.” *American Journal of International Law* 93(1): 12–22.
Sikkink, Kathryn. 2011. *The Justice Cascade: How Human Rights Prosecutions are Changing World Politics*. New York: W.W. Norton.
Sikkink, Kathryn and Kim, Hun Joon. 2013. “The justice cascade: The origins and effectiveness of prosecutions of human rights violations.” *Annual Review of Law and Science* 9: 269–285.
Simmons, Beth A. and Allison Danner. 2010. “Credible commitments and the International Criminal Court.” *International Organization* 64(X): 225–256.
Sloane, Robert D. 2010. “The expressive capacity of international punishment: The limits of the national law analogy and the potential of international criminal law.” In *Globalization of Criminal Justice*, ed. Michael Bohlander. New York: Routledge.
Snyder, Jack and Leslie Vinjamuri. 2003. “Trials and errors: Principle and pragmatism in strategies of international justice.” *International Security* 28(3): 5–44.
Sriram, Chandra Lekha. 2013. *Globalizing Justice for Mass Atrocities: A Revolution in Accountability*. New York: Routledge.
Straus, Scott. 2012. “Retreating from the brink: Theorizing mass violence and the dynamics of restraint.” *Perspectives on Politics* 10(2): 343–362.
Sundberg, Ralph and Erik Melander. 2013. “Introducing the UCDP Georeferenced Event Dataset.” *Journal of Peace Research* 50(4): 523–532.
Sundberg, Ralph, Kristine Eck, and Joakim Kreutz. 2012. “Introducing the UNCDP Non-State Conflict Dataset.” *Journal of Peace Research* 49(2): 351–362.

Thoms, Oskar N.T., James Ron, and Roland Paris. 2010. "State-level effects of transitional justice: What do we know?" *International Journal of Transitional Justice* 4(3): 329–354.
United Nations. 1999. Rome Statute of the International Criminal Court (as corrected by the process-verbaux of 10 November 1998 and 12 July 1999). https://legal.un.org/icc/statute/99_corr/preamble.htm
United Nations. 2002. "'There Must Be No Relenting' in Fight Against Impunity, Says Secretary-General as International Criminal Court Rome Statute Comes into Force." Press Release SG/SM/8293 (July 1). https://www.un.org/press/en/2002/sgsm8293.doc.htm
Valentino, Benjamin A. 2014. "Why we kill: The political science of political violence against civilians." *Annual Review of Political Science* 17: 89–103.
Verdeja, Ernesto. 2016. "Predicting genocide and mass atrocities." *Genocide Studies and Prevention: An International Journal* 9(3): 13–32.
Vinjamuri, Leslie. 2010. "Deterrence, democracy, and the pursuit of International Justice." *Ethics & International Affairs* 24(2): 191–211.
Wegner, Patrick. 2016. *The International Criminal Court in Ongoing Intrastate Conflicts: Navigating the Peace-Justice Divide*. Cambridge: Cambridge University Press.
Wippman, David. 1999. "Atrocities, Deterrence, and the Limits of International Justice." *Fordham International Law.*
Wood, Reed M and Mark Gibney (2010). "The Political Terror Scale: A re-introduction and comparison to CIRI." *Human Rights Quarterly* 32(2): 367–400.
World Bank. 2010. World Development Indicators. https://datacatalog.worldbank.org/dataset/world-development-indicators

20. Strategic deference of the European Court of Justice

Economic influences on judicial decision-making

Joshua Boston and Dino Hadzic

Courts are often unable to compel compliance with their decisions. Given this inability, compliance can be viewed as "voluntary" when undertaken by a litigant against whom a decision has been issued. This is particularly problematic when a court issues an adverse ruling against an incumbent government (Carrubba and Gabel, 2014). In that case, the government is presented with a choice: either (a) change behavior and practices to implement the court's decision or (b) ignore the court and disregard the decision. When democratically elected officeholders would pay a significant cost with the public for acquiescing to a court decision, those officials are forced to consider the latter option of defiance (Carrubba et al., 2012; Helmke, 2002).

Given noncompliance, courts can pay significant costs: first, in the case at hand, the court does not achieve its preferred outcome; and second, in the longer term, the court may diminish in its public support, or legitimacy (e.g., Gibson and Caldeira, 1995). Such a loss of legitimacy may then place compliance with future decisions in jeopardy: "…noncompliance by a policymaker today may begin to undermine the general perception that court decisions must be respected, and thus induce more and more noncompliance as citizens and political elites become less likely to react when policymakers fail to adhere to judicial rulings" (Staton and Vanberg, 2008, 507). For these reasons, it is important for a court to engage in strategic anticipation—determining whether it will achieve compliance whenever it can issue a decision against a government (Staton and Vanberg, 2008; Gould, 1973).

The discussion above begs several questions: under what conditions is a court more likely to strategically defer and opt to not decide against the government? What factors enable a court to better anticipate noncompliance? In turn, do judges modify their behavior to preclude noncompliance by not deciding against the government? Scholars have paid significant attention to compliance with judicial orders in the context of separation of powers (e.g., Clark, 2009), federalism (e.g., Schorpp, 2012), bureaucratic enforcement (e.g., Spriggs, 1997), polarized mass publics (e.g., Gibson, 2007; Nicholson and Hansford, 2014; Armaly and Enders, 2021), among other institutional arrangements. Indeed, judges often attempt to employ various strategies to engender compliance among certain audiences (Black et al., 2016; Stiansen, 2021).

This study contributes to the already substantial work examining the European Court of Justice (ECJ) (Carrubba et al., 2012; Carrubba et al., 2008; Sweet and Brunell, 2012; Alter, 1998). One of the important questions in this literature is how judges consider the preferences and interests of litigants—in this case, European Union (EU) member states. We specifically build on Carrubba et al. (2008), who examine the risks of noncompliance with ECJ decisions, and the strategic choices of and anticipation by the ECJ in the face of potential defiance from EU members (Garrett et al., 1998; Hermansen, 2020; Cheruvu and Krehbiel, 2022).

In examining this supranational court—facing heightened constraints due to the nature of governance across the EU—we supplement existing theories of compliance by considering the significant role of economic constraints, which are a central concern in European politics. We argue that as an EU member state's prior year gross domestic product (GDP) growth is increasingly poor, the ECJ will be more likely to be deferential and not rule against the member state. Given poor performance, a member state will be less able or willing to bear both the economic and political costs of compliance with an antagonistic ECJ order. In anticipating noncompliance, the ECJ will be less likely to decide against that government than it would be if the government was presiding over a well-performing economy. We extend our argument to consider the moderating effects of additional economic and political factors: (a) trade dependence and (b) membership duration.

We use data on ECJ issue-level dispositions from 1960 to 1999 from Carrubba and Gabel (2014), which we supplement with data on member states' economic performance, trade dependence, and EU membership duration. Our analysis presents evidence supporting our expectation regarding economic performance: the ECJ is more likely to rule in favor of a member state when prior year GDP growth is lower. Moreover, the effect of economic performance on the likelihood that a member state receives a positive disposition increases in magnitude as that member's (a) trade dependence and (b) membership duration increase. Overall, our findings are consistent with a strategic interpretation of ECJ decision-making, where a member state's economic performance is a key factor in determining when the ECJ is likely to defer.

JUDICIAL INSTITUTIONS AND STRATEGIC ANTICIPATION

This study contributes to several substantial literatures that consider strategic behavior in judicial institutions. Scholars of American courts frequently focus on judges' anticipatory behavior in the separation of powers context (e.g., Segal, 1997; Owens, 2010). Strategic accounts of judicial behavior have significantly expanded to span the American–comparative divide (e.g., Vanberg, 2000; Krehbiel, 2016). Even more, some scholarship has endeavored to consider the constraints imposed on courts by federal and transnational systems of government (e.g., Schorpp, 2012; Chen, 2003; Carrubba et al., 2008). Research also considers a role for economic considerations in judicial decision-making—a topic we examine further below. In reviewing some of the existing contributions across these relationships, we lay the groundwork for a theory of economically constrained judicial institutions within transnational governments—a theory that has important implications for understanding the nature of judicial power.

Across country contexts, courts face many of the same opportunities and constraints in establishing and building their power, such that they would be able to induce compliance among elites and the mass public. Within the separation of powers framework, scholars point to both exogenous (i.e., lack of deference to judicial institutions is costly) and endogenous (i.e., deference to judicial institutions derives a benefit to elites) explanations for why democracies facilitate seemingly non-democratic judicial authority.[1] Exogenous explanations argue

1 For a thorough overview of scholarship in these areas, see Vanberg (2015).

that judicial institutions maintain a broad reservoir of public support, and that noncompliance would lead to some decrease in public support for other branches of government (e.g., Gibson et al., 1998).

Endogenous explanations take multiple forms. First, independent courts provide direct informational benefits to democratic elites, where judicial processes can reveal *ex post* information about how policies lead to outcomes (e.g., Rogers, 2001). In this way, elites can use judicial review to make policy course corrections. Second, independent courts provide long-term policy entrenchment for incumbent governments. Insurance theory is a mechanism for mutual restraint across regimes, whereby elected officials who fear losing office endow courts with independent power and authority (e.g., Stephenson, 2003) in order to protect and preserve their policies: "Leaders have strong incentives to empower the courts with greater levels of independence when they are threatened politically or when they believe that they will no longer remain in power" (Randazzo et al., 2016, 2).

These theories broadly speak to legislative and executive deference to independent judicial institutions. That deference depends on a cost–benefit calculation made by political elites: democratically elected officeholders "respect judicial authority only as long as, on balance, the presence of independent courts provides sufficient benefits or subverting them is too costly" (Vanberg, 2015, 179).

How do judges behave in the context of this cost–benefit calculation made by legislators, executives, or other governments? The literature on strategic decision-making in judicial institutions has left little question that judges individually and collectively acquiesce to external constraints. To be sure, judges have sincere preferences, and those preferences drive decision-making, especially in the absence of significant external constraints (Segal and Spaeth, 2002). Still, court outputs are "interdependent"; if judges desire "to see their favored policies become the law of the land, they must take into account the preferences of other actors and the actions they expect them to take" (Epstein and Knight, 1997, 14–15). A judge's desire to achieve ideal policy is constrained on multiple fronts. First, courts and judges are generally incapable of enforcing their own rulings (e.g., Rosenberg, 2008). Second, court outputs speak to a variety of different audiences inside and outside of government (Black et al., 2016). Those audiences vary in their willingness to engage in (a) noncompliance or defiance (e.g., McGuire and Stimson, 2004; Black et al., 2016), or (b) court-curbing behavior (e.g., Clark, 2009).

In this way, judges may find themselves at odds with litigants, regional governments, co-equal branches of government, or certain factions of the mass public. These external actors constrain judges, who must consider when their preferred outcomes would be at odds with the preferences of different extra-judicial actors. In the American context, congressional and executive preferences can cause the Supreme Court and lower courts to alter their decisions (Bergara et al., 2003; Hansford and Damore, 2000; Carrubba and Zorn, 2010), or, at the very least, to alter the language used to write an adverse decision (Owens et al., 2013). The mass public can likewise act as a constraint on courts, though empirical findings are inconsistent, and some research suggests a highly independent Supreme Court (Mishler and Sheehan, 1993; Epstein and Martin, 2010; Casillas et al., 2011; Johnson and Strother, 2021). To be sure, while many actors can express their direct (dis-)approval of judicial actions, democratically accountable institutions also interact with and filter public sentiment to condition judicial authority (Ura and Wohlfarth, 2010).

Studies of courts outside the narrow American context suggest similar maneuvering in response to opportunities and constraints. From developing to consolidated democracies, judges must consider where potential court decisions fall in the range of preferences among extra-judicial actors (Epstein et al., 2001). When a hypothetical decision would fall outside any possible intersection of preferences and when the court is relatively low in public support, judges should avoid addressing the controversial legal issue to avoid possible noncompliance. But when courts have the public on their side, strategic judges can use their legitimacy to induce compliance; evidence from the German Federal Constitutional Court shows that public hearings are a tool to engender compliance among other government actors (Krehbiel, 2016). Judges also exploit strategic openings to draw the mass public's attention to judicial decisions that would further enhance judicial authority and independence (Staton, 2006).

But when courts find themselves in a weakened position, they can be reticent to exercise their power or authority, as is often the case in nascent regimes (e.g., Graber, 1998). In particular, judicial institutionalization, which develops over time, allows judges to expand their ability to create and enforce judicial rules (e.g., McGuire, 2004). Theoretically, the same is true among sovereign governments who use courts to enforce obligations in a federal system or regulatory regime (Carrubba, 2009); before fully earning the public's trust, courts will tend toward their narrow authority to enforce some rules. In the section that follows, we consider how these pressures—along with economic constraints—can be felt by judges on the ECJ.

CONSTRAINED JUDICIAL BEHAVIOR ON THE ECJ

The dynamic relationship between courts and extra-judicial actors yields an array of circumstances in which judges might find themselves anticipating noncompliance. In the broadest sense, potential noncompliance increases when extra-judicial actors (a) do not yield significant benefits from, or (b) must pay substantial costs for compliance with, a judicial order. Indeed, these considerations are exacerbated with supranational courts such as the ECJ, where the goal of achieving sufficient European integration does not always align with member states' respective interests (Alter, 1996).

To be sure, the EU and its institutions provide wide-ranging benefits to member states. The ECJ allows actors to credibly commit to their agreements, and when violations arise the ECJ acts as an information clearinghouse, where member states can gain information about defections (Carrubba, 2005). However, the informational benefits of ECJ litigation do not always lead to judicial remedies. Indeed, the information might reveal that defection from EU treaty obligations stemmed from the significant costs associated with compliance. EU member states have frequent opportunities and substantial incentives to deviate from or violate their obligations; what is in the interests of the bloc is not always in the interests of an individual member state.

> [W]hile there are incentives for [national] governments to argue against decisions that declare national practices to be illegal restrictions of EU trade [...], this does not mean that governments invariably want to ignore ECJ rulings once they are made. Rather, governments must weigh the costs of accepting the court's decision against the benefits derived from having an effective legal system in the EU [...]. The costs of acquiescence vary with the economic size and political clout of the adversely affected sectors. The benefits of accepting a decision are a function of the magnitude of the country's economic gains from the internal market (Garrett, 1995, 172).

The degree of strategic interdependence between the ECJ and member states goes even further. Carrubba et al. (2012) provide evidence that ECJ judges perceive potential threats of noncompliance or overrides from member states. Those threats—measured through (a) potential overrides by the European Council (i.e., share of council votes) or (b) magnitude of member states opposing a particular litigant—significantly alter the behavior of ECJ judges, who acquiesce. Larsson and Naurin (2016) expand on these findings by studying ECJ *Reports for the Hearing*, some of which included member state observations—a mechanism for national governments to formally signal their preferences on the legal issues at hand. Empirical evidence reveals that member state preferences—whether in favor of greater European integration or preserved national sovereignty—significantly impact ECJ dispositions.

Taking a step further, the process of influencing ECJ decision-making need not operate directly through blatant threats of noncompliance or override. To that point, Blauberger et al. (2018) examine ECJ responsiveness to the changing nature of debate regarding EU citizenship and access to social benefits across member states. Studying how the increasing politicization in these debates impacts judicial decision-making, Blauberger et al. (2018) find that both the magnitude and negative tone of newspaper articles on free movement across member states coincided with pivotal ECJ decisions like *Dano v Jobcenter Leipzig*, wherein the ECJ surprised many by deciding against a Romanian national's claim for unemployment benefits in Germany.

THEORY AND HYPOTHESES: ECONOMIC CONSIDERATIONS IN JUDICIAL STRATEGY

That judicial actors are attuned to the tenor of public mood on salient issues suggests that other important national issues—for example, the economy—might impact judicial decision-making. Political scientists have long focused on the direct and indirect effects of economic considerations on mass political preferences (e.g., Duch and Stevenson, 2008; Powell and Whitten, 1993). Indeed, the influence of the economy on politics is pervasive; it is well established that economic performance can structure elites' strategic behavior to win and retain office (e.g., Vavreck, 2009).

The fundamental characterization of economic voting boils down to voters' perceptions of past, present, and future economic performance: an "economic voter uses personal experience or the current health of the economy as a signal of the incumbent's economic competence, which will affect the nation's and the voter's economic prosperity in the future" (Erikson et al., 2002, 80).

But few studies extend economic theories into scholarly understanding of judicial behavior. Perhaps this stems from judicial actors' lack of accountability for economic performance, though—as consumers of politics—judges are perceptive community members who can condemn or commend incumbent officeholders for their handling of the economy. Brennan et al. (2009a) find evidence of this dynamic at the U.S. Supreme Court, where justices behave analogously to mass voters: "Justices seem to be responding positively to (their perceptions of) competent economic management" by rewarding the incumbent government with favorable outcomes in taxation cases (Brennan et al., 2009a, 1220). The opposite is also true—that justices tend to punish incumbent governments with adverse decisions during poor economic performance attributable to poor governance. When the economy deteriorates more so than it does during typical recessions—for example, the Great Depression—judicial support for the government increases in order to help the incumbents thwart the crisis. Additional research suggests that the willingness of the Court to reward or punish the incumbent government for economic performance is complex; Brennan et al. (2009b) find evidence that the justices tend to give less deference to the U.S. Solicitor General when the economy performs poorly.

While U.S. Supreme Court justices are effectively insulated from removal, many U.S. state court judges are not so protected, with many facing periodic partisan or retention elections. Such accountability mechanisms bolster questions of economic responsiveness among state judicial actors. Rice (2014) examines economic responsiveness resulting from variations in judicial selection mechanisms. Across U.S. states in economic cases, unelected high court judges are more likely to cast pro-government votes as the economy worsens (i.e., when unemployment increases), whereas elected high court judges are more likely to punish the incumbent government with votes against the state as the economy worsens. These findings expand upon Duch and Stevenson (2008), which differentiates between electorally and non-electorally dependent decision-makers and how voters punish the former for how they handle the economy. Myers (2020) finds similar political economy dynamics in analyses of the High Court of Australia.

It is well established that—as an agent of European economic integration—the ECJ works to enforce treaty obligations that generate "the economic benefit of belonging to the EU in the first place" (Carrubba et al., 2008, 439). Those obligations—rooted in the Treaty of Rome—range trade-related issues. For instance, as Gabel et al. (2012) document, European Economic Community Treaty articles 30 and 34 call for the elimination of import and export restrictions: "[T]he ECJ's primary responsibility in its first three decades was to resolve cases involving the free movement of goods, broadly construed" (Gabel et al., 2012, 1128).

Why then would ECJ judges—whose objective and purpose is to promote Eurocentric economic values—ever defer to member states? We argue that the ECJ has a significant informational advantage relative to other actors (e.g., Carrubba, 2005; Larsson and Naurin, 2016; Blauberger et al., 2018). As such, the ECJ judges can strategically anticipate how member states engage in the cost–benefit analysis as it pertains to compliance. When the ECJ anticipates a higher probability of noncompliance by a member state, it may be the case that the ECJ is better off defecting from Eurocentric principles, but in favor of maintaining the court's legitimacy (e.g., Staton and Vanberg, 2008). Otherwise, noncompliance could significantly harm the court's legitimacy. When courts prioritize their reputation over preference-based outcomes, that preserves their downstream ability to achieve acquiescence (Garrett, 1995).

Economic Growth Hypothesis: As a member state's prior year GDP growth decreases, the ECJ will be more likely to decide in favor of the member state.

We expect a member state's prior economic performance to be a signal to the ECJ of the member state's ability or willingness to comply with a potential judicial order. We specify our expectation in our *Economic Growth Hypothesis* and its complement: when economic performance (i.e., lagged GDP growth) is strong, the risk of noncompliance by the member state is relatively low. But when member state economic performance is poor, an adverse ECJ ruling could impose greater commerce- and trade-based burdens on member states that are already struggling economically. In these circumstances, the potential for noncompliance increases.

We use Duch and Stevenson (2008) as a foundation for our theoretical story. Economic theories of voting argue that voters can recognize and understand economic trends, and, furthermore, they are able to assign appropriate credit or blame to those responsible. Electorally dependent decision-makers are blamed for poor economic performance when those actors are responsible for the economy. As elected decision-makers become less responsible for the economy, and control is gained by non-electorally dependent decision-makers, those in elected office are punished less. When national economic performance becomes increasingly dependent on international trade, attributing blame through democratic institutions for poor economic performance becomes increasingly difficult for voters.

In the case of an adverse ECJ ruling, a member state may side with its voters, who are eager to blame one political actor or another for poor economic management. Though Duch and Stevenson (2008) suggest that globalization confuses determinations of accountability, European voters frequently blame the EU for their woes (e.g., Hobolt and Tilley, 2014). A strategic court that is primarily concerned with maintaining institutional legitimacy is eager to avoid the ire of the mass public.

We condition our *Economic Growth Hypothesis* by considering a role for (a) trade dependence, and (b) a country's EU membership duration. We believe these economic and political phenomena moderate the effects of economic growth on ECJ decision-making, though trade and membership duration operate through different means on ECJ judges. First, our *Trade Dependence Moderation Hypothesis* considers how ECJ judges differentiate between member states based on the importance of trade to their national economies. Trade is an issue of paramount importance in EU politics. As stated above and throughout the ECJ literature, the court finds purpose in maintaining the free movement of goods throughout the EU.

Trade Dependence Moderation Hypothesis: When a member state is increasingly trade dependent and that member state's economy is performing poorly, the ECJ will be more likely to decide in favor of the member state.

We contend, given the informational advantage of the ECJ, that a member state's trade dependence exacerbates the costs of compliance with an ECJ ruling. Given that the legal issues the ECJ encounters are often trade-related, it is likely that complying with an adverse ECJ ruling will, on average, be particularly costly if the member state is heavily trade dependent. For that reason, we expect economic underperformance to have an especially pronounced effect among more trade-dependent members. In other words, if a member state's prior economic performance can be a signal to the ECJ of that member's ability or willingness to comply, then that signal should be especially informative when it comes from members that are heavily trade dependent.

Second, our *Membership Duration Moderation Hypothesis* considers how ECJ judges differentiate between member states based on the length of their EU membership. Earlier accession into the EU—that is, the founding six member states (i.e., Belgium, France, Italy, Luxembourg, the Netherlands, and West Germany) and those who followed in 1973 (i.e., Denmark, Ireland, and the United Kingdom)—suggests that national governments have largely come to terms with baseline compliance with EU treaty obligations; any enduring issues are more significant and member states might be intransigent, especially when a national economy is performing poorly.

Membership Moderation Hypothesis: When a member state has a longer EU membership and that member state's economy is performing poorly, the ECJ will be more likely to decide in favor of the member state.

The complement to our *Membership Duration Moderation Hypothesis* argues that newer members are obliged to align themselves with their newfound obligations to EU treaties. While compliance with ECJ orders directing member states to adjust their national policies has significant costs, newer members are willing to bear those costs due to their desire to benefit from their newer membership in the economic community.

DATA: MEASURING ECJ DECISIONS AND ECONOMIC CONSTRAINTS

The data for our study originate from multiple sources, but the primary dataset is from Carrubba and Gabel (2014). These data, as detailed in Table 20.1, include 15 EU member states: the founding six members (Belgium, France, Italy, Luxembourg, the Netherlands, and West Germany), and those with accessions between 1973 and 1995 (1973: Denmark, Ireland, and the United Kingdom; 1981: Greece; 1986: Portugal and Spain; 1995: Austria, Finland, and Sweden). The ECJ decision data, spanning 1960 to 1999, precede the accession of the remaining 13 member states which joined in 2004, 2007, and 2013.

Table 20.1 Summary statistics for economic constraints and ECJ dispositions

Variable	Obs.	Mean	Median	Std. Dev.	Min.	Max.
GDP Growth	1,696	2.577	2.505	1.970	−2.259	10.904
Trade Dependence	1,668	67.070	45.282	37.255	26.945	232.890
Membership Duration	1,708	25.355	27	10.982	1	41

Member State Wins	Obs.	Wins	Losses	% Wins
All Member States	1,666	527	1,139	32
	11	4	7	36
	285	99	186	35
	30	13	17	43
	8	4	4	50
	180	68	112	38
	215	73	142	34
	141	29	112	21
	55	14	41	25
	355	88	267	25
	38	10	28	26
	152	70	82	46
	19	7	12	37
	70	13	57	19
	12	4	8	33
	95	31	64	33

For the purposes of this study, we limit our data only to those observations involving a single EU member state as a plaintiff or defendant, which leaves 1,666 total observations.[2] From this, we construct our outcome variable, *Member State Wins*, as a binary indicator for whether the

[2] Due to data availability for our explanatory variables, some of our regression estimations in the following section vary in the number of included observations.

ECJ rules in favor of the member state on a particular legal issue—whether the member state is a plaintiff or defendant. The level of analysis across all model estimations is the legal issue, the level at which ECJ rulings are made (or more specifically, the legal issue-year level).

Of the 1,666 total observations/issues in our dataset, the ECJ ruled in favor of the member state 527 times (roughly 32 percent of the time). However, we do observe significant across-country variation in win rate, with Finland winning on four of its eight legal issues addressed by the ECJ (50 percent win rate) and the Netherlands winning on 70 of its 152 legal issues (46 percent win rate). That is juxtaposed with the least likely winners: Spain, with 13 wins across 70 legal issues (19 percent win rate); and Greece, with 29 wins across 141 legal issues (21 percent win rate).

We further supplement our data to help construct our main explanatory variable of interest and the two moderator variables, which we detail in Table 20.1. First, we utilize GDP growth data published by the World Bank. *GDP Growth*—which is measured at the country-year level—is lagged by one year. The mean growth rate across observations is 2.577, with a minimum of −2.259 and a maximum of 10.904. Next, *Trade Dependence* is also constructed using World Bank data and measures trade as a percentage of GDP in the year the ECJ ruling was issued. *Trade Dependence* has a mean of 67.070 and a minimum and maximum of 26.945 and 232.890, respectively. Finally, *Membership Duration* measures the number of years for which the state had been a member of the EU the year a particular ruling was issued. The mean of *Membership Duration* is 25.355, while the minimum is 1 and the maximum is 41. For more detailed summary statistics of the key variables, see Table 20.1.

In the regression estimations that follow below in our empirical and appendix sections, we employ multiple modeling strategies and specifications to account for variation across member states, within particular legal issues, and within cases (i.e., across legal issues within a given dispute heard by the ECJ). Our most straightforward models employ logit estimations with *GDP Growth* as our primary explanatory variable for whether a member state wins on a particular issue—our outcome variable. We supplement our logit models with multilevel specifications, which include several different levels to account for the possibility that our model parameters vary within the levels we discuss above. We employ similar approaches across our main regression estimations in Table 20.2, which provides a test of our *Economic Growth Hypothesis*, and Table 20.4, which interacts variables for *Membership Duration* and *Trade Dependence* with *GDP Growth* to examine our moderation hypotheses.

RESULTS: RELATING ECONOMIC PERFORMANCE AND ECJ DEFERENCE

To reiterate our expectations before delving into our empirical tests, our *Economic Growth Hypothesis* relates prior year GDP growth at the member state level to the likelihood that the ECJ will rule for or against the member state. As lagged growth increases, the ECJ perceives a member state's economy to be healthier, and therefore, the member state has lower costs of implementing an ECJ decision, even if the member state or its citizens do not like the decision. On the other hand, when lagged growth decreases (or is at lower levels), the ECJ anticipates potential noncompliance by the member state, as the ECJ decision might impose a greater economic burden on the member state. As such the ECJ defers to the position of the member state, and decides in its favor, which also preserves the ECJ's reputation and legitimacy.

Our *Trade Dependence Moderation Hypothesis* works in concert with our existing theoretical mechanism, where a member state's dependence on trade suggests an increasing imbalance in the cost–benefit calculation by the member state. Specifically, as a member's trade dependence increases and the potential costs of compliance do so as well, members that are underperforming economically will be especially unlikely to comply (therefore increasing ECJ deference). On the other hand, our *Membership Duration Moderation Hypothesis* expects ECJ deference to member states who have been EU members longer but have poorly performing economies. Newer members receive less ECJ deference stemming from the need to align those member states with the parameters of EU membership. Newer members often have stronger preferences for compliance so that their citizens benefit from the EU.

Table 20.2 Understanding the relationship between member state economic performance and ECJ decision-making

	DV = Member State Wins			
	(1)	(2)	(3)	(4)
GDP Growth	−0.051*	−0.054*	−0.048*	−0.050
	(0.027)	(0.031)	(0.028)	(0.031)
Intercept	−0.643***	−0.790***	−0.639***	−0.748***
	(0.086)	(0.110)	(0.133)	(0.146)
Estimation:	Logit	2-level Logit L1: Issue L2: Case	2-level Logit L1: Issue L2: Country	3-level Logit L1: Issue L2: Case L3: Country
N	1,654	1,654	1,654	1,654
AIC	2,063	2,050	2,048	2,039

Notes:
Cell entries represent unstandardized coefficient estimates with standard errors in parentheses. Model 1 reports results from a simple logit regression. Models 2 and 3 report results from 2-level logit regressions with legal issues nested within cases and countries, respectively. Model 4 reports results from a 3-level logit regression with legal issues nested within cases and cases nested within countries.
* $p<0.10$, ** $p<0.05$, *** $p<0.01$.

In Table 20.2, we begin by testing our *Economic Growth Hypothesis*—that the ECJ is less likely to rule against a member state that is underperforming economically. We present results across four model specifications in Table 20.2, where our outcome across all models is *Member State Wins* (1 = wins, 0 = loses). Our primary explanatory variable of interest is *GDP Growth.* As we observe in Column (1) of Table 20.2, a negative and statistically significant coefficient on *GDP Growth* indicates higher levels of growth correspond to a lower probability that the ECJ rules in the member state's favor.

Column (1) presents the simplest estimation, a bivariate logit regression, while Columns (2), (3), and (4) are multilevel logit regressions. For Columns (2) and (3), legal issues are nested within cases and countries, respectively. Column (4) presents results from a three-level logit where legal issues are nested within cases and cases within countries. As the results presented in Table 20.2 show, we find tentative support for the *Economic Growth Hypothesis* across three of the four model specifications. The coefficient estimate for *GDP Growth* is negative and significant at the 90 percent level in the models across Columns (1), (2), and (3). While not significant for Column (4) (*p-value* = 0.109), the estimate is still in the anticipated direction.

Table 20.3 *Predicted probabilities of member state winning across levels of GDP growth*

	Member State GDP Quantiles:				
	Minimum	25th	Median	75th	Maximum
	–2.259	1.544	2.505	3.781	10.904
Pr(Member State Wins)	0.371	0.327	0.316	0.302	0.231

For a substantive interpretation of the results, consider Table 20.3, which presents predicted probabilities derived from Table 20.2's Column (1) model. At the minimum value of *GDP Growth* (–2.259), the predicted probability of the ECJ ruling in the member state's favor is 0.371. The probability of a favorable ECJ ruling, in turn, decreases as growth increases. In other words, improving member state economies makes adverse ECJ rulings more likely. At the maximum value of *GDP Growth* (10.904), the predicted probability of a favorable ECJ ruling stands at 0.231. Our results suggest that when moving from the minimum to the maximum observed values of GDP growth in the data, the probability that the member state achieves a favorable outcome decreases by 0.14. This is a substantively meaningful change and, ultimately, we interpret these results as providing suggestive support for the *Economic Growth Hypothesis*.

Next, we proceed to examine our *Membership Duration Moderation Hypothesis* and *Trade Dependence Moderation Hypothesis* in Columns (1) and (2), respectively, of Table 20.4. Our choice of model specification remains identical to those discussed above for Table 20.2, though we reserve our multi-level models for presentation in the appendix below. Table 20.4 considers the moderating effect of *Membership Duration* and *Trade Dependence* in the relationship between *GDP Growth* and whether a *Member State Wins*. As such, we employ interaction terms between *GDP Growth* and the relevant moderator.

Column (1) of Table 20.4 reveals statistical and substantive support for our *Membership Duration Moderation Hypothesis*—that newer EU members are more likely to receive an adverse ECJ ruling despite potential poor economic performance, whereas longer EU members receive more deferential treatment given economic performance. Holding constant the effect of *GDP Growth*, we observe that increasing *Membership Duration* increases the likelihood that a *Member State Wins* a legal issue at the ECJ. The interactive effect of *GDP Growth* and *Membership Duration* reveals a statistically significant dynamic that benefits long-term EU members. As *Membership Duration* increases and *GDP Growth* increases, the member state is less likely to win its legal issue. But lower levels of economic growth for long-term member states lead to more ECJ deference, and a higher probability that the member state will win its legal issue when compared with countries that have shorter EU membership duration.

We further examine this interactive effect in Panel (a) of Figure 20.1. The x-axis plots *Membership Duration* in ten-year increments, while the y-axis plots the marginal effect of prior year GDP growth on the likelihood of a favorable ECJ ruling (i.e., the coefficient from Column (1) of Table 20.4). At low values of *Membership Duration, GDP Growth* does not appear to influence ECJ behavior. But this changes as the moderator increases; for states that have been EU members for 20 years or more, the effect of *GDP Growth* becomes negative and significant.

Column (2) of Table 20.4 reveals statistical and substantive support for our *Trade Dependence Moderation Hypothesis*—that EU member states that are more dependent on trade for economic growth are more likely to receive a favorable ECJ ruling given poor economic growth.

Table 20.4 *Understanding the relationship between member state economic performance and ECJ decision-making, moderating effect of membership duration and trade dependence*

	DV = Member State Wins	
	(1)	(2)
GDP Growth	0.090	0.088
	(0.063)	(0.057)
Membership Duration	0.221***	
	(0.083)	
GDP Growth × Membership Duration	−0.066**	
	(0.027)	
Trade Dependence		0.777***
		(0.241)
GDP Growth × Trade Dependence		−0.184***
		(0.067)
Intercept	−1.162***	−1.192***
	(0.222)	(0.191)
N	1,654	1,625
AIC	2,059	2,024

Notes:
Cell entries represent unstandardized coefficient estimates with standard errors in parentheses. Models are estimated with logit regressions. Table 20A.1 and Table 20A.2 in the appendix report supplementary models with (1) results from 2-level logit regressions with legal issues nested within (a) cases and (b) countries, and (2) results from a 3-level logit regression with legal issues nested within cases and cases nested within countries.
* p<0.10, ** p<0.05, *** p<0.01.

Holding constant the effect of *GDP Growth*, we observe that increasing *Trade Dependence* significantly increases the likelihood that a *Member State Wins* a legal issue at the ECJ. The interactive effect of *GDP Growth* and *Trade Dependence* is also statistically significant. The interactive dynamic shows that higher *GDP Growth* and higher *Trade Dependence* lead to lower likelihoods of winning on a given legal issue. Once again, the complementary dynamic shows that lower levels of economic growth for trade-dependent member states lead to more ECJ deference, and a higher likelihood for the member state to win its legal issue when compared with countries that are less trade dependent.

Panel (b) of Figure 20.1 plots the logit estimation from Column (2) of Table 20.4. The graph details the dynamic relationship between *Trade Dependence* and the marginal effect of prior year GDP growth on the likelihood of a favorable ECJ ruling. At low levels of *Trade Dependence*, we observe a null relationship between *GDP Growth* and the likelihood of a favorable ECJ ruling. However, as *Trade Dependence* increases, the marginal effect of *GDP Growth* on *Member State Wins* decreases, providing evidence that lower levels of economic growth among highly trade-dependent member states are more likely to produce a favorable ECJ ruling.

In Tables 20A.1 and 20A.2 of the appendix, we examine alternative model specifications with corresponding figures (Figures 20A.1 and 20A.2) to further test our *Trade Dependence Moderation Hypothesis* and *Membership Duration Moderation Hypothesis*. Those model specifications, which are largely consistent with the results we present in Table 20.4 and Figure 20.1, include multilevel models similar to those we present in our main regression estimations in Table 20.2. Overall, we regard our empirical results as largely supporting a story of strategic judicial behavior.

(a) The Effects of GDP Growth on ECJ Decisions as Moderated by Membership Duration

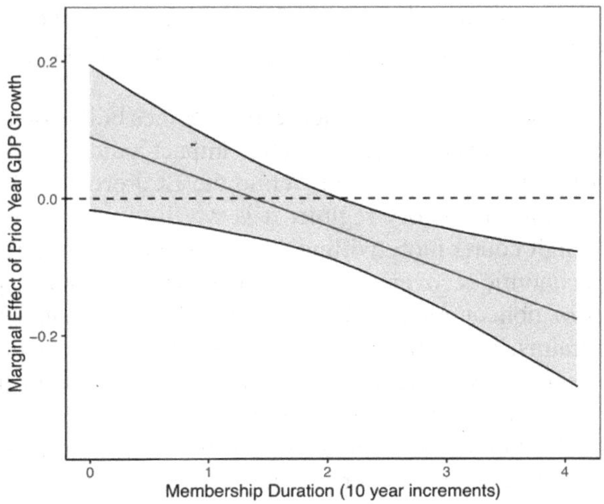

(b) The Effects of GDP Growth on ECJ Decisions as Moderated by Trade Dependence

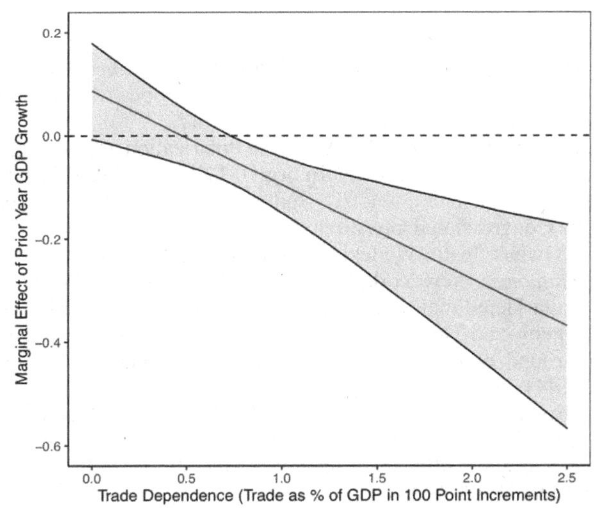

Figure 20.1 *The effect of GDP growth across membership duration and trade dependence*

DISCUSSION: ECONOMIC CONSTRAINTS AND JUDICIAL INSTITUTIONS

Our study provides further evidence of strategic deference among ECJ judges and builds on a great deal of prior work (e.g., Carrubba et al., 2012; Larsson and Naurin, 2016; Cheruvu and Krehbiel, 2022). It is not merely the case that judges acquiesce to avert threats to judicial legitimacy and independence. Legislative and executive preferences certainly matter in predicting the likelihood of compliance with judicial orders. But our contribution goes further. As Blauberger et al. (2018) argue and we agree, judges are astute consumers of social, political, and economic information. While we narrowly focus on economic factors and related moderating effects, all these factors—often external to specific legal disputes and issues—can weigh on judges.

Our evidence of economic constraints on judicial outcomes builds on the important judicial strategy literature that considers how external factors impact judicial behavior. However, there is certainly room for more work to be done. While the ECJ provides legal remedies within the context of an economic regulatory regime, it is worth examining this dynamic in other contexts. Are federal high courts more willing to tolerate policy experimentation in regional governments during economic recoveries? Do regimes that subscribe to particular ideologies exacerbate the threat of noncompliance due to economic performance? Generalizing away from economic constraints, do high courts fear regional noncompliance during periods of backlash against the central government? Do courts ultimately correct rulings once economic constraints diminish, or do they maintain prior precedents? While few scholars have directly considered a role for economic voting in judicial decision-making, we believe there is substantial room to develop this line of inquiry across courts, countries, and legal issues.

REFERENCES

Alter, Karen J. 1996. "The European Court's Political Power." *West European Politics* 19(3): 458–487.

Alter, Karen J. 1998. "Who are the 'Masters of the Treaty'?: European Governments and the European Court of Justice." *International Organization* 52(1): 121–147.

Armaly, Miles T. and Adam M. Enders. 2021. "Affective Polarization and Support for the U.S. Supreme Court." *Political Research Quarterly*, https://doi.org/10.1177/10659129211006196.

Bergara, Mario, Barak Richman and Pablo T. Spiller. 2003. "Modeling Supreme Court Strategic Decision Making: The Congressional Constraint." *Legislative Studies Quarterly* 28(2): 247–280.

Black, Ryan C., Ryan J. Owens, Justin Wedeking and Patrick C. Wohlfarth. 2016. *U.S. Supreme Court Opinions and Their Audiences*. New York, NY: Cambridge University Press.

Blauberger, Michael, Anita Heindlmaier, Dion Kramer, Dorte Sindbjerg Martinsen, Jessica Sampson Thierry, Angelika Schenk and Benjamin Werner. 2018. "ECJ Judges Read the Morning Papers. Explaining the Turnaround of European Citizenship Jurisprudence." *Journal of European Public Policy* 25(10): 1422–1441.

Brennan, Thomas, Lee Epstein and Nancy Staudt. 2009a. "Economic Trends and Judicial Outcomes: A Macrotheory of the Court." *Duke Law Journal* 58(7): 1191–1230.

Brennan, Thomas, Lee Epstein and Nancy Staudt. 2009b. "The Political Economy of Judging." *Minnesota Law Review* 93: 1503–1534.

Carrubba, Clifford J. 2005. "Courts and Compliance in International Regulatory Regimes." *Journal of Politics* 67(3): 669–689.

Carrubba, Clifford J. 2009. "A Model of the Endogenous Development of Judicial Institutions in Federal and International Systems." *Journal of Politics* 71(1): 55–69.

Carrubba, Clifford J. and Matthew Gabel. 2014. *International Courts and the Performance of International Agreements: A General Theory with Evidence from the European Union*. New York, NY: Cambridge University Press.

Carrubba, Clifford J., Matthew Gabel and Charles Hankla. 2008. "Judicial Behavior under Political Constraints: Evidence from the European Court of Justice." *American Political Science Review* 102(4): 435–452.

Carrubba, Clifford J., Matthew Gabel and Charles Hankla. 2012. "Understanding the Role of the European Court of Justice in European Integration." *American Political Science Review* 106(1): 214–223.

Carrubba, Clifford J. and Christopher Zorn. 2010. "Executive Discretion, Judicial Decision Making, and Separation of Powers in the United States." *Journal of Politics* 72(3): 812–824.

Casillas, Christopher J., Peter K. Enns and Patrick C. Wohlfarth. 2011. "How Public Opinion Constrains the U.S. Supreme Court." *American Journal of Political Science* 55(1): 74–88.

Chen, Paul. 2003. "The Institutional Sources of State Success in Federalism Litigation before the Supreme Court." *Law and Policy* 25(4): 455–472.

Cheruvu, Sivaram and Jay N. Krehbiel. 2022. "Delegation, Compliance, and Judicial Decision-making in the Court of Justice of the European Union." *Journal of Law and Courts*, https://doi.org/10.1086/718496.

Clark, Tom S. 2009. "The Separation of Powers, Court Curbing, and Judicial Legitimacy." *American Journal of Political Science* 53(4): 971–989.

Duch, Raymond M. and Randolph T. Stevenson. 2008. *The Economic Vote: How Political and Economic Institutions Condition Election Results*. New York: Cambridge University Press.

Epstein, Lee and Jack Knight. 1997. *The Choices Justices Make*. Washington, DC: Sage.

Epstein, Lee, Jack Knight and Olga Shvetsova. 2001. "The Role of Constitutional Courts in the Establishment and Maintenance of Democratic Systems of Government." *Law and Society Review* 35(1): 117–164.

Epstein, Lee and Andrew D. Martin. 2010. "Does Public Opinion Influence the Supreme Court? Possibly Yes (But We're Not Sure Why)." *University of Pennsylvania Journal of Constitutional Law* 13(2): 263–281.

Erikson, Robert S., Michael B. MacKuen and James A. Stimson. 2002. *The Macro Polity*. New York, NY: Cambridge University Press.

Gabel, Matthew J., Clifford J. Carrubba, Caitlin Ainsley and Donald M. Beaudette. 2012. "Of Courts and Commerce." *Journal of Politics* 74(4): 1125–1137.

Garrett, Geoffrey. 1995. "The Politics of Legal Integration in the European Union." *International Organization* 49(1): 171–181.

Garrett, Geoffrey, R. Daniel Kelemen and Heiner Schulz. 1998. "The European Court of Justice, National Governments, and Legal Integration in the European Union." *International Organization* 52(1): 149–176.

Gibson, James L. 2007. "The Legitimacy of the U.S. Supreme Court in a Polarized Polity." *Journal of Empirical Legal Studies* 4(3): 507–538.

Gibson, James L. and Gregory A. Caldeira. 1995. "The Legitimacy of Transnational Legal Institutions: Compliance, Support, and the European Court of Justice." *American Journal of Political Science* 39(2): 459–489.

Gibson, James L., Gregory A. Caldeira and Vanessa A. Baird. 1998. "On the Legitimacy of National High Courts." *American Political Science Review* 92(2): 343–358.

Gould, John P. 1973. "The Economics of Legal Conflicts." *Journal of Legal Studies* 2(2): 279–300.

Graber, Mark A. 1998. "Establishing Judicial Review? Schooner Peggy and the Early Marshall Court." *Political Research Quarterly* 51(1): 221–239.

Hansford, Thomas G. and David F. Damore. 2000. "Congressional Preferences, Perceptions of Threat, and Supreme Court Decision Making." *American Politics Quarterly* 28(4): 490–510.

Helmke, Gretchen. 2002. "The Logic of Strategic Defection: Court-Executive Relations in Argentina under Dictatorship and Democracy." *American Political Science Review* 96(2): 291–303.

Hermansen, Silje Synnøve Lyder. 2020. "Building Legitimacy: Strategic Case Allocations in the Court of Justice of the European Union." *Journal of European Public Policy* 27(8): 1215–1235.

Hobolt, Sara B. and James Tilley. 2014. *Blaming Europe?: Responsibility Without Accountability in the European Union*. New York: Oxford University Press.

Johnson, Ben and Logan Strother. 2021. The Least Responsive Branch: Supreme Court Justices Do Not Respond to Public Opinion. In *Proceedings of the Midwest Political Science Association Annual Meeting*.

Krehbiel, Jay N. 2016. "The Politics of Judicial Procedures: The Role of Public Oral Hearings in the German Constitutional Court." *American Journal of Political Science* 60(4): 990–1005.

Larsson, Olof and Daniel Naurin. 2016. "Judicial Independence and Political Uncertainty: How the Risk of Override Affects the Court of Justice of the EU." *International Organization* 70(2): 377–408.

McGuire, Kevin T. 2004. "The Institutionalization of the U.S. Supreme Court." *Political Analysis* 12(2): 128–142.
McGuire, Kevin T. and James A. Stimson. 2004. "The Least Dangerous Branch Revisited: New Evidence on Supreme Court Responsiveness to Public Preferences." *Journal of Politics* 66(4): 1018–1035.
Mishler, William and Reginald S. Sheehan. 1993. "The Supreme Court as a Countermajoritarian Institution? The Impact of Public Opinion on Supreme Court Decisions." *American Political Science Review* 87(1): 87–101.
Myers, William M. 2020. "Judging Government Economic Performance." *Australian Journal of Political Science* 55(1): 38–54.
Nicholson, Stephen P. and Thomas G. Hansford. 2014. "Partisans in Robes: Party Cues and Public Acceptance of Supreme Court Decisions." *American Journal of Political Science* 58(3): 620–636.
Owens, Ryan J. 2010. "The Separation of Powers and Supreme Court Agenda Setting." *American Journal of Political Science* 54(2): 412–427.
Owens, Ryan J., Justin Wedeking and Patrick C. Wohlfarth. 2013. "How the Supreme Court Alters Opinion Language to Evade Congressional Review." *Journal of Law and Courts* 1(1): 35–59.
Powell Jr., G. Bingham and Guy D. Whitten. 1993. "A Cross-National Analysis of Economic Voting: Taking Account of the Political Context." *American Journal of Political Science* 37(2): 391–414.
Randazzo, Kirk A., Douglas M. Gibler and Rebecca Reid. 2016. "Examining the Development of Judicial Independence." *Political Research Quarterly* 69(3): 583–593.
Rice, Douglas. 2014. "On Courts and Pocketbooks: Macroeconomic Judicial Behavior across Methods of Judicial Selection." *Journal of Law and Courts* 2(2): 327–347.
Rogers, James R. 2001. "Information and Judicial Review: A Signaling Game of Legislative-Judicial Interaction." *American Journal of Political Science* 45(1): 84–99.
Rosenberg, Gerald N. 2008. *The Hollow Hope: Can Courts Bring About Social Change?* Chicago, IL: University of Chicago Press.
Schorpp, Susanne. 2012. "Strategic Anticipation of Noncompliant Governors: State Supreme Court Behavior in Response to the Political Environment." *Justice System Journal* 33(3): 275–293.
Segal, Jeffrey A. 1997. "Separation-of-Powers Games in the Positive Theory of Congress and Courts." *American Political Science Review* 97(1): 28–44.
Segal, Jeffrey A. and Harold J. Spaeth. 2002. *The Supreme Court and the Attitudinal Model Revisited.* New York, NY: Cambridge University Press.
Spriggs, James F. 1997. "Explaining Federal Bureaucratic Compliance with Supreme Court Opinions." *Political Research Quarterly* 50(3): 567–593.
Staton, Jeffrey K. 2006. "Constitutional Review and the Selective Promotion of Case Results." *American Journal of Political Science* 50(1): 98–112.
Staton, Jeffrey K. and Georg Vanberg. 2008. "The Value of Vagueness: Delegation, Defiance, and Judicial Opinions." *American Journal of Political Science* 52(3): 504–519.
Stephenson, Matthew C. 2003. "'When the Devil Turns…': The Political Foundations of Independent Judicial Review." *Journal of Legal Studies* 32(1): 59–89.
Stiansen, Øyvind. 2021. "Directing Compliance? Remedial Approach and Compliance with European Court of Human Rights Judgments." *British Journal of Political Science* 51(2): 899–907.
Sweet, Alec Stone and Thomas L. Brunell. 2012. "The European Court of Justice, State Noncompliance, and the Politics of Override." *American Political Science Review* 106(1): 204–213.
Ura, Joseph Daniel and Patrick C. Wohlfarth. 2010. "'An Appeal to the People': Public Opinion and Congressional Support for the Supreme Court." *Journal of Politics* 72(4): 939–956.
Vanberg, Georg. 2000. "Establishing Judicial Independence in West Germany: The Impact of Opinion Leadership and the Separation of Powers." *Comparative Politics* 32(3): 333–353.
Vanberg, Georg. 2015. "Constitutional Courts in Comparative Perspective: A Theoretical Assessment." *Annual Review of Political Science* 18: 167–185.
Vavreck, Lynn. 2009. *The Message Matters: The Economy and Presidential Campaigns.* Princeton, NJ: Princeton University Press.

APPENDIX 20A

Table 20A.1 *Understanding the relationship between member state economic performance and ECJ decision-making, moderating effect of trade dependence*

	DV = Member State Wins			
	(1)	(2)	(3)	(4)
GDP Growth	0.088	0.088	0.060	0.062
	(0.057)	(0.064)	(0.061)	(0.066)
Trade Dependence	0.777***	0.783***	0.407	0.446
	(0.241)	(0.273)	(0.402)	(0.419)
GDP Growth ×	–0.184***	–0.186***	–0.144*	–0.148*
	(0.067)	(0.074)	(0.074)	(0.079)
Intercept	–1.192***	–1.329***	–0.922***	–1.056***
	(0.191)	(0.220)	(0.306)	(0.323)
Estimation:	Logit	2-level	2-level	3-level
		Logit	Logit	Logit
		L1: Issue	L1: Issue	L1: Issue
		L2: Case	L2: Country	L2: Case
				L3: Country
N	1,625	1,625	1,625	1,625
AIC	2,024	2,014	2,016	2,008

Notes:
Cell entries represent unstandardized coefficient estimates with standard errors in parentheses. Model 1 reports results from a simple logit regression. Models 2 and 3 report results from 2-level logit regressions with legal issues nested within cases and countries, respectively. Model 4 reports results from a 3-level logit regression with legal issues nested within cases and cases nested within countries.
* $p<0.10$, ** $p<0.05$, *** $p<0.01$.

Table 20A.2 *Understanding the relationship between member state economic performance and ECJ decision-making, moderating effect of membership duration*

	DV = Member State Wins			
	(1)	(2)	(3)	(4)
GDP Growth	0.090	0.107	0.079	0.095
	(0.063)	(0.073)	(0.067)	(0.074)
Membership Duration	0.221***	0.244**	0.140	0.164
	(0.083)	(0.096)	(0.104)	(0.114)
GDP Growth ×	–0.066**	–0.074**	–0.060**	–0.068**
	(0.027)	(0.031)	(0.028)	(0.031)
Intercept	–1.162***	–1.361***	–0.948***	–1.111***
	(0.222)	(0.263)	(0.275)	(0.306)
Estimation:	Logit	2-level	2-level	3-level
		Logit	Logit	Logit
		L1: Issue	L1: Issue	L1: Issue
		L2: Case	L2: Country	L2: Case
				L3: Country

	DV = Member State Wins			
	(1)	(2)	(3)	(4)
N	1,654	1,654	1,654	1,654
AIC	2,059	2,047	2,047	2,038

Notes:
Cell entries represent unstandardized coefficient estimates with standard errors in parentheses. Model 1 reports results from a simple logit regression. Models 2 and 3 report results from 2-level logit regressions with legal issues nested within cases and countries, respectively. Model 4 reports results from a 3-level logit regression with legal issues nested within cases and cases nested within countries.
* p<0.10, ** p<0.05, *** p<0.01.

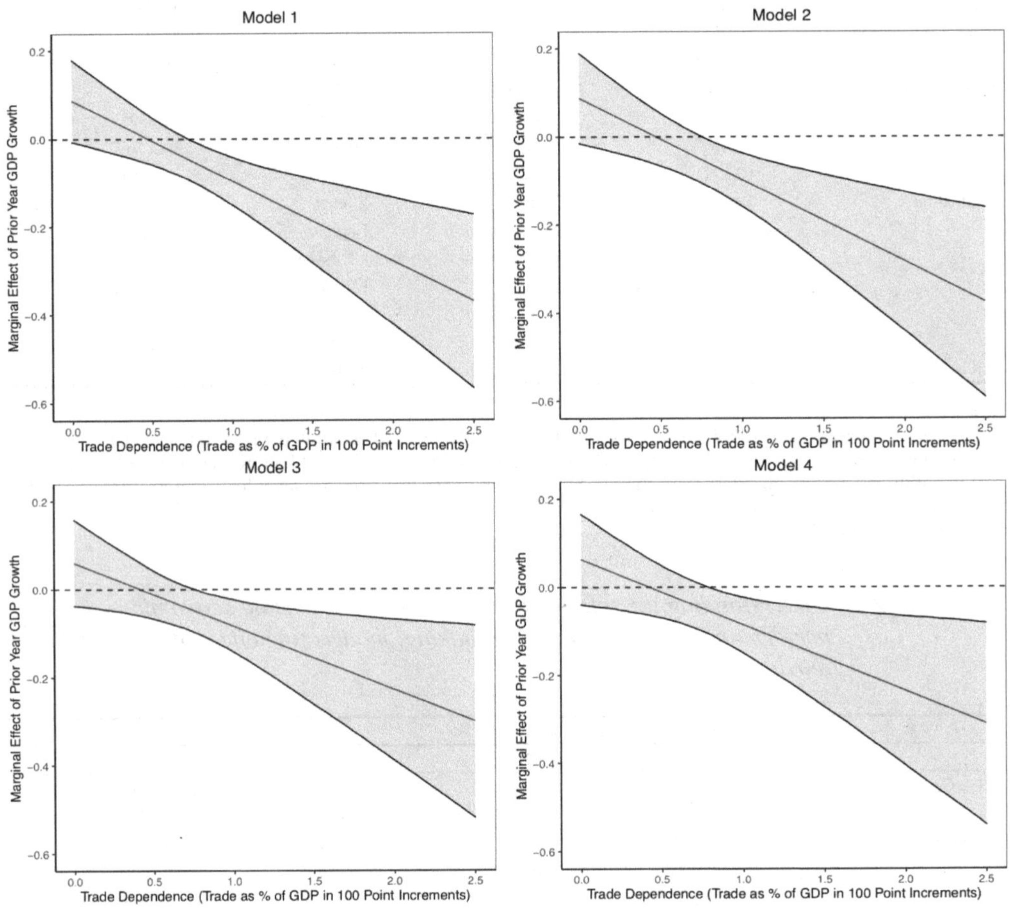

Figure 20A.1 The effect of GDP growth across trade dependence

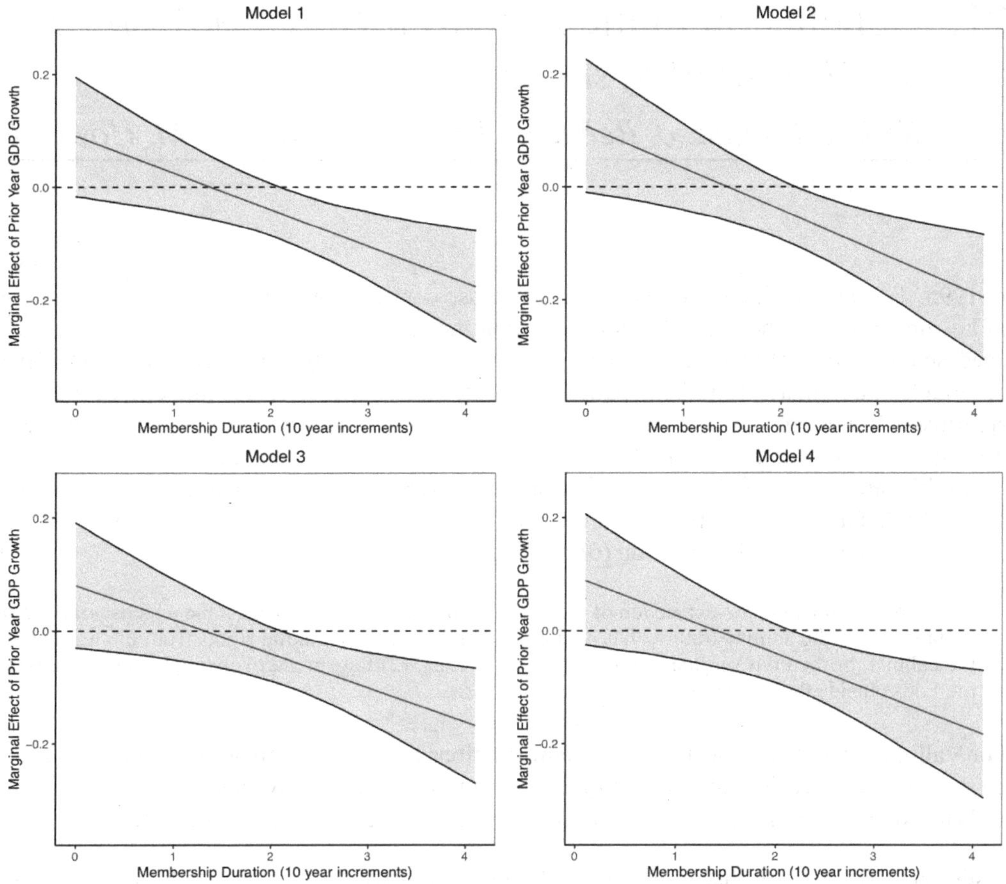

Figure 20A.2 The effect of GDP growth across membership duration

21. Conclusion to the *Research Handbook on Law and Political Systems*

Kirk A. Randazzo, Rebecca A. Reid, and Robert M. Howard

In 1995, Tate and Vallinder edited a volume whose contributions focused on the intersection of law and politics. They called this intersection the "judicialization of politics" and encouraged scholars to continue exploring how each aspect mutually influences the other. They accurately stated that "the judicialization of politics may be or may become one of the most significant trends in late-twentieth and early-twenty-first-century government. It deserves careful description, analysis, and evaluation" (Tate and Vallinder 1995, 5).

Additionally, each of the editors contributed a separate chapter that expounded on the phrase "judicialization of politics" in an effort to provide more definition and clarity. Vallinder (1995, 13) stated that judicialization (of politics):

> should mean either (1) the expansion of the province of the courts or judges at the expense of the politicians and/or the administrators, that is, the transfer of decision-making rights from the legislature, the cabinet, or the civil service to the courts, or, at least, (2) the spread of judicial decision-making methods outside the judicial province proper.

For Vallinder, one of the most obvious manifestations of the "judicialization of politics" could be seen in the increasing utilization of judicial review over legislative and executive actions.

Tate expanded on this perspective by stating that scholars needed to better understand:

> the political conditions that appear to promote the judicialization of politics and logically [analyze] how those conditions interact with the values of those who are the prime actors in the process, the judges, to determine whether or not the judicialization of politics is likely to occur in a particular setting (Tate 1995, 27).

He identified some of the most likely conditions under which the judicialization of politics could manifest. These included democratic consolidation, a separation of powers governmental framework, a recognition of individual rights (especially for members of minority groups), use of litigation by interest groups or political opposition parties, ineffective majoritarian institutions and public perceptions of these institutions, and the delegation of political issues by majoritarian institutions (Tate 1995, 28–32; Tate and Vallinder 1995).

After over 25 years, we ask the question again. How has the "judicialization of politics" manifested and evolved? We examine this question by focusing on the intersections of law, courts, and political systems. This focus involves chapters that explore single-country dynamics, regional or cross-national influences, and transnational systems. Based on the analyses offered across the 19 chapters in this handbook, several themes emerge that expand our understanding of the "judicialization of politics" and the intersections of law and political systems.

At its core, judicialization reflects the dynamic nature of how law, courts, and political systems evolve in tandem through contestation, (re)negotiation, and collaboration. The expansion of judicial activity and power, increased judicial activism and judicial review to curb legislative and executive actions, transfer of authority and decision-making from political actors to courts, legalization of politics, and politicization of courts all reflect how political systems and courts reimagine their role within changing conditions and contexts. Each chapter offers insight into these crosscutting themes of judicialization and explores the conditions under which judicialization occurs (or not). These chapters thus reveal how political systems are reinforced and reflected in judiciaries, and how courts impact political systems in turn.

JUDICIALIZATION AS JUDICIAL ACTIVISM: ASSERTIVENESS VERSUS DEFERENCE

The definition offered by Vallinder implies that there is a dividing line between law and politics, about which the "judicialization" occurs—either when the courts "expand their province at the expense of politicians" or when judges exercise their decision-making "outside the judicial province proper" (1995, 13). Where exactly is this line located?

Graham tackles this question head on. As he notes, politicians and pundits often use the term "judicial activism" when they decry a judgment with which they disagree. Yet judges are often asked to rule on controversial issues upon which the public has conflicting beliefs and upon ambiguous statutory language, such as what constitutes "a reasonable period" or "compelling reasons" or "exceptional public interest." While accusations of judicial activism span across countries and legal systems, the paradox in the UK is that this accusation of judges acting politically arises despite the simultaneous view of judges as "old guard conservatives" where senior judges are perceived as "traditional," "part of the establishment," and "on the right of the political spectrum." Graham argues that "there has been a something of a shift to a vision of the judiciary as a more liberal institution," particularly due to the rise in human rights, immigration, and EU issues. In this context of shifting regional integration, populism, and international pressures on domestic politics, Graham examines what it means for judges to be political based upon the most prevalent criticisms of UK judges. Most of these criticisms involve judges going beyond simply applying the law—a sentiment that seemingly echoes the original definition offered by Vallinder in 1995. However, Graham correctly notes that no matter how appealing this idea might be, "it is difficult to suggest that it reflects reality. Very few could seriously argue that judges in the UK *only ever* declare what the law is and apply it to the facts before them" (emphasis in original). Indeed, he asserts that "judges might operate in a 'political' space" but this does not mean that "their actions in that space are themselves politically motivated." Further, Graham demonstrates that UK courts are largely deferential on the grounds of democratic, parliamentary legitimacy and expertise. This contestation of (the presence of) judicial activism reflects the opportunity and constraints for judicialization across shifting political contexts domestically and internationally.

Similarly, judicial activism often fall hand in hand with queries of judicial review. Rosenthal and Talmor address judicialization in this regard, where increased judicial activism is conceptualized as increased utilization of judicial review, following Vallinder's (1995) definition. They examine the Israeli Supreme Court (ISC) in light of concerns "that their judicial review is regarded as an individual effort rather than reflecting a legal system," thereby developing a perception of "a law of judges rather than a law of court." They thus investigate "whether the judicialization of politics is an outcome of a collective effort of courts, or an outcome of the purposeful action of specific judges who consistently pursue the implementation of their desired political ideologies." What they discover is that the judicialization of politics in Israel is not related to individuals or to courts, but rather to factions within the ISC. They demonstrate:

> Over time, there are judges from the different factions we identified as being a part of the same composition of judges. Hence, while the court sets judicial policy and promotes it, it does so with various voices within it. The way these factions interpret and sustain the law is based on an ongoing conversation within the different parts of the Israeli party represented on the court.

Hence, judicialization in Israel is pursued by dynamically changing judicial factions within the politically moderate ISC, where no faction takes over the Court. Judicialization, then, is not driven by individual judge partisan ideologies; nor is it a cohesive effort by the Court as a whole. Rather, judicialization, in this political context, has emerged through the shifting judicial factions in response to the political questions they are asked to adjudicate via judicial review.

Similarly, Castillejos-Aragón's examination of judicial behavior during times of emergency reflects judicialization as judicial activism. During the initial stages of the COVID-19 pandemic, the Constitutional Chamber and Salvadorian magistrates played a "visible" yet "incremental" role in monitoring the executive's response to the pandemic. As the pandemic progressed, however, the Chamber increasingly asserted its authority and struck down measures implemented by the Bukele administration. These judges also engaged in activism through creating new judicial remedies to protect citizens against arbitrary arrests and expanding the scope of constitutional interpretation to better protect citizen rights and liberties. Yet this activism is not purely at the expense of the executive and legislative branches. Rather, the Constitutional Chamber of El Salvador has served as a beacon, guiding executive actions to better manage the pandemic, outlining constitutional options available to the executive, and promoting better inter-institutional dialogue among branches of government.

In contrast, judicial deference is typically considered the absence of judicialization, where courts reinforce judicial boundaries by constraining their decision-making and avoiding potential political issues. Yet the decision not to act, or to act in a constrained manner, is also a political act. In addition, these instances of judicial constraint and deference often occur when the courts are placed within the political disputes between other institutions, reflecting the judicialization of politics as courts are being (increasingly) asked to determine political issues involving conflicts between political institutions.

For example, Johnson examines judicial behavior in response to the federal Freedom of Information Act (FOIA). Signed in 1966 by President Lyndon B. Johnson, this statute is designed to "facilitate government transparency through proactive disclosures of information, and the disclosure of records upon request." However, Congress also recognized instances in which records should remain secret, and therefore included several exceptions to the general transparency principle outlined in the FOIA statute. These exemptions include matters related to national security, internal rules and practices of an agency, trade secrets, inter- or intra-agency memoranda, personnel or medical files, information compiled for law enforcement purposes, etc. Additionally, the U.S. Congress "has amended FOIA multiple times in direct response to judicial decision-making when courts were seemingly too deferential to executive branch preferences." That Congress felt the need to amend the statute following court decisions that were too deferential to the executive—contrary to congressional intent—

reflects the "judicialization of politics," where the courts are asked to resolve disputes between congressional and executive institutions.

JUDICIALIZATION AS JUDICIAL POWER: IMPACT AND COMPLIANCE

Judicialization can also be conceptualized as the expansion of court power, where existing courts take on new issue areas and/or new courts are created to tackle political problems that become legalized and placed within judicial purview. Yet the degree to which courts are effective in these areas depends on how their decisions are received. In short, judicial power depends not only upon the creation or expansion of *de jure* powers and jurisdiction, but upon the extent to which judicial decisions achieve compliance and have meaningful impact. The degree to which judicial power is realized in these new terrains influences the possibilities for future judicialization and court empowerment.

For example, a perennial question remains regarding the impact of the International Criminal Court (ICC). In light of mixed empirical results of previous scholarship, Broache investigates whether the ICC has had a deterrent effect on violence against civilians. He notes how the ICC possesses limited jurisdiction and is dependent "on state cooperation to conduct investigations and enforce arrest warrants," which may hinder its ability to deter atrocities. He finds that the ICC has no effect on country-level civilian deaths in its first decade of its operation, implying that there are no deterrent effects on violence against civilians (at least in the aggregate, state-level and across conflict types). On the other hand, he finds evidence against the claims that the ICC has exacerbated such atrocities.

In the face of limited state cooperation and potential compliance, Boston and Hadzic evaluate how international courts like the European Court of Justice (ECJ) engage in strategic deference in order to avoid noncompliance. Specifically, the ECJ is strategically deferential to EU member states that experience lower levels of economic growth. As reduced economic resources limit states' willingness or ability to comply with ECJ orders, the ECJ takes into consideration the economic conditions of states as a proxy for likelihood of compliance. When states are unlikely to comply, the ECJ strategically defers so as to not rule against the state. This strategic use of judicial power protects the ECJ by maintaining its institutional legitimacy, avoids the ire of irritated publics and political officials, and averts threats to judicial authority.

These relatively nascent international courts themselves reflect judicialization as the expansion of courts, law, and judges entering into the international political realm. Issues that traditionally fell squarely within the political realm (e.g., human rights, war, trade, and economic integration) have become legalized and judicialized. In response to this judicialization of international politics, states in the international system created international and regional courts to adjudicate these issues. Nonetheless, these courts face changing political dynamics and limited enforcement capacities akin to domestic courts. As such, we see mixed evidence of compliance and impact, as well as evidence of strategic behavior as courts navigate the Scylla and Charybdis of noncompliance and irrelevance across diverse state interests and political systems.

JUDICIALIZATION DURING TRANSITION: COLONIALISM, CONSTITUTIONALISM, AND INTERVENTION

Opportunities for judicialization depend upon the institutional arrangements entrenched by, and entrenching, political systems. As such, constitution-making and amending frame the boundaries and codify the expectations within which courts are able to maneuver. Indeed, constitutions and formal judicial powers evolve from the political conditions of their origin. Thus, the potential for judicialization arises from political conditions at each state's constitutional origin, where constitutions formalize political systems and distributions of power. Yet constitutional and political contexts change over time, creating shifting opportunities and constraints for judicialization.

As constitution-making in democratic transitions defines the legal architecture within which judicialization may be possible, Pastor y Camarasa examines the transnational dimensions of constitution-making in Tunisia. She focuses on the key interactions between transnational and domestic actors in Tunisia's 2014 constitution, showing that the new constitutional legal order and domestic political systems are built with the normative preferences and expertise of foreign actors. The Western liberal constitutionalism that is replicated by transnational experts can create domestic or local tensions with the imposed legal and political systems. These political and legal systems distribute power across different—often polarized—local groups and impose particular (Western) understandings of human rights, governance structures, international standards, and "best practices" that frequently dismiss local traditions, histories, and power asymmetries. Indeed, these tensions are likely due to the very nature that foreign experts are sought by the assumption that they (and their expertise) are neutral, apolitical, and without the "taint" of a political agenda due to their foreign-ness—which is desirable because of the extant polarization that leads to the inability to coordinate viable solutions domestically. Yet, as Pastor y Camarasa correctly notes, expertise and knowledge are inherently political. Thus, Tunisia also represents an example of how legal reforms and constitution-making can be limited by the political systems within which they are imposed or implemented. Despite the democratic 2014 constitution, Tunisia is experiencing threats of democratic backsliding, rights violations, and presidential attacks on the judiciary, creating a political environment unsupportive of judicialization and the rule of law.

Similarly, Shen emphasizes that:

> the moment of constitutional design is an encounter between domestic and international politics. Particularly with the development of human rights in constitutional texts since the mid-20th century, constitution-making responds to the exigencies of local politics, but also to transnational legal standards of constitutionalism, incorporating discourses regarding rights, democracy, and the rule of law.

Shen analyzes this dynamic in Cambodia and the challenges faced from the implementation of the Paris Agreements of 1991. Though several international actors helped the process toward democratic consolidation, the end result was a weak constitution that promised liberal democracy but only delivered a single-party regime. As Shen describes, the initial regime:

> rested on the strong, but temporary, institutions of the [United Nations]: the peacekeepers and the electoral staff. Once these were no longer part of the political framework, the institutions that had been built by that framework began to falter, and the actors who had successfully held onto power

during the intervention were able to overwhelm those who had chosen to give up power based on good faith dealings with the UN.

Hence, Cambodia reflects another example of how, despite best intentions, the intervention of transnational actors can impose constitutional models and political structures that distort the political reality and are unequipped to effectively implement constitutional provisions. Without the political systems to support them, constitution-making and formal judicial empowerment lack the ability to instill judicialization, the rule of law, and democratic consolidation.

Young also approaches his chapter from the insight that constitutions and formal judicial powers evolve from the political conditions of their origin. Young analyzes how colonial origins and transnational/foreign actors can impact judicialization. Specifically, he explores how colonization continues to impact courts and judicial systems through how incorporating former colonial power undermines sovereignty and possibilities for judicialization. Young investigates how several Caribbean states constitutionalized colonial laws and chose to retain the British Judicial Committee of the Privy Council (JCPC) as the highest appellate court after independence, rather than accede to the newly established Caribbean Court of Justice (CCJ). Akin to the experiences of Tunisia and Cambodia, the foreign-ness of the British JCPC lends it a "hallmark of credibility" to domestic and international actors, as well as domestic Caribbean perceptions of independence and legitimacy. Despite their tumultuous histories with British colonialism and strong evidence that the CCJ is similarly independent, many Caribbean political actors view the JCPC as preferable to the CCJ, where the JCPC offers domestic judicial and political systems legitimacy through the colonial entrenchment of perceptions of (British/white/foreign) superiority—thereby perpetuating colonization that has direct and concrete effects on domestic judicial systems. Not only does the CCJ have the difficult task of overcoming the colonial shadow of the JCPC, but the JCPC continues to determine Caribbean jurisprudence in ways that hinder regional sovereignty, rights protections, and judicialization. For example, JCPC jurisprudence on the death penalty causes Caribbean backlash and criticism over "judicial imperialism" and "over-legalization" of human rights commitments. This backlash may persuade some Caribbean actors to become more likely to accede to the CCJ. However, the parallel fear that the CCJ would then become a "hangman's court" due to the regional popularity of the death penalty would also make rights-oriented political actors less likely to transition to the CCJ. Thus, judicialization within the context of human rights and colonization informs domestic judicial hierarchies and systems as well as creating boundaries for the possibility of Caribbean judicialization within the CCJ, which is incentivized to follow JCPC precedent and be ever conscientious of regional policy preferences to protect its nascent credibility, public support, and legitimacy.

OPPORTUNITIES FOR JUDICIALIZATION

One of the fundamental factors that can enable or enhance judicialization is public and institutional support, judicial legitimacy, and legal system structures themselves. At its most fundamental, judicialization requires perceptions of legitimacy for the court and legal system(s). Without this legitimacy to incur trust and support for judicial processes and law-based decision-making, the transfer of political issues to courts, legalization of political issues, and expansion of judicial power cannot be realized. In essence, without legitimacy, courts remain (perceived as) ineffective at resolving issues such that the expansion of their jurisdiction, agency, and power are precluded.

For example, Truscott and Wilhelm argue that the United States judiciary is not independent, but is "tied to decisions made by Congress." Congress strategically supports the judiciary to reinforce and constitutionalize its own decisions and policymaking. Indeed, they argue that the development of the U.S. judiciary is due to congressional support. Their 220-year analysis of political and economic trends throughout U.S. history demonstrates relatively stable support for the entire federal judiciary, compared with more volatility for the U.S. Supreme Court. American judicialization, then, occurs through stable congressional support. Congressional support has led to the expansion of agenda control for federal judges and jurisdictional scope, as well as judicial power through enforcement and compliance with its decisions. Thus, stable judicial support with the legislature, enabled by strategic congressional preferences for its own institutional power and policymaking, has created the opportunity for—and directly promoted—judicialization.

Similarly, Romano and Curry demonstrate that judges cannot be separated from political systems, where judges are representatives for particular constituent audiences (at least in functioning democracies). This chapter questions longstanding assumptions and norms of judicial independence and sources of judicial legitimacy by asserting that judicial legitimacy is derived from popular sovereignty, that judges are (direct or indirect) representatives like other democratic politicians, and that courts are inherently political institutions. The implication is therefore that judicialization depends upon the level of public support for their judicial representatives. Knowing this, judges (as representatives) communicate strategically with their constituent audience through their decision-making, opinion-writing, and public communications.

Meyer takes this notion further to illustrate how judges can increase their public support through efforts to promote transparency and "open justice" principles requiring judicial processes to be visible. Transparency promotes public trust, where Meyer shows that increases in "open justice" practices in European countries have a positive impact on citizen trust in their legal system. This increased trust enhances public support for the court, which can assist in protecting the court from court-curbing and increase compliance, but also creates additional opportunities for judicialization. Trusted legal systems and courts enjoying public support authorize judicialization, where courts become trusted democratic institutions upon which political issues and conflicts can be addressed. Furthermore, courts and judges are not passive agents in judicialization; rather, they can strategically engage in practices and behavior to promote public support to further their institutional authority and enable judicialization.

However, the possibilities of judicialization and public support may not be equally enjoyed. Dumas and Mannix take a deeper dive into the intersection of political systems and the judicialization of politics when they examine the selection system used by Alabama, where there is a two-tiered system in which judges in the state trial courts are elected in partisan, district-wide contests but appellate judges compete in partisan statewide elections. Judge composition on the bench may determine the degree to which judicialization and public support can be realized. Specifically, Dumas and Mannix examine how judge gender, race, and political affiliation interact with these state institutional arrangements to shape the judicial process. Minority judges are subject to more judicial scrutiny in the form of reversals—despite similar decision outcomes—suggesting that judicial composition may influence not only the judicial process but also judicialization opportunities where public support falters for individual judges due to minoritized identities. This chapter also suggests that while diversification of the bench may improve public support for the court as an institution, this effect does not necessarily translate to individual judges, where demographic and political identities can make the public view minority judges as less legitimate or competent. The descriptive representation of judges, then, does not have consistent effects in improving public support for courts or in creating spaces for judicialization.

Beyond representation and judicial support, opportunities for judicialization can also arise from courts' role as dispute resolution mechanisms. Munir and Munir highlight judicial roles in curbing social unrest by providing an institutional mechanism and avenue through which dissatisfied citizens can protect their interests and express their grievances. Courts enjoying perceptions of judicial legitimacy can quell protests, especially non-violent protests. This mechanism can create new spaces for judicialization where a legitimate court may be increasingly asked to adjudicate on political issues in order to reduce social unrest, political opposition, and other grievances against the state or regime. By transferring these political issues to courts and empowering them, regimes can benefit from public support from the delegation of power away from the regime and commitment to law-based responses to citizen grievances, reduce the likelihood of protests and social unrest, and reinforce formal institutional mechanisms that provide the regime information and administrative control necessary to ensure political survival. A court that is interested in maintaining or expanding its institutional power would similarly seek to maintain public support and perceptions of legitimacy, which are necessary in order for citizens to use the courts for their grievances. These strategic considerations can create spaces for judicialization across regime types.

Driscoll and Gandur examine public support for courts even further, questioning the assumptions necessary for arguments that public support for courts can protect them from attacks and court-curbing via electoral support. Specifically, Driscoll and Gandur investigate whether there are electoral costs to noncompliance with judicial decisions, arguing that noncompliance has a very small influence on vote choice. This empirical reality suggests that this assumption underpinning foundational scholarship and inquiry is actually quite fragile and deserving of more attention. These authors outline how future research can better examine how the public monitors noncompliance, attributes responsibility for noncompliance, understands judicial decisions, engages with political leader cues, and weighs or balances multiple policy preferences and issue areas in elections. The implication of these arguments is, then: if judicial noncompliance does not reliably incur electoral costs, there is potentially little consequence for noncompliance (even in democracies). If there is little cost, public support may not be sufficient for enabling or maintaining judicialization and court empowerment. Therefore, the expansion of the province of courts and judges, as well as the perpetuation of judicialized systems, requires additional factors beyond public support and legitimacy.

Finally, Kabo examines the effects of legal pluralism, often generated from colonial experiences, transnational intervention, and local political histories, on economic development. In this chapter, Kabo expands upon previous scholarship by investigating the prevalent assumption of legal singularity (i.e., a singular system of law). Kabo notes that 45% of states around the world, many of which are often the target of development programs, are legally pluralist, with multiple legal and normative orders within the same territorial space. Taking this reality into account, Kabo evaluates how legally pluralist "rule of laws" political systems impact economic development in the form of foreign direct investment (FDI), finding that legal pluralism does not attract or hinder FDI. Yet underlying this chapter is judicialization, where it is judicialization that promotes economic development via court empowerment and expansion of courts to determine property rights, enforce contracts, and other protections for investments. It is the shift away from political actors to the courts that provides the credible commitment to potential investors that the state is safe and stable for investment. Legally pluralist political systems can create uncertainty in these commitments as there are multiple rules of the game, some of which may be contradictory, not made public, and determined outside of state judicial institutions. Legal pluralism, then, can create a diffused or decentralized (*de facto*) judicial system that goes beyond the formal state institutions, creating new opportunities for judicialization through transferring authority to non-state and quasi-judicial actors, or "outside of the judicial province proper" (Vallinder 1995, 13).

CONSTRAINTS ON JUDICIALIZATION: POLITICIZATION, LEGAL WEAPONIZATION, AND COURT-CURBING

While the factors that create opportunities for judicialization are crucial, it is equally important to examine potential constraints that limit or hinder the possibility of judicialization. As previous chapters have indicated, political systems and law must be self-reinforcing in order for judicialization to have the chance to arise. Yet political systems can also leverage law to prohibit the possibility of judicialization.

For instance, Trochev and Juzgenbayez identify the lack of judicialization in Kazakhstan, Kyrgyzstan, Tajikistan, Turkmenistan, and Uzbekistan. They address the emergence of new constitutional courts following the collapse of the Soviet Union within authoritarian presidentialist regimes. As they note:

> judges of newly created constitutional courts have agency – they make the decision rules for the newly created courts and shape the ways in which these courts choose to decide or not to decide cases... However, once presidents consolidated their personalist regimes, eliminated rival patron–client pyramids and gained full control over judicial appointments, constitutional courts lost their assertiveness and switched to offering services to the patrons-in-chief, like approving the constitutionality of constitutional amendments, which the president had sponsored, extending the incumbent's terms of office, and dismissing all cases which could threaten their patrons.

As a result, constitutional courts enjoyed relatively short periods of autonomy and independence, which were later reined in as presidents consolidated their positions and authority. Thus, despite the formal empowerment of constitutional courts, Trochev and Juzgenbayez suggest that judicialization requires a political context where courts are not unilaterally appointed or controlled by patron executives and the presence of competing patrons or multiple patron–client pyramids. Rather, in these states, courts have been "instrumentalized to preserve the power of the patron through shifting expectations about the rigidity of constitutional texts and shifting blame for unpopular decisions in the eyes of domestic and international audiences." In other words, the constitutional empowerment of courts has led to their instrumentalization of constitutional review to preserve autocratic regimes rather than leading judicialization. In sum, political systems determine the degree to which constitutions impact judicialization, where the same constitutional provisions of judicial empowerment can lead to different trajectories of courts. As the authors astutely note, "On paper, constitutional tribunals may gain more powers and become more accessible, yet this does not, by itself, translate into greater judicial power or promote judicialization of distribution of power because formal and informal relations, in which judges are embedded, facilitate their instrumentalization by the powers that be."

Similarly, Aydin-Cakir reminds us that authoritarian rulers often:

> use laws to curtail the power of democratic institutions… that by changing the constitution or issuing specific laws, elected authoritarian leaders can remove the political opposition, weaken or pack the courts, and establish government control over the media and other vital institutions (Landau 2013, 194). As a result, by using legal means, authoritarian leaders try to consolidate power, remain in office, construct a more authoritarian order, and protect their self-interests.

Using Turkey as a case study, Aydin-Cakir demonstrates "that an elected authoritarian leader usually prefers to use formal legal means to curtail the power of the judiciary. But coercion mechanisms will be preferred when there is an imminent threat against the government and when the potential for public backlash is low." Thus, the law is weaponized to ensure authoritarian leader political survival; and the law is most easily weaponized through constitutional reforms when there are few veto players and ideological congruence with legislative majorities to ensure its passage. Reiterating other author observations, Aydin-Cakir notes that high levels of public support for the judiciary do not prevent a regime from curtailing judicial independence—they only affect the mechanism by which the regime suppresses the courts. Hence, the possibilities for judicialization are limited in authoritarian regimes facing political threats from opposition. Easy legal reform procedures or minimal requirements, as well as ideological congruence/limited veto players, allow regimes to use the law as a legitimate court-curbing device to restrict court power and curtail judicialization.

Popova and Rothmayr Allison expand our notion of the judicialization of politics by also focusing on the weaponization of law, particularly in the transitioning democracies or hybrid regimes of Eastern Europe. They note that the weaponization of law can be viewed as "a mid-point on the spectrum between a politically relevant, powerful, and activist judiciary in a liberal democratic setting and a politically subservient judiciary in an autocratic setting." It can manifest itself in a variety of ways, from the politicization of judicial careers to large numbers of lawsuits involving political actors to extensive media coverage of the courts that focuses on a lack of good-faith litigation. As they note:

> weaponization straddles the fine line between using the law aggressively and abusing it. Savvy political actors could find opportunities to weaponize without violating the letter of the law. The result is a legally sound case pursued in bad faith. But often weaponization involves varying levels of abuse of the law.

As they conclude, a "weaponized legal system is a specific style of politics that might be facilitated in certain political and institutional contexts, but that needs actors that initiate strategies of politicization and others that contribute to fuel such strategies." Hence, we see similar uses of "lawfare" in these states as in Turkey, where authoritarian regimes use law to politicize courts, undermine their legitimacy, and constrain them using legal and constitutional reforms. By changing the rules of the game and limiting judicial power in these areas, regimes can undermine political opposition, consolidate power, and ensure their political survival. This strategic politicization of courts inhibits the possibility of judicialization.

FINAL THOUGHTS

Over 25 years ago Tate and Vallinder stated that "the judicialization of politics may be or may become one of the most significant trends in late-twentieth and early-twenty-first-century government. It deserves careful description, analysis, and evaluation." Inspired by their conclusions, we ask: how has the "judicialization of politics" manifested and evolved? We examine this question by focusing on the intersection of law and political systems. This focus involves chapters that explore single-country dynamics, regional or cross-national influences, and transnational systems. The chapters offered in this handbook remind us to remain cognizant of the line between law and politics (which is often not clear), to remain sensitive to examinations of judges versus courts, and to consider how political systems manifest across levels of analysis. Indeed, law, courts, and political systems reflect, reinforce, and mutually constitute each other. These chapters reveal the close, symbiotic (but not nonconflictual) relationships between law and political systems across regime types and across time. To be sure, the constellations of legal and colonial histories, shifting political contexts, eras of conflict and transition, foreign interventions, and fluctuating public support and legitimacy all influence the opportunities and constraints for judicialization. As Tate (1995) suggests, we hope scholars continue to examine "the political conditions that appear to promote the judicialization of politics and logically [analyze] how those conditions interact with the values of those who are the prime actors in the process, the judges, to determine whether or not the judicialization of politics is likely to occur in a particular setting" (27). As these chapters reveal, there is much left to be discovered.

REFERENCES

Tate, C. N. 1995. "Why the Expansion of Judicial Power?" In Tate, C. N., and T. Vallinder. 1995. *The Global Expansion of Judicial Power*. New York University Press, pp. 27–38.

Tate, C. N., and T. Vallinder. 1995. *The Global Expansion of Judicial Power*. New York University Press.

Vallinder, T. 1995 "When the Courts Go Marching In." In Tate, C. N., and T. Vallinder. 1995. *The Global Expansion of Judicial Power*. New York University Press, pp. 13–26.

Index

Achour, Y. B. 191, 193
activist judges 57
adjudication 66–8
Administrative Procedure Act (APA): Section 3 72
Affordable Care Act (ACA) 216
AfroBarometer survey 219–20
agency success in Federal Court
  litigation 75
  separation of powers 75–6
  transparency disputes 76
Agreement of Dickenson Bay 292
Akayev, A. 151–2
Albiston, C. R. 258
Alemanno, A. 237
Allison, C. R. 4, 354
American Bar Association (ABA) ratings 48–9
American political development
  judicial representation and 34–7
Americas Barometer survey 219–20
Annan, K. 307
Anthony, K. D. 290, 296
anti-people regime of Bakiev 152
Appel, B. 312, 314, 316
Appellate Jurisdiction Act (1876) 291
April Revolution (2010) 153
Arab Spring 187
armed conflict dataset (ACD) 312
Atambayev 153–5, 162
audience democracy 30–31
authoritarian populism 8
autocratic constitutions 103
autocratic legalism *vs.* weaponized legalism 174
autoregressive distributed lag (ARDL) 131
Aydin-Cakir, A. 2, 354

Baekova 151–2, 162
Baimakhanov, M. 147–8
Bakiev, K. 152
Banić, S. 197–8
Barak (Judge) 96–7
Barnes, J. 123
Barrow, D. J. 46
Bartels, B. L. 216–17
Basch, F. 224
battle deaths 317, 320
Beasley, C. 25
Begum, S. 63
Beinish (President) 97
Belaïd, C. 192
Benesh, S. C. 247
Bentham, J. 234, 250
Berlusconi, S. 174
Bertelsmann Transformation Index (BTI) 260
Biden, J. 81–2
Black judges 49
Black, R. C. 75
Black women judges 47–8
Blass, A. 143, 157
Blauberger, M. 184, 330
blueprint constitutions 102
Blume, L. 274
Bonneau, C. W. 44, 56
Boston, J. 6, 348
Bouazizi, M. 191
Brahmi, M. 192
Brennan, T. 330–31
Breyer, S. 33, 39
Brinks, D. M. 143, 157
Britt, C. L. 46
Broache, M. P. 6, 310, 348
Browne-Wilkinson (Lord) 60
Buddhist Liberal Democratic Party (BLDP) 105–6
Bukele, N. 200–201, 204–10, 347

Caldeira, G. A. 239
Cambodian Constitution 99–101
  antecedent conditions 114–15
    external pressure and cultural unfamiliarity 117–18
    political institutions without Paris and UNTAC 115–16
  autocratic constitutions 103
  billboard 102
  blueprint constitutions 102
  constitutional malice 103–4
  design 99
  diffusion 99
    billboard and window-dressing constitutions 102
    blueprint constitutions 102
    constitutional weakness and 101–5
    incorporation of international politics 101–2
    local actors 99–100
  external pressure and cultural unfamiliarity 117–18

international actors 118
Paris Agreements *see* Paris Agreements
peacebuilding and constitution-making 100–101
BLDP 106–7
CPP 105–6
DPK 106
factions 105–7
FUNCINPEC 106
goals of peace process 107–8
negotiation to constitutional ratification 107–10
peace process 104
political institutions without Paris and UNTAC 115–16
post-election clouds 113–14
rule of law and constitutionalism 103
window-dressing 102
Cambodian People's Party (CPP) 105–6, 113
Canon, B. 226
Cardozo, B. 67
Caribbean Basin 290
Caribbean Community (CARICOM) 290
Caribbean Court of Justice (CCJ) 6, 290, 292, 350
challenges 293–9
Belize International Services Limited v. The Attorney General of Belize [2020] 299
death penalty 295
ex officio membership 293
JCPC 293–9
Maxo Tido v. The Queen 295
Pratt and Morgan v. Attorney General of Jamaica and Other 295
JCPC 290–92, 301–2
justices 299–300
Caribbean Free Trade Association (CARIFTA) 292
Carlin, R. E. 220, 223
Carrubba, C. J. 215, 326–7, 330, 333
Castillejos-Aragón, M. 4, 347
Castro, M. G. 202
Central Asia *see* instrumentalization of constitutional law (Central Asia)
Chakrapong, N. 108
Chancellor (Lord) 65
Chapultepec Peace Accords (1992) 203
Choudhry, S. 197
Christenson, D. P. 216–17
Cingranelli-Richards (CIRI) Physical Integrity Rights Index 312
civilian deaths 315, 318
Clark, T. S. 18, 123–4
Clinton, B. 45
Coase, R. H. 274
Collins, P. M. 26, 31
Committee of Political Reform 191
communal property rights 281
Comparative Manifestos Project 92
compliance with high courts 326
as democratic value 216–17
and diffuse support 218–19
electoral costs to noncompliance 221–3
and instrumentalism 215–16
and public attitude formation 223
five "Ws" of compliance 223–7
monitoring, problem of 227–9
strategy, question of 229–31
surveys around world, compliance-related questions on 219–20
see also public support and compliance with high courts
conflict 317
history 317, 320
termination 317
congressional support for federal judiciary 134–5
ARDL *see* autoregressive distributed lag (ARDL)
conceptualization of institutional development 122
economic considerations 124
model and results 131–4
operationalization 126
autonomy 127–8
differentiation 127
durability 127
dynamic index of judicial institutionalization, construction 128–31
political considerations 125–6
Constitutional Chamber of El Salvador 201–2, 210–11
centros de contención 210
as constitutional beacon 206–10
exception regimes, alternative process for 208–9
habeas corpus procedural rules 209–10
judicial enforcement and executing judge 210
rights limitation and suspension and exception regimes 206–8
state of emergency declaration 208
creation 203–4
inconstitucionalidad 10–2020 209
inconstitucionalidad 21–2020 206
inconstitucionalidad 63–2020 208
Constitutional Court Act (Uzbekistan) 158
constitutional malice concept 103–4
constitution-making (Tunisia) 186–9, 198–9

2014 Tunisian constitution drafting *see* Tunisian constitution (2014) drafting
Arab Spring 187
drafting 2014 Tunisian constitution 191–2
institutional documentation 188
politics of transnational legal expertise in political legal reforms 189–90
transnational actors 187–8
transnational dimension of 187
Consumer Product Safety Act 79
court-curbing mechanism 8–9, 184, 353–4
AKP government, under rule of 12–14
costs 16–17
clientelistic strategies 17–18
judicial appointment and removal procedures 18
political opposition 18
public backlash 18–20
defined 8
judicial politics literature 11–12
literature review 9–12
strategic model
benefits 14–15
cost 16–19
judiciary and ruling party, relationship between 14–15
opposition parties, closing down 14
subservient judiciary 15
Courtney, W. 148
courts functioning in El Salvador 200–202, 210–11
Constitutional Chamber 201–2
as constitutional beacon 206–10
creation 203–4
COVID-19 pandemic, executive response to 204–6
emergencies 200–201
institutionalization of administration of justice 202–3
COVID-19 pandemic (El Salvador) 204–6
Crenshaw, K. 46
Curry, T. A. 2, 351
customary-dominant law 287–8

Dahl, R. A. 30
Dancy, G. 312
Darville, R. B. 293, 295
Das, C. J. 267
Deforge, Q. 190
democracy 316
Democracy Reporting International (DRI) 194–5
Democratic Choice of Kazakhstan movement 150
Democratic Party of Kampuchea (DPK) 105–6
democratization 317
Department of Interior's (DOI)
Exemption 5 76–7
deterrence hypothesis 308
Dicker, R. 307
difference-in-differences (DiD) approach 307, 318
dissent 317
Driscoll, A. 5, 221, 353
Duch, R. M. 331, 332
Dumas, T. 2, 351
Durrsma, A. 311
Duysheev, K. 154–5
Dyson, M. R. 62

economic development and legal pluralism 272–3
data 282–4
description 284
Huber-White standard errors 286
inflation 286
juriglobe categorization 283
model and estimation 284–5
results 285–7
trade openness 286
WGIs' "rule of law" 283–4
FDI 282
practical challenges
customary law 281
dynamic nature of law 281
FDI 282
private property 280–81
well-functioning judiciary 281
theoretical challenges and law as tool 278–80
see also law and development literature
Edelman 258
Eisinger, P. K. 255
Elena, S. 240–41
Ellett, R. 182
El Mozote Massacre 203
El Salvador courts functioning *see* courts functioning in El Salvador
Emomali, R. 157
Ennahda (Islamist party) 191
Environmental Protection Agency (EPA) 71
Equal Employment Opportunity Commission (EEOC) 45
Erdoğan, R. T. 12–14, 174
European Convention on Human Rights 64
European Court of Justice (ECJ) 326–7, 348
compliance 326
constrained judicial behavior on 329–30
decisions and economic constraints: data 333–4
economic considerations in judicial strategy
ECJ judges 331
economic growth hypothesis 331–2
Great Depression 331

membership duration moderation hypothesis 332–3
trade dependence moderation hypothesis 332
U.S. Supreme Court justices 331
voting 330
economic constraints and judicial institutions 338–9
economic performance and deference: results 334–8
judicial institutions and strategic anticipation
cost–benefit calculation, judges behaviour in 328
judges 328–9
powers framework, separation of 327–8
noncompliance 326
European Social Survey (ESS) 236
Evans, G. 110

Faculty of Legal, Political and Social Sciences of Tunis (Faculty) 193
fairness 26
Federal Aviation Act
Section 1104 74
Federal Communications Commission (FCC) 80
Fedtke, J. 198
female judges 44–5
Flanagan, F. 197
Floyd, G. 25
FOIA Improvement Act 72, 81
Ford (President) 74
foreign direct investment (FDI) 273, 352
Freedom of Information Act (FOIA) 3, 81–2, 347
EPA v. Mink 73–4
Exemption 1 74
Exemption 3 74
Exemption 5 71, 76–7
Exemption 7C 78–9
Federal Aviation Administration v. Robertson 74
records exempt from disclosure under 72–3
Supreme Court and 76–7
cases by court 79–81
pattern of deference 77–8
unanimity 78–9
Freedom of Occupation (Israel Basic Laws) 91
Freedom in the World Report (2019) 8
Free National Movement (FNM) 295
Frendo, M. 197
Friedman, P. 175
Friedrich Ebert Foundation 191
Friedrich Naumann Foundation 191

Gabei, M. 326–7, 330, 333
Galanter, M. 281
Gandhi, J. 102
Gandur, M. 5, 352
Garoupa, N. 180, 238–9, 246–7
Georeferenced Event Dataset 315
Ghandi, I. 267
Gibson, J. L. 181, 217, 239
Gil-Garcia, J. R. 240–41
Ginsburg, T. 75, 197
Glennon, C. 257
Glick, D. M. 216–17
good governance 275
Gostojić 240–41, 245
governance and institutions 274–6
Government Employees Salary Reform Act (1964) 123
government transparency and judicial deference 71–2
agency success in federal court 75–6
Department of Justice 81–2
federal agencies and judicial outcomes 75–6
FOIA *see* Freedom of Information Act (FOIA)
Supreme Court and FOIA 76–7
cases by court 79–81
pattern of deference 77–8
unanimity 78–9
Graham, L. 3, 346
Griffiths, J. 277, 280, 283, 287
gross domestic product (GDP) per capita 317, 320
Grzymala-Busse, A. 183

habeas corpus procedural rules 209–10
Hadzic, D. 6, 348
Hale, H. E. 163
Hamilton, A. 5
Hans Seidel Foundation 191
Harvey, A. K. 239
Hawkins, D. 224
Hazare, A. 267, 269
Helmke, G. 11
Hess, B. 239
Hilbink, L. 201
Hillebrecht, C. 224, 311
Hirschl, R. 177–8
Hubert, A. 295
Huber-White standard errors 285–6
Hughes, D. A. 123
Human Dignity and Freedom (Israel Basic Laws) 91
human rights 64–6
Human Rights Act 1998 (HRA) 64–5
Hungary autocratic legalism 174

incentives 275–6
independent judiciary 256, 317

India 267–71
 India Against Corruption movement 269
 judicial legitimacy
  index, negative score on 268–9
  levels in India (1996–2017) 268
  perceptions of 270–71
  and protests in India (1996–2017) 270
 PIL 269
 protest movements 267
 rape and sexual assault cases 269–70
 Supreme Court 267–8
India Against Corruption movement 269
inevitable flip side of judicialization phenomenon 177–8
instrumentalization of constitutional law (Central Asia) 139–43, 163–4
 activist rulings proportion by constitutional tribunals 141
 clientelist structure and appointment procedure of constitutional tribunals 141
 constitutional amendments in post-Soviet Central Asia 140
 constitutional courts as "regime allies" and "sidelined" courts 143
 genuine judicialization, instead of 145–6
 judicialized politics, outcomes of 143–5
 Kazakhstan, constitutional review
  approval of voters 148–9
  cancellation of vote 148
  Kvyatkovskaya decision 147–8
  "one person – one vote" principle 148
  political uncertainty 150
 Kyrgyzstan's constitutional review 151–5
 political context and activism of constitutional courts 161
 Tajikistan's constitutional court 155–7
 trajectories of politics and 159–63
 Uzbekistan: stable sidelined constitutional court 157–9
International Criminal Court (ICC) 306–7, 348
 atrocities prevention and 307–9
 jurisdiction 309
International Institute for Democracy and Electoral Assistance (International IDEA) 187
International Justice Program at Human Rights Watch 307
Islamic Renaissance Party of Tajikistan 156
Ismatov, A. 158
Israel High Court of Justice Executive Branch Merits Decisions (IHCJE) dataset 92
Israeli Declaration of Independence (1948) 91
Israeli's HCJ and judicialization of politics in Israel 85–7
 Basic Laws 90–91
 IHCJE dataset 92–3
 judges 85
 judicial activism between collective and personal effort 87–90
 MARPOR *see* Manifesto Research on Political Representation (MARPOR) project
 reasonableness doctrine 91
 variables
  judges' decisions 92
  political petitions and ideological contexts 92–3
Israeli Supreme Court (ISC) 346

Jackson, A. B. 81
Jackson, D. W. 203, 206
Jacoby, W. 224
Jamadar (Justice) 299
Jebali, H. 191
Jeenbekov (President) 154–5
Jo, H. 308, 310, 312–13, 320
Johnson, C. 226
Johnson, G. E. 3, 75
Johnson, L. B. 72, 347
Johnston, C. D. 216–17
Joireman, S. 281
Jones, B. 190
Jubran (Judge) 97
judges 40–42
 civil trial courts 56
 data and methods
  appeals and reversal rates 54
  case outcomes by judges' race, gender, and party ID 52–6
  civil litigation 52
  state trial court data 50
  tort reform 51–2
 gender and race 43–4
  female judges 44–5
  intersectional discrimination, effects of 46–7
  and judging 43–7
  judicial competence perceptions 47–9
  sex discrimination cases 44
  verdicts 45
  White and Black judges 45–6
 ideology and judicial decision-making 42–3
 institutional structure of Alabama courts 56
  ABA ratings for federal judges 48–9
  decision to overrule lower court judge 49
  discrimination 47–8
  general public evaluation of judges 49–50

opinion assignment and citations 49
minority 41
previous literature
gender, race, and judging 43–7
gender, race, and judicial competence perceptions 47–9
ideology and judicial decision-making 42–3
and public tend 29
trial court rulings 55
see also judges and politics in UK courts
judges and politics in UK courts 57–8
acting politically
going beyond applying the law 59–60
government's actions, review of 60–62
human rights, dealing with sensitive questions relating to 64–6
political figures deemed to have legitimacy or expertise 62–4
activist judges 57
adjudication 66–8
criticisms 68–70
government's actions, judicial review of 60–62
human rights, acting politically when dealing with sensitive questions relating to
adjudication 66
HRA 64–5
jurisprudence of ECHR 65–6
qualified rights 65
not acting politically, judges 59
"judges as umpires" theory 26
judicial activism 346–8
Judicial Committee Act (1833) 291
Judicial Committee Act (1844) 291
Judicial Committee of the Privy Council (JCPC) 6, 290–92, 350
judicial competence perception, gender and race
judicialization
constraints on 353–4
judicial activism, as 346–8
judicial power, as 346–8
opportunities for 350–53
of politics 1, 345, 355
transition, during 349–50
judicialization of politics 1, 345, 355
Central Asia 143–5
authoritarian patron–client regimes 145
issue-specific 144–5
politically salient issues 145
Israel
consistent in judicial decisions 89
court of judges 90
court of law 89
judges 85–6
judicial factions 97
no consistency in judicial decisions 87–9
judicial legitimacy 256–8
impartiality 257
independent judiciary defined 256
minority groups 258
protests *see* protests
public legitimacy defined 257
judicial representation
and American political development 34–5
appointment systems 35–7
authorization constituency 35
Missouri Plan 37
partisan and nonpartisan electoral systems 35
selection and retention systems for state courts of last resort (2020) 36
audience democracy 30–32
described 28
female and minority judges 29–30
judges and public tend 29
policy-making process 30
treatments of 28–9
judicial websites
evaluation to measure open justice 240–41
investigation of open justice on European high court 242–5
and open judicial data 240
Juzgenbayev, A. 4, 353

Kabo, V. 5, 352
Kapiszewski, D. 201, 226
Kastellec, J. P. 18
Kazakhstan
instrumentalization of constitutional review 147–50
professional backgrounds of members of KCCl 162
Kazakhstani Constitutional Council (KCCl) 142, 149–50
professional backgrounds of members of 162
Kazakhstani Constitutional Court (KCCt) 141–2, 147–9
Keith (Lord) 61
Kekilbayev 148
Kelemen, R. D. 184
Kennedy, D. 189
Kenyatta, U. 309
Kersten, M. 311
Kim, H. 308, 312
Kirby, M. 67
Kirkpatrick, J. 30, 47
Kirschner, N. 10

Klamath Native American Tribes 76–7
Klein, B. 41, 52
Konrad Adenauer Foundation 191
Krcmaric, D. 312
Krönke, M. 220
Kvyatkovskaya, T. 147
Kyrgyzstani Constitutional Chamber (KyrCCh) 142, 153–4

Larsson, O. 330
law and development literature
    governance and institutions
        good governance 275
        government institutions 276
        incentives 275–6
        NIE 274–5
        WGIs 275
        World Bank 275
    rule of law 273–4
    singularity 276–7
law and political systems 1–2
    court-curbing mechanisms 2
    multinational and transnational analyses 4
lefty human rights lawyers 57
legal pluralism
    concept 277–8
    customary-dominant law 287–8
    defined 277
    strong 277
    weak 277
legitimacy, judicial *see* judicial legitimacy
Levi, E. (Judge) 88
Levin (Judge) 97
Levitsky, S. 11
Lührmann, A. 20
Lundy, P. 190

Mabrouk, S. 194
Mackay (Lord) 65
Magalhães, P. C. 235, 238–9, 246–7
majoritarians in robes 25–7, 37–9
    judges as political representatives 39
    "judges as umpires" theory 26
    judicial representation
        and American political development 34–7
        audience democracy 30–32
        described 28
        female and minority judges 29–30
        judges and public tend 29
        policy-making process 30
        treatments of 28–9
    justification 32–3
    persuasion 33
    selection, retention, and audience representation 32–3, 37–8
Mamyrov (Judge) 153–4
Mamyrov Manifesto Research on Political Representation (MARPOR) project
    categories 94–5
    described 92–3
    HCJ's judges' right–left RILE scores 96–7
    judges' support patterns across dimensions 94
    petition proportion 93
    policy topics distribution 94
    usage of scheme 93
Manifestos Research Group 92
Manin, B. 30
Mannix, A. 2, 351
Mansbridge, J. 28
Markcović 240–41, 245
Mart, S. N. 75
Marzouki, M. 191
Mason, D. 202
Mass Mobilization dataset 259, 264, 270
Max Planck Foundation 193
Mazmanyan, A. 143
McAllister, J. R. 308
McGovern, M. 190
McGuire, K. T. 122–3, 126–9, 132–4
Mebazaa, F. 191
Meernik, J. 312
Meltzer (Judge) 97
merit selection 35
Meyer, P. 5, 351
Millennium Development Goals 191
Milligan 258
minority judges 47
Mirziyoev, S. 159
Missouri Plan 35, 37
Møller, J. 276
Mondak, J. J. 217
Montanaro, L. 31
Moore, S. 248
Moreno-Ocampo, L. 308
Morgan, I. 294
Moustafa, T. 102
Muammar al-Qaddafi 311
Mubarak (President) 102
Mudde, C. 182
Muhammad III as-Sadiq 186
Muller, T. R. 311
Munir, H. 5, 352
Munir, S. R. 5, 352
Myers, W. M. 331

Narmada Bachao Andolan case (2000) 269

National United Front for an Independent, Neutral and Peaceful Cambodia (FUNCINPEC) 105–6, 113–15
Naurin, D. 330
Nazarbayev (President) 147–50, 156, 159, 162
Ndulo, M. 279
Nelson, M. J. 181, 217, 221
Neuberger (Lord) 65
neutrality 26
Newey-standard errors 285
new institutional economics (NIE) 274–5
NOMINATE methodology 125
noncompliance 326
nonpartisan electoral systems 35
non-standard judges 47
non-violent protest 264–6
North, D. 274
Nownes, A. J. 257

O'Donnell, G. A. 11
Office of Government Information Services 73
Office of the Solicitor General (OSG) 75
ONUSAL 202
open justice 234–6
  accessibility 237
  approach to measuring 239
    evaluation of judicial websites to measure open justice 240–41
    judicial websites and open judicial data 240
    measuring open justice 241–2
  claims 234
  concept 236–9
  consequences and incentives of 238–9
  data defined 240
  defined 236–7
  European high court websites, investigation on 242–5
  judicial websites
    evaluation to measure open justice 240–41
    and open judicial data 240
  measurement 241–2
  openness 234, 237
  public trust, influence on
    analysis and discussion 247–50
    data and methods 246–7
  transparency 234–5, 237
Orban, V. 171, 174
O'Shaughnessy, L. N. 203, 206
Oskonbayev (Judge) 154
Owens, R. J. 75
ownership, location, internalization (OLI) paradigm 282

Paris Accords 114
Paris Agreements 3, 105, 107, 109, 115–16, 349
  Annex 3 110
  Annex 5 110–11
  implementation, divergent responses to 111–13
  legal framework 110–11
Parkin, M. 240
partisan electoral systems 35
Pastor y Camarasa, A. 4, 349
Patterson, P. J. 296
Penn World Tables 260
People's Movement of Kyrgyzstan 152
Peretti, T. J. 38
Perlin, P. 75
Persad-Bissessar, K. 296
persuasion 33
Pitkin, H. F. 28, 32
political behavior, defined 62
politicization of courts (Europe) 169, 185, 353–4
  definition of politicization 169
  explanations for 176–7
    judicialization, reversing or limiting 177–9
    low trust in courts and social networks 180–82
    populism, rise of 182–4
  strategies
    ad hoc proactive 175–6
    ad hoc reactive 175
    systematic formal 176
    systematic informal 176
  weaponized legalism 185
    anti-corruption prosecutions 173
    autocratic legalism vs. 174
    corruption prosecutions 173
    dimensions of politicization 170–71
    judicial reform measures 171
    political actors 172–3
    political competitors 172–3
    public discourse 173
Popova, M. 4, 354
population 317, 320
populism in Europe
  backlash against ECJ 184
  defined 182
  politicization of courts 184
  populist governments and backlash 183
  weaponized legalism 183–4
Porta,D. 182
Posner, E. 200
Pratt, E. 294
Priest, G. I. 41, 52
Problem of Social Cost, The 274
promissory 28

Prorok 312
protests
  described 255–6
  judicial legitimacy and 258–9
    BTI 260
    child mortality 261
    high levels of judicial legitimacy associated with fewer protests 259
    India 267–71
    legal mobilization 258–9
    Mass Mobilization dataset 259
    PolityIV scores 260
    poverty and human well-being challenges 261
    research design 259–61
    results and discussion 261–4
    Rule of Law Index 260
    WGI dataset 260
  violent and non-violent 264–6
public attitudes and compliance with high courts
  empirical evaluations of
    concepts or consequence 218–19
    electoral costs to noncompliance 221–3
    empirical evaluations of 217–18
    surveys around world, compliance-related questions on 219–20
  monitoring, problem of 227–9
  and public attitude formation 223–31
  strategy, question of 229–31
public interest litigation (PIL) 269
public legitimacy
  defined 257
public support and compliance with high courts 212–15
  cooperation enhancement 215–16
  coordination enhancement 216–17
  democratic value, compliance as 216–17
  instrumentalism 215–16
  public attitudes
    concepts or consequence 218–19
    electoral costs to noncompliance 221–3
    empirical evaluations of 217–23
    five "Ws" of compliance 223–7, 232
    monitoring, problem of 227–9
    strategy, question of 229–31
    surveys around world, compliance-related questions on 219–20
public trust, influence of open justice on
  analysis and discussion 247–50
  data and methods
    legal tradition and highest court type 246
    trust in the legal system 246
    years of education, age and gender 246–7

Radtke, M. 310
Rakhmon, E. 156–7
Ramsey, A. 238, 247
Ranariddh 106, 108
ratification 316, 318
Raz, J. 279
R (Begum) v Special Immigration Appeals Commission case 63
reasonableness doctrine 91
Rehfeld, A. 35
Rehnquist Court 79–80
Reid (Lord) 59
representation, judicial *see* judicial representation
Resnik, J. 237
Rice, H. M. 44, 56
right–left policy positions (RILE) 93, 97
  HCJ's judges' right-left RILE scores 96–7
Ringhand, L. A. 26, 31
Roberts, J. 26, 80
Rodman, K. A. 311
Romano, M. K. 2, 351
Romero, A. 224
Rome Statute 316, 318
Rooney, B. 20
Rosenthal, M. 3, 346
Rouge, K. 105, 108, 112, 115–16
Rove, C. 52
rule of law 273–4
Ryder, E. 237

Sage, C. 288
Salvadoran Constitution
  Article 186 200
Salzman, R. 238, 247
Samphan, K. 106
Sandoval-Almazan, R. 240–41
Sann, S. 106
Sarkozy, N. 174
Saunders, C. 186
Saward, M. 32
Scalia, A. 27, 30, 77
Scheppele, K. L. 103, 174
Schmitter, P. C. 11
Segal, J. A. 55
Seider, R. 203
Sen, H. 115
Sharp, D. 190
Shawcross, W. 109
Shen, K. 3, 349
Sihanouk, N. 111, 113
Sikkink, K. 308, 312

Simmons, B. A. 308, 310, 312–13, 320
situational jurisdiction 316, 318
Skaaning, S-E. 276
Slate, D. 173
slot machine jurisprudence 59
Smithey, S. I. 217
Smith, J. H. 291
Solberg, N. (Judge) 89
Soros, G. 171
Soubert, S. 106
Sriram, C. 189–90
Staton, J. K. 12, 224, 230
Stefan, O. 237
Steffensmeier, D. 46
Stephenson, M. C. 215
Stevenson, R. T. 331–2
Stevens, R. 58
Stiansen, Ø. 184
strong legal pluralism 277
Stykow, P. 157
Supreme Court
 congressional support for 123–4
 FOIA and 76–7
  cases by court 79–81
  pattern of deference 77–8
  unanimity 78–9
Svolik, M. 12, 145

Tajikistan's constitutional court 155–7
Talmor, S. 3, 346
Tamanaha, B. 278
Tate, C. N. 1, 345, 355
Tax Division 80
Taylor, M. 201, 226
Thomassen, W. 197
Tokayev, K-Z. 150
Toktogazieva, S. 148
Toma, E. 123
trade openness 286
Trade Secrets Act 79
Trochev, A. 4, 182, 353
Trump, D. 81–2, 175, 181
Truscott, J. 4
Tulip Revolution 152
Tunisian constitution (1861) 186
Tunisian constitution (2014) drafting
 described 191–2
 transnational expertise 192
  awareness, raising 194–5
  constitutional drafts, commenting on 195–8
  neutral and technical expertise 193–4
Turner, B. 278, 280
Tusk, D. 171
Tyler, T. R. 257

UCDP One-Sided Violence (OSV) dataset 312–13
UN-brokered power-sharing agreement 155
United Nations Development Programme (UNDP) 187
United Nations Transitional Authority in Cambodia 100
UN Mission or ONUSAL 202
UNTAC mission 114
UN Transitional Authority in Cambodia 3
Uppsala Conflict Data Program (UCDP) 312
Ura, J. D. 124, 126–7, 129
U.T. Transitional Authority in Cambodia's (UNTAC) 106, 115–16
Uzbekistan: stable sidelined constitutional court 157–9

Vallinder, T. 1, 345–6, 355
Vanberg, G. 12, 212, 228, 230–31, 257
van Doeveren, V. 274
Vannucci, A. 183
van Schalkwyk, F. 240–41
Varol, O., L. D. 20
Venice Commission 156, 187, 197
Verkuil, P. R. 75
Vermeule, A. 200
Vermeulen, B. 197
Vietnamese-backed regime (1980) 106
Vining, R. L. 123
violence against civilians 321–2
 control variables
  country-level indicators of conflict and contestation 317
  country-level structures 316–17
 data structure 314–15
 dependent variable 315
 empirical literature review
  cross-national comparative findings 311–14
  single case studies 310–11
 ICC *see* International Criminal Court (ICC)
 independent variable 316
 justice cascade 306
 ratification 316
 situational jurisdiction 316
 statistical modeling strategy and results 318–21
violent protest 264–6
Voeten, E. 178–9, 183–4, 257
Voight, S. 274
Volkansek 181
von Benda-Beckmann, K. 278, 280
Voting Rights Act 44

Walker, T. G. 46

weak legal pluralism 277, 283
weaponization of law 354
weaponized legalism (Europe)
    anti-corruption prosecutions 173
    autocratic legalism vs. 174
    corruption prosecutions 173
    dimensions of politicization 170–71
    judicial reform measures 171
    political actors 172–3
    political competitors 172–3
    public discourse 173
Wedeking, J. 240
Wegner, P. 310–11
White judges 49
Wider Caribbean 290
Wiebelhaus-Brahm, E. 312
Wilhelm, T. 4, 123
window-dressing constitutions 102
Witt (Justice) 297
Wohlfarth, P. C. 124, 126–7, 129
Woolcock, M. 288
'Work! Freedom! National dignity!' motto 191
World Bank 275
World Governance Indicators (WGIs) 260, 275
World Health Organization 205
World Values Survey (2005–2009) 17
Wright (Lord) 67

Yasushi, A. 118
Yates, J. 75
Yeazell, S. 51
Yeltsin, B. 148, 151
Yilmaz, Z. 19
Young, H. 6, 350

Zamir (Judge) 97
Zhaparov, S. 155
Ziblatt, D. 11
Zorkin, V. 147